PENGUIN ACADEMICS

DRAMA
A Pocket Anthology

CANADIAN EDITION

Edited by **R. S. GWYNN** *Lamar University*

WANDA CAMPBELL *Acadia University*

PEARSON
Longman

Toronto

National Library of Canada Cataloguing in Publication

Drama : a pocket anthology / edited by R.S. Gwynn, Wanda Campbell. — Canadian ed.

Includes bibliographical references and index.
ISBN 0-321-17050-4

1. Drama—Collections. I. Gwynn, R. S. II. Campbell, Wanda, 1963–

PN6112.D69 2003   808.82   C2003-904632-X

Original edition published by Pearson Education, Inc. Copyright © 2002. This edition is authorized for sale only in Canada.

Copyright © 2004 Pearson Education Canada Inc., Toronto, Ontario

ISBN 0-321-17050-4

Vice-President, Editorial Director: Michael J. Young
Acquisitions Editor: Marianne Minaker
Marketing Manager: Toivo Pajo
Signing Representative: Ryan St. Peters
Supervising Developmental Editor: Suzanne Schaan
Production Editor: Charlotte Morrison-Reed
Copy Editor: Sharon Kirsch
Production Manager: Wendy Moran
Page Layout: B.J. Weckerle
Permissions Research: Beth McAuley
Art Director: Mary Opper
Cover Design: Michelle Bellemare
Cover Image: Katherine Knight

1 2 3 4 5   08 07 06 05 04

Printed and bound in Canada.

PENGUIN
ACADEMICS

PEARSON
Longman

Contents

Drama 37

Preface

When the *Pocket Anthology* series first appeared a decade ago, the chief aim was to offer a clear alternative to the anthologies of fiction, poetry, and drama that were available at the time. We are very pleased to offer new Canadian editions of the *Pocket Anthology* series. This volume, *Drama: A Pocket Anthology*, has been published concurrently with its two companion volumes, *Fiction: A Pocket Anthology*, and *Poetry: A Pocket Anthology*, and the three volumes are also published together in a combined edition, *Literature: A Pocket Anthology*.

  Drama addresses the four wishes and concerns most commonly expressed by both instructors and students. First, of course, is the **variety** of selections it contains. The contents of *Drama* have been shaped by the advice of experienced instructors who have cited the plays and playwrights that are most often taught and that possess proven appeal to students. Admittedly, a pocket anthology has to be very selective in its contents, so we are especially proud that the plays in this book include both established canonical writers as well as newer voices such as Judith Thompson who reflect the diversity of gender, ethnic background, and national origin that is essential to any study of contemporary literature. In addition, the website for the original Longman edition at www.ablongman.com/gwynn contains online versions of the medieval morality play *Everyman* and Oscar Wilde's comedy of manners *The Importance of Being Earnest*, as well as links to some classic plays, including works by Aphra Behn, Oliver Goldsmith, and George Bernard Shaw.

  Our second aim is **flexibility**—a book that can be used as either a primary or supplemental text in a variety of courses, ranging from introduction to drama to advanced courses in theatre or playwriting. When combined with one of its companion volumes, *Fiction* or *Poetry*, or with novels, collections of short stories or poems by individual authors, or other plays, *Drama* may also be used in introductory literature courses. In addition to its generous selection of poems, *Poetry* contains biographical headnotes for authors, an introduction that covers the techniques and terminology of the genre, and a concise section on writing about poetry and on research procedures. A *Question Book* for the Canadian edition, available to instructors on request, offers ideas for discussion questions or writing topics. As a further aid to instructors and students, the website cited above provides a number of resources that may be of interest to users of the Canadian edition.

The third goal is **affordability.** The Canadian edition of *Drama* reflects the original claims of the Pocket Anthology series, that these books represent "a new standard of value." Because of its affordability, *Drama* may be easily supplemented in individual courses with texts on the history of the theatre, guides to playwriting, handbooks of grammar and usage, or manuals of style.

Finally, we stress **portability.** A semester is a short time, and few courses can cover more than a fraction of the material that many bulkier collections contain. For instructors who focus on a single genre at a time, *Drama* and its companion volumes, *Fiction* and *Poetry*, offer compact yet self-contained editions. While *Drama* still may be a snug fit in most pockets, we trust that instructors and their students will be grateful for a book that is more manageable.

In closing, we would like to express our gratitude to the instructors who reviewed all or part of the Canadian *Pocket Anthology* series and offered invaluable recommendations for improvements:

Julia Denholm, Langara College
Cecily Devereux, University of Alberta
Fraser Easton, University of Waterloo
Thomas Ezzy, Dawson College
Melanie Fahlman Reid, Capilano College
Gordon Fulton, University of Victoria
Christopher E. Gittings, University of Alberta
Kathleen Irwin, University of Regina
Tobi Kazakewich, University of Ottawa
Christine Kerr, Champlain Regional College
Ric Knowles, University of Guelph
Jean-François Leroux, University of Ottawa

Kathy McConnell, Dalhousie University
Ninian Mellamphy, University of Western Ontario
Paul Milton, Okanagan University College
Paul Matthew St. Pierre, Simon Fraser University
Dawn Neill, University of Victoria
Catherine Nelson-McDermott, University of British Columbia
Mary Silcox, McMaster University
Cheryl Suzack, University of Alberta
Paul Tyndall, University of British Columbia
Lynn Wells, University of Regina
Patricia Whiting, University of Ottawa

R.S. Gwynn
Lamar University

Wanda Campbell
Acadia University

R. S. Gwynn has edited several other books, including *Poetry: A Pocket Anthology*, *Literature: A Pocket Anthology*, *Fiction: A Pocket Anthology*, *The Longman Anthology of Short Fiction* (with Dana Gioia), and two volumes of *The Dictionary of Literary Biography*. He has also authored five collections of poetry, including *No Word of Farewell: Selected Poems: 1970–2000*.

Professor Gwynn teaches at Lamar University in Beaumont, Texas.

Wanda Campbell has edited several other books including *The Poetry of John Strachan* and *Hidden Rooms: Early Canadian Women Poets*. She has authored two collections of poetry, *Sky Fishing* and *Haw [Thorn]* and has published academic articles, fiction, and poetry in journals across Canada. She teaches Literature and Creative Writing at Acadia University in Wolfville, Nova Scotia.

Introduction

The Play's the Thing

The theatre, located in the heart of a fading downtown business district, is a relic of the silent movie era that has been restored to something approaching its former glory. Although only a few members of tonight's audience can actually remember it in its heyday, the expertise of the organist seated at the antique Wurlitzer instills a sense of false nostalgia in the crowd, now settling by twos and threes into red, plush-covered seats and looking around in search of familiar faces. Just as the setting is somewhat out of the ordinary, so is this group. Unlike movie audiences, they are for the most part older and less casually dressed. Few small children are present, and even the teenagers seem to be on their best behaviour. Oddly, no one is eating popcorn or noisily drawing on a soda straw. A mood of seriousness and anticipation hovers over the theatre, and those who have lived in the town long enough can spot the spouse or companion of one of the principal actors nervously folding a program or checking a watch.

As the organ magically descends into the recesses of the orchestra pit, the lights dim, a hush falls over the crowd, and the curtain creakily rises. There is a general murmur of approval at the ingenuity and many hours of hard work that have transformed empty space into a remarkable semblance of a turn-of-the-century upper-class drawing room. Dressed as a domestic servant, a young woman, known by face to the audience from her frequent appearances in local television commercials, enters and begins to dust a table. She hums softly to herself. A tall young man, in reality a junior partner in a local law firm, wanders in, carrying a tennis racket. The maid turns, sees him, and catches her breath, startled. "Why Mr. Fenton!" she exclaims. . . .

And the world begins.

The full experience of drama—whether at an amateur production like the little theatre performance described here or at a huge Broadway playhouse—is much more complex than that of any other form of literature. The word **drama** itself comes from a Greek word meaning "a thing that is done," and the roots of both **theatre** and **audience** call to mind the acts of seeing and hearing, respectively. Like other communal public activities—such as religious services, sporting events, and meetings of political or fraternal organizations—drama's own set of customs, rituals, and rules has evolved over many centuries. The exact shape of these characteristics—**dramatic conventions**—may differ from country to country or from period to period, but they all have one aim in common, namely to define and govern an art form whose essence is to be found in public performances of written texts. No other form of literature shares this primary goal. Before we can discuss drama purely as literature, we should first ponder some aspects of its unique status as "a thing that is done."

It is worth noting that dramatists are also called playwrights. Note the spelling; a "wright" is a maker, as old family names like Cartwright or Boatwright attest. If a play is in fact *made* rather than written, then a playwright is similar to an architect who has designed a unique building. The concept may be his or hers, but the construction project requires the contributions of many other hands before the sparkling steel and glass tower alters the city's skyline. In the case of a new play, money must be raised by a producer, a director must be chosen, a cast and a crew found, a set designed and built, and many hours of rehearsal completed before the curtain can be raised for the first time. Along the way, modifications to the original play may become necessary, and it is possible that the author will listen to advice from the actors, director, or stage manager and incorporate these opinions into any revisions. Professional theatre is, after all, a branch of show business, and no play will survive much beyond its premiere if it does not attract paying crowds. The dramatists we read and study so reverently today managed to reach large popular audiences in their time. Even ancient Greek playwrights like Sophocles and Euripides must have stood by surreptitiously "counting the house" as the open-air seats slowly filled, and Shakespeare prospered as part-owner of the Globe theatre to the extent that he was able to retire to his hometown at the ripe old age of forty-seven.

When compared with this rich communal experience, the solitary act of reading a play seems a poor substitute, contrary to the play's very nature (only a small category known as **closet drama** comprises plays intended to be read instead of acted). Yet dramatists like Shakespeare and Ibsen are counted among the giants of world literature, and their works are annually read by far more people than actually see these plays performed. In reading a play, we are forced to pay close attention to such matters as **set description**, particularly with a playwright like Ibsen who lavishes great attention on the design of his set; references to **properties,** or "props," that will figure in the action of the play; physical description of characters and costumes; **stage directions** indicating the movements and gestures made by actors in scenes; and any other **stage business,** that is, action without dialogue. Many modern dramatists are very scrupulous in detailing these matters; writers of earlier periods, however, provided little or no instruction. In reading Sophocles or Shakespeare, we are forced to concentrate on the characters' words to envision how actions and other characters were originally conceived. Reading aloud, alone or in a group, or following along in the text while listening to a recorded performance is particularly recommended for verse plays like *Oedipus the King* or *Othello*. Also, versions of many of the plays contained in this book are currently available on videotape or DVD. Although viewing a film is an experience of a different kind from seeing a live performance, film versions obviously provide a convenient insight into the ways in which great actors have interpreted their roles. Seeing the joy in the face of Laurence Fishburne when, as Othello, he lands triumphantly in Cyprus and rejoins his bride makes his tragic fall even more poignant.

Origins of Drama

No consensus exists about the exact date of the birth of drama but, according to most authorities, it originated in Greece over 2500 years ago as an outgrowth of the worship of the god Dionysus, who was associated with fertility, agriculture (especially the cultivation of vineyards), and seasonal renewal. In these Dionysian festivals, a group of fifty citizens of Athens, known as a **chorus,** outfitted and trained by a leader, or **choragos,** would perform hymns of praise to the god, known as **dithyrambic poetry.** The celebration concluded with the ritual sacrifice of a goat, or *tragos.* The two main genres of drama originally took their names from these rituals. The word comedy comes from *kômos,* the Greek term for a festivity. These primitive revels were invariably accompanied by a union of the sexes (*gamos* in Greek, a word that survives in English words like "monogamy"), perhaps in the symbolic form of a dance celebrating fertility and continuance of the race. This is an ancient custom still symbolically observed in the "fade-out kiss" that concludes most comedies. The word tragedy literally means "song of the goat," taking its name from the *tragos* that was killed on the altar (**thymele**), cooked, and shared by the celebrants with their god.

Around 600 B.C. certain refinements took place. In the middle of the sixth century B.C. an official springtime festival, known as the Greater or City Dionysia, was established in Athens, and prizes for the best dithyrambic poems were first awarded. At about the same time a special **orchestra,** or "dancing place," was constructed, a circular area surrounding the altar, and permanent seats, or a **theatron** ("seeing place"), arranged in a semicircle around the orchestra were added. At the back of the orchestra the facade of a temple (the **skene**) and a raised "porch" in front of it (the **proskenion,** in later theatres the **proscenium**) served as a backdrop, usually representing the palace of the ruler; walls extending to either side of the skene, the **parodoi,** served to conceal backstage activity from the audience. Behind the *skene* a crane-like device called a **mechane** could be used to lower a god from the heavens or represent a spectacular effect like the flying chariot drawn by dragons at the conclusion of Euripides's *Medea.*

Around 535 B.C. a writer named Thespis won the annual competition with a startling innovation. Thespis separated one member of the chorus (called a *hypocrites,* or "actor") and had him engage in **dialogue,** spoken lines representing conversation, with the remaining members. If we define drama primarily as a story related through live action and recited dialogue, then Thespis may rightly be called the father of drama, and his name endures in "thespian," a synonym for actor.

The century after Thespis, from 500 to 400 B.C., saw many refinements in the way tragedies were performed and is considered the golden age of Greek drama. In that century, the careers of the three great tragic playwrights—Aeschylus (525–456 B.C.), Sophocles (c. 496–406 B.C.), and Euripides (c. 485–408 B.C.)—and the greatest comic playwright, Aristophanes (448–380 B.C.), overlapped. It is no coincidence that in this remarkable period Athens, under the leadership of the general Pericles (d. 429 B.C.), reached the height of its wealth, influence, and cultural development and was home to the philosophers Socrates (470–399 B.C.) and Plato (427–327 B.C.). Aristotle (384–322 B.C.), the third of the great Athenian philosophers, was also a literary critic who wrote the first extended analysis of drama.

Aristotle on Tragedy

In his *Poetics*, the earliest work of literary criticism in Western civilization, Aristotle attempts to define and classify the different literary **genres** that use rhythm, language, and harmony. He identifies four genres—epic poetry, dithyrambic poetry, comedy, and tragedy— which have in common their attempts at imitation, or *mimesis*, of various types of human activity.

Aristotle comments most fully on tragedy, and his definition of the genre demands close examination:

> *A tragedy, then, is the imitation of an action that is serious and also, as having magnitude, complete in itself; in language with pleasurable accessories, each kind brought in separately in the parts of the work; in a dramatic, not in a narrative form; with incidents arousing pity and fear, wherewith to accomplish its catharsis of such emotions.*

First we should note that the imitation here is of *action*. Later in the passage, when Aristotle differentiates between narrative and dramatic forms of literature, it is clear that he is referring to tragedy as a type of literature written primarily for public performance. Furthermore, tragedy must be serious and must have magnitude. By this, Aristotle implies that issues of life and death must be involved and that these issues must be of public import. In many Greek tragedies the fate of the *polis*, or city, of which the chorus is the voice, is bound up with the actions taken by the main character in the play. Despite their rudimentary form of democracy, the people of Athens would have been perplexed by a tragedy with an ordinary citizen at its centre; the magnitude of tragedy demands that only the affairs of persons of high rank are of sufficient importance for tragedy. Aristotle further requires that this imitated action possess a sense of completeness. At no point does he say that a tragedy has to end with a death or even in a state of unhappiness; he does require, however, that the audience sense that after the last words are spoken no further story cries out to be told.

The next part of the passage may confuse the modern reader. By "language with pleasurable accessories" Aristotle means the poetic devices of rhythm and, in the choral parts of the tragedy, music and dance as well. Reading the choral passages in a Greek tragedy, we are likely to forget that these passages were intended to be chanted or sung ("chorus" and "choir" share the same root word in Greek) and danced ("choreography" comes from this root as well).

The rest of Aristotle's definition dwells on the emotional effects of tragedy on the audience. Pity and fear are to be evoked—pity because we must care for the characters and to some extent empathize with them, fear because we come to realize that the fate they endure involves actions that civilized men and women most abhor; in *Oedipus the King*, these actions involve murder, incest, suicide, and self-mutilation. Finally, Aristotle's word **catharsis** has proven controversial over the centuries. The word literally means "a purging," but readers have debated whether Aristotle is referring to a release of harmful emotions or a transformation of them. In either case, the implication is that viewing a tragedy has a beneficial effect on an audience, perhaps because the viewers' deepest fears are brought to light in a make-believe setting. How many of us, at the end of some particularly wrenching film, have turned to a companion and said, "Thank god, it was only a movie"? The sacrificial animal from whom tragedy took its name was, after all, only a stand-in whose blood was offered to the gods as a substitute for a human subject. The protagonist of a tragedy remains, in many ways, a "scapegoat" on whose head we project our own unconscious terrors. Aristotle identifies six elements of a tragedy, and these elements are still useful in analyzing not only tragedies but other types of plays as well. In order of importance they are **plot, characterization, theme, diction, melody,** and **spectacle.** Despite the fact that *Poetics* is over two thousand years old, Aristotle's elements still provide a useful way of understanding how plays work.

Plot

Aristotle considers plot the chief element of a play, and it is easy to see this when we consider that in discussing a film with a friend we usually give a brief summary, or **synopsis,** of the plot, stopping just short of "giving it away" by telling how the story concludes. Aristotle defines plot as "the combination of incidents, or things done in the story," going on to give the famous formulation that a plot "is that which has beginning, middle, and end." Aristotle notes that the best plots are selective in their use of material and have an internal coherence and logic. Aristotle seems to favour plays with a unified plot, that is, one that takes place in a single day; in a short play with a **unified plot** like Gwen Pharis Ringwood's *Still Stands the House*, the action is continuous and imitates the amount of time that the events would have taken in real life. By **episodic plot** we mean one that spreads its action out over a longer period of time. A play that has a unified plot, a single setting, and no subplots is said to observe the **three unities,** which critics in some past eras have virtually insisted on as ironclad rules. Although most plots are chronological, playwrights in the last half-century have experimented, sometimes radically, with such straight-forward progression through time. Arthur Miller's *Death of a Salesman* effectively blends **flashbacks** to past events with his main action, as does Judith Thompson's *Sled*.

Two other important elements of plots that Aristotle considers most successful are **reversal** (*peripeteia* in Greek, also known as **peripety**), and **recognition** (*anagnorisis* in Greek, also known as **discovery**). By reversal he means a change "from one state of things within the play to its opposite." Aristotle cites one example from *Oedipus the King*: "the Messenger, who, coming to gladden Oedipus and to remove his fears as to his mother, reveals the secret of his birth"; but an earlier reversal in the same play occurs when Iocastê, attempting to alleviate Oedipus's fears of prophecies, inadvertently mentions the "place where three roads meet," where Oedipus killed a man he took as a stranger. Most plays have more than a single reversal; each episode or act builds on the main character's hopes that his or her problems will be solved, only to dash those expectations as the play proceeds. Recognition, the second term, is perhaps more properly an element of characterization because it involves a character's "change from ignorance to knowledge." If the events of the plot have not served to illuminate the character about his or her failings, then the audience is likely to feel that the story lacks depth. The kind of self-knowledge that tragedies provide is invariably accompanied by suffering and is won at great emotional cost, whereas in comedies reversals may bring relief to the characters, and recognition may bring about the happy conclusion of the play.

As with fiction, a typical plot may be broken down into several components. First comes the **exposition,** which provides the audience with essential information—who, what, when, where—that it needs to know before the play can continue. A novelist or short-story writer can present information directly with some sort of variation on the "Once upon a time" opening. But dramatists have particular problems with exposition because facts must be presented in the form of dialogue and action. Greek dramatists used the first two parts of a tragedy, a prologue and the first appearance of the chorus, to refresh the audience's familiarity with the myths being retold and to set up the initial situation of the play. Other types of drama use a single character to provide expository material. Medieval morality plays often use a "heavenly messenger" to deliver the opening speech, and some of Shakespeare's plays employ a single character named "Chorus" who speaks an introductory prologue and sets the scene for later portions of the plays as well (the film *Shakespeare in Love* captures this memorably). Occasionally, we encounter the least elegant solution to the problem of dramatic exposition, employing minor characters whose sole function is to provide background information in the play's opening scene. Countless drawing-room comedies have raised the curtain on a pair of servants in the midst of a gossipy conversation that catches the audience up on the doings of the family members who make up the rest of the cast.

The second part of a plot is called the **complication,** the interjection of some circumstance or event that shakes up the stable situation that has existed before the play's opening and begins the **rising action** of the play, during which the audience's tension and expectations become tightly intertwined and involved with the characters and the events they experience. Complication in a play may be both external and internal. A plague, a threatened invasion, or a conclusion of a war is a typical example of an external complication, an outside event that affects the characters' lives. However, many plays rely primarily on an internal complication, a single character's weakness in his or her personality. Often the complication is heightened by **conflict** between two characters whom events have forced into collision with each other. In Arthur Miller's *Death of a Salesman*, for example, the external complication stems from Willy's troubles with his boss, the internal complication is his growing depression and suicidal tendencies, and the chief conflict is with his son Biff. No matter how it is presented, the complication of the plot usually introduces a problem that the characters cannot avoid. The rising action, which constitutes the body of the play, usually contains a number of moments of **crisis**, when solutions crop up momentarily but quickly disappear. These critical moments in the scenes may take the form of the kinds of reversals discussed above, and the audience's emotional involvement in the plot generally hinges on the characters' rising and falling hopes.

The central moment of crisis in the play is the **climax**, or the moment of greatest tension, which initiates the **falling action** of the plot. Perhaps "moments" of greatest tension would be a more exact phrase, for skillful playwrights know how to wring as much tension as possible from the audience. In the best plots everything in earlier parts of the play has pointed to this scene—a duel, a suicide, a murder—and the play's highest pitch of emotion.

The final part of a plot is the **resolution**, or **dénouement**. This French word literally refers to the untying of a knot, the release of the tension that has built up during the play. The dénouement returns the play and its characters to a stable situation, though not the same one that existed at the beginning of the play, and gives some indication of what the future holds for them. A dénouement may be either closed or open. A **closed dénouement** ties up everything neatly and explains all unanswered questions the audience might have; an **open dénouement** leaves a few tantalizing loose ends.

Several other plot terms should also be noted. Aristotle mentions, not altogether favourably, plots with "double issues." The most common word for this is **subplot**, a less important story involving minor characters that may mirror the main plot of the play. Some plays, like Shakespeare's *A Midsummer Night's Dream*, may even have more than one subplot. Occasionally, a playwright finds it necessary to drop hints about coming events in the plot, perhaps to keep the audience from complaining that certain incidents have happened "out of the blue." This is called **foreshadowing.** If a climactic incident that helps to resolve the plot has not been adequately prepared for, the playwright may be accused of having resorted to a ***deus ex machina*** ending, which takes its name from the *mechane* that once literally lowered a god or goddess into the midst of the dramatic proceedings. An ending of this sort, like that of an old western movie in which the cavalry arrives just as the wagon train is about to be annihilated, is rarely satisfactory.

Finally the difference between **suspense** and **dramatic irony** should be addressed. Both of these devices generate tension in the audience, although through opposite means—suspense when the audience does not know what is about to happen, dramatic irony, paradoxically, when it does. Much of our pleasure in reading a new play lies in speculating about what will happen next, but in Greek tragedy the original audience would be fully familiar with the basic outlines of the mythic story before the action even began. Dramatic irony thus occurs at moments when the audience is more knowledgeable about events than the onstage characters are. In *Oedipus the King*, the audience knows who the murderer of Laïos is, and in *Othello* we are continually reminded that Iago is lying to Othello. In some plays, our foreknowledge of certain events is so strong that we may want to cry out a warning to the characters.

Characterization

The Greek word ***agon*** means "debate" and refers to the central issue or conflict of a play. From *agon* we derive two words commonly used to denote the chief characters in a play: **protagonist,** literally the "first speaker," and **antagonist,** one who speaks against him. Often the word "hero" is used as a synonym for protagonist, and it is difficult not to think of Oedipus or Othello as tragic heroes. In many modern plays it may be more appropriate to speak of the protagonist as an **anti-hero** because he or she may possess few, if any, of the traditional attributes of a hero, a point that Arthur Miller discusses in his essay "Tragedy and the Common Man." Similarly, the word "villain" may bring to mind a sinister, sneering character in a top hat and opera cloak from an old-fashioned **melodrama** (a play whose complications are solved happily at the last minute by the "triumph of good over evil") and usually has little application to the complex characters one encounters in a serious play.

Aristotle, in his discussion of characterization, stresses the complexity that marks the personages in the greatest plays. Nothing grows tiresome more quickly than a perfectly virtuous man or woman at the centre of a play, and nothing is more offensive to the audience than seeing absolute innocence despoiled. Although Aristotle stresses that a successful protagonist must be better than ordinary men and women, he also insists that the protagonist be somewhat less than perfect:

> *There remains, then, the intermediate kind of personage, a man not pre-eminently virtuous and just, whose misfortune, however, is brought upon him not by vice and depravity but by some error of judgment. . . .*

Aristotle's word for this error is **hamartia,** which is commonly translated as "tragic flaw" but might more properly be termed a "great error." Whether he means some innate flaw, like a psychological defect, or simply a great mistake is open to question, but writers of tragedies have traditionally created deeply flawed protagonists. In ordinary circumstances, the protagonist's strength of character may allow him to prosper, but under the pressure of events he may crack as one small chink in his armour widens and leaves him vulnerable. A typical flaw in tragedies is **hubris,** arrogance or excessive pride, which leads the protagonist into errors that might have been avoided if he had listened to the advice of others. Oedipus, for example, is adequately warned by Teiresias not to pursue his investigation into Laïos's death, but he is too stubborn to listen. Although he does not use the term himself, Aristotle touches here on the concept of **poetic justice,** the audience's sense that virtue and vice have been fairly dealt with in the play and that the protagonist's punishment is to some degree deserved.

We should bear in mind that the greatest burden of characterization in drama falls on the actor or actress who undertakes a role. No matter how well-written a part is, in the hands of an incompetent or inappropriate performer the character will not be credible. Vocal inflection, gesture, and even the strategic use of silence are the stock in trade of actors, for it is up to them to convince us that we are involved in the sufferings and joys of real human beings. No two actors will play the same part in the same manner. The role of Othello has been played in film versions by actors as various as Orson Welles, Laurence Olivier, Anthony Hopkins, and Laurence Fishburne. Comparing these performances provides a wonderful short course in the validity of radically different approaches to the same role. In reading, there are several points to keep in mind about main characters. Physical description, while it may be minimal at best, is worth paying close attention to. To cite one example from the plays contained in this edition, Shakespeare identifies Othello simply as a "Moor," a native of North Africa. Racialization is an important cause of conflict in the play, but through the years the part has been played with equal success by both black and white actors. The central issue in *Othello* is that the tragic hero is a cultural misfit in the Venetian society from which he takes a wife; he is a widely respected military leader but an outsider all the same. Shakespeare provides us with few other details of Othello's appearance, but we can probably assume that he is a large and powerful warrior, capable of commanding men by his mere presence. Sometimes an author will give a character a name that is an indicator of his or her personality and appearance. Oedipus's name, in Greek, refers to his scarred feet. Willy Loman, the failed protagonist of Arthur Miller's *Death of a Salesman*, bears a surname ("low man") which contains a pun on his character, a device called a **characternym.**

Character motivation is another point of characterization to ponder. Why do characters act in a certain manner? What do they hope to gain from their actions? In some cases, these motives are clear enough and may be discussed openly by the characters. In other plays, motivation is more elusive, as the playwright deliberately mystifies the audience by presenting characters who perhaps are not fully aware of the reasons for their compulsions. Modern dramatists, influenced by advances in psychology, have often refused to reduce characters' actions to simple equations of cause and effect.

Two conventions that the playwright may employ in revealing motivation are **soliloquy** and **aside.** A soliloquy is a speech made by a single character on stage alone. Hamlet's soliloquies, among them some of the most famous passages in all drama, show us the process of his mind as he toys with various plans of revenge but delays putting them into action. The aside is a brief remark (traditionally delivered to the side of a raised hand) that an actor makes directly to the audience and that the other characters on stage cannot hear. Occasionally an aside reveals a reason for a character's behaviour in a scene. Neither of these devices is as widely used in today's theatre as in earlier periods, but they remain part of the dramatist's collection of techniques.

Minor characters are also of great importance in a successful play, and several different traditional types exist. A **foil,** a minor character with whom a major character sharply contrasts, is used primarily as a sounding board for ideas, as in the way Iago banters with the foolish Roderigo in *Othello.* A **confidant,** like Nora Helmer's friend Dr. Rank in Ibsen's *A Doll's House,* is a trusted friend or servant to whom a major character speaks frankly and openly; confidants fulfill in some respects one role that the chorus plays in Greek tragedy. **Stock characters** are stereotypes that are useful for advancing the plot and fleshing out the scenes, particularly in comedies. Hundreds of plays have employed a pair of innocent young lovers, sharp-tongued servants, and/or meddling mothers-in-law as part of their casts. **Allegorical characters** in morality plays like *Everyman* are clearly labelled by their names and, for the most part, are personifications of human attributes (Beauty, Good Deeds) or of theological concepts (Confession). **Comic relief** in a tragedy may be provided by minor characters like Shakespeare's fools or clowns.

Theme

Aristotle has relatively little to say about the theme of a play, simply noting that "Thought of the personages is shown in everything to be effected by their language." Because he focuses to such a large degree on the emotional side of tragedy—its stimulation of pity and fear—he seems to give less importance to the role of drama as a serious forum for the discussion of ideas, referring his readers to another of his works, *The Art of Rhetoric,* where these matters have greater prominence. Nevertheless, **theme,** the central idea or ideas that a play discusses, is important in Greek tragedy and in the subsequent history of the theatre. The trilogies of early playwrights were thematically unified around an *aition,* a Greek word for the origin of a custom; today one might find the origin of the holiday custom of gift-giving in a Nativity play.

Some dramas are explicitly **didactic** in their intent, existing with the specific aim of instructing the audience in ethical, religious, or political areas. A **morality play,** a popular type of drama in the late

Middle Ages, is essentially a sermon on sin and redemption rendered in dramatic terms. More subtle in its didacticism is the **problem play** of the late nineteenth century, popularized by Ibsen, which uses the theatre as a forum for the serious debate of social issues like industrial pollution or women's rights. The **drama of ideas** of playwrights like George Bernard Shaw does not merely present social problems; it goes further, actually advancing programs of reform. In the United States during the Great Depression, Broadway theatres featured a great deal of **social drama,** in which radical social and political programs were openly propagandized. In the ensuing decades the theatre has remained a popular forum for debating issues of class, gender, and racialization, as the success of Tomson Highway's *The Rez Sisters*, and many other plays, will attest. Keep in mind, however, that plays are not primarily religious or political forums. If we are not entertained and moved by a play's language, action, and plot, then it is unlikely that we will respond to its message. The author who must resort to long sermons from a *raisonneur* (like Cléante, the protagonist's brother-in-law in Molière's famous comedy *Tartuffe*) who serves primarily as the voice of reason, that is, the mouthpiece for the playwright's opinions, is not likely to hold the audience's sympathy or attention for long. The best plays are complex enough that they cannot be reduced to simple "thesis statements" that sum up their meaning in a few words.

Diction

Aristotle was also the author of the first important manual of public speaking, *The Art of Rhetoric*, so it should come as no surprise that he devotes considerable attention in the *Poetics* to the precise words, either alone or in combinations, that playwrights use. Instead of "diction," we would probably speak today of a playwright's "style" or discuss his or her handling of various levels of idiom in the dialogue. Although much of what Aristotle has to say about parts of speech and the sounds of words in Greek is of little interest to us, his emphasis on clarity and originality in the choice of words remains relevant. For Aristotle, the language of tragedy should be "poetic" in the best sense, somehow elevated above the level of ordinary speech but not so ornate that it loses the power to communicate feelings and ideas to an audience. Realism in speech is largely a matter of illusion, and close inspection of the actual lines of modern dramatists like Miller reveal a discrepancy between the carefully chosen words that characters speak in plays, often making up lengthy **monologues,** and the halting, often inarticulate ("Like ya know what I mean?") manner in which we may express ourselves in everyday life. The language of the theatre has always been an artificial one. The idiom of plays, whether by William Shakespeare or by Judith Thompson, *imitates* the language of life; it does not duplicate it.

Ancient Greek is a language with a relatively small vocabulary and, even in translation, we encounter a great deal of repetition of key words. *Polis,* the Greek word for city, appears many times in Sophocles' plays, stressing the communal fate that the protagonist and the chorus, representing the citizens, share. Shakespeare's use of the full resources of the English language has been the standard against which all subsequent writers in the language have had to measure themselves. However, Shakespeare's language presents some special difficulties for the modern reader. His vocabulary is essentially the same as ours, but many words have changed in meaning or become obsolete over the last four hundred years. Shakespeare is also a master of different **levels of diction.** In the space of a few lines he can range from self-consciously flowery heights ("If after every tempest come such calms,/May the winds blow till they have waken'd death!/And let the labouring bark climb hills of seas/Olympus-high and duck again as low/As hell's to heaven!" exults Othello on being reunited with his bride in Cyprus) to the slangy level of the streets—he is a master of the off-colour joke and the sarcastic put-down. Responding to Roderigo's threat to drown himself, Iago says, "Come, be a man. Drown thyself! drown cats and blind puppies." We should remember that Shakespeare's poetic drama lavishly uses figurative language; his lines abound with similes, metaphors, personifications, and hyperboles, all characteristic devices of the language of poetry. Shakespeare's theatre had little in the way of scenery and no "special effects," so a passage from *Hamlet* like "But, look, the morn, in russet mantle clad/Walks o'er the dew of yon high eastward hill" is not merely pretty or picturesque; it has the dramatic function of helping the audience visualize the welcome end of a long, fearful night.

It is true that playwrights since the middle of the nineteenth century have striven for more fidelity to reality, more verisimilitude, in the language their characters use, but even realistic dramatists often rise to rhetorical peaks that have little relationship to the way people actually speak. Ibsen began his career as a poet and, surprisingly, the first draft of Arthur Miller's "realistic" tragedy *Death of a Salesman* was largely written in verse.

Melody

Greek tragedy was accompanied by music. None of this music survives, and we cannot be certain how it was integrated into the drama. Certainly the choral parts of the play were sung and danced, and it is likely that even the dialogue involved highly rhythmical chanting, especially in passages employing **stichomythia,** rapid alternation of single lines between two actors, a device often encountered during moments of high dramatic tension. In the original language, the different poetic rhythms used in Greek tragedy are still evident, although these are for the most part lost in English translation. At any rate, it is apparent that the skillful manipulation of a variety of **poetic metres,** combinations of line lengths and rhythms, for different types of scenes was an important part of the tragic poet's repertoire.

Both tragedies and comedies have been written in verse throughout the ages, often employing rhyme as well as rhythm. *Oedipus the King* is written in a variety of poetic metres, with some of them appropriate for dialogue between actors and others for the choral odes. Shakespeare's *Othello* is composed, like all of his plays, largely in **blank verse,** that is, unrhymed lines of iambic pentameter (lines of ten syllables, alternating unstressed and stressed syllables). He also uses rhymed pairs of lines called **couplets,** particularly for emphasis at the close of scenes; songs (there are three in *Othello*); and even prose passages, especially when dealing with comic or "low" characters. A study of Shakespeare's versification is beyond the scope of this discussion, but suffice it to say that a trained actor must be aware of the rhythmical patterns that Shakespeare utilized if he or she is to deliver the lines with anything approaching accuracy.

Of course, not only verse drama has rhythm. Judith Thompson's play *Sled* is punctuated with the singing of Annie Delaney, and whether in lyrics or dialogue, Thompson seeks to "celebrate the music of the human voice." The ancient verse heritage of tragedy lingers on in the modern theatre and has proven resistant even to the prosaic rhythms of contemporary life.

Spectacle

Spectacle (sometimes called *mise en scène,* French for "putting on stage") is the last of Aristotle's elements of tragedy and, in his view, the least important. By spectacle we mean the purely visual dimension of a play; in ancient Greece, this meant costumes, a few props, and effects carried out by the use of the mechane. Costumes in Greek tragedy were simple but impressive. The tragic mask, or *persona,* and a high-heeled boot (*cothurnus*), were apparently designed to give characters a larger-than-life appearance. Historians also speculate that the mask might have additionally served as a crude megaphone to amplify the actors' voices, a necessary feature when we consider that the open air theatre in Athens could seat over ten thousand spectators. Other elements of set decoration were kept to a minimum, although playwrights occasionally employed a few well-chosen spectacular effects like the triumphant entrance of the victorious king in Aeschylus's Agamemnon, which involves a horse-drawn chariot and brilliant red carpet on which Agamemnon walks to his death. Elizabethan drama likewise relied little on spectacular stage effects. Shakespeare's plays call for few props, and little attempt was made at historical accuracy in costumes, a noble patron's cast-off clothing dressing Caesar one week, Othello the next.

Advances in technology since Shakespeare's day have obviously facilitated more elaborate effects in what we now call **staging** than patrons of earlier centuries could have envisioned. In the nineteenth century, first gas and then electric lighting not only made effects like sunrises possible but also, through the use of different combinations of colour, added atmosphere to certain scenes. By Ibsen's day, realistic **box sets** were designed to resemble, in the smallest details, interiors of houses and apartments with an invisible "fourth wall" nearest the audience. Modern theatre has experimented in all directions with set design, from the bare stage to barely suggested walls and furnishings, from revolving stages to scenes that "break the plane" by involving the audience in the drama. Samuel Beckett is famous for the spareness of his sets, from the lone tree of *Waiting for Godot* to the "Desert. Dazzling light." of *Act Without Words I: A Mime for One Player.* Tomson Highway's *The Rez Sisters* employs music, mime, dancing, "lighting magic," and the transformation of the entire theatre into a bingo palace with Nanabush as the Bingo Master. It is fitting that Wasaychigan, the name of the fictional Reserve where the play is set, means "window" in Ojibway, as Highway uses a variety of theatrical techniques to provide us a window into the dreams and realities of life on the Rez. In today's Broadway productions, the most impressive uses of spectacle may represent anything from the catacombs beneath the Paris Opera House in *Phantom of the Opera* to ten-metre-high street barricades manned by soldiers firing muskets in *Les Misérables*. Modern technology can create virtually any sort of stage illusion; the only limitations in today's professional theatre are imagination and budget.

Before we leave our preliminary discussion, one further element should be mentioned—**setting.** Particular locales—Thebes, Corinth, and Mycenæ—are the sites of different tragedies, and each city has its own history; in the case of Thebes, this history involves a family curse that touches the members of three generations. But for the most part specific locales in the greatest plays are less important than the universal currents that are touched. If we are interested in the particular features of middle-class marriage in Oslo in the late nineteenth century, we would perhaps do better going to sociology texts than to Ibsen's *A Doll's House*. Still, every play implies a larger sense of setting, a sense of history that is called the **enveloping action.** Life on the prairies may not be as desperate as it was during the Depression years, the context for Gwen Pharis Ringwood's *Still Stands the House*, and yet farmers continue to face similar struggles. Even though a play from the past may still speak eloquently today, it also provides a time capsule whose contents tell us how people lived and what they most valued during the period when the play was written and first performed.

Brief History and Description of Dramatic Conventions

Greek Tragedy

By the time of Sophocles, tragedy had evolved into an art form with a complex set of conventions. Each playwright would submit a **tetralogy,** or set of four plays, to the yearly competition. The first three plays, or **trilogy,** would be tragedies, perhaps unified like those of Aeschylus's *Oresteia*, which deals with Agamemnon's tragic homecoming from the Trojan War. The fourth, called a **satyr-play,** was comic, with a chorus of goat-men engaging in bawdy revels that, oddly, mocked the serious content of the preceding tragedies. Only one complete trilogy, the *Oresteia* by Aeschylus, and one satyr-play, *The Cyclops* by Euripides, have survived. Three plays by Sophocles on the myths surrounding Oedipus and his family—*Oedipus the King, Oedipus at Colonus,* and *Antigone*—are still performed and read, but they were written at separate times and accompanied by other tragedies that are now lost. As tragedy developed in this period, it seems clear that playwrights thought increasingly of individual plays as complete in themselves; *Oedipus the King* does not leave the audience with the feeling that there is more to be told, even though Oedipus is still alive at the end of the play.

Each tragedy was composed according to a prescribed formula, as ritualized as the order of worship in a contemporary church service. The tragedy begins with a **prologue** (*prologos*), "that which is said first." The prologue is an introductory scene that tells the audience important information about the play's setting, characters, and events immediately preceding the opening of the drama. The second part of the tragedy is called the *parodos,* the first appearance of the chorus in the play. As the members of the chorus enter the orchestra, they dance and sing more generally of the situation in which the city finds itself. Choral parts in some translations are divided into sections called **strophes** and **antistrophes,** indicating choral movements to left and right, respectively. The body of the play is made up of two types of alternating scenes. The first, an episode (*episodos*) is a passage of dialogue between two or more actors or between actors and the chorus. Each of these "acts" of the tragedy is separated from the rest by a choral **ode** (*stasimon;* pl. *stasima*) during which the chorus is alone on the orchestra, commenting, as the voice of public opinion, about the course of action being taken by the main characters. Typically there are four pairs of episodes and odes in the play. The final scene of the play is called the *exodos*. During this part, the climax occurs out of sight of the audience, and a vivid description of this usually violent scene is sometimes given by a messenger or other witness. After the messenger's speech, the protagonist reappears and the resolution of his fate is determined. In some plays, a wheeled platform called an *eccyclema* was used to move this fatal tableau into the view of the spectators. A tragedy concludes with the exit of the main characters, sometimes leaving the chorus to deliver a brief speech, or **epilogue,** a final summing up of the play's meaning.

Although we may at first find such complicated rituals bizarre, we should keep in mind that dramatic conventions are primarily customary and artificial and have little to do with "reality" as we usually experience it. The role of the chorus (set by the time of Sophocles at fifteen members) may seem puzzling to modern readers, but in many ways the conventions of Greek tragedy are no stranger than those of contemporary musical comedy like *Grease*, in which a pair of teenage lovers burst into a duet and dance, soon to be joined by a host of other cast members. What is most remarkable about the history of drama is not how much these conventions have changed but how remarkably similar they have remained for over twenty-five centuries.

Medieval Drama

Drama flourished during Greek and Roman times, but after the fall of the Roman Empire (A.D. 476) it went into four centuries of eclipse, kept alive throughout Europe only by wandering troupes of actors performing various types of **folk drama.** The "Punch and Judy" puppet show, still popular in parts of Europe, is a late survivor of this tradition, as are the ancient slapstick routines of circus clowns. Even though drama was officially discouraged by the Church for a long period, when it did re-emerge it was as an outgrowth of the Roman Catholic mass, in the form of **liturgical drama.** Around the ninth century, short passages of sung dialogue between the priest and choir, called **tropes,** were added on special holidays to commemorate the event. These tropes grew more elaborate over the years until full-fledged religious pageants were being performed in front of the altar. In 1210, Pope Innocent III, wishing to restore the dignity of the services, banned such performances from the interior of the church. Moving them outside, first to the church porch and later entirely off church property, provided greater opportunity for inventiveness in action and staging.

In the fourteenth and fifteenth centuries, much of the work of putting on plays passed to the guilds, organizations of skilled craftsmen, and their productions became part of city-wide festivals in many Continental and British cities. Several types of plays evolved. **Mystery plays** were derived from holy scripture. **Passion plays** (some of which survive unchanged today) focused on the crucifixion of Christ. **Miracle plays** dramatized the lives of the saints. The last and most complex, **morality plays,** were dramatized sermons with allegorical characters

(Everyman, Death, Good Deeds) representing various generalized aspects of human life.

Elizabethan Drama

Although the older morality plays were still performed throughout the sixteenth century, during the time of Queen Elizabeth I (b. 1533, reigned 1558–1603) a new type of drama, typical in many ways of other innovative types of literature developed in the Renaissance, began to be produced professionally by companies of actors not affiliated with any religious institutions. This **secular drama,** beginning in short pieces called **interludes,** which may have been designed for entertainment during banquets or other public celebrations, eventually evolved into full-length tragedies and comedies designed for performance in large outdoor theatres like Shakespeare's famous Globe.

A full history of this fertile period would take many pages, but a few of its dramatic conventions are worth noting. We have already mentioned blank verse, the poetic line perfected by Shakespeare's contemporary Christopher Marlowe (1564–1593). Shakespeare wrote tragedies, comedies, and historical dramas with equal success, all characterized by passages that remain the greatest examples of poetic expression in English.

The raised platform stage in an Elizabethan theatre used little or no scenery, but relied on the author's descriptive talents to set the scene and indicate lighting and weather. The stage itself had two supporting columns, which might be used to represent trees or hiding places; a raised area at the rear, which could represent a balcony or upper story of a house; a small curtained alcove at its base; and a trap door, which could serve as a grave or hiding place. In contrast to the relatively bare stage, costumes were elaborate and acting was highly stylized, with the blank verse lines delivered at high volume and with broad gestures. Female roles were played by young boys, and the same actor might play several different minor roles in the same play.

A few more brief words about Shakespeare's plays may be in order. First, drama in Shakespeare's time was intended for performance, with publication being of only secondary importance. The texts of many of Shakespeare's plays were published in cheap editions called **quartos,** which are full of misprints and often contain widely different versions of the same play. Any play by Shakespeare contains words and passages that different editors have trouble agreeing on. Second, originality, in the sense we prize it, meant little to a playwright in a time before copyright laws; virtually every one of Shakespeare's plays is derived from an earlier source—Greek myth, history, another play or, in the case of *Othello*, an Italian short story of questionable literary merit. The true test of Shakespeare's genius rests in his ability to transform these raw materials into art. Finally, we should keep in mind that Shakespeare's plays were designed to appeal to a wide audience— educated aristocrats and slovenly "groundlings" filled the theatre—and this fact may account for the great diversity of tones and levels of language in the plays. Purists of later eras might have been dismayed by some of Shakespeare's wheezy clowns and bad puns, but for us the mixture of "high" and "low" elements gives his plays their remarkable texture.

The Comic Genres

Shakespeare's ability to move easily between "high" and "low," between tragic and comic, should be a reminder that comedy has developed along lines parallel to tragedy and never wholly separate from it. Most of Aristotle's remarks on comedy are lost, but he does make the observation that comedy differs from tragedy in that comedy depicts men and women as worse than they are, whereas tragedy generally stresses their best qualities. During the great age of Greek tragedy, comedies were regularly performed at Athenian festivals. The greatest of the early comic playwrights was Aristophanes (c. 450–380 B.C.). The plays of Aristophanes are classified as **Old Comedy** and shared many of the same structural elements as tragedy, with scenes alternating with choral parts. Old Comedy was always satirical and usually obscene; in *Lysistrata*, written during the devastating Athenian wars with Sparta, the men of both sides are brought to their knees by the women of the two cities, who engage in a sex strike until the men relent. **New Comedy,** which evolved in the century after Aristophanes, tended to observe more traditional moral values and stressed romance. The New Comedy of Greece greatly influenced the writings of Roman playwrights like Plautus (254–184 B.C.) and Terence (190–59 B.C.). Plautus's *Miles Gloriosus* still finds favour in its modern musical adaptation, *A Funny Thing Happened on the Way to the Forum.*

Like other forms of drama, comedy virtually vanished during the early Middle Ages. Its spirit was kept alive primarily by roving companies of actors who staged improvisational dramas in the squares of towns throughout Europe. The popularity of these plays is evidenced by certain elements in the religious dramas of the same period: the *Second Shepherd's Play* (c. 1450) involves a sheep-rustler with three shepherds in an uproarious parody of the Nativity that still evokes laughter today. Even a serious play such as *Everyman* contains satirical elements in the complicated excuses that Goods and other characters contrive for not accompanying the protagonist on his journey with Death.

On the Continent, a highly stylized form of improvisational drama appeared in sixteenth century Italy, apparently an evolution from earlier types of folk drama. ***Commedia dell'arte*** involved a cast of masked stock characters (the miserly old man, the young wife, the ardent seducer) in situations involving mistaken identity and cuckoldry. Because it was an improvisational form, *commedia dell'arte* does not survive in written texts, but its popularity influenced the direction that comedy would take in the next century. The great French comic playwright Molière (1622–1673) incorporated many of its elements into his own plays, which combine elements of **farce,** a type of comedy that hinges on broadly drawn characters and embarrassing situations usually involving sexual misconduct, with serious social satire. Comedy such as Molière's, which exposes the hypocrisy and pretensions of people in social situations, is called **comedy of manners;** as Molière put it, the main purpose of his plays was "the correction of mankind's vices."

Other types of comedy have also been popular in different eras. Shakespeare's comedies begin with the farcical complications of *The Comedy of Errors*, progress through romantic **pastoral** comedies, such as *As You Like It*, which present an idealized view of rural life, and end with the philosophical comedies of his final period, of which *The Tempest* is the greatest example. His contemporary Ben Jonson (1572–1637) favoured a type known as **comedy of humours,** a type of comedy of manners in which the conduct of the characters is determined by their underlying dominant trait (the four humours were thought to be bodily fluids whose proportions determined personality). English plays of the late seventeenth and early eighteenth centuries tended to combine the hard-edged satire of comedy of manners with varying amounts of sentimental romance. A play of this type, usually hinging on matters of inheritance and marriage, is known as a **drawing-room comedy,** and its popularity, while peaking in the mid-nineteenth century, endures today.

Modern comedy in English can be said to begin with Oscar Wilde (1854–1900) and George Bernard Shaw (1856–1950). Wilde's brilliant wit and skillful incorporation of paradoxical **epigrams,** witty sayings that have made him one of the most quoted authors of the nineteenth century, have rarely been equalled. Shaw, who began his career as a drama critic, admired both Wilde and Ibsen, and succeeded in combining the best elements of the comedy of manners and the problem play in his works. *Major Barbara* (1905), a typical **comedy of ideas,** frames serious discussion of war, religion, and poverty with a search for an heir to a millionaire's fortune and a suitable husband for one of his daughters. One striking development of comedy in recent times lies in its deliberate harshness. So-called **black humour,** an extreme type of satire in which barriers of taste are assaulted and pain seems the constant companion of laughter, has characterized much of the work of playwrights like Samuel Beckett (1906–1989), Eugene Ionesco (1909–1994), and Edward Albee (b. 1928).

Realistic Drama, the Modern Stage, and Beyond

Realism is a term that is loosely employed as a synonym for "true to life," but in literary history it denotes a style of writing that developed in the mid-nineteenth century, first in the novels of such masters as Charles Dickens, Gustave Flaubert, and Count Lev Nikolaevich Tolstoy, and later in the dramas of Ibsen and Chekhov. Many of the aspects of dramatic realism have to do with staging and acting. The box set, with its invisible "fourth wall" facing the audience, could, with the added subtleties of artificial lighting, successfully mimic the interior of a typical middle-class home. Realistic prose drama dropped devices like the soliloquy in favour of more natural means of acting, such as those championed by Konstantin Stanislavsky (1863–1938). This Russian director worked closely with Anton Chekhov (1860–1904) to perfect a method whereby actors learned to identify with their characters' psychological problems from "inside out." This "method" acting often tries, as is the case in Chekhov's plays and, later, those of Arthur Miller, to develop a play's **subtext,** the crucial issue in the play that no one can bear to address directly. Stanislavsky's theories have influenced several generations of actors and have become standard throughout the world of the theatre. Ibsen's plays, which in fact ushered in the modern era of the theatre, are often called **problem plays** because they deal with serious, even controversial or taboo, issues in society. Shaw said that Ibsen's great originality as a playwright lay in his ability to shock the members of the audience into thinking about their own lives. As the barriers of censorship have fallen over the years, the capacity of the theatre to shock has perhaps been diminished, but writers still find it a forum admirably suited for debating the controversial issues that divide society.

World drama in this century has gone far beyond realism to experiment with the dreamlike atmosphere of **expressionism** (which, like the invisible walls in Miller's *Death of a Salesman*, employs distorted sets to mirror the troubled, perhaps even unbalanced, psyches of the play's characters) or **theatre of the absurd,** which depicts a world without meaning in which everything seems ridiculous. Nevertheless, realism is still the dominant style of today's theatre, even if our definition of it has to be modified to take into account plays as diverse as *Death of a Salesman* and *Sled*.

Film Versions: A Note

Nothing can equal the experience of an actual stage production, but the many fine film versions of the plays in this anthology offer instructors and students the opportunity, in some cases, to explore two or three different cinematic approaches to the same material. I regularly teach a course in drama and film, and I have found that the differences between print and film versions of plays offer students many challenging topics for discussion, analysis, and writing. Of course, the two media differ radically; in some cases noted below, the film versions, especially those from past decades, badly compromise the original plays. To cite one notorious instance regarding a play not in this anthology, Elia Kazan's celebrated film of Tennessee Williams's *A Streetcar Named Desire*, so wonderful in its sets, direction, and the performances of Marlon Brando and Vivien Leigh, tampers with the play's ending (on orders from the Hollywood Production Code office) to give the impression that Stella will take her child and leave Stanley. Williams himself wrote the screenplay, and he was aware of, if not exactly happy with, the moral standards of the times.

The late O. B. Hardison, director of the Folger Shakespeare Library, once observed two important differences between plays and films. The first is that attending a play is a social function; the audience members and the performers are aware of one another's presence, and laughter in the wrong place can signal the beginning of a disaster. But film is largely a private experience; it was with good reason that one film critic titled a collection of her reviews *A Year in the Dark*. The other chief difference, Hardison notes, is that drama is a realistic medium, whereas film is surrealistic. Watching a play, we see real persons who have a physical reality, and we see them from a uniform perspective. But film has conditioned us to its own complex vocabulary of close-ups, jump cuts, and panoramas, and we view the action from a variety of perspectives. These differences, as fundamental as they seem, are rarely noted by students (unless they have taken a film course) until they are pointed out. Still, film versions provide us with a wonderful time capsule in which many treasures of drama's past have been preserved. A reasoned list of some of these, most of them available on video or DVD, follows.

Oedipus the King

Tyrone Guthrie's 1957 version, *Oedipus Rex*, is a filmed record of his famous Stratford, Ontario, production and retains the masks and choral movements of ancient Greek tragedy. Guthrie uses the William Butler Yeats translation, which sacrifices literal fidelity to poetic grandeur. Douglas Campbell and Eleanor Stuart are impressive as Oedipus and Iocastê, and the messenger is played by Douglas Rain, the voice of the HAL computer in *2001: A Space Odyssey*. The youthful William Shatner, hidden behind a mask, is a member of the chorus. Philip Savile's 1968 version, starring Christopher Plummer, is also worthwhile; this version opens up the play with scenes beautifully photographed in ancient settings. Orson Welles's performance as Teiresias is particularly striking, though some may protest at actually having to watch Oedipus blind himself while listening to the messenger's voiceover narration.

The Tragedy of Othello, the Moor of Venice

Othello has proved one of Shakespeare's most popular plays on film. Orson Welles's 1952 version, thought lost for many years, was lovingly restored by his daughter Rebecca Welles and features a re-mastered soundtrack that remedies most of the original complaints about the poor quality of sound in the film. A fascinating film-noir study in Shakespeare, it features a bravura performance by Welles and an affecting one by Suzanne Cloutier as Desdemona. Less successful is Laurence Olivier's 1966 version, essentially a filmed version of his acclaimed Royal Shakespeare Company production. Olivier's controversial performance, which mimics West Indian speech patterns, and that of Maggie Smith as Desdemona are worth seeing, but Olivier's stage makeup, unconvincing in film close-ups, and minimal production values mar the effort. The 1980 version, starring Anthony Hopkins as Othello and Bob Hoskins as Iago, features interesting performances from the principals, despite Hopkins's distracting hairpiece. This uncut version was part of the PBS Shakespeare series and is widely available in libraries. The 1995 film, directed by Oliver Parker, has excellent performances by Laurence Fishburne and Kenneth Branagh and a sumptuous, erotic style. Contemporary students will probably find it the most satisfying of the four. The high school basketball drama "O," directed by Tim Blake Nelson and released in 2001, is based on Othello.

A Doll's House

For some inexplicable reason *A Doll's House* was made into two films in the same year, 1973. Patrick Garland's version stars Clair Bloom as Nora and Anthony Hopkins as Torvald. Sir Ralph Richardson essays the role of Dr. Rank, and the reliable Denholm Elliott plays Krogstad. Joseph Losey's version features Jane Fonda as an energetic (and very young) Nora, David Warner as Torvald, and Trevor Howard as Dr. Rank. Most critics felt that the Losey version, which includes actual scenes that Ibsen only hints at, tried too obviously to make the play relevant to contemporary audiences. The 1993 Iranian film *Sara*, directed by Dariush Mehrjui and starring Niki Karimi, is an award-winning adaptation of Ibsen's play.

Death of a Salesman

Miller was not pleased with the 1951 film, in which Fredric March overacted badly as Willy Loman. Still, Mildred Dunnock, Kevin McCarthy, and Cameron Mitchell provided excellent support. Volker

Schlöndorff's 1985 version has been widely acclaimed, though some viewers have found Dustin Hoffman ill-suited to the role that Miller wrote with the large-boned Lee J. Cobb in mind. John Malkovich and Kate Reid are very good, and Schlöndorff's impressionistic set designs and seamless handling of flashbacks are very impressive. A videotape of the final performance of the award-winning 1999 Broadway revival, starring Brian Dennehy and Elizabeth Franz, aired on Showtime in 2000. Dennehy brought a magnitude to the role of Willy Loman that many critics found impressive.

Act Without Words I: A Mime for One Player

This short piece was made into an animated film by Pyramid Film Productions in 1970 and was performed on film by Barry Smith's Theatre of Puppets in 1982. More recently, *Act Without Words I* was filmed as part of the ambitious Beckett on Film project, in which all nineteen plays have been filmed by noted directors and actors. More about this project, including interviews with the participants, can be found at **www.beckettonfilm.com**. *Act Without Words I* was directed by Karl Reisz, director of such films as *The French Lieutenant's Woman* (1980) and *Sweet Dreams* (1990), and stars Sean Foley, a trained clown, who co-founded the comedy act Right Size. Of the twenty-minute film that features action and music, Reisz said, "As always with Beckett, in the agony there is pity, understanding and humanity. By using repetition, Beckett was trying to make sense of his own experience of the world."

The Rez Sisters

Excerpts from the play that formed part of a cabaret performance were included in the documentary *Thank You for the Love You Gave: The Life & Times of Tomson Highway*, which first aired on CBC television in 1997.

Writing About Drama

Writing assignments vary widely and your teacher's instructions may range from general ("Discuss any two scenes in the plays we have read") to very specific ("Write an explication, in not less than 1000 words, on Shakespeare's use of imagery and figurative language in Othello's speech to the Venetian Senate in which he describes his courtship of Desdemona"). Such processes as choosing, limiting, and developing a topic; "brainstorming" by taking notes on random ideas and refining those ideas further through group discussion or conferences with your instructor; using the library and the Internet to locate supporting secondary sources; and revising a first draft in light of critical remarks are undoubtedly techniques you have practised in other composition classes. Basic types of organizational schemes learned in "theme-writing" courses can also be applied to writing about drama. Formal assignments of these types should avoid contractions and jargon, and should be written in a clear, straightforward style. Most literary essays are not of the personal experience type, and you should follow common sense in avoiding the first person and slang. It goes without saying that you should carefully proofread your rough and final drafts to eliminate errors in spelling, punctuation, usage, and grammar.

Typical writing assignments on plays fall into four main categories: review, explication or close reading, analysis, and comparison-contrast. A review, an evaluation of an actual performance of a play, will focus less on the play itself, particularly if it is a well-known one, than on the actors' performances, the overall direction of the production, and the elements of staging. Because a review is primarily a news story, basic information about the time and place of production should be given at the beginning of the review. A short summary of the play's plot may follow, with perhaps some remarks on its stage history, and subsequent paragraphs will evaluate the performers and the production. Remember that a review is both a *report* and a *recommendation,* either positive or negative, to readers. You should strive for accuracy in such matters as spelling the actors' names correctly, and you should also try to be fair in pointing out the strong and weak points of the production. It is essential to support any general statements about the play's successes or shortcomings with specific references to the production, so it is a good idea to take notes during the performance. Because film versions of most of the plays in this book, sometimes in several different versions, are available on videotape or DVD, you might also be asked to review one of these films, paying attention perhaps to the innovative way in which a director like Orson Welles or Volker Schlöndorff has "opened up" the action of a play by utilizing the more complex technical resources of motion pictures. Reference sources providing examples of professional drama and film reviews are *The New York Times Theater Reviews, The New York Times Film Reviews, The Canadian Theatre Review,* and *Theatre Research in Canada.* Of course, *The New York Times, The Globe and Mail,* and other big-city newspapers may be searched online for reviews of recent productions. Popular magazines containing drama reviews include *Time, The New Yorker, Maclean's,* and others. Numerous reviews and Web sites for recent productions can also be found on the Internet.

An explication assignment, on the other hand, requires that you pay close attention to selected passages, giving a detailed account of all the nuances of a speech from a play you have read. Because Shakespeare's poetry is often full of figurative language that may not be fully understood until it has been subjected to an "unfolding" (the literal meaning of explication), individual sections of *Othello*—speeches, scenes, soliloquies—would be likely choices for writing assignments. For example, you might be asked to compare the four different accounts of Othello's courtship of Desdemona—first by Iago and Roderigo, next by her father, Brabantio, then by Othello and Desdemona themselves— that we hear in the first act of the play. Other passages that might yield more meaning under close reading include Iago's various explanations for his hatred of Othello or the several different references in the play to reputation and "good name."

Analysis assignments typically turn on definition and illustration, focusing on only one of the main elements of the play, such as plot or characterization. You might be required to explain Aristotle's statements about peripety and then apply his terminology to a twentieth-century play like *Death of a Salesman*. Here you would attempt to locate relevant passages from the play to support Aristotle's contentions about the importance of these reversals in the best plots. Or you might be asked to provide a summary of his comments about the tragic hero and then apply this definition to a character like Willy Loman. In doing so, you might use other supporting materials such as Arthur Miller's essay "Tragedy and the Common Man," in which the author discusses the modern notion that the tragic hero need not be drawn from the upper strata of society.

Comparison-contrast assignments are also popular. You might be assigned to compare two or more characters in a single play (Willy Loman's sons, Biff and Happy, for example, or male and female attitudes expressed by Annie Delaney and her husband, Jack, in Judith Thompson's *Sled*), or to contrast characters in two different plays (Oedipus and Othello as undeserving victims of fate, perhaps, or Willy Loman and Gwen Pharis Ringwood's Hester Warren as protagonists embittered by failed dreams). Comparison-contrast assignments require careful planning, and it is essential to find both significant similarities and differences to support your thesis. Obviously, a proposed topic about two characters who have almost nothing in common would have little discernable purpose.

Supporting your statements about a play is necessary, either by quoting directly from the play or, if required, by using outside sources for additional critical opinion. You may be required to use secondary sources from the library or Internet in writing your paper. A subject search through your library's books is a good starting place, especially for older playwrights who have attracted extensive critical attention. Reference books like *Twentieth Century Authors*, *Contemporary Authors*, and the *Dictionary of Literary Biography* provide compact overviews of playwrights' careers. *Contemporary Literary Criticism*, *Critical Survey of Drama*, and *Drama Criticism* contain both original evaluations and excerpts from critical pieces on published works, and the *MLA Index* will direct you to articles on drama in scholarly journals. We have already mentioned the reference books from *The New York*

Times as an excellent source of drama reviews. One scholarly journal that focuses on individual passages from literary works, the *Explicator*, is also worth inspecting. In recent years, the Internet has facilitated the chores of research, and many online databases, reference works, and periodicals may be quickly located using search engines like Google (**www.google.com**). The Internet also holds a wealth of information, ranging from corporate Web sites promoting play productions to sites on individual authors, many of which are run by universities or organizations. Navigating the Internet can be a forbidding task, and a book like Lester Faigley's *The Longman Guide to the Web* is an invaluable traveller's companion. Students should be aware, however, that Web sites vary widely in quality. Some are legitimate academic sources displaying sound scholarship; others are little more than "fan pages" that may contain erroneous or misleading information.

Careful documentation of your sources is essential; if you use any material other than what is termed "common knowledge," you must cite it in your paper. Common knowledge includes biographical information; an author's publications, prizes, and awards received; and other information that can be found in more than one reference book. Anything else—direct quotes or material you have put in your own words by paraphrasing—requires both a parenthetical citation in the body of your paper and an entry on your works cited pages. Doing less than this is to commit an act of plagiarism, for which the penalties are usually severe. Internet materials, which are so easily cut and pasted into a manuscript, provide an easy temptation but are immediately noticeable. Nothing is easier to spot in a paper than an uncited "lift" from a source; in most cases the vocabulary and sentence structure will be radically different from the rest of the paper.

The current edition of the *MLA Handbook for Writers of Research Papers*, which is available in the reference section of almost any library and which, if you plan to write papers for other English or drama courses, is a good addition to your personal library, contains formats for bibliographies and manuscript form that most instructors consider standard; indeed, most of the handbooks of grammar and usage commonly used in university courses follow MLA style and may be sufficient for your needs. If you have doubts, ask your instructor about what format is preferred. The type of parenthetical citation used today is simple to learn and dispenses with such time-consuming and repetitive chores as footnotes and endnotes. In using parenthetical citations remember that your goal is to direct your reader from the quoted passage in the paper to its source in your bibliography and from there, if necessary, to the book or periodical from which the quote is taken. A good parenthetical citation gives only the *minimal* information needed to accomplish this. Here are a few examples from student papers on *Othello*:

> In a disarming display of modesty before the
> Venetian senators, Othello readily admits that his
> military background has not prepared him to act as an
> eloquent spokesman in his own defence: "[...] little of
> this great world can I speak / More than pertains to feats
> of broils and battle; / And therefore little shall I grace
> my cause / In speaking for myself" (1.3.86-89).

Quotations from Shakespeare's plays are cited by act, scene, and line numbers instead of by page numbers. Note that short quotes from poetic dramas require that line breaks be indicated by the virgule (/) or slash; quotes longer than five lines should be indented ten spaces and formatted to duplicate the line breaks of the original. Here, the reader knows that Shakespeare is the author, so the citation will simply direct him or her to anthology or the collected or single edition of Shakespeare listed in the works cited section at the end of the paper:

> Shakespeare, William. <u>Complete Works of Shakespeare</u>. Ed.
>   Hardin Craig. New York: Scott, 1961.
> Shakespeare, William. <u>Othello</u>. Ed. David Bevington. New
>   York: Bantam, 1988.
> Shakespeare, William. <u>The Tragedy of Othello, the Moor of
>   Venice. Literature: An Introduction to Fiction,
>   Poetry, and Drama</u>. 7th ed. Eds. X. J. Kennedy and
>   Dana Gioia. New York: Longman, 1999. 1303-1400.

If, on the other hand, you are quoting from a prose drama, you would probably indicate a page number.

> In <u>A Doll's House</u>, Ibsen wants to demonstrate
> immediately that Nora and Helmer share almost childlike

attitudes towards each other. "Is that my little lark
twittering out there?" is Helmer's initial line in the
play (43).

The citation directs the reader to the works cited entry:

Ibsen, Henrik. <u>Four Major Plays</u>. Trans. Rolf Fjelde.
New York: Signet, 1965.

Similarly, quotes from secondary critical sources should follow the same
rules of common sense.

One critic, providing a classic estimate of
Shakespeare's skill in conceiving Othello's antagonist,
notes, "Evil has nowhere else been portrayed with such
mastery as in the character of Iago" (Bradley 173).

In this case, the critic is not named in the paper, so his name must be
included in the parenthetical citation. The reader knows where to look
in the works cited:

Bradley, A. C. <u>Shakespearean Tragedy</u>. New York: Fawcett,
1967.

If the writer provides the critic's name ("A. C. Bradley, providing a
classic estimate . . ."), then the parentheses should contain only the
page number.

Of course, different types of sources—reference book entries, articles
in periodicals, newspaper reviews of plays—require different
bibliographical information, so be sure to check the *MLA Handbook* if
you have questions. Here are a few more of the most commonly used
formats:

An Edited Collection of Essays

Kolin, Philip C., ed. Othello: <u>New Critical Essays</u>. New
York: Routledge, 2002.

A CASEBOOK

Murphy, Brenda and Susan C. W. Abbotson. <u>Understanding Death of a Salesman: A Student Casebook to Issues, Sources, and Historical Documents</u>. Westport, CT: Greenwood, 1999.

PLAY REPRINTED IN AN ANTHOLOGY OR TEXTBOOK

Ringwood, Gwen Pharis. Still <u>Stands the House</u>. <u>Encounter: Canadian Drama in Four Media</u>. Ed. Eugene Benson. Toronto: Methuen, 1973. 30-53.

ARTICLE IN A REFERENCE BOOK

"Judith Thompson." <u>Encyclopedia of Literature in Canada</u>. Ed. W. H. New. Toronto: U of Toronto P, 2002. 1111-13.

ARTICLE IN A SCHOLARLY JOURNAL

Perkins, Lina. "Remembering the Trickster in Tomson Highway's <u>The Rez Sisters</u>." <u>Modern Drama</u>. 45.2 (2002): 259-69.

REVIEW IN A NEWSPAPER

St. Germain, Pat. "Bingo Play <u>Rez Sisters</u> Is a Winner." <u>Winnipeg Sun</u>, p. 17. 9 March 2003.

ONLINE ARTICLE OR REVIEW

Anthony, Geraldine. "Gwen Pharis Ringwood: Biocritical Essay." <http://www.ucalgary.ca/library/SpecColl/ringbioc.htm>.

ONLINE AUTHOR WEB SITE

The Samuel Beckett Endpage. <http://beckett.english.ucsb.edu/>.

ONLINE REFERENCE WORK

"Sophocles." Encyclopædia Britannica Online. 10 July 2003. <http://search.eb.com/eb/article?eu=118260>.

Drama

Sophocles (496?–406 B.C.) *lived in Athens in the age of Pericles, during the city's greatest period of culture, power, and influence. Sophocles distinguished himself as an athlete, a musician, a military adviser, a politician and, most important, a dramatist. At sixteen, he was chosen to lead a chorus in reciting a poem on the Greek naval victory over the Persians at Salamis, and he won his first prizes as a playwright before he was thirty. Although both Aeschylus, his senior, and Euripides, his younger rival, have their champions, Sophocles, whose career spanned so long a period that he competed against both of them, is generally considered to be the most important Greek writer of tragedies; his thirty victories in the City Dionysia surpass the combined totals of his two great colleagues. Of his 123 plays, only seven survive intact, including two other plays relating to Oedipus and his children,* Antigone *and* Oedipus at Colonus, *which was produced after Sophocles' death by his grandson. He is generally credited with expanding the technical possibilities of drama by introducing a third actor in certain scenes (Aeschylus used only two) and by both reducing the number of lines given to the chorus and increasing its integration into his plays. Sophocles was intimately involved in both civic and military affairs, twice serving as a chief adviser to Pericles, and his sense of duty to the* polis *(Greek for city) is apparent in many of his plays.* Oedipus the King *was first performed in Athens in about 430 B.C. Its importance can be judged by the many references that Aristotle makes to it in his discussion of tragedy in the* Poetics.

Sophocles

Oedipus the King

CHARACTERS °

Oedipus
A Priest
Creon
Teiresias
Iocastê
Messenger
Shepherd of Laïos
Second Messenger
Chorus of Theban Elders

Characters: Some of the characters' names are usually Anglicized: Jocasta, Laius. This translation uses spelling that reflects the original Greek.

Translated by Dudley Fitts and Robert Fitzgerald

Scene: *Before the palace of Oedipus, King of Thebes. A central door and two lateral doors open onto a platform which runs the length of the façade. On the platform, right and left, are altars; and three steps lead down into the "orchestra," or chorus-ground. At the beginning of the action these steps are crowded by suppliants° who have brought branches and chaplets of olive leaves and who lie in various attitudes of despair. Oedipus enters.*

PROLOGUE°

OEDIPUS: My children, generations of the living
In the line of Kadmos,° nursed at his ancient hearth:
Why have you strewn yourself before these altars
In supplication, with your boughs and garlands?
The breath of incense rises from the city   *5*
With a sound of prayer and lamentation.
                                                    Children,
I would not have you speak through messengers,
And therefore I have come myself to hear you—
I, Oedipus, who bear the famous name.
(*To a Priest.*) You, there, since you are eldest in the company,   *10*
Speak for them all, tell me what preys upon you,
Whether you come in dread, or crave some blessing:
Tell me, and never doubt that I will help you
In every way I can; I should be heartless
Were I not moved to find you suppliant here.   *15*
PRIEST: Great Oedipus, O powerful King of Thebes!
You see how all the ages of our people
Cling to your altar steps: here are boys
Who can barely stand alone, and here are priests
By weight of age, as I am a priest of God,   *20*
And young men chosen from those yet unmarried;
As for the others, all that multitude,

---

suppliants persons who come to ask a favour.   **Prologue** first part of a tragedy, containing the exposition.   **2 line of Kadmos** Thebes had been founded by Cadmus.

They wait with olive chaplets in the squares,
At the two shrines of Pallas,° and where Apollo°
Speaks in the glowing embers.
Your own eyes   25
Must tell you: Thebes is tossed on a murdering sea
And can not lift her head from the death surge.
A rust consumes the buds and fruits of the earth;
The herds are sick; children die unborn,
And labor is vain. The god of plague and pyre   30
Raids like detestable lightning through the city,
And all the house of Kadmos is laid waste,
All emptied, and all darkened: Death alone
Battens upon the misery of Thebes.
You are not one of the immortal gods, we know;   35
Yet we have come to you to make our prayer
As to the man surest in mortal ways
And wisest in the ways of God. You saved us
From the Sphinx, that flinty singer, and the tribute
We paid to her so long; yet you were never   40
Better informed than we, nor could we teach you:
It was some god breathed in you to set us free.
Therefore, O mighty King, we turn to you:
Find us our safety, find us a remedy,
Whether by counsel of the gods or men.   45
A king of wisdom tested in the past
Can act in a time of troubles, and act well.
Noblest of men, restore
Life to your city! Think how all men call you
Liberator for your triumph long ago;   50
Ah, when your years of kingship are remembered,
Let them not say *We rose, but later fell*—
Keep the State from going down in the storm!
Once, years ago, with happy augury,
You brought us fortune; be the same again!   55

---

24 Pallas Athena, goddess of wisdom.   **Apollo** here the god of prophecy. At his shrine at Delphi, the future could be divined.

No man questions your power to rule the land:
But rule over men, not over a dead city!
Ships are only hulls, citadels are nothing,
When no life moves in the empty passageways.

OEDIPUS: Poor children! You may be sure I know   60
All that you longed for in your coming here.
I know that you are deathly sick; and yet,
Sick as you are, not one is as sick as I.
Each of you suffers in himself alone
His anguish, not another's; but my spirit   65
Groans for the city, for myself, for you.
I was not sleeping, you are not waking me.
No, I have been in tears for a long while
And in my restless thought walked many ways.
In all my search, I found one helpful course,   70
And that I have taken: I have sent Creon,
Son of Menoikeus, brother of the Queen,
To Delphi, Apollo's place of revelation,
To learn there, if he can,
What act or pledge of mine may save the city.   75
I have counted the days, and now, this very day,
I am troubled, for he has overstayed his time.
What is he doing? He has been gone too long.
Yet whenever he comes back, I should do ill
To scant whatever duty God reveals.   80

PRIEST: It is a timely promise. At this instant
They tell me Creon is here.

OEDIPUS: O Lord Apollo!
May his news be fair as his face is radiant!

PRIEST: It could not be otherwise: he is crowned with bay,
The chaplet is thick with berries.

OEDIPUS: We shall soon know;   85
He is near enough to hear us now.

Enter Creon.

                    O Prince:

Brother: son of Menoikeus:
What answer do you bring us from the god?
CREON: A strong one. I can tell you, great afflictions
Will turn out well, if they are taken well.   *90*
OEDIPUS: What was the oracle? These vague words
Leave me still hanging between hope and fear.
CREON: Is it your pleasure to hear me with all these
Gathered around us? I am prepared to speak,
But should we not go in?
OEDIPUS: Let them all hear it   *95*
It is for them I suffer, more than for myself.
CREON: Then I will tell you what I heard at Delphi.
In plain words
The god commands us to expel from the land of Thebes
An old defilement we are sheltering.   *100*
It is a deathly thing, beyond cure.
We must not let it feed upon us longer.
OEDIPUS: What defilement? How shall we rid ourselves of it?
CREON: By exile or death, blood for blood. It was
Murder that brought the plague-wind on the city.   *105*
OEDIPUS: Murder of whom? Surely the god has named him?
CREON: My lord: long ago Laïos was our king,
Before you came to govern us.
OEDIPUS: I know;
I learned of him from others; I never saw him.
CREON: He was murdered; and Apollo commands us now   *110*
To take revenge upon whoever killed him.
OEDIPUS: Upon whom? Where are they? Where shall we
find a clue
To solve that crime, after so many years?
CREON: Here in this land, he said.
                                        If we make enquiry,
We may touch things that otherwise escape us.   *115*
OEDIPUS: Tell me: Was Laïos murdered in his house,
Or in the fields, or in some foreign country?
CREON: He said he planned to make a pilgrimage.
He did not come home again.

OEDIPUS: And was there no one,
No witness, no companion, to tell what happened?   *120*
CREON: They were all killed but one, and he got away
So frightened that he could remember one thing only.
OEDIPUS: What was that one thing? One may be the key
To everything, if we resolve to use it.
CREON: He said that a band of highwaymen attacked them,   *125*
Outnumbered them, and overwhelmed the King.
OEDIPUS: Strange, that a highwayman should be so daring—
Unless some faction here bribed him to do it.
CREON: We thought of that. But after Laïos' death
New troubles arose and we had no avenger.   *130*
OEDIPUS: What troubles could prevent your hunting down the
killers?
CREON: The riddling Sphinx's song
Made us deaf to all mysteries but her own.
OEDIPUS: Then once more I must bring what is dark to light.
It is most fitting that Apollo shows,   *135*
As you do, this compunction for the dead.
You shall see how I stand by you, as I should,
To avenge the city and the city's god,
And not as though it were for some distant friend,
But for my own sake, to be rid of evil.   *140*
Whoever killed King Laïos might—who knows?—
Decide at any moment to kill me as well.
By avenging the murdered king I protect myself.
Come, then, my children: leave the altar steps,
Lift up your olive boughs!
One of you go   *145*
And summon the people of Kadmos to gather here.
I will do all that I can; you may tell them that.

Exit a Page.

So, with the help of God,
We shall be saved—or else indeed we are lost.
PRIEST: Let us rise, children. It was for this we came,   *150*
And now the King has promised it himself.

Phoibos° has sent us an oracle; may he descend
Himself to save us and drive out the plague.

*Exeunt Oedipus and Creon into the palace by the central
door. The Priest and the Suppliants disperse right and left.
After a short pause the Chorus enters the orchestra.*

PÁRODOS °

STROPHE° 1

CHORUS: What is God singing in his profound
Delphi of gold and shadow?
What oracle for Thebes, the sunwhipped city?
Fear unjoints me, the roots of my heart tremble.
Now I remember, O Healer, your power, and wonder: 5
Will you send doom like a sudden cloud, or weave it
Like nightfall of the past?
Speak, speak to us, issue of holy sound:
Dearest to our expectancy: be tender!

ANTISTROPHE° 1

Let me pray to Athenê, the immortal daughter of Zeus,   10
And to Artemis her sister
Who keeps her famous throne in the market ring,
And to Apollo, bowman at the far butts of heaven—
O gods, descend! Like three streams leap against
The fires of our grief, the fires of darkness;   15
Be swift to bring us rest!
As in the old time from the brilliant house
Of air you stepped to save us, come again!

---

152 Phoibos that is, Apollo.
Párodos chanted by the chorus on its first entrance.   **A strophe** was chanted while the chorus
danced from stage right to stage left.   An **antistrophe** was chanted while the chorus danced from
left to right.

STROPHE 2

Now our afflictions have no end,
Now all our stricken host lies down   *20*
And no man fights off death with his mind;
The noble plowland bears no grain,
And groaning mothers can not bear—
See, how our lives like birds take wing,
Like sparks that fly when a fire soars,   *25*
To the shore of the god of evening.

ANTISTROPHE 2

The plague burns on, it is pitiless,
Though pallid children laden with death
Lie unwept in the stony ways,
And old gray women by every path   *30*
Flock to the strand about the altars
There to strike their breasts and cry
Worship of Phoibos in wailing prayers:
Be kind, God's golden child!

STROPHE 3

There are no swords in this attack by fire,   *35*
No shields, but we are ringed with cries.
Send the besieger plunging from our homes
Into the vast sea-room of the Atlantic
Or into the waves that foam eastward of Thrace—
For the day ravages what the night spares—   *40*
Destroy our enemy, lord of the thunder!
Let him be riven by lightning from heaven!

ANTISTROPHE 3

Phoibos Apollo, stretch the sun's bowstring,
That golden cord, until it sing for us,
Flashing arrows in heaven!
                    Artemis,° Huntress,   *45*
Race with flaring lights upon our mountains!

45 Artemis goddess of the hunt and female chastity.

O scarlet god, O golden-banded brow,
O Theban Bacchos in a storm of Maenads,°

Enter Oedipus, center.

Whirl upon Death, that all the Undying hate!
Come with blinding torches, come in joy!   *50*

SCENE I°

OEDIPUS: Is this your prayer? It may be answered. Come,
  Listen to me, act as the crisis demands,
  And you shall have relief from all these evils.
  Until now I was a stranger to this tale,
  As I had been a stranger to the crime.   *5*
  Could I track down the murderer without a clue?
  But now, friends,
  As one who became a citizen after the murder,
  I make this proclamation to all Thebans:
  If any man knows by whose hand Laïos, son of Labdakos,   *10*
  Met his death, I direct that man to tell me everything,
  No matter what he fears for having so long withheld it.
  Let it stand as promised that no further trouble
  Will come to him, but he may leave the land in safety.
  Moreover: If anyone knows the murderer to be foreign,   *15*
  Let him not keep silent: he shall have his reward from me.
  However, if he does conceal it; if any man
  Fearing for his friend or for himself disobeys this edict,
  Hear what I propose to do:
  I solemnly forbid the people of this country,   *20*
  Where power and throne are mine, ever to receive that man
  Or speak to him, no matter who he is, or let him
  Join in sacrifice, lustration, or in prayer.
  I decree that he be driven from every house,
  Being, as he is, corruption itself to us: the Delphic   *25*
  Voice of Zeus has pronounced this revelation.
  Thus I associate myself with the oracle

---

48 Bacchos . . . Maenads god of wine and his priestesses.   **Scene** in Greek, *episodos.*

And take the side of the murdered king.
As for the criminal, I pray to God—
Whether it be a lurking thief, or one of a number—   30
I pray that that man's life be consumed in evil and
wretchedness.
And as for me, this curse applies no less
If it should turn out that the culprit is my guest here,
Sharing my hearth.
                              You have heard the penalty.
I lay it on you now to attend to this   35
For my sake, for Apollo's, for the sick
Sterile city that heaven has abandoned.
Suppose the oracle had given you no command:
Should this defilement go uncleansed for ever?
You should have found the murderer: your king,   40
A noble king, had been destroyed!
                              Now I,
Having the power that he held before me,
Having his bed, begetting children there
Upon his wife, as he would have, had he lived—
Their son would have been my children's brother,   45
If Laïos had had luck in fatherhood!
(But surely ill luck rushed upon his reign)—
I say I take the son's part, just as though
I were his son, to press the fight for him
And see it won! I'll find the hand that brought   50
Death to Labdakos' and Polydoros' child,
Heir of Kadmos' and Agenor's line.
And as for those who fail me,
May the gods deny them the fruit of the earth,
Fruit of the womb, and may they rot utterly!   55
Let them be wretched as we are wretched, and worse!
For you, for loyal Thebans, and for all
Who find my actions right, I pray the favor
Of justice, and of all the immortal gods.

CHORAGOS°:   Since I am under oath, my lord, I swear   *60*
   I did not do the murder, I can not name
   The murderer. Might not the oracle
   That has ordained the search tell where to find him?
OEDIPUS: An honest question. But no man in the world
   Can make the gods do more than the gods will.   *65*
CHORAGOS: There is one last expedient—
OEDIPUS: Tell me what it is.
   Though it seem slight, you must not hold it back.
CHORAGOS: A lord clairvoyant to the lord Apollo,
   As we all know, is the skilled Teiresias.
   One might learn much about this from him, Oedipus.   *70*
OEDIPUS: I am not wasting time:
   Creon spoke of this, and I have sent for him—
   Twice, in fact; it is strange that he is not here.
CHORAGOS: The other matter—that old report—seems useless.
OEDIPUS: Tell me. I am interested in all reports.   *75*
CHORAGOS: The King was said to have been killed by
   highwaymen.
OEDIPUS: I know. But we have no witnesses to that.
CHORAGOS: If the killer can feel a particle of dread,
   Your curse will bring him out of hiding!
OEDIPUS: No.
   The man who dared that act will fear no curse.   *80*

Enter the blind seer Teiresias, led by a Page.

CHORAGOS: But there is one man who may detect the criminal.
   This is Teiresias, this is the holy prophet
   In whom, alone of all men, truth was born.
OEDIPUS: Teiresias: seer: student of mysteries,
   Of all that's taught and all that no man tells,   *85*
   Secrets of Heaven and secrets of the earth:
   Blind though you are, you know the city lies
   Sick with plague; and from this plague, my lord,
   We find that you alone can guard or save us.
   Possibly you did not hear the messengers?   *90*

60 Choragos leader of the chorus.

Apollo, when we sent to him,
Sent us back word that this great pestilence
Would lift, but only if we established clearly
The identity of those who murdered Laïos.
They must be killed or exiled.

Can you use   95

Birdflight or any art of divination
To purify yourself, and Thebes, and me
From this contagion? We are in your hands.
There is no fairer duty
Than that of helping others in distress.   *100*

TEIRESIAS: How dreadful knowledge of the truth can be
When there's no help in truth! I knew this well,
But made myself forget. I should not have come.

OEDIPUS: What is troubling you? Why are your eyes so cold?

TEIRESIAS: Let me go home. Bear your own fate, and I'll   *105*
Bear mine. It is better so: trust what I say.

OEDIPUS: What you say is ungracious and unhelpful
To your native country. Do not refuse to speak.

TEIRESIAS: When it comes to speech, your own is neither
temperate
Nor opportune. I wish to be more prudent.   *110*

OEDIPUS: In God's name, we all beg you—

TEIRESIAS: You are all ignorant.
No; I will never tell you what I know.
Now it is my misery; then, it would be yours.

OEDIPUS: What! You do know something, and will not
tell us?
You would betray us all and wreck the State?   *115*

TEIRESIAS: I do not intend to torture myself, or you.
Why persist in asking? You will not persuade me.

OEDIPUS: What a wicked old man you are! You'd try a stone's
Patience! Out with it! Have you no feeling at all?

TEIRESIAS: You call me unfeeling. If you could only see   *120*
The nature of your own feelings . . .

OEDIPUS: Why,
Who would not feel as I do? Who could endure
Your arrogance toward the city?

TEIRESIAS: What does it matter!
  Whether I speak or not; it is bound to come.
OEDIPUS: Then, if "it" is bound to come, you are bound to
  tell me.   *125*
TEIRESIAS: No, I will not go on. Rage as you please.
OEDIPUS: Rage? Why not!
                         And I'll tell you what I think:
  You planned it, you had it done, you all but
  Killed him with your own hands: if you had eyes,
  I'd say the crime was yours, and yours alone.   *130*
TEIRESIAS: So? I charge you, then,
  Abide by the proclamation you have made:
  From this day forth
  Never speak again to these men or to me;
  You yourself are the pollution of this country.   *135*
OEDIPUS: You dare say that! Can you possibly think you have
  Some way of going free, after such insolence?
TEIRESIAS: I have gone free. It is the truth sustains me.
OEDIPUS: Who taught you shamelessness? It was not your
  craft.
TEIRESIAS: You did. You made me speak. I did not want to.   *140*
OEDIPUS: Speak what? Let me hear it again more clearly.
TEIRESIAS: Was it not clear before? Are you tempting me?
OEDIPUS: I did not understand it. Say it again.
TEIRESIAS: I say that you are the murderer whom you seek.
OEDIPUS: Now twice you have spat out infamy. You'll pay
  for it!   *145*
TEIRESIAS: Would you care for more? Do you wish to be really
  angry?
OEDIPUS: Say what you will. Whatever you say is worthless.
TEIRESIAS: I say you live in hideous shame with those
  Most dear to you. You can not see the evil.
OEDIPUS: It seems you can go on mouthing like this for ever. *150*
TEIRESIAS: I can, if there is power in truth.
OEDIPUS: There is:
  But not for you, not for you,
  You sightless, witless, senseless, mad old man!

TEIRESIAS: You are the madman. There is no one here
    Who will not curse you soon, as you curse me.   *155*
OEDIPUS: You child of endless night! You can not hurt me
    Or any other man who sees the sun.
TEIRESIAS: True: it is not from me your fate will come.
    That lies within Apollo's competence,
    As it is his concern.
OEDIPUS: Tell me: *160*
    Are you speaking for Creon, or for yourself?
TEIRESIAS: Creon is no threat. You weave your own doom.
OEDIPUS: Wealth, power, craft of statesmanship!
    Kingly position, everywhere admired!
    What savage envy is stored up against these,   *165*
    If Creon, whom I trusted, Creon my friend,
    For this great office which the city once
    Put in my hands unsought—if for this power
    Creon desires in secret to destroy me!
    He has brought this decrepit fortune-teller, this   *170*
    Collector of dirty pennies, this prophet fraud—
    Why, he is no more clairvoyant than I am!
                       Tell us:
    Has your mystic mummery ever approached the truth?
    When that hellcat the Sphinx was performing here,
    What help were you to these people?   *175*
    Her magic was not for the first man who came along:
    It demanded a real exorcist. Your birds—
    What good were they? or the gods, for the matter of that?
    But I came by,
    Oedipus, the simple man, who knows nothing—   *180*
    I thought it out for myself, no birds helped me!
    And this is the man you think you can destroy,
    That you may be close to Creon when he's king!
    Well, you and your friend Creon, it seems to me,
    Will suffer most. If you were not an old man,   *185*
    You would have paid already for your plot.
CHORAGOS: We can not see that his words or yours
    Have been spoken except in anger, Oedipus,

And of anger we have no need. How can God's will
Be accomplished best? That is what most concerns us.   190
TEIRESIAS: You are a king. But where argument's concerned
    I am your man, as much a king as you.
    I am not your servant, but Apollo's.
    I have no need of Creon to speak for me.
    Listen to me. You mock my blindness, do you?   195
    But I say that you, with both your eyes, are blind:
    You can not see the wretchedness of your life,
    Nor in whose house you live, no, nor with whom.
    Who are your father and mother? Can you tell me?
    You do not even know the blind wrongs   200
    That you have done them, on earth and in the world below.
    But the double lash of your parents' curse will whip you
    Out of this land some day, with only night
    Upon your precious eyes.
    Your cries then—where will they not be heard?   205
    What fastness of Kithairon° will not echo them?
    And that bridal-descant of yours—you'll know it then,
    The song they sang when you came here to Thebes
    And found your misguided berthing.
    All this, and more, that you can not guess at now,   210
    Will bring you to yourself among your children.
    Be angry, then. Curse Creon. Curse my words.
    I tell you, no man that walks upon the earth
    Shall be rooted out more horribly than you.
OEDIPUS: Am I to bear this from him?—Damnation   215
    Take you! Out of this place! Out of my sight!
TEIRESIAS: I would not have come at all if you had not
    asked me.
OEDIPUS: Could I have told that you'd talk nonsense, that
    You'd come here to make a fool of yourself, and of me?
TEIRESIAS: A fool? Your parents thought me sane enough.   220
OEDIPUS: My parents again!—Wait: who were my parents?
TEIRESIAS: This day will give you a father, and break your
    heart.

206 Kithairon a mountain near Thebes.

OEDIPUS: Your infantile riddles! Your damned abracadabra!

TEIRESIAS: You were a great man once at solving riddles.

OEDIPUS: Mock me with that if you like; you will find it true.   *225*

TEIRESIAS: It was true enough. It brought about your ruin.

OEDIPUS: But if it saved this town?

TEIRESIAS (*to the Page*):   Boy, give me your hand.

OEDIPUS: Yes, boy; lead him away.

                        —While you are here

We can do nothing. Go; leave us in peace.

TEIRESIAS: I will go when I have said what I have to say.   *230*

How can you hurt me? And I tell you again:

The man you have been looking for all this time,

The damned man, the murderer of Laïos,

That man is in Thebes. To your mind he is foreignborn,

But it will soon be shown that he is a Theban,   *235*

A revelation that will fail to please.

                            A blind man,

Who has his eyes now; a penniless man, who is rich now;

And he will go tapping the strange earth with his staff;

To the children with whom he lives now he will be

Brother and father—the very same; to her   *240*

Who bore him, son and husband—the very same

Who came to his father's bed, wet with his father's blood.

Enough. Go think that over.

If later you find error in what I have said,

You may say that I have no skill in prophecy.   *245*

> *Exit Teiresias, led by his Page.*
> *Oedipus goes into the palace.*

ODE° I

STROPHE 1

CHORUS: The Delphic stone of prophecies
      Remembers ancient regicide
      And a still bloody hand.

Ode also known as *stasimon*, a choral interlude.

That killer's hour of flight has come.
He must be stronger than riderless   5
Coursers of untiring wind,
For the son of Zeus° armed with his father's thunder
Leaps in lightning after him;
And the Furies° follow him, the sad Furies.

ANTISTROPHE 1

Holy Parnassos' peak of snow   10
Flashes and blinds that secret man,
That all shall hunt him down:
Though he may roam the forest shade
Like a bull gone wild from pasture
To rage through glooms of stone.   15
Doom comes down on him; flight will not avail him;
For the world's heart calls him desolate,
And the immortal Furies follow, for ever follow.

STROPHE 2

But now a wilder thing is heard
From the old man skilled at hearing Fate in the wingbeat
of a bird.   20
Bewildered as a blown bird, my soul hovers and can not find
Foothold in this debate, or any reason or rest of mind.
But no man ever brought—none can bring
Proof of strife between Thebes' royal house,
Labdakos' line,° and the son of Polybos;°   25
And never until now has any man brought word
Of Laïos' dark death staining Oedipus the King.

ANTISTROPHE 2

Divine Zeus and Apollo hold
Perfect intelligence alone of all tales ever told;
And well though this diviner works, he works in his own night;   30

---

7 son of Zeus Apollo.   **9 Furies** three female spirits who punished evildoers.   **25 Labdakos' line** descendants of Laïos.   **Polybos** King of Corinth who adopted Oedipus.

No man can judge that rough unknown or trust in second sight,
For wisdom changes hands among the wise.
Shall I believe my great lord criminal
At a raging word that a blind old man let fall?
I saw him, when the carrion woman faced him of old,   35
Prove his heroic mind! These evil words are lies.

SCENE II

CREON: Men of Thebes:
    I am told that heavy accusations
    Have been brought against me by King Oedipus.
    I am not the kind of man to bear this tamely.
    If in these present difficulties   5
    He holds me accountable for any harm to him
    Through anything I have said or done—why, then,
    I do not value life in this dishonor.
    It is not as though this rumor touched upon
    Some private indiscretion. The matter is grave.   10
    The fact is that I am being called disloyal
    To the State, to my fellow citizens, to my friends.
CHORAGOS: He may have spoken in anger, not from his mind.
CREON: But did you not hear him say I was the one
    Who seduced the old prophet into lying?   15
CHORAGOS: The thing was said; I do not know how seriously.
CREON: But you were watching him! Were his eyes steady?
    Did he look like a man in his right mind?
CHORAGOS: I do not know.
    I can not judge the behavior of great men.
    But here is the King himself.

    Enter Oedipus.

OEDIPUS: So you dared come back.   20
    Why? How brazen of you to come to my house,
    You murderer!
            Do you think I do not know
    That you plotted to kill me, plotted to steal my throne?

Tell me, in God's name: am I a coward, a fool,
That you should dream you could accomplish this?   25
A fool who could not see your slippery game?
A coward, not to fight back when I saw it?
You are the fool, Creon, are you not? hoping
Without support or friends to get a throne?
Thrones may be won or bought: you could do neither.   30
CREON: Now listen to me. You have talked; let me talk, too.
You can not judge unless you know the facts.
OEDIPUS: You speak well: there is one fact; but I find it hard
To learn from the deadliest enemy I have.
CREON: That above all I must dispute with you.   35
OEDIPUS: That above all I will not hear you deny.
CREON: If you think there is anything good in being stubborn
Against all reason, then I say you are wrong.
OEDIPUS: If you think a man can sin against his own kind
And not be punished for it, I say you are mad.   40
CREON: I agree. But tell me: what have I done to you?
OEDIPUS: You advised me to send for that wizard, did you not?
CREON: I did. I should do it again.
OEDIPUS: Very well. Now tell me:
How long has it been since Laïos—
CREON: What of Laïos?
OEDIPUS: Since he vanished in that onset by the road?   45
CREON: It was long ago, a long time.
OEDIPUS: And this prophet,
Was he practicing here then?
CREON: He was; and with honor, as now.
OEDIPUS: Did he speak of me at that time?
CREON: He never did;
At least, not when I was present.
OEDIPUS: But . . . the enquiry?
I suppose you held one?
CREON: We did, but we learned nothing.   50
OEDIPUS: Why did the prophet not speak against me then?
CREON: I do not know; and I am the kind of man
Who holds his tongue when he has no facts to go on.
OEDIPUS: There's one fact that you know, and you could tell it.

CREON: What fact is that? If I know it, you shall have it.   55

OEDIPUS: If he were not involved with you, he could not say
   That it was I who murdered Laïos.

CREON: If he says that, you are the one that knows it!—
   But now it is my turn to question you.

OEDIPUS: Put your questions. I am no murderer.   60

CREON: First then: You married my sister?

OEDIPUS: I married your sister.

CREON: And you rule the kingdom equally with her?

OEDIPUS: Everything that she wants she has from me.

CREON: And I am the third, equal to both of you?

OEDIPUS: That is why I call you a bad friend.   65

CREON: No. Reason it out, as I have done.
   Think of this first: Would any sane man prefer
   Power, with all a king's anxieties,
   To that same power and the grace of sleep?
   Certainly not I.   70
   I have never longed for the king's power—only his rights.
   Would any wise man differ from me in this?
   As matters stand, I have my way in everything
   With your consent, and no responsibilities.
   If I were king, I should be a slave to policy.   75
   How could I desire a scepter more
   Than what is now mine—untroubled influence?
   No, I have not gone mad; I need no honors,
   Except those with the perquisites I have now.
   I am welcome everywhere; every man salutes me,   80
   And those who want your favor seek my ear,
   Since I know how to manage what they ask.
   Should I exchange this ease for that anxiety?
   Besides, no sober mind is treasonable.
   I hate anarchy   85
   And never would deal with any man who likes it.
   Test what I have said. Go to the priestess
   At Delphi, ask if I quoted her correctly.
   And as for this other thing: if I am found
   Guilty of treason with Teiresias,   90
   Then sentence me to death! You have my word

It is a sentence I should cast my vote for—
But not without evidence!
                                    You do wrong
When you take good men for bad, bad men for good.
A true friend thrown aside—why, life itself   95
Is not more precious!
                                    In time you will know this well:
For time, and time alone, will show the just man,
Though scoundrels are discovered in a day.
CHORAGOS: This is well said, and a prudent man would
ponder it.
Judgments too quickly formed are dangerous.   100
OEDIPUS: But is he not quick in his duplicity?
And shall I not be quick to parry him?
Would you have me stand still, hold my peace, and let
This man win everything, through my inaction?
CREON: And you want—what is it, then? To banish me?   105
OEDIPUS: No, not exile. It is your death I want,
So that all the world may see what treason means.
CREON: You will persist, then? You will not believe me?
OEDIPUS: How can I believe you?
CREON: Then you are a fool.
OEDIPUS: To save myself?
CREON: In justice, think of me.   110
OEDIPUS: You are evil incarnate.
CREON: But suppose that you are
wrong?
OEDIPUS: Still I must rule.
CREON: But not if you rule badly.
OEDIPUS: O city, city!
CREON: It is my city, too!
CHORAGOS: Now, my lords, be still. I see the Queen,
Iocastê, coming from her palace chambers;   115
And it is time she came, for the sake of you both.
This dreadful quarrel can be resolved through her.

Enter Iocastê.

IOCASTÊ: Poor foolish men, what wicked din is this?
With Thebes sick to death, is it not shameful
That you should rake some private quarrel up?   *120*
(*To Oedipus.*) Come into the house.

                     —And you, Creon,
go now:
Let us have no more of this tumult over nothing.
CREON: Nothing? No, sister: what your husband plans for me
Is one of two great evils: exile or death.
OEDIPUS: He is right.

                     Why, woman, I have caught him squarely   *125*
Plotting against my life.
CREON: No! Let me die
Accurst if ever I have wished you harm!
IOCASTÊ: Ah, believe it, Oedipus!
In the name of the gods, respect this oath of his
For my sake, for the sake of these people here!   *130*

STROPHE 1

CHORAGOS: Open your mind to her, my lord. Be ruled by her, I
beg you!
OEDIPUS: What would you have me do?
CHORAGOS: Respect Creon's word. He has never spoken like
a fool,
And now he has sworn an oath.
OEDIPUS: You know what you ask?
CHORAGOS: I do.
OEDIPUS: Speak on, then.
CHORAGOS: A friend so sworn should not be baited so,   *135*
In blind malice, and without final proof.
OEDIPUS: You are aware, I hope, that what you say
Means death for me, or exile at the least.

STROPHE 2

CHORAGOS: No, I swear by Helios, first in Heaven!
May I die friendless and accurst,   *140*
The worst of deaths, if ever I meant that!

It is the withering fields
That hurt my sick heart:
Must we bear all these ills,
And now your bad blood as well? 145

OEDIPUS: Then let him go. And let me die, if I must,
Or be driven by him in shame from the land of Thebes.
It is your unhappiness, and not his talk,
That touches me.
As for him—
Wherever he goes, hatred will follow him. 150

CREON: Ugly in yielding, as you were ugly in rage!
Natures like yours chiefly torment themselves.

OEDIPUS: Can you not go? Can you not leave me?

CREON: I can.
You do not know me; but the city knows me,
And in its eyes I am just, if not in yours. 155

Exit Creon.

ANTISTROPHE 1

CHORAGOS: Lady Iocastê, did you not ask the King to go to his
chambers?

IOCASTÊ: First tell me what has happened.

CHORAGOS: There was suspicion without evidence; yet it rankled
As even false charges will.

IOCASTÊ: On both sides?

CHORAGOS: On both.

IOCASTÊ: But what was said?

CHORAGOS: Oh let it rest, let it be done with! 160
Have we not suffered enough?

OEDIPUS: You see to what your decency has brought you:
You have made difficulties where my heart saw none.

ANTISTROPHE 2

CHORAGOS: Oedipus, it is not once only I have told you—
You must know I should count myself unwise 165
To the point of madness, should I now forsake you—
You, under whose hand,

In the storm of another time,
Our dear land sailed out free.
But now stand fast at the helm!   170
IOCASTÊ: In God's name, Oedipus, inform your wife as well:
Why are you so set in this hard anger?
OEDIPUS: I will tell you, for none of these men deserves
My confidence as you do. It is Creon's work,
His treachery, his plotting against me.   175
IOCASTÊ: Go on, if you can make this clear to me.
OEDIPUS: He charges me with the murder of Laïos.
IOCASTÊ: Has he some knowledge? Or does he speak from
hearsay?
OEDIPUS: He would not commit himself to such a charge,
But he has brought in that damnable soothsayer   180
To tell his story.
IOCASTÊ: Set your mind at rest.
If it is a question of soothsayers, I tell you
That you will find no man whose craft gives knowledge
Of the unknowable.
                    Here is my proof:
An oracle was reported to Laïos once   185
(I will not say from Phoibos himself, but from
His appointed ministers, at any rate)
That his doom would be death at the hands of his own son—
His son, born of his flesh and of mine!
Now, you remember the story: Laïos was killed   190
By marauding strangers where three highways meet;
But his child had not been three days in this world
Before the King had pierced the baby's ankles
And left him to die on a lonely mountainside.
Thus, Apollo never caused that child   195
To kill his father, and it was not Laïos' fate
To die at the hands of his son, as he had feared.
This is what prophets and prophecies are worth!
Have no dread of them.
                    It is God himself
Who can show us what he wills, in his own way.   200

OEDIPUS: How strange a shadowy memory crossed my mind,
 Just now while you were speaking; it chilled my heart.
IOCASTÊ: What do you mean? What memory do you speak of?
OEDIPUS: If I understand you, Laïos was killed
 At a place where three roads meet.
IOCASTÊ: So it was said;   *205*
 We have no later story.
OEDIPUS: Where did it happen?
IOCASTÊ: Phokis, it is called: at a place where the Theban Way
 Divides into the roads toward Delphi and Daulia.
OEDIPUS: When?
IOCASTÊ: We had the news not long before you came
 And proved the right to your succession here.   *210*
OEDIPUS: Ah, what net has God been weaving for me?
IOCASTÊ: Oedipus! Why does this trouble you?
OEDIPUS: Do not ask
 me yet.
 First, tell me how Laïos looked, and tell me
 How old he was.
IOCASTÊ: He was tall, his hair just touched
 With white; his form was not unlike your own.   *215*
OEDIPUS: I think that I myself may be accurst
 By my own ignorant edict.
IOCASTÊ: You speak strangely.
 It makes me tremble to look at you, my King.
OEDIPUS: I am not sure that the blind man can not see.
 But I should know better if you were to tell me—   *220*
IOCASTÊ: Anything—though I dread to hear you ask it.
OEDIPUS: Was the King lightly escorted, or did he ride
 With a large company, as a ruler should?
IOCASTÊ: There were five men with him in all: one was a
 herald,
 And a single chariot, which he was driving.   *225*
OEDIPUS: Alas, that makes it plain enough!
                         But who—
 Who told you how it happened?
IOCASTÊ: A household servant,
 The only one to escape.

OEDIPUS: And is he still
   A servant of ours?
IOCASTÊ: No; for when he came back at last
   And found you enthroned in the place of the dead king,   *230*
   He came to me, touched my hand with his, and begged
   That I would send him away to the frontier district
   Where only the shepherds go—
   As far away from the city as I could send him.
   I granted his prayer; for although the man was a slave,   *235*
   He had earned more than this favor at my hands.
OEDIPUS: Can he be called back quickly?
IOCASTÊ: Easily.
   But why?
OEDIPUS: I have taken too much upon myself
   Without enquiry; therefore I wish to consult him.
IOCASTÊ: Then he shall come.
                              But am I not one also   *240*
   To whom you might confide these fears of yours?
OEDIPUS: That is your right; it will not be denied you,
   Now least of all; for I have reached a pitch
   Of wild foreboding. Is there anyone
   To whom I should sooner speak?   *245*
   Polybos of Corinth is my father.
   My mother is a Dorian: Meropê.
   I grew up chief among the men of Corinth
   Until a strange thing happened—
   Not worth my passion, it may be, but strange.   *250*
   At a feast, a drunken man maundering in his cups
   Cries out that I am not my father's son!
   I contained myself that night, though I felt anger
   And a sinking heart. The next day I visited
   My father and mother, and questioned them. They stormed,   *255*
   Calling it all the slanderous rant of a fool;
   And this relieved me. Yet the suspicion
   Remained always aching in my mind;
   I knew there was talk; I could not rest;
   And finally, saying nothing to my parents,   *260*
   I went to the shrine at Delphi.

The god dismissed my question without reply;
He spoke of other things.

                Some were clear,
Full of wretchedness, dreadful, unbearable:
As, that I should lie with my own mother, breed   *265*
Children from whom all men would turn their eyes;
And that I should be my father's murderer.
I heard all this, and fled. And from that day
Corinth to me was only in the stars
Descending in that quarter of the sky,   *270*
As I wandered farther and farther on my way
To a land where I should never see the evil
Sung by the oracle. And I came to this country
Where, so you say, King Laïos was killed.
I will tell you all that happened there, my lady.   *275*
There were three highways
Coming together at a place I passed;
And there a herald came towards me, and a chariot
Drawn by horses, with a man such as you describe
Seated in it. The groom leading the horses   *280*
Forced me off the road at his lord's command;
But as this charioteer lurched over towards me
I struck him in my rage. The old man saw me
And brought his double goad down upon my head
As I came abreast.

                He was paid back, and more!   *285*
Swinging my club in this right hand I knocked him
Out of his car, and he rolled on the ground.

                          I killed him.
I killed them all.
Now if that stranger and Laïos were—kin,
Where is a man more miserable than I?   *290*
More hated by the gods? Citizen and alien alike
Must never shelter me or speak to me—
I must be shunned by all.

                And I myself
Pronounced this malediction upon myself!
Think of it: I have touched you with these hands,   *295*

These hands that killed your husband. What defilement!
Am I all evil, then? It must be so,
Since I must flee from Thebes, yet never again
See my own countrymen, my own country,
For fear of joining my mother in marriage   *300*
And killing Polybos, my father.
                                        Ah,
If I was created so, born to this fate,
Who could deny the savagery of God?
O holy majesty of heavenly powers!
May I never see that day! Never!   *305*
Rather let me vanish from the race of men
Than know the abomination destined me!

CHORAGOS: We too, my lord, have felt dismay at this.
   But there is hope: you have yet to hear the shepherd.

OEDIPUS: Indeed, I fear no other hope is left me.   *310*

IOCASTÊ: What do you hope from him when he
   comes?

OEDIPUS: This much:
   If his account of the murder tallies with yours,
   Then I am cleared.

IOCASTÊ: What was it that I said
   Of such importance?

OEDIPUS: Why, "marauders," you said,
   Killed the King, according to this man's story.   *315*
   If he maintains that still, if there were several,
   Clearly the guilt is not mine: I was alone.
   But if he says one man, singlehanded, did it,
   Then the evidence all points to me.

IOCASTÊ: You may be sure that he said there were several;   *320*
   And can he call back that story now? He cannot.
   The whole city heard it as plainly as I.
   But suppose he alters some detail of it:
   He can not ever show that Laïos' death
   Fulfilled the oracle: for Apollo said   *325*
   My child was doomed to kill him; and my child—
   Poor baby!—it was my child that died first.

No. From now on, where oracles are concerned,
I would not waste a second thought on any.
OEDIPUS: You may be right.

                              But come: let someone go   *330*
For the shepherd at once. This matter must be settled.
IOCASTÊ: I will send for him.

     I would not wish to cross you in anything,
And surely not in this.—Let us go in.

                              Exeunt into the palace.

ODE II

STROPHE 1

CHORUS: Let me be reverent in the ways of right,
     Lowly the paths I journey on;
     Let all my words and actions keep
     The laws of the pure universe
     From highest Heaven handed down.   *5*
     For Heaven is their bright nurse,
     Those generations of the realms of light;
     Ah, never of mortal kind were they begot,
     Nor are they slaves of memory, lost in sleep:
     Their Father is greater than Time, and ages not.   *10*

ANTISTROPHE 1

     The tyrant is a child of Pride
     Who drinks from his great sickening cup
     Recklessness and vanity,
     Until from his high crest headlong
     He plummets to the dust of hope.   *15*
     That strong man is not strong.
     But let no fair ambition be denied;
     May God protect the wrestler for the State
     In government, in comely policy,
     Who will fear God, and on His ordinance wait.   *20*

STROPHE 2

Haughtiness and the high hand of disdain
Tempt and outrage God's holy law;
And any mortal who dares hold
No immortal Power in awe
Will be caught up in a net of pain: 25
The price for which his levity is sold.
Let each man take due earnings, then,
And keep his hands from holy things,
And from blasphemy stand apart—
Else the crackling blast of heaven   30
Blows on his head, and on his desperate heart;
Though fools will honor impious men,
In their cities no tragic poet sings.

ANTISTROPHE 2

Shall we lose faith in Delphi's obscurities,
We who have heard the world's core   35
Discredited, and the sacred wood
Of Zeus at Elis praised no more?
The deeds and the strange prophecies
Must make a pattern yet to be understood.
Zeus, if indeed you are lord of all,   40
Throned in light over night and day,
Mirror this in your endless mind:
Our masters call the oracle
Words on the wind, and the Delphic vision blind!
Their hearts no longer know Apollo,   45
And reverence for the gods has died away.

SCENE III

Enter Iocastê.

IOCASTÊ: Princes of Thebes, it has occurred to me
   To visit the altars of the gods, bearing
   These branches as a suppliant, and this incense.

Our King is not himself: his noble soul
Is overwrought with fantasies of dread,   5
Else he would consider
The new prophecies in the light of the old.
He will listen to any voice that speaks disaster,
And my advice goes for nothing.

She approaches the altar, right.

                To you, then, Apollo,
Lycean lord, since you are nearest, I turn in prayer.   10
Receive these offerings, and grant us deliverance
From defilement. Our hearts are heavy with fear
When we see our leader distracted, as helpless sailors
Are terrified by the confusion of their helmsman.

Enter Messenger.

MESSENGER: Friends, no doubt you can direct me: 15
    Where shall I find the house of Oedipus,
    Or, better still, where is the King himself?
CHORAGOS: It is this very place, stranger; he is inside.
    This is his wife and mother of his children.
MESSENGER: I wish her happiness in a happy house,   20
    Blest in all the fulfillment of her marriage.
IOCASTÊ: I wish as much for you: your courtesy
    Deserves a like good fortune. But now, tell me:
    Why have you come? What have you to say to us?
MESSENGER: Good news, my lady, for your house and your
    husband.   25
IOCASTÊ: What news? Who sent you here?
MESSENGER: I am from Corinth.
    The news I bring ought to mean joy for you,
    Though it may be you will find some grief in it.
IOCASTÊ: What is it? How can it touch us in both ways?
MESSENGER: The word is that the people of the Isthmus   30
    Intend to call Oedipus to be their king.
IOCASTÊ: But old King Polybos—is he not reigning still?
MESSENGER: No. Death holds him in his sepulchre.
IOCASTÊ: What are you saying? Polybos is dead?

MESSENGER: If I am not telling the truth, may I die myself. 35

IOCASTÊ (*to a Maidservant*): Go in, go quickly; tell this to your
master.

O riddlers of God's will, where are you now!
This was the man whom Oedipus, long ago,
Feared so, fled so, in dread of destroying him—
But it was another fate by which he died. 40

Enter Oedipus, center.

OEDIPUS: Dearest Iocastê, why have you sent for me?

IOCASTÊ: Listen to what this man says, and then tell me
What has become of the solemn prophecies.

OEDIPUS: Who is this man? What is his news for me?

IOCASTÊ: He has come from Corinth to announce your father's
death! 45

OEDIPUS: Is it true, stranger? Tell me in your own words.

MESSENGER: I can not say it more clearly: the King is dead.

OEDIPUS: Was it by treason? Or by an attack of illness?

MESSENGER: A little thing brings old men to their rest.

OEDIPUS: It was sickness, then?

MESSENGER: Yes, and his many years. 50

OEDIPUS: Ah!

Why should a man respect the Pythian hearth,° or
Give heed to the birds that jangle above his head?
They prophesied that I should kill Polybos,
Kill my own father; but he is dead and buried, 55
And I am here—I never touched him, never,
Unless he died of grief for my departure,
And thus, in a sense, through me. No. Polybos
Has packed the oracles off with him underground.
They are empty words.

IOCASTÊ: Had I not told you so? 60

OEDIPUS: You had; it was my faint heart that betrayed me

IOCASTÊ: From now on never think of those things again.

OEDIPUS: And yet—must I not fear my mother's bed?

IOCASTÊ: Why should anyone in this world be afraid,

52 Pythian hearth where burnt offerings were made at Delphi.

Since Fate rules us and nothing can be foreseen? 65
A man should live only for the present day.
Have no more fear of sleeping with your mother:
How many men, in dreams, have lain with their mothers!
No reasonable man is troubled by such things.

OEDIPUS: That is true; only— 70
If only my mother were not still alive!
But she is alive. I can not help my dread.

IOCASTÊ: Yet this news of your father's death is wonderful.

OEDIPUS: Wonderful. But I fear the living woman.

MESSENGER: Tell me, who is this woman that you fear? 75

OEDIPUS: It is Meropê, man; the wife of King Polybos.

MESSENGER: Meropê? Why should you be afraid of her?

OEDIPUS: An oracle of the gods, a dreadful saying.

MESSENGER: Can you tell me about it or are you sworn to
silence?

OEDIPUS: I can tell you, and I will. 80
Apollo said through his prophet that I was the man
Who should marry his own mother, shed his father's blood
With his own hands. And so, for all these years
I have kept clear of Corinth, and no harm has come—
Though it would have been sweet to see my parents again. 85

MESSENGER: And is this the fear that drove you out of
Corinth?

OEDIPUS: Would you have me kill my father?

MESSENGER: As for that
You must be reassured by the news I gave you.

OEDIPUS: If you could reassure me, I would reward you.

MESSENGER: I had that in mind, I will confess: I thought 90
I could count on you when you returned to Corinth.

OEDIPUS: No: I will never go near my parents again.

MESSENGER: Ah, son, you still do not know what you are
doing—

OEDIPUS: What do you mean? In the name of God tell me!

MESSENGER: —If these are your reasons for not going home. 95

OEDIPUS: I tell you, I fear the oracle may come true.

MESSENGER: And guilt may come upon you through your
parents?

OEDIPUS: That is the dread that is always in my heart.

MESSENGER: Can you not see that all your fears are
groundless?

OEDIPUS: How can you say that? They are my parents, surely?   *100*

MESSENGER: Polybos was not your father.

OEDIPUS: Not my father?

MESSENGER: No more your father than the man speaking to
you.

OEDIPUS: But you are nothing to me!

MESSENGER: ·   Neither was he.

OEDIPUS: Then why did he call me son?

MESSENGER: I will tell you:
Long ago he had you from my hands, as a gift.   *105*

OEDIPUS: Then how could he love me so, if I was not his?

MESSENGER: He had no children, and his heart turned to you.

OEDIPUS: What of you? Did you buy me? Did you find me by
chance?

MESSENGER: I came upon you in the crooked pass of
Kithairon.

OEDIPUS: And what were you doing there?

MESSENGER: Tending my flocks.   *110*

OEDIPUS: A wandering shepherd?

MESSENGER: But your savior, son, that day.

OEDIPUS: From what did you save me?

MESSENGER: Your ankles should tell
you that.

OEDIPUS: Ah, stranger, why do you speak of that childhood
pain?

MESSENGER: I cut the bonds that tied your ankles together.

OEDIPUS: I have had the mark as long as I can remember.   *115*

MESSENGER: That was why you were given the name you
bear.

OEDIPUS: God! Was it my father or my mother who did it?
Tell me!

MESSENGER: I do not know. The man who gave you to me
Can tell you better than I.   *120*

OEDIPUS: It was not you that found me, but another?

MESSENGER: It was another shepherd gave you to me.

OEDIPUS: Who was he? Can you tell me who he was?

MESSENGER: I think he was said to be one of Laïos' people.

OEDIPUS: You mean the Laïos who was king here years ago?   *125*

MESSENGER: Yes; King Laïos; and the man was one of his
    herdsmen.

OEDIPUS: Is he still alive? Can I see him?

MESSENGER: These men here
    Know best about such things.

OEDIPUS: Does anyone here
    Know this shepherd that he is talking about?
    Have you seen him in the fields, or in the town?   *130*
    If you have, tell me. It is time things were made plain.

CHORAGOS: I think the man he means is that same shepherd
    You have already asked to see. Iocastê perhaps
    Could tell you something.

OEDIPUS: Do you know anything
    About him, Lady? Is he the man we have summoned?   *135*
    Is that the man this shepherd means?

IOCASTÊ: Why think of him?
    Forget this herdsman. Forget it all.
    This talk is a waste of time.

OEDIPUS: How can you say that,
    When the clues to my true birth are in my hands?

IOCASTÊ: For God's love, let us have no more questioning!   *140*
    Is your life nothing to you?
    My own is pain enough for me to bear.

OEDIPUS: You need not worry. Suppose my mother a slave,
    And born of slaves: no baseness can touch you.

IOCASTÊ: Listen to me, I beg you: do not do this thing!   *145*

OEDIPUS: I will not listen; the truth must be made known.

IOCASTÊ: Everything that I say is for your own good!

OEDIPUS: My own
    good
    Snaps my patience, then; I want none of it.

IOCASTÊ: You are fatally wrong! May you never learn who
    you are!

OEDIPUS: Go, one of you, and bring the shepherd here.   *150*
    Let us leave this woman to brag of her royal name.

IOCASTÊ: Ah, miserable!
That is the only word I have for you now.
That is the only word I can ever have.

Exit into the palace.

CHORAGOS: Why has she left us, Oedipus? Why has she gone   155
In such a passion of sorrow? I fear this silence:
Something dreadful may come of it.
OEDIPUS: Let it come!
However base my birth, I must know about it.
The Queen, like a woman, is perhaps ashamed
To think of my low origin. But I   160
Am a child of Luck; I can not be dishonored.
Luck is my mother; the passing months, my brothers,
Have seen me rich and poor.
                              If this is so,
How could I wish that I were someone else?
How could I not be glad to know my birth?   165

ODE III

STROPHE

CHORUS: If ever the coming time were known
To my heart's pondering,
Kithairon, now by Heaven I see the torches
At the festival of the next full moon,
And see the dance, and hear the choir sing   5
A grace to your gentle shade:
Mountain where Oedipus was found,
O mountain guard of a noble race!
May the god who heals us lend his aid,
And let that glory come to pass   10
For our king's cradling-ground.

ANTISTROPHE

Of the nymphs that flower beyond the years,
Who bore you, royal child,

To Pan of the hills or the timberline Apollo,
Cold in delight where the upland clears, 15
Or Hermês for whom Kyllenê's° heights are piled?
Or flushed as evening cloud,
Great Dionysos, roamer of mountains,
He—was it he who found you there,
And caught you up in his own proud 20
Arms from the sweet god-ravisher
Who laughed by the Muses' fountains?

SCENE IV

OEDIPUS: Sirs: though I do not know the man,
   I think I see him coming, this shepherd we want:
   He is old, like our friend here, and the men
   Bringing him seem to be servants of my house.
   But you can tell, if you have ever seen him. 5

Enter Shepherd escorted by servants.

CHORAGOS: I know him, he was Laïos' man. You can trust
him.
OEDIPUS: Tell me first, you from Corinth: is this the shepherd
   We were discussing?
MESSENGER: This is the very man.
OEDIPUS (*to Shepherd*):   Come here. No, look at me. You must
   answer
   Everything I ask.—You belonged to Laïos? 10
SHEPHERD: Yes: born his slave, brought up in his house.
OEDIPUS: Tell me: what kind of work did you do for him?
SHEPHERD: I was a shepherd of his, most of my life.
OEDIPUS: Where mainly did you go for pasturage?
SHEPHERD: Sometimes Kithairon, sometimes the hills near-by. 15
OEDIPUS: Do you remember ever seeing this man out there?
SHEPHERD: What would he be doing there? This man?
OEDIPUS: This man standing here. Have you ever seen him
   before?

16 Kyllenê a sacred mountain of Hermês, the messenger of the gods.

SHEPHERD: No. At least, not to my recollection.

MESSENGER: And that is not strange, my lord. But I'll refresh   20
His memory: he must remember when we two
Spent three whole seasons together, March to September,
On Kithairon or thereabouts. He had two flocks;
I had one. Each autumn I'd drive mine home
And he would go back with his to Laïos' sheepfold.—   25
Is this not true, just as I have described it?

SHEPHERD: True, yes; but it was all so long ago.

MESSENGER: Well, then: do you remember, back in those days
That you gave me a baby boy to bring up as my own?

SHEPHERD: What if I did? What are you trying to say?   30

MESSENGER: King Oedipus was once that little child.

SHEPHERD: Damn you, hold your tongue!

OEDIPUS: No more of that!
It is your tongue needs watching, not this man's.

SHEPHERD: My King, my Master, what is it I have done wrong?

OEDIPUS: You have not answered his question about the boy.   35

SHEPHERD: He does not know . . . He is only making
trouble . . .

OEDIPUS: Come, speak plainly, or it will go hard with you.

SHEPHERD: In God's name, do not torture an old man!

OEDIPUS: Come here, one of you; bind his arms behind him.

SHEPHERD: Unhappy king! What more do you wish to learn?   40

OEDIPUS: Did you give this man the child he speaks of?

SHEPHERD: I did.
And I would to God I had died that very day.

OEDIPUS: You will die now unless you speak the truth.

SHEPHERD: Yet if I speak the truth, I am worse than dead.

OEDIPUS: Very well; since you insist upon delaying—   45

SHEPHERD: No! I have told you already that I gave him the
boy.

OEDIPUS: Where did you get him? From your house? From
somewhere else?

SHEPHERD: Not from mine, no. A man gave him to me.

OEDIPUS: Is that man here? Do you know whose slave he was?

SHEPHERD: For God's love, my King, do not ask me any more!   50

OEDIPUS: You are a dead man if I have to ask you again.

SHEPHERD: Then . . . Then the child was from the palace of
    Laïos.
OEDIPUS: A slave child? or a child of his own line?
SHEPHERD: Ah, I am on the brink of dreadful speech!
OEDIPUS: And I of dreadful hearing. Yet I must hear.   *55*
SHEPHERD: If you must be told, then . . .

                                   They said it was
    Laïos' child;
    But it is your wife who can tell you about that.
OEDIPUS: My wife!—Did she give it to you?
SHEPHERD: My lord, she did.
OEDIPUS: Do you know why?
SHEPHERD: I was told to get rid of it.
OEDIPUS: An unspeakable mother!
SHEPHERD: There had been
    prophecies . . .   *60*
OEDIPUS: Tell me.
SHEPHERD: It was said that the boy would kill his own father.
OEDIPUS: Then why did you give him over to this old man?
SHEPHERD: I pitied the baby, my King,
    And I thought that this man would take him far away   *65*
    To his own country.
    He saved him—but for what a fate!
    For if you are what this man says you are,
    No man living is more wretched than Oedipus.
OEDIPUS: Ah God!
    It was true!
    All the prophecies!
    —Now,   *70*
    O Light, may I look on you for the last time!
    I, Oedipus,
    Oedipus, damned in his birth, in his marriage damned,
    Damned in the blood he shed with his own hand!

                              He rushes into the palace.

Ode IV

STROPHE 1

CHORUS: Alas for the seed of men.
What measure shall I give these generations
That breathe on the void and are void
And exist and do not exist?
Who bears more weight of joy   5
Than mass of sunlight shifting in images,
Or who shall make his thought stay on
That down time drifts away?
Your splendor is all fallen.
O naked brow of wrath and tears,   10
O change of Oedipus!
I who saw your days call no man blest—
Your great days like ghosts gone.

ANTISTROPHE 1

That mind was a strong bow.
Deep, how deep you drew it then, hard archer,   15
At a dim fearful range,
And brought dear glory down!
You overcame the stranger—
The virgin with her hooking lion claws—
And though death sang, stood like a tower   20
To make pale Thebes take heart.
Fortress against our sorrow!
True king, giver of laws,
Majestic Oedipus!
No prince in Thebes had ever such renown,   25
No prince won such grace of power.

STROPHE 2

And now of all men ever known
Most pitiful is this man's story:
His fortunes are most changed, his state
Fallen to a low slave's   30

Ground under bitter fate.
O Oedipus, most royal one!
The great door that expelled you to the light
Gave at night—ah, gave night to your glory:
As to the father, to the fathering son.   35
All understood too late.
How could that queen whom Laïos won,
The garden that he harrowed at his height,
Be silent when that act was done?

ANTISTROPHE 2

But all eyes fail before time's eye,   40
All actions come to justice there.
Though never willed, though far down the deep past,
Your bed, your dread sirings,
Are brought to book at last.
Child by Laïos doomed to die,   45
Then doomed to lose that fortunate little death,
Would God you never took breath in this air
That with my wailing lips I take to cry:
For I weep the world's outcast.
I was blind, and now I can tell why: 50
Asleep, for you had given ease of breath
To Thebes, while the false years went by.

ÉXODOS °

Enter, from the palace, Second Messenger.

SECOND MESSENGER: Elders of Thebes, most honored in this
land,
What horrors are yours to see and hear, what weight
Of sorrow to be endured, if, true to your birth,
You venerate the line of Labdakos!
I think neither Istros nor Phasis, those great rivers,   5
Could purify this place of the corruption

Éxodos final scene (or *episodos*).

It shelters now, or soon must bring to light—
Evil not done unconsciously, but willed.
The greatest griefs are those we cause ourselves.

CHORAGOS: Surely, friend, we have grief enough already;   *10*
What new sorrow do you mean?
SECOND MESSENGER: The Queen is dead.
CHORAGOS: Iocastê? Dead? But at whose hand?
SECOND MESSENGER: Her own.
The full horror of what happened, you can not know,
For you did not see it; but I, who did, will tell you
As clearly as I can how she met her death.   *15*

When she had left us,
In passionate silence, passing through the court,
She ran to her apartment in the house,
Her hair clutched by the fingers of both hands.
She closed the doors behind her; then, by that bed   *20*
Where long ago the fatal son was conceived—
That son who should bring about his father's death—
We heard her call upon Laïos, dead so many years,
And heard her wail for the double fruit of her marriage,
A husband by her husband, children by her child.   *25*

Exactly how she died I do not know:
For Oedipus burst in moaning and would not let us
Keep vigil to the end: it was by him
As he stormed about the room that our eyes were caught.
From one to another of us he went, begging a sword,   *30*
Cursing the wife who was not his wife, the mother
Whose womb had carried his own children and himself.
I do not know: it was none of us aided him,
But surely one of the gods was in control!
For with a dreadful cry   *35*
He hurled his weight, as though wrenched out of himself,
At the twin doors: the bolts gave, and he rushed in.
And there we saw her hanging, her body swaying
From the cruel cord she had noosed about her neck.
A great sob broke from him, heartbreaking to hear,   *40*
As he loosed the rope and lowered her to the ground.

I would blot out from my mind what happened next!
For the King ripped from her gown the golden brooches
That were her ornament, and raised them, and plunged
them down
Straight into his own eyeballs, crying, "No more,   45
No more shall you look on the misery about me,
The horrors of my own doing! Too long you have known
The faces of those whom I should never have seen,
Too long been blind to those for whom I was searching!
From this hour, go in darkness!" And as he spoke,   50
He struck at his eyes—not once, but many times;
And the blood spattered his beard,
Bursting from his ruined sockets like red hail.

So from the unhappiness of two this evil has sprung,
A curse on the man and woman alike. The old   55
Happiness of the house of Labdakos
Was happiness enough: where is it today?
It is all wailing and ruin, disgrace, death—all
The misery of mankind that has a name—
And it is wholly and for ever theirs.   60
CHORAGOS: Is he in agony still? Is there no rest for him?
SECOND MESSENGER: He is calling for someone to lead him
to the gates
So that all the children of Kadmos may look upon
His father's murderer, his mother's—no,
I can not say it!
And then he will leave Thebes,   65
Self-exiled, in order that the curse
Which he himself pronounced may depart from the house.
He is weak, and there is none to lead him,
So terrible is his suffering.
But you will see:
Look, the doors are opening; in a moment   70
You will see a thing that would crush a heart of stone.

The central door is opened; Oedipus, blinded, is led in.

CHORAGOS: Dreadful indeed for men to see.
      Never have my own eyes
      Looked on a sight so full of fear.
      Oedipus!   75
      What madness came upon you, what daemon
      Leaped on your life with heavier
      Punishment than a mortal man can bear?
      No: I can not even
      Look at you, poor ruined one.   80
      And I would speak, question, ponder,
      If I were able. No.
      You make me shudder.
OEDIPUS: God. God.
      Is there a sorrow greater?   85
      Where shall I find harbor in this world?
      My voice is hurled far on a dark wind.
      What has God done to me?
CHORAGOS: Too terrible to think of, or to see.

STROPHE 1

OEDIPUS: O cloud of night,   90
      Never to be turned away: night coming on,
      I can not tell how: night like a shroud!
      My fair winds brought me here.
                                    Oh God. Again
      The pain of the spikes where I had sight,
      The flooding pain   95
      Of memory, never to be gouged out.
CHORAGOS: This is not strange.
      You suffer it all twice over, remorse in pain,
      Pain in remorse.

ANTISTROPHE 1

OEDIPUS: Ah dear friend   100
      Are you faithful even yet, you alone?
      Are you still standing near me, will you stay here,
      Patient, to care for the blind?

The blind man!

Yet even blind I know who it is attends me,
By the voice's tone—   105
Though my new darkness hide the comforter.
CHORAGOS: Oh fearful act!
What god was it drove you to rake black
Night across your eyes?

STROPHE 2

OEDIPUS: Apollo. Apollo. Dear   110
Children, the god was Apollo.
He brought my sick, sick fate upon me.
But the blinding hand was my own!
How could I bear to see
When all my sight was horror everywhere?   115
CHORAGOS: Everywhere; that is true.
OEDIPUS: And now what is left?
Images? Love? A greeting even,
Sweet to the senses? Is there anything?
Ah, no, friends: lead me away.   120
Lead me away from Thebes.

Lead the great wreck

And hell of Oedipus, whom the gods hate.
CHORAGOS: Your fate is clear, you are not blind to that.
Would God you had never found it out!

ANTISTROPHE 2

OEDIPUS: Death take the man who unbound   125
My feet on that hillside
And delivered me from death to life! What life?
If only I had died,
This weight of monstrous doom
Could not have dragged me and my darlings down.   130
CHORAGOS: I would have wished the same.
OEDIPUS: Oh never to have come here
With my father's blood upon me! Never
To have been the man they call his mother's husband!

Oh accurst! Oh child of evil, 135
To have entered that wretched bed—
              the selfsame one!
More primal than sin itself, this fell to me.
CHORAGOS: I do not know how I can answer you.
You were better dead than alive and blind.
OEDIPUS: Do not counsel me any more. This punishment 140
That I have laid upon myself is just.
If I had eyes,
I do not know how I could bear the sight
Of my father, when I came to the house of Death,
Or my mother: for I have sinned against them both 145
So vilely that I could not make my peace
By strangling my own life.
                  Or do you think my children,
Born as they were born, would be sweet to my eyes?
Ah never, never! Nor this town with its high walls,
Nor the holy images of the gods.
                For I, 150
Thrice miserable!—Oedipus, noblest of all the line
Of Kadmos, have condemned myself to enjoy
These things no more, by my own malediction
Expelling that man whom the gods declared
To be a defilement in the house of Laïos. 155
After exposing the rankness of my own guilt,
How could I look men frankly in the eyes?
No, I swear it,
If I could have stifled my hearing at its source,
I would have done it and made all this body 160
A tight cell of misery, blank to light and sound:
So I should have been safe in a dark agony
Beyond all recollection.
               Ah Kithairon!
Why did you shelter me? When I was cast upon you,
Why did I not die? Then I should never 165
Have shown the world my execrable birth.
Ah Polybos! Corinth, city that I believed
The ancient seat of my ancestors: how fair

I seemed, your child! And all the while this evil
Was cancerous within me!
                          For I am sick   170
In my daily life, sick in my origin.
O three roads, dark ravine, woodland and way
Where three roads met: you, drinking my father's blood,
My own blood, spilled by my own hand: can you remember
The unspeakable things I did there, and the things   175
I went on from there to do?
                          O marriage, marriage!
The act that engendered me, and again the act
Performed by the son in the same bed—
                                    Ah, the net
Of incest, mingling fathers, brothers, sons,
With brides, wives, mothers: the last evil   180
That can be known by men: no tongue can say
How evil!
          No. For the love of God, conceal me
Somewhere far from Thebes; or kill me; or hurl me
Into the sea, away from men's eyes for ever.
Come, lead me. You need not fear to touch me.   185
Of all men, I alone can bear this guilt.

Enter Creon.

CHORAGOS: We are not the ones to decide; but Creon here
    May fitly judge of what you ask. He only
    Is left to protect the city in your place.
OEDIPUS: Alas, how can I speak to him? What right have I   190
    To beg his courtesy whom I have deeply wronged?
CREON: I have not come to mock you, Oedipus,
    Or to reproach you, either.
    (*To Attendants.*)   —You, standing there:
    If you have lost all respect for man's dignity,
    At least respect the flame of Lord Helios: 195
    Do not allow this pollution to show itself
    Openly here, an affront to the earth
    And Heaven's rain and the light of day. No, take him
    Into the house as quickly as you can.

For it is proper 200
That only the close kindred see his grief.

OEDIPUS: I pray you in God's name, since your courtesy
Ignores my dark expectation, visiting
With mercy this man of all men most execrable:
Give me what I ask—for your good, not for mine. 205

CREON: And what is it that you would have me do?

OEDIPUS: Drive me out of this country as quickly as may be
To a place where no human voice can ever greet me.

CREON: I should have done that before now—only,
God's will had not been wholly revealed to me. 210

OEDIPUS: But his command is plain: the parricide
Must be destroyed. I am that evil man.

CREON: That is the sense of it, yes; but as things are,
We had best discover clearly what is to be done.

OEDIPUS: You would learn more about a man like me? 215

CREON: You are ready now to listen to the god.

OEDIPUS: I will listen. But it is to you
That I must turn for help. I beg you, hear me.
The woman in there—
Give her whatever funeral you think proper: 220
She is your sister.
                    —But let me go, Creon!
Let me purge my father's Thebes of the pollution
Of my living here, and go out to the wild hills,
To Kithairon, that has won such fame with me,
The tomb my mother and father appointed for me, 225
And let me die there, as they willed I should.
And yet I know
Death will not ever come to me through sickness
Or in any natural way: I have been preserved
For some unthinkable fate. But let that be. 230
As for my sons, you need not care for them.
They are men, they will find some way to live.
But my poor daughters, who have shared my table,
Who never before have been parted from their father—
Take care of them, Creon; do this for me. 235
And will you let me touch them with my hands

A last time, and let us weep together?
Be kind, my lord,
Great prince, be kind!
                Could I but touch them,
They would be mine again, as when I had my eyes.   *240*

Enter Antigonê and Ismene, attended.

Ah, God!
Is it my dearest children I hear weeping?
Has Creon pitied me and sent my daughters?
CREON: Yes, Oedipus: I knew that they were dear to you
In the old days, and know you must love them still.   *245*
OEDIPUS: May God bless you for this—and be a friendlier
Guardian to you than he has been to me!
Children, where are you?
Come quickly to my hands: they are your brother's—
Hands that have brought your father's once clear eyes   *250*
To this way of seeing—
                Ah dearest ones,
I had neither sight nor knowledge then, your father
By the woman who was the source of his own life!
And I weep for you—having no strength to see you—,
I weep for you when I think of the bitterness   *255*
That men will visit upon you all your lives.
What homes, what festivals can you attend
Without being forced to depart again in tears?
And when you come to marriageable age,
Where is the man, my daughters, who would dare   *260*
Risk the bane that lies on all my children?
Is there any evil wanting? Your father killed
His father; sowed the womb of her who bore him;
Engendered you at the fount of his own existence!
That is what they will say of you.
                Then, whom   *265*
Can you ever marry? There are no bridegrooms for you,
And your lives must wither away in sterile dreaming.
O Creon, son of Menoikeus!
You are the only father my daughters have,

Since we, their parents, are both of us gone for ever.   *270*
They are your own blood: you will not let them
Fall into beggary and loneliness;
You will keep them from the miseries that are mine!
Take pity on them; see, they are only children,
Friendless except for you. Promise me this,   *275*
Great Prince, and give me your hand in token of it.

Creon clasps his right hand.

Children:
I could say much, if you could understand me,
But as it is, I have only this prayer for you:
Live where you can, be as happy as you can—   *280*
Happier, please God, than God has made your father!

CREON: Enough. You have wept enough. Now go within.
OEDIPUS: I must; but it is hard.
CREON: Time eases all things.
OEDIPUS: But you must promise—
CREON: Say what you desire.
OEDIPUS: Send me from Thebes!
CREON: God grant that I may!   *285*
OEDIPUS: But since God hates me . . .
CREON: No, he will grant your
wish.
OEDIPUS: You promise?
CREON: I cannot speak beyond my knowledge.
OEDIPUS: Then lead me in.
CREON: Come now, and leave your children.
OEDIPUS: No! Do not take them from me!
CREON: Think no longer
That you are in command here, but rather think   *290*
How, when you were, you served your own destruction.

*Exeunt into the house all but the Chorus; the Choragos
chants directly to the audience.*

CHORAGOS: Men of Thebes: look upon Oedipus.
This is the king who solved the famous riddle
And towered up, most powerful of men.

No mortal eyes but looked on him with envy,   295
Yet in the end ruin swept over him.
Let every man in mankind's frailty
Consider his last day; and let none
Presume on his good fortune until he find
Life, at his death, a memory without pain.   300

—*c. 430 B.C.*

William Shakespeare (1564–1616), the supreme writer of English, was born, baptized, and buried in the market town of Stratford-on-Avon, eighty miles from London. Son of a glove maker and merchant who was high bailiff (or mayor) of the town, he probably attended grammar school and learned to read Latin authors in the original. At eighteen he married Anne Hathaway, twenty-six, by whom he had three children, including twins. By 1592 he had become well-known and envied as an actor and playwright in London. From 1594 until he retired, he belonged to the same theatrical company, the Lord Chamberlain's Men (later renamed the King's Men in honour of their patron, James I), for whom he wrote thirty-six plays —some of them, such as Hamlet *and* King Lear, *profound reworkings of old plays. As an actor, Shakespeare is believed to have played supporting roles, such as Hamlet's father's ghost. The company prospered, moved into the Globe Theatre in 1599, and in 1608 bought the fashionable Blackfriars as well; Shakespeare owned an interest in both theatres. When plagues shut down the theatres from 1592 to 1594, Shakespeare turned to story poems; his great* sonnets *(published only in 1609) probably also date from the 1590s. Plays were regarded as entertainments of little literary merit and Shakespeare did not bother to supervise their publication. After* The Tempest *(1611), the last play entirely from his hand, he retired to Stratford, where since 1597 he had owned the second-largest house in town. Most critics agree that when he wrote* Othello *(c. 1604), Shakespeare was at the height of his powers.*

William Shakespeare
The Tragedy of Othello, The Moor of Venice

CHARACTERS

Othello, the Moor
Brabantio, [a senator,] father to Desdemona
Cassio, an honorable lieutenant [to Othello]
Iago, [Othello's ancient,] a villain

NOTE ON THE TEXT: This text of *Othello* is based on that of the First Folio, or large collection, of Shakespeare's plays (1623). But there are many differences between the Folio text and that of the play's first printing in the Quarto, or small volume, of 1621 (eighteen or nineteen years after the play's first performance). Some readings from the Quarto are included. For the reader's convenience, some material has been added by the editor, David Bevington (some indications of scene, some stage directions). Such additions are enclosed in brackets. Mr. Bevington's text and notes were prepared for his book, *The Complete Works of Shakespeare*, 4th ed. (New York: HarperCollins, 1992).

Edited by David Bevington

Roderigo, a gulled gentleman
Duke of Venice
Senators [of Venice]
Montano, governor of Cyprus
Gentlemen of Cyprus
Lodovico and Gratiano, [kinsmen to Brabantio,] two noble Venetians
Sailors
Clown
Desdemona, [daughter to Brabantio and] wife to Othello
Emilia, wife to Iago
Bianca, a courtesan [and mistress to Cassio]
[*A Messenger*
A Herald
A Musician
Servants, Attendants, Officers, Senators, Musicians, Gentlemen]

[Scene: *Venice; a seaport in Cyprus*]

ACT I

SCENE I [VENICE. A STREET.]

Enter Roderigo and Iago.

RODERIGO: Tush, never tell me!° I take it much unkindly
   That thou, Iago, who hast had my purse
   As if the strings were thine, shouldst know of this.°
IAGO: 'Sblood,° but you'll not hear me.
   If ever I did dream of such a matter,   5
   Abhor me.
RODERIGO: Thou toldst me thou didst hold him in thy hate.
IAGO: Despise me
   If I do not. Three great ones of the city,
   In personal suit to make me his lieutenant,   10
   Off-capped to him;° and by the faith of man,

---

1 never tell me (An expression of incredulity, like "tell me another one.")   **3 this** i.e., Desdemona's
elopement   **4 'Sblood** by His (Christ's) blood   **11 him** i.e., Othello

I know my price, I am worth no worse a place.
But he, as loving his own pride and purposes,
Evades them with a bombast circumstance°
Horribly stuffed with epithets of war,°   15
And, in conclusion,
Nonsuits° my mediators. For, "Certes,"° says he,
"I have already chose my officer."
And what was he?
Forsooth, a great arithmetician,°   20
One Michael Cassio, a Florentine,
A fellow almost damned in a fair wife,°
That never set a squadron in the field
Nor the division of a battle° knows
More than a spinster°—unless the bookish theoric,°   25
Wherein the togaed° consuls° can propose°
As masterly as he. Mere prattle without practice
Is all his soldiership. But he, sir, had th' election;
And I, of whom his° eyes had seen the proof
At Rhodes, at Cyprus, and on other grounds   30
Christened° and heathen, must be beleed and calmed°
By debitor and creditor.° This countercaster,°
He, in good time,° must his lieutenant be,
And I—God bless the mark!°—his Moorship's ancient.°
RODERIGO: By heaven, I rather would have been his hangman.°   35
IAGO: Why, there's no remedy. 'Tis the curse of service;
    Preferment° goes by letter and affection,°

---

14 bombast circumstance wordy evasion. (Bombast is cotton padding.)   **15 epithets of war** military expressions   **17 Nonsuits** rejects the petition of.   **Certes** certainly   **20 arithmetician** i.e., a man whose military knowledge is merely theoretical, based on books of tactics   **22 A . . . wife** (Cassio does not seem to be married, but his counterpart in Shakespeare's source does have a woman in his house. See also Act IV, Scene i, line 127.)   **24 division of a battle** disposition of a military unit   **25 a spinster** i.e., a housewife, one whose regular occupation is spinning.   **theoric** theory   **26 togaed** wearing the toga.   **consuls** counsellors, senators.   **propose** discuss   **29 his** i.e., Othello's   **31 Christened** Christian.   **beleed and calmed** left to leeward without wind, becalmed. (A sailing metaphor.)   **32 debitor and creditor** (A name for a system of bookkeeping, here used as a contemptuous nickname for Cassio.)   **countercaster** i.e., bookkeeper, one who tallies with *counters*, or "metal disks." (Said contemptuously.)   **33 in good time** opportunely, i.e., forsooth   **34 God bless the mark** (Perhaps originally a formula to ward off evil; here an expression of impatience.)   **ancient** standard-bearer, ensign   **35 his hangman** the executioner of him   **37 Preferment** promotion.   **letter and affection** personal influence and favouritism

And not by old gradation,° where each second
Stood heir to th' first. Now, sir, be judge yourself
Whether I in any just term° am affined°   *40*
To love the Moor.

RODERIGO: I would not follow him then.

IAGO: O sir, content you.°
I follow him to serve my turn upon him.
We cannot all be masters, nor all masters   *45*
Cannot be truly° followed. You shall mark
Many a duteous and knee-crooking knave
That, doting on his own obsequious bondage,
Wears out his time, much like his master's ass,
For naught but provender, and when he's old, cashiered.°   *50*
Whip me° such honest knaves. Others there are
Who, trimmed in forms and visages of duty,°
Keep yet their hearts attending on themselves,
And, throwing but shows of service on their lords,
Do well thrive by them, and when they have lined their coats,° *55*
Do themselves homage.° These fellows have some soul,
And such a one do I profess myself. For, sir,
It is as sure as you are Roderigo,
Were I the Moor I would not be Iago.°
In following him, I follow but myself—   *60*
Heaven is my judge, not I for love and duty,
But seeming so for my peculiar° end.
For when my outward action doth demonstrate
The native° act and figure° of my heart
In compliment extern,° 'tis not long after   *65*
But I will wear my heart upon my sleeve
For daws° to peck at. I am not what I am.°

---

38 old gradation step-by-step seniority, the traditional way   **40 term** respect.   **affined** bound
43 content you don't you worry about that   **46 truly** faithfully   **50 cashiered** dismissed from service   **51 Whip me** whip, as far as I'm concerned   **52 trimmed . . . duty** dressed up in the mere form and show of dutifulness   **55 lined their coats** i.e., stuffed their purses   **56 Do themselves homage** i.e., attend to self-interest solely   **59 Were . . . Iago** i.e., if I were able to assume command, I certainly would not choose to remain a subordinate, or, I would keep a suspicious eye on a flattering subordinate   **62 peculiar** particular, personal   **64 native** innate.   **figure** shape, intent   **65 compliment extern** outward show. (Conforming in this case to the inner workings and intention of the heart.)   **67 daws** small crowlike birds, proverbially stupid and avaricious.   **I am not what I am** i.e., I am not one who wears his heart on his sleeve.

RODERIGO: What a full° fortune does the thick-lips° owe°
    If he can carry 't thus!°
IAGO: Call up her father.
    Rouse him, make after him, poison his delight,   *70*
    Proclaim him in the streets; incense her kinsmen,
    And, though he in a fertile climate dwell,
    Plague him with flies.° Though that his joy be joy,°
    Yet throw such changes of vexation° on 't
    As it may° lose some color.°   *75*
RODERIGO: Here is her father's house. I'll call aloud.
IAGO: Do, with like timorous° accent and dire yell
    As when, by night and negligence,° the fire
    Is spied in populous cities.
RODERIGO: What ho, Brabantio! Signor Brabantio, ho!   *80*
IAGO: Awake! What ho, Brabantio! Thieves, thieves, thieves!
    Look to your house, your daughter, and your bags!
    Thieves, thieves!

Brabantio [enters] above [at a window].°

BRABANTIO: What is the reason of this terrible summons?
    What is the matter° there?   *85*
RODERIGO: Signor, is all your family within?
IAGO: Are your doors locked?
BRABANTIO: Why, wherefore ask you this?
IAGO: Zounds,° sir, you're robbed. For shame, put on your gown!
    Your heart is burst; you have lost half your soul.
    Even now, now, very now, an old black ram   *90*
    Is tupping° your white ewe. Arise, arise!
    Awake the snorting° citizens with the bell,
    Or else the devil° will make a grandsire of you.
    Arise, I say!

---

68 full swelling.   **thick-lips** (Elizabethans often applied the term "Moor" to Negroes.)   **owe** own
69 carry 't thus carry this off   **72–73 though . . . flies** though he seems prosperous and happy
now, vex him with misery   **73 Though . . . be joy** although he seems fortunate and happy.
(Repeats the idea of line 72.)   **74 changes of vexation** vexing changes   **75 As it may** that may
cause it to.   **some color** some of its fresh gloss   **77 timorous** frightening   **78 and negligence**
i.e., by negligence   **83 [s.d.] at a window** (This stage direction, from the Quarto, probably calls for
an appearance on the gallery above and rearstage.)   **85 the matter** your business   **88 Zounds** by
His (Christ's) wounds   **91 tupping** covering, copulating with. (Said of sheep.)   **92 snorting** snor-
ing   **93 the devil** (The devil was conventionally pictured as black.)

BRABANTIO: What, have you lost your wits?

RODERIGO: Most reverend signor, do you know my voice?   *95*

BRABANTIO: Not I. What are you?

RODERIGO: My name is Roderigo.

BRABANTIO: The worser welcome.

I have charged thee not to haunt about my doors.
In honest plainness thou hast heard me say   *100*
My daughter is not for thee; and now, in madness,
Being full of supper and distempering° drafts,
Upon malicious bravery° dost thou come
To start° my quiet.

RODERIGO: Sir, sir, sir—

BRABANTIO: But thou must needs be sure   *105*
My spirits and my place° have in° their power
To make this bitter to thee.

RODERIGO: Patience, good sir.

BRABANTIO: What tell'st thou me of robbing? This is Venice;
My house is not a grange.°

RODERIGO: Most grave Brabantio,
In simple° and pure soul I come to you.   *110*

IAGO: Zounds, sir, you are one of those that will not serve God
if the devil bid you. Because we come to do you service and
you think we are ruffians, you'll have your daughter covered
with a Barbary° horse; you'll have your nephews° neigh to
you; you'll have coursers° for cousins° and jennets° for germans.°   *115*

BRABANTIO: What profane wretch art thou?

IAGO: I am one, sir, that comes to tell you your daughter and
the Moor are now making the beast with two backs.

BRABANTIO: Thou art a villain.

IAGO: You are—a senator.°

BRABANTIO: This thou shalt answer.° I know thee, Roderigo.

---

102 distempering intoxicating   **103 Upon malicious bravery** with hostile intent to defy me
104 start startle, disrupt   **106 My spirits and my place** my temperament and my authority of office.   **have in** have it in   **109 grange** isolated country house   **110 simple** sincere   **113 Barbary**
from northern Africa (and hence associated with Othello).   **nephews** i.e., grandsons
114 coursers powerful horses.   **cousins** kinsmen.   **jennets** small Spanish horses.   **germans** near
relatives   **118 a senator** (Said with mock politeness, as though the word itself were an insult.)
119 answer be held accountable for

RODERIGO: Sir, I will answer anything. But I beseech you,   *120*
 If't be your pleasure and most wise° consent—
 As partly I find it is—that your fair daughter,
 At this odd-even° and dull watch o' the night,
 Transported with° no worse nor better guard
 But with a knave° of common hire, a gondolier,   *125*
 To the gross clasps of a lascivious Moor—
 If this be known to you and your allowance°
 We then have done you bold and saucy° wrongs.
 But if you know not this, my manners tell me
 We have your wrong rebuke. Do not believe   *130*
 That, from° the sense of all civility,°
 I thus would play and trifle with your reverence.°
 Your daughter, if you have not given her leave,
 I say again, hath made a gross revolt,
 Tying her duty, beauty, wit,° and fortunes   *135*
 In an extravagant° and wheeling° stranger°
 Of here and everywhere. Straight° satisfy yourself.
 If she be in her chamber or your house,
 Let loose on me the justice of the state
 For thus deluding you.   *140*
BRABANTIO: Strike on the tinder,° ho!
 Give me a taper! Call up all my people!
 This accident° is not unlike my dream.
 Belief of it oppresses me already.
 Light, I say, light!   *Exit [above].*
IAGO: Farewell, for I must leave you.   *145*
 It seems not meet° nor wholesome to my place°
 To be producted°—as, if I stay, I shall—
 Against the Moor. For I do know the state,
 However this may gall° him with some check,°

---

121 **wise** well-informed   123 **odd-even** between one day and the next, i.e., about midnight
124 **with** by   125 **But with a knave** than by a low fellow, a servant   127 **allowance** permission
128 **saucy** insolent   131 **from** contrary to.   **civility** good manners, decency   132 **your reverence**
the respect due to you   135 **wit** intelligence   136 **extravagant** expatriate, wandering far from
home.   **wheeling** roving about, vagabond.   **stranger** foreigner   137 **Straight** straightway
141 **tinder** charred linen ignited by a spark from flint and steel, used to light torches or tapers (lines
142, 167)   143 **accident** occurrence, event   146 **meet** fitting.   **place** position (as ensign)
147 **producted** produced (as a witness)   149 **gall** rub; oppress.   **check** rebuke

Cannot with safety cast° him, for he's embarked°   150
With such loud reason° to the Cyprus wars,
Which even now stands in act,° that, for their souls,°
Another of his fathom° they have none
To lead their business; in which regard,°
Though I do hate him as I do hell pains,   155
Yet for necessity of present life°
I must show out a flag and sign of love,
Which is indeed but sign. That you shall surely find him,
Lead to the Sagittary° the raisèd search,°
And there will I be with him. So farewell.   *Exit.*   160

*Enter [below] Brabantio [in his nightgown°] with servants
and torches.*

BRABANTIO: It is too true an evil. Gone she is;
And what's to come of my despisèd time°
Is naught but bitterness. Now, Roderigo,
Where didst thou see her?—O unhappy girl!—
With the Moor, sayst thou?—Who would be a father!—   165
How didst thou know 'twas she?—O, she deceives me
Past thought!—What said she to you?—Get more tapers.
Raise all my kindred.—Are they married, think you?
RODERIGO: Truly, I think they are.
BRABANTIO: O heaven! How got she out? O treason of the
blood!   170
Fathers, from hence trust not your daughters' minds
By what you see them act. Is there not charms°
By which the property° of youth and maidhood
May be abused?° Have you not read, Roderigo,
Of some such thing?
RODERIGO: Yes, sir, I have indeed.   175

---

150 cast dismiss.   **embarked** engaged   **151 loud reason** unanimous shout of confirmation (in the Senate)   **152 stands in act** are going on.   **for their souls** to save themselves   **153 fathom** i.e., ability, depth of experience   **154 in which regard** out of regard for which   **156 life** livelihood   **159 Sagittary** (An inn or house where Othello and Desdemona are staying, named for its sign of Sagittarius, or Centaur.)   **raisèd search** search party roused out of sleep   **160 [s.d.] nightgown** dressing gown. (This costuming is specified in the Quarto text.)   **162 time** i.e., remainder of life   **172 charms** spells   **173 property** special quality, nature   **174 abused** deceived

BRABANTIO: Call up my brother.—O, would you had had her!—
Some one way, some another.—Do you know
Where we may apprehend her and the Moor?
RODERIGO: I think I can discover° him, if you please
To get good guard and go along with me.   *180*
BRABANTIO: Pray you, lead on. At every house I'll call;
I may command° at most.—Get weapons, ho!
And raise some special officers of night.—
On, good Roderigo. I will deserve° your pains.

Exeunt.

Scene II [Venice. Another Street, Before Othello's Lodgings.]

Enter Othello, Iago, attendants with torches.

IAGO: Though in the trade of war I have slain men,
Yet do I hold it very stuff° o' the conscience
To do no contrived° murder. I lack iniquity
Sometimes to do me service. Nine or ten times
I had thought t' have yerked° him° here under the ribs.   *5*
OTHELLO: 'Tis better as it is.
IAGO: Nay, but he prated,
And spoke such scurvy and provoking terms
Against your honor
That, with the little godliness I have,
I did full hard forbear him.° But, I pray you, sir,   *10*
Are you fast married? Be assured of this,
That the magnifico° is much beloved,
And hath in his effect° a voice potential°
As double as the Duke's. He will divorce you,
Or put upon you what restraint or grievance   *15*
The law, with all his might to enforce it on,
Will give him cable.°

---

179 discover reveal, uncover   **182 command** demand assistance   **184 deserve** show gratitude for
2 very stuff essence, basic material (continuing the metaphor of *trade* from line 1)   **3 contrived**
premeditated   **5 yerked** stabbed.   **him** i.e., Roderigo   **10 I . . . him** I restrained myself with
great difficulty from assaulting him   **12 magnifico** Venetian grandee, i.e., Brabantio   **13 in his**
effect at his command.   **potential** powerful   **17 cable** i.e., scope

OTHELLO:　　　　　　Let him do his spite.
My services which I have done the seigniory°
Shall out-tongue his complaints. 'Tis yet to know°—
Which, when I know that boasting is an honor,　　　　　　*20*
I shall promulgate—I fetch my life and being
From men of royal siege,° and my demerits°
May speak unbonneted° to as proud a fortune
As this that I have reached. For know, Iago,
But that I love the gentle Desdemona,　　　　　　*25*
I would not my unhousèd° free condition
Put into circumscription and confine°
For the sea's worth.° But look, what lights come yond?

Enter Cassio [and certain officers°] with torches.

IAGO:　Those are the raisèd father and his friends.
You were best go in.

OTHELLO:　　　　　　Not I. I must be found.　　　　　　*30*
My parts, my title, and my perfect soul°
Shall manifest me rightly. Is it they?

IAGO:　By Janus,° I think no.

OTHELLO:　The servants of the Duke? And my lieutenant?
The goodness of the night upon you, friends!　　　　　　*35*
What is the news?

CASSIO:　　　　　　The Duke does greet you, General,
And he requires your haste-post-haste appearance
Even on the instant.

OTHELLO:　　　　　　What is the matter,° think you?

CASSIO:　Something from Cyprus, as I may divine.°
It is a business of some heat.° The galleys　　　　　　*40*
Have sent a dozen sequent° messengers
This very night at one another's heels,

---

18 seigniory Venetian government　　**19 yet to know** not yet widely known　　**22 siege** i.e., rank.
(Literally, a seat used by a person of distinction.)　　**demerits** deserts　　**23 unbonneted** without removing the hat, i.e., on equal terms (? Or "with hat off," "in all due modesty.")　　**26 unhousèd** un-
confined, undomesticated　　**27 circumscription and confine** restriction and confinement　　**28 the
sea's worth** all the riches at the bottom of the sea.　　[**s.d.**] **officers** (The Quarto text calls for "Cassio
with lights, officers with torches.")　　**31 My . . . soul** my natural gifts, my position or reputation,
and my unflawed conscience　　**33 Janus** Roman two-faced god of beginnings　　**38 matter** business
39 divine guess　　**40 heat** urgency　　**41 sequent** successive

And many of the consuls,° raised and met,
Are at the Duke's already. You have been hotly called for;
When, being not at your lodging to be found,   45
The Senate hath sent about° three several° quests
To search you out.
OTHELLO: 'Tis well I am found by you.
I will but spend a word here in the house
And go with you.   [*Exit.*]
CASSIO: Ancient, what makes° he here?
IAGO: Faith, he tonight hath boarded° a land carrack.°   50
If it prove lawful prize,° he's made forever.
CASSIO: I do not understand.
IAGO: He's married.
CASSIO: To who?

[*Enter Othello.*]

IAGO: Marry,° to—Come, Captain, will you go?
OTHELLO: Have with you.°
CASSIO: Here comes another troop to seek for you.   55

Enter Brabantio, Roderigo, with officers and torches.°

IAGO: It is Brabantio. General, be advised.°
He comes to bad intent.
OTHELLO: Holla! Stand there!
RODERIGO: Signor, it is the Moor.
BRABANTIO: Down with him, thief!

[*They draw on both sides.*]

IAGO: You, Roderigo! Come, sir, I am for you.
OTHELLO: Keep up° your bright swords, for the dew will rust
them.   60
Good signor, you shall more command with years
Than with your weapons.

---

43 **consuls** senators   46 **about** all over the city.   **several** separate   49 **makes** does
50 **boarded** gone aboard and seized as an act of piracy (with sexual suggestion).   **carrack** large
merchant ship   51 **prize** booty   53 **Marry** (An oath, originally "by the Virgin Mary"; here used
with wordplay on *married.*)   54 **Have with you** i.e., let's go   55 [**s.d.**] **officers and torches** (The
Quarto text calls for "others with lights and weapons.")   56 **be advised** be on your guard
60 **Keep up** keep in the sheath

BRABANTIO: O thou foul thief, where hast thou stowed my
daughter?
Damned as thou art, thou hast enchanted her!
For I'll refer me° to all things of sense,° 65
If she in chains of magic were not bound
Whether a maid so tender, fair, and happy,
So opposite to marriage that she shunned
The wealthy curlèd darlings of our nation,
Would ever have, t' incur a general mock, 70
Run from her guardage° to the sooty bosom
Of such a thing as thou—to fear, not to delight.
Judge me the world if 'tis not gross in sense°
That thou hast practiced on her with foul charms,
Abused her delicate youth with drugs or minerals° 75
That weakens motion.° I'll have 't disputed on;°
'Tis probable and palpable to thinking.
I therefore apprehend and do attach° thee
For an abuser of the world, a practicer
Of arts inhibited° and out of warrant.°— 80
Lay hold upon him! If he do resist,
Subdue him at his peril.

OTHELLO: Hold your hands,
Both you of my inclining° and the rest.
Were it my cue to fight, I should have known it
Without a prompter.—Whither will you that I go 85
To answer this your charge?

BRABANTIO: To prison, till fit time
Of law and course of direct session°
Call thee to answer.

OTHELLO: What if I do obey?
How may the Duke be therewith satisfied, 90
Whose messengers are here about my side
Upon some present business of the state

---

65 refer me submit my case.   **things of sense** commonsense understandings, or, creatures possess-
ing common sense   **71 her guardage** my guardianship of her   **73 gross in sense** obvious
75 minerals i.e., poisons   **76 weakens motion** impair the vital faculties.   **disputed on** argued in
court by professional counsel, debated by experts   **78 attach** arrest   **80 arts inhibited** prohibited
arts, black magic.   **out of warrant** illegal   **83 inclining** following, party   **88 course of direct
session** regular or specially convened legal proceedings

To bring me to him?

OFFICER: 'Tis true, most worthy signor.

The Duke's in council, and your noble self,

I am sure, is sent for.

BRABANTIO: How? The Duke in council?   95

In this time of the night? Bring him away.°

Mine's not an idle° cause. The Duke himself,

Or any of my brothers of the state,

Cannot but feel this wrong as 'twere their own;

For if such actions may have passage free,°   100

Bondslaves and pagans shall our statesmen be.

Exeunt.

SCENE III [VENICE. A COUNCIL CHAMBER.]

*Enter Duke [and] Senators [and sit at a table, with lights],
and Officers.° [The Duke and Senators are reading dispatches.]*

DUKE: There is no composition° in these news

That gives them credit.

FIRST SENATOR: Indeed, they are disproportioned.°

My letters say a hundred and seven galleys.

DUKE: And mine, a hundred forty.

SECOND SENATOR: And mine, two hundred.   5

But though they jump° not on a just° account—

As in these cases, where the aim° reports

'Tis oft with difference—yet do they all confirm

A Turkish fleet, and bearing up to Cyprus.

DUKE: Nay, it is possible enough to judgment.   10

I do not so secure me in the error

But the main article I do approve°

In fearful sense.

SAILOR (*within*):   What ho, what ho, what ho!

---

96 away right along   **97 idle** trifling   **100 have passage free** are allowed to go unchecked
[s.d.] Enter . . . Officers (The Quarto text calls for the Duke and senators to "sit at a table with
lights and attendants.")
1 composition consistency   **3 disproportioned** inconsistent   **6 jump** agree.   **just** exact   **7 the
aim** conjecture   **11–12 I do not . . . approve** I do not take such (false) comfort in the discrepan-
cies that I fail to perceive the main point, i.e., that the Turkish fleet is threatening

Enter Sailor.

OFFICER: A messenger from the galleys.
DUKE: Now, what's the business?   *15*
SAILOR: The Turkish preparation° makes for Rhodes.
    So was I bid report here to the state
    By Signor Angelo.
DUKE: How say you by° this change?
FIRST SENATOR: This cannot be
    By no assay° of reason. 'Tis a pageant°   *20*
    To keep us in false gaze.° When we consider
    Th' importancy of Cyprus to the Turk,
    And let ourselves again but understand
    That, as it more concerns the Turk than Rhodes,
    So may he with more facile question bear it,°   *25*
    For that° it stands not in such warlike brace,°
    But altogether lacks th' abilities°
    That Rhodes is dressed in°—if we make thought of this,
    We must not think the Turk is so unskillful°
    To leave that latest° which concerns him first,   *30*
    Neglecting an attempt of ease and gain
    To wake° and wage° a danger profitless.
DUKE: Nay, in all confidence, he's not for Rhodes.
OFFICER: Here is more news.

Enter a Messenger.

MESSENGER: The Ottomites, reverend and gracious,   *35*
    Steering with due course toward the isle of Rhodes,
    Have there injointed them° with an after° fleet.
FIRST SENATOR: Ay, so I thought. How many, as you guess?
MESSENGER: Of thirty sail; and now they do restem
    Their backward course,° bearing with frank appearance°   *40*
    Their purposes toward Cyprus. Signor Montano,

---

16 preparation fleet prepared for battle   **19 by** about   **20 assay** test.   **pageant** mere show
21 in false gaze looking the wrong way   **25 So may . . . it** so also he (the Turk) can more easily
capture it (Cyprus)   **26 For that** since.   **brace** state of defence   **27 abilities** means of self-
defence   **28 dressed in** equipped with   **29 unskillful** deficient in judgment   **30 latest** last
32 wake stir up.   **wage** risk   **37 injointed them** joined themselves.   **after** second, following
39-40 restem . . . course retrace their original course   **40 frank appearance** undisguised intent

Your trusty and most valiant servitor,°
With his free duty° recommends° you thus,
And prays you to believe him.

DUKE: 'Tis certain then for Cyprus.   *45*
Marcus Luccicos, is not he in town?

FIRST SENATOR: He's now in Florence.

DUKE: Write from us to him, post-post-haste. Dispatch.

FIRST SENATOR: Here comes Brabantio and the valiant Moor.

*Enter Brabantio, Othello, Cassio, Iago, Roderigo, and offi-
cers.*

DUKE: Valiant Othello, we must straight° employ you   *50*
Against the general enemy° Ottoman.
[*To Brabantio.*] I did not see you; welcome, gentle° signor.
We lacked your counsel and your help tonight.

BRABANTIO: So did I yours. Good Your Grace, pardon me;
Neither my place° nor aught I heard of business   *55*
Hath raised me from my bed, nor doth the general care
Take hold on me, for my particular° grief
Is of so floodgate° and o'erbearing nature
That it engluts° and swallows other sorrows
And it is still itself.°

DUKE: Why, what's the matter?   *60*

BRABANTIO: My daughter! O, my daughter!

DUKE AND SENATORS: Dead?

BRABANTIO: Ay, to me.
She is abused,° stol'n from me, and corrupted
By spells and medicines bought of mountebanks;
For nature so preposterously to err,
Being not deficient,° blind, or lame of sense,°   *65*
Sans° witchcraft could not.

DUKE: Whoe'er he be that in this foul proceeding
Hath thus beguiled your daughter of herself,

---

42 servitor officer under your command   **43 free duty** freely given and loyal service.
recommends commends himself and reports to 50   **straight** straightway   **51 general enemy** universal enemy to all Christendom   **52 gentle** noble   **55 place** official position   **57 particular** personal   **58 floodgate** i.e., overwhelming (as when floodgates are opened)   **59 engluts** engulfs
60 is still itself remains undiminished   **62 abused** deceived   **65 deficient** defective.   **lame of**
sense deficient in sensory perception   **66 Sans** without

And you of her, the bloody book of law
You shall yourself read in the bitter letter   70
After your own sense°—yea, though our proper° son
Stood in your action.°
BRABANTIO: Humbly I thank Your Grace.
Here is the man, this Moor, whom now it seems
Your special mandate for the state affairs
Hath hither brought.
ALL: We are very sorry for 't.   75
DUKE [*to Othello*]:   What, in your own part, can you say to
this?
BRABANTIO: Nothing, but this is so.
OTHELLO: Most potent, grave, and reverend signors,
My very noble and approved° good masters:
That I have ta'en away this old man's daughter,   80
It is most true; true, I have married her.
The very head and front° of my offending
Hath this extent, no more. Rude° am I in my speech,
And little blessed with the soft phrase of peace;
For since these arms of mine had seven years' pith,°   85
Till now some nine moons wasted,° they have used
Their dearest° action in the tented field;
And little of this great world can I speak
More than pertains to feats of broils and battle,
And therefore little shall I grace my cause   90
In speaking for myself. Yet, by your gracious patience,
I will a round° unvarnished tale deliver
Of my whole course of love—what drugs, what charms,
What conjuration, and what mighty magic,
For such proceeding I am charged withal,°   95
I won his daughter.
BRABANTIO: A maiden never bold;
Of spirit so still and quiet that her motion

---

71 After . . . sense according to your own interpretation.   **our proper** my own   **72 Stood . . .
action** were under your accusation   **79 approved** proved, esteemed   **82 head and front** height
and breadth, entire extent   **83 Rude** unpolished   **85 since . . . pith** i.e., since I was seven.   **pith**
strength, vigour   **86 Till . . . wasted** until some nine months ago (since when Othello has evidently
not been on active duty, but in Venice)   **87 dearest** most valuable   **92 round** plain   **95 withal**
with

Blushed at herself;° and she, in spite of nature,
Of years,° of country, credit,° everything,
To fall in love with what she feared to look on!   *100*
It is a judgment maimed and most imperfect
That will confess° perfection so could err
Against all rules of nature, and must be driven
To find out practices° of cunning hell
Why this should be. I therefore vouch° again   *105*
That with some mixtures powerful o'er the blood,°
Or with some dram conjured to this effect,°
He wrought upon her.

DUKE: To vouch this is no proof,
Without more wider° and more overt test°
Than these thin habits° and poor likelihoods°   *110*
Of modern seeming° do prefer° against him.

FIRST SENATOR: But Othello, speak.
Did you by indirect and forcèd courses°
Subdue and poison this young maid's affections?
Or came it by request and such fair question°   *115*
As soul to soul affordeth?

OTHELLO: I do beseech you,
Send for the lady to the Sagittary
And let her speak of me before her father.
If you do find me foul in her report,
The trust, the office I do hold of you   *120*
Not only take away, but let your sentence
Even fall upon my life.

DUKE: Fetch Desdemona hither.

OTHELLO: Ancient, conduct them. You best know the place.

[*Exeunt Iago and attendants.*]

And, till she come, as truly as to heaven

97–98 her . . . herself i.e., she blushed easily at herself. (*Motion* can suggest the impulse of the soul
or of the emotions, or physical movement.)   **99 years** i.e., difference in age.   **credit** virtuous reputation   **102 confess** concede (that)   **104 practices** plots   **105 vouch** assert   **106 blood** passions   **107 dram . . . effect** dose made by magical spells to have this effect   **109 more wider**
fuller.   **test** testimony   **110 habits** garments, i.e., appearances.   **poor likelihoods** weak infer-
ences   **111 modern seeming** commonplace assumption.   **prefer** bring forth   **113 forcèd**
courses means used against her will   **115 question** conversation

I do confess the vices of my blood,° 125
So justly° to your grave ears I'll present
How I did thrive in this fair lady's love,
And she in mine.

DUKE: Say it, Othello.

OTHELLO: Her father loved me, oft invited me, 130
Still° questioned me the story of my life
From year to year—the battles, sieges, fortunes
That I have passed.
I ran it through, even from my boyish days
To th' very moment that he bade me tell it, 135
Wherein I spoke of most disastrous chances,
Of moving accidents° by flood and field,
Of hairbreadth scapes i' th' imminent deadly breach,°
Of being taken by the insolent foe
And sold to slavery, of my redemption thence, 140
And portance° in my travels' history,
Wherein of antres° vast and deserts idle,°
Rough quarries,° rocks, and hills whose heads touch heaven,
It was my hint° to speak—such was my process—
And of the Cannibals that each other eat, 145
The Anthropophagi,° and men whose heads
Do grow beneath their shoulders. These things to hear
Would Desdemona seriously incline;
But still the house affairs would draw her thence,
Which ever as she could with haste dispatch 150
She'd come again, and with a greedy ear
Devour up my discourse. Which I, observing,
Took once a pliant° hour, and found good means
To draw from her a prayer of earnest heart
That I would all my pilgrimage dilate,° 155
Whereof by parcels° she had something heard,

125 blood passions, human nature   **126 justly** truthfully, accurately   **131 Still** continually
137 moving accidents stirring happenings   **138 imminent . . . breach** death-threatening gaps
made in a fortification   **141 portance** conduct   **142 antres** caverns.   **idle** barren, desolate
143 Rough quarries rugged rock formations   **144 hint** occasion, opportunity
146 Anthropophagi man-eaters. (A term from Pliny's *Natural History*.)   **153 pliant** well-suiting
155 dilate relate in detail   **156 by parcels** piecemeal

But not intentively.° I did consent,
And often did beguile her of her tears,
When I did speak of some distressful stroke
That my youth suffered. My story being done,   160
She gave me for my pains a world of sighs.
She swore, in faith, 'twas strange, 'twas passing° strange,
'Twas pitiful, 'twas wondrous pitiful.
She wished she had not heard it, yet she wished
That heaven had made her° such a man. She thanked me,   165
And bade me, if I had a friend that loved her,
I should but teach him how to tell my story,
And that would woo her. Upon this hint° I spake.
She loved me for the dangers I had passed,
And I loved her that she did pity them.   170
This only is the witchcraft I have used.
Here comes the lady. Let her witness it.

Enter Desdemona, Iago, [and] attendants.

DUKE: I think this tale would win my daughter too.
Good Brabantio,
Take up this mangled matter at the best.°   175
Men do their broken weapons rather use
Than their bare hands.
BRABANTIO: I pray you, hear her speak.
If she confess that she was half the wooer,
Destruction on my head if my bad blame
Light on the man!—Come hither, gentle mistress.   180
Do you perceive in all this noble company
Where most you owe obedience?
DESDEMONA: My noble Father,
I do perceive here a divided duty.
To you I am bound for life and education;°
My life and education both do learn° me   185
How to respect you. You are the lord of duty;°

---

157 intentively with full attention, continuously   **162 passing** exceedingly   **165 made her** created her to be   **168 hint** opportunity. (Othello does not mean that she was dropping hints.)
175 Take . . . best make the best of a bad bargain   **184 education** upbringing   **185 learn** teach
186 of duty to whom duty is due

I am hitherto your daughter. But here's my husband,
And so much duty as my mother showed
To you, preferring you before her father,
So much I challenge° that I may profess   *190*
Due to the Moor my lord.

BRABANTIO: God be with you! I have done.
Please it Your Grace, on to the state affairs.
I had rather to adopt a child than get° it.
Come hither, Moor.   *195*

[He joins the hands of Othello and Desdemona.]

I here do give thee that with all my heart°
Which, but thou hast already, with all my heart°
I would keep from thee.—For your sake,° jewel,
I am glad at soul I have no other child,
For thy escape° would teach me tyranny,   *200*
To hang clogs° on them.—I have done, my lord.

DUKE: Let me speak like yourself,° and lay a sentence°
Which, as a grece° or step, may help these lovers
Into your favor.
When remedies° are past, the griefs are ended   *205*
By seeing the worst, which late on hopes depended.°
To mourn a mischief° that is past and gone
Is the next° way to draw new mischief on.
What° cannot be preserved when fortune takes,
Patience her injury a mockery makes.°   *210*
The robbed that smiles steals something from the thief;
He robs himself that spends a bootless grief.°

BRABANTIO: So let the Turk of Cyprus us beguile,
We lose it not, so long as we can smile.
He bears the sentence well that nothing bears   *215*

---

190 **challenge** claim   194 **get** beget   196 **with all my heart** wherein my whole affection has been engaged   197 **with all my heart** willingly, gladly   198 **For your sake** on your account   200 **escape** elopement   201 **clogs** (Literally, blocks of wood fastened to the legs of criminals or convicts to inhibit escape.)   202 **like yourself** i.e., as you would, in your proper temper.   **lay a sentence** apply a maxim   203 **grece** step   205 **remedies** hopes of remedy   206 **which . . . depended** which griefs were sustained until recently by hopeful anticipation   207 **mischief** misfortune, injury   208 **next** nearest   209 **What** whatever   210 **Patience . . . makes** patience laughs at the injury inflicted by fortune (and thus eases the pain)   212 **spends a bootless grief** indulges in unavailing grief

But the free comfort which from thence he hears,
But he bears both the sentence and the sorrow
That, to pay grief, must of poor patience borrow.°
These sentences, to sugar or to gall,
Being strong on both sides, are equivocal.°   220
But words are words. I never yet did hear
That the bruisèd heart was piercèd through the ear.°
I humbly beseech you, proceed to th' affairs of state.

DUKE: The Turk with a most mighty preparation makes for
Cyprus. Othello, the fortitude° of the place is best known to
you; and though we have there a substitute° of most al-
lowed° sufficiency, yet opinion, a sovereign mistress of effects, throws a more safer voice on you.° You must therefore
be content to slubber° the gloss of your new fortunes with
this more stubborn° and boisterous expedition.

OTHELLO: The tyrant custom, most grave senators,   230
Hath made the flinty and steel couch of war
My thrice—driven° bed of down. I do agnize°
A natural and prompt alacrity
I find in hardness,° and do undertake
These present wars against the Ottomites.   235
Most humbly therefore bending to your state,°
I crave fit disposition for my wife,
Due reference of place and exhibition,°
With such accommodation° and besort°
As levels° with her breeding.°   240

DUKE: Why, at her father's.

BRABANTIO: I will not have it so.

OTHELLO: Nor I.

215–218 He bears . . . borrow a person well bears out your maxim who can enjoy its platitudinous
comfort, free of all genuine sorrow, but anyone whose grief bankrupts his poor patience is left with
your saying and his sorrow, too. (*Bears the sentence* also plays on the meaning, "receives judicial sentence.")   **219–220 These . . . equivocal** these fine maxims are equivocal, either sweet or bitter in
their application   **222 piercèd . . . ear** i.e., surgically lanced and cured by mere words of advice
225 fortitude strength   **226 substitute** deputy.   **allowed** acknowledged   **226–227 opinion . . .
on you** general opinion, an important determiner of affairs, chooses you as the best man
228 slubber soil, sully.   **229 stubborn** harsh, rough   **232 thrice-driven** thrice sifted, winnowed.
agnize know in myself, acknowledge   **234 hardness** hardship   **236 bending . . . state** bowing or
kneeling to your authority   **238 reference . . . exhibition** provision of appropriate place to live
and allowance of money   **239 accommodation** suitable provision.   **besort** attendance
240 levels equals, suits.   **breeding** social position, upbringing

DESDEMONA: Nor I. I would not there reside,
   To put my father in impatient thoughts
   By being in his eye. Most gracious Duke,
   To my unfolding° lend your prosperous° ear,   *245*
   And let me find a charter° in your voice,
   T' assist my simpleness.
DUKE: What would you, Desdemona?
DESDEMONA: That I did love the Moor to live with him,
   My downright violence and storm of fortunes°   *250*
   May trumpet to the world. My heart's subdued
   Even to the very quality of my lord.°
   I saw Othello's visage in his mind,
   And to his honors and his valiant parts°
   Did I my soul and fortunes consecrate.   *255*
   So that, dear lords, if I be left behind
   A moth° of peace, and he go to the war,
   The rites° for why I love him are bereft me,
   And I a heavy interim shall support
   By his dear° absence. Let me go with him.   *260*
OTHELLO: Let her have your voice.°
   Vouch with me, heaven, I therefor beg it not
   To please the palate of my appetite,
   Nor to comply with heat°—the young affects°
   In me defunct—and proper° satisfaction,   *265*
   But to be free° and bounteous to her mind.
   And heaven defend° your good souls that you think°
   I will your serious and great business scant
   When she is with me. No, when light-winged toys
   Of feathered Cupid seel° with wanton dullness   *270*
   My speculative and officed instruments,°

---

245 unfolding explanation, proposal.   **prosperous** propitious   **246 charter** privilege, authoriza-
tion   **250 My . . . fortunes** my plain and total breach of social custom, taking my future by storm
and disrupting my whole life   **251-252 My heart's . . . lord** my heart is brought wholly into accord
with Othello's virtues; I love him for his virtues   **254 parts** qualities   **257 moth** i.e., one who consumes merely   **258 rites** rites of love (with a suggestion, too, of "rights," sharing)   **260 dear** (1)
heartfelt (2) costly   **261 voice** consent   **264 heat** sexual passion.   **young affects** passions of
youth, desires   **265 proper** personal   **266 free** generous   **267 defend** forbid.   **think** should
think   **270 seel** i.e., make blind (as in falconry, by sewing up the eyes of the hawk during training)
271 speculative . . . instruments eyes and other faculties used in the performance of duty

That° my disports° corrupt and taint° my business,
Let huswives make a skillet of my helm,
And all indign° and base adversities
Make head° against my estimation!°   275
DUKE: Be it as you shall privately determine,
  Either for her stay or going. Th' affair cries haste,
  And speed must answer it.
A SENATOR: You must away tonight.
DESDEMONA: Tonight, my lord?
DUKE: This night.
OTHELLO: With all my heart.
DUKE: At nine i' the morning here we'll meet again.   280
  Othello, leave some officer behind,
  And he shall our commission bring to you,
  With such things else of quality and respect°
  As doth import° you.
OTHELLO: So please Your Grace, my ancient;
  A man he is of honesty and trust.   285
  To his conveyance I assign my wife,
  With what else needful Your Good Grace shall think
  To be sent after me.
DUKE: Let it be so.
  Good night to everyone. [*To Brabantio.*] And, noble signor,
  If virtue no delighted° beauty lack,   290
  Your son-in-law is far more fair than black.
FIRST SENATOR: Adieu, brave Moor. Use Desdemona well.
BRABANTIO: Look to her, Moor, if thou hast eyes to see.
  She has deceived her father, and may thee.

  Exeunt [*Duke, Brabantio, Cassio, Senators, and officers*].

OTHELLO: My life upon her faith! Honest Iago,   295
  My Desdemona must I leave to thee.
  I prithee, let thy wife attend on her,
  And bring them after in the best advantage.°

---

272 **That** so that. **disports** sexual pastimes. **taint** impair 274 **indign** unworthy, shameful
275 **Make head** raise an army. **estimation** reputation 283 **of quality and respect** of importance and relevance 284 **import** concern 290 **delighted** capable of delighting 298 **in . . . ad-**
vantage at the most favourable opportunity

Come, Desdemona. I have but an hour
Of love, of worldly matters and direction,° 300
To spend with thee. We must obey the time.°

Exit [with Desdemona].

RODERIGO: Iago—
IAGO: What sayst thou, noble heart?
RODERIGO: What will I do, think'st thou?
IAGO: Why, go to bed and sleep. 305
RODERIGO: I will incontinently° drown myself.
IAGO: If thou dost, I shall never love thee after. Why, thou silly
gentleman?
RODERIGO: It is silliness to live when to live is torment; and
then have we a prescription° to die when death is our physi-
cian.
IAGO: O villainous!° I have looked upon the world for four
times seven years, and, since I could distinguish betwixt a 310
benefit and an injury, I never found man that knew how to
love himself. Ere I would say I would drown myself for the
love of a guinea hen,° I would change my humanity with a
baboon.
RODERIGO: What should I do? I confess it is my shame to be
so fond,° but it is not in my virtue° to amend it. 315
IAGO: Virtue? A fig!° 'Tis in ourselves that we are thus or thus.
Our bodies are our gardens, to the which our wills are gar-
deners; so that if we will plant nettles or sow lettuce, set hys-
sop° and weed up thyme, supply it with one gender° of herbs
or distract it with° many, either to have it sterile with idle-
ness° or manured with industry—why, the power and corrigible authority° of this lies in our wills. If the beam° of our 320
lives had not one scale of reason to poise° another of sensuality,

---

300 direction instructions   **301 the time** the urgency of the present crisis   **306 incontinently** immediately, without self-restraint   **308–309 prescription** (1) right based on long-established custom
(2) doctor's prescription   **310 villainous** i.e., what perfect nonsense   **313 guinea hen** (A slang
term for a prostitute.)   **314 fond** infatuated   **315 virtue** strength, nature   **316 fig** (To give a fig is
to thrust the thumb between the first and second fingers in a vulgar and insulting gesture.)
318 hyssop an herb of the mint family   **319 gender** kind.   **distract it with** divide it among.
320 idleness want of cultivation.   **corrigible authority** power to correct   **321 beam** balance.
322 poise counterbalance.

the blood° and baseness of our natures would conduct us to most preposterous conclusions. But we have reason to cool our raging motions,° our carnal stings, our unbitted° lusts, whereof I take this that you call love to be a sect or scion.°

RODERIGO: It cannot be.   325

IAGO: It is merely a lust of the blood and a permission of the will. Come, be a man. Drown thyself? Drown cats and blind puppies. I have professed me thy friend, and I confess me knit to thy deserving with cables of perdurable° toughness. I could never better stead° thee than now. Put money in thy purse. Follow thou the wars; defeat thy favor° with an usurped° beard. I say, put money in thy purse. It cannot be   330 long that Desdemona should continue her love to the Moor— put money in thy purse—nor he his to her. It was a violent commencement in her, and thou shalt see an answerable sequestration°—put but money in thy purse. These Moors are changeable in their wills°—fill thy purse with money. The   335 food that to him now is as luscious as locusts° shall be to him shortly as bitter as coloquintida.° She must change for youth; when she is sated with his body, she will find the error of her choice. She must have change, she must. Therefore put money in thy purse. If thou wilt needs damn thyself, do it a more delicate way than drowning. Make° all the money thou canst. If sanctimony° and a frail vow betwixt an erring°   340 barbarian and a supersubtle Venetian be not too hard for my wits and all the tribe of hell, thou shalt enjoy her. Therefore make money. A pox of drowning thyself! It is clean out of the way.° Seek thou rather to be hanged in compassing° thy joy than to be drowned and go without her.

                                                                345

---

blood natural passions   **324 motions** appetites.   **unbitted** unbridled, uncontrolled   **325 sect or scion** cutting or offshoot   **329 perdurable** very durable   **330 stead** assist   **331 defeat thy favor** disguise your face.   **usurped** (The suggestion is that Roderigo is not man enough to have a beard of his own.)   **334–335 an answerable sequestration** a corresponding separation or estrangement   **336 wills** carnal appetites   **337 locusts** fruit of the carob tree (see Matthew 3:4), or perhaps honeysuckle.   **coloquintida** colocynth or bitter apple, a purgative   **341 Make** raise, collect.   **sanctimony** sacred ceremony   **342 erring** wandering, vagabond, unsteady   **344 clean . . . way** entirely unsuitable as a course of action   **compassing** encompassing, embracing

RODERIGO: Wilt thou be fast° to my hopes if I depend on the issue?°

IAGO: Thou art sure of me. Go, make money. I have told thee often, and I retell thee again and again, I hate the Moor. My cause is hearted;° thine hath no less reason. Let us be conjunctive° in our revenge against him. If thou canst cuckold him, thou dost thyself a pleasure, me a sport. There are many events in the womb of time which will be delivered. Traverse,° go, provide thy money. We will have more of this tomorrow. Adieu.

RODERIGO: Where shall we meet i' the morning?

IAGO: At my lodging.

RODERIGO: I'll be with thee betimes.° [*He starts to leave.*]   355

IAGO: Go to, farewell.—Do you hear, Roderigo?

RODERIGO: What say you?

IAGO: No more of drowning, do you hear?

RODERIGO: I am changed.

IAGO: Go to, farewell. Put money enough in your purse.   360

RODERIGO: I'll sell all my land.   *Exit.*

IAGO: Thus do I ever make my fool my purse;
For I mine own gained knowledge should profane
If I would time expend with such a snipe°
But for my sport and profit. I hate the Moor;   365
And it is thought abroad° that twixt my sheets
He's done my office.° I know not if 't be true;
But I, for mere suspicion in that kind,
Will do as if for surety.° He holds me well;°
The better shall my purpose work on him.   370
Cassio's a proper° man. Let me see now:
To get his place and to plume up° my will
In double knavery—How, how?—Let's see:
After some time, to abuse° Othello's ear
That he° is too familiar with his wife.   375

---

346 fast true.   **issue** (successful) outcome   **348 hearted** fixed in the heart, heartfelt
349 conjunctive united   **351 Traverse** (A military marching term.)   **355 betimes** early
364 snipe woodcock, i.e., fool   **366 it is thought abroad** it is rumored   **367 my office** i.e., my
sexual function as husband   **369 do . . . surety** act as if on certain knowledge.   **holds me well**
regards me favourably   **371 proper** handsome   **372 plume up** put a feather in the cap of, i.e.,
glorify, gratify   **374 abuse** deceive   **375 he** i.e., Cassio

He hath a person and a smooth dispose°
To be suspected, framed to make women false.
The Moor is of a free° and open° nature,
That thinks men honest that but seem to be so,
And will as tenderly° be led by the nose   380
As asses are.
I have 't. It is engendered. Hell and night
Must bring this monstrous birth to the world's light.

                                            [*Exit.*]

ACT II

SCENE I [A SEAPORT IN CYPRUS. AN OPEN PLACE NEAR THE QUAY.]

Enter Montano and two Gentlemen.

MONTANO: What from the cape can you discern at sea?
FIRST GENTLEMAN: Nothing at all. It is a high-wrought
flood.°
I cannot, twixt the heaven and the main,°
Descry a sail.
MONTANO: Methinks the wind hath spoke aloud at land;   5
A fuller blast ne'er shook our battlements.
If it hath ruffianed° so upon the sea,
What ribs of oak, when mountains° melt on them,
Can hold the mortise?° What shall we hear of this?
SECOND GENTLEMAN: A segregation° of the Turkish fleet.   10
For do but stand upon the foaming shore,
The chidden° billow seems to pelt the clouds;
The wind-shaked surge, with high and monstrous mane,°
Seems to cast water on the burning Bear°

---

376 **dispose** disposition   378 **free** frank, generous.   **open** unsuspicious   380 **tenderly** readily
2 **high-wrought flood** very agitated sea   3 **main** ocean (also at line 41)   7 **ruffianed** raged
8 **mountains** i.e., of water   9 **hold the mortise** hold their joints together. (A *mortise* is the socket
hollowed out in fitting timbers.)   10 **segregation** dispersal   12 **chidden** i.e., rebuked, repelled (by
the shore), and thus shot into the air   13 **monstrous mane** (The surf is like the mane of a wild
beast.)   14 **the burning Bear** i.e., the constellation Ursa Minor or the Little Bear, which includes
the polestar (and hence regarded as the guards of *th' ever-fixèd pole* in the next line; sometimes the
term *guards* is applied to the two "pointers" of the Big Bear or Dipper, which may be intended here.)

And quench the guards of th' ever-fixèd pole.   15
I never did like molestation° view
On the enchafèd° flood.
MONTANO: If that° the Turkish fleet
Be not ensheltered and embayed,° they are drowned;
It is impossible to bear it out.°   20

Enter a [Third] Gentleman.

THIRD GENTLEMAN: News, lads! Our wars are done.
The desperate tempest hath so banged the Turks
That their designment° halts.° A noble ship of Venice
Hath seen a grievous wreck° and sufferance°
On most part of their fleet.   25
MONTANO: How? Is this true?
THIRD GENTLEMAN: The ship is here put in,
A Veronesa;° Michael Cassio,
Lieutenant to the warlike Moor Othello,
Is come on shore; the Moor himself at sea,   30
And is in full commission here for Cyprus.
MONTANO: I am glad on 't. 'Tis a worthy governor.
THIRD GENTLEMAN: But this same Cassio, though he speak
  of comfort
Touching the Turkish loss, yet he looks sadly°
And prays the Moor be safe, for they were parted   35
With foul and violent tempest.
MONTANO: Pray heaven he be,
For I have served him, and the man commands
Like a full° soldier. Let's to the seaside, ho!
As well to see the vessel that's come in
As to throw out our eyes for brave Othello,   40
Even till we make the main and th' aerial blue°
An indistinct regard.°
THIRD GENTLEMAN: Come, let's do so,

---

16 **like molestation** comparable disturbance   17 **enchafèd** angry   18 **If that** if   19 **embayed**
sheltered by a bay   20 **bear it out** survive, weather the storm   23 **designment** design, enterprise.
halts is lame   24 **wreck** shipwreck.   **sufferance** damage, disaster   28 **Veronesa** i.e., fitted out in
Verona for Venetian service, or possibly *Verennessa* (the Folio spelling), i.e., *verrinessa*, a cutter (from
verrinare, "to cut through")   34 **sadly** gravely   38 **full** perfect   41 **the main . . . blue** the sea
and the sky   42 **An indistinct regard** indistinguishable in our view

For every minute is expectancy°
Of more arrivance.°

Enter Cassio.

CASSIO: Thanks, you the valiant of this warlike isle,   45
That so approve° the Moor! O, let the heavens
Give him defense against the elements,
For I have lost him on a dangerous sea.
MONTANO: Is he well shipped?
CASSIO: His bark is stoutly timbered, and his pilot   50
Of very expert and approved allowance;°
Therefore my hopes, not surfeited to death,°
Stand in bold cure.°
                    [*A cry*] *within*: "A sail, a sail, a sail!"
CASSIO: What noise?
A GENTLEMAN: The town is empty. On the brow o' the sea°   55
Stand ranks of people, and they cry "A sail!"
CASSIO: My hopes do shape him for° the governor.

                                        [*A shot within.*]

SECOND GENTLEMAN: They do discharge their shot of
courtesy;°
Our friends at least.
CASSIO: I pray you, sir, go forth,
And give us truth who 'tis that is arrived.   60
SECOND GENTLEMAN: I shall.   *Exit.*
MONTANO: But, good Lieutenant, is your general wived?
CASSIO: Most fortunately. He hath achieved a maid
That paragons° description and wild fame,°
One that excels the quirks° of blazoning° pens,   65
And in th' essential vesture of creation

---

43 is expectancy gives expectation   **44 arrivance** arrival   **46 approve** admire, honour
51 approved allowance tested reputation   **52 surfeited to death** i.e., overextended, worn thin
through repeated application or delayed fulfillment   **53 in bold cure** in strong hopes of fulfillment
55 brow o' the sea cliff-edge   **57 My . . . for** I hope it is   **58 discharge . . . courtesy** fire a
salute in token of respect and courtesy   **64 paragons** surpasses.   **wild fame** extravagant report
65 quirks witty conceits.   **blazoning** setting forth as though in heraldic language

Does tire the enginer.°

Enter [Second] Gentleman.°

   How now? Who has put in?°

SECOND GENTLEMAN: 'Tis one Iago, ancient to the General.

CASSIO: He's had most favorable and happy speed.
 Tempests themselves, high seas, and howling winds,   *70*
 The guttered° rocks and congregated sands—
 Traitors ensteeped° to clog the guiltless keel—
 As° having sense of beauty, do omit°
 Their mortal° natures, letting go safely by
 The divine Desdemona.

MONTANO: What is she?   *75*

CASSIO: She that I spake of, our great captain's captain,
 Left in the conduct of the bold Iago,
 Whose footing° here anticipates our thoughts
 A sennight's° speed. Great Jove, Othello guard,
 And swell his sail with thine own powerful breath,   *80*
 That he may bless this bay with his tall° ship,
 Make love's quick pants in Desdemona's arms,
 Give renewed fire to our extincted spirits,
 And bring all Cyprus comfort!

Enter Desdemona, Iago, Roderigo, and Emilia.

        O, behold,
 The riches of the ship is come on shore!   *85*
 You men of Cyprus, let her have your knees.

[The gentlemen make curtsy to Desdemona.]

 Hail to thee, lady! And the grace of heaven
 Before, behind thee, and on every hand
 Enwheel thee round!

66–67 in . . . enginer in her real, God-given, beauty, (she) defeats any attempt to praise her.
enginer engineer, i.e., poet, one who devises. **[s.d.]** *Second Gentleman* (So identified in the Quarto
text here and in lines 58, 61, 68, and 96; the Folio calls him a gentleman.) **67 put in** i.e., to
harbour **71 guttered** jagged, trenched **72 ensteeped** lying under water **73 As** as if. **omit**
forbear to exercise **74 mortal** deadly **78 footing** landing **79 sennight's** week's **81 tall** splendid, gallant

DESDEMONA: I thank you, valiant Cassio.
  What tidings can you tell me of my lord?   *90*
CASSIO: He is not yet arrived, nor know I aught
  But that he's well and will be shortly here.
DESDEMONA: O, but I fear—How lost you company?
CASSIO: The great contention of the sea and skies
  Parted our fellowship.
              [*Within*] "A sail, a sail!" [*A shot.*]
              But hark. A sail!   *95*
SECOND GENTLEMAN: They give their greeting to the citadel.
  This likewise is a friend.
CASSIO: See for the news.

              [*Exit Second Gentleman.*]

  Good Ancient, you are welcome. [*Kissing Emilia.*] Welcome,
  mistress.
  Let it not gall your patience, good Iago,
  That I extend° my manners; 'tis my breeding°   *100*
  That gives me this bold show of courtesy.
IAGO: Sir, would she give you so much of her lips
  As of her tongue she oft bestows on me,
  You would have enough.
DESDEMONA: Alas, she has no speech!°   *105*
IAGO: In faith, too much.
  I find it still,° when I have list° to sleep.
  Marry, before your ladyship, I grant,
  She puts her tongue a little in her heart
  And chides with thinking.°
EMILIA: You have little cause to say so.   *110*
IAGO: Come on, come on. You are pictures out of doors,°
  Bells° in your parlors, wildcats in your kitchens,°
  Saints° in your injuries, devils being offended,
  Players° in your huswifery,° and huswives° in your beds.

---

100 **extend** give scope to.   **breeding** training in the niceties of etiquette   105 **she has no speech**
i.e., she's not a chatterbox, as you allege   107 **still** always.   **list** desire   110 **with thinking** i.e., in
her thoughts only   111 **pictures out of doors** i.e., silent and well-behaved in public   112 **Bells** i.e.,
jangling, noisy, and brazen.   **in your kitchens** i.e., in domestic affairs. (Ladies would not do the
cooking.)   113 **Saints** martyrs   114 **Players** idlers, triflers, or deceivers.   **huswifery** housekeeping.   **huswives** hussies (i.e., women are "busy" in bed, or unduly thrifty in dispensing sexual favours)

DESDEMONA: O, fie upon thee, slanderer!   *115*
IAGO: Nay, it is true, or else I am a Turk.°
  You rise to play, and go to bed to work.
EMILIA: You shall not write my praise.
IAGO: No, let me not.
DESDEMONA: What wouldst write of me, if thou shouldst
  praise me?
IAGO: O gentle lady, do not put me to 't,   *120*
  For I am nothing if not critical.°
DESDEMONA: Come on, essay.°—There's one gone to the
  harbor?
IAGO: Ay, madam.
DESDEMONA: I am not merry, but I do beguile
  The thing I am° by seeming otherwise.   *125*
  Come, how wouldst thou praise me?
IAGO: I am about it, but indeed my invention
  Comes from my pate as birdlime° does from frieze°—
  It plucks out brains and all. But my Muse labors,°
  And thus she is delivered: *130*
  If she be fair and wise, fairness and wit,
  The one's for use, the other useth it.°
DESDEMONA: Well praised! How if she be black° and witty?
IAGO: If she be black, and thereto have a wit,
  She'll find a white° that shall her blackness fit.°   *135*
DESDEMONA: Worse and worse.
EMILIA: How if fair and foolish?
IAGO: She never yet was foolish that was fair,
  For even her folly° helped her to an heir.°
DESDEMONA: These are old fond° paradoxes to make fools
  laugh i' th' alehouse.
  What miserable praise hast thou for her that's foul and
  foolish?   *140*

---

116 a Turk an infidel, not to be believed   **121 critical** censorious   **122 essay** try   **125 The thing I am** i.e., my anxious self   **128 birdlime** sticky substance used to catch small birds.   **frieze** coarse woolen cloth   **129 labors** (1) exerts herself (2) prepares to deliver a child (with a following pun on *delivered* in line 130)   **132 The one's . . . it** i.e., her cleverness will make use of her beauty   **133 black** dark-complexioned, brunette   **135 a white** a fair person (with word-play on "wight," a person).   **fit** (with sexual suggestion of mating)   **138 folly** (with added meaning of "lechery, wantonness").   **to an heir** i.e., to bear a child   **139 fond** foolish

IAGO: There's none so foul° and foolish thereunto,°
    But does foul° pranks which fair and wise ones do.

DESDEMONA: O heavy ignorance! Thou praisest the worst best. But what praise couldst thou bestow on a deserving woman indeed, one that, in the authority of her merit, did justly put on the vouch° of very malice itself?   *145*

IAGO: She that was ever fair, and never proud,
    Had tongue at will, and yet was never loud,
    Never lacked gold and yet went never gay,°
    Fled from her wish, and yet said, "Now I may,"°
    She that being angered, her revenge being nigh,   *150*
    Bade her wrong stay° and her displeasure fly,
    She that in wisdom never was so frail
    To change the cod's head for the salmon's tail,°
    She that could think and ne'er disclose her mind,
    See suitors following and not look behind,   *155*
    She was a wight, if ever such wight were—

DESDEMONA: To do what?

IAGO: To suckle fools° and chronicle small beer.°

DESDEMONA: O most lame and impotent conclusion! Do not learn of him, Emilia, though he be thy husband. How say   *160* you, Cassio? Is he not a most profane° and liberal° counselor?

CASSIO: He speaks home,° madam. You may relish° him more in° the soldier than in the scholar.

    [*Cassio and Desdemona stand together, conversing intimately.*]

IAGO [*aside*]: He takes her by the palm. Ay, well said,° whisper. With as little a web as this will I ensnare as great a fly as   *165* Cassio. Ay, smile upon her, do; I will gyve° thee in thine own

---

141 **foul** ugly. **thereunto** in addition   142 **foul** sluttish   145 **put . . . vouch** compel the approval   148 **gay** extravagantly clothed   149 **Fled . . . may** avoided temptation where the choice was hers   151 **Bade . . . stay** i.e., resolved to put up with her injury patiently   153 **To . . . tail** i.e., to exchange a lackluster husband for a sexy lover (?) (**Cod's head** is slang for "penis," and tail, for "pudendum.")   158 **suckle fools** breastfeed babies.   **chronicle small beer** i.e., keep petty household accounts, keep track of trivial matters   161 **profane** irreverent, ribald.   **liberal** licentious, free-spoken   162 **home** right to the target. (A term from fencing.)   **relish** appreciate   **in** in the character of   164 **well said** well done   166 **gyve** fetter, shackle.

courtship.° You say true;° 'tis so, indeed. If such tricks as these strip you out of your lieutenantry, it had been better you had not kissed your three fingers so oft, which now again you are most apt to play the sir° in. Very good; well kissed! An excellent courtesy! 'Tis so, indeed. Yet again your fingers to your lips? Would they were clyster pipes° for your sake! [*Trumpet within.*] The Moor! I know his trumpet.

CASSIO: 'Tis truly so.

DESDEMONA: Let's meet him and receive him.

CASSIO: Lo, where he comes!

Enter Othello and attendants.

OTHELLO: O my fair warrior!

DESDEMONA: My dear Othello!   *175*

OTHELLO: It gives me wonder great as my content
To see you here before me. O my soul's joy,
If after every tempest come such calms,
May the winds blow till they have wakened death,
And let the laboring bark climb hills of seas   *180*
Olympus-high, and duck again as low
As hell's from heaven! If it were now to die,
'Twere now to be most happy, for I fear
My soul hath her content so absolute
That not another comfort like to this   *185*
Succeeds in unknown fate.°

DESDEMONA: The heavens forbid
But that our loves and comforts should increase
Even as our days do grow!

OTHELLO: Amen to that, sweet powers!
I cannot speak enough of this content.   *190*
It stops me here; it is too much of joy.
And this, and this, the greatest discords be

[*They kiss.*]°

---

courtship courtesy, show of courtly manners.   **You say true** i.e., that's right, go ahead   **169 the sir** i.e., the fine gentleman   **170 clyster pipes** tubes used for enemas and douches   **186 Succeeds . . . fate** i.e., can follow in the unknown future   **192 [s.d.] They kiss** (The direction is from the Quarto.)

That e'er our hearts shall make!

IAGO [*aside*]:   O, you are well tuned now!
But I'll set down° the pegs that make this music,   *195*
As honest as I am.°

OTHELLO: Come, let us to the castle.
News, friends! Our wars are done, the Turks are drowned.
How does my old acquaintance of this isle?—
Honey, you shall be well desired° in Cyprus;   *200*
I have found great love amongst them. O my sweet,
I prattle out of fashion,° and I dote
In mine own comforts.—I prithee, good Iago,
Go to the bay and disembark my coffers.°
Bring thou the master° to the citadel;   *205*
He is a good one, and his worthiness
Does challenge° much respect.—Come, Desdemona.—
Once more, well met at Cyprus!

> *Exeunt Othello and Desdemona [and all*
> *but Iago and Roderigo].*

IAGO [*to an attendant*]:   Do thou meet me presently at the harbor. [*To Roderigo.*] Come hither. If thou be'st valiant—as,
they say, base men° being in love have then a nobility in
their natures more than is native to them—list° me. The
Lieutenant tonight watches on the court of guard.° First, I
must tell thee this: Desdemona is directly in love with him.

RODERIGO: With him? Why, 'tis not possible.

IAGO: Lay thy finger thus,° and let thy soul be instructed.
Mark me with what violence she first loved the Moor, but°
for bragging and telling her fantastical lies. To love him still
for prating? Let not thy discreet heart think it. Her eye must
be fed; and what delight shall she have to look on the devil?
When the blood is made dull with the act of sport,° there

---

195 set down loosen (and hence untune the instrument)   **196 As . . . I am** for all my supposed
honesty   **200 desired** welcomed   **202 out of fashion** irrelevantly, incoherently (?)   **204 coffers**
chests, baggage   **205 master** ship's captain   **207 challenge** lay claim to, deserve   **210 base men**
even lowly born men   **211 list** listen to   **212 court of guard** guardhouse. (Cassio is in charge of
the watch.)   **215 thus** i.e., on your lips   **216 but** only   **219 the act of sport** sex

should be, again to inflame it and to give satiety a fresh appetite, loveliness in favor,° sympathy° in years, manners, and beauties—all which the Moor is defective in. Now, for want of these required conveniences,° her delicate tenderness will find itself abused,° begin to heave the gorge,° disrelish and abhor the Moor. Very nature° will instruct her in it and compel her to some second choice. Now, sir, this granted—as it is a most pregnant° and unforced position— who stands so eminent in the degree of° this fortune as Cassio does? A knave very voluble,° no further conscionable° than in putting on the mere form of civil and humane° seeming for the better compassing of his salt° and most hidden loose affection.° Why, none, why, none. A slipper° and subtle knave, a finder out of occasions, that has an eye can stamp° and counterfeit advantages,° though true advantage never present itself; a devilish knave. Besides, the knave is handsome, young, and hath all those requisites in him that folly° and green° minds look after. A pestilent complete knave, and the woman hath found him° already.

RODERIGO: I cannot believe that in her. She's full of most blessed condition.°

IAGO: Blessed fig's end!° The wine she drinks is made of grapes. If she had been blessed, she would never have loved the Moor. Blessed pudding!° Didst thou not see her paddle with the palm of his hand? Didst not mark that?

RODERIGO: Yes, that I did; but that was but courtesy.

IAGO: Lechery, by this hand. An index° and obscure° prologue to the history of lust and foul thoughts. They met so near with their lips that their breaths embraced together. Villainous thoughts, Roderigo! When these mutualities° so

220

225

230

235

240

---

220 favor appearance. **sympathy** correspondence, similarity **222 required conveniences** things conducive to sexual compatibility **223 abused** cheated, revolted. **heave the gorge** experience nausea **224 Very nature** her very instincts **225 pregnant** evident, cogent **226 in . . . of** as next in line for **227 voluble** facile, glib. **conscionable** conscientious, conscience-bound **228 humane** polite, courteous. **salt** licentious **229 affection** passion. **slipper** slippery **230 an eye can stamp** an eye that can coin, create **231 advantages** favourable opportunities **233 folly** wantonness. **green** immature **234 found him** sized him up, perceived his intent **235 condition** disposition **236 fig's end** (See Act I, Scene iii, line 316 for the vulgar gesture of the fig.) **237 pudding** sausage **240 index** table of contents. **obscure** (i.e., the *lust and foul thoughts* in line 241 are secret, hidden from view) **243 mutualities** exchanges, intimacies.

marshal the way, hard at hand° comes the master and main exercise, th' incorporate° conclusion. Pish! But, sir, be you ruled by me. I have brought you from Venice. Watch you° 245 tonight; for the command, I'll lay 't upon you.° Cassio knows you not. I'll not be far from you. Do you find some occasion to anger Cassio, either by speaking too loud, or tainting° his discipline, or from what other course you please, which the time shall more favorably minister.°

RODERIGO: Well.   250

IAGO: Sir, he's rash and very sudden in choler,° and haply° may strike at you. Provoke him that he may, for even out of that will I cause these of Cyprus to mutiny,° whose qualification° shall come into no true taste° again but by the displanting of Cassio. So shall you have a shorter journey to your desires by the means I shall then have to prefer° them, 255 and the impediment most profitably removed, without the which there were no expectation of our prosperity.

RODERIGO: I will do this, if you can bring it to any opportunity.

IAGO: I warrant° thee. Meet me by and by° at the citadel. I must fetch his necessaries ashore. Farewell.   260

RODERIGO: Adieu.   *Exit.*

IAGO: That Cassio loves her, I do well believe 't;
That she loves him, 'tis apt° and of great credit.°
The Moor, howbeit that I endure him not,
Is of a constant, loving, noble nature,   265
And I dare think he'll prove to Desdemona
A most dear husband. Now, I do love her too,
Not out of absolute lust—though peradventure
I stand accountant° for as great a sin—
But partly led to diet° my revenge   270
For that I do suspect the lusty Moor
Hath leaped into my seat, the thought whereof

---

hard at hand closely following   **244 incorporate** carnal   **245 Watch you** stand watch   **245–246 for the command . . . you** I'll arrange for you to be appointed, given orders   **247 tainting** disparaging   **249 minister** provide   **251 choler** wrath   **haply** perhaps   **253 mutiny** riot. **qualification** appeasement.   **true taste** i.e., acceptable state   **255 prefer** advance   **259 warrant** assure.   **by and by** immediately   **263 apt** probable.   **credit** credibility   **269 accountant** accountable   **270 diet** feed

Doth, like a poisonous mineral, gnaw my innards;
And nothing can or shall content my soul
Till I am evened with him, wife for wife,   275
Or failing so, yet that I put the Moor
At least into a jealousy so strong
That judgment cannot cure. Which thing to do,
If this poor trash of Venice, whom I trace°
For° his quick hunting, stand the putting on,°   280
I'll have our Michael Cassio on the hip,°
Abuse° him to the Moor in the rank garb—°
For I fear Cassio with my nightcap° too—
Make the Moor thank me, love me, and reward me
For making him egregiously an ass   285
And practicing upon° his peace and quiet
Even to madness. 'Tis here, but yet confused.
Knavery's plain face is never seen till used.

Exit.

SCENE II [CYPRUS. A STREET.]

Enter Othello's Herald with a proclamation.

HERALD: It is Othello's pleasure, our noble and valiant general, that, upon certain tidings now arrived, importing the
mere perdition° of the Turkish fleet, every man put himself
into triumph:° some to dance, some to make bonfires, each
man to what sport and revels his addiction° leads him. For,
besides these beneficial news, it is the celebration of his nup-
tial. So much was his pleasure should be proclaimed. All of-   5
fices° are open, and there is full liberty of feasting from this

---

279 **trace** i.e., train, or follow (?), or perhaps *trash*, a hunting term, meaning to put weights on a
hunting dog in order to slow him down   280 **For** to make more eager.   **stand . . . on** respond
properly when I incite him to quarrel   281 **on the hip** at my mercy, where I can throw him. (A
wrestling term.)   282 **Abuse** slander.   **rank garb** coarse manner, gross fashion   283 **with my
nightcap** i.e., as a rival in my bed, as one who gives me cuckold's horns   286 **practicing upon**
plotting against
2 **mere perdition** complete destruction   3 **triumph** public celebration   4 **addiction** inclination
6 **offices** rooms where food and drink are kept

present hour of five till the bell have told eleven. Heaven bless the isle of Cyprus and our noble general Othello!

Exit.

SCENE III [CYPRUS. THE CITADEL.]

Enter Othello, Desdemona, Cassio, and attendants.

OTHELLO: Good Michael, look you to the guard tonight.
Let's teach ourselves that honorable stop°
Not to outsport° discretion.

CASSIO: Iago hath direction what to do,
But notwithstanding, with my personal eye   5
Will I look to 't.

OTHELLO: Iago is most honest.
Michael, good night. Tomorrow with your earliest°
Let me have speech with you. [*To Desdemona.*]
   Come, my dear love,
The purchase made, the fruits are to ensue;
That profit's yet to come 'tween me and you.°—   10
Good night.

Exit [Othello, with Desdemona and attendants].

Enter Iago.

CASSIO: Welcome, Iago. We must to the watch.

IAGO: Not this hour,° Lieutenant; 'tis not yet ten o' the clock.
Our general cast° us thus early for the love of his
Desdemona; who° let us not therefore blame. He hath not yet
made wanton the night with her, and she is sport for Jove.   15

CASSIO: She's a most exquisite lady.

IAGO: And, I'll warrant her, full of game.

CASSIO: Indeed, she's a most fresh and delicate creature.

IAGO: What an eye she has! Methinks it sounds a parley° to
provocation.

---

2 stop restraint   **3 outsport** celebrate beyond the bounds of   **7 with your earliest** at your earliest convenience   **9-10 The purchase . . . you** i.e., though married, we haven't yet consummated our love   **13 Not this hour** not for an hour yet.   **cast** dismissed   **14 who** i.e., Othello   **19 sounds a parley** calls for a conference, issues an invitation

CASSIO: An inviting eye, and yet methinks right modest.　　*20*

IAGO: And when she speaks, is it not an alarum° to love?

CASSIO: She is indeed perfection.

IAGO: Well, happiness to their sheets! Come, Lieutenant, I have a stoup° of wine, and here without° are a brace° of Cyprus gallants that would fain have a measure° to the health of　　*25* black Othello.

CASSIO: Not tonight, good Iago. I have very poor and unhappy brains for drinking. I could well wish courtesy would invent some other custom of entertainment.

IAGO: O, they are our friends. But one cup! I'll drink for you.°

CASSIO: I have drunk but one cup tonight, and that was craftily qualified° too, and behold what innovation° it makes　　*30* here.° I am unfortunate in the infirmity and dare not task my weakness with any more.

IAGO: What, man? 'Tis a night of revels. The gallants desire it.

CASSIO: Where are they?

IAGO: Here at the door. I pray you, call them in.

CASSIO: I'll do 't, but it dislikes me.°　　　　　　　*Exit.*　　*35*

IAGO: If I can fasten but one cup upon him,
　　With that which he hath drunk tonight already,
　　He'll be as full of quarrel and offense°
　　As my young mistress' dog. Now, my sick fool Roderigo,
　　Whom love hath turned almost the wrong side out,　　*40*
　　To Desdemona hath tonight caroused°
　　Potations pottle-deep;° and he's to watch.°
　　Three lads of Cyprus—noble swelling° spirits,
　　That hold their honors in a wary distance,°
　　The very elements° of this warlike isle—　　　　　*45*
　　Have I tonight flustered with flowing cups,
　　And they watch° too. Now, 'mongst this flock of drunkards

---

21 alarum signal calling men to arms (continuing the military metaphor of *parley*, line 19)
23 stoup measure of liquor, two quarts　**24 without** outside.　**brace** pair　**24–25 fain have a measure** gladly drink a toast　**28 for you** in your place. (Iago will do the steady drinking to keep the gallants company while Cassio has only one cup.)　**29 qualified** diluted　**30 innovation** disturbance, insurrection.　**here** i.e., in my head　**35 it dislikes me** i.e., I'm reluctant　**38 offense** readiness to take offence　**41 caroused** drunk off　**42 pottle-deep** to the bottom of the tankard. **watch** stand watch　**43 swelling** proud　**44 hold . . . distance** i.e., are extremely sensitive of their honour　**45 very elements** typical sort　**47 watch** are members of the guard

Am I to put our Cassio in some action
That may offend the isle.—But here they come.

Enter Cassio, Montano, and gentlemen; [servants following with wine].

If consequence do but approve my dream,°   50
My boat sails freely both with wind and stream.°

CASSIO: 'Fore God, they have given me a rouse° already.

MONTANO: Good faith, a little one; not past a pint, as I am a
soldier.

IAGO: Some wine, ho! [*He sings.*]

>   "And let me the cannikin° clink, clink,   55
>   And let me the cannikin clink.
>   A soldier's a man,
>   O, man's life's but a span;°
>   Why, then, let a soldier drink."

Some wine, boys!   60

CASSIO: 'Fore God, an excellent song.

IAGO: I learned it in England, where indeed they are most potent in potting.° Your Dane, your German, and your swag-
bellied Hollander—drink, ho!—are nothing to your English.

CASSIO: Is your Englishman so exquisite in his drinking?   65

IAGO: Why, he drinks you,° with facility, your Dane° dead
drunk; he sweats not° to overthrow your Almain;° he gives
your Hollander a vomit ere the next pottle can be filled.

CASSIO: To the health of our general!

MONTANO: I am for it, Lieutenant, and I'll do you justice.°   70

IAGO: O sweet England! [*He sings.*]

>   "King Stephen was and—a worthy peer,
>   His breeches cost him but a crown;
>   He held them sixpence all too dear,
>   With that he called the tailor lown.°   75

---

50 If . . . dream if subsequent events will only substantiate my scheme   **51 stream** current
52 rouse full draft of liquor   **55 cannikin** small drinking vessel   **58 span** brief span of time.
(Compare Psalm 39:6 as rendered in the 1928 *Book of Common Prayer:* "Thou hast made my days as
it were a span long.")   **62 potting** drinking   **66 drinks you** drinks. **your Dane** your typical
Dane. **sweats not** i.e., need not exert himself   **67 Almain** German   **70 I'll . . . justice** i.e., I'll
drink as much as you   **75 lown** lout, rascal

> He was a wight of high renown,
>> And thou art but of low degree.
> 'Tis pride° that pulls the country down;
>> Then take thy auld° cloak about thee."

Some wine, ho!   *80*

CASSIO: 'Fore God, this is a more exquisite song than the other.

IAGO: Will you hear 't again?

CASSIO: No, for I hold him to be unworthy of his place that does those things. Well, God's above all; and there be souls must be saved, and there be souls must not be saved.   *85*

IAGO: It's true, good Lieutenant.

CASSIO: For mine own part—no offense to the General, nor any man of quality°—I hope to be saved.

IAGO: And so do I too, Lieutenant.

CASSIO: Ay, but, by your leave, not before me; the lieutenant is   *90*
to be saved before the ancient. Let's have no more of this; let's to our affairs.—God forgive us our sins!—Gentlemen, let's look to our business. Do not think, gentlemen, I am drunk. This is my ancient; this is my right hand, and this is my left. I am not drunk now. I can stand well enough, and speak well enough.   *95*

GENTLEMEN: Excellent well.

CASSIO: Why, very well then; you must not think then that I am drunk.   *Exit.*

MONTANO: To th' platform, masters. Come, let's set the watch.°

[Exeunt Gentlemen.]

IAGO: You see this fellow that is gone before.
> He's a soldier fit to stand by Caesar
> And give direction; and do but see his vice.   *100*
> 'Tis to his virtue a just equinox,°
> The one as long as th' other. 'Tis pity of him.

---

78 pride i.e., extravagance in dress   **79 auld** old   **88 quality** rank   **97 set the watch** mount the guard   **101 just equinox** exact counterpart. (*Equinox* is a day on which daylight and nighttime hours are equal.)

I fear the trust Othello puts him in,
On some odd time of his infirmity,
Will shake this island.

MONTANO: But is he often thus?   *105*

IAGO: 'Tis evermore the prologue to his sleep.
He'll watch the horologe a double set,°
If drink rock not his cradle.

MONTANO: It were well
The General were put in mind of it.
Perhaps he sees it not, or his good nature   *110*
Prizes the virtue that appears in Cassio
And looks not on his evils. Is not this true?

Enter Roderigo.

IAGO [*aside to him*]:   How now, Roderigo?
I pray you, after the Lieutenant; go.   [*Exit Roderigo.*]

MONTANO: And 'tis great pity that the noble Moor   *115*
Should hazard such a place as his own second
With° one of an engraffed° infirmity.
It were an honest action to say so
To the Moor.

IAGO: Not I, for this fair island.
I do love Cassio well and would do much   *120*
To cure him of this evil.   [*Cry within:* "Help! Help!"]
                              But, hark! What noise?

Enter Cassio, pursuing° Roderigo.

CASSIO: Zounds, you rogue! You rascal!

MONTANO: What's the matter, Lieutenant?

CASSIO: A knave teach me my duty? I'll beat the knave into a
    twiggen° bottle.

RODERIGO: Beat me?   *125*

CASSIO: Dost thou prate, rogue? [*He strikes Roderigo.*]

---

107 watch . . . set stay awake twice around the clock or *horologe*   **116–117 hazard . . . With** risk giving such an important position as his second in command to   **117 engraffed** engrafted, inveterate   **121 [s.d.] pursuing** (The Quarto text reads, "driving in.")   **124 twiggen** wicker-covered. (Cassio vows to assail Roderigo until his skin resembles wickerwork or until he has driven Roderigo through the holes in a wickerwork.)

MONTANO: Nay, good Lieutenant. [*Restraining him.*] I pray
you, sir, hold your hand.

CASSIO: Let me go, sir, or I'll knock you o'er the mazard.°

MONTANO: Come, come, you're drunk.

CASSIO: Drunk? [*They fight.*] 130

IAGO [*aside to Roderigo*]: Away, I say. Go out and cry a
mutiny.°

[*Exit Roderigo.*]

Nay, good Lieutenant—God's will, gentlemen—
Help, ho!—Lieutenant—sir—Montano—sir—
Help, masters!°—Here's a goodly watch indeed!

[*A bell rings.*]°

Who's that which rings the bell?—Diablo,° ho! 135
The town will rise.° God's will, Lieutenant, hold!
You'll be ashamed forever.

Enter Othello and attendants [*with weapons*].

OTHELLO: What is the matter here?

MONTANO: Zounds, I bleed still.
I am hurt to th' death. He dies! [*He thrusts at Cassio.*]

OTHELLO: Hold, for your lives!

IAGO: Hold, ho! Lieutenant—sir—Montano—gentlemen— 140
Have you forgot all sense of place and duty?
Hold! The General speaks to you. Hold, for shame!

OTHELLO: Why, how now, ho! From whence ariseth this?
Are we turned Turks, and to ourselves do that
Which heaven hath forbid the Ottomites?° 145
For Christian shame, put by this barbarous brawl!
He that stirs next to carve for° his own rage
Holds his soul light;° he dies upon his motion.°
Silence that dreadful bell. It frights the isle

---

128 mazard i.e., head. (Literally, a drinking vessel.) **131 mutiny** riot **134 masters** sirs. **s.d. A bell rings** (This direction is from the Quarto, as are *Exit Roderigo* at line 114, *They fight* at line 130, and *with weapons* at line 137.) **135 Diablo** the devil **136 rise** grow riotous **144–145 to ourselves . . . Ottomites** inflict on ourselves the harm that heaven has prevented the Turks from doing (by destroying their fleet) **147 carve for** i.e., indulge, satisfy with his sword **148 Holds . . . light** i.e., places little value on his life. **upon his motion** if he moves

From her propriety.° What is the matter, masters?   *150*
Honest Iago, that looks dead with grieving,
Speak. Who began this? On thy love, I charge thee.

IAGO: I do not know. Friends all but now, even now,
In quarter° and in terms° like bride and groom
Devesting them° for bed; and then, but now—   *155*
As if some planet had unwitted men—
Swords out, and tilting one at others' breasts
In opposition bloody. I cannot speak°
Any beginning to this peevish odds;°
And would in action glorious I had lost   *160*
Those legs that brought me to a part of it!

OTHELLO: How comes it, Michael, you are thus forgot?°

CASSIO: I pray you, pardon me. I cannot speak.

OTHELLO: Worthy Montano, you were wont be° civil;
The gravity and stillness° of your youth   *165*
The world hath noted, and your name is great
In mouths of wisest censure.° What's the matter
That you unlace° your reputation thus
And spend your rich opinion° for the name
Of a night-brawler? Give me answer to it.   *170*

MONTANO: Worthy Othello, I am hurt to danger.
Your officer, Iago, can inform you—
While I spare speech, which something° now offends° me—
Of all that I do know; nor know I aught
By me that's said or done amiss this night,   *175*
Unless self-charity be sometimes a vice,
And to defend ourselves it be a sin
When violence assails us.

OTHELLO: Now, by heaven,
My blood° begins my safer guides° to rule,
And passion, having my best judgment collied,°   *180*

---

150 propriety proper state or condition   **154 In quarter** in friendly conduct, within bounds.   **in terms** on good terms   **155 Devesting them** undressing themselves   **158 speak** explain   **159 peevish odds** childish quarrel   **162 are thus forgot** have forgotten yourself thus   **164 wont** be accustomed to be   **165 stillness** sobriety   **167 censure** judgment   **168 unlace** undo, lay open (as one might loose the strings of a purse containing reputation)   **169 opinion** reputation   **173 something** somewhat.   **offends** pains   **179 blood** passion (of anger).   **guides** i.e., reason   **180 collied** darkened

Essays° to lead the way. Zounds, if I stir,
Or do but lift this arm, the best of you
Shall sink in my rebuke. Give me to know
How this foul rout° began, who set it on;
And he that is approved in° this offense,   185
Though he had twinned with me, both at a birth,
Shall lose me. What? In a town of° war
Yet wild, the people's hearts brim full of fear,
To manage° private and domestic quarrel?
In night, and on the court and guard of safety?°   190
'Tis monstrous. Iago, who began 't?

MONTANO [*to Iago*]:   If partially affined,° or leagued in office,°
Thou dost deliver more or less than truth,
Thou art no soldier.

IAGO: Touch me not so near.
I had rather have this tongue cut from my mouth   195
Than it should do offense to Michael Cassio;
Yet, I persuade myself, to speak the truth
Shall nothing wrong him. Thus it is, General.
Montano and myself being in speech,
There comes a fellow crying out for help,   200
And Cassio following him with determined sword
To execute° upon him. Sir, this gentleman

[*indicating Montano*]

Steps in to Cassio and entreats his pause.°
Myself the crying fellow did pursue,
Lest by his clamor—as it so fell out—   205
The town might fall in fright. He, swift of foot,
Outran my purpose, and I returned, the rather°
For that I heard the clink and fall of swords
And Cassio high in oath, which till tonight
I ne'er might say before. When I came back—   210

---

181 Essays undertakes   **184 rout** riot   **185 approved in** found guilty of   **187 town of** town garrisoned for   **189 manage** undertake   **190 on . . . safety** at the main guardhouse or headquarters and on watch   **192 partially affined** made partial by some personal relationship.   **leagued in office** in league as fellow officers   **202 execute** give effect to (his anger)   **203 his pause** him to stop   **207 rather** sooner

For this was brief—I found them close together
At blow and thrust, even as again they were
When you yourself did part them.
More of this matter cannot I report.
But men are men; the best sometimes forget.°   215
Though Cassio did some little wrong to him,
As men in rage strike those that wish them best,°
Yet surely Cassio, I believe, received
From him that fled some strange indignity,
Which patience could not pass.°

OTHELLO: I know, Iago,   220
Thy honesty and love doth mince this matter,
Making it light to Cassio. Cassio, I love thee,
But nevermore be officer of mine.

Enter Desdemona, attended.

Look if my gentle love be not raised up.
I'll make thee an example.   225
DESDEMONA: What is the matter, dear?
OTHELLO: All's well now,
sweeting;
Come away to bed. [*To Montano.*] Sir, for your hurts,
Myself will be your surgeon.°—Lead him off.

[*Montano is led off.*]

Iago, look with care about the town
And silence those whom this vile brawl distracted.   230
Come, Desdemona. 'Tis the soldiers' life
To have their balmy slumbers waked with strife.

Exit [with all but Iago and Cassio].

IAGO: What, are you hurt, Lieutenant?
CASSIO: Ay, past all surgery.
IAGO: Marry, God forbid!   235

---

215 forget forget themselves **217 those . . . best** i.e., even those who are well disposed **220 pass** pass over, overlook **228 be your surgeon** i.e., make sure you receive medical attention

CASSIO: Reputation, reputation, reputation! O, I have lost my reputation! I have lost the immortal part of myself, and what remains is bestial. My reputation, Iago, my reputation!

IAGO: As I am an honest man, I thought you had received some bodily wound; there is more sense in that than in reputation. Reputation is an idle and most false imposition,° oft got without merit and lost without deserving. You have lost no reputation at all, unless you repute yourself such a loser. What, man, there are more ways to recover° the General again. You are but now cast in his mood°—a punishment more in policy° than in malice, even so as one would beat his offenseless dog to affright an imperious lion.° Sue° to him again and he's yours.

CASSIO: I will rather sue to be despised than to deceive so good a commander with so slight,° so drunken, and so indiscreet an officer. Drunk? And speak parrot?° And squabble? Swagger? Swear? And discourse fustian with one's own shadow? O thou invisible spirit of wine, if thou hast no name to be known by, let us call thee devil!

IAGO: What was he that you followed with your sword? What had he done to you?

CASSIO: I know not.

IAGO: Is 't possible?

CASSIO: I remember a mass of things, but nothing distinctly; a quarrel, but nothing wherefore.° O God, that men should put an enemy in their mouths to steal away their brains! That we should, with joy, pleasance, revel, and applause° transform ourselves into beasts!

IAGO: Why, but you are now well enough. How came you thus recovered?

CASSIO: It hath pleased the devil drunkenness to give place to the devil wrath. One unperfectness shows me another, to make me frankly despise myself.

241 false imposition thing artificially imposed and of no real value   243 recover regain favour with   244 cast in his mood dismissed in a moment of anger.   in policy done for expediency's sake and as a public gesture   245 would . . . lion i.e., would make an example of a minor offender in order to deter more important and dangerous offenders   246 Sue petition   248 slight worthless   248-249 speak parrot talk nonsense, rant   256 wherefore why   258 applause desire for applause

IAGO: Come, you are too severe a moraler.° As the time, the place, and the condition of this country stands, I could heartily wish this had not befallen; but since it is as it is, mend it for your own good.

CASSIO: I will ask him for my place again; he shall tell me I am a drunkard. Had I as many mouths as Hydra,° such an answer would stop them all. To be now a sensible man, by and by a fool, and presently a beast! O, strange! Every inordinate cup is unblessed, and the ingredient is a devil.

IAGO: Come, come, good wine is a good familiar creature, if it be well used. Exclaim no more against it. And, good Lieutenant, I think you think I love you.

CASSIO: I have well approved° it, sir. I drunk!

IAGO: You or any man living may be drunk at a time,° man. I'll tell you what you shall do. Our general's wife is now the general—I may say so in this respect, for that° he hath devoted and given up himself to the contemplation, mark, and denotement° of her parts° and graces. Confess yourself freely to her; importune her help to put you in your place again. She is of so free,° so kind, so apt, so blessed a disposition, she holds it a vice in her goodness not to do more than she is requested. This broken joint between you and her husband entreat her to splinter;° and, my fortunes against any lay° worth naming, this crack of your love shall grow stronger than it was before.

CASSIO: You advise me well.

IAGO: I protest,° in the sincerity of love and honest kindness.

CASSIO: I think it freely;° and betimes in the morning I will beseech the virtuous Desdemona to undertake for me. I am desperate of my fortunes if they check° me here.

IAGO: You are in the right. Good night, Lieutenant. I must to the watch.

CASSIO: Good night, honest Iago. *Exit Cassio.*

IAGO: And what's he then that says I play the villain,

265

270

275

280

285

---

262 moraler moralizer   **266 Hydra** the Lernaean Hydra, a monster with many heads and the ability to grow two heads when one was cut off, slain by Hercules as the second of his twelve labours   **272 approved** proved   **273 at a time** at one time or another   **274–275 in . . . that** in view of this fact, that   **275–276 mark, and denotement** (Both words mean "observation.")   **276 parts** qualities   **277 free** generous   **280 splinter** bind with splints.   **lay** stake, wager   **283 protest** insist, declare   **284 freely** unreservedly   **286 check** repulse

When this advice is free° I give, and honest,   290
Probal° to thinking, and indeed the course
To win the Moor again? For 'tis most easy
Th' inclining° Desdemona to subdue°
In any honest suit; she's framed as fruitful°
As the free elements.° And then for her   295
To win the Moor—were 't to renounce his baptism,
All seals and symbols of redeemèd sin—
His soul is so enfettered to her love
That she may make, unmake, do what she list,
Even as her appetite° shall play the god   300
With his weak function.° How am I then a villain,
To counsel Cassio to this parallel° course
Directly to his good? Divinity of hell!°
When devils will the blackest sins put on,°
They do suggest° at first with heavenly shows,   305
As I do now. For whiles this honest fool
Plies Desdemona to repair his fortune,
And she for him pleads strongly to the Moor,
I'll pour this pestilence into his ear,
That she repeals him° for her body's lust;   310
And by how much she strives to do him good,
She shall undo her credit with the Moor.
So will I turn her virtue into pitch,°
And out of her own goodness make the net
That shall enmesh them all.

Enter Roderigo.

                            How now, Roderigo?   315

RODERIGO: I do follow here in the chase, not like a hound that
hunts, but one that fills up the cry.° My money is almost

---

290 free (1) free from guile (2) freely given   **291 Probal** probable, reasonable   **293 inclining** favourably disposed. **subdue** persuade   **294 framed as fruitful** created as generous   **295 free elements** i.e., earth, air, fire, and water, unrestrained and spontaneous   **300 her appetite** her desire, or, perhaps, his desire for her   **301 function** exercise of faculties (weakened by his fondness for her)   **302 parallel** corresponding to these facts and to his best interests   **303 Divinity of hell** inverted theology of hell (which seduces the soul to its damnation)   **304 put on** further, instigate   **305 suggest** tempt   **310 repeals him** attempts to get him restored   **313 pitch** i.e., (1) foul blackness (2) a snaring substance   **317 fills up the cry** merely takes part as one of the pack

spent; I have been tonight exceedingly well cudgeled; and I
think the issue will be I shall have so much° experience for
my pains, and so, with no money at all and a little more wit,
return again to Venice.

IAGO: How poor are they that have not patience!
What wound did ever heal but by degrees?
Thou know'st we work by wit, and not by witchcraft,
And wit depends on dilatory time.
Does 't not go well? Cassio hath beaten thee,   *325*
And thou, by that small hurt, hast cashiered° Cassio.
Though other things grow fair against the sun,
Yet fruits that blossom first will first be ripe.°
Content thyself awhile. By the Mass, 'tis morning!
Pleasure and action make the hours seem short.   *330*
Retire thee; go where thou art billeted.
Away, I say! Thou shalt know more hereafter.
Nay, get thee gone.   *Exit Roderigo.*
                    Two things are to be done.
My wife must move° for Cassio to her mistress;
I'll set her on;   *335*
Myself the while to draw the Moor apart
And bring him jump° when he may Cassio find
Soliciting his wife. Ay, that's the way.
Dull not device° by coldness° and delay.   *Exit.*

ACT III

SCENE I [BEFORE THE CHAMBER OF OTHELLO AND DESDEMONA.]

Enter Cassio [and] Musicians.

CASSIO: Masters, play here—I will content your pains°—
Something that's brief, and bid "Good morrow, General."
[*They play.*]

---

318 so much just so much and no more   **326 cashiered** dismissed from service   **327–328 Though
. . . ripe** i.e., plans that are well-prepared and set expeditiously in motion will soonest ripen into success   **334 move** plead   **337 jump** precisely   **339 device** plot.   **coldness** lack of zeal
1 content your pains reward your efforts

[*Enter*] *Clown.*

CLOWN: Why, masters, have your instruments been in Naples, that they speak i' the nose° thus?

A MUSICIAN: How, sir, how? 5

CLOWN: Are these, I pray you, wind instruments?

A MUSICIAN: Ay, marry, are they, sir.

CLOWN: O, thereby hangs a tail.

A MUSICIAN: Whereby hangs a tale, sir?

CLOWN: Marry, sir, by many a wind instrument° that I know. 10 But, masters, here's money for you. [*He gives money.*] And the General so likes your music that he desires you, for love's sake,° to make no more noise with it.

A MUSICIAN: Well, sir, we will not.

CLOWN: If you have any music that may not° be heard, to 't again; but, as they say, to hear music the General does not greatly care. 15

A MUSICIAN: We have none such, sir.

CLOWN: Then put up your pipes in your bag, for I'll away.° Go, vanish into air, away! *Exeunt Musicians.*

CASSIO: Dost thou hear, mine honest friend?

CLOWN: No, I hear not your honest friend; I hear you. 20

CASSIO: Prithee, keep up° thy quillets.° There's a poor piece of gold for thee. [*He gives money.*] If the gentle-woman that attends the General's wife be stirring, tell her there's one Cassio entreats her a little favor of speech.° Wilt thou do this?

CLOWN: She is stirring, sir. If she will stir° hither, I shall seem° to notify unto her. 25

CASSIO: Do, good my friend. *Exit Clown.*

Enter Iago.

3-4 speak i' the nose (1) sound nasal (2) sound like one whose nose has been attacked by syphilis. (Naples was popularly supposed to have a high incidence of venereal disease.) **10 wind instrument** (With a joke on flatulence. The *tail*, line 8, that hangs nearby the *wind instrument* suggests the penis.) **12 for love's sake** (1) out of friendship and affection (2) for the sake of lovemaking in Othello's marriage **14 may not** cannot **17 I'll away** (Possibly a misprint, or a snatch of song?) **21 keep up** do not bring out, do not use. **quillets** quibbles, puns **23 a little . . . speech** the favor of a brief talk **25 stir** bestir herself (with a play on *stirring*, "rousing herself from rest") **seem** deem it good, think fit

In happy time,° Iago.

IAGO: You have not been abed, then?

CASSIO: Why, no. The day had broke
Before we parted. I have made bold, Iago,
To send in to your wife. My suit to her   *30*
Is that she will to virtuous Desdemona
Procure me some access.

IAGO: I'll send her to you presently;
And I'll devise a means to draw the Moor
Out of the way, that your converse and business   *35*
May be more free.

CASSIO: I humbly thank you for 't.   *Exit* [*Iago*].
                                        I never knew
A Florentine° more kind and honest.

Enter Emilia.

EMILIA: Good morrow, good Lieutenant. I am sorry
For your displeasure;° but all will sure be well.   *40*
The General and his wife are talking of it,
And she speaks for you stoutly.° The Moor replies
That he you hurt is of great fame° in Cyprus
And great affinity,° and that in wholesome wisdom
He might not but refuse you; but he protests° he loves you   *45*
And needs no other suitor but his likings
To take the safest occasion by the front°
To bring you in again.

CASSIO: Yet I beseech you,
If you think fit, or that it may be done,
Give me advantage of some brief discourse   *50*
With Desdemon alone.

EMILIA: Pray you, come in.
I will bestow you where you shall have time
To speak your bosom° freely.

CASSIO: I am much bound to you.   [*Exeunt.*]

---

26 In happy time i.e., well-met   **38 Florentine** i.e., even a fellow Florentine. (Iago is a Venetian;
Cassio is a Florentine.)   **40 displeasure** fall from favour   **42 stoutly** spiritedly   **43 fame** reputation, importance   **44 affinity** kindred, family connection   **45 protests** insists   **47 occasion . . .
front** opportunity by the forelock   **53 bosom** inmost thoughts

Scene II [The Citadel.]

Enter Othello, Iago, and Gentlemen.

OTHELLO [*giving letters*]: These letters give, Iago, to the pilot,
And by him do my duties° to the Senate.
That done, I will be walking on the works;°
Repair° there to me.
IAGO: Well, my good lord, I'll do 't.
OTHELLO: This fortification, gentlemen, shall we see 't?   5
GENTLEMEN: We'll wait upon° your lordship.   *Exeunt.*

Scene III [The Garden of the Citadel.]

Enter Desdemona, Cassio, and Emilia.

DESDEMONA: Be thou assured, good Cassio, I will do
All my abilities in thy behalf.
EMILIA: Good madam, do. I warrant it grieves my husband
As if the cause were his.
DESDEMONA: O, that's an honest fellow. Do not doubt, Cassio,   5
But I will have my lord and you again
As friendly as you were.
CASSIO: Bounteous madam,
Whatever shall become of Michael Cassio,
He's never anything but your true servant.
DESDEMONA: I know 't. I thank you. You do love my lord;   10
You have known him long, and be you well assured
He shall in strangeness° stand no farther off
Than in a politic° distance.
CASSIO: Ay, but, lady,
That policy may either last so long,
Or feed upon such nice and waterish diet,°   15
Or breed itself so out of circumstance,°
That, I being absent and my place supplied,°

---

2 do my duties convey my respects   **3 works** breastworks, fortifications   **4 Repair** return, come
6 wait upon attend
12 strangeness aloofness   **13 politic** required by wise policy   **15 Or . . . diet** or sustain itself at
length upon such trivial and meager technicalities   **16 breed . . . circumstance** continually renew
itself so out of chance events, or yield so few chances for my being pardoned   **17 supplied** filled by
another person

My general will forget my love and service.

DESDEMONA: Do not doubt° that. Before Emilia here
I give thee warrant° of thy place. Assure thee, 20
If I do vow a friendship I'll perform it
To the last article. My lord shall never rest.
I'll watch him tame° and talk him out of patience;°
His bed shall seem a school, his board° a shrift;°
I'll intermingle everything he does 25
With Cassio's suit. Therefore be merry, Cassio,
For thy solicitor° shall rather die
Than give thy cause away.°

Enter Othello and Iago [at a distance].

EMILIA: Madam, here comes my lord.

CASSIO: Madam, I'll take my leave. 30

DESDEMONA: Why, stay, and hear me speak.

CASSIO: Madam, not now. I am very ill at ease,
Unfit for mine own purposes.

DESDEMONA: Well, do your discretion.° *Exit Cassio.*

IAGO: Ha? I like not that. 35

OTHELLO: What dost thou say?

IAGO: Nothing, my lord; or if—I know not what.

OTHELLO: Was not that Cassio parted from my wife?

IAGO: Cassio, my lord? No, sure, I cannot think it,
That he would steal away so guiltylike, 40
Seeing you coming.

OTHELLO: I do believe 'twas he.

DESDEMONA: How now, my lord?
I have been talking with a suitor here,
A man that languishes in your displeasure. 45

OTHELLO: Who is 't you mean?

DESDEMONA: Why, your lieutenant, Cassio. Good my lord,
If I have any grace or power to move you,
His present reconciliation take;°

---

19 doubt fear   **20 warrant** guarantee   **23 watch him tame** tame him by keeping him from sleeping. (A term from falconry.)   **out of patience** past his endurance   **24 board** dining table.   **shrift**
confessional   **27 solicitor** advocate   **28 away** up   **34 do your discretion** act according to your
own discretion   **49 His . . . take** let him be reconciled to you right away

For if he be not one that truly loves you,   50
That errs in ignorance and not in cunning,°
I have no judgment in an honest face.
I prithee, call him back.
OTHELLO: Went he hence now?
DESDEMONA: Yes, faith, so humbled   55
That he hath left part of his grief with me
To suffer with him. Good love, call him back.
OTHELLO: Not now, sweet Desdemon. Some other time.
DESDEMONA: But shall 't be shortly?
OTHELLO: The sooner, sweet, for you.   60
DESDEMONA: Shall 't be tonight at supper?
OTHELLO: No, not tonight.
DESDEMONA: Tomorrow dinner,° then?
OTHELLO: I shall not dine at home.
I meet the captains at the citadel.   65
DESDEMONA: Why, then, tomorrow night, or Tuesday morn,
On Tuesday noon, or night, on Wednesday morn.
I prithee, name the time, but let it not
Exceed three days. In faith, he's penitent;
And yet his trespass, in our common reason°—   70
Save that, they say, the wars must make example
Out of her best°—is not almost° a fault
T' incur a private check.° When shall he come?
Tell me, Othello. I wonder in my soul
What you would ask me that I should deny,   75
Or stand so mammering on.° What? Michael Cassio,
That came a-wooing with you, and so many a time,
When I have spoke of you dispraisingly,
Hath ta'en your part—to have so much to do
To bring him in!° By 'r Lady, I could do much—   80
OTHELLO: Prithee, no more. Let him come when he will;
I will deny thee nothing.

---

51 in cunning wittingly   **63 dinner** (The noontime meal.)   **70 common reason** everyday judgments   **71–72 Save . . . best** were it not that, as the saying goes, military discipline requires making an example of the very best men. (*Her* refers to wars as a singular concept.)   **72 not almost** scarcely   **73 private check** even a private reprimand   **76 mammering on** wavering about   **80 bring him in** restore him to favour

DESDEMONA: Why, this is not a boon.
　'Tis as I should entreat you wear your gloves,
　Or feed on nourishing dishes, or keep you warm,　　　　　　　85
　Or sue to you to do a peculiar° profit
　To your own person. Nay, when I have a suit
　Wherein I mean to touch° your love indeed,
　It shall be full of poise° and difficult weight,
　And fearful to be granted.　　　　　　　　　　　　　　　90
OTHELLO: I will deny thee nothing.
　Whereon,° I do beseech thee, grant me this,
　To leave me but a little to myself.
DESDEMONA: Shall I deny you? No. Farewell, my lord.
OTHELLO: Farewell, my Desdemona. I'll come to thee straight.°　95
DESDEMONA: Emilia, come.—Be as your fancies° teach you;
　Whate'er you be, I am obedient.　　　　*Exit [with Emilia].*
OTHELLO: Excellent wretch!° Perdition catch my soul
　But I do love thee! And when I love thee not,
　Chaos is come again.°　　　　　　　　　　　　　　　　100
IAGO: My noble lord—
OTHELLO: What dost thou say, Iago?
IAGO: Did Michael Cassio, when you wooed my lady,
　Know of your love?
OTHELLO: He did, from first to last. Why dost thou ask?　　105
IAGO: But for a satisfaction of my thought;
　No further harm.
OTHELLO:　　　　Why of thy thought, Iago?
IAGO: I did not think he had been acquainted with her.
OTHELLO: O, yes, and went between us very oft.
IAGO: Indeed?　　　　　　　　　　　　　　　　　　110
OTHELLO: Indeed? Ay, indeed. Discern'st thou aught in that?
　Is he not honest?
IAGO: Honest, my lord?
OTHELLO: Honest. Ay, honest.

---

86 peculiar particular, personal　**88 touch** test　**89 poise** weight, heaviness; or equipoise, delicate balance involving hard choice　**92 Whereon** in return for which　**95 straight** straightway
96 fancies inclinations　**98 wretch** (A term of affectionate endearment.)　**99–100 And . . . again** i.e., my love for you will last forever, until the end of time when chaos will return. (But with an unconscious, ironic suggestion that, if anything should induce Othello to cease loving Desdemona, the result would be chaos.)

IAGO: My lord, for aught I know. 115

OTHELLO: What dost thou think?

IAGO: Think, my lord?

OTHELLO: "Think, my lord?" By heaven, thou echo'st me,
As if there were some monster in thy thought
Too hideous to be shown. Thou dost mean something. 120
I heard thee say even now, thou lik'st not that,
When Cassio left my wife. What didst not like?
And when I told thee he was of my counsel°
In my whole course of wooing, thou criedst "Indeed?"
And didst contract and purse° thy brow together 125
As if thou then hadst shut up in thy brain
Some horrible conceit.° If thou dost love me,
Show me thy thought.

IAGO: My lord, you know I love you.

OTHELLO: I think thou dost; 130
And, for° I know thou'rt full of love and honesty,
And weigh'st thy words before thou giv'st them breath,
Therefore these stops° of thine fright me the more;
For such things in a false disloyal knave
Are tricks of custom,° but in a man that's just 135
They're close dilations,° working from the heart
That passion cannot rule.°

IAGO: For° Michael Cassio,
I dare be sworn I think that he is honest.

OTHELLO: I think so too.

IAGO: Men should be what they seem;
Or those that be not, would they might seem none!° 140

OTHELLO: Certain, men should be what they seem.

IAGO: Why, then, I think Cassio's an honest man.

OTHELLO: Nay, yet there's more in this.
I prithee, speak to me as to thy thinkings,
As thou dost ruminate, and give thy worst of thoughts 145
The worst of words.

---

123 of my counsel in my confidence   **125 purse** knit   **127 conceit** fancy   **131 for** because
133 stops pauses   **135 of custom** customary   **136 close dilations** secret or involuntary expressions or delays   **137 That passion cannot rule** i.e., that are too passionately strong to be restrained (referring to the workings), or . . . that cannot rule its own passions (referring to the heart).
137 For as for   **140 none** i.e., not to be men, or not seem to be honest

IAGO: Good my lord, pardon me.
   Though I am bound to every act of duty,
   I am not bound to that° all slaves are free to.°
   Utter my thoughts? Why, say they are vile and false,
   As where's the palace whereinto foul things   *150*
   Sometimes intrude not? Who has that breast so pure
   But some uncleanly apprehensions
   Keep leets and law days,° and in sessions sit
   With° meditations lawful?°

OTHELLO: Thou dost conspire against thy friend,° Iago,   *155*
   If thou but think'st him wronged and mak'st his ear
   A stranger to thy thoughts.

IAGO: I do beseech you,
   Though I perchance am vicious° in my guess—
   As I confess it is my nature's plague
   To spy into abuses, and oft my jealousy°   *160*
   Shapes faults that are not—that your wisdom then,°
   From one° that so imperfectly conceits,°
   Would take no notice, nor build yourself a trouble
   Out of his scattering° and unsure observance.
   It were not for your quiet nor your good,   *165*
   Nor for my manhood, honesty, and wisdom,
   To let you know my thoughts.

OTHELLO: What dost thou mean?

IAGO: Good name in man and woman, dear my lord,
   Is the immediate° jewel of their souls.
   Who steals my purse steals trash; 'tis something, nothing;   *170*
   'Twas mine, 'tis his, and has been slave to thousands;
   But he that filches from me my good name
   Robs me of that which not enriches him
   And makes me poor indeed.

OTHELLO: By heaven, I'll know thy thoughts.   *175*

---

148 that that which. **free to** free with respect to   **153 Keep leets and law days** i.e., hold court,
set up their authority in one's heart. (*Leets* are a kind of manor court; *law days* are the days courts sit
in session, or those sessions.)   **154 With** along with. **lawful** innocent   **155 thy friend** i.e.,
Othello   **158 vicious** wrong   **160 jealousy** suspicious nature   **161 then** on that account
162 one i.e., myself, Iago. **conceits** judges, conjectures   **164 scattering** random
169 immediate essential, most precious

IAGO: You cannot, if° my heart were in your hand,
    Nor shall not, whilst 'tis in my custody.
OTHELLO: Ha?
IAGO: O, beware, my lord, of jealousy.
    It is the green-eyed monster which doth mock
    The meat it feeds on.° That cuckold lives in bliss   *180*
    Who, certain of his fate, loves not his wronger;°
    But O, what damnèd minutes tells° he o'er
    Who dotes, yet doubts, suspects, yet fondly loves!
OTHELLO: O misery!
IAGO: Poor and content is rich, and rich enough,°   *185*
    But riches fineless° is as poor as winter
    To him that ever fears he shall be poor.
    Good God, the souls of all my tribe defend
    From jealousy!
OTHELLO: Why, why is this?   *190*
    Think'st thou I'd make a life of jealousy,
    To follow still the changes of the moon
    With fresh suspicions?° No! To be once in doubt
    Is once° to be resolved.° Exchange me for a goat
    When I shall turn the business of my soul   *195*
    To such exsufflicate and blown° surmises
    Matching thy inference.° 'Tis not to make me jealous
    To say my wife is fair, feeds well, loves company,
    Is free of speech, sings, plays, and dances well;
    Where virtue is, these are more virtuous.   *200*
    Nor from mine own weak merits will I draw
    The smallest fear or doubt of her revolt.°
    For she had eyes, and chose me. No, Iago,
    I'll see before I doubt; when I doubt, prove;
    And on the proof, there is no more but this—   *205*

---

176 if even if   **179-180 doth mock . . . on** mocks and torments the heart of its victim, the man who suffers jealousy   **181 his wronger** i.e., his faithless wife. (The unsuspecting cuckold is spared the misery of loving his wife only to discover she is cheating on him.)   **182 tells** counts   **185 Poor . . . enough** to be content with what little one has is the greatest wealth of all. (Proverbial.)   **186 fineless** boundless   **192-193 To follow . . . suspicions** to be constantly imagining new causes for suspicion, changing incessantly like the moon   **194 once** once and for all.   **resolved** free of doubt, having settled the matter   **196 exsufflicate and blown** inflated and blown up, rumoured about, or, spat out and flyblown, hence, loathsome, disgusting   **197 inference** description or allegation   **202 doubt . . . revolt** fear of her unfaithfulness

Away at once with love or jealousy.

IAGO: I am glad of this, for now I shall have reason
To show the love and duty that I bear you
With franker spirit. Therefore, as I am bound,
Receive it from me. I speak not yet of proof.   210
Look to your wife; observe her well with Cassio.
Wear your eyes thus, not° jealous nor secure.°
I would not have your free and noble nature,
Out of self-bounty,° be abused.° Look to 't.
I know our country disposition well;   215
In Venice they do let God see the pranks
They dare not show their husbands; their best conscience
Is not to leave 't undone, but keep 't unknown.
Othello: Dost thou say so?

IAGO: She did deceive her father, marrying you;   220
And when she seemed to shake and fear your looks,
She loved them most.

OTHELLO: And so she did.

IAGO: Why, go to,° then!
She that, so young, could give out such a seeming,°
To seel° her father's eyes up close as oak,°
He thought 'twas witchcraft! But I am much to blame.   225
I humbly do beseech you of your pardon
For too much loving you.

OTHELLO: I am bound° to thee forever.

IAGO: I see this hath a little dashed your spirits.

OTHELLO: Not a jot, not a jot.

IAGO: I' faith, I fear it has.   230
I hope you will consider what is spoke
Comes from my love. But I do see you're moved.
I am to pray you not to strain my speech
To grosser issues° nor to larger reach°
Than to suspicion.   235

OTHELLO: I will not.

---

212 **not** neither.   **secure** free from uncertainty   214 **self-bounty** inherent or natural goodness and generosity.   **abused** deceived   222 **go to** (An expression of impatience.)   223 **seeming** false appearance   224 **seel** blind. (A term from falconry.)   **oak** (A close-grained wood.)   228 **bound** indebted (but perhaps with ironic sense of "tied")   234 **issues** significances.   **reach** meaning, scope

IAGO: Should you do so, my lord,
    My speech should fall into such vile success°
    Which my thoughts aimed not. Cassio's my worthy friend.
    My lord, I see you're moved.
OTHELLO: No, not much moved.   240
    I do not think but Desdemona's honest.°
IAGO: Long live she so! And long live you to think so!
OTHELLO: And yet, how nature erring from itself—
IAGO: Ay, there's the point! As—to be bold with you—
    Not to affect° many proposèd matches   245
    Of her own clime, complexion, and degree,°
    Whereto we see in all things nature tends—
    Foh! One may smell in such a will° most rank,
    Foul disproportion,° thoughts unnatural.
    But pardon me. I do not in position°   250
    Distinctly speak of her, though I may fear
    Her will, recoiling° to her better° judgment,
    May fall to match you with her country forms°
    And happily° repent.
OTHELLO: Farewell, farewell!
    If more thou dost perceive, let me know more.   255
    Set on thy wife to observe. Leave me, Iago.
IAGO [*going*]:   My lord, I take my leave.
OTHELLO: Why did I marry? This honest creature doubtless
    Sees and knows more, much more, than he unfolds.
IAGO [*returning*]:   My Lord, I would I might entreat your honor   260
    To scan° this thing no farther. Leave it to time.
    Although 'tis fit that Cassio have his place—
    For, sure, he fills it up with great ability—
    Yet, if you please to hold him off awhile,
    You shall by that perceive him and his means.°   265
    Note if your lady strain his entertainment°
    With any strong or vehement importunity;

---

238 success effect, result   **241 honest** chaste   **245 affect** prefer, desire   **246 clime . . . degree** country, colour, and social position   **248 will** sensuality, appetite   **249 disproportion** abnormality   **250 position** argument, proposition   **252 recoiling** reverting.   **better** i.e., more natural and reconsidered   **253 fall . . . forms** undertake to compare you with Venetian norms of handsomeness   **254 happily repent** perhaps repent her marriage   **261 scan** scrutinize   **265 his means** the method he uses (to regain his post)   **266 strain his entertainment** urge his reinstatement

Much will be seen in that. In the meantime,
Let me be thought too busy° in my fears—
As worthy cause I have to fear I am—   270
And hold her free,° I do beseech your honor.

OTHELLO: Fear not my government.°

IAGO: I once more take my leave.   *Exit.*

OTHELLO: This fellow's of exceeding honesty,
And knows all qualities,° with a learnèd spirit,   275
Of human dealings. If I do prove her haggard,°
Though that her jesses° were my dear heartstrings,
I'd whistle her off and let her down the wind°
To prey at fortune.° Haply, for° I am black
And have not those soft parts of conversation°   280
That chamberers° have, or for I am declined
Into the vale of years—yet that's not much—
She's gone. I am abused,° and my relief
Must be to loathe her. O curse of marriage,
That we can call these delicate creatures ours   285
And not their appetites! I had rather be a toad
And live upon the vapor of a dungeon
Than keep a corner in the thing I love
For others' uses. Yet, 'tis the plague of great ones;
Prerogatived° are they less than the base.°   290
'Tis destiny unshunnable, like death.
Even then this forkèd° plague is fated to us
When we do quicken.° Look where she comes.

Enter Desdemona and Emilia.

If she be false, O, then heaven mocks itself!
I'll not believe 't.

---

269 busy interfering   **271 hold her free** regard her as innocent   **272 government** self-control, conduct   **275 qualities** natures, types   **276 haggard** wild (like a wild female hawk)   **277 jesses** straps fastened around the legs of a trained hawk   **278 I'd . . . wind** i.e., I'd let her go forever. (To release a hawk downwind was to invite it not to return.)   **279 prey at fortune** fend for herself in the wild.   **Haply, for** perhaps because   **280 soft . . . conversation** pleasing graces of social behaviour   **281 chamberers** gallants   **283 abused** deceived   **290 Prerogatived** privileged (to have honest wives).   **the base** ordinary citizens. (Socially prominent men are especially prone to the unavoidable destiny of being cuckolded and to the public shame that goes with it.)   **292 forkèd** (An allusion to the horns of the cuckold.)   **293 quicken** receive life. (Quicken may also mean to swarm with maggots as the body festers, as in Act IV, Scene ii, line 69, in which case lines 292-293 suggest that *even then*, in death, we are cuckolded by *forkèd* worms.)

DESDEMONA: How now, my dear Othello?   *295*
    Your dinner, and the generous° islanders
    By you invited, do attend° your presence.
OTHELLO: I am to blame.
DESDEMONA: Why do you speak so faintly?
    Are you not well?
OTHELLO: I have a pain upon my forehead here.   *300*
DESDEMONA: Faith, that's with watching.° 'Twill away again.

[She offers her handkerchief.]

    Let me but bind it hard, within this hour
    It will be well.
OTHELLO: Your napkin° is too little.
    Let it alone.° Come, I'll go in with you.

[He puts the handkerchief from him, and it drops.]

DESDEMONA: I am very sorry that you are not well.   *305*

                                        Exit [with Othello].

EMILIA *[picking up the handkerchief]:*   I am glad I have found
    this napkin.
    This was her first remembrance from the Moor.
    My wayward° husband hath a hundred times
    Wooed me to steal it, but she so loves the token—
    For he conjured her she should ever keep it—   *310*
    That she reserves it evermore about her
    To kiss and talk to. I'll have the work ta'en out,°
    And give 't Iago. What he will do with it
    Heaven knows, not I;
    I nothing but to please his fantasy.°   *315*

Enter Iago.

IAGO: How now? What do you here alone?
EMILIA: Do not you chide. I have a thing for you.

---

296 generous noble   **297 attend** await   **301 watching** too little sleep   **303 napkin** handkerchief
304 Let it alone i.e., never mind   **308 wayward** capricious   **312 work ta'en out** design of the
embroidery copied   **315 fantasy** whim

IAGO: You have a thing for me? It is a common thing°—
EMILIA: Ha?
IAGO: To have a foolish wife.   320
EMILIA: O, is that all? What will you give me now
   For that same handkerchief?
IAGO: What handkerchief?
EMILIA: What handkerchief?
   Why, that the Moor first gave to Desdemona;   325
   That which so often you did bid me steal.
IAGO: Hast stolen it from her?
EMILIA: No, faith. She let it drop by negligence,
   And to th' advantage° I, being here, took 't up.
   Look, here 'tis.
IAGO: A good wench! Give it me.   330
EMILIA: What will you do with 't, that you have been so
   earnest
   To have me filch it?
IAGO [*snatching it*]:   Why, what is that to you?
EMILIA: If it be not for some purpose of import,
   Give 't me again. Poor lady, she'll run mad
   When she shall lack° it.
IAGO: Be not acknown on 't.°   335
   I have use for it. Go, leave me.   *Exit Emilia.*
   I will in Cassio's lodging lose° this napkin
   And let him find it. Trifles light as air
   Are to the jealous confirmations strong
   As proofs of Holy Writ. This may do something.   340
   The Moor already changes with my poison.
   Dangerous conceits° are in their natures poisons,
   Which at the first are scarce found to distaste,°
   But with a little act° upon the blood
   Burn like the mines of sulfur.

   Enter Othello.

---

318 common thing (With bawdy suggestion; *common* suggests coarseness and availability to all com-
ers, and *thing* is a slang term for the pudendum.)   **329 to th' advantage** taking the opportunity
335 lack miss.   **Be . . . on't** do not confess knowledge of it   **337 lose** (The Folio spelling, *loose*, is
a normal spelling for "lose," but it may also contain the idea of "let go," "release.")   **342 conceits**
fancies, ideas   **343 distaste** be distasteful   **344 act** action, working

I did say so.
Look where he comes! Not poppy nor mandragora°
Nor all the drowsy syrups of the world
Shall ever medicine thee to that sweet sleep
Which thou owedst° yesterday.

OTHELLO: Ha, ha, false to me?

IAGO: Why, how now, General? No more of that. 350

OTHELLO: Avaunt! Begone! Thou hast set me on the rack.
I swear 'tis better to be much abused
Than but to know 't a little.

IAGO: How now, my lord?

OTHELLO: What sense had I of her stolen hours of lust?
I saw 't not, thought it not, it harmed not me. 355
I slept the next night well, fed well, was free° and merry;
I found not Cassio's kisses on her lips.
He that is robbed, not wanting° what is stolen,
Let him not know 't and he's not robbed at all.

IAGO: I am sorry to hear this. 360

OTHELLO: I had been happy if the general camp,
Pioners° and all, had tasted her sweet body,
So° I had nothing known. O, now, forever
Farewell the tranquil mind! Farewell content!
Farewell the plumèd troops and the big° wars 365
That makes ambition virtue! O, farewell!
Farewell the neighing steed and the shrill trump,
The spirit-stirring drum, th' ear-piercing fife,
The royal banner, and all quality,°
Pride,° pomp, and circumstance° of glorious war! 370
And O, you mortal engines,° whose rude throats
Th' immortal Jove's dread clamors° counterfeit,
Farewell! Othello's occupation's gone.

IAGO: Is 't possible, my lord?

OTHELLO: Villain, be sure thou prove my love a whore! 375

---

346 **mandragora** an opiate made of the mandrake root   349 **thou owedst** you did own   356 **free** carefree   358 **wanting** missing   362 **Pioners** diggers of mines, the lowest grade of soldiers   363 **So** provided   365 **big** stately   369 **quality** character, essential nature   370 **Pride** rich display.   **circumstance** pageantry   371 **mortal engines** i.e., cannon. (*Mortal* means "deadly.")   372 **Jove's dread clamors** i.e., thunder

Be sure of it. Give me the ocular proof,
Or, by the worth of mine eternal soul,
Thou hadst been better have been born a dog
Than answer my waked wrath!

IAGO: Is 't come to this?

OTHELLO: Make me to see 't, or at the least so prove it   *380*
That the probation° bear no hinge nor loop
To hang a doubt on, or woe upon thy life!

IAGO: My noble lord—

OTHELLO: If thou dost slander her and torture me,
Never pray more; abandon all remorse;°   *385*
On horror's head horrors accumulate;°
Do deeds to make heaven weep, all earth amazed;°
For nothing canst thou to damnation add
Greater than that.

IAGO: O grace! O heaven forgive me!
Are you a man? Have you a soul or sense?   *390*
God b' wi' you; take mine office. O wretched fool,°
That lov'st to make thine honesty a vice!°
O monstrous world! Take note, take note, O world,
To be direct and honest is not safe.
I thank you for this profit,° and from hence°   *395*
I'll love no friend, sith° love breeds such offense.°

OTHELLO: Nay, stay. Thou shouldst be° honest.

IAGO: I should be wise, for honesty's a fool
And loses that° it works for.

OTHELLO: By the world,
I think my wife be honest and think she is not;   *400*
I think that thou art just and think thou art not.
I'll have some proof. My name, that was as fresh
As Dian's° visage, is now begrimed and black
As mine own face. If there be cords, or knives,
Poison, or fire, or suffocating streams,   *405*

---

381 probation proof   **385 remorse** pity, penitent hope for salvation   **386 horrors accumulate**
add still more horrors   **387 amazed** confounded with horror   **391 O wretched fool** (Iago addresses
himself as a fool for having carried honesty too far.)   **392 vice** failing, something overdone
395 profit profitable instruction.   **hence** henceforth   **396 sith** since.   **offense** i.e., harm to the one
who offers help and friendship   **397 Thou shouldst be** it appears that you are. (But Iago replies in
the sense of "ought to be.")   **399 that** what   **403 Dian** Diana, goddess of the moon and of chastity

I'll not endure it. Would I were satisfied!

IAGO: I see, sir, you are eaten up with passion.
I do repent me that I put it to you.
You would be satisfied?

OTHELLO: Would? Nay, and I will.

IAGO: And may; but how? How satisfied, my lord?   *410*
Would you, the supervisor,° grossly gape on?
Behold her topped?

OTHELLO: Death and damnation! O!

IAGO: It were a tedious difficulty, I think,
To bring them to that prospect. Damn them then,°
If ever mortal eyes do see them bolster°   *415*
More° than their own.° What then? How then?
What shall I say? Where's satisfaction?
It is impossible you should see this,
Were they as prime° as goats, as hot as monkeys,
As salt° as wolves in pride,° and fools as gross   *420*
As ignorance made drunk. But yet I say,
If imputation and strong circumstances°
Which lead directly to the door of truth
Will give you satisfaction, you might have 't.

OTHELLO: Give me a living reason she's disloyal.   *425*

IAGO: I do not like the office.
But sith° I am entered in this cause so far,
Pricked° to 't by foolish honesty and love,
I will go on. I lay with Cassio lately,
And being troubled with a raging tooth   *430*
I could not sleep. There are a kind of men
So loose of soul that in their sleeps will mutter
Their affairs. One of this kind is Cassio.
In sleep I heard him say, "Sweet Desdemona,
Let us be wary, let us hide our loves!"   *435*
And then, sir, would he grip and wring my hand,
Cry "O sweet creature!", then kiss me hard,

---

411 supervisor onlooker   **414 Damn them then** i.e., they would have to be really incorrigible
415 bolster go to bed together, share a bolster   **416 More** other.   **own** own eyes   **419 prime**
lustful   **420 salt** wanton, sensual.   **pride** heat   **422 imputation . . . circumstances** strong cir-
cumstantial evidence   **427 sith** since   **428 Pricked** spurred

As if he plucked up kisses by the roots
That grew upon my lips; then laid his leg
Over my thigh, and sighed, and kissed, and then   *440*
Cried, "Cursèd fate that gave thee to the Moor!"

OTHELLO: O monstrous! Monstrous!

IAGO: Nay, this was but his
dream.

OTHELLO: But this denoted a foregone conclusion.°
'Tis a shrewd doubt,° though it be but a dream.

IAGO: And this may help to thicken other proofs   *445*
That do demonstrate thinly.

OTHELLO: I'll tear her all to pieces.

IAGO: Nay, but be wise. Yet we see nothing done;
She may be honest yet. Tell me but this:
Have you not sometimes seen a handkerchief
Spotted with strawberries° in your wife's hand?   *450*

OTHELLO: I gave her such a one. 'Twas my first gift.
Iago: I know not that; but such a handkerchief—
I am sure it was your wife's—did I today
See Cassio wipe his beard with.

OTHELLO: If it be that—

IAGO: If it be that, or any that was hers,   *455*
It speaks against her with the other proofs.

OTHELLO: O, that the slave° had forty thousand lives!
One is too poor, too weak for my revenge.
Now do I see 'tis true. Look here, Iago,
All my fond° love thus do I blow to heaven.   *460*
'Tis gone.
Arise, black vengeance, from the hollow hell!
Yield up, O love, thy crown and hearted° throne
To tyrannous hate! Swell, bosom, with thy freight,°
For 'tis of aspics'° tongues!   *465*

IAGO: Yet be content.°

OTHELLO: O, blood, blood, blood!

---

443 foregone conclusion concluded experience or action   **444 shrewd doubt** suspicious circumstance   **450 Spotted with strawberries** embroidered with a strawberry pattern   **457 the slave** i.e., Cassio   **460 fond** foolish (but also suggesting "affectionate")   **463 hearted** fixed in the heart   **464 freight** burden   **465 aspics'** venomous serpents'   **466 content** calm

IAGO: Patience, I say. Your mind perhaps may change.

OTHELLO: Never, Iago. Like to the Pontic Sea,°

    Whose icy current and compulsive course 470

    Ne'er feels retiring ebb, but keeps due on

    To the Propontic° and the Hellespont,°

    Even so my bloody thoughts with violent pace

    Shall ne'er look back, ne'er ebb to humble love,

    I that a capable° and wide revenge 475

    Swallow them up. Now, by yond marble° heaven,

    [*Kneeling*] In the due reverence of a sacred vow

    I here engage my words.

IAGO: Do not rise yet.

    [*He kneels.*]° Witness, you ever-burning lights above,

    You elements that clip° us round about, 480

    Witness that here Iago doth give up

    The execution° of his wit,° hands, heart,

    To wronged Othello's service. Let him command,

    And to obey shall be in me remorse,°

    What bloody business ever.° [*They rise.*]

OTHELLO: I greet thy love, 485

    Not with vain thanks, but with acceptance bounteous,

    And will upon the instant put thee to 't.°

    Within these three days let me hear thee say

    That Cassio's not alive.

IAGO: My friend is dead;

    'Tis done at your request. But let her live. 490

OTHELLO: Damn her, lewd minx!° O, damn her, damn her!

    Come, go with me apart. I will withdraw

    To furnish me with some swift means of death

    For the fair devil. Now art thou my lieutenant.

IAGO: I am your own forever.   *Exeunt.* 495

---

469 Pontic Sea Black Sea   **472 Propontic** Sea of Marmara, between the Black Sea and the Aegean. **Helllespont** Dardanelles, straits where the Sea of Marmara joins with the Aegean   **475 capable** ample, comprehensive   **476 marble** i.e., gleaming like marble and unrelenting   **479 [s.d.] He kneels** (In the Quarto text, Iago kneels here after Othello has knelt at line 477.)   **480 clip** encompass   **482 execution** exercise, action. **wit** mind   **484 remorse** pity (for Othello's wrongs) **485 ever** soever   **487 to 't** to the proof   **491 minx** wanton

Scene IV [Before the Citadel.]

Enter Desdemona, Emilia, and Clown.

DESDEMONA: Do you know, sirrah,° where Lieutenant Cassio lies?°

CLOWN: I dare not say he lies anywhere.

DESDEMONA: Why, man?

CLOWN: He's a soldier, and for me to say a soldier lies, 'tis stabbing.

DESDEMONA: Go to. Where lodges he? 5

CLOWN: To tell you where he lodges is to tell you where I lie.

DESDEMONA: Can anything be made of this?

CLOWN: I know not where he lodges, and for me to devise a lodging and say he lies here, or he lies there, were to lie in mine own throat.°

DESDEMONA: Can you inquire him out, and be edified by report? 10

CLOWN: I will catechize the world for him; that is, make questions, and by them answer.

DESDEMONA: Seek him, bid him come hither. Tell him I have moved° my lord on his behalf and hope all will be well.

CLOWN: To do this is within the compass of man's wit, and therefore I will attempt the doing it. *Exit Clown.* 15

DESDEMONA: Where should I lose that handkerchief, Emilia?

EMILIA: I know not, madam.

DESDEMONA: Believe me, I had rather have lost my purse
Full of crusadoes;° and but my noble Moor 20
Is true of mind and made of no such baseness
As jealous creatures are, it were enough
To put him to ill thinking.

EMILIA: Is he not jealous?

DESDEMONA: Who, he? I think the sun where he was born
Drew all such humors° from him.

EMILIA: Look where he comes. 25

---

1 sirrah (A form of address to an inferior.)   **lies** lodges. (But the Clown makes the obvious pun.)
9 lie . . . throat (1) lie egregiously and deliberately (2) use the windpipe to speak a lie   **13 moved**
petitioned   **20 crusadoes** Portuguese gold coins   **25 humors** (Refers to the four bodily fluids
thought to determine temperament.)

Enter Othello.

DESDEMONA: I will not leave him now till Cassio
Be called to him.—How is 't with you, my lord?
OTHELLO: Well, my good lady. [*Aside.*] O, hardness to
dissemble!—
How do you, Desdemona?
DESDEMONA: Well, my good lord.
OTHELLO: Give me your hand. [*She gives her hand.*] This hand is
moist, my lady.   30
DESDEMONA: It yet hath felt no age nor known no sorrow.
OTHELLO: This argues° fruitfulness° and liberal° heart.
Hot, hot, and moist. This hand of yours requires
A sequester° from liberty, fasting and prayer,
Much castigation,° exercise devout;°   35
For here's a young and sweating devil here
That commonly rebels. 'Tis a good hand,
A frank° one.
DESDEMONA: You may indeed say so,
For 'twas that hand that gave away my heart.
OTHELLO: A liberal hand. The hearts of old gave hands,°   40
But our new heraldry is hands, not hearts.°
DESDEMONA: I cannot speak of this. Come now, your
promise.
OTHELLO: What promise, chuck?°
DESDEMONA: I have sent to bid Cassio come speak with you.
OTHELLO: I have a salt and sorry rheum° offends me;   45
Lend me thy handkerchief.
DESDEMONA: Here, my lord. [*She offers a handkerchief.*]
OTHELLO: That which I gave you.
DESDEMONA: I have it not about me.
OTHELLO: Not?

---

32 argues gives evidence of.   **fruitfulness** generosity, amorousness, and fecundity.   **liberal** generous and sexually free   **34 sequester** separation, sequestration   **35 castigation** corrective discipline.   **exercise devout** i.e., prayer, religious meditation, etc.   **38 frank** generous, open (with sexual suggestion)   **40 The hearts . . . hands** i.e., in former times, people would give their hearts
when they gave their hands to something   **41 But . . . hearts** i.e., in our decadent times, the joining
of hands is no longer a badge to signify the giving of hearts   **43 chuck** (A term of endearment.)
45 salt . . . rheum distressful head cold or watering of the eyes

DESDEMONA: No, faith, my lord.   50
OTHELLO: That's a fault. That handkerchief
Did an Egyptian to my mother give.
She was a charmer,° and could almost read
The thoughts of people. She told her, while she kept it
'Twould make her amiable° and subdue my father   55
Entirely to her love, but if she lost it
Or made a gift of it, my father's eye
Should hold her loathèd and his spirits should hunt
After new fancies.° She, dying, gave it me,
And bid me, when my fate would have me wived,   60
To give it her.° I did so; and take heed on 't;
Make it a darling like your precious eye.
To lose 't or give 't away were such perdition°
As nothing else could match.
DESDEMONA: Is 't possible?
OTHELLO: 'Tis true. There's magic in the web° of it.   65
A sibyl, that had numbered in the world
The sun to course two hundred compasses,°
In her prophetic fury° sewed the work;°
The worms were hallowed that did breed the silk,
And it was dyed in mummy° which the skillful   70
Conserved of° maidens' hearts.
DESDEMONA: I' faith! Is 't true?
OTHELLO: Most veritable. Therefore look to 't well.
DESDEMONA: Then would to God that I had never seen 't!
OTHELLO: Ha? Wherefore?
DESDEMONA: Why do you speak so startingly and rash?°   75
OTHELLO: Is 't lost? Is 't gone? Speak, is 't out o' the way?°
DESDEMONA: Heaven bless us!
OTHELLO: Say you?
DESDEMONA: It is not lost; but what an if° it were?
OTHELLO: How?   80

---

53 charmer sorceress   **55 amiable** desirable   **59 fancies** loves   **61 her** i.e., to my wife
63 perdition loss   **65 web** fabric, weaving   **67 compasses** annual circlings. (The *sibyl*, or
prophetess, was two-hundred years old.)   **68 prophetic fury** frenzy of prophetic inspiration.
work embroidered pattern   **70 mummy** medicinal or magical preparation drained from mummified
bodies   **71 Conserved of** prepared or preserved out of   **75 startingly and rash** disjointedly and
impetuously, excitedly   **76 out o' the way** lost, misplaced   **79 an if** if

DESDEMONA: I say it is not lost.

OTHELLO: Fetch 't, let me see 't.

DESDEMONA: Why, so I can, sir, but I will not now.
This is a trick to put me from my suit.
Pray you, let Cassio be received again.

OTHELLO: Fetch me the handkerchief! My mind misgives.   85

DESDEMONA: Come, come,
You'll never meet a more sufficient° man.

OTHELLO: The handkerchief!

DESDEMONA: I pray, talk° me of Cassio.

OTHELLO: The handkerchief!

DESDEMONA: A man that all his time°
Hath founded his good fortunes on your love,   90
Shared dangers with you—

OTHELLO: The handkerchief!

DESDEMONA: I' faith, you are to blame.

OTHELLO: Zounds!   *Exit Othello.*

EMILIA: Is not this man jealous?   95

DESDEMONA: I ne'er saw this before.
Sure, there's some wonder in this handkerchief.
I am most unhappy in the loss of it.

EMILIA: 'Tis not a year or two shows us a man.°
They are all but stomachs, and we all but° food;   100
They eat us hungerly,° and when they are full
They belch us.

Enter Iago and Cassio.

                         Look you, Cassio and my husband.

IAGO [*to Cassio*]: There is no other way; 'tis she must do 't.
And, lo, the happiness!° Go and importune her.

DESDEMONA: How now, good Cassio? What's the news with
you?

CASSIO: Madam, my former suit. I do beseech you
That by your virtuous° means I may again

---

87 sufficient able, complete   **88 talk** talk to   **89 all his time** throughout his career   **99 'Tis . . . man** i.e., you can't really know a man even in a year or two of experience (?), or, real men come along seldom (?)   **100 but** nothing but   **101 hungerly** hungrily   **104 the happiness** in happy time, fortunately met   **107 virtuous** efficacious

Exist and be a member of his love
Whom I, with all the office° of my heart,
Entirely honor. I would not be delayed.　　　　　　　*110*
If my offense be of such mortal° kind
That nor my service past, nor° present sorrows,
Nor purposed merit in futurity
Can ransom me into his love again,
But to know so must be my benefit;°　　　　　　　*115*
So shall I clothe me in a forced content,
And shut myself up in° some other course,
To fortune's alms.°

DESDEMONA:　　　　　　　Alas, thrice-gentle Cassio,
My advocation° is not now in tune.
My lord is not my lord; nor should I know him,　　　*120*
Were he in favor° as in humor° altered.
So help me every spirit sanctified
As I have spoken for you all my best
And stood within the blank° of his displeasure
For my free speech! You must awhile be patient.　　*125*
What I can do I will, and more I will
Than for myself I dare. Let that suffice you.

IAGO:　Is my lord angry?

EMILIA:　　　　　　　He went hence but now,
And certainly in strange unquietness.

IAGO:　Can he be angry? I have seen the cannon　　*130*
When it hath blown his ranks into the air,
And like the devil from his very arm
Puffed his own brother—and is he angry?
Something of moment° then. I will go meet him.
There's matter in 't indeed, if he be angry.　　　　*135*

DESDEMONA:　I prithee, do so.　　　　　　*Exit [Iago].*
　　　　　　　　Something, sure, of state,°

---

109 office loyal service　**111 mortal** fatal　**112 nor . . . nor** neither . . . nor　**115 But . . .
benefit** merely to know that my case is hopeless will have to content me (and will be better than
uncertainty)　**117 shut . . . in** confine myself to　**118 To fortune's alms** throwing myself on
the mercy of fortune　**119 advocation** advocacy　**121 favor** appearance.　**humor** mood
124 within the blank within point-blank range. (The *blank* is the center of the target.)
134 of moment of immediate importance, momentous　**136 of state** concerning state affairs

Either from Venice, or some unhatched practice°
Made demonstrable here in Cyprus to him,
Hath puddled° his clear spirit; and in such cases
Men's natures wrangle with inferior things,   *140*
Though great ones are their object. 'Tis even so;
For let our finger ache, and it indues°
Our other, healthful members even to a sense
Of pain. Nay, we must think men are not gods,
Nor of them look for such observancy°   *145*
As fits the bridal.° Beshrew me° much, Emilia,
I was, unhandsome° warrior as I am,
Arraigning his unkindness with° my soul;
But now I find I had suborned the witness,°
And he's indicted falsely.

EMILIA: Pray heaven it be   *150*
State matters, as you think, and no conception
Nor no jealous toy° concerning you.

DESDEMONA: Alas the day! I never gave him cause.

EMILIA: But jealous souls will not be answered so;
They are not ever jealous for the cause,   *155*
But jealous for° they're jealous. It is a monster
Begot upon itself,° born on itself.

DESDEMONA: Heaven keep that monster from Othello's mind!

EMILIA: Lady, amen.

DESDEMONA: I will go seek him. Cassio, walk hereabout.   *160*
If I do find him fit, I'll move your suit
And seek to effect it to my uttermost.

CASSIO: I humbly thank your ladyship.

Exit [Desdemona with Emilia].

Enter Bianca.

BIANCA: Save° you, friend Cassio!

---

137 unhatched practice as yet unexecuted or undiscovered plot   **139 puddled** muddied
142 indues brings to the same condition   **145 observancy** attentiveness   **146 bridal** wedding
(when a bridegroom is newly attentive to his bride).   **Beshrew me** (A mild oath.)
147 unhandsome insufficient, unskillful   **148 with** before the bar of   **149 suborned the witness**
induced the witness to give false testimony   **152 toy** fancy   **156 for** because   **157 Begot upon itself** generated solely from itself   **164 Save** God save.

CASSIO: What make° you from home?
　　How is 't with you, my most fair Bianca?   165
　　I' faith, sweet love, I was coming to your house.
BIANCA:　And I was going to your lodging, Cassio.
　　What, keep a week away? Seven days and nights?
　　Eightscore-eight° hours? And lovers' absent hours
　　More tedious than the dial° eightscore times?   170
　　O weary reckoning!
CASSIO: Pardon me, Bianca.
　　I have this while with leaden thoughts been pressed;
　　But I shall, in a more continuate° time,
　　Strike off this score° of absence. Sweet Bianca,

　　[*giving her Desdemona's handkerchief*]

　　Take me this work out.°
BIANCA: O Cassio, whence came this?   175
　　This is some token from a newer friend.°
　　To the felt absence now I feel a cause.
　　Is 't come to this? Well, well.
CASSIO: Go to, woman!
　　Throw your vile guesses in the devil's teeth,
　　From whence you have them. You are jealous now   180
　　That this is from some mistress, some remembrance.
　　No, by my faith, Bianca.
BIANCA: Why, whose is it?
CASSIO:　I know not, neither. I found it in my chamber.
　　I like the work well. Ere it be demanded°—
　　As like° enough it will—I would have it copied.   185
　　Take it and do 't, and leave me for this time.
BIANCA:　Leave you? Wherefore?
CASSIO:　I do attend here on the General,
　　And think it no addition,° nor my wish,
　　To have him see me womaned.   190
BIANCA:　Why, I pray you?

---

make do　**169 Eightscore-eight** one hundred sixty-eight, the number of hours in a week　**170 the
dial** a complete revolution of the clock　**173 continuate** uninterrupted　**174 Strike . . . score** settle this account　**175 Take . . . out** copy this embroidery for me　**176 friend** mistress
184 demanded inquired for　**185 like** likely　**189 addition** i.e., addition to my reputation

CASSIO: Not that I love you not.
BIANCA: But that you do not love me.
  I pray you, bring° me on the way a little,
  And say if I shall see you soon at night.   *195*
CASSIO: 'Tis but a little way that I can bring you,
  For I attend here; but I'll see you soon.
BIANCA: 'Tis very good. I must be circumstanced.°

Exeunt omnes.

ACT IV

SCENE I [BEFORE THE CITADEL.]

Enter Othello and Iago.

IAGO: Will you think so?
OTHELLO: Think so, Iago?
IAGO: What,
  To kiss in private?
OTHELLO: An unauthorized kiss!
IAGO: Or to be naked with her friend in bed
  An hour or more, not meaning any harm?
OTHELLO: Naked in bed, Iago, and not mean harm?   *5*
  It is hypocrisy against the devil.
  They that mean virtuously and yet do so,
  The devil their virtue tempts, and they tempt heaven.
IAGO: If they do nothing, 'tis a venial° slip.
  But if I give my wife a handkerchief—   *10*
OTHELLO: What then?
IAGO: Why then, 'tis hers, my lord, and being hers,
  She may, I think, bestow 't on any man.
OTHELLO: She is protectress of her honor too.
  May she give that?   *15*
IAGO: Her honor is an essence that's not seen;
  They have it° very oft that have it not.

---

194 bring accompany   **198 be circumstanced** be governed by circumstance, yield to your conditions
9 venial pardonable   **17 They have it** i.e., they enjoy a reputation for it

But, for the handkerchief—
OTHELLO: By heaven, I would most gladly have forgot it.
    Thou saidst—O, it comes o'er my memory   *20*
    As doth the raven o'er the infectious house,°
    Boding to all—he had my handkerchief.
IAGO: Ay, what of that?
OTHELLO: That's not so good now.
IAGO: What
    If I had said I had seen him do you wrong?
    Or heard him say—as knaves be such abroad,°   *25*
    Who having, by their own importunate suit,
    Or voluntary dotage° of some mistress,
    Convincèd or supplied° them, cannot choose
    But they must blab—
OTHELLO: Hath he said anything?
IAGO: He hath, my lord; but, be you well assured,   *30*
    No more than he'll unswear.
OTHELLO: What hath he said?
IAGO: Faith, that he did—I know not what he did.
OTHELLO: What? What?
IAGO: Lie—
OTHELLO: With her?
IAGO: With her, on her; what you will.
OTHELLO: Lie with her? Lie on her? We say "lie on her" when
    they belie° her. Lie with her? Zounds, that's fulsome.°—   *35*
    Handkerchief—confessions—handkerchief!—To confess and
    be hanged for his labor—first to be hanged and then to con-
    fess.°—I tremble at it. Nature would not invest herself in
    such shadowing passion without some instruction.° It is not
    words° that shakes me thus. Pish! Noses, ears, and lips.—Is
    't possible?—Confess—handkerchief!—O devil!   *40*

---

21 raven . . . house (Allusion to the belief that the raven hovered over a house of sickness or infection, such as one visited by the plague.)   **25 abroad** around about   **27 voluntary dotage** willing infatuation   **28 Convincèd or supplied** seduced or sexually gratified   **35 belie** slander **36 fulsome** foul   **37–38 first . . . to confess** (Othello reverses the proverbial *confess* and *be hanged*; Cassio is to be given no time to confess before he dies.)   **38–39 Nature . . . instruction** i.e., without some foundation in fact, nature would not have dressed herself in such an overwhelming passion that comes over me now and fills my mind with images, or in such a lifelike fantasy as Cassio had in his dream of lying with Desdemona   **39 words** mere words

Falls in a trance.

IAGO: Work on,
My medicine, work! Thus credulous fools are caught,
And many worthy and chaste dames even thus,
All guiltless, meet reproach.—What, ho! My lord!   *45*
My lord, I say! Othello!

Enter Cassio.

How now, Cassio?
CASSIO: What's the matter?
IAGO: My lord is fall'n into an epilepsy.
This is his second fit. He had one yesterday.
CASSIO: Rub him about the temples.
IAGO: No, forbear.   *50*
The lethargy° must have his° quiet course.
If not, he foams at mouth, and by and by
Breaks out to savage madness. Look, he stirs.
Do you withdraw yourself a little while.
He will recover straight. When he is gone,   *55*
I would on great occasion° speak with you.

                                        [*Exit Cassio.*]

How is it, General? Have you not hurt your head?
OTHELLO: Dost thou mock me?°
IAGO: I mock you not, by heaven.
Would you would bear your fortune like a man!
OTHELLO: A hornèd man's a monster and a beast.   *60*
IAGO: There's many a beast then in a populous city,
And many a civil° monster.
OTHELLO: Did he confess it?
IAGO: Good sir, be a man.
Think every bearded fellow that's but yoked°   *65*
May draw with you.° There's millions now alive

---

51 lethargy coma. **his** its **56 on great occasion** on a matter of great importance **58 mock me** (Othello takes Iago's question about hurting his head to be a mocking reference to the cuckold's horns.) **62 civil** i.e., dwelling in a city **65 yoked** (1) married (2) put into the yoke of infamy and cuckoldry **66 draw with you** pull as you do, like oxen who are yoked, i.e., share your fate as cuckold

That nightly lie in those unproper° beds
Which they dare swear peculiar.° Your case is better.°
O, 'tis the spite of hell, the fiend's arch-mock,
To lip° a wanton in a secure° couch   70
And to suppose her chaste! No, let me know,
And knowing what I am,° I know what she shall be.°

OTHELLO: O, thou art wise. 'Tis certain.

IAGO: Stand you awhile apart;
  Confine yourself but in a patient list.°   75
  Whilst you were here o'erwhelmèd with your grief—
  A passion most unsuiting such a man—
  Cassio came hither. I shifted him away,°
  And laid good 'scuse upon your ecstasy,°
  Bade him anon return and here speak with me,   80
  The which he promised. Do but encave° yourself
  And mark the fleers,° the gibes, and notable° scorns
  That dwell in every region of his face;
  For I will make him tell the tale anew,
  Where, how, how oft, how long ago, and when   85
  He hath and is again to cope° your wife.
  I say, but mark his gesture. Marry, patience!
  Or I shall say you're all-in-all in spleen,°
  And nothing of a man.

OTHELLO: Dost thou hear, Iago?
  I will be found most cunning in my patience;   90
  But—dost thou hear?—most bloody.

IAGO: That's not amiss;
  But yet keep time° in all. Will you withdraw?

  [*Othello stands apart.*]

  Now will I question Cassio of Bianca,
  A huswife° that by selling her desires
  Buys herself bread and clothes. It is a creature   95

---

67 **unproper** not exclusively their own   68 **peculiar** private, their own.   **better** i.e., because you
know the truth   70 **lip** kiss.   **secure** free from suspicion   72 **what I am** i.e., a cuckold.   **she
shall be** will happen to her   75 **in . . . list** within the bounds of patience   78 **shifted him away**
used a dodge to get rid of him   79 **ecstasy** trance   81 **encave** conceal   82 **fleers** sneers.
notable obvious   86 **cope** encounter with, have sex with   88 **all-in-all in spleen** utterly governed
by passionate impulses   92 **keep time** keep yourself steady (as in music)   94 **huswife** hussy

That dotes on Cassio—as 'tis the strumpet's plague
To beguile many and be beguiled by one.
He, when he hears of her, cannot restrain°
From the excess of laughter. Here he comes.

Enter Cassio.

As he shall smile, Othello shall go mad;   *100*
And his unbookish° jealousy must conster°
Poor Cassio's smiles, gestures, and light behaviors
Quite in the wrong.—How do you now, Lieutenant?
CASSIO: The worser that you give me the addition°
Whose want° even kills me.   *105*
IAGO: Ply Desdemona well and you are sure on 't.
[*Speaking lower.*] Now, if this suit lay in Bianca's power,
How quickly should you speed!
CASSIO [*laughing*]: Alas, poor caitiff!°
OTHELLO [*aside*]: Look how he laughs already!   *110*
IAGO: I never knew a woman love man so.
CASSIO: Alas, poor rogue! I think, i' faith, she loves me.
OTHELLO: Now he denies it faintly, and laughs it out.
IAGO: Do you hear, Cassio?
OTHELLO: Now he importunes him
To tell it o'er. Go to!° Well said,° well said.   *115*
IAGO: She gives it out that you shall marry her.
Do you intend it?
CASSIO: Ha, ha, ha!
OTHELLO: Do you triumph, Roman?° Do you triumph?
CASSIO: I marry her? What? A customer?° Prithee, bear some   *120*
charity to my wit;° do not think it so unwholesome. Ha,
ha, ha!
OTHELLO: So, so, so, so! They laugh that win.°
IAGO: Faith, the cry° goes that you shall marry her.
CASSIO: Prithee, say true.

---

98 restrain refrain   **101 unbookish** uninstructed.   **conster** construe   **104 addition** title
105 Whose want the lack of which   **109 caitiff** wretch   **115 Go to** (An expression of remonstrance.)   **Well said** well done   **119 Roman** (The Romans were noted for their *triumphs* or tri-
umphal processions.)   **120 customer** i.e., prostitute.   **bear . . . wit** be more charitable to my
judgment   **122 They . . . win** i.e., they that laugh last laugh best   **123 cry** rumour

IAGO: I am a very villain else.°   125

OTHELLO: Have you scored me?° Well.

CASSIO: This is the monkey's own giving out. She is persuaded
I will marry her out of her own love and flattery,° not out of
my promise.

OTHELLO: Iago beckons me.° Now he begins the story.

CASSIO: She was here even now; she haunts me in every place.   130
I was the other day talking on the seabank° with certain
Venetians, and thither comes the bauble,° and, by this
hand,° she falls me thus about my neck—

[*He embraces Iago.*]

OTHELLO: Crying, "O dear Cassio!" as it were; his gesture
imports it.

CASSIO: So hangs and lolls and weep upon me, so shakes and
pulls me. Ha, ha, ha!

OTHELLO: Now he tells how she plucked him to my chamber.   135
O, I see that nose of yours, but not that dog I shall throw
it to.°

CASSIO: Well, I must leave her company.

IAGO: Before me,° look where she comes.

Enter Bianca [with Othello's handkerchief].

CASSIO: 'Tis such another fitchew!° Marry, a perfumed one.—
What do you mean by this haunting of me?   140

BIANCA: Let the devil and his dam° haunt you! What did you
mean by that same handkerchief you gave me even now? I
was a fine fool to take it. I must take out the work? A likely
piece of work,° that you should find it in your chamber and
know not who left it there! This is some minx's token, and I
must take out the work? There; give it your hobbyhorse.°   145

---

125 I . . . else call me a complete rogue if I'm not telling the truth   **126 scored me** scored off me,
beaten me, made up my reckoning, branded me   **128 flattery** self-flattery, self-deception
129 beckons signals   **131 seabank** seashore   **132 bauble** plaything   **by this hand** I make my
vow   **136 not . . . to** (Othello imagines himself cutting off Cassio's nose and throwing it to a dog.)
138 Before me i.e., on my soul   **139 'Tis . . . fitchew** what a polecat she is! Just like all the others.
(Polecats were often compared with prostitutes because of their rank smell and presumed lechery.)
141 dam mother   **143 A likely . . . work** a fine story   **145 hobbyhorse** harlot

[*She gives him the handkerchief.*] Wheresoever you had it, I'll take out no work on 't.

CASSIO: How now, my sweet Bianca? How now? How now?

OTHELLO: By heaven, that should be° my handkerchief!

BIANCA: If you'll come to supper tonight, you may; if you will not, come when you are next prepared for.° 150

Exit.

IAGO: After her, after her.

CASSIO: Faith, I must. She'll rail in the streets else.

IAGO: Will you sup there?

CASSIO: Faith, I intend so.

IAGO: Well, I may chance to see you, for I would very fain speak with you. 155

CASSIO: Prithee, come. Will you?

IAGO: Go to.° Say no more. [*Exit Cassio.*]

OTHELLO [*advancing*]: How shall I murder him, Iago?

IAGO: Did you perceive how he laughed at his vice?

OTHELLO: O, Iago! 160

IAGO: And did you see the handkerchief?

OTHELLO: Was that mine?

IAGO: Yours, by this hand. And to see how he prizes the foolish woman your wife! She gave it him, and he hath given it his whore.

OTHELLO: I would have him nine years a-killing. A fine woman! A fair woman! A sweet woman! 165

IAGO: Nay, you must forget that.

OTHELLO: Ay, let her rot and perish, and be damned tonight, for she shall not live. No, my heart is turned to stone; I strike it, and it hurts my hand. O, the world hath not a sweeter creature! She might lie by an emperor's side and command 170 him tasks.

IAGO: Nay, that's not your way.°

OTHELLO: Hang her! I do but say what she is. So delicate with her needle! An admirable musician! O, she will sing the sav-

148 should be must be **149–150 when . . . for** when I'm ready for you (i.e., never) **157 Go to** (An expression of remonstrance.) **172 your way** i.e., the way you should think of her

ageness out of a bear. Of so high and plenteous wit and in-
vention!°   *175*

IAGO: She's the worse for all this.

OTHELLO: O, a thousand, a thousand times! And then, of so
gentle a condition!°

IAGO: Ay, too gentle.°

OTHELLO: Nay, that's certain. But yet the pity of it, Iago! O,
Iago, the pity of it, Iago!   *180*

IAGO: If you are so fond° over her iniquity, give her patent° to
offend, for if it touch not you it comes near nobody.

OTHELLO: I will chop her into messes.° Cuckold me?

IAGO: O, 'tis foul in her.

OTHELLO: With mine officer?   *185*

IAGO: That's fouler.

OTHELLO: Get me some poison, Iago, this night. I'll not ex-
postulate with her, lest her body and beauty unprovide° my
mind again. This night, Iago.

IAGO: Do it not with poison. Strangle her in her bed, even the
bed she hath contaminated.   *190*

OTHELLO: Good, good! The justice of it pleases. Very good.

IAGO: And for Cassio, let me be his undertaker.° You shall hear
more by midnight.

OTHELLO: Excellent good. [*A trumpet within.*] What trumpet
is that same?

IAGO: I warrant, something from Venice.

Enter Lodovico, Desdemona, and attendants.

'Tis Lodovico. This comes from the Duke.   *195*
See, your wife's with him.

LODOVICO: God save you, worthy General!

OTHELLO: With all my heart,° sir.

LODOVICO [*giving him a letter*]: The Duke and the senators of
Venice greet you.

OTHELLO: I kiss the instrument of their pleasures.

---

175 invention imagination   **177 gentle a condition** well-born and well-bred   **178 gentle** generous, yielding (to other men)   **181 fond** foolish.   **patent** licence   **183 messes** portions of meat,
i.e., bits   **188 unprovide** weaken, render unfit   **192 be his undertaker** undertake to dispatch him
197 With all my heart i.e., I thank you most heartily

[*He opens the letter, and reads.*]

DESDEMONA: And what's the news, good cousin Lodovico?   *200*
IAGO: I am very glad to see you, signor.
   Welcome to Cyprus.
LODOVICO: I thank you. How does Lieutenant Cassio?
IAGO: Lives, sir.
DESDEMONA: Cousin, there's fall'n between him and my lord   *205*
   An unkind° breach; but you shall make all well.
OTHELLO: Are you sure of that?
DESDEMONA: My lord?
OTHELLO [*reads*]:   "This fail you not to do, as you will—"
LODOVICO: He did not call; he's busy in the paper.   *210*
   Is there division twixt my lord and Cassio?
DESDEMONA: A most unhappy one. I would do much
   T' atone° them, for the love I bear to Cassio.
OTHELLO: Fire and brimstone!
DESDEMONA: My lord?   *215*
OTHELLO: Are you wise?
DESDEMONA: What, is he angry?
LODOVICO: Maybe the letter moved him;
   For, as I think, they do command him home,
   Deputing Cassio in his government.°
DESDEMONA: By my troth, I am glad on 't.°   *220*
OTHELLO: Indeed?
DESDEMONA: My lord?
OTHELLO: I am glad to see you mad.°
DESDEMONA: Why, sweet Othello—
OTHELLO [*striking her*]:   Devil!   *225*
DESDEMONA: I have not deserved this.
LODOVICO: My lord, this would not be believed in Venice,
   Though I should swear I saw 't. 'Tis very much.°
   Make her amends; she weeps.
OTHELLO: O devil, devil!

---

206 unkind unnatural, contrary to their natures; hurtful   **213 atone** reconcile   **219 government** office   **220 on 't** of it   **223 I am . . . mad** i.e., I am glad to see that you are insane enough to rejoice in Cassio's promotion (? Othello bitterly plays on Desdemona's *I am glad.*)   **228 very much** too much, outrageous

If that the earth could teem° with woman's tears,   230
Each drop she falls would prove a crocodile.°
Out of my sight!
DESDEMONA: I will not stay to offend you. [*Going.*]
LODOVICO: Truly, an obedient lady.
   I do beseech your lordship, call her back.
OTHELLO: Mistress!   235
DESDEMONA [*returning*]:   My lord?
OTHELLO: What would you with her, sir?°
LODOVICO: Who, I, my lord?
OTHELLO: Ay, you did wish that I would make her turn.
   Sir, she can turn, and turn, and yet go on   240
   And turn again; and she can weep, sir, weep;
   And she's obedient,° as you say, obedient,
   Very obedient.—Proceed you in your tears.—
   Concerning this, sir—O well-painted passion!°—
   I am commanded home.—Get you away;   245
   I'll send for you anon.—Sir, I obey the mandate
   And will return to Venice.—Hence, avaunt!

                          [*Exit Desdemona.*]

   Cassio shall have my place. And, sir, tonight
   I do entreat that we may sup together.
   You are welcome, sir, to Cyprus.—Goats and monkeys!° *Exit.*   250
LODOVICO: Is this the noble Moor whom our full Senate
   Call all in all sufficient? Is this the nature
   Whom passion could not shake? Whose solid virtue
   The shot of accident nor dart of chance
   Could neither graze nor pierce?
IAGO: He is much changed.   255
LODOVICO: Are his wits safe? Is he not light of brain?
IAGO: He's that he is. I may not breathe my censure
   What he might be. If what he might he is not,

---

230 teem breed, be impregnated   **231 falls . . . crocodile** (Crocodiles were supposed to weep hypo-critical tears for their victims.)   **237 What . . . sir** (Othello implies that Desdemona is pliant and will do a *turn*, lines 239-241, for any man.)   **242 obedient** (With much the same sexual connota-tion as *turn* in lines 239-241.)   **244 passion** i.e., grief   **250 Goats and monkeys** (See Act III, Scene iii, line 419.)

I would to heaven he were!°
LODOVICO: What, strike his wife?
IAGO: Faith, that was not so well; yet would I knew   *260*
That stroke would prove the worst!
LODOVICO: Is it his use?°
Or did the letters work upon his blood°
And new-create his fault?
IAGO: Alas, alas!
It is not honesty in me to speak
What I have seen and known. You shall observe him,   *265*
And his own courses will denote° him so
That I may save my speech. Do but go after,
And mark how he continues.
LODOVICO: I am sorry that I am deceived in him.   *Exeunt.*

SCENE II [THE CITADEL.]

Enter Othello and Emilia.

OTHELLO: You have seen nothing then?
EMILIA: Nor ever heard, nor ever did suspect.
OTHELLO: Yes, you have seen Cassio and she together.
EMILIA: But then I saw no harm, and then I heard
Each syllable that breath made up between them.   *5*
OTHELLO: What, did they never whisper?
EMILIA: Never, my lord.
OTHELLO: Nor send you out o' the way?
EMILIA: Never.
OTHELLO: To fetch her fan, her gloves, her mask, nor nothing?   *10*
EMILIA: Never, my lord.
OTHELLO: That's strange.
EMILIA: I durst, my lord, to wager she is honest,
Lay down my soul at stake.° If you think other,
Remove your thought; it doth abuse your bosom.°   *15*

257-259 I may . . . were i.e., I dare not venture an opinion as to whether he's of unsound mind, as you suggest, but, if he isn't, then it might be better to wish he were in fact insane, since only that could excuse his wild behaviour   **261 use** custom   **262 blood** passions   **266 courses will denote** actions will reveal
14 at stake as the wager   **15 abuse your bosom** deceive you

If any wretch have put this in your head,
Let heaven requite it with the serpent's curse!°
For if she be not honest, chaste, and true,
There's no man happy; the purest of their wives
Is foul as slander.

OTHELLO: Bid her come hither. Go.   20

Exit Emilia.

She says enough; yet she's a simple bawd
That cannot say as much.° This° is a subtle whore,
A closet lock and key° of villainous secrets.
And yet she'll kneel and pray; I have seen her do 't.

Enter Desdemona and Emilia.

DESDEMONA: My lord, what is your will?   25
OTHELLO: Pray you, chuck, come hither.
DESDEMONA: What is your pleasure?
OTHELLO: Let me see your eyes.
Look in my face.
DESDEMONA: What horrible fancy's this?
OTHELLO [*to Emilia*]:   Some of your function,° mistress.
Leave procreants° alone and shut the door;   30
Cough or cry "hem" if anybody come.
Your mystery, your mystery!° Nay, dispatch.

Exit Emilia.

DESDEMONA [*kneeling*]:   Upon my knees, what doth your
speech import?
I understand a fury in your words,
But not the words.   35
OTHELLO: Why, what art thou?
DESDEMONA: Your wife, my lord, your true
And loyal wife.

---

17 the serpent's curse the curse pronounced by God on the serpent for deceiving Eve, just as some
man has done to Othello and Desdemona. (See Genesis 3:14.)   **21–22 she's . . . much** i.e., any pro-
curess or go-between who couldn't make up as plausible a story as Emilia's would have to be pretty
stupid   **22 This** i.e., Desdemona   **23 closet lock and key** i.e., concealer   **29 Some . . . function**
i.e., practise your chosen profession, that of bawd (by guarding the door)   **30 procreants** mating
couples   **32 mystery** trade, occupation

OTHELLO: Come, swear it, damn thyself,
Lest, being like one of heaven,° the devils themselves
Should fear to seize thee. Therefore be double damned:
Swear thou art honest.
DESDEMONA: Heaven doth truly know it. 40
OTHELLO: Heaven truly knows that thou art false as hell.
DESDEMONA: To whom, my lord? With whom? How am I
false?
OTHELLO [*weeping*]: Ah, Desdemon! Away, away, away!
DESDEMONA: Alas the heavy day! Why do you weep?
Am I the motive° of these tears, my lord? 45
If haply you my father do suspect
An instrument of this your calling back,
Lay not your blame on me. If you have lost him,
I have lost him too.
OTHELLO: Had it pleased heaven
To try me with affliction, had they° rained 50
All kinds of sores and shames on my bare head,
Steeped me in poverty to the very lips,
Given to captivity me and my utmost hopes,
I should have found in some place of my soul
A drop of patience. But, alas, to make me 55
A fixèd figure for the time of scorn°
To point his° slow and moving finger° at!
Yet could I bear that too, well, very well.
But there where I have garnered° up my heart,
Where either I must live or bear no life, 60
The fountain° from the which my current runs
Or else dries up—to be discarded thence!
Or keep it as a cistern° for foul toads
To knot° and gender° in! Turn thy complexion there,°
Patience, thou young and rose-lipped cherubin— 65

---

38 being . . . heaven looking like an angel   **45 motive** cause   **50 they** i.e., heavenly powers
56 time of scorn i.e., scornful world   **57 his** its.   **slow and moving finger** i.e., hour hand of the
clock, moving so slowly it seems hardly to move at all. (Othello envisages himself as being eternally
pointed at by the scornful world as the numbers on a clock are pointed at by the hour hand.)
59 garnered stored   **61 fountain** spring   **63 cistern** cesspool   **64 knot** couple.   **gender** engen-
der.   **Turn . . . there** change your color, grow pale, at such a sight

Ay, there look grim as hell!°
DESDEMONA: I hope my noble lord esteems me honest.°
OTHELLO: O, ay, as summer flies are in the shambles,°
    That quicken° even with blowing.° O thou weed,
    Who art so lovely fair and smell'st so sweet   70
    That the sense aches at thee, would thou hadst ne'er been
    born!
DESDEMONA: Alas, what ignorant° sin have I committed?
OTHELLO: Was this fair paper, this most goodly book,
    Made to write "whore" upon? What committed?
    Committed? O thou public commoner!°   75
    I should make very forges of my cheeks,
    That would to cinders burn up modesty,
    Did I but speak thy deeds. What committed?
    Heaven stops the nose at it and the moon winks;°
    The bawdy° wind, that kisses all it meets,   80
    Is hushed within the hollow mine° of earth
    And will not hear 't. What committed?
    Impudent strumpet!
DESDEMONA: By heaven, you do me wrong.
OTHELLO: Are not you a strumpet?
DESDEMONA: No, as I am a Christian.   85
    If to preserve this vessel° for my lord
    From any other foul unlawful touch
    Be not to be a strumpet, I am none.
OTHELLO: What, not a whore?
DESDEMONA: No, as I shall be saved.   90
OTHELLO: Is 't possible?
DESDEMONA: O, heaven forgive us!
OTHELLO: I cry you mercy,° then.
    I took you for that cunning whore of Venice
    That married with Othello. [*Calling out.*] You, mistress,
    That have the office opposite to Saint Peter   95

65–66 Patience . . . hell (Even Patience, that rose-lipped cherub, will look grim and pale at this spectacle.)   **67 honest** chaste   **68 shambles** slaughterhouse   **69 quicken** come to life.   **with blowing** i.e., with the puffing up of something rotten in which maggots are breeding   **72 ignorant sin** sin in ignorance   **75 commoner** prostitute   **79 winks** closes her eyes. (The moon symbolizes chastity.)   **80 bawdy** kissing one and all   **81 mine** cave (where the winds were thought to dwell)   **86 vessel** body   **92 cry you mercy** beg your pardon

And keep the gate of hell!

Enter Emilia.

You, you, ay, you!
We have done our course.° There's money for your
pains.[*He gives money.*]
I pray you, turn the key and keep our counsel.   *Exit.*
EMILIA: Alas, what does this gentleman conceive?°
How do you, madam? How do you, my good lady?   *100*
DESDEMONA: Faith, half asleep.°
EMILIA: Good madam, what's the matter with my lord?
DESDEMONA: With who?
EMILIA: Why, with my lord, madam.
DESDEMONA: Who is thy lord?
EMILIA: He that is yours, sweet lady.   *105*
DESDEMONA: I have none. Do not talk to me, Emilia.
I cannot weep, nor answers have I none
But what should go by water.° Prithee, tonight
Lay on my bed my wedding sheets, remember;
And call thy husband hither.   *110*
EMILIA: Here's a change indeed!   *Exit.*
DESDEMONA: 'Tis meet I should be used so, very meet.°
How have I been behaved, that he might stick°
The small'st opinion° on my least misuse?°

Enter Iago and Emilia.

IAGO: What is your pleasure, madam? How is 't with you?   *115*
DESDEMONA: I cannot tell. Those that do teach young babes
Do it with gentle means and easy tasks.
He might have chid me so, for, in good faith,
I am a child to chiding.
IAGO: What is the matter, lady?   *120*
EMILIA: Alas, Iago, my lord hath so bewhored her,
Thrown such despite and heavy terms upon her,
That true hearts cannot bear it.

---

97 course business (with an indecent suggestion of "trick," turn at sex)   **99 conceive** suppose, think   **101 half asleep** i.e., dazed   **108 go by water** be expressed by tears   **112 meet** fitting   **113 stick** attach   **114 opinion** censure.   **least misuse** slightest misconduct

DESDEMONA: Am I that name, Iago?

IAGO: What name, fair lady?   125

DESDEMONA: Such as she said my lord did say I was.

EMILIA: He called her whore. A beggar in his drink
   Could not have laid such terms upon his callet.°

IAGO: Why did he so?

DESDEMONA [*weeping*]: I do not know. I am sure I am none
   such.   130

IAGO: Do not weep, do not weep. Alas the day!

EMILIA: Hath she forsook so many noble matches,
   Her father and her country and her friends,
   To be called whore? Would it not make one weep?

DESDEMONA: It is my wretched fortune.

IAGO: Beshrew° him for 't!   135
   How comes this trick° upon him?

DESDEMONA: Nay, heaven doth know.

EMILIA: I will be hanged if some eternal° villain,
   Some busy and insinuating° rogue,
   Some cogging,° cozening° slave, to get some office,
   Have not devised this slander. I will be hanged else.   140

IAGO: Fie, there is no such man. It is impossible.

DESDEMONA: If any such there be, heaven pardon him!

EMILIA: A halter° pardon him! And hell gnaw his bones!
   Why should he call her whore? Who keeps her company?
   What place? What time? What form?° What likelihood?   145
   The Moor's abused by some most villainous knave,
   Some base notorious knave, some scurvy fellow.
   O heaven, that° such companions° thou'dst unfold,°
   And put in every honest hand a whip
   To lash the rascals naked through the world   150
   Even from the east to th' west!

IAGO: Speak within door.°

EMILIA: O, fie upon them! Some such squire° he was

---

128 callet whore   **135 Beshrew** curse   **136 trick** strange behaviour, delusion   **137 eternal** inveterate   **138 insinuating** ingratiating, fawning, wheedling   **139 cogging** cheating.   **cozening** de-
frauding   **143 halter** hangman's noose   **145 form** appearance, circumstance   **148 that** would that.
companions fellows.   **unfold** expose   **151 within door** i.e., not so loud   **152 squire** fellow

That turned your wit the seamy side without°
And made you to suspect me with the Moor.

IAGO: You are a fool. Go to.°

DESDEMONA: Alas, Iago,   *155*
What shall I do to win my lord again?
Good friend, go to him; for, by this light of heaven,
I know not how I lost him. Here I kneel. [*She kneels.*]
If e'er my will did trespass 'gainst his love,
Either in discourse° of thought or actual deed,   *160*
Or that° mine eyes, mine ears, or any sense
Delighted them° in any other form;
Or that I do not yet,° and ever did,
And ever will—though he do shake me off
To beggarly divorcement—love him dearly,   *165*
Comfort forswear° me! Unkindness may do much,
And his unkindness may defeat° my life,
But never taint my love. I cannot say "whore."
It does abhor° me now I speak the word;
To do the act that might the addition° earn   *170*
Not the world's mass of vanity° could make me.

[*She rises.*]

IAGO: I pray you, be content. 'Tis but his humor.°
The business of the state does him offense,
And he does chide with you.

DESDEMONA: If 'twere no other—   *175*

IAGO: It is but so, I warrant. [*Trumpets within.*]
Hark, how these instruments summon you to supper!
The messengers of Venice stays the meat.°
Go in, and weep not. All things shall be well.

                     Exeunt Desdemona and Emilia.

Enter Roderigo.

---

153 seamy side without wrong side out   **155 Go to** i.e., that's enough   **160 discourse of thought**
process of thinking   **161 that** if. (Also in line 163.)   **162 Delighted them** took delight   **163 yet**
still   **166 Comfort forswear** may heavenly comfort forsake   **167 defeat** destroy   **169 abhor** (1)
fill me with abhorrence (2) make me whorelike   **170 addition** title   **171 vanity** showy splendour
172 humor mood   **178 stays the meat** are waiting to dine

How now, Roderigo?   *180*

RODERIGO: I do not find that thou deal'st justly with me.

IAGO: What in the contrary?

RODERIGO: Every day thou daff'st me° with some device,°
Iago, and rather, as it seems to me now, keep'st from me all
conveniency° than suppliest me with the least advantage° of   *185*
hope. I will indeed no longer endure it, nor am I yet persuaded to put up° in peace what already I have foolishly suffered.

IAGO: Will you hear me, Roderigo?

RODERIGO: Faith, I have heard too much, for your words and
performances are no kin together.

IAGO: You charge me most unjustly.   *190*

RODERIGO: With naught but truth. I have wasted myself out
of my means. The jewels you have had from me to deliver°
Desdemona would half have corrupted a votarist.° You have
told me she hath received them and returned me expectations and comforts of sudden respect° and acquaintance, but
I find none.   *195*

IAGO: Well, go to, very well.

RODERIGO: "Very well"! "Go to"! I cannot go to,° man, nor
'tis not very well. By this hand, I think it is scurvy, and begin
to find myself fopped° in it.

IAGO: Very well.

RODERIGO: I tell you 'tis not very well.° I will make myself   *200*
known to Desdemona. If she will return me my jewels, I will
give over my suit and repent my unlawful solicitation; if not,
assure yourself I will seek satisfaction° of you.

IAGO: You have said now?°

RODERIGO: Ay, and said nothing but what I protest
intendment° of doing.

---

183 thou daff'st me you put me off.   **device** excuse, trick   **184 conveniency** advantage, opportunity   **185 advantage** increase   **186 put up** submit to, tolerate   **192 deliver** deliver to
193 votarist nun   **194 sudden respect** immediate consideration   **197 I cannot go to** (Roderigo
changes Iago's go to, an expression urging patience, to *I cannot go to*, "I have no opportunity for success in wooing.")   **198 fopped** fooled, duped   **200 not very well** (Roderigo changes Iago's *very
well*, "all right, then," to *not very well*, "not at all good.")   **202 satisfaction** repayment. (The term
normally means settling of accounts in a duel.)   **203 You . . . now** have you finished?
204 intendment intention

IAGO: Why, now I see there's mettle in thee, and even from this   *205*
instant do build on thee a better opinion than ever before.
Give me thy hand, Roderigo. Thou hast taken against me a
most just exception; but yet I protest I have dealt most directly in thy affair.

RODERIGO: It hath not appeared.

IAGO: I grant indeed it hath not appeared, and your suspicion   *210*
is not without wit and judgment. But, Roderigo, if thou hast
that in thee indeed which I have greater reason to believe
now than ever—I mean purpose, courage, and valor—this
night show it. If thou the next night following enjoy not
Desdemona, take me from this world with treachery and   *215*
devise engines for° my life.

RODERIGO: Well, what is it? Is it within reason and compass?

IAGO: Sir, there is especial commission come from Venice to de-
pute Cassio in Othello's place.

RODERIGO: Is that true? Why, then Othello and Desdemona
return again to Venice.   *220*

IAGO: O, no; he goes into Mauritania and takes away with him
the fair Desdemona, unless his abode be lingered here by
some accident; wherein none can be so determinate° as the
removing of Cassio.

RODERIGO: How do you mean, removing of him?

IAGO: Why, by making him uncapable of Othello's place—   *225*
knocking out his brains.

RODERIGO: And that you would have me to do?

IAGO: Ay, if you dare do yourself a profit and a right. He sups
tonight with a harlotry,° and thither will I go to him. He
knows not yet of his honorable fortune. If you will watch his
going thence, which I will fashion to fall out° between twelve   *230*
and one, you may take him at your pleasure. I will be near to
second your attempt, and he shall fall between us. Come,
stand not amazed at it, but go along with me. I will show
you such a necessity in his death that you shall think

---

214 engines for plots against   **223 determinate** conclusive   **229 harlotry** slut   **230 fall out**
occur

yourself bound to put it on him. It is now high° suppertime,
and the night grows to waste.° About it.   235
RODERIGO: I will hear further reason for this.
IAGO: And you shall be satisfied.   *Exeunt.*

SCENE III [THE CITADEL.]

*Enter Othello, Lodovico, Desdemona, Emilia, and atten-
dants.*

LODOVICO: I do beseech you, sir, trouble yourself no further.
OTHELLO: O, pardon me; 'twill do me good to walk.
LODOVICO: Madam, good night. I humbly thank your
ladyship.
DESDEMONA: Your honor is most welcome.
OTHELLO: Will you walk, sir?
O, Desdemona!   5
DESDEMONA: My lord?
OTHELLO: Get you to bed on th' instant.
I will be returned forthwith. Dismiss your attendant there.
Look 't be done.
DESDEMONA: I will, my lord.   10

Exit [Othello, with Lodovico and attendants].

EMILIA: How goes it now? He looks gentler than he did.
DESDEMONA: He says he will return incontinent,°
And hath commanded me to go to bed,
And bid me to dismiss you.
EMILIA: Dismiss me?   15
DESDEMONA: It was his bidding. Therefore, good Emilia,
Give me my nightly wearing, and adieu.
We must not now displease him.
EMILIA: I would you had never seen him!
DESDEMONA: So would not I. My love doth so approve him   20
That even his stubbornness,° his checks,° his frowns—
Prithee, unpin me—have grace and favor in them.

---

234 high fully   **235 grows to waste** wastes away
12 incontinent immediately   **21 stubbornness** roughness   **checks** rebukes

[*Emilia prepares Desdemona for bed.*]

EMILIA: I have laid those sheets you bade me on the bed.

DESDEMONA: All's one.° Good faith, how foolish are our minds!
If I do die before thee, prithee shroud me   *25*
In one of these same sheets.

EMILIA: Come, come, you talk.°

DESDEMONA: My mother had a maid called Barbary.
She was in love, and he she loved proved mad°
And did forsake her. She had a song of "Willow."
An old thing 'twas, but it expressed her fortune,   *30*
And she died singing it. That song tonight
Will not go from my mind; I have much to do
But to go hang° my head all at one side
And sing it like poor Barbary. Prithee, dispatch.

EMILIA: Shall I go fetch your nightgown?°   *35*

DESDEMONA: No, unpin me here.
This Lodovico is a proper° man.

EMILIA: A very handsome man.

DESDEMONA: He speaks well.

EMILIA: I know a lady in Venice would have walked barefoot *40*
to Palestine for a touch of his nether lip.

DESDEMONA [*singing*]:
    "The poor soul sat sighing by a sycamore tree,
    Sing all a green willow;°
    Her hand on her bosom, her head on her knee,
    Sing willow, willow, willow.   *45*
    The fresh streams ran by her and murmured her moans;
    Sing willow, willow, willow;
    Her salt tears fell from her, and softened the stones—"
    Lay by these.
        [*Singing.*] "Sing willow, willow, willow—"   *50*
    Prithee, hie thee.° He'll come anon.°

---

24 All's one all right. It doesn't really matter   **26 talk** i.e., prattle   **28 mad** wild, i.e., faithless
32–33 I . . . hang I can scarcely keep myself from hanging   **35 nightgown** dressing gown
37 proper handsome   **43 willow** (A conventional emblem of disappointed love.)   **51 hie thee**
hurry.   **anon** right away

[*Singing.*] "Sing all a green willow must be my
garland.
　Let nobody blame him; his scorn I approve—"
Nay, that's not next.—Hark! Who is 't that knocks?

EMILIA: It's the wind.

DESDEMONA [*singing*]:
　"I called my love false love; but what said he then?　　　55
　Sing willow, willow, willow;
　If I court more women, you'll couch with more men."
So, get thee gone. Good night. Mine eyes do itch;
Doth that bode weeping?

EMILIA:　　　　　　　　　　'Tis neither here nor there.　　　60

DESDEMONA: I have heard it said so. O, these men, these
men!
Dost thou in conscience think—tell me, Emilia—
That there be women do abuse° their husbands
In such gross kind?

EMILIA:　　　　　　There be some such, no question.

DESDEMONA: Wouldst thou do such a deed for all the world?　　　65

EMILIA: Why, would not you?

DESDEMONA:　　　　　　　No, by this heavenly light!

EMILIA: Nor I neither by this heavenly light;
I might do 't as well i' the dark.

DESDEMONA: Wouldst thou do such a deed for all the world?

EMILIA: The world's a huge thing. It is a great price　　　70
For a small vice.

DESDEMONA: Good troth, I think thou wouldst not.

EMILIA: By my troth, I think I should, and undo 't when I had
done. Marry, I would not do such a thing for a joint ring,°
nor for measures of lawn,° nor for gowns, petticoats, nor
caps, nor any petty exhibition.° But for all the whole world!　　　75
Uds° pity, who would not make her husband a cuckold to
make him a monarch? I should venture purgatory for 't.

DESDEMONA: Beshrew me if I would do such a wrong
For the whole world.

---

63 abuse deceive　**74 joint ring** a ring made in separate halves.　　**lawn** fine linen　**75 exhibition**
gift　**76 Uds** God's

EMILIA: Why, the wrong is but a wrong i' the world, and having the world for your labor, 'tis a wrong in your own world,
and you might quickly make it right.

DESDEMONA: I do not think there is any such woman.

EMILIA: Yes, a dozen, and as many
To th' vantage° as would store° the world they played° for.   *85*
But I do think it is their husbands' faults
If wives do fall. Say that they slack their duties°
And pour our treasures into foreign laps,°
Or else break out in peevish jealousies,
Throwing restraint upon us? Or say they strike us,°   *90*
Or scant our former having in despite?°
Why, we have galls,° and though we have some grace,
Yet have we some revenge. Let husbands know
Their wives have sense° like them. They see, and smell,
And have their palates both for sweet and sour,   *95*
As husbands have. What is it that they do
When they change us for others? Is it sport?°
I think it is. And doth affection° breed it?
I think it doth. Is 't frailty that thus errs?
It is so, too. And have not we affections,   *100*
Desires for sport, and frailty, as men have?
Then let them use us well; else let them know,
The ills we do, their ills instruct us so.

DESDEMONA: Good night, good night. God me such uses° send
Not to pick bad from bad, but by bad mend!°   *105*

Exeunt.

---

85 To th' vantage in addition, to boot.   **store** populate.   **played** (1) gambled (2) sported sexually
87 duties marital duties   **88 pour . . . laps** i.e., are unfaithful, give what is rightfully ours (semen)
to other women   **90 Throwing . . . us** i.e., jealously restricting our freedom to see other men
91 scant . . . despite reduce our allowance to spite us   **92 have galls** i.e., are capable of resenting
injury and insult   **94 sense** physical sense   **97 sport** sexual pastime   **98 affection** passion
104 uses habit, practice   **105 Not . . . mend** i.e., not to learn bad conduct from others' badness (as
Emilia has suggested women learn from men), but to mend my ways by perceiving what badness is,
making spiritual benefit out of evil and adversity

ACT V

SCENE I [A STREET IN CYPRUS.]

Enter Iago and Roderigo.

IAGO: Here stand behind this bulk.° Straight will he come.
Wear thy good rapier bare,° and put it home.
Quick, quick! Fear nothing. I'll be at thy elbow.
It makes us or it mars us. Think on that,
And fix most firm thy resolution.   5
RODERIGO: Be near at hand. I may miscarry in 't.
IAGO: Here, at thy hand. Be bold, and take thy stand.

[*Iago stands aside. Roderigo conceals himself.*]

RODERIGO: I have no great devotion to the deed;
And yet he hath given me satisfying reasons.
'Tis but a man gone. Forth, my sword! He dies.   10

[*He draws.*]

IAGO: I have rubbed this young quat° almost to the sense,°
And he grows angry. Now, whether he kill Cassio
Or Cassio him, or each do kill the other,
Every way makes my gain. Live Roderigo,°
He calls me to a restitution large   15
Of gold and jewels that I bobbed° from him
As gifts to Desdemona.
It must not be. If Cassio do remain,
He hath a daily beauty in his life
That makes me ugly; and besides, the Moor   20
May unfold° me to him; there stand I in much peril.
No, he must die. Be 't so. I hear him coming.

Enter Cassio.

RODERIGO [*coming forth*]: I know his gait, 'tis he.—Villain,
thou diest!

---

1 bulk framework projecting from the front of a shop   **2 bare** unsheathed   **11 quat** pimple, pustule.   **to the sense** to the quick   **14 Live Roderigo** if Roderigo lives   **16 bobbed** swindled
21 unfold expose

[*He attacks Cassio.*]

CASSIO: That thrust had been mine enemy indeed,
But that my coat° is better than thou know'st.   25
I will make proof° of thine.

[*He draws, and wounds Roderigo.*]

RODERIGO: O, I am slain! [*He falls.*]

[*Iago, from behind, wounds Cassio in the leg, and exits.*]

CASSIO: I am maimed forever. Help, ho! Murder! Murder!

Enter Othello.

OTHELLO: The voice of Cassio! Iago keeps his word.
RODERIGO: O, villain that I am!
OTHELLO: It is even so. ·   30
CASSIO: O, help, ho! Light! A surgeon!
OTHELLO: 'Tis he. O brave Iago, honest and just,
That hast such noble sense of thy friend's wrong!
Thou teachest me. Minion,° your dear lies dead,
And your unblest fate hies.° Strumpet, I come.   35
Forth of° my heart those charms, thine eyes, are blotted;
Thy bed, lust-stained, shall with lust's blood be spotted.

                                        Exit Othello.

Enter Lodovico and Gratiano.

CASSIO: What ho! No watch? No passage?° Murder! Murder!
GRATIANO: 'Tis some mischance. The voice is very direful.
CASSIO: O, help!   40
LODOVICO: Hark!
RODERIGO: O wretched villain!
LODOVICO: Two or three groan. 'Tis heavy° night;
These may be counterfeits. Let's think 't unsafe
To come in to° the cry without more help.   45

---

25 **coat** (Possibly a garment of mail under the outer clothing, or simply a tougher coat than Roderigo expected.)   26 **proof** a test   34 **Minion** hussy (i.e., Desdemona)   35 **hies** hastens on   36 **Forth of** from out   38 **passage** people passing by   43 **heavy** thick, dark   45 **come in to** approach

[*They remain near the entrance.*]

RODERIGO: Nobody come? Then shall I bleed to death.

Enter Iago [*in his shirtsleeves, with a light*].

LODOVICO: Hark!

GRATIANO: Here's one comes in his shirt, with light and weapons.

IAGO: Who's there? Whose noise is this that cries on° murder?

LODOVICO: We do not know.

IAGO: Did not you hear a cry?   50

CASSIO: Here, here! For heaven's sake, help me!

IAGO: What's the matter?

[*He moves toward Cassio.*]

GRATIANO [*to Lodovico*]:   This is Othello's ancient, as I take it.

LODOVICO [*to Gratiano*]:   The same indeed, a very valiant fellow.

IAGO [*to Cassio*]:   What° are you here that cry so grievously?

CASSIO: Iago? O, I am spoiled,° undone by villains!   55
Give me some help.

IAGO: O me, Lieutenant! What villains have done this?

CASSIO: I think that one of them is hereabout,
And cannot make° away.

IAGO: O treacherous villains!

[*To Lodovico and Gratiano.*]

What are you there? Come in, and give some help. [*They
advance.*]   60

RODERIGO: O, help me there!

CASSIO: That's one of them.

IAGO: O murderous slave! O villain!

[*He stabs Roderigo.*]

RODERIGO: O damned Iago! O inhuman dog!

---

49 cries on cries out   **54 What** who (also at lines 60 and 66)   **55 spoiled** ruined, done for
59 make get

IAGO: Kill men i' the dark?—Where be these bloody
    thieves?—
    How silent is this town!—Ho! Murder, murder!—   65
    [*To Lodovico and Gratiano.*] What may you be? Are you of
    good or evil?
LODOVICO: As you shall prove us, praise° us.
IAGO: Signor Lodovico?
LODOVICO: He, sir.
IAGO: I cry you mercy.° Here's Cassio hurt by villains.   70
GRATIANO: Cassio?
IAGO: How is 't, brother?
CASSIO: My leg is cut in two.
IAGO: Marry, heaven forbid!
    Light, gentlemen! I'll bind it with my shirt.   75

[*He hands them the light, and tends to Cassio's wound.*]

Enter Bianca.

BIANCA: What is the matter, ho? Who is 't that cried?
IAGO: Who is 't that cried?
BIANCA: O my dear Cassio!
    My sweet Cassio! O Cassio, Cassio, Cassio!
IAGO: O notable strumpet! Cassio, may you suspect
    Who they should be that have thus mangled you?   80
CASSIO: No.
GRATIANO: I am sorry to find you thus. I have been to seek
    you.
IAGO: Lend me a garter. [*He applies a tourniquet.*] So.—O,
    for a chair,°
    To bear him easily hence!
BIANCA: Alas, he faints! O Cassio, Cassio, Cassio!   85
IAGO: Gentlemen all, I do suspect this trash
    To be a party in this injury.—
    Patience awhile, good Cassio.—Come, come;
    Lend me a light. [*He shines the light on Roderigo.*] Know
    we this face or no?

67 praise appraise   **70 I cry you mercy** I beg your pardon   **83 chair** litter

Alas, my friend and my dear countryman 90
Roderigo! No.—Yes, sure.—O heaven! Roderigo!

GRATIANO: What, of Venice?

IAGO: Even he, sir. Did you know him?

GRATIANO: Know him? Ay.

IAGO: Signor Gratiano? I cry your gentle° pardon. 95
These bloody accidents° must excuse my manners
That so neglected you.

GRATIANO: I am glad to see you.

IAGO: How do you, Cassio? O, a chair, a chair!

GRATIANO: Roderigo!

IAGO: He, he, 'tis he. [*A litter is brought in.*] O, that's well
said;° the chair. 100
Some good man bear him carefully from hence;
I'll fetch the General's surgeon. [*To Bianca.*] For you,
mistress,
Save you your labor.°—He that lies slain here, Cassio,
Was my dear friend. What malice° was between you?

CASSIO: None in the world, nor do I know the man. 105

IAGO [*to Bianca*]: What, look you pale?—O, bear him out o'
th' air.°

[*Cassio and Roderigo are borne off.*]

Stay you,° good gentlemen.—Look you pale, mistress?—
Do you perceive the gastness° of her eye?—
Nay, if you stare,° we shall hear more anon.—
Behold her well; I pray you, look upon her. 110
Do you see, gentlemen? Nay, guiltiness
Will speak, though tongues were out of use.

[*Enter Emilia.*]

EMILIA: 'Las, what's the matter? What's the matter, husband?

IAGO: Cassio hath here been set on in the dark

---

95 gentle noble **96 accidents** sudden events **100 well said** well done **103 Save . . . labor**
i.e., never you mind tending Cassio **104 malice** enmity **106 bear . . . air** (Fresh air was thought
to be dangerous for a wound.) **107 Stay you** (Lodovico and Gratiano are evidently about to leave.)
108 gastness terror **109 stare** (Iago pretends to interpret Bianca's wild looks as an involuntary
confession of guilt.)

By Roderigo and fellows that are scaped.   *115*
He's almost slain, and Roderigo dead.
EMILIA: Alas, good gentleman! Alas, good Cassio!
IAGO: This is the fruits of whoring. Prithee, Emilia,
Go know° of Cassio where he supped tonight.
[*To Bianca.*] What, do you shake at that?   *120*
BIANCA: He supped at my house, but I therefore shake not.
IAGO: O, did he so? I charge you go with me.
EMILIA: O, fie upon thee, strumpet!
BIANCA: I am no strumpet, but of life as honest°
As you that thus abuse me.   *125*
EMILIA: As I? Faugh! Fie upon thee!
IAGO: Kind gentlemen, let's go see poor Cassio dressed.°—
Come, mistress, you must tell's another tale.
Emilia, run you to the citadel
And tell my lord and lady what hath happed.—   *130*
Will you go on afore? [*Aside.*] This is the night
That either makes me or fordoes° me quite.   *Exeunt.*

SCENE II [A BEDCHAMBER IN THE CITADEL.]

Enter Othello [with a light], and Desdemona in her bed.°

OTHELLO: It is the cause,° it is the cause, my soul.
Let me not name it to you, you chaste stars!
It is the cause. Yet I'll not shed her blood,
Nor scar that whiter skin of hers than snow,
And smooth as monumental° alabaster.   *5*
Yet she must die, else she'll betray more men.
Put out the light, and then put out the light.°
If I quench thee, thou flaming minister,°
I can again thy former light restore,
Should I repent me;° but once put out thy light,   *10*
Thou cunning'st pattern° of excelling nature,

---

119 know learn   **124 honest** chaste   **127 Cassio dressed** Cassio's wounds dressed   **132 fordoes**
undoes, ruins
[s.d.] in her bed (Either the curtains are drawn back to reveal the bed in a recessed area backstage,
or the bed is "thrust out" onstage as the scene begins.)   **1 cause** i.e., cause of justice, the offence itself, which Othello must correct as an agent of justice   **5 monumental** i.e., used in making tombs
and funeral monuments   **7 the light . . . light** the torch or lamp . . . Desdemona's life   **8 flaming
minister** torch or lamp that serves me   **10 repent me** change my mind

I know not where is that Promethean heat°
That can thy light relume.° When I have plucked thy rose,
I cannot give it vital growth again;
It needs must wither. I'll smell thee on the tree.   15

[He kisses her.]

O balmy breath, that dost almost persuade
Justice to break her sword! One more, one more.
Be thus when thou art dead, and I will kill thee,
And love thee after. One more, and that's the last.

[He kisses her.]

So sweet was ne'er so fatal. I must weep,   20
But they are cruel° tears. This sorrow's heavenly;
It strikes where it doth love.° She wakes.
DESDEMONA: Who's there? Othello?
OTHELLO: Ay, Desdemona.
DESDEMONA: Will you come to bed, my lord?   25
OTHELLO: Have you prayed tonight, Desdemon?
DESDEMONA: Ay, my lord.
OTHELLO: If you bethink yourself of any crime°
Unreconciled as yet to heaven and grace,
Solicit° for it straight.°   30
DESDEMONA: Alack, my lord, what may you mean by that?
OTHELLO: Well, do it, and be brief. I will walk by.
I would not kill thy unpreparèd spirit.
No, heaven forfend!° I would not kill thy soul.
DESDEMONA: Talk you of killing?
OTHELLO: Ay, I do.
DESDEMONA: Then heaven   35
Have mercy on me!
OTHELLO: Amen, with all my heart!
DESDEMONA: If you say so, I hope you will not kill me.
OTHELLO: Humh!

---

11 Thou . . . pattern you skillfully wrought perfect example   **12 Promethean heat** divine fire.
(Alluding to the theft of fire from heaven by Prometheus.)   **13 relume** rekindle   **21 cruel** unrelenting   **22 It . . . love** (Compare Hebrews 12:6: "For whom the Lord loveth he chasteneth.")
28 crime sin   **30 Solicit** petition, pray.   **straight** immediately   **34 forfend** forbid

DESDEMONA: And yet I fear you; for you're fatal then
When your eyes roll so. Why I should fear I know not,   *40*
Since guiltiness I know not; but yet I feel I fear.
OTHELLO: Think on thy sins.
DESDEMONA: They are loves I bear to you.°
OTHELLO: Ay, and for that thou diest.
DESDEMONA: That death's unnatural that kills for loving.
Alas, why gnaw you so your nether lip?   *45*
Some bloody passion shakes your very frame.
These are portents; but yet I hope, I hope,
They do not point on° me.
OTHELLO: Peace, and be still!
DESDEMONA: I will so. What's the matter?   *50*
OTHELLO: That handkerchief which I so loved and gave thee
Thou gav'st to Cassio.
DESDEMONA: No, by my life and soul!
Send for the man and ask him.
OTHELLO: Sweet soul, take heed, take heed of perjury.
Thou art on thy deathbed.   *55*
DESDEMONA: Ay, but not yet to die.
OTHELLO: Yes, presently.°
Therefore confess thee freely of thy sin;
For to deny each article with oath
Cannot remove nor choke the strong conception°
That I do groan withal.° Thou art to die.   *60*
DESDEMONA: Then Lord have mercy on me!
OTHELLO: I say, amen.
DESDEMONA: And have you mercy too! I never did
Offend° you in my life; never loved Cassio
But with such general warranty° of heaven
As I might love. I never gave him token.   *65*
OTHELLO: By heaven, I saw my handkerchief in 's hand.
O perjured woman! Thou dost stone° my heart,
And makes me call what I intend to do

---

42 **They are . . . you** i.e., if I sinned, it was in loving you more than my father or more than God
48 **point on** point at, predict what is to happen to   56 **presently** immediately   59 **conception** (1)
belief in your guilt (2) plan in my mind   60 **groan withal** (1) groan at in sorrow (2) as in giving
birth   63 **Offend** wrong   64 **warranty** sanction   67 **stone** turn to stone, harden

A murder, which I thought a sacrifice.
I saw the handkerchief.

DESDEMONA: He found it, then.   70
I never gave it him. Send for him hither;
Let him confess a truth.

OTHELLO: He hath confessed.

DESDEMONA: What, my lord?

OTHELLO: That he hath used thee.

DESDEMONA: How? Unlawfully?

OTHELLO: Ay.

DESDEMONA: He will not say so.

OTHELLO: No, his mouth is stopped;   75
Honest Iago hath ta'en order° for 't.

DESDEMONA: O, my fear interprets. What, is he dead?

OTHELLO: Had all his hairs been lives, my great revenge
Had stomach for them all.

DESDEMONA: Alas, he is betrayed and I undone! [*She weeps.*]   80

OTHELLO: Out, strumpet! Weep'st thou for him to my face?

DESDEMONA: O, banish me, my lord, but kill me not!

OTHELLO: Down, strumpet!

DESDEMONA: Kill me tomorrow; let me live tonight!

OTHELLO: Nay, if you strive—   85

DESDEMONA: But half an hour!

OTHELLO: Being done,° there is no pause.

DESDEMONA: But while I say one prayer!

OTHELLO: It is too late.

Smothers her.

EMILIA [*at the door*]: My lord, my lord! What, ho! My lord,
my lord!

OTHELLO: What noise is this? Not dead? Not yet quite dead?
I that am cruel am yet merciful;   90
I would not have thee linger in thy pain.

[*He dispatches her.*]

---

76 ta'en order taken measures   **86 Being done** i.e., since justice has begun its relentless course

So, so.

EMILIA [*within*]:   What, ho! My lord, my lord!

OTHELLO: Who's there?

EMILIA [*within*]:   O, good my lord, I would speak a word with
you!

OTHELLO: Yes, 'tis Emilia.—By and by.—She's dead.
'Tis like° she comes to speak of Cassio's death.—   95
The noise was here.° Ha! No more moving?
Still as the grave. Shall she come in? Were 't good?—
I think she stirs again. No. What's best to do?
If she come in, she'll sure speak to my wife.
My wife! My wife! What wife? I have no wife.   100
O, insupportable! O heavy hour!
Methinks it should be now a huge eclipse
Of sun and moon, and that th' affrighted globe
Should yawn° at alteration.°

EMILIA [*within*]:   I do beseech you
That I may speak with you, O, good my lord!   105

OTHELLO: I had forgot thee. O, come in, Emilia.—
Soft,° by and by. Let me the curtains draw.—

[*He closes the bed-curtains and opens the door.*]

Where art thou?

Enter Emilia.

What's the matter with thee now?

EMILIA: O, my good lord, yonder's foul murders done!

OTHELLO: What, now?   110

EMILIA: But now, my lord.

OTHELLO: It is the very error° of the moon;
She comes more nearer earth than she was wont,
And makes men mad.

EMILIA: Cassio, my lord, hath killed a young Venetian   115

---

95 like likely that   **96 here** (The Folio's *high* is possible, suggesting that the commotion of the attack on Cassio was loud.)   **104 yawn** gape in amazement. i.e., move in an earthquake. (According to Pliny, earthquakes often happen during eclipses.)   **at alteration** at these cataclysmic events in nature, well-suited to express the horror of Desdemona's death   **107 Soft** wait a minute   **112 error** aberration, irregularity

Called Roderigo.

OTHELLO:　　　　Roderigo killed?
And Cassio killed?

EMILIA:　　　　　　No, Cassio is not killed.

OTHELLO:　Not Cassio killed? Then murder's out of tune,
And sweet revenge grows harsh.

DESDEMONA:　O, falsely, falsely murdered!　　　　　　　　*120*

EMILIA:　O Lord, what cry is that?

OTHELLO:　That? What?

EMILIA:　Out° and alas, that was my lady's voice.

[She opens the bed-curtains.]

Help, help, ho, help! O lady, speak again!
Sweet Desdemona! O sweet mistress, speak!　　　　　　*125*

DESDEMONA:　A guiltless death I die.

EMILIA:　O, who hath done this deed?

DESDEMONA:　Nobody; I myself. Farewell.
Commend me to my kind lord. O, farewell!　　　*[She dies.]*

OTHELLO:　Why, how should she be murdered?

EMILIA:　　　　　　　　　　　　Alas, who knows?　*130*

OTHELLO:　You heard her say herself it was not I.

EMILIA:　She said so. I must needs report the truth.

OTHELLO:　She's like a liar gone to burning hell!
'Twas I that killed her.

EMILIA:　　　　　　O, the more angel she,
And you the blacker devil!　　　　　　　　　　*135*

OTHELLO:　She turned to folly,° and she was a whore.

EMILIA:　Thou dost belie° her, and thou art a devil.

OTHELLO:　She was false as water.

EMILIA:　Thou art rash as fire to say
That she was false. O, she was heavenly true!　　　*140*

OTHELLO:　Cassio did top her. Ask thy husband else.°
O, I were damned beneath all depth in hell
But that I did proceed upon just grounds
To this extremity. Thy husband knew it all.

---

123 Out (A cry of dismay, intensifying *alas.*)　**136 folly** i.e., wantonness, fleshly sin　**137 belie** slander　**141 else** i.e., if you don't believe me

EMILIA: My husband?   *145*
OTHELLO: Thy husband.
EMILIA: That she was false to wedlock?
OTHELLO: Ay, with Cassio. Nay, had she been true,
  If heaven would make me such another world
  Of one entire and perfect chrysolite,°   *150*
  I'd not have sold her for it.
EMILIA: My husband?
OTHELLO: Ay, 'twas he that told me on her first.
  An honest man he is, and hates the slime
  That sticks on filthy deeds.   *155*
EMILIA: My husband?
OTHELLO: What needs this iterance,° woman? I say thy
  husband.
EMILIA: O mistress, villainy hath made mocks with° love!
  My husband say she was false?
OTHELLO: He, woman;
  I say thy husband. Dost understand the word?   *160*
  My friend, thy husband, honest, honest Iago.
EMILIA: If he say so, may his pernicious soul
  Rot half a grain a day! He lies to th' heart.
  She was too fond of her most filthy bargain.
OTHELLO: Ha?   *[He draws.]*   *165*
EMILIA: Do thy worst!
  This deed of thine is no more worthy heaven
  Than thou wast worthy her.
OTHELLO: Peace, you were best.°
EMILIA: Thou hast not half that power to do me harm
  As I have to be hurt.° O gull!° O dolt!   *170*
  As ignorant as dirt! Thou hast done a deed—
  I care not for thy sword; I'll make thee known,
  Though I lost twenty lives.—Help! Help, ho, help!
  The Moor hath killed my mistress! Murder, murder!

Enter Montano, Gratiano, and Iago.

---

150 **chrysolite** precious topaz   157 **iterance** iteration, repetition   158 **made mocks with** derided, made sport of   168 **you were best** it would be best for you   170 **to be hurt** i.e., to endure hurt. **gull** dupe

MONTANO: What is the matter? How now, General?   *175*
EMILIA: O, are you come, Iago? You have done well,
That men must lay their murders on your neck.
GRATIANO: What is the matter?
EMILIA [*to Iago*]: Disprove this villain, if thou be'st a man.
He says thou toldst him that his wife was false.   *180*
I know thou didst not; thou'rt not such a villain.
Speak, for my heart is full.
IAGO: I told him what I thought, and told no more
Than what he found himself was apt° and true.
EMILIA: But did you ever tell him she was false?   *185*
IAGO: I did.
EMILIA: You told a lie, an odious, damnèd lie!
Upon my soul, a lie, a wicked lie.
She false with Cassio? Did you say with Cassio?
IAGO: With Cassio, mistress. Go to, charm° your tongue.   *190*
EMILIA: I will not charm my tongue; I am bound to speak.
My mistress here lies murdered in her bed—
ALL: O heavens forfend!
EMILIA: And your reports have set the murder on.
OTHELLO: Nay, stare not, masters. It is true indeed.   *195*
GRATIANO: 'Tis a strange truth.
MONTANO: O monstrous act!
EMILIA: Villainy, villainy, villainy!
I think upon 't—I think I smell 't! O villainy!
I thought so then°—I'll kill myself for grief—
O villainy, villainy!   *200*
IAGO: What, are you mad? I charge you, get you home.
EMILIA: Good gentlemen, let me have leave to speak.
'Tis proper I obey him, but not now.
Perchance, Iago, I will ne'er go home.
Othello: O! O! O!   [*Othello falls on the bed.*°]
EMILIA: Nay, lay thee down and roar,   *205*
For thou hast killed the sweetest innocent

---

184 apt plausible   **190 charm** keep silent (as though by a magic spell)   **199 then** (Perhaps at Act III, Scene iii, lines 331-332 and Act IV, Scene ii, lines 137-154.)   **205 [s.d.] Othello . . . bed** (This direction is from the Quarto, as also *He kisses her* at line 19 and *She dies* at line 129.)

That e'er did lift up eye.°
OTHELLO [*rising*]:   O, she was foul!
  I scarce did know you, uncle. There lies your niece,
  Whose breath indeed these hands have newly stopped.
  I know this act shows° horrible and grim.   *210*
GRATIANO: Poor Desdemon! I am glad thy father's dead.
  Thy match was mortal to him, and pure grief
  Shore his old thread° in twain. Did he live now,
  This sight would make him do a desperate turn,°
  Yea, curse his better angel from his side,   *215*
  And fall to reprobance.°
OTHELLO: 'Tis pitiful. But yet Iago knows
  That she with Cassio hath the act of shame
  A thousand times committed. Cassio confessed it;
  And she did gratify° his amorous works   *220*
  With that recognizance° and pledge of love
  Which I first gave her. I saw it in his hand;
  It was a handkerchief, an antique token
  My father gave my mother.
EMILIA: O God! O heavenly God!   *225*
IAGO: Zounds, hold your peace.
EMILIA: 'Twill out, 'twill out! I peace?
  No, I will speak as liberal as the north.°
  Let heaven and men and devils, let them all,
  All, all, cry shame against me, yet I'll speak.
IAGO: Be wise, and get you home.
EMILIA: I will not.

  [*Iago threatens Emilia.*]

GRATIANO: Fie   *230*
  Your sword upon a woman?
EMILIA: O thou dull Moor! That handkerchief thou speak'st of
  I found by fortune and did give my husband;
  For often, with a solemn earnestness,

---

207 lift up eye i.e., lift her eyes to heaven   **210 shows** looks   **213 Shore . . . thread** sheared the
thread of his old age (as Atropos, one of the three Fates, was thought to do)   **214 turn** deed
216 reprobance damnation, i.e., suicide   **220 gratify** reward   **221 recognizance** token
227 liberal as the north freely as the north wind (blows)

More than indeed belonged° to such a trifle,   235
He begged of me to steal 't.
IAGO: Villainous whore!
EMILIA: She give it Cassio? No, alas! I found it,
And I did give 't my husband.
IAGO: Filth, thou liest!
EMILIA: By heaven, I do not, I do not, gentlemen.
O murderous coxcomb!° What should such a fool   240
Do with so good a wife?
OTHELLO: Are there no stones° in heaven
But what serves for the thunder?—Precious° villain!

[He runs at Iago; Montano disarms Othello. Iago, from be-
hind, stabs Emilia.°]

GRATIANO: The woman falls! Sure he hath killed his wife.
EMILIA: Ay, ay. O, lay me by my mistress' side.   245

Exit [Iago.]

GRATIANO: He's gone, but his wife's killed.
MONTANO: 'Tis a notorious villain. Take you this weapon,
Which I have here recovered from the Moor.
Come, guard the door without. Let him not pass,
But kill him rather. I'll after that same villain,   250
For 'tis a damnèd slave.

Exit [with all but Othello and Emilia, who has been laid by
                              Desdemona's side].

OTHELLO: I am not valiant neither,
But every puny whipster° gets my sword.
But why should honor° outlive honesty?°
Let it go all.
EMILIA: What did thy song bode, lady?   255
Hark, canst thou hear me? I will play the swan,

---

235 belonged was appropriate   **240 coxcomb** fool. (Addressed to Othello.)   **242 stones** bolts, such as those used for thunderbolts   **243 Precious** i.e., arrant, utter   **[s.d.] He . . . Emilia** (The Quarto text reads, "The Moor runs at Iago. Iago kills his wife." The Quarto also specifies the exit of Iago at line 245 and the death of Emilia at line 260.)   **253 whipster** contemptible fellow (one who is always ready to whip out his sword)   **254 honor** i.e., the bravery for which one enjoys a soldier's reputation   **honesty** true integrity

And die in music. [*She sings.*] "Willow, willow, willow."
Moor, she was chaste. She loved thee, cruel Moor.
So come my soul to bliss as I speak true.
So speaking as I think, alas, I die.   [*She dies.*]   *260*

OTHELLO: I have another weapon in this chamber;
It was a sword of Spain, the ice-brook's temper°—
O, here it is. [*He finds a sword.*] Uncle, I must come forth.

GRATIANO [*within*]:   If thou attempt it, it will cost thee dear.
Thou hast no weapon, and perforce must suffer.   *265*

OTHELLO: Look in upon me then and speak with me,
Or, naked° as I am, I will assault thee.

[*Enter Gratiano.*]

GRATIANO: What is the matter?
OTHELLO: Behold, I have a weapon;
A better never did itself sustain
Upon a soldier's thigh. I have seen the day   *270*
That, with this little arm and this good sword,
I have made my way through more impediments
Than twenty times your stop.° But O, vain boast!
Who can control his fate? 'Tis not so now.
Be not afraid, though you do see me weaponed;   *275*
Here is my journey's end, here is my butt°
And very seamark° of my utmost sail.

[*Gratiano steps back.*]

Do you go back dismayed? 'Tis a lost° fear;
Man but a rush° against Othello's breast
And he retires. Where should Othello go?   *280*

[*He turns to Desdemona.*]

Now, how dost thou look now? O ill-starred wench!
Pale as thy smock! When we shall meet at compt,°
This look of thine will hurl my soul from heaven,

---

262 the ice-brook's temper tempered in ice-cold water   **267 naked** unarmed   **273 stop** power
(to stop)   **276 butt** goal, limit. (An archery term.)   **277 seamark** beacon (marking his destination
or limit)   **278 lost** wasted, unneeded   **279 Man . . . rush** wield no more than a reed   **282 compt**
account, judgment day

And fiends will snatch at it. Cold, cold, my girl?
Even like thy chastity. O cursèd, cursèd slave!°   285
Whip me, ye devils,
From the possession of this heavenly sight!
Blow me about in winds! Roast me in sulfur!
Wash me in steep-down gulfs of liquid fire!
O Desdemon! Dead, Desdemon! Dead! O! O!   290

Enter Lodovico, Cassio [carried in a litter°], Montano, and
Iago [prisoner], with officers.

LODOVICO: Where is this rash and most unfortunate man?
OTHELLO: That's he that was Othello. Here I am.
LODOVICO: Where is that viper? Bring the villain forth.

[Iago is led forward.]

OTHELLO: I look down towards his feet;° but that's a fable.
If that thou be'st a devil, I cannot kill thee.   295

[He wounds Iago.]

LODOVICO: Wrench his sword from him.

[Othello is disarmed.]

IAGO: I bleed, sir, but not
killed.
OTHELLO: I am not sorry neither. I'd have thee live,
For in my sense° 'tis happiness to die.
LODOVICO: O thou Othello, that was once so good,
Fall'n in the practice° of a cursèd slave,°   300
What shall be said to thee?
OTHELLO: Why, anything.
An honorable murderer, if you will,
For naught I did in hate, but all in honor.
LODOVICO: This wretch hath part confessed his villainy.
Did you and he consent° in Cassio's death?   305

---

285 slave i.e., Othello himself   **290 [s.d.] in a litter** (The Quarto specifies that Cassio is "in a
chair.")   **294 towards his feet** i.e., to see if they are cloven, as the devil's are fabled to be   **298 in
my sense** to one who feels as I do   **300 in the practice** through the plotting, into the snare.   **slave**
villain   **305 consent** agree

OTHELLO: Ay.

CASSIO: Dear General, I never gave you cause.

OTHELLO: I do believe it, and I ask your pardon.
Will you, I pray, demand that demi-devil
Why he hath thus ensnared my soul and body?   *310*

IAGO: Demand me nothing. What you know, you know.
From this time forth I never will speak word.

LODOVICO: What, not to pray?

GRATIANO: Torments° will ope your lips.

OTHELLO: Well, thou dost best.   *315*

LODOVICO: Sir, you shall understand what hath befall'n,
Which, as I think, you know not. Here is a letter
Found in the pocket of the slain Roderigo;
And here another. [*He produces letters.*] The one of them
imports
The death of Cassio, to be undertook   *320*
By Roderigo.

OTHELLO: O villain!

CASSIO: Most heathenish and most gross!°

LODOVICO [*showing another paper*]: Now here's another
discontented° paper
Found in his pocket too. And this, it seems,
Roderigo meant t' have sent this damnèd villain;   *325*
But that belike° Iago in the interim
Came in and satisfied him.°

OTHELLO: O thou pernicious caitiff!—
How came you, Cassio, by that handkerchief
That was my wife's?

CASSIO: I found it in my chamber;   *330*
And he himself confessed but even now
That there he dropped it for a special purpose
Which wrought to his desire.°

OTHELLO: O fool, fool, fool!

CASSIO: There is besides in Roderigo's letter

---

314 Torments torture   **322 gross** monstrous   **323 discontented** full of discontent   **326 belike**
most likely   **327 Came . . . him** interposed and gave him satisfactory explanation   **333 wrought**
. . . desire worked out as he wished, fitted in with his plan

How he upbraids Iago, that he made him   335
Brave° me upon the watch, whereon it came°
That I was cast;° and even but now he spake,
After long seeming dead, Iago hurt him,
Iago set him on.
LODOVICO [*to Othello*]:   You must forsake this room and go
with us.
Your power and your command is taken off,°
And Cassio rules in Cyprus. For this slave,
If there be any cunning cruelty
That can torment him much and hold him long,°
It shall be his. You shall close prisoner rest°   345
Till that the nature of your fault be known
To the Venetian state.—Come, bring away.
OTHELLO: Soft you;° a word or two before you go.
I have done the state some service, and they know 't.
No more of that. I pray you, in your letters,   350
When you shall these unlucky° deeds relate,
Speak of me as I am; nothing extenuate,
Nor set down aught in malice. Then must you speak
Of one that loved not wisely but too well;
Of one not easily jealous but, being wrought,°   355
Perplexed° in the extreme; of one whose hand,
Like the base Indian,° threw a pearl away
Richer than all his tribe; of one whose subdued° eyes,
Albeit unusèd to the melting mood,
Drops tears as fast as the Arabian trees   360
Their medicinable gum.° Set you down this;
And say besides that in Aleppo once,
Where a malignant and a turbaned Turk
Beat a Venetian and traduced the state,
I took by th' throat the circumcisèd dog   365

---

336 Brave defy.   **whereon it came** whereof it came about   **337 cast** dismissed   **341 taken off**
taken away   **344 hold him long** keep him alive a long time (during his torture)   **345 rest** remain
348 Soft you one moment   **351 unlucky** unfortunate   **355 wrought** worked upon, worked into a
frenzy   **356 Perplexed** distraught   **357 Indian** (This reading from the Quarto pictures an ignorant savage who cannot recognize the value of a precious jewel. The Folio reading, *Iudean* or *Judean*,
i.e., infidel or disbeliever, may refer to Herod, who slew Miriamne in a fit of jealousy, or to Judas
Iscariot, the betrayer of Christ.)   **358 subdued** i.e., overcome by grief   **361 gum** i.e., myrrh

And smote him, thus.   [*He stabs himself.*°]
LODOVICO: O bloody period!°
GRATIANO: All that is spoke is marred.
OTHELLO: I kissed thee ere I killed thee. No way but this,
Killing myself, to die upon a kiss.   370

[*He kisses Desdemona and dies.*]

CASSIO: This did I fear, but thought he had no weapon;
For he was great of heart.
LODOVICO [*to Iago*]:   O Spartan dog,°
More fell° than anguish, hunger, or the sea!
Look on the tragic loading of this bed.
This is thy work. The object poisons sight;   375
Let it be hid.° Gratiano, keep° the house,

[*The bed curtains are drawn*]

And seize upon° the fortunes of the Moor,
For they succeed on° you. [*To Cassio.*] To you, Lord
Governor,
Remains the censure° of this hellish villain,
The time, the place, the torture. O, enforce it!   380
Myself will straight aboard, and to the state
This heavy act with heavy heart relate.   *Exeunt.*

                                                        —1604?

---

366 [s.d.] **He stabs himself** (This direction is in the Quarto text.)   **367 period** termination, conclusion   **372 Spartan dog** (Spartan dogs were noted for their savagery and silence.)   **373 fell** cruel   **376 Let it be hid** i.e., draw the bed curtains. (No stage direction specifies that the dead are to be carried offstage at the end of the play.)   **keep** remain in   **377 seize upon** take legal possession of   **378 succeed on** pass as though by inheritance to   **379 censure** sentencing

Henrik Ibsen (1828–1906), universally acknowledged as the first of the great modern playwrights, was born in Skien, a small town in Norway, the son of a merchant who went bankrupt during Ibsen's childhood. Ibsen first trained for a medical career, but drifted into the theatre, gaining, like Shakespeare and Molière, important dramatic training through a decade's service as a stage manager and director. Ibsen was unsuccessful in establishing a theatre in Oslo, and he spent almost thirty years living and writing in Germany and Italy. The fame he won through early poetic dramas like Peer Gynt *(1867), which is considered the supreme exploration of the Norwegian national character, was overshadowed by the realistic prose plays he began writing with* Pillars of Society *(1877).* A Doll's House *(1879), and* Ghosts *(1881), which deal, respectively, with a woman's struggle for independence and self-respect and with the taboo subject of venereal disease, made Ibsen an internationally famous, if controversial, figure. Although Ibsen's type of realism, displayed in "problem plays" such as these and later psychological dramas like* The Wild Duck *(1885) and* Hedda Gabler *(1890), has become so fully assimilated into our literary heritage that now it is difficult to think of him as an innovator, his marriage of the tightly constructed plots of the conventional "well-made play" to serious discussion of social issues was one of the most significant developments in the history of drama. Interestingly, the conclusion of* A Doll's House *proved so unsettling that Ibsen was forced to write an alternative ending, in which Nora states her case but does not slam the door on her marriage. His most influential advocate in English-speaking countries was George Bernard Shaw, whose* The Quintessence of Ibsenism *(1891) is one of the earliest and most influential studies of Ibsen's dramatic methods and ideas.*

Henrik Ibsen
A Doll's House

[Et dukkehjem]

PLAY IN THREE ACTS

CHARACTERS

Torvald Helmer, a lawyer
Nora, his wife
Dr. Rank

Translated by James McFarlane

Mrs. Kristine Linde
Nils Krogstad
Anne Marie, *the nursemaid*
Helene, *the maid*
The Helmers' three children
A porter

The action takes place in the Helmers' flat.

Act I

A pleasant room, tastefully but not expensively furnished. On the back wall, one door on the right leads to the entrance hall, a second door on the left leads to Helmer's study. Between these two doors, a piano. In the middle of the left wall, a door; and downstage from it, a window. Near the window a round table with armchairs and a small sofa. In the right wall, upstage, a door; and on the same wall downstage, a porcelain stove with a couple of armchairs and a rocking-chair. Between the stove and the door a small table. Etchings on the walls. A whatnot with china and other small objets d'art; a small bookcase with books in handsome bindings. Carpet on the floor; a fire burns in the stove. A winter's day.

The front door-bell rings in the hall; a moment later, there is the sound of the front door being opened. Nora comes into the room, happily humming to herself. She is dressed in her outdoor things, and is carrying lots of parcels which she then puts down on the table, right. She leaves the door into the hall standing open; a Porter can be seen outside holding a Christmas tree and a basket; he hands them to the Maid who has opened the door for them.

NORA: Hide the Christmas tree away carefully, Helene. The children mustn't see it till this evening when it's decorated. [*To the Porter, taking out her purse.*] How much?
PORTER: Fifty öre.
NORA: There's a crown. Keep the change.

[*The Porter thanks her and goes. Nora shuts the door. She continues to laugh quietly and happily to herself as she takes off her things. She takes a bag of macaroons out of her pocket and eats one or two; then she walks stealthily across and listens at her husband's door.*]

NORA: Yes, he's in.

[*She begins humming again as she walks over to the table, right.*]

HELMER [*in his study*]: Is that my little sky-lark chirruping out there?

NORA [*busy opening some of the parcels*]: Yes, it is.

HELMER: Is that my little squirrel frisking about?

NORA: Yes!

HELMER: When did my little squirrel get home?

NORA: Just this minute. [*She stuffs the bag of macaroons in her pocket and wipes her mouth.*] Come on out, Torvald, and see what I've bought.

HELMER: I don't want to be disturbed! [*A moment later, he opens the door and looks out, his pen in his hand.*] 'Bought', did you say? All that? Has my little spendthrift been out squandering money again?

NORA: But, Torvald, surely this year we can spread ourselves just a little. This is the first Christmas we haven't had to go carefully.

HELMER: Ah, but that doesn't mean we can afford to be extravagant, you know.

NORA: Oh yes, Torvald, surely we can afford to be just a little bit extravagant now, can't we? Just a teeny-weeny bit. You are getting quite a good salary now, and you are going to earn lots and lots of money.

HELMER: Yes, after the New Year. But it's going to be three whole months before the first pay cheque comes in.

NORA: Pooh! We can always borrow in the meantime.

HELMER: Nora! [*Crosses to her and takes her playfully by the ear.*] Here we go again, you and your frivolous ideas! Suppose I went and borrowed a thousand crowns today, and you went and spent it all over Christmas, then on New Year's Eve a slate fell and hit me on the head and there I was. . . .

NORA [*putting her hand over his mouth*]: Sh! Don't say such horrid things.

HELMER: Yes, but supposing something like that did happen . . . what then?

NORA: If anything as awful as that did happen, I wouldn't care if I owed anybody anything or not.

HELMER: Yes, but what about the people I'd borrowed from?

NORA: Them? Who cares about them! They are only strangers!

HELMER: Nora, Nora! Just like a woman! Seriously though, Nora, you know what I think about these things. No debts! Never borrow! There's always something inhibited, something unpleasant, about a home built on credit and borrowed money. We two have managed to stick it out so far, and that's the way we'll go on for the little time that remains.

NORA [*walks over to the stove*]:   Very well, just as you say, Torvald.

HELMER [*following her*]:   There, there! My little singing bird mustn't go drooping her wings, eh? Has it got the sulks, that little squirrel of mine? [*Takes out his wallet.*] Nora, what do you think I've got here?

NORA [*quickly turning round*]:   Money!

HELMER: There! [*He hands her some notes.*] Good heavens, I know only too well how Christmas runs away with the housekeeping.

NORA [*counts*]:   Ten, twenty, thirty, forty. Oh, thank you, thank you, Torvald! This will see me quite a long way.

HELMER: Yes, it'll have to.

NORA: Yes, yes, I'll see that it does. But come over here, I want to show you all the things I've bought. And so cheap! Look, some new clothes for Ivar . . . and a little sword. There's a horse and a trumpet for Bob. And a doll and a doll's cot for Emmy. They are not very grand but she'll have them all broken before long anyway. And I've got some dress material and some handkerchiefs for the maids. Though, really, dear old Anne Marie should have had something better.

HELMER: And what's in this parcel here?

NORA [*shrieking*]:   No, Torvald! You mustn't see that till tonight!

HELMER: All right. But tell me now, what did my little spendthrift fancy for herself?

NORA: For me? Puh, I don't really want anything.

HELMER: Of course you do. Anything reasonable that you think you might like, just tell me.

NORA: Well, I don't really know. As a matter of fact, though, Torvald . . .

HELMER: Well?

NORA [*toying with his coat buttons, and without looking at him*]: If you did want to give me something, you could . . . you could always . . .

HELMER: Well, well, out with it!

NORA [*quickly*]: You could always give me money, Torvald. Only what you think you could spare. And then I could buy myself something with it later on.

HELMER: But Nora. . . .

NORA: Oh, please, Torvald dear! Please! I beg you. Then I'd wrap the money up in some pretty gilt paper and hang it on the Christmas tree. Wouldn't that be fun?

HELMER: What do we call my pretty little pet when it runs away with all the money?

NORA: I know, I know, we call it a spendthrift. But please let's do what I said, Torvald. Then I'll have a bit of time to think about what I need most. Isn't that awfully sensible, now, eh?

HELMER [*smiling*]: Yes, it is indeed—that is, if only you really could hold on to the money I gave you, and really did buy something for yourself with it. But it just gets mixed up with the housekeeping and frittered away on all sorts of useless things, and then I have to dig into my pocket all over again.

NORA: Oh but, Torvald. . . .

HELMER: You can't deny it, Nora dear. [*Puts his arm around her waist.*] My pretty little pet is very sweet, but it runs away with an awful lot of money. It's incredible how expensive it is for a man to keep such a pet.

NORA: For shame! How can you say such a thing? As a matter of fact I save everything I can.

HELMER [*laughs*]: Yes, you are right there. Everything you *can*. But you simply can't.

NORA [*hums and smiles quietly and happily*]: Ah, if you only knew how many expenses the likes of us sky-larks and squirrels have, Torvald!

HELMER: What a funny little one you are! Just like your father. Always on the look-out for money, wherever you can lay your hands on it; but as soon as you've got it, it just seems to slip through your fingers. You never seem to know what you've done with it. Well, one must accept you as you are. It's in the blood. Oh yes, it is, Nora. That sort of thing is hereditary.

NORA: Oh, I only wish I'd inherited a few more of Daddy's qualities.

HELMER: And I wouldn't want my pretty little song-bird to be the least bit different from what she is now. But come to think of it, you look rather . . . rather . . . how shall I put it? . . . rather guilty today. . . .

NORA: Do I?

HELMER: Yes, you do indeed. Look me straight in the eye.

NORA [*looks at him*]: Well?

HELMER [*wagging his finger at her*]: My little sweet-tooth surely didn't forget herself in town today?

NORA: No, whatever makes you think that?

HELMER: She didn't just pop into the confectioner's for a moment?

NORA: No, I assure you, Torvald. . . !

HELMER: Didn't try sampling the preserves?

NORA: No, really I didn't.

HELMER: Didn't go nibbling a macaroon or two?

NORA: No, Torvald, honestly, you must believe me. . . !

HELMER: All right then! It's really just my little joke. . . .

NORA [*crosses to the table*]: I would never dream of doing anything you didn't want me to.

HELMER: Of course not, I know that. And then you've given me your word. . . . [*Crosses to her.*] Well then, Nora dearest, you shall keep your little Christmas secrets. They'll all come out tonight, I dare say, when we light the tree.

NORA: Did you remember to invite Dr. Rank?

HELMER: No. But there's really no need. Of course he'll come and have dinner with us. Anyway, I can ask him when he looks in this morning. I've ordered some good wine. Nora, you can't imagine how I am looking forward to this evening.

NORA: So am I. And won't the children enjoy it, Torvald!

HELMER: Oh, what a glorious feeling it is, knowing you've got a nice, safe job, and a good fat income. Don't you agree? Isn't it wonderful, just thinking about it?

NORA: Oh, it's marvellous!

HELMER: Do you remember last Christmas? Three whole weeks beforehand you shut yourself up every evening till after midnight making flowers for the Christmas tree and all the other splendid things you wanted to surprise us with. Ugh, I never felt so bored in all my life.

NORA: I wasn't the least bit bored.

HELMER [*smiling*]: But it turned out a bit of an anticlimax, Nora.

NORA: Oh, you are not going to tease me about that again! How was I to know the cat would get in and pull everything to bits?

HELMER: No, of course you weren't. Poor little Nora! All you wanted was for us to have a nice time—and it's the thought behind it that counts, after all. All the same, it's a good thing we've seen the back of those lean times.

NORA: Yes, really it's marvellous.

HELMER: Now there's no need for me to sit here all on my own, bored to tears. And you don't have to strain your dear little eyes, and work those dainty little fingers to the bone. . . .

NORA [*clapping her hands*]: No, Torvald, I don't, do I? Not any more. Oh, how marvellous it is to hear that! [*Takes his arm.*] Now I want to tell you how I've been thinking we might arrange things, Torvald. As soon as Christmas is over. . . . [*The door-bell rings in the hall.*] Oh, there's the bell. [*Tidies one or two things in the room.*] It's probably a visitor. What a nuisance!

HELMER: Remember I'm not at home to callers.

MAID [*in the doorway*]: There's a lady to see you, ma'am.

NORA: Show her in, please.

MAID [*to Helmer*]: And the doctor's just arrived, too, sir.

HELMER: Did he go straight into my room?

MAID: Yes, he did, sir.

[*Helmer goes into his study. The Maid shows in Mrs. Linde, who is in travelling clothes, and closes the door after her.*]

MRS. LINDE [*subdued and rather hesitantly*]: How do you do, Nora?

NORA [*uncertainly*]: How do you do?

MRS. LINDE: I'm afraid you don't recognize me.

NORA: No, I don't think I . . . And yet I seem to. . . . [*Bursts out suddenly.*] Why! Kristine! Is it really you?

MRS. LINDE: Yes, it's me.

NORA: Kristine! Fancy not recognizing you again! But how was I to, when . . . [*Gently.*] How you've changed, Kristine!

MRS. LINDE: I dare say I have. In nine . . . ten years. . . .

NORA: Is it so long since we last saw each other? Yes, it must be. Oh, believe me these last eight years have been such a happy time. And now you've come up to town, too? All that long journey in wintertime. That took courage.

MRS. LINDE: I just arrived this morning on the steamer.

NORA: To enjoy yourself over Christmas, of course. How lovely! Oh, we'll have such fun, you'll see. Do take off your things. You are not cold, are you? [*Helps her.*] There now! Now let's sit down here in comfort beside the stove. No, here, you take the armchair, I'll sit here on the rocking-chair. [*Takes her hands.*] Ah, now you look a bit more like your old self again. It was just that when I first saw you. . . . But you are a little paler, Kristine . . . and perhaps even a bit thinner!

MRS. LINDE: And much, much older, Nora.

NORA: Yes, perhaps a little older . . . very, very little, not really very much. [*Stops suddenly and looks serious.*] Oh, what a thoughtless creature I am, sitting here chattering on like this! Dear, sweet Kristine, can you forgive me?

MRS. LINDE: What do you mean, Nora?

NORA [*gently*]: Poor Kristine, of course you're a widow now.

MRS. LINDE: Yes, my husband died three years ago.

NORA: Oh, I remember now. I read about it in the papers. Oh, Kristine, believe me I often thought at the time of writing to you. But I kept putting it off, something always seemed to crop up.

MRS. LINDE: My dear Nora, I understand so well.

NORA: No, it wasn't very nice of me, Kristine. Oh, you poor thing, what you must have gone through. And didn't he leave you anything?

MRS. LINDE: No.

NORA: And no children?

MRS. LINDE: No.

NORA: Absolutely nothing?

MRS. LINDE: Nothing at all . . . not even a broken heart to grieve over.

NORA [*looks at her incredulously*]: But, Kristine, is that possible?

MRS. LINDE [*smiles sadly and strokes Nora's hair*]: Oh, it sometimes happens, Nora.

NORA: So utterly alone. How terribly sad that must be for you. I have three lovely children. You can't see them for the moment, because they're out with their nanny. But now you must tell me all about yourself. . . .

MRS. LINDE: No, no, I want to hear about you.

NORA: No, you start. I won't be selfish today. I must think only about your affairs today. But there's just one thing I really must tell you. Have you heard about the great stroke of luck we've had in the last few days?

MRS. LINDE: No. What is it?

NORA: What do you think? My husband has just been made Bank Manager!

MRS. LINDE: Your husband? How splendid!

NORA: Isn't it tremendous! It's not a very steady way of making a living, you know, being a lawyer, especially if he refuses to take on anything that's the least bit shady—which of course is what Torvald does, and I think he's quite right. You can imagine how pleased we are! He starts at the Bank straight after New Year, and he's getting a big salary and lots of commission. From now on we'll be able to live quite differently . . . we'll do just what we want. Oh, Kristine, I'm so happy and relieved. I must say it's lovely to have plenty of money and not have to worry. Isn't it?

MRS. LINDE: Yes. It must be nice to have enough, at any rate.

NORA: No, not just enough, but pots and pots of money.

MRS. LINDE [*smiles*]: Nora, Nora, haven't you learned any sense yet? At school you used to be an awful spendthrift.

NORA: Yes, Torvald still says I am. [*Wags her finger.*] But little Nora isn't as stupid as everybody thinks. Oh, we haven't really been in a position where I could afford to spend a lot of money. We've both had to work.

MRS. LINDE: You too?

NORA: Yes, odd jobs—sewing, crochet-work, embroidery and things like that. [*Casually.*] And one or two other things, besides. I suppose you know that Torvald left the Ministry when we got married. There weren't any prospects of promotion in his department, and of course he needed to earn more money than he had before. But the first year he wore himself out completely. He had to take on all kinds of extra jobs, you know, and he found himself working all hours of the day and night. But he couldn't go on like that; and he became seriously ill. The doctors said it was essential for him to go South.

MRS. LINDE: Yes, I believe you spent a whole year in Italy, didn't you?

NORA: That's right. It wasn't easy to get away, I can tell you. It was just after I'd had Ivar. But of course we had to go. Oh, it was an absolutely marvellous trip. And it saved Torvald's life. But it cost an awful lot of money, Kristine.

MRS. LINDE: That I can well imagine.

NORA: Twelve hundred dollars. Four thousand eight hundred crowns. That's a lot of money, Kristine.

MRS. LINDE: Yes, but in such circumstances, one is very lucky if one has it.

NORA: Well, we got it from Daddy, you see.

MRS. LINDE: Ah, that was it. It was just about then your father died, I believe, wasn't it?

NORA: Yes, Kristine, just about then. And do you know, I couldn't even go and look after him. Here was I expecting Ivar any day. And I also had poor Torvald, gravely ill, on my hands. Dear, kind Daddy! I never saw him again, Kristine. Oh, that's the saddest thing that has happened to me in all my married life.

MRS. LINDE: I know you were very fond of him. But after that you left for Italy?

NORA: Yes, we had the money then, and the doctors said it was urgent. We left a month later.

MRS. LINDE: And your husband came back completely cured?

NORA: Fit as a fiddle!

MRS. LINDE: But . . . what about the doctor?

NORA: How do you mean?

MRS. LINDE: I thought the maid said something about the gentleman who came at the same time as me being a doctor.

NORA: Yes, that was Dr. Rank. But this isn't a professional visit. He's our best friend and he always looks in at least once a day. No, Torvald has never had a day's illness since. And the children are fit and healthy, and so am I. [*Jumps up and claps her hands.*] Oh God, oh God, isn't it marvellous to be alive, and to be happy, Kristine! . . . Oh, but I ought to be ashamed of myself. . . Here I go on talking about nothing but myself. [*She sits on a low stool near Mrs. Linde and lays her arms on her lap.*] Oh, please, you mustn't be angry with me! Tell me, is it really true that you didn't love your husband? What made you marry him, then?

MRS. LINDE: My mother was still alive; she was bedridden and helpless. And then I had my two young brothers to look after as well. I didn't think I would be justified in refusing him.

NORA: No, I dare say you are right. I suppose he was fairly wealthy then?

MRS. LINDE: He was quite well off, I believe. But the business was shaky. When he died, it went all to pieces, and there just wasn't anything left.

NORA: What then?

MRS. LINDE: Well, I had to fend for myself, opening a little shop, running a little school, anything I could turn my hand to. These last three years have been one long relentless drudge. But now it's finished, Nora. My poor dear mother doesn't need me any more, she's passed away. Nor the boys either; they're at work now, they can look after themselves.

NORA: What a relief you must find it. . . .

MRS. LINDE: No, Nora! Just unutterably empty. Nobody to live for any more. [*Stands up restlessly.*] That's why I couldn't stand it any longer being cut off up there. Surely it must be a bit easier here to find something to occupy your mind. If only I could manage to find a steady job of some kind, in an office perhaps. . . .

NORA: But, Kristine, that's terribly exhausting; and you look so worn out even before you start. The best thing for you would be a little holiday at some quiet little resort.

MRS. LINDE [*crosses to the window*]: I haven't any father I can fall back on for the money, Nora.

NORA [*rises*]: Oh, please, you mustn't be angry with me!

MRS. LINDE [*goes to her*]: My dear Nora, you mustn't be angry with me either. That's the worst thing about people in my position, they become so bitter. One has nobody to work for, yet one has to be on the look-out all the time. Life has to go on, and one starts thinking only of oneself. Believe it or not, when you told me the good news

about your step up, I was pleased not so much for your sake as for
mine.

NORA: How do you mean? Ah, I see. You think Torvald might be able
to do something for you.

MRS. LINDE: Yes, that's exactly what I thought.

NORA: And so he shall, Kristine. Just leave things to me. I'll bring it
up so cleverly . . . I'll think up something to put him in a good
mood. Oh, I do so much want to help you.

MRS. LINDE: It is awfully kind of you, Nora, offering to do all this for
me, particularly in your case, where you haven't known much trouble or hardship in your own life.

NORA: When I . . .? I haven't known much . . .?

MRS. LINDE [*smiling*]: Well, good heavens, a little bit of sewing to do
and a few things like that. What a child you are, Nora!

NORA [*tosses her head and walks across the room*]: I wouldn't be too
sure of that, if I were you.

MRS. LINDE: Oh?

NORA: You're just like the rest of them. You all think I'm useless when
it comes to anything really serious. . . .

MRS. LINDE: Come, come. . . .

NORA: You think I've never had anything much to contend with in
this hard world.

MRS. LINDE: Nora dear, you've only just been telling me all the things
you've had to put up with.

NORA: Pooh! They were just trivialities! [*Softly.*] I haven't told you
about the really big thing.

MRS. LINDE: What big thing? What do you mean?

NORA: I know you rather tend to look down on me, Kristine. But you
shouldn't, you know. You are proud of having worked so hard and
so long for your mother.

MRS. LINDE: I'm sure I don't look down on anybody. But it's true
what you say: I am both proud and happy when I think of how I
was able to make Mother's life a little easier towards the end.

NORA: And you are proud when you think of what you have done for
your brothers, too.

MRS. LINDE: I think I have every right to be.

NORA: I think so too. But now I'm going to tell you something,
Kristine. I too have something to be proud and happy about.

MRS. LINDE: I don't doubt that. But what is it you mean?

NORA: Not so loud. Imagine if Torvald were to hear! He must never on any account . . . nobody must know about it, Kristine, nobody but you.

MRS. LINDE: But what is it?

NORA: Come over here. [*She pulls her down on the sofa beside her.*] Yes, Kristine, I too have something to be proud and happy about. I was the one who saved Torvald's life.

MRS. LINDE: Saved . . . ? How . . . ?

NORA: I told you about our trip to Italy. Torvald would never have recovered but for that. . . .

MRS. LINDE: Well? Your father gave you what money was necessary. . . .

NORA [*smiles*]: That's what Torvald thinks, and everybody else. But . . .

MRS. LINDE: But . . . ?

NORA: Daddy never gave us a penny. I was the one who raised the money.

MRS. LINDE: You? All that money?

NORA: Twelve hundred dollars. Four thousand eight hundred crowns. What do you say to that!

MRS. LINDE: But, Nora, how was it possible? Had you won a sweepstake or something?

NORA [*contemptuously*]: A sweepstake? Pooh! There would have been nothing to it then.

MRS. LINDE: Where did you get it from, then?

NORA [*hums and smiles secretively*]: H'm, tra-la-la!

MRS. LINDE: Because what you couldn't do was borrow it.

NORA: Oh? Why not?

MRS. LINDE: Well, a wife can't borrow without her husband's consent.

NORA [*tossing her head*]: Ah, but when it happens to be a wife with a bit of a sense for business . . . a wife who knows her way about things, then. . . .

MRS. LINDE: But, Nora, I just don't understand. . . .

NORA: You don't have to. I haven't said I did borrow the money. I might have got it some other way. [*Throws herself back on the sofa.*] I might even have got it from some admirer. Anyone as reasonably attractive as I am. . . .

MRS. LINDE: Don't be so silly!

NORA: Now you must be dying of curiosity, Kristine.

MRS. LINDE: Listen to me now, Nora dear—you haven't done anything rash, have you?

NORA [*sitting up again*]: Is it rash to save your husband's life?

MRS. LINDE: I think it was rash to do anything without telling him. . . .

NORA: But the whole point was that he mustn't know anything. Good heavens, can't you see! He wasn't even supposed to know how desperately ill he was. It was me the doctors came and told his life was in danger, that the only way to save him was to go South for a while. Do you think I didn't try talking him into it first? I began dropping hints about how nice it would be if I could be taken on a little trip abroad, like other young wives. I wept, I pleaded. I told him he ought to show some consideration for my condition, and let me have a bit of my own way. And then I suggested he might take out a loan. But at that he nearly lost his temper, Kristine. He said I was being frivolous, that it was his duty as a husband not to give in to all these whims and fancies of mine—as I do believe he called them. All right, I thought, somehow you've got to be saved. And it was then I found a way. . . .

MRS. LINDE: Did your husband never find out from your father that the money hadn't come from him?

NORA: No, never. It was just about the time Daddy died. I'd intended letting him into the secret and asking him not to give me away. But when he was so ill . . . I'm sorry to say it never became necessary.

MRS. LINDE: And you never confided in your husband?

NORA: Good heavens, how could you ever imagine such a thing! When he's so strict about such matters! Besides, Torvald is a man with a good deal of pride—it would be terribly embarrassing and humiliating for him if he thought he owed anything to me. It would spoil everything between us; this happy home of ours would never be the same again.

MRS. LINDE: Are you never going to tell him?

NORA [*reflectively, half-smiling*]: Oh yes, some day perhaps . . . in many years time, when I'm no longer as pretty as I am now. You mustn't laugh! What I mean of course is when Torvald isn't quite so much in love with me as he is now, when he's lost interest in watching me dance, or get dressed up, or recite. Then it might be a good thing to have something in reserve. . . . [*Breaks off.*] What nonsense! That day will never come. Well, what have you got to say to my big secret, Kristine? Still think I'm not much good for anything? One thing, though, it's meant a lot of worry for me, I can tell you. It hasn't always been easy to meet my obligations when the time came. You know in business there is something called quarterly interest, and other things called instalments, and these are always terribly difficult things to cope with. So what I've had to do is save a little here and there, you see, wherever I could. I couldn't really save anything out of the housekeeping, because Torvald has to live in decent style. I couldn't let the children go about badly dressed either—I felt any money I got for them had to go on them alone. Such sweet little things!

MRS. LINDE: Poor Nora! So it had to come out of your own allowance?

NORA: Of course. After all, I was the one it concerned most. Whenever Torvald gave me money for new clothes and such-like, I never spent more than half. And always I bought the simplest and cheapest things. It's a blessing most things look well on me, so Torvald never noticed anything. But sometimes I did feel it was a bit hard, Kristine, because it is nice to be well dressed, isn't it?

MRS. LINDE: Yes, I suppose it is.

NORA: I have had some other sources of income, of course. Last winter I was lucky enough to get quite a bit of copying to do. So I shut myself up every night and sat and wrote through to the small hours of the morning. Oh, sometimes I was so tired, so tired. But it was tremendous fun all the same, sitting there working and earning money like that. It was almost like being a man.

MRS. LINDE: And how much have you been able to pay off like this?

NORA: Well, I can't tell exactly. It's not easy to know where you are with transactions of this kind, you understand. All I know is I've paid off just as much as I could scrape together. Many's the time I was at my wit's end. [*Smiles.*] Then I used to sit here and pretend that some rich old gentleman had fallen in love with me. . . .

MRS. LINDE: What! What gentleman?

NORA: Oh, rubbish! . . . and that now he had died, and when they opened his will, there in big letters were the words: "My entire fortune is to be paid over, immediately and in cash, to charming Mrs. Nora Helmer."

MRS. LINDE: But my dear Nora—who is this man?

NORA: Good heavens, don't you understand? There never was any old gentleman; it was just something I used to sit here pretending, time and time again, when I didn't know where to turn next for money. But it doesn't make very much difference; as far as I'm concerned, the old boy can do what he likes, I'm tired of him; I can't be bothered any more with him or his will. Because now all my worries are over. [*Jumping up.*] Oh God, what a glorious thought, Kristine! No more worries! Just think of being without a care in the world . . . being able to romp with the children, and making the house nice and attractive, and having things just as Torvald likes to have them! And then spring will soon be here, and blue skies. And maybe we can go away somewhere. I might even see something of the sea again. Oh yes! When you're happy, life is a wonderful thing!

[*The door-bell is heard in the hall.*]

MRS. LINDE [*gets up*]: There's the bell. Perhaps I'd better go.

NORA: No, do stay, please. I don't suppose it's for me; it's probably somebody for Torvald. . . .

MAID [*in the doorway*]: Excuse me, ma'am, but there's a gentleman here wants to see Mr. Helmer, and I didn't quite know . . . because the Doctor is in there. . . .

NORA: Who is the gentleman?

KROGSTAD [*in the doorway*]: It's me, Mrs. Helmer.

[*Mrs. Linde starts, then turns away to the window.*]

NORA [*tense, takes a step towards him and speaks in a low voice*]: You? What is it? What do you want to talk to my husband about?

KROGSTAD: Bank matters . . . in a manner of speaking. I work at the bank, and I hear your husband is to be the new manager. . . .

NORA: So it's . . .

KROGSTAD: Just routine business matters, Mrs. Helmer. Absolutely nothing else.

NORA: Well then, please go into his study.

[*She nods impassively and shuts the hall door behind him; then she walks across and sees to the stove.*]

MRS. LINDE: Nora . . . who was that man?

NORA: His name is Krogstad.

MRS. LINDE: So it really was him.

NORA: Do you know the man?

MRS. LINDE: I used to know him . . . a good many years ago. He was a solicitor's clerk in our district for a while.

NORA: Yes, so he was.

MRS. LINDE: How he's changed!

NORA: His marriage wasn't a very happy one, I believe.

MRS. LINDE: He's a widower now, isn't he?

NORA: With a lot of children. There, it'll burn better now.

[*She closes the stove door and moves the rocking-chair a little to one side.*]

MRS. LINDE: He does a certain amount of business on the side, they say?

NORA: Oh? Yes, it's always possible. I just don't know. . . . But let's not think about business . . . it's all so dull.

[*Dr. Rank comes in from Helmer's study.*]

RANK [*still in the doorway*]: No, no, Torvald, I won't intrude. I'll just look in on your wife for a moment. [*Shuts the door and notices Mrs. Linde.*] Oh, I beg your pardon. I'm afraid I'm intruding here as well.

NORA: No, not at all! [*Introduces them.*] Dr. Rank . . . Mrs. Linde.

RANK: Ah! A name I've often heard mentioned in this house. I believe I came past you on the stairs as I came in.

MRS. LINDE: I have to take things slowly going upstairs. I find it rather a trial.

RANK: Ah, some little disability somewhere, eh?

MRS. LINDE: Just a bit run down, I think, actually.

RANK: Is that all? Then I suppose you've come to town for a good rest—doing the rounds of the parties?

MRS. LINDE: I have come to look for work.

RANK: Is that supposed to be some kind of sovereign remedy for being run down?

MRS. LINDE: One must live, Doctor.

RANK: Yes, it's generally thought to be necessary.

NORA: Come, come, Dr. Rank. You are quite as keen to live as anybody.

RANK: Quite keen, yes. Miserable as I am, I'm quite ready to let things drag on as long as possible. All my patients are the same. Even those with a moral affliction are no different. As a matter of fact, there's a bad case of that kind in talking with Helmer at this very moment. . . .

MRS. LINDE [*softly*]: Ah!

NORA: Whom do you mean?

RANK: A person called Krogstad—nobody you would know. He's rotten to the core. But even he began talking about having to *live*, as though it were something terribly important.

NORA: Oh? And what did he want to talk to Torvald about?

RANK: I honestly don't know. All I heard was something about the Bank.

NORA: I didn't know that Krog . . . that this Mr. Krogstad had anything to do with the Bank.

RANK: Oh yes, he's got some kind of job down there. [*To Mrs. Linde.*] I wonder if you've got people in your part of the country too who go rushing round sniffing out cases of moral corruption, and then installing the individuals concerned in nice, well-paid jobs where they can keep them under observation. Sound, decent people have to be content to stay out in the cold.

MRS. LINDE: Yet surely it's the sick who most need to be brought in.

RANK [*shrugs his shoulders*]: Well, there we have it. It's that attitude that's turning society into a clinic.

[*Nora, lost in her own thoughts, breaks into smothered laughter and claps her hands.*]

RANK: Why are you laughing at that? Do you know in fact what society is?

NORA: What do I care about your silly old society? I was laughing about something quite different . . . something frightfully funny. Tell me, Dr. Rank, are all the people who work at the Bank dependent on Torvald now?

RANK: Is *that* what you find so frightfully funny?

NORA [*smiles and hums*]: Never you mind! Never you mind! [*Walks about the room.*] Yes, it really is terribly amusing to think that we . . . that Torvald now has power over so many people. [*She takes the bag out of her pocket.*] Dr. Rank, what about a little macaroon?

RANK: Look at this, eh? Macaroons. I thought they were forbidden here.

NORA: Yes, but these are some Kristine gave me.

MRS. LINDE: What? I . . . ?

NORA: Now, now, you needn't be alarmed. You weren't to know that Torvald had forbidden them. He's worried in case they ruin my teeth, you know. Still . . . what's it matter once in a while! Don't you think so, Dr. Rank? Here! [*She pops a macaroon into his mouth.*] And you too, Kristine. And I shall have one as well; just a little one . . . or two at the most. [*She walks about the room again.*] Really I am so happy. There's just one little thing I'd love to do now.

RANK: What's that?

NORA: Something I'd love to say in front of Torvald.

RANK: Then why can't you?

NORA: No, I daren't. It's not very nice.

MRS. LINDE: Not very nice?

RANK: Well, in that case it might not be wise. But to us, I don't see why. . . . What is this you would love to say in front of Helmer?

NORA: I would simply love to say: 'Damn'.

RANK: Are you mad!

MRS. LINDE: Good gracious, Nora. . . !

RANK: Say it! Here he is!

NORA [*hiding the bag of macaroons*]: Sh! Sh!

[*Helmer comes out of his room, his overcoat over his arm and his hat in his hand.*]

NORA [*going over to him*]: Well, Torvald dear, did you get rid of him?

HELMER: Yes, he's just gone.

NORA: Let me introduce you. This is Kristine, who has just arrived in town. . . .

HELMER: Kristine. . . ? You must forgive me, but I don't think I know . . .

NORA: Mrs. Linde, Torvald dear. Kristine Linde.

HELMER: Ah, indeed. A school-friend of my wife's, presumably.

MRS. LINDE: Yes, we were girls together.

NORA: Fancy, Torvald, she's come all this long way just to have a word with you.

HELMER: How is that?

MRS. LINDE: Well, it wasn't really. . . .

NORA: The thing is, Kristine is terribly clever at office work, and she's frightfully keen on finding a job with some efficient man, so that she can learn even more. . . .

HELMER: Very sensible, Mrs. Linde.

NORA: And then when she heard you'd been made Bank Manager— there was a bit in the paper about it—she set off at once. Torvald please! You *will* try and do something for Kristine, won't you? For my sake?

HELMER: Well, that's not altogether impossible. You are a widow, I presume?

MRS. LINDE: Yes.

HELMER: And you've had some experience in business?

MRS. LINDE: A fair amount.

HELMER: Well, it's quite probable I can find you a job, I think. . . .

NORA [*clapping her hands*]: There, you see!

HELMER: You have come at a fortunate moment, Mrs. Linde. . . .

MRS. LINDE: Oh, how can I ever thank you. . . ?

HELMER: Not a bit. [*He puts on his overcoat.*] But for the present I must ask you to excuse me. . . .

RANK: Wait. I'm coming with you.

[*He fetches his fur coat from the hall and warms it at the stove.*]

NORA: Don't be long, Torvald dear.

HELMER: Not more than an hour, that's all.

NORA: Are you leaving too, Kristine?

MRS. LINDE [*putting on her things*]: Yes, I must go and see if I can't find myself a room.

HELMER: Perhaps we can all walk down the road together.

NORA [*helping her*]: What a nuisance we are so limited for space here. I'm afraid it just isn't possible. . . .

MRS. LINDE: Oh, you mustn't dream of it! Goodbye, Nora dear, and thanks for everything.

NORA: Goodbye for the present. But . . . you'll be coming back this evening, of course. And you too, Dr. Rank? What's that? If you are up to it? Of course you'll be up to it. Just wrap yourself up well.

[*They go out, talking, into the hall; children's voices can be heard on the stairs.*]

NORA: Here they are! Here they are! [*She runs to the front door and opens it. Anne Marie, the nursemaid, enters with the children.*] Come in! Come in! [*She bends down and kisses them.*] Ah! my sweet little darlings. . . . You see them, Kristine? Aren't they lovely!

RANK: Don't stand here chattering in this draught!

HELMER: Come along, Mrs. Linde. The place now becomes unbearable for anybody except mothers.

[*Dr. Rank, Helmer and Mrs. Linde go down the stairs: the Nursemaid comes into the room with the children, then Nora, shutting the door behind her.*]

NORA: How fresh and bright you look! My, what red cheeks you've got! Like apples and roses. [*During the following, the children keep chattering away to her.*] Have you had a nice time? That's splendid. And you gave Emmy and Bob a ride on your sledge? Did you now! Both together! Fancy that! There's a clever boy, Ivar. Oh, let me take her a little while, Anne Marie. There's my sweet little baby-doll! [*She takes the youngest of the children from the Nursemaid and dances with her.*] All right, Mummy will dance with Bobby too. What? You've been throwing snowballs? Oh, I wish I'd been there. No, don't bother, Anne Marie, I'll help them off with their things. No, please, let me—I like doing it. You go on in, you look frozen. You'll find some hot coffee on the stove. [*The Nursemaid goes into the room, left. Nora takes off the children's coats and hats and throws them down anywhere, while the children all talk at once.*] Really! A great big dog came running after you? But he didn't bite. No, the doggies wouldn't bite my pretty little dollies. You mustn't touch the parcels, Ivar! What are they? Wouldn't you like to know! No, no, that's nasty. Now? Shall we play something? What shall we play? Hide and seek? Yes, let's play hide and seek. Bob can hide first. Me first? All right, let me hide first.

[*She and the children play, laughing and shrieking, in this room and in the adjacent room on the right. Finally Nora hides under the table; the children come rushing in to look for her but cannot find her; they hear her stifled laughter, rush to the table, lift up the tablecloth and find her. Tremendous shouts of delight. She creeps out and pretends to frighten them. More shouts. Meanwhile there has been a knock at the front door, which nobody has heard. The door half opens, and Krogstad can be seen. He waits a little; the game continues.*]

KROGSTAD: I beg your pardon, Mrs. Helmer. . . .

NORA [*turns with a stifled cry and half jumps up*]: Ah! What do you want?

KROGSTAD: Excuse me. The front door was standing open. Somebody must have forgotten to shut it. . . .

NORA [*standing up*]: My husband isn't at home, Mr. Krogstad.

KROGSTAD: I know.

NORA: Well . . . what are you doing here?

KROGSTAD: I want a word with you.

NORA: With. . . ? [*Quietly, to the children.*] Go to Anne Marie. What? No, the strange man won't do anything to Mummy. When he's gone we'll have another game. [*She leads the children into the room, left, and shuts the door after them; tense and uneasy.*] You want to speak to me?

KROGSTAD: Yes, I do.

NORA: Today? But it isn't the first of the month yet. . . .

KROGSTAD: No, it's Christmas Eve. It depends entirely on you what sort of Christmas you have.

NORA: What do you want? Today I can't possibly . . .

KROGSTAD: Let's not talk about that for the moment. It's something else. You've got a moment to spare?

NORA: Yes, I suppose so, though . . .

KROGSTAD: Good. I was sitting in Olsen's café, and I saw your husband go down the road . . .

NORA: Did you?

KROGSTAD: . . . with a lady.

NORA: Well?

KROGSTAD: May I be so bold as to ask whether that lady was a Mrs. Linde?

NORA: Yes.

KROGSTAD: Just arrived in town?

NORA: Yes, today.

KROGSTAD: And she's a good friend of yours?

NORA: Yes, she is. But I can't see. . .

KROGSTAD: I also knew her once.

NORA: I know.

KROGSTAD: Oh? So you know all about it. I thought as much. Well, I want to ask you straight: is Mrs. Linde getting a job in the Bank?

NORA: How dare you cross-examine me like this, Mr. Krogstad? You, one of my husband's subordinates? But since you've asked me, I'll tell you. Yes, Mrs. Linde *has* got a job. And I'm the one who got it for her, Mr. Krogstad. Now you know.

KROGSTAD: So my guess was right.

NORA [*walking up and down*]: Oh, I think I can say that some of us have a little influence now and again. Just because one happens to be a woman, that doesn't mean. . . . People in subordinate positions, ought to take care they don't offend anybody . . . who . . hm . . .

KROGSTAD: . . . has influence?

NORA: Exactly.

KROGSTAD [*changing his tone*]: Mrs. Helmer, will you have the goodness to use your influence on my behalf?

NORA: What? What do you mean?

KROGSTAD: Will you be so good as to see that I keep my modest little job at the Bank?

NORA: What do you mean? Who wants to take it away from you?

KROGSTAD: Oh, you needn't try and pretend to me you don't know. I can quite see that this friend of yours isn't particularly anxious to bump up against me. And I can also see now whom I can thank for being given the sack.

NORA: But I assure you. . . .

KROGSTAD: All right, all right. But to come to the point: there's still time. And I advise you to use your influence to stop it.

NORA: But, Mr. Krogstad, I *have* no influence.

KROGSTAD: Haven't you? I thought just now you said yourself . . .

NORA: I didn't mean it that way, of course. Me? What makes you think I've got any influence of that kind over my husband?

KROGSTAD: I know your husband from our student days. I don't suppose he is any more steadfast than other married men.

NORA: You speak disrespectfully of my husband like that and I'll show you the door.

KROGSTAD: So the lady's got courage.

NORA: I'm not frightened of you any more. After New Year I'll soon be finished with the whole business.

KROGSTAD [*controlling himself*]: Listen to me, Mrs. Helmer. If necessary I shall fight for my little job in the Bank as if I were fighting for my life.

NORA: So it seems.

KROGSTAD: It's not just for the money, that's the last thing I care about. There's something else . . . well, I might as well out with it. You see it's like this. You know as well as anybody that some years ago I got myself mixed up in a bit of trouble.

NORA: I believe I've heard something of the sort.

KROGSTAD: It never got as far as the courts; but immediately it was as if all paths were barred to me. So I started going in for the sort of business you know about. I had to do something, and I think I can say I haven't been one of the worst. But now I have to get out of it. My sons are growing up; for their sake I must try and win back what respectability I can. That job in the Bank was like the first step on the ladder for me. And now your husband wants to kick me off the ladder again, back into the mud.

NORA: But in God's name, Mr. Krogstad, it's quite beyond my power to help you.

KROGSTAD: That's because you haven't the will to help me. But I have ways of making you.

NORA: You wouldn't go and tell my husband I owe you money?

KROGSTAD: Suppose I did tell him?

NORA: It would be a rotten shame. [*Half choking with tears.*] That secret is all my pride and joy—why should he have to hear about it in this nasty, horrid way . . . hear about it from *you.* You would make things horribly unpleasant for me. . . .

KROGSTAD: Merely unpleasant?

NORA [*vehemently*]: Go on, do it then! It'll be all the worse for you. Because then my husband will see for himself what a bad man you are, and then you certainly won't be able to keep your job.

KROGSTAD: I asked whether it was only a bit of domestic unpleasantness you were afraid of?

NORA: If my husband gets to know about it, he'll pay off what's owing at once. And then we'd have nothing more to do with you.

KROGSTAD [*taking a pace towards her*]: Listen, Mrs. Helmer, either you haven't a very good memory, or else you don't understand much about business. I'd better make the position a little bit clearer for you.

NORA: How do you mean?

KROGSTAD: When your husband was ill, you came to me for the loan of twelve hundred dollars.

NORA: I didn't know of anybody else.

KROGSTAD: I promised to find you the money. . . .

NORA: And you did find it.

KROGSTAD: I promised to find you the money on certain conditions. At the time you were so concerned about your husband's illness, and so anxious to get the money for going away with, that I don't think you paid very much attention to all the incidentals. So there is perhaps some point in reminding you of them. Well, I promised to find you the money against an IOU which I drew up for you.

NORA: Yes, and which I signed.

KROGSTAD: Very good. But below that I added a few lines, by which your father was to stand security. This your father was to sign.

NORA: Was to . . . ? He did sign it.

KROGSTAD: I had left the date blank. The idea was that your father was to add the date himself when he signed it. Remember?

NORA: Yes, I think. . . .

KROGSTAD: I then gave you the IOU to post to your father. Wasn't that so?

NORA: Yes.

KROGSTAD: Which of course you did at once. Because only about five or six days later you brought it back to me with your father's signature. I then paid out the money.

NORA: Well? Haven't I paid the instalments regularly?

KROGSTAD: Yes, fairly. But . . . coming back to what we were talking about . . . that was a pretty bad period you were going through then, Mrs. Helmer.

NORA: Yes, it was.

KROGSTAD: Your father was seriously ill, I believe.

NORA: He was very near the end.

KROGSTAD: And died shortly afterwards?

NORA: Yes.

KROGSTAD: Tell me, Mrs. Helmer, do you happen to remember which day your father died? The exact date, I mean.

NORA: Daddy died on 29 September.

KROGSTAD: Quite correct. I made some inquiries. Which brings up a rather curious point [*takes out a paper*] which I simply cannot explain.

NORA: Curious . . .? I don't know . . .

KROGSTAD: The curious thing is, Mrs. Helmer, that your father signed this document three days after his death.

NORA: What? I don't understand. . . .

KROGSTAD: Your father died on 29 September. But look here. Your father has dated his signature 2 October. Isn't that rather curious, Mrs. Helmer? [*Nora remains silent.*] It's also remarkable that the words "2 October" and the year are not in your father's handwriting, but in a handwriting I rather think I recognize. Well, perhaps that could be explained. Your father might have forgotten to date his signature, and then somebody else might have made a guess at the date later, before the fact of your father's death was known. There is nothing wrong in that. What really matters is the signature. And *that* is of course genuine, Mrs. Helmer? It really was your father who wrote his name here?

NORA [*after a moment's silence, throws her head back and looks at him defiantly*]: No, it wasn't. It was me who signed father's name.

KROGSTAD: Listen to me. I suppose you realize that that is a very dangerous confession?

NORA: Why? You'll soon have all your money back.

KROGSTAD: Let me ask you a question: why didn't you send that document to your father?

NORA: It was impossible. Daddy was ill. If I'd asked him for his signature, I'd have had to tell him what the money was for. Don't you see, when he was as ill as that I couldn't go and tell him that my husband's life was in danger. It was simply impossible.

KROGSTAD: It would have been better for you if you had abandoned the whole trip.

NORA: No, that was impossible. This was the thing that was to save my husband's life. I couldn't give it up.

KROGSTAD: But did it never strike you that this was fraudulent. . . ?

NORA: That wouldn't have meant anything to me. Why should I worry about you? I couldn't stand you, not when you insisted on going through with all those cold-blooded formalities, knowing all the time what a critical state my husband was in.

KROGSTAD: Mrs. Helmer, it's quite clear you still haven't the faintest idea what it is you've committed. But let me tell you, my own offence was no more and no worse than that, and it ruined my entire reputation.

NORA: You? Are you trying to tell me that you once risked everything to save your wife's life?

KROGSTAD: The law takes no account of motives.

NORA: Then they must be very bad laws.

KROGSTAD: Bad or not, if I produce this document in court, you'll be condemned according to them.

NORA: I don't believe it. Isn't a daughter entitled to try and save her father from worry and anxiety on his deathbed? Isn't a wife entitled to save her husband's life? I might not know very much about the law, but I feel sure of one thing: it must say somewhere that things like this are allowed. You mean to say you don't know that—you, when it's your job? You must be a rotten lawyer, Mr. Krogstad.

KROGSTAD: That may be. But when it comes to business transactions—like the sort between us two—perhaps you'll admit I know something about *them*? Good. Now you must please yourself. But I tell you this: if I'm pitched out a second time, you are going to keep me company.

[*He bows and goes out through the hall.*]

NORA [*stands thoughtfully for a moment, then tosses her head*]: Rubbish! He's just trying to scare me. I'm not such a fool as all that. [*Begins gathering up the children's clothes; after a moment she stops.*] Yet . . . ? No, it's impossible! I did it for love, didn't I?

THE CHILDREN [*in the doorway, left*]: Mummy, the gentleman's just gone out of the gate.

NORA: Yes, I know. But you mustn't say anything to anybody about that gentleman. You hear? Not even to Daddy!

THE CHILDREN: All right, Mummy. Are you going to play again?

NORA: No, not just now.

THE CHILDREN: But Mummy, you promised!

NORA: Yes, but I can't just now. Off you go now, I have a lot to do. Off you go, my darlings. [*She herds them carefully into the other room and shuts the door behind them. She sits down on the sofa, picks up her embroidery and works a few stitches, but soon stops.*] No! [*She flings her work down, stands up, goes to the hall door and calls out.*] Helene! Fetch the tree in for me, please. [*She walks across to the table, left, and opens the drawer; again pauses.*] No, really, it's quite impossible!

MAID [*with the Christmas tree*]: Where shall I put it, ma'am?

NORA: On the floor there, in the middle.

MAID: Anything else you want me to bring?

NORA: No, thank you. I've got what I want.

[*The Maid has put the tree down and goes out.*]

NORA [*busy decorating the tree*]: Candles here . . . and flowers here.—Revolting man! It's all nonsense! There's nothing to worry about. We'll have a lovely Christmas tree. And I'll do anything you want me to, Torvald; I'll sing for you, dance for you. . . .

[*Helmer, with a bundle of documents under his arm, comes in by the hall door.*]

NORA: Ah, back again already?

HELMER: Yes. Anybody been?

NORA: Here? No.

HELMER: That's funny. I just saw Krogstad leave the house.

NORA: Oh? O yes, that's right. Krogstad was here a minute.

HELMER: Nora, I can tell by your face he's been asking you to put a good word in for him.

NORA: Yes.

HELMER: And you were to pretend it was your own idea? You were to keep quiet about his having been here. He asked you to do that as well, didn't he?

NORA: Yes, Torvald. But . . .

HELMER: Nora, Nora, what possessed you to do a thing like that? Talking to a person like him, making him promises? And then on top of everything, to tell me a lie!

NORA: A lie. . . ?

HELMER: Didn't you say that nobody had been here? [*Wagging his finger at her.*] Never again must my little song-bird do a thing like that! Little song-birds must keep their pretty little beaks out of mischief; no chirruping out of tune! [*Puts his arm round her waist.*] Isn't that the way we want things to be? Yes, of course it is. [*Lets her go.*] So let's say no more about it. [*Sits down by the stove.*] Ah, nice and cosy here!

[*He glances through his papers.*]

NORA [*busy with the Christmas tree, after a short pause*]: Torvald!
HELMER: Yes.
NORA: I'm so looking forward to the fancy dress ball at the Stenborgs on Boxing Day.
HELMER: And I'm terribly curious to see what sort of surprise you've got for me.
NORA: Oh, it's too silly.
HELMER: Oh?
NORA: I just can't think of anything suitable. Everything seems so absurd, so pointless.
HELMER: Has my little Nora come to *that* conclusion?
NORA [*behind his chair, her arms on the chairback*]: Are you very busy, Torvald?
HELMER: Oh. . . .
NORA: What are all those papers?
HELMER: Bank matters.
NORA: Already?
HELMER: I have persuaded the retiring manager to give me authority to make any changes in organization or personnel I think necessary. I have to work on it over the Christmas week. I want everything straight by the New Year.
NORA: So that was why that poor Krogstad. . . .
HELMER: Hm!
NORA [*still leaning against the back of the chair, running her fingers through his hair*]: If you hadn't been so busy, Torvald, I'd have asked you to do me an awfully big favour.
HELMER: Let me hear it. What's it to be?
NORA: Nobody's got such good taste as you. And the thing is I do so want to look my best at the fancy dress ball. Torvald, couldn't you

give me some advice and tell me what you think I ought to go as
and how I should arrange my costume?

HELMER: Aha! So my impulsive little woman is asking for somebody
to come to her rescue, eh?

NORA: Please, Torvald, I never get anywhere without your help.

HELMER: Very well, I'll think about it. We'll find something.

NORA: That's sweet of you. [*She goes across to the tree again;
pauses.*] How pretty these red flowers look.—Tell me, was it really
something terribly wrong this man Krogstad did?

HELMER: Forgery. Have you any idea what that means?

NORA: Perhaps circumstances left him no choice?

HELMER: Maybe. Or perhaps, like so many others, he just didn't
think. I am not so heartless that I would necessarily want to con-
demn a man for a single mistake like that.

NORA: Oh no, Torvald, of course not!

HELMER: Many a man might be able to redeem himself, if he honestly
confessed his guilt and took his punishment.

NORA: Punishment?

HELMER: But that wasn't the way Krogstad chose. He dodged what
was due to him by a cunning trick. And that's what has been the
cause of his corruption.

NORA: Do you think it would . . . ?

HELMER: Just think how a man with a thing like that on his conscience will always be having to lie and cheat and dissemble; he can
never drop the mask, not even with his own wife and children. And
the children—*that's* the most terrible part of it, Nora.

NORA: Why?

HELMER: A fog of lies like that in a household, and it spreads disease
and infection to every part of it. Every breath the children take in
that kind of house is reeking with evil germs.

NORA [*closer behind him*]: Are you sure of that?

HELMER: My dear Nora, as a lawyer I know what I'm talking about.
Practically all juvenile delinquents come from homes where the
mother is dishonest.

NORA: Why mothers particularly?

HELMER: It's generally traceable to the mothers, but of course fathers
can have the same influence. Every lawyer knows that only too
well. And yet there's Krogstad been poisoning his own children for

years with lies and deceit. That's the reason I call him morally depraved. [*Holds out his hands to her.*] That's why my sweet little Nora must promise me not to try putting in any more good words for him. Shake hands on it. Well? What's this? Give me your hand. There now! That's settled. I assure you I would have found it impossible to work with him. I quite literally feel physically sick in the presence of such people.

NORA [*draws her hand away and walks over to the other side of the Christmas tree*]: How hot it is in here! And I still have such a lot to do.

HELMER [*stands up and collects his papers together*]: Yes, I'd better think of getting some of this read before dinner. I must also think about your costume. And I might even be able to lay my hands on something to wrap in gold paper and hang on the Christmas tree. [*He lays his hand on her head.*] My precious little singing bird.

[*He goes into his study and shuts the door behind him.*]

NORA [*quietly, after a pause*]: Nonsense! It can't be. It's impossible. It *must* be impossible.

MAID [*in the doorway, left*]: The children keep asking so nicely if they can come in and see Mummy.

NORA: No, no, don't let them in! You stay with them, Anne Marie.

MAID: Very well, ma'am.

[*She shuts the door.*]

NORA [*pale with terror*]: Corrupt my children . . . ! Poison my home? [*Short pause; she throws back her head.*] It's not true! It could never, never be true!

ACT TWO

The same room. In the corner beside the piano stands the Christmas tree, stripped, bedraggled and with its candles burnt out. Nora's outdoor things lie on the sofa. Nora, alone there, walks about restlessly; at last she stops by the sofa and picks up her coat.

NORA [*putting her coat down again*]: Somebody's coming! [*Crosses to the door, listens.*] No, it's nobody. Nobody will come today, of

course, Christmas Day—nor tomorrow, either. But perhaps. . . .
[*She opens the door and looks out.*] No, nothing in the letter box;
quite empty. [*Comes forward.*] Oh, nonsense! He didn't mean it
seriously. Things like that *can't* happen. It's impossible. Why, I
have three small children.

[*The Nursemaid comes from the room, left, carrying a big card-
board box.*]

NURSEMAID: I finally found it, the box with the fancy dress costumes.

NORA: Thank you. Put it on the table, please.

NURSEMAID [*does this*]: But I'm afraid they are in an awful mess.

NORA: Oh, if only I could rip them up into a thousand pieces!

NURSEMAID: Good heavens, they can be mended all right, with a bit
of patience.

NORA: Yes, I'll go over and get Mrs. Linde to help me.

NURSEMAID: Out again? In this terrible weather? You'll catch your
death of cold, Ma'am.

NORA: Oh, worse things might happen.—How are the children?

NURSEMAID: Playing with their Christmas presents, poor little things,
but . . .

NORA: Do they keep asking for me?

NURSEMAID: They are so used to being with their Mummy.

NORA: Yes, Anne Marie, from now on I can't be with them as often as
I was before.

NURSEMAID: Ah well, children get used to anything in time.

NORA: Do you think so? Do you think they would forget their Mummy
if she went away for good?

NURSEMAID: Good gracious—for good?

NORA: Tell me, Anne Marie—I've often wondered—how on earth
could you bear to hand your child over to strangers?

NURSEMAID: Well, there was nothing else for it when I had to come
and nurse my little Nora.

NORA: Yes but . . . how could you *bring* yourself to do it?

NURSEMAID: When I had the chance of such a good place? When a
poor girl's been in trouble she must make the best of things.
Because *he* didn't help, the rotter.

NORA: But your daughter will have forgotten you.

NURSEMAID: Oh no, she hasn't. She wrote to me when she got confirmed, and again when she got married.

NORA [*putting her arms round her neck*]: Dear old Anne Marie, you were a good mother to me when I was little.

NURSEMAID: My poor little Nora never had any other mother but me.

NORA: And if my little ones only had you, I know you would. . . . Oh, what am I talking about! [*She opens the box.*] Go in to them. I must . . . Tomorrow I'll let you see how pretty I am going to look.

NURSEMAID: Ah, there'll be nobody at the ball as pretty as my Nora.

[She goes into the room, left.]

NORA [*begins unpacking the box, but soon throws it down*]: Oh, if only I dare go out. If only I could be sure nobody would come. And that nothing would happen in the meantime here at home. Rubbish—nobody's going to come. I mustn't think about it. Brush this muff. Pretty gloves, pretty gloves! I'll put it right out of my mind. One, two, three, four, five, six. . . . [*Screams.*] Ah, they are coming. . . . [*She starts towards the door, but stops irresolute. Mrs. Linde comes from the hall, where she has taken off her things.*] Oh, it's you, Kristine. There's nobody else out there, is there? I'm so glad you've come.

MRS. LINDE: I heard you'd been over looking for me.

NORA: Yes, I was just passing. There's something you must help me with. Come and sit beside me on the sofa here. You see, the Stenborgs are having a fancy dress party upstairs tomorrow evening, and now Torvald wants me to go as a Neapolitan fisher lass and dance the tarantella. I learned it in Capri, you know.

MRS. LINDE: Well, well! So you are going to do a party piece?

NORA: Torvald says I should. Look, here's the costume, Torvald had it made for me down there. But it's got all torn and I simply don't know. . . .

MRS. LINDE: We'll soon have that put right. It's only the trimming come away here and there. Got a needle and thread? Ah, here's what we are after.

NORA: It's awfully kind of you.

MRS. LINDE: So you are going to be all dressed up tomorrow, Nora? Tell you what—I'll pop over for a minute to see you in all your finery. But I'm quite forgetting to thank you for the pleasant time we had last night.

NORA [*gets up and walks across the room*]:   Somehow I didn't think yesterday was as nice as things generally are.—You should have come to town a little earlier, Kristine.—Yes, Torvald certainly knows how to make things pleasant about the place.

MRS. LINDE: You too, I should say. You are not your father's daughter for nothing. But tell me, is Dr. Rank always as depressed as he was last night?

NORA: No, last night it was rather obvious. He's got something seriously wrong with him, you know. Tuberculosis of the spine, poor fellow. His father was a horrible man, who used to have mistresses and things like that. That's why the son was always ailing, right from being a child.

MRS. LINDE [*lowering her sewing*]:   But my dear Nora, how do you come to know about things like that?

NORA [*walking about the room*]:   Huh! When you've got three children, you get these visits from . . . women who have had a certain amount of medical training. And you hear all sorts of things from them.

MRS. LINDE [*begins sewing again; short silence*]:   Does Dr. Rank call in every day?

NORA: Every single day. He was Torvald's best friend as a boy, and he's a good friend of *mine*, too. Dr. Rank is almost like one of the family.

MRS. LINDE: But tell me—is he really genuine? What I mean is: doesn't he sometimes rather turn on the charm?

NORA: No, on the contrary. What makes you think that?

MRS. LINDE: When you introduced me yesterday, he claimed he'd often heard my name in this house. But afterwards I noticed your husband hadn't the faintest idea who I was. Then how is it that Dr Rank should. . . .

NORA: Oh yes, it was quite right what he said, Kristine. You see Torvald is so terribly in love with me that he says he wants me all to himself. When we were first married, it even used to make him sort of jealous if I only as much as mentioned any of my old friends from back home. So of course I stopped doing it. But I often talk to Dr. Rank about such things. He likes hearing about them.

MRS. LINDE: Listen, Nora! In lots of ways you are still a child. Now, I'm a good deal older than you, and a bit more experienced. I'll tell you something: I think you ought to give up all this business with Dr. Rank.

NORA: Give up what business?

MRS. LINDE: The whole thing, I should say. Weren't you saying yesterday something about a rich admirer who was to provide you with money. . . .

NORA: One who's never existed, I regret to say. But what of it?

MRS. LINDE: Has Dr. Rank money?

NORA: Yes, he has.

MRS. LINDE: And no dependents?

NORA: No, nobody. But . . . ?

MRS. LINDE: And he comes to the house every day?

NORA: Yes, I told you.

MRS. LINDE: But how can a man of his position want to pester you like this?

NORA: I simply don't understand.

MRS. LINDE: Don't pretend, Nora. Do you think I don't see now who you borrowed the twelve hundred from?

NORA: Are you out of your mind? Do you really think that? A friend of ours who comes here every day? The whole situation would have been absolutely intolerable.

MRS. LINDE: It *really* isn't him?

NORA: No, I give you my word. It would never have occurred to me for one moment. . . . Anyway, he didn't have the money to lend then. He didn't inherit it till later.

MRS. LINDE: Just as well for you, I'd say, my dear Nora.

NORA: No, it would never have occurred to me to ask Dr. Rank. . . . All the same I'm pretty certain if I were to ask him . . .

MRS. LINDE: But of course you won't.

NORA: No, of course not. I can't ever imagine it being necessary. But I'm quite certain if ever I were to mention it to Dr. Rank. . . .

MRS. LINDE: Behind your husband's back?

NORA: I have to get myself out of that other business. That's also behind his back. I *must* get myself out of that.

MRS. LINDE: Yes, that's what I said yesterday. But . . .

NORA [*walking up and down*]:   A man's better at coping with these things than a woman. . . .

MRS. LINDE: Your own husband, yes.

NORA: Nonsense! [*Stops.*]   When you've paid everything you owe, you do get your IOU back again, don't you?

MRS. LINDE: Of course.

NORA: And you can tear it up into a thousand pieces and burn it—the nasty, filthy thing!

MRS. LINDE [*looking fixedly at her, puts down her sewing and slowly rises*]:   Nora, you are hiding something from me.

NORA: Is it so obvious?

MRS. LINDE: Something has happened to you since yesterday morning. Nora, what is it?

NORA [*going towards her*]:   Kristine! [*Listens.*] Hush! There's Torvald back. Look, you go and sit in there beside the children for the time being. Torvald can't stand the sight of mending lying about. Get Anne Marie to help you.

MRS. LINDE [*gathering a lot of the things together*]:   All right, but I'm not leaving until we have thrashed this thing out.

[*She goes into the room, left; at the same time Helmer comes in from the hall.*]

NORA [*goes to meet him*]:   I've been longing for you to be back, Torvald, dear.

HELMER: Was that the dressmaker . . . ?

NORA: No, it was Kristine; she's helping me with my costume. I think it's going to look very nice . . .

HELMER: Wasn't that a good idea of mine, now?

NORA: Wonderful! But wasn't it also nice of me to let you have your way?

HELMER [*taking her under the chin*]:   Nice of you—because you let your husband have his way? All right, you little rogue, I know you didn't mean it that way. But I don't want to disturb you. You'll be wanting to try the costume on, I suppose.

NORA: And I dare say you've got work to do?

HELMER: Yes. [*Shows her a bundle of papers.*] Look at this. I've been down at the Bank. . . .

[He turns to go into his study.]

NORA: Torvald!

HELMER [*stopping*]: Yes.

NORA: If a little squirrel were to ask ever so nicely. . . ?

HELMER: Well?

NORA: Would you do something for it?

HELMER: Naturally I would first have to know what it is.

NORA: Please, if only you would let it have its way, and do what it wants, it'd scamper about and do all sorts of marvellous tricks.

HELMER: What is it?

NORA: And the pretty little sky-lark would sing all day long. . . .

HELMER: Huh! It does that anyway.

NORA: I'd pretend I was an elfin child and dance a moonlight dance for you, Torvald.

HELMER: Nora—I hope it's not that business you started on this morning?

NORA [*coming closer*]: Yes, it is, Torvald. I implore you!

HELMER: You have the nerve to bring that up again?

NORA: Yes, yes, you *must* listen to me. You must let Krogstad keep his job at the Bank.

HELMER: My dear Nora, I'm giving his job to Mrs. Linde.

NORA: Yes, it's awfully sweet of you. But couldn't you get rid of somebody else in the office instead of Krogstad?

HELMER: This really is the most incredible obstinacy! Just because you go and make some thoughtless promise to put in a good word for him, you expect me . . .

NORA: It's not that, Torvald. It's for your own sake. That man writes in all the nastiest papers, you told me that yourself. He can do you no end of harm. He terrifies me to death. . . .

HELMER: Aha, now I see. It's your memories of what happened before that are frightening you.

NORA: What do you mean?

HELMER: It's your father you are thinking of.

NORA: Yes . . . yes, that's right. You remember all the nasty insinuations those wicked people put in the papers about Daddy? I honestly think they would have had him dismissed if the Ministry hadn't sent you down to investigate, and you hadn't been so kind and helpful.

HELMER: My dear little Nora, there is a considerable difference between your father and me. Your father's professional conduct was not entirely above suspicion. Mine is. And I hope it's going to stay that way as long as I hold this position.

NORA: But nobody knows what some of these evil people are capable of. Things could be so nice and pleasant for us here, in the peace and quiet of our home—you and me and the children, Torvald! That's why I implore you. . . .

HELMER: The more you plead for him, the more impossible you make it for me to keep him on. It's already known down at the Bank that I am going to give Krogstad his notice. If it ever got around that the new manager had been talked over by his wife. . . .

NORA: What of it?

HELMER: Oh, nothing! As long as the little woman gets her own stubborn way . . . ! Do you want me to make myself a laughing stock in the office? . . . Give people the idea that I am susceptible to any kind of outside pressure? You can imagine how soon I'd feel the consequences of that! Anyway, there's one other consideration that makes it impossible to have Krogstad in the Bank as long as I am manager.

NORA: What's that?

HELMER: At a pinch I might have overlooked his past lapses. . . .

NORA: Of course you could, Torvald!

HELMER: And I'm told he's not bad at his job, either. But we knew each other rather well when we were younger. It was one of those rather rash friendships that prove embarrassing in later life. There's no reason why you shouldn't know we were once on terms of some familiarity. And he, in his tactless way, makes no attempt to hide the fact, particularly when other people are present. On the contrary, he thinks he has every right to treat me as an equal, with his 'Torvald this' and 'Torvald that' every time he opens his mouth. I find it extremely irritating, I can tell you. He would make my position at the Bank absolutely intolerable.

NORA: Torvald, surely you aren't serious?

HELMER: Oh? Why not?

NORA: Well, it's all so petty.

HELMER: What's that you say? Petty? Do you think I'm petty?

NORA: No, not at all, Torvald dear! And that's why . . .

HELMER: Doesn't make any difference! . . . You call my motives petty; so I must be petty too. Petty! Indeed! Well, we'll put a stop to that, once and for all. [*He opens the hall door and calls.*] Helene!

NORA: What are you going to do?

HELMER [*searching among his papers*]: Settle things. [*The Maid comes in.*] See this letter? I want you to take it down at once. Get hold of a messenger and get him to deliver it. Quickly. The address is on the outside. There's the money.

MAID: Very good, sir.

[*She goes with the letter.*]

HELMER [*putting his papers together*]: There now, my stubborn little miss.

NORA [*breathless*]: Torvald . . . what was that letter?

HELMER: Krogstad's notice.

NORA: Get it back, Torvald! There's still time! Oh, Torvald, get it back! Please for my sake, for your sake, for the sake of the children! Listen, Torvald, please! You don't realize what it can do to us.

HELMER: Too late.

NORA: Yes, too late.

HELMER: My dear Nora, I forgive you this anxiety of yours, although it is actually a bit of an insult. Oh, but it is, I tell you! It's hardly flattering to suppose that anything this miserable pen-pusher wrote could frighten *me!* But I forgive you all the same, because it is rather a sweet way of showing how much you love me. [*He takes her in his arms.*] This is how things must be, my own darling Nora. When it comes to the point, I've enough strength and enough courage, believe me, for whatever happens. You'll find I'm man enough to take everything on myself.

NORA [*terrified*]: What do you mean?

HELMER: Everything, I said. . . .

NORA [*in command of herself*]: That is something you shall never, never do.

HELMER: All right, then we'll share it, Nora—as man and wife. That's what we'll do. [*Caressing her.*] Does that make you happy now? There, there, don't look at me with those eyes, like a little frightened dove. The whole thing is sheer imagination.—Why don't you run through the tarantella and try out the tambourine? I'll go into my study and shut both the doors, then I won't hear anything. You can make all the noise you want. [*Turns in the doorway.*] And when Rank comes, tell him where he can find me.

[*He nods to her, goes with his papers into his room, and shuts the door behind him.*]

NORA [*wild-eyed with terror, stands as though transfixed*]:   He's quite capable of doing it! He would do it! No matter what, he'd do it.— No, never in this world! Anything but that! Help? Some way out . . . ? [*The door-bell rings in the hall.*] Dr. Rank. . . ! Anything but that, anything! [*She brushes her hands over her face, pulls herself together and opens the door into the hall. Dr. Rank is standing outside hanging up his fur coat. During what follows it begins to grow dark.*] Hello, Dr. Rank. I recognized your ring. Do you mind not going in to Torvald just yet, I think he's busy.

RANK: And you?

[*Dr. Rank comes into the room and she closes the door behind him.*]

NORA: Oh, you know very well I've always got time for you.

RANK: Thank you. A privilege I shall take advantage of as long as I am able.

NORA: What do you mean—as long as you are able?

RANK: Does that frighten you?

NORA: Well, it's just that it sounds so strange. Is anything likely to happen?

RANK: Only what I have long expected. But I didn't think it would come quite so soon.

NORA [*catching at his arm*]:   What have you found out? Dr. Rank, you must tell me!

RANK: I'm slowly sinking. There's nothing to be done about it.

NORA [*with a sigh of relief*]:   Oh, it's *you* you're . . . ?

RANK: Who else? No point in deceiving oneself. I am the most wretched of all my patients, Mrs. Helmer. These last few days I've made a careful analysis of my internal economy. Bankrupt! Within a month I shall probably be lying rotting up there in the churchyard.

NORA: Come now, what a ghastly thing to say!

RANK: The whole damned thing is ghastly. But the worst thing is all the ghastliness that has to be gone through first. I only have one more test to make; and when that's done I'll know pretty well when the final disintegration will start. There's something I want to ask you. Helmer is a sensitive soul; he loathes anything that's ugly. I don't want him visiting me. . . .

NORA: But Dr. Rank. . . .

RANK: On no account must he. I won't have it. I'll lock the door on him.—As soon as I'm absolutely certain of the worst, I'll send you my visiting card with a black cross on it. You'll know then the final horrible disintegration has begun.

NORA: Really, you are being quite absurd today. And here was I hoping you would be in a thoroughly good mood.

RANK: With death staring me in the face? Why should I suffer for another man's sins? What justice is there in that? Somewhere, somehow, every single family must be suffering some such cruel retribution. . . .

NORA [*stopping up her ears*]: Rubbish! Do cheer up!

RANK: Yes, really the whole thing's nothing but a huge joke. My poor innocent spine must do penance for my father's gay subaltern life.

NORA [*by the table, left*]: Wasn't he rather partial to asparagus and *pâté de foie gras?*

RANK: Yes, he was. And truffles.

NORA: Truffles, yes. And oysters, too, I believe?

RANK: Yes, oysters, oysters, of course.

NORA: And all the port and champagne that goes with them. It does seem a pity all these delicious things should attack the spine.

RANK: Especially when they attack a poor spine that never had any fun out of them.

NORA: Yes, that is an awful pity.

RANK [*looks at her sharply*]: Hm. . . .

NORA [*after a pause*]: Why did you smile?

RANK: No, it was you who laughed.

NORA: No, it was you who smiled, Dr. Rank!

RANK [*getting up*]:   You are a bigger rascal than I thought you were.

NORA: I feel full of mischief today.

RANK: So it seems.

NORA [*putting her hands on his shoulders*]:   Dear, dear Dr. Rank, you mustn't go and die on Torvald and me.

RANK: You wouldn't miss me for long. When you are gone, you are soon forgotten.

NORA [*looking at him anxiously*]:   Do you think so?

RANK: People make new contacts, then . . .

NORA: Who make new contacts?

RANK: Both you and Helmer will, when I'm gone. You yourself are already well on the way, it seems to me. What was this Mrs. Linde doing here last night?

NORA: Surely you aren't jealous of poor Kristine?

RANK: Yes, I am. She'll be my successor in this house. When I'm done for, I can see this woman. . . .

NORA: Hush! Don't talk so loud, she's in there.

RANK: Today as well? There you are, you see!

NORA: Just to do some sewing on my dress. Good Lord, how absurd you are! [*She sits down on the sofa.*] Now Dr. Rank, cheer up. You'll see tomorrow how nicely I can dance. And you can pretend I'm doing it just for you—and for Torvald as well, of course. [*She takes various things out of the box.*] Come here, Dr. Rank. I want to show you something.

RANK [*sits*]:   What is it?

NORA: Look!

RANK: Silk stockings.

NORA: Flesh-coloured! Aren't they lovely! Of course, it's dark here now, but tomorrow. . . . No, no, no, you can only look at the feet. Oh well, you might as well see a bit higher up, too.

RANK: Hm. . . .

NORA: Why are you looking so critical? Don't you think they'll fit?

RANK: I couldn't possibly offer any informed opinion about that.

NORA [*looks at him for a moment*]:   Shame on you. [*Hits him lightly across the ear with the stockings.*] Take that! [*Folds them up again.*]

RANK: And what other delights am I to be allowed to see?

NORA: Not another thing. You are too naughty. [*She hums a little and searches among her things.*]

RANK [*after a short pause*]: Sitting here so intimately like this with you, I can't imagine . . . I simply cannot conceive what would have become of me if I had never come to this house.

NORA [*smiles*]: Yes, I rather think you do enjoy coming here.

RANK [*in a low voice, looking fixedly ahead*]: And the thought of having to leave it all. . .

NORA: Nonsense. You aren't leaving.

RANK [*in the same tone*]: . . . without being able to leave behind even the slightest token of gratitude, hardly a fleeting regret even . . . nothing but an empty place to be filled by the first person that comes along.

NORA: Supposing I were to ask you to . . . ? No . . .

RANK: What?

NORA: . . . to show me the extent of your friendship . . .

RANK: Yes?

NORA: I mean . . . to do me a tremendous favour. . . .

RANK: Would you really, for once, give me that pleasure?

NORA: You have no idea what it is.

RANK: All right, tell me.

NORA: No, really I can't, Dr. Rank. It's altogether too much to ask . . . because I need your advice and help as well. . . .

RANK: The more the better. I cannot imagine what you have in mind. But tell me anyway. You do trust me, don't you?

NORA: Yes, I trust you more than anybody I know. You are my best and my most faithful friend. I know that. So I will tell you. Well then, Dr. Rank, there is something you must help me to prevent. You know how deeply, how passionately Torvald is in love with me. He would never hesitate for a moment to sacrifice his life for my sake.

RANK [*bending towards her*]: Nora . . . do you think he's the only one who . . . ?

NORA [*stiffening slightly*]: Who . . . ?

RANK: Who wouldn't gladly give his life for your sake.

NORA [*sadly*]: Oh!

RANK: I swore to myself you would know before I went. I'll never have a better opportunity. Well, Nora! Now you know. And now you know too that you can confide in me as in nobody else.

NORA [*rises and speaks evenly and calmly*]: Let me past.

RANK [*makes way for her, but remains seated*]: Nora. . . .

NORA [*in the hall doorway*]: Helene, bring the lamp in, please. [*Walks over to the stove.*] Oh, my dear Dr. Rank, that really was rather horrid of you.

RANK [*getting up*]: That I have loved you every bit as much as anybody? Is *that* horrid?

NORA: No, but that you had to go and tell me. When it was all so unnecessary. . . .

RANK: What do you mean? Did you know . . . ?

[*The Maid comes in with the lamp, puts it on the table, and goes out again.*]

RANK: Nora . . . Mrs. Helmer . . . I'm asking you if you knew?

NORA: How can I tell whether I did or didn't. I simply can't tell you. . . . Oh, how could you be so clumsy, Dr. Rank! When everything was so nice.

RANK: Anyway, you know now that I'm at your service, body and soul. So you can speak out.

NORA [*looking at him*]: After this?

RANK: I beg you to tell me what it is.

NORA: I can tell you nothing now.

RANK: You must. You can't torment me like this. Give me a chance— I'll do anything that's humanly possible.

NORA: You can do nothing for me now. Actually, I don't really need any help. It's all just my imagination, really it is. Of course! [*She sits down in the rocking-chair, looks at him and smiles.*] I must say, you are a nice one, Dr. Rank! Don't you feel ashamed of yourself, now the lamp's been brought in?

RANK: No, not exactly. But perhaps I ought to go—for good?

NORA: No, you mustn't do that. You must keep coming just as you've always done. You know very well Torvald would miss you terribly.

RANK: And *you*?

NORA: I always think it's tremendous fun having you.

RANK: That's exactly what gave me wrong ideas. I just can't puzzle you out. I often used to feel you'd just as soon be with me as with Helmer.

NORA: Well, you see, there are those people you love and those people you'd almost rather *be* with.

RANK: Yes, there's something in that.

NORA: When I was a girl at home, I loved Daddy best, of course. But I also thought it great fun if I could slip into the maids' room. For one thing they never preached at me. And they always talked about such exciting things.

RANK: Aha! So it's their role I've taken over!

NORA [*jumps up and crosses to him*]: Oh, my dear, kind Dr. Rank, I didn't mean that at all. But you can see how it's a bit with Torvald as it was with Daddy. . . .

[*The Maid comes in from the hall.*]

MAID: Please, ma'am. . . !

[*She whispers and hands her a card.*]

NORA [*glances at the card*]: Ah!

[*She puts it in her pocket.*]

RANK: Anything wrong?

NORA: No, no, not at all. It's just . . . it's my new costume. . . .

RANK: How is that? There's your costume in there.

NORA: That one, yes. But this is another one. I've ordered it. Torvald mustn't hear about it. . . .

RANK: Ah, so that's the big secret, is it!

NORA: Yes, that's right. Just go in and see him, will you? He's in the study. Keep him occupied for the time being. . . .

RANK: Don't worry. He shan't escape me.

[*He goes into Helmer's study.*]

NORA [*to the Maid*]: Is he waiting in the kitchen?

MAID: Yes, he came up the back stairs. . . .

NORA: But didn't you tell him somebody was here?

MAID: Yes, but it was no good.

NORA: Won't he go?

MAID: No, he won't till he's seen you.

NORA: Let him in, then. But quietly. Helene, you mustn't tell anybody about this. It's a surprise for my husband.

MAID. I understand, ma'am. . . .

[*She goes out.*]

NORA: Here it comes! What I've been dreading! No, no, it can't happen, it *can't* happen.

[*She walks over and bolts Helmer's door. The Maid opens the hall door for Krogstad and shuts it again behind him. He is wearing a fur coat, over-shoes, and a fur cap.*]

NORA [*goes towards him*]: Keep your voice down, my husband is at home.

KROGSTAD: What if he is?

NORA: What do you want with me?

KROGSTAD: To find out something.

NORA: Hurry, then. What is it?

KROGSTAD: You know I've been given notice.

NORA: I couldn't prevent it, Mr. Krogstad, I did my utmost for you, but it was no use.

KROGSTAD: Has your husband so little affection for you? He knows what I can do to you, yet he dares. . . .

NORA: You don't imagine he knows about it!

KROGSTAD: No, I didn't imagine he did. It didn't seem a bit like my good friend Torvald Helmer to show that much courage. . . .

NORA: Mr. Krogstad, I must ask you to show some respect for my husband.

KROGSTAD: Oh, sure! All due respect! But since you are so anxious to keep this business quiet, Mrs. Helmer, I take it you now have a rather clearer idea of just what it is you've done, than you had yesterday.

NORA: Clearer than *you* could ever have given me.

KROGSTAD: Yes, being as I am such a rotten lawyer. . . .

NORA: What do you want with me?

KROGSTAD: I just wanted to see how things stood, Mrs. Helmer. I've been thinking about you all day. Even a mere money-lender, a hack journalist, a—well, even somebody like me has a bit of what you might call feeling.

NORA: Show it then. Think of my little children.

KROGSTAD: Did you or your husband think of mine? But what does it matter now? There was just one thing I wanted to say: you needn't take this business too seriously. I shan't start any proceedings, for the present.

NORA: Ah, I knew you wouldn't.

KROGSTAD: The whole thing can be arranged quite amicably. Nobody need know. Just the three of us.

NORA: My husband must never know.

KROGSTAD: How can you prevent it? Can you pay off the balance?

NORA: No, not immediately.

KROGSTAD: Perhaps you've some way of getting hold of the money in the next few days.

NORA: None I want to make use of.

KROGSTAD: Well, it wouldn't have been very much help to you if you had. Even if you stood there with the cash in your hand and to spare, you still wouldn't get your IOU back from me now.

NORA: What are you going to do with it?

KROGSTAD: Just keep it—have it in my possession. Nobody who isn't implicated need know about it. So if you are thinking of trying any desperate remedies . . .

NORA: Which I am. . . .

KROGSTAD: . . . if you happen to be thinking of running away. . .

NORA: Which I am!

KROGSTAD: . . . or anything worse . . .

NORA: How did you know?

KROGSTAD: . . . forget it!

NORA: How did you know I was thinking of *that*?

KROGSTAD: Most of us think of *that*, to begin with. I did, too; but I didn't have the courage. . . .

NORA [*tonelessly*]: I haven't either.

KROGSTAD [*relieved*]: So you haven't the courage either, eh?

NORA: No, I haven't! I haven't!

KROGSTAD: It would also be very stupid. There'd only be the first domestic storm to get over. . . . I've got a letter to your husband in my pocket here. . . .

NORA: And it's all in there?

KROGSTAD: In as tactful a way as possible.

NORA [*quickly*]: He must never read that letter. Tear it up. I'll find the money somehow.

KROGSTAD: Excuse me, Mrs. Helmer, but I've just told you. . . .

NORA: I'm not talking about the money I owe you. I want to know how much you are demanding from my husband, and I'll get the money.

KROGSTAD: I want no money from your husband.

NORA: What do you want?

KROGSTAD: I'll tell you. I want to get on my feet again, Mrs. Helmer; I want to get to the top. And your husband is going to help me. For the last eighteen months I've gone straight; all that time it's been hard going; I was content to work my way up, step by step. Now I'm being kicked out, and I won't stand for being taken back again as an act of charity. I'm going to get to the top, I tell you. I'm going back into that Bank—with a better job. Your husband is going to create a new vacancy, just for me. . . .

NORA: He'll never do that!

KROGSTAD: He will do it. I know him. He'll do it without so much as a whimper. And once I'm in there with him, you'll see what's what. In less than a year I'll be his right-hand man. It'll be Nils Krogstad, not Torvald Helmer, who'll be running that Bank.

NORA: You'll never live to see that day!

KROGSTAD: You mean you . . . ?

NORA: Now I have the courage.

KROGSTAD: You can't frighten me! A precious pampered little thing like you. . . .

NORA: I'll show you! I'll show you!

KROGSTAD: Under the ice, maybe? Down in the cold, black water? Then being washed up in the spring, bloated, hairless, unrecognizable. . . .

NORA: You can't frighten me.

KROGSTAD: You can't frighten me, either. People don't do that sort of thing, Mrs. Helmer. There wouldn't be any point to it, anyway. I'd still have him right in my pocket.

NORA: Afterwards? When I'm no longer. . .

KROGSTAD: Aren't you forgetting that your reputation would then be entirely in my hands? [*Nora stands looking at him, speechless.*] Well, I've warned you. Don't do anything silly. When Helmer gets my letter, I expect to hear from him. And don't forget: it's him who is forcing me off the straight and narrow again, your own husband! That's something I'll never forgive him for. Goodbye, Mrs. Helmer.

[*He goes out through the hall. Nora crosses to the door, opens it slightly, and listens.*]

NORA: He's going. He hasn't left the letter. No, no, that would be impossible! [*Opens the door further and further.*] What's he doing? He's stopped outside. He's not going down the stairs. Has he changed his mind? Is he . . .? [*A letter falls into the letter-box. Then Krogstad's footsteps are heard receding as he walks downstairs. Nora gives a stifled cry, runs across the room to the sofa table; pause.*] In the letter-box! [*She creeps stealthily across to the hall door.*] There it is! Torvald, Torvald! It's hopeless now!

MRS. LINDE. [*comes into the room, left, carrying the costume*]: There, I think that's everything. Shall we try it on?

NORA [*in a low, hoarse voice*]: Kristine, come here.

MRS. LINDE [*throws the dress down on the sofa*]: What's wrong with you? You look upset.

NORA: Come here. Do you see that letter? *There*, look! Through the glass in the letter-box.

MRS. LINDE: Yes, yes, I can see it.

NORA: It's a letter from Krogstad.

MRS. LINDE: Nora! It was Krogstad who lent you the money!

NORA: Yes. And now Torvald will get to know everything.

MRS. LINDE: Believe me, Nora, it's best for you both.

NORA: But there's more to it than that. I forged a signature. . . .

MRS. LINDE: Heavens above!

NORA: Listen, I want to tell you something, Kristine, so you can be my witness.

MRS. LINDE: What do you mean "witness"? What do you want me to . . . ?

NORA: If I should go mad . . . which might easily happen . . .

MRS. LINDE: Nora!

NORA: Or if anything happened to me . . . which meant I couldn't be here. . . .

MRS. LINDE: Nora, Nora! Are you out of your mind?

NORA: And if somebody else wanted to take it all upon himself, the whole blame, you understand. . . .

MRS. LINDE: Yes, yes. But what makes you think . . . ?

NORA: Then you must testify that it isn't true, Kristine. I'm not out of my mind; I'm quite sane now. And I tell you this: nobody else knew anything, I alone was responsible for the whole thing. Remember that!

MRS. LINDE: I will. But I don't understand a word of it.

NORA: Why should you? You see something miraculous is going to happen.

MRS. LINDE: Something miraculous?

NORA: Yes, a miracle. But something so terrible as well, Kristine—oh, it must *never* happen, not for anything.

MRS. LINDE: I'm going straight over to talk to Krogstad.

NORA: Don't go. He'll only do you harm.

MRS. LINDE: There was a time when he would have done anything for me.

NORA: Him!

MRS. LINDE: Where does he live?

NORA: How do I know. . . ? Wait a minute. [*She feels in her pocket.*] Here's his card. But the letter, the letter . . . !

HELMER [*from his study, knocking on the door*]: Nora!

NORA [*cries out in terror*]: What's that? What do you want?

HELMER: Don't be frightened. We're not coming in. You've locked the door. Are you trying on?

NORA: Yes, yes, I'm trying on. It looks so nice on me, Torvald.

MRS. LINDE [*who has read the card*]: He lives just round the corner.

NORA: It's no use. It's hopeless. The letter is there in the box.

MRS. LINDE: Your husband keeps the key?

NORA: Always.

MRS. LINDE: Krogstad must ask for his letter back unread, he must find some sort of excuse. . . .

NORA: But this is just the time that Torvald generally . . .

MRS. LINDE: Put him off! Go in and keep him busy. I'll be back as soon as I can.

[*She goes out hastily by the hall door. Nora walks over to Helmer's door, opens it and peeps in.*]

NORA: Torvald!

HELMER [*in the study*]: Well, can a man get into his own living-room again now? Come along, Rank, now we'll see . . . [*In the doorway.*] But what's this?

NORA: What, Torvald dear?

HELMER: Rank led me to expect some kind of marvellous transformation.

RANK [*in the doorway*]: That's what I thought too, but I must have been mistaken.

NORA: I'm not showing myself off to anybody before tomorrow.

HELMER: Nora dear, you look tired. You haven't been practising too hard?

NORA: No, I haven't practised at all yet.

HELMER: You'll have to, though.

NORA: Yes, I certainly must, Torvald. But I just can't get anywhere without your help: I've completely forgotten it.

HELMER: We'll soon polish it up.

NORA: Yes, do help me, Torvald. Promise? I'm so nervous. All those people. . . . You must devote yourself exclusively to me this evening. Pens away! Forget all about the office! Promise me, Torvald dear!

HELMER: I promise. This evening I am wholly and entirely at your service . . . helpless little thing that you are. Oh, but while I remember, I'll just look first . . .

[*He goes towards the hall door.*]

NORA: What do you want out there?

HELMER: Just want to see if there are any letters.

NORA: No, don't, Torvald!

HELMER: Why not?

NORA: Torvald, *please!* There aren't any.

HELMER: Just let me see.

[*He starts to go. Nora, at the piano, plays the opening bars of the tarantella.*]

HELMER [*at the door, stops*]:   Aha!

NORA: I shan't be able to dance tomorrow if I don't rehearse it with you.

HELMER [*walks to her*]:   Are you really so nervous, Nora dear?

NORA: Terribly nervous. Let me run through it now. There's still time before supper. Come and sit here and play for me, Torvald dear. Tell me what to do, keep me right—as you always do.

HELMER: Certainly, with pleasure, if that's what you want.

[*He sits at the piano. Nora snatches the tambourine out of the box, and also a long gaily-coloured shawl which she drapes round herself, then with a bound she leaps forward.*]

NORA [*shouts*]:   Now play for me! Now I'll dance!

[*Helmer plays and Nora dances; Dr. Rank stands at the piano behind Helmer and looks on.*]

HELMER [*playing*]:   Not so fast! Not so fast!

NORA: I can't help it.

HELMER: Not so wild, Nora!

NORA: This is how it has to be.

HELMER [*stops*]:   No, no, that won't do at all.

NORA [*laughs and swings the tambourine*]:   Didn't I tell you?

RANK: Let me play for her.

HELMER [*gets up*]:   Yes, do. Then I'll be better able to tell her what to do.

[*Dr. Rank sits down at the piano and plays. Nora dances more and more wildly. Helmer stands by the stove giving her repeated directions as she dances; she does not seem to hear them. Her hair comes undone and falls about her shoulders; she pays no attention and goes on dancing. Mrs. Linde enters.*]

MRS. LINDE [*standing as though spellbound in the doorway*]:   Ah . . . !

NORA [*dancing*]:   See what fun we are having, Kristine.

HELMER: But my dear darling Nora, you are dancing as though your life depended on it.

NORA: It does.

HELMER: Stop, Rank! This is sheer madness. Stop, I say.

[*Dr. Rank stops playing and Nora comes to a sudden halt.*]

HELMER [*crosses to her*]: I would never have believed it. You have forgotten everything I ever taught you.

NORA [*throwing away the tambourine*]: There you are, you see.

HELMER: Well, some more instruction is certainly needed there.

NORA: Yes, you see how necessary it is. You must go on coaching me right up to the last minute. Promise me, Torvald?

HELMER: You can rely on me.

NORA: You mustn't think about anything else but me until after tomorrow . . . mustn't open any letters . . . mustn't touch the letter-box.

HELMER: Ah, you are still frightened of what that man might . . .

NORA: Yes, yes, I am.

HELMER: I can see from your face there's already a letter there from him.

NORA: I don't know. I think so. But you mustn't read anything like that now. We don't want anything horrid coming between us until all this is over.

RANK [*softly to Helmer*]: I shouldn't cross her.

HELMER [*puts his arm round her*]: The child must have her way. But tomorrow night, when your dance is done. . . .

NORA: Then you are free.

MAID [*in the doorway, right*]: Dinner is served, madam.

NORA: We'll have champagne, Helene.

MAID: Very good, madam.

[*She goes.*]

HELMER: Aha! It's to be quite a banquet, eh?

NORA: With champagne flowing until dawn. [*Shouts.*] And some macaroons, Helene . . . lots of them, for once in a while.

HELMER [*seizing her hands*]: Now, now, not so wild and excitable! Let me see you being my own little singing bird again.

NORA: Oh yes, I will. And if you'll just go in . . . you, too, Dr. Rank. Kristine, you must help me to do my hair.

RANK [*Softly, as they leave*]: There isn't anything . . . anything as it were, impending, is there?

HELMER: No, not at all, my dear fellow. It's nothing but these childish fears I was telling you about.

[*They go out to the right.*]

NORA: Well?

MRS. LINDE: He's left town.

NORA: I saw it in your face.

MRS. LINDE: He's coming back tomorrow evening. I left a note for him.

NORA: You shouldn't have done that. You must let things take their course. Because really it's a case for rejoicing, waiting like this for the miracle.

MRS. LINDE: What is it you are waiting for?

NORA: Oh, you wouldn't understand. Go and join the other two. I'll be there in a minute.

[*Mrs. Linde goes into the dining-room. Nora stands for a moment as though to collect herself, then looks at her watch.*]

NORA: Five. Seven hours to midnight. Then twenty-four hours till the next midnight. Then the tarantella will be over. Twenty-four and seven? Thirty-one hours to live.

HELMER [*in the doorway, right*]:   What's happened to our little sky-lark?

NORA [*running towards him with open arms*]:   Here she is!

ACT THREE

The same room. The round table has been moved to the centre of the room, and the chairs placed round it. A lamp is burning on the table. The door to the hall stands open. Dance music can be heard coming from the floor above. Mrs. Linde is sitting by the table, idly turning over the pages of a book; she tries to read, but does not seem able to concentrate. Once or twice she listens, tensely, for a sound at the front door.

MRS. LINDE [*looking at her watch*]:   Still not here. There isn't much time left. I only hope he hasn't . . . [*She listens again.*] Ah, there he is. [*She goes out into the hall, and cautiously opens the front door.*

Soft footsteps can be heard on the stairs. She whispers.] Come in. There's nobody here.

KROGSTAD [*in the doorway*]:   I found a note from you at home. What does it all mean?

MRS. LINDE: I *had* to talk to you.

KROGSTAD: Oh? And did it have to be here, in this house?

MRS. LINDE: It wasn't possible over at my place, it hasn't a separate entrance. Come in. We are quite alone. The maid's asleep and the Helmers are at a party upstairs.

KROGSTAD [*comes into the room*]:   Well, well! So the Helmers are out dancing tonight! Really?

MRS. LINDE: Yes, why not?

KROGSTAD: Why not indeed!

MRS. LINDE: Well then, Nils. Let's talk.

KROGSTAD: Have we two anything more to talk about?

MRS. LINDE: We have a great deal to talk about.

KROGSTAD: I shouldn't have thought so.

MRS. LINDE: That's because you never really understood me.

KROGSTAD: What else was there to understand, apart from the old, old story? A heartless woman throws a man over the moment something more profitable offers itself.

MRS. LINDE: Do you really think I'm so heartless? Do you think I found it easy to break it off.

KROGSTAD: Didn't you?

MRS. LINDE: You didn't really believe that?

KROGSTAD: If that wasn't the case, why did you write to me as you did?

MRS. LINDE: There was nothing else I could do. If I had to make the break, I felt in duty bound to destroy any feeling that you had for me.

KROGSTAD [*clenching his hands*]:   So that's how it was. And all that . . . was for money!

MRS. LINDE: You mustn't forget I had a helpless mother and two young brothers. We couldn't wait for you, Nils. At that time you hadn't much immediate prospect of anything.

KROGSTAD: That may be. But you had no right to throw me over for somebody else.

MRS. LINDE: Well, I don't know. Many's the time I've asked myself whether I was justified.

KROGSTAD [*more quietly*]: When I lost you, it was just as if the ground had slipped away from under my feet. Look at me now: a broken man clinging to the wreck of his life.

MRS. LINDE: Help might be near.

KROGSTAD: It was near. Then you came along and got in the way.

MRS. LINDE: Quite without knowing, Nils. I only heard today it's you I'm supposed to be replacing at the Bank.

KROGSTAD: If you say so, I believe you. But now you do know, aren't you going to withdraw?

MRS. LINDE: No, that wouldn't benefit you in the slightest.

KROGSTAD: Benefit, benefit. . . . ! I would do it just the same.

MRS. LINDE: I have learned to go carefully. Life and hard, bitter necessity have taught me that.

KROGSTAD: And life has taught me not to believe in pretty speeches.

MRS. LINDE: Then life has taught you a very sensible thing. But deeds are something you surely must believe in?

KROGSTAD: How do you mean?

MRS. LINDE: You said you were like a broken man clinging to the wreck of his life.

KROGSTAD: And I said it with good reason.

MRS. LINDE: And I am like a broken woman clinging to the wreck of her life. Nobody to care about, and nobody to care for.

KROGSTAD: It was your own choice.

MRS. LINDE: At the time there was no other choice.

KROGSTAD: Well, what of it?

MRS. LINDE: Nils, what about us two castaways joining forces.

KROGSTAD: What's that you say?

MRS. LINDE: Two of us on *one* wreck surely stand a better chance than each on his own.

KROGSTAD: Kristine!

MRS. LINDE: Why do you suppose I came to town?

KROGSTAD: You mean, you thought of me?

MRS. LINDE: Without work I couldn't live. All my life I have worked, for as long as I can remember; that has always been my one great joy. But now I'm completely alone in the world, and feeling horribly empty and forlorn. There's no pleasure in working only for yourself. Nils, give me somebody and something to work for.

KROGSTAD: I don't believe all this. It's only a woman's hysteria, wanting to be all magnanimous and self-sacrificing.

MRS. LINDE: Have you ever known me hysterical before?

KROGSTAD: Would you really do this? Tell me—do you know all about my past?

MRS. LINDE: Yes.

KROGSTAD: And you know what people think about me?

MRS. LINDE: Just now you hinted you thought you might have been a different person with me.

KROGSTAD: I'm convinced I would.

MRS. LINDE: Couldn't it still happen?

KROGSTAD: Kristine! You know what you are saying, don't you? Yes, you do. I can see you do. Have you really the courage . . . ?

MRS. LINDE: I need someone to mother, and your children need a mother. We two need each other. Nils, I have faith in what, deep down, you are. With you I can face anything.

KROGSTAD [*seizing her hands*]: Thank you, thank you, Kristine. And I'll soon have everybody looking up to me, or I'll know the reason why. Ah, but I was forgetting. . . .

MRS. LINDE: Hush! The tarantella! You must go!

KROGSTAD: Why? What is it?

MRS. LINDE: You hear that dance upstairs? When it's finished they'll be coming.

KROGSTAD: Yes, I'll go. It's too late to do anything. Of course, you know nothing about what steps I've taken against the Helmers.

MRS. LINDE: Yes, Nils, I do know.

KROGSTAD: Yet you still want to go on. . . .

MRS. LINDE: I know how far a man like you can be driven by despair.

KROGSTAD: Oh, if only I could undo what I've done!

MRS. LINDE: You still can. Your letter is still there in the box.

KROGSTAD: Are you sure?

MRS. LINDE: Quite sure. But . . .

KROGSTAD [*regards her searchingly*]: Is that how things are? You want to save your friend at any price? Tell me straight. Is that it?

MRS. LINDE: When you've sold yourself *once* for other people's sake, you don't do it again.

KROGSTAD: I shall demand my letter back.

MRS. LINDE: No, no.

KROGSTAD: Of course I will, I'll wait here till Helmer comes. I'll tell him he has to give me my letter back . . . that it's only about my notice . . . that he mustn't read it . . .

MRS. LINDE: No, Nils, don't ask for it back.

KROGSTAD: But wasn't that the very reason you got me here?

MRS. LINDE: Yes, that was my first terrified reaction. But that was yesterday, and it's quite incredible the things I've witnessed in this house in the last twenty-four hours. Helmer must know everything. This unhappy secret must come out. Those two must have the whole thing out between them. All this secrecy and deception, it just can't go on.

KROGSTAD: Well, if you want to risk it. . . . But one thing I can do, and I'll do it at once. . . .

MRS. LINDE [*listening*]: Hurry! Go, go! The dance has stopped. We aren't safe a moment longer.

KROGSTAD: I'll wait for you downstairs.

MRS. LINDE: Yes, do. You must see me home.

KROGSTAD: I've never been so incredibly happy before.

[*He goes out by the front door. The door out into the hall remains standing open.*]

MRS. LINDE [*tidies the room a little and gets her hat and coat ready*]: How things change! How things change! Somebody to work for . . . to live for. A home to bring happiness into. Just let me get down to it. . . . I wish they'd come. . . . [*Listens.*] Ah, there they are. . . . Get my things.

[*She takes her coat and hat. The voices of Helmer and Nora are heard outside. A key is turned and Helmer pushes Nora almost forcibly into the hall. She is dressed in the Italian costume, with a big black shawl over it. He is in evening dress, and over it a black cloak, open.*]

NORA [*still in the doorway, reluctantly*]: No, no, not in here! I want to go back up again. I don't want to leave so early.

HELMER: But my dearest Nora . . .

NORA: Oh, please, Torvald, I beg you. . . . *Please*, just for another hour.

HELMER: Not another minute, Nora my sweet. You remember what we agreed. There now, come along in. You'll catch cold standing there.

[*He leads her, in spite of her resistance, gently but firmly into the room.*]

MRS. LINDE: Good evening.

NORA: Kristine!

HELMER: Why, Mrs. Linde. You here so late?

MRS. LINDE: Yes. You must forgive me but I did so want to see Nora all dressed up.

NORA: Have you been sitting here waiting for me?

MRS. LINDE: Yes, I'm afraid I wasn't in time to catch you before you went upstairs. And I felt I couldn't leave again without seeing you.

HELMER [*removing Nora's shawl*]: Well take a good look at her. I think I can say she's worth looking at. Isn't she lovely, Mrs. Linde?

MRS. LINDE: Yes, I must say. . . .

HELMER: Isn't she quite extraordinarily lovely? That's what everybody at the party thought, too. But she's dreadfully stubborn . . . the sweet little thing! And what shall we do about that? Would you believe it, I nearly had to use force to get her away.

NORA: Oh Torvald, you'll be sorry you didn't let me stay, even for half an hour.

HELMER: You hear that, Mrs. Linde? She dances her tarantella, there's wild applause—which was well deserved, although the performance was perhaps rather realistic . . . I mean, rather more so than was strictly necessary from the artistic point of view. But anyway! The main thing is she was a success, a tremendous success. Was I supposed to let her stay after that? Spoil the effect? No thank you! I took my lovely little Capri girl—my capricious little Capri girl, I might say—by the arm, whisked her once round the room, a curtsey all round, and then—as they say in novels—the beautiful vision vanished. An exit should always be effective, Mrs. Linde. But I just can't get Nora to see that. Phew! It's warm in here. [*He throws his cloak over a chair and opens the door to his study.*] What? It's dark. Oh yes, of course. Excuse me. . . .

[*He goes in and lights a few candles.*]

NORA [*quickly, in a breathless whisper*]: Well?

MRS. LINDE [*Softly*]: I've spoken to him.

NORA: And . . . ?

MRS. LINDE: Nora . . . you must tell your husband everything.

NORA [*tonelessly*]: I knew it.

MRS. LINDE: You've got nothing to fear from Krogstad. But you must speak.

NORA: I won't.

MRS. LINDE: Then the letter will.

NORA: Thank you, Kristine. Now I know what's to be done. Hush . . . !

HELMER [*comes in again*]: Well, Mrs. Linde, have you finished admiring her?

MRS. LINDE: Yes. And now I must say good night.

HELMER: Oh, already? Is this yours, this knitting?

MRS. LINDE [*takes it*]: Yes, thank you. I nearly forgot it.

HELMER: So you knit, eh?

MRS. LINDE: Yes.

HELMER: You should embroider instead, you know.

MRS. LINDE: Oh? Why?

HELMER: So much prettier. Watch! You hold the embroidery like this in the left hand, and then you take the needle in the right hand, like this, and you describe a long, graceful curve. Isn't that right?

MRS. LINDE: Yes, I suppose so. . . .

HELMER: Whereas knitting on the other hand just can't help being ugly. Look! Arms pressed into the sides, the knitting needles going up and down—there's something Chinese about it. . . . Ah, that was marvellous champagne they served tonight.

MRS. LINDE: Well, good night, Nora! And stop being so stubborn.

HELMER: Well said, Mrs. Linde!

MRS. LINDE: Good night, Mr. Helmer.

HELMER [*accompanying her to the door*]: Good night, good night! You'll get home all right, I hope? I'd be only too pleased to . . . But you haven't far to walk. Good night, good night! [*She goes; he shuts the door behind her and comes in again.*] There we are, got rid of her at last. She's a frightful bore, that woman.

NORA: Aren't you very tired, Torvald?

HELMER: Not in the least.

NORA: Not sleepy?

HELMER. Not at all. On the contrary, I feel extremely lively. What about you? Yes, you look quite tired and sleepy.

NORA: Yes, I'm very tired. I just want to fall straight off to sleep.

HELMER: There you are, you see! Wasn't I right in thinking we shouldn't stay any longer?

NORA: Oh, everything you do is right.

HELMER [*kissing her forehead*]: There's my little sky-lark talking common sense. Did you notice how gay Rank was this evening?

NORA: Oh, was he? I didn't get a chance to talk to him.

HELMER: I hardly did either. But it's a long time since I saw him in such a good mood. [*Looks at Nora for a moment or two, then comes nearer her.*] Ah, it's wonderful to be back in our own home again, and quite alone with you. How irresistibly lovely you are, Nora!

NORA: Don't look at me like that, Torvald!

HELMER: Can't I look at my most treasured possession? At all this loveliness that's mine and mine alone, completely and utterly mine.

NORA [*walks round to the other side of the table*]: You mustn't talk to me like that tonight.

HELMER [*following her*]: You still have the tarantella in your blood, I see. And that makes you even more desirable. Listen! The guests are beginning to leave now. [*Softly.*] Nora . . . soon the whole house will be silent.

NORA: I should hope so.

HELMER: Of course you do, don't you, Nora my darling? You know, whenever I'm out at a party with you . . . do you know why I never talk to you very much, why I always stand away from you and only steal a quick glance at you now and then . . . do you know why I do that? It's because I'm pretending we are secretly in love, secretly engaged and nobody suspects there is anything between us.

NORA: Yes, yes. I know your thoughts are always with me, of course.

HELMER: And when it's time to go, and I lay your shawl round those shapely, young shoulders, round the exquisite curve of your neck . . . I pretend that you are my young bride, that we are just leaving our wedding, that I am taking you to our new home for the first time . . . to be alone with you for the first time . . . quite alone with your young and trembling loveliness! All evening I've been longing for you, and nothing else. And as I watched you darting and swaying in the tarantella, my blood was on fire . . . I couldn't bear it any longer . . . and that's why I brought you down here with me so early. . . .

NORA: Go away, Torvald! Please leave me alone. I won't have it.

HELMER: What's this? It's just your little game isn't it, my little Nora. Won't! Won't! Am I not your husband . . . ?

[*There is a knock on the front door.*]

NORA [*startled*]: Listen . . . !

HELMER [*going towards the hall*]: Who's there?

RANK [*outside*]: It's me. Can I come in for a minute?

HELMER [*in a low voice, annoyed*]: Oh, what does he want now? [*Aloud.*] Wait a moment. [*He walks across and opens the door.*] How nice of you to look in on your way out.

RANK: I fancied I heard your voice and I thought I would just look in. [*He takes a quick glance round.*] Ah yes, this dear, familiar old place! How cosy and comfortable you've got things here, you two.

HELMER: You seemed to be having a pretty good time upstairs yourself.

RANK: Capital! Why shouldn't I? Why not make the most of things in this world? At least as much as one can, and for as long as one can. The wine was excellent. . . .

HELMER: Especially the champagne.

RANK: You noticed that too, did you? It's incredible the amount I was able to put away.

NORA: Torvald also drank a lot of champagne this evening.

RANK: Oh?

NORA: Yes, and that always makes him quite merry.

RANK: Well, why shouldn't a man allow himself a jolly evening after a day well spent?

HELMER: Well spent? I'm afraid I can't exactly claim that.

RANK [*clapping him on the shoulder*]: But I can, you see!

NORA: Dr. Rank, am I right in thinking you carried out a certain laboratory test today?

RANK: Exactly.

HELMER: Look at our little Nora talking about laboratory tests!

NORA: And may I congratulate you on the result?

RANK: You may indeed.

NORA: So it was good?

RANK: The best possible, for both doctor and patient—certainty!

NORA [*quickly and searchingly*]: Certainty?

RANK: Absolute certainty. So why shouldn't I allow myself a jolly evening after that?

NORA: Quite right, Dr. Rank.

HELMER: I quite agree. As long as you don't suffer for it in the morning.

RANK: Well, you never get anything for nothing in this life.

NORA: Dr. Rank . . . you are very fond of masquerades, aren't you?

RANK: Yes, when there are plenty of amusing disguises. . . .

NORA: Tell me, what shall we two go as next time?

HELMER: There's frivolity, for you . . . thinking about the next time already!

RANK: We two? I'll tell you. You must go as Lady Luck. . . .

HELMER: Yes, but how do you find a costume to suggest *that?*

RANK: Your wife could simply go in her everyday clothes. . . .

HELMER: That was nicely said. But don't you know what you would be?

RANK: Yes, my dear friend, I know exactly what I shall be.

HELMER: Well?

RANK: At the next masquerade, I shall be invisible.

HELMER: That's a funny idea!

RANK: There's a big black cloak . . . haven't you heard of the cloak of invisibility? That comes right down over you, and then nobody can see you.

HELMER [*suppressing a smile*]: Of course, that's right.

RANK: But I'm clean forgetting what I came for. Helmer, give me a cigar, one of the dark Havanas.

HELMER: With the greatest of pleasure.

[*He offers his case.*]

RANK [*takes one and cuts the end off*]: Thanks.

NORA [*strikes a match*]: Let me give you a light.

RANK: Thank you. [*She holds out the match and he lights his cigar.*] And now, goodbye!

HELMER: Goodbye, goodbye, my dear fellow!

NORA: Sleep well, Dr. Rank.

RANK: Thank you for that wish.

NORA: Wish me the same.

RANK: You? All right, if you want me to. . . . Sleep well. And thanks for the light.

[*He nods to them both, and goes.*]

HELMER [*subdued*]: He's had a lot to drink.

NORA [*absently*]: Very likely.

[*Helmer takes a bunch of keys out of his pocket and goes out into the hall.*]

NORA: Torvald . . . what do you want there?

HELMER: I must empty the letter-box, it's quite full. There'll be no room for the papers in the morning. . . .

NORA: Are you going to work tonight?

HELMER: You know very well I'm not. Hello, what's this? Somebody's been at the lock.

NORA: At the lock?

HELMER: Yes, I'm sure of it. Why should that be? I'd hardly have thought the maids . . . ? Here's a broken hair-pin. Nora, it's one of yours. . . .

NORA [*quickly*]: It must have been the children. . . .

HELMER: Then you'd better tell them not to. Ah . . . there . . . I've managed to get it open. [*He takes the things out and shouts into the kitchen.*] Helene! . . . Helene, put the light out in the hall. [*He comes into the room again with the letters in his hand and shuts the hall door.*] Look how it all mounts up. [*Runs through them.*] What's this?

NORA: The letter! Oh no, Torvald, no!

HELMER: Two visiting cards . . . from Dr. Rank.

NORA: From Dr. Rank?

HELMER [*looking at them*]: Dr. Rank, Medical Practitioner. They were on top. He must have put them in as he left.

NORA: Is there anything on them?

HELMER: There's a black cross above his name. Look. What an uncanny idea. It's just as if he were announcing his own death.

NORA: He is.

HELMER: What? What do you know about it? Has he said anything to you?

NORA: Yes. He said when these cards came, he would have taken his last leave of us. He was going to shut himself up and die.

HELMER: Poor fellow! Of course I knew we couldn't keep him with us very long. But so soon. . . . And hiding himself away like a wounded animal.

NORA: When it has to happen, it's best that it should happen without words. Don't you think so, Torvald?

HELMER [*walking up and down*]: He had grown so close to us. I don't think I can imagine him gone. His suffering and his loneliness seemed almost to provide a background of dark cloud to the sunshine of our lives. Well, perhaps it's all for the best. For him at any rate. [*Pauses.*] And maybe for us as well, Nora. Now there's just the two of us. [*Puts his arms round her.*] Oh, my darling wife, I can't hold you close enough. You know, Nora . . . many's the time I wish you were threatened by some terrible danger so I could risk everything, body and soul, for your sake.

NORA [*tears herself free and says firmly and decisively*]: Now you must read your letters, Torvald.

HELMER: No, no, not tonight. I want to be with you, my darling wife.

NORA: Knowing all the time your friend is dying . . . ?

HELMER: You are right. It's been a shock to both of us. This ugly thing has come between us . . . thoughts of death and decay. We must try to free ourselves from it. Until then . . . we shall go our separate ways.

NORA [*her arms round his neck*]: Torvald . . . good night! Good night!

HELMER [*kisses her forehead*]: Goodnight, my little singing bird. Sleep well, Nora, I'll just read through my letters.

[*He takes the letters into his room and shuts the door behind him.*]

NORA [*gropes around her, wild-eyed, seizes Helmer's cloak, wraps it round herself, and whispers quickly, hoarsely, spasmodically*]: Never see him again. Never, never, never. [*Throws her shawl over her head.*] And never see the children again either. Never, never. Oh, that black icy water. Oh, that bottomless . . . ! If only it were all

over! He's got it now. Now he's reading it. Oh no, no! Not yet!
Torvald, goodbye . . . and my children. . . .

[*She rushes out in the direction of the hall; at the same moment
Helmer flings open his door and stands there with an open letter in
his hand.*]

HELMER: Nora!

NORA [*shrieks*]: Ah!

HELMER: What is this? Do you know what is in this letter?

NORA: Yes, I know. Let me go! Let me out!

HELMER [*holds her back*]: Where are you going?

NORA [*trying to tear herself free*]: You mustn't try to save me,
Torvald!

HELMER [*reels back*]: True! Is it true what he writes? How dreadful!
No, no, it can't possibly be true.

NORA: It *is* true. I loved you more than anything else in the world.

HELMER: Don't come to me with a lot of paltry excuses!

NORA [*taking a step towards him*]: Torvald . . . !

HELMER: Miserable woman . . . what is this you have done?

NORA: Let me go. I won't have you taking the blame for me. You
mustn't take it on yourself.

HELMER: Stop play-acting! [*Locks the front door.*] You are staying
here to give an account of yourself. Do you understand what you
have done? Answer me! Do you understand?

NORA [*looking fixedly at him, her face hardening*]: Yes, now I'm
really beginning to understand.

HELMER [*walking up and down*]: Oh, what a terrible awakening this
is. All these eight years . . . this woman who was my pride and joy
. . . a hypocrite, a liar, worse than that, a criminal! Oh, how utterly
squalid it all is! Ugh! Ugh! [*Nora remains silent and looks fixedly
at him.*] I should have realized something like this would happen. I
should have seen it coming. All your father's irresponsible ways. . . .
Quiet! All your father's irresponsible ways are coming out in you.
No religion, no morals, no sense of duty. . . . Oh, this is my punishment for turning a blind eye to him. It was for your sake I did it,
and this is what I get for it.

NORA: Yes, this.

HELMER: Now you have ruined my entire happiness, jeopardized my whole future. It's terrible to think of. Here I am, at the mercy of a thoroughly unscrupulous person; he can do whatever he likes with me, demand anything he wants, order me about just as he chooses . . . and I daren't even whimper. I'm done for, a miserable failure, and it's all the fault of a feather-brained woman!

NORA: When I've left this world behind, you will be free.

HELMER: Oh, stop pretending! Your father was just the same, always ready with fine phrases. What good would it do me if you left this world behind, as you put it? Not the slightest bit of good. He can still let it all come out, if he likes; and if he does, people might even suspect me of being an accomplice in these criminal acts of yours. They might even think I was the one behind it all, that it was I who pushed you into it! And it's you I have to thank for this . . . and when I've taken such good care of you, all our married life. Now do you understand what you have done to me?

NORA [*coldly and calmly*]: Yes.

HELMER: I just can't understand it, it's so incredible. But we must see about putting things right. Take that shawl off. Take it off, I tell you! I must see if I can't find some way or other of appeasing him. The thing must be hushed up at all costs. And as far as you and I are concerned, things must appear to go on exactly as before. But only in the eyes of the world, of course. In other words you'll go on living here; that's understood. But you will not be allowed to bring up the children, I can't trust you with them. . . . Oh, that I should have to say this to the woman I loved so dearly, the woman I still. . . . Well, that must be all over and done with. From now on, there can be no question of happiness. All we can do is save the bits and pieces from the wreck, preserve appearances. . . . [*The front door-bell rings. Helmer gives a start.*] What's that? So late? How terrible, supposing. . . . If he should . . . ? Hide, Nora! Say you are not well.

[*Nora stands motionless. Helmer walks across and opens the door into the hall.*]

MAID [*half dressed, in the hall*]: It's a note for Mrs. Helmer.

HELMER: Give it to me. [*He snatches the note and shuts the door.*] Yes, it's from him. You can't have it. I want to read it myself.

NORA: You read it then.

HELMER [*by the lamp*]: I hardly dare. Perhaps this is the end, for both of us. Well, I *must* know. [*He opens the note hurriedly, reads a few lines, looks at another enclosed sheet, and gives a cry of joy.*] Nora! [*Nora looks at him inquiringly.*] Nora! I must read it again. Yes, yes, it's true! I am saved! Nora, I am saved!

NORA: And me?

HELMER: You too, of course, we are both saved, you as well as me. Look, he's sent your IOU back. He sends his regrets and apologies for what he has done. . . . His luck has changed. . . . Oh, what does it matter what he says. We are saved, Nora! Nobody can do anything to you now. Oh, Nora, Nora . . . but let's get rid of this disgusting thing first. Let me see. . . . [*He glances at the IOU.*] No, I don't want to see it. I don't want it to be anything but a dream. [*He tears up the IOU and both letters, throws all the pieces into the stove and watches them burn.*] Well, that's the end of that. He said in his note you'd known since Christmas Eve. . . . You must have had three terrible days of it, Nora.

NORA: These three days haven't been easy.

HELMER: The agonies you must have gone through! When the only way out seemed to be. . . . No, let's forget the whole ghastly thing. We can rejoice and say: It's all over! It's all over! Listen to me, Nora! You don't seem to understand: it's all over! Why this grim look on your face? Oh, poor little Nora, of course I understand. You can't bring yourself to believe I've forgiven you. But I have, Nora, I swear it. I forgive you everything. I know you did what you did because you loved me.

NORA: That's true.

HELMER: You loved me as a wife should love her husband. It was simply that you didn't have the experience to judge what was the best way of going about things. But do you think I love you any the less for that; just because you don't know how to act on your own responsibility? No, no, you just lean on me, I shall give you all the advice and guidance you need. I wouldn't be a proper man if I didn't find a woman doubly attractive for being so obviously helpless. You mustn't dwell on the harsh things I said in that first moment of horror, when I thought everything was going to come crashing down about my ears. I have forgiven you, Nora, I swear it! I have forgiven you!

NORA: Thank you for your forgiveness.

[*She goes out through the door, right.*]

HELMER: No, don't go! [*He looks through the doorway.*] What are you doing in the spare room?

NORA: Taking off this fancy dress.

HELMER [*standing at the open door*]. Yes, do. You try and get some rest, and set your mind at peace again, my frightened little songbird. Have a good long sleep; you know you are safe and sound under my wing. [*Walks up and down near the door.*] What a nice, cosy little home we have here, Nora! Here you can find refuge. Here I shall hold you like a hunted dove I have rescued unscathed from the cruel talons of the hawk, and calm your poor beating heart. And that will come, gradually, Nora, believe me. Tomorrow you'll see everything quite differently. Soon everything will be just as it was before. You won't need me to keep on telling you I've forgiven you; you'll feel convinced of it in your own heart. You don't really imagine me ever thinking of turning you out, or even of reproaching you? Oh, a real man isn't made that way, you know, Nora. For a man, there's something indescribably moving and very satisfying in knowing that he has forgiven his wife—forgiven her, completely and genuinely, from the depths of his heart. It's as though it made her his property in a double sense: he has, as it were, given her a new life, and she becomes in a way both his wife and at the same time his child. That is how you will seem to me after today, helpless, perplexed little thing that you are. Don't you worry your pretty little head about anything, Nora. Just you be frank with me, and I'll take all the decisions for you. . . . What's this? Not in bed? You've changed your things?

NORA [*in her everyday dress*]: Yes, Torvald, I've changed.

HELMER: What for? It's late.

NORA: I shan't sleep tonight.

HELMER: But my dear Nora. . . .

NORA [*looks at her watch*]: It's not so terribly late. Sit down, Torvald. We two have a lot to talk about.

[*She sits down at one side of the table.*]

HELMER: Nora, what is all this? Why so grim?

NORA: Sit down. It'll take some time. I have a lot to say to you.

HELMER [*sits down at the table opposite her*]: You frighten me, Nora. I don't understand you.

NORA: Exactly. You don't understand me. And I have never understood you, either—until tonight. No, don't interrupt. I just want you to listen to what I have to say. We are going to have things out, Torvald.

HELMER: What do you mean?

NORA: Isn't there anything that strikes you about the way we two are sitting here?

HELMER: What's that?

NORA: We have now been married eight years. Hasn't it struck you this is the first time you and I, man and wife, have had a serious talk together?

HELMER: Depends what you mean by "serious."

NORA: Eight whole years—no, more, ever since we first knew each other—and never have we exchanged one serious word about serious things.

HELMER: What did you want me to do? Get you involved in worries that you couldn't possibly help me to bear?

NORA: I'm not talking about worries. I say we've never once sat down together and seriously tried to get to the bottom of anything.

HELMER: But, my dear Nora, would that have been a thing for you?

NORA: That's just it. You have never understood me . . . I've been greatly wronged, Torvald. First by my father, and then by you.

HELMER: What! Us two! The two people who loved you more than anybody?

NORA [*shakes her head*]: You two never loved me. You only thought how nice it was to be in love with me.

HELMER: But, Nora, what's this you are saying?

NORA: It's right, you know, Torvald. At home, Daddy used to tell me what he thought, then I thought the same. And if I thought differently, I kept quiet about it, because he wouldn't have liked it. He used to call me his baby doll, and he played with me as I used to play with my dolls. Then I came to live in your house. . . .

HELMER: What way is that to talk about our marriage?

NORA [*imperturbably*]: What I mean is: I passed out of Daddy's hands into yours. You arranged everything to your tastes, and I acquired the same tastes. Or I pretended to . . . I don't really know . . . I think it was a bit of both, sometimes one thing and sometimes the other. When I look back, it seems to me I have been living here like a beggar, from hand to mouth. I lived by doing tricks for you, Torvald. But that's the way you wanted it. You and Daddy did me a great wrong. It's your fault that I've never made anything of my life.

HELMER: Nora, how unreasonable . . . how ungrateful you are! Haven't you been happy here?

NORA: No, never. I thought I was, but I wasn't really.

HELMER: Not . . . not happy!

NORA: No, just gay. And you've always been so kind to me. But our house has never been anything but a play-room. I have been your doll wife, just as at home I was Daddy's doll child. And the children in turn have been my dolls. I thought it was fun when you came and played with me, just as they thought it was fun when I went and played with them. That's been our marriage, Torvald.

HELMER: There is some truth in what you say, exaggerated and hysterical though it is. But from now on it will be different. Play-time is over; now comes the time for lessons.

NORA: Whose lessons? Mine or the children's?

HELMER: Both yours and the children's, my dear Nora.

NORA: Ah, Torvald, you are not the man to teach me to be a good wife for you.

HELMER: How can you say that?

NORA: And what sort of qualifications have I to teach the children?

HELMER: Nora!

NORA: Didn't you say yourself, a minute or two ago, that you couldn't trust me with that job.

HELMER: In the heat of the moment! You shouldn't pay any attention to that.

NORA: On the contrary, you were quite right. I'm not up to it. There's another problem needs solving first. I must take steps to educate myself. You are not the man to help me there. That's something I must do on my own. That's why I'm leaving you.

HELMER [*jumps up*]: What did you say?

NORA: If I'm ever to reach any understanding of myself and the things around me, I must learn to stand alone. That's why I can't stay here with you any longer.

HELMER: Nora! Nora!

NORA: I'm leaving here at once. I dare say Kristine will put me up for tonight. . . .

HELMER: You are out of your mind! I won't let you! I forbid you!

NORA: It's no use forbidding me anything now. I'm taking with me my own personal belongings. I don't want anything of yours, either now or later.

HELMER: This is madness!

NORA: Tomorrow I'm going home—to what used to be my home, I mean. It will be easier for me to find something to do there.

HELMER: Oh, you blind, inexperienced . . .

NORA: I must set about *getting* experience, Torvald.

HELMER: And leave your home, your husband and your children? Don't you care what people will say?

NORA: That's no concern of mine. All I know is that this is necessary for *me*.

HELMER: This is outrageous! You are betraying your most sacred duty.

NORA: And what do you consider to be my most sacred duty?

HELMER: Does it take me to tell you that? Isn't it your duty to your husband and your children?

NORA: I have another duty equally sacred.

HELMER: You have not. What duty might *that* be?

NORA: My duty to myself.

HELMER: First and foremost, you are a wife and mother.

NORA: That I don't believe any more. I believe that first and foremost I am an individual, just as much as you are—or at least I'm going to try to be. I know most people agree with you, Torvald, and that's also what it says in books. But I'm not content any more with what most people say, or with what it says in books. I have to think things out for myself, and get things clear.

HELMER: Surely you are clear about your position in your own home? Haven't you an infallible guide in questions like these? Haven't you your religion?

NORA: Oh, Torvald, I don't really know what religion is.

HELMER: What do you say!

NORA: All I know is what Pastor Hansen said when I was confirmed. He said religion was this, that and the other. When I'm away from all this and on my own, I'll go into that, too. I want to find out whether what Pastor Hansen told me was right—or at least whether it's right for *me*.

HELMER: This is incredible talk from a young woman! But if religion cannot keep you on the right path, let me at least stir your conscience. I suppose you do have some moral sense? Or tell me—perhaps you don't?

NORA: Well, Torvald, that's not easy to say. I simply don't know. I'm really very confused about such things. All I know is my ideas about such things are very different from yours. I've also learnt that the law is different from what I thought; but I simply can't get it into my head that that particular law is right. Apparently a woman has no right to spare her old father on his death-bed, or to save her husband's life, even. I just don't believe it.

HELMER: You are talking like a child. You understand nothing about the society you live in.

NORA: No, I don't. But I shall go into that too. I must try to discover who is right, society or me.

HELMER: You are ill, Nora. You are delirious. I'm half inclined to think you are out of your mind.

NORA: Never have I felt so calm and collected as I do tonight.

HELMER: Calm and collected enough to leave your husband and children?

NORA: Yes.

HELMER: Then only one explanation is possible.

NORA: And that is?

HELMER: You don't love me any more.

NORA: Exactly.

HELMER: Nora! Can you say that!

NORA: I'm desperately sorry, Torvald. Because you have always been so kind to me. But I can't help it. I don't love you any more.

HELMER [*struggling to keep his composure*]: Is that also a "calm and collected" decision you've made?

NORA: Yes, absolutely calm and collected. That's why I don't want to stay here.

HELMER: And can you also account for how I forfeited your love?

NORA: Yes, very easily. It was tonight, when the miracle didn't happen. It was then I realized you weren't the man I thought you were.

HELMER: Explain yourself more clearly. I don't understand.

NORA: For eight years I have been patiently waiting. Because, heavens, I knew miracles didn't happen every day. Then this devastating business started, and I became absolutely convinced the miracle *would* happen. All the time Krogstad's letter lay there, it never so much as crossed my mind that you would ever submit to that man's conditions. I was absolutely convinced you would say to him: Tell the whole wide world if you like. And when that was done . . .

HELMER: Yes, then what? After I had exposed my own wife to dishonour and shame . . . !

NORA: When that was done, I was absolutely convinced you would come forward and take everything on yourself, and say: I am the guilty one.

HELMER: Nora!

NORA: You mean I'd never let you make such a sacrifice for my sake? Of course not. But what would my story have counted for against yours?—That was the miracle I went in hope and dread of. It was to prevent it that I was ready to end my life.

HELMER: I would gladly toil day and night for you, Nora, enduring all manner of sorrow and distress. But nobody sacrifices his *honour* for the one he loves.

NORA: Hundreds and thousands of women have.

HELMER: Oh, you think and talk like a stupid child.

NORA: All right. But you neither think nor talk like the man I would want to share my life with. When you had got over your fright— and you weren't concerned about me but only about what might happen to you—and when all danger was past, you acted as though nothing had happened. I was your little sky-lark again, your little doll, exactly as before; except you would have to protect it twice as carefully as before, now that it had shown itself to be so weak and fragile. [*Rises.*] Torvald, that was the moment I realised that for eight years I'd been living with a stranger, and had borne him three children. . . . Oh, I can't bear to think about it! I could tear myself to shreds.

HELMER [*sadly*]: I see. I see. There is a tremendous gulf dividing us. But, Nora, is there no way we might bridge it?

NORA: As I am now, I am no wife for you.

HELMER: I still have it in me to change.

NORA: Perhaps . . . if you have your doll taken away.

HELMER: And be separated from you! No, no, Nora, the very thought of it is inconceivable.

NORA [*goes into the room, right*]: All the more reason why it must be done.

[*She comes back with her outdoor things and a small travelling bag which she puts on the chair beside the table.*]

HELMER: Nora, Nora, not now! Wait till the morning.

NORA [*putting on her coat*]: I can't spend the night in a strange man's room.

HELMER: Couldn't we go on living here like brother and sister . . . ?

NORA [*tying on her hat*]: You know very well that wouldn't last. [*She draws the shawl round her.*] Goodbye, Torvald. I don't want to see the children. I know they are in better hands than mine. As I am now, I can never be anything to them.

HELMER: But some day, Nora, some day . . . ?

NORA: How should I know? I've no idea what I might turn out to be.

HELMER: But you are my wife, whatever you are.

NORA: Listen, Torvald, from what I've heard, when a wife leaves her husband's house as I am doing now, he is absolved by law of all responsibility for her. I can at any rate free you from all responsibility. You must not feel in any way bound, any more than I shall. There must be full freedom on both sides. Look, here's your ring back. Give me mine.

HELMER: That too?

NORA: That too.

HELMER: There it is.

NORA: Well, that's the end of that. I'll put the keys down here. The maids know where everything is in the house—better than I do, in fact. Kristine will come in the morning after I've left to pack up the few things I brought with me from home. I want them sent on.

HELMER: The end! Nora, will you never think of me?

NORA: I dare say I'll often think about you and the children and this house.

HELMER: May I write to you, Nora?

NORA: No, never. I won't let you.

HELMER: But surely I can send you . . .

NORA: Nothing, nothing.

HELMER: Can't I help you if ever you need it?

NORA: I said "no." I don't accept things from strangers.

HELMER: Nora, can I never be anything more to you than a stranger?

NORA [*takes her bag*]: Ah, Torvald, only by a miracle of miracles. . . .

HELMER: Name it, this miracle of miracles!

NORA: Both you and I would have to change to the point where . . . Oh, Torvald, I don't believe in miracles any more.

HELMER: But I *will* believe. Name it! Change to the point where . . . ?

NORA: Where we could make a real marriage of our lives together. Goodbye!

[*She goes out through the hall door.*]

HELMER [*sinks down on a chair near the door, and covers his face with his hands*]: Nora! Nora! [*He rises and looks round.*] Empty! She's gone! [*With sudden hope.*] The miracle of miracles . . . ?

[*The heavy sound of a door being slammed is heard from below.*]

—*1879*

Gwen Pharis Ringwood (1910–1984) was born in Anatone in the state of Washington but moved at the age of three to a farm in southern Alberta. She studied both at the University of Montana and the University of Alberta, graduating with a B.A. in 1934. She worked for Elizabeth Sterling Haynes, co-founder of the Banff School of the Theatre, and it was there that her first stage play, The Dragons of Kent, *was produced in 1935. A Rockefeller Fellowship took her to the University of North Carolina where a number of "folk" plays, including her famous one-act work,* Still Stands the House, *and* Pasque Flower *(developed into her first full-length play,* Dark Harvest*), were first produced by the Carolina Playmakers. In 1939, Pharis married Dr. J. B. Ringwood and moved to northern Saskatchewan, and in 1941 she received the Governor General's Award for her outstanding service to Canadian drama. She continued to write plays representing the life of the regions in which she lived, including* A Fine Coloured Easter Egg *(1948), a Native trilogy entitled* Drum Song, *a musical, and several plays for children. In 1968, she moved to Williams Lake, British Columbia, where she continued to write and teach, and where the Gwen Pharis Ringwood Civic Theatre was opened in her honour. In addition to the prize-winning* Still Stands the House, *which was widely performed and anthologized, she wrote more than sixty plays, including* A Remembrance of Miracles *(1976) and* The Garage Sale *(1981). Her* Collected Plays *were published in 1982, and she died of cancer in 1984.*

Gwen Pharis Ringwood
Still Stands the House

CAST OF CHARACTERS

Ruth Warren
Arthur Manning
Hester Warren
Bruce Warren

Scene: *A living room.*

The icy wind of a northern blizzard sweeps across the prairie, lashes about the old Warren farmhouse, and howls insistently at the door and windows. But the Warren house was built to withstand the menace of the Canadian winter and scornfully suffers the storm to shriek about the chimney corner, to knock at the door and rattle the windows in a wild attempt to force an entrance.

The living-room of this house has about it a faded austerity, a decayed elegance that is as remote and cheerless as a hearth in which no fire is ever laid. The room has made a stern and solemn pact with the past. Once it held the warm surge of life: but as the years have gone by, it has settled in a rigid pattern of neat, uncompromising severity.

As if in defiance of the room, the frost has covered the window in the rear wall with a wild and exotic design. Beside the window is an imposing leather armchair, turned toward the handsome coal stove in the Right corner. A footstool is near the chair. A door at the Centre of the rear wall leads to the snow-sheeted world outside. Along the Left wall, between a closed door to a bedroom (now unused) and an open door to the kitchen, is a mahogany sideboard. Above it is a portrait of old Martin Warren, who built this house and lived in it until his death. The portrait is of a stern and handsome man in his early fifties, and in the expression of the eyes the artist has caught something of his unconquerable will.

An open staircase, winding to the bedrooms upstairs, extends into the room at Right. There is a rocking chair by the stove with a small stand-table beside it. A mahogany dining table and two matching chairs are placed at a convenient distance from the side-board and the kitchen door. The figured wall paper is cracked and faded. The dark rug, the heavy curtains, and the tablecloth show signs of much wear, but there is nothing of cheapness about them.

Two coal oil lanterns have been left beside the kitchen door. Blooming bravely on the table, in contrast to its surroundings, is a pot of lavender hyacinths.

(Ruth Warren is standing near the outside door, talking to Arthur Manning, who is about to leave. Ruth is small, fair-haired, and pretty, twenty-five or twenty-six years of age. There is more strength in her than her rather delicate appearance would indicate. She wears a soft blue house-dress, with a light wool cardigan over it. Manning is a middle-aged man of prosperous appearance. He wears a heavy overcoat over a dark business suit. His hat, gloves and scarf are on the armchair.)

RUTH: Do you think you'd better try to go back tonight, Mr. Manning? The roads may be drifted.

MANNING: It's a bad blizzard, all right, but I don't think I'll have any trouble. There's a heater in the car, and I've just had the engine checked over.

RUTH: You'll be welcome if you care to spend the night.

MANNING: Thank you, but I'm afraid I've got to get back to town. I'd hate to try it in an old car, but this one of mine can pull through anything.

RUTH: I've never seen a storm come up so quickly.

MANNING: These prairie blizzards are no joke. One of my sheep-herders got lost in one last year, just half a mile from the house. He froze to death out there trying to find his way.

RUTH: How frightful!

MANNING: One of the ranch hands found him the next morning. Poor old fellow—he'd herded for me for twenty years. I never knew how he came to be out in a storm like that.

RUTH: They say when a person gets lost he begins to go round in a circle, although it seems straight ahead.

MANNING: Yes, I've always heard that. The winters are the one thing I've got against this country.

RUTH *(Wistfully)*: I used to like them in town. We went skating on the river and tobogganing. But out here it's different.

MANNING: If Bruce sells the farm and takes this irrigated place near town, you won't notice the winter so much, Mrs. Warren.

RUTH: No. I hope he does take your offer, Mr. Manning. I want him to.

MANNING: He'll never get a better. Five thousand dollars and an irri-gated quarter is a good price for a dryland farm these days.

RUTH: If only we didn't have to decide so soon.

MANNING: I talked it all over with Bruce in town a couple of weeks ago, and I think he's pretty well made up his mind. All he needs to do is sign the papers.

RUTH: I thought he'd have until spring to decide.

MANNING: I've got orders to close the deal before I go South next week. You tell Bruce I'll come by tomorrow or the next day, and we can get it all settled.

RUTH: I'll tell him. I hope he does take it, Mr. Manning.

MANNING: I know you do and you're right. I think all he needs is a little persuading. He's had a hard time here these dry years.

RUTH: I don't know what Hester will say.

MANNING: I understand she's very much attached to the place. Is it true that she never leaves the farm?

RUTH: Not often.

MANNING: She'd be better off where she could get out more.

RUTH: I don't know.

MANNING: I suppose all those years out here, keeping house for Bruce and her father, were pretty hard on her.

RUTH: The house has come to mean so much to her. But maybe she won't mind. (*Smiling hopefully.*) We'll see.

The door to the bedroom, Left, is opened quietly, and Hester Warren enters the room. She closes and locks the door behind her and stands looking at the two in the room with cold surmise. Hester is forty years old. She is tall, dark and unsmiling. The stern rigidity of her body, the bitter austerity of her mouth, and the almost arrogant dignity of her carriage seem to make her a part of the room she enters. There is bitter resentment in her dark eyes as she confronts Ruth and Manning. She holds a leather-bound Bible close to her breast.

RUTH *(Startled)*: Why, Hester! I thought you never unlocked that door.

HESTER *(Quietly)*: No. I keep Father's room as it was.

RUTH: Then why were you—

HESTER: I was reading in Father's room. I heard a stranger.

RUTH: You know Mr. Manning, Hester.

MANNING *(With forced friendliness)*: I don't suppose you remember me, Miss Warren.

HESTER *(Without moving)*: How do you do?

MANNING *(Embarrassed at her coldness and anxious to get away)*: Well, I'll be getting on home. I'll leave these papers for Bruce to sign, Mrs. Warren. Tell him I'll come by tomorrow. He'll find it's all there, just as we talked about it. (*He lays the document on the table.*)

RUTH: Thank you, Mr. Manning.

MANNING *(Turning to go)*:   Take care of yourselves. Good-night. *(To Hester.)* Good-night, Miss Warren.

(Hester barely nods.)

RUTH: You're sure you ought to try it in the storm?

MANNING: Sure. There's no danger if I go right away. *(He goes out.)*

RUTH *(Calling after him as she shuts the door)*:   Good-night.

(Hester watches Manning out and, as Ruth returns, she looks at her suspiciously. There is a silence which Hester finally breaks.)

HESTER: What did he want here?

RUTH *(Uncomfortable under Hester's scrutiny)*:   He just left some papers for Bruce to look over, Hester. He was in a hurry so he didn't wait to see Bruce.

HESTER: I see. What has Arthur Manning got to do with Bruce?

RUTH: It's something to do with the farm, Hester. I'll put these away. *(She starts to take up the document on the table, but Hester is before her.)*

HESTER *(After a long look at the document)*:   A deed of sale. *(Turning angrily upon Ruth.)* So this is what you've been hiding from me.

RUTH *(Quickly)*:   Oh, no! Nothing's settled, Hester. Mr. Manning made an offer, and Bruce wants to think it over. That's all.

HESTER *(Her eyes betraying her intense agitation)*:   Bruce isn't going to sell this place!

RUTH: It's just an offer. Nothing has been decided.

HESTER: Your hand's in this! You've been after him to leave here.

RUTH *(Trying to conciliate her)*:   Let's not quarrel. You can talk to Bruce about it, Hester.

HESTER: You hate this house, I know that.

RUTH: No. *(Facing Hester firmly.)* But I think Bruce ought to sell.

HESTER: You married him. You made your choice.

RUTH *(Quietly)*:   I've not regretted that. It's just that we're so cut off and lonely here; and this is the best offer we could get. But let me put these away. *(Indicating the deed of sale.)* We'll talk about it later, the three of us.

HESTER *(Allowing Ruth to take the papers)*:   You may as well burn them. He isn't going to sell.

RUTH: Please, Hester—we'll discuss it when Bruce comes. *(She places the document on the sideboard, then crosses to the stove.)* I'll build up the fire.

HESTER *(Takes the Bible to the sideboard and places it under her father's portrait. She stands looking up at the portrait)*: This house will not be sold. I won't allow it.

RUTH *(Puts some coal on the fire. Shivering)*: It's so cold it almost frightens me. The thermometer has dropped ten degrees within the hour.

HESTER: I hope Bruce knows enough to get the stock in. They'll freeze where they stand if they're left out tonight. *(She moves to the window and takes her knitting from the ledge.)*

RUTH: He'll have them in. *(Crossing to the table.)* Look, Hester, how the hyacinths have bloomed. I could smell them when I came in the room just now.

HESTER: Hyacinths always seem like death to me.

RUTH *(Her voice is young and vibrant)*: Oh, no. They're birth, they're spring! They say in Greece you find them growing wild in April. *(She takes an old Wedgwood bowl from the sideboard, preparing to set the pot of hyacinths in it.)*

HESTER *(In a dry, unfriendly tone)*: I've asked you not to use that Wedgwood bowl. It was my grandmother's. I don't want it broken.

RUTH: I'm sorry. *(Replacing the bowl, she gets a plain one from inside the sideboard.)* I thought the hyacinths would look so pretty in it, but I'll use the plain one.

HESTER: You've gone to as much trouble for that plant as if it were a child. *(Hester sits in the rocking chair by the stove.)*

RUTH *(Placing the hyacinths in the bowl)*: They're so sweet. I like to touch them.

HESTER: They'll freeze tonight, I'm thinking.

RUTH: Not in here. We'll have to keep the fire up anyway. *(Leaving the bowl of hyacinths on the table, Ruth returns to the sideboard, taking some bright chintz from the drawer. She holds it up for Hester to see.)* I've almost finished the curtains, Hester.

HESTER *(Tonelessly)*: You have?

RUTH: Don't you think they'll make this room more cheerful?

HESTER: The ones we have seem good enough to me.

RUTH: But they're so old.

HESTER *(Coldly)*:   Old things have beauty when you've eyes to see it. That velvet has a richness that you can't buy now.

RUTH *(Moving to the window)*:   I want to make the room gay and happy for the spring. You'll see how much difference these will make.

HESTER: I've no doubt. *(Hester rises and goes to the table to avoid looking at the curtains.)*

RUTH *(Measuring the chintz with the curtains at the window)*:   I wonder if I have them wide enough.

(The Wind rises.)

(As if the sound had quelled her pleasure in the bright curtains, Ruth turns slowly away from the window. A touch of hysteria creeps into her voice.) The wind swirls and shrieks and raises such queer echoes in this old house! It seems to laugh at us in here, thinking we're safe, hugging the stove! As if it knew it could blow out the light and the fire and— *(Getting hold of herself.)* I've never seen a blizzard when it was as cold as this. Have you, Hester?

HESTER *(Knitting)*:   Bruce was born on a night like this.

(Throughout this scene Hester seldom looks at Ruth but gives all her attention to her knitting. She seems reluctant to talk and yet impelled to do so.)

RUTH: I didn't know.

HESTER: Father had to ride for the doctor while I stayed here with Mother.

RUTH: Alone?

HESTER: Yes. I was rubbing Father's hands with snow when we heard the baby crying. Then we helped the doctor bathe him.

RUTH: You were such a little girl to do so much.

HESTER: After Mother died I did it all.

RUTH: I know, but it was too hard for a child. I don't see how you managed.

HESTER: Father always helped me with the washing.

RUTH: Not many men would stay in from the field to do that.

HESTER: No. *(Her knitting drops to her lap, and for a moment she is lost in the past.)* "We'll have to lean on one another now,

Daughter."—Those were his words.—And that's the way it was. I was beside him until—I never left him.

RUTH *(At Hester's side)*: You've never talked of him like this before.

HESTER *(Unconscious of Ruth)*: He always liked the snow. *(Her eyes are on the portrait of her father.)* He called it a moving shroud, a winding-sheet that the wind lifts and raises and lets fall again.

RUTH: It is like that.

HESTER: He'd come in and say, "The snow lies deep on the summer fallow, Hester. That means a good crop next year."

RUTH: I know. It's glorious in the fall with the wheat like gold on the hills. No wonder he loved it.

HESTER *(Called out of her dream, she abruptly resumes her knitting)*: There hasn't been much wheat out there these last years.

RUTH: That isn't Bruce's fault, Hester.

HESTER: You have to love a place to make things grow. The land knows when you don't care about it, and Bruce doesn't care about it any more. Not like Father did.

RUTH *(Her hands raised to touch the portrait above the sideboard)*: I wish I'd known your father.

HESTER *(Rising and facing Ruth with a sudden and terrible anger)*: Don't touch that picture. It's mine.

RUTH *(Startled, she faces Hester)*: Why, Hester—

HESTER: Can't I have anything of my own? Must you put your fingers on everything I have?

RUTH *(Moving to Hester)*: Hester, you know I didn't mean—What is the matter with you?

HESTER: I won't have you touch it.

RUTH *(Gently)*: Do you hate my being here so much?

HESTER *(Turning away)*: You've more right here than I have now, I suppose.

RUTH *(Crossing over to the stove)*: You make me feel that I've no right at all.

HESTER *(A martyr now)*: I'm sorry if you don't approve my ways. I can go, if that's what you want.

RUTH *(Pleading)*: Please—I've never had a sister, and when Bruce told me he had one, I thought we'd be such friends—

HESTER *(Sitting in the chair by the stove)*: We're not a family to put words to everything we feel. *(She resumes her knitting.)*

RUTH *(Trying to bridge the gulf between them)*: I get too excited over things: I know it. Bruce tells me I sound affected when I say too much about the way I feel, the way I like people—or the sky in the evening. I—

HESTER *(Without looking up)*: Did you get the separator put up? Or shall I do it?

RUTH *(Discouraged, Ruth turns away, and going to the table, sits down with her sewing)*: It's ready for the milk when Bruce brings it. I put it together this morning.

HESTER: The lanterns are empty.

RUTH: I'll fill them in a minute.

HESTER: When I managed this house, I always filled the lanterns right after supper. Then they were ready.

RUTH *(Impatiently)*: I said I'd fill them, Hester, and I will. They're both there in the corner. *(She indicates the lanterns at the end of the sideboard.)*

HESTER: Bruce didn't take one, then?

RUTH: No.

HESTER: You'd better put a lamp in the window.

RUTH *(Lights a small lamp on the sideboard and takes it to the window)*: I wish he'd come. It's strange how women feel safer when their men are near, close enough to touch, isn't it? No matter how strong you think you are. *(As she speaks, Ruth drapes some of the chintz over the armchair.)*

HESTER: I can't say that I need my strength from Bruce, or could get it if I needed it.

RUTH: That's because he's still a little boy to you. *(A pause. Then Ruth speaks hesitantly.)* Hester—

HESTER: Yes?

RUTH: Will you mind the baby in the house?

HESTER *(After a silence, constrainedly)*: No, I won't mind. I'll keep out of the way.

RUTH *(Warmly, commanding a response)*: I don't want you to. You'll love him, Hester.

HESTER *(Harshly)*: I loved Bruce, but I got no thanks for it. He feels I stand in his way now.

RUTH *(Suddenly aware that Hester has needed and wanted love)*: You mustn't say that. It isn't true.

HESTER: When he was little, after Mother died, he'd come tugging at my hand—He'd get hold of my little finger and say, "Come, Hettie—come and look." Everything was "Hettie" then.

RUTH *(Eagerly, moving to Hester)*: It will be like that again. This baby will be almost like your own.

HESTER *(As if Ruth's words were an implied reproach)*: I could have married, and married well if I'd had a mind to.

RUTH: I know that. I've wondered why you didn't, Hester.

HESTER: The young men used to ride over here on Sunday, but I stopped that. *(A pause.)* I never saw a man I'd let touch me. Maybe you don't mind that kind of thing. I do.

RUTH *(Involuntarily; it is a cry)*: No! *(Attempting to put her arms around Hester.)* What hurt you?

HESTER *(Rising)*: Don't try your soft ways on me. *(She moves behind the armchair, her hand falls caressingly on the back of the chair.)* I couldn't leave Bruce and Father here alone. My duty was here in this house. So I stayed. *(Hester notices the chintz material draped over the chair and, taking it up, turns to Ruth angrily.)* What do you intend to do with this?

RUTH: I thought—there's enough left to make covers for the chair to match the curtains—

HESTER *(Throwing the chintz down)*: This is Father's chair. I won't have it changed.

RUTH: I'm sorry, Hester. *(With spirit.)* Must we keep everything the same forever?

HESTER: There's nothing in this house that isn't good, that wasn't bought with care and pride by one of us who loved it. This stuff is cheap and gaudy.

RUTH: It isn't dull and falling apart with age.

HESTER: Before my father died, when he was ill, he sat here in this chair where he could see them threshing from the window. It was the first time since he came here that he'd not been in the fields at harvest. Now you come—you who never knew him, who never saw him—and you won't rest until—

RUTH: Hester!

HESTER: You've got no right to touch it! *(Her hands grip the back of the old chair as she stands rigid, her eyes blazing.)*

(Bruce Warren enters from outside, carrying a pail of milk. He is tall and dark, about thirty years old, sensitive and bitter. His vain struggle to make the farm pay since his father's death has left him with an oppressive sense of failure. He is proud and quick to resent an imagined reproach. He has dark hair, his shoulders are a little stooped, and he moves restlessly and abruptly. Despite his moodiness, he is extremely likeable. He is dressed warmly in dark trousers, a sweater under his heavy leather coat; he wears gloves, cap and high boots. He brushes the snow from his coat as he enters.)

BRUCE *(Carrying the milk into the kitchen)*:   Is the separator up, Ruth?

RUTH: Yes, it's all ready, Bruce. Wait, I'll help you. *(She follows him into the kitchen.)*

(Hester stands at the chair a moment after they have gone; her eyes fall on the plant on the table. Slowly she goes toward it, as if drawn by something she hated. She looks down at the lavender blooms for a moment. Then with a quick, angry gesture, she crushes one of the stalks. She turns away and is winding up her wool when Bruce and Ruth return.)

You must be frozen.

BRUCE *(Taking off his coat and gloves)*:   I'm cold, all right. God, it's a blizzard: thirty-eight below, and a high wind. *(He throws his coat over a chair at the table.)*

RUTH *(With pride)*:   Did you see the hyacinths? They've bloomed since yesterday.

BRUCE *(Smiling)*:   Yes, they're pretty. *(Touching them, he notices the broken stalk.)* Looks like one of them's broken.

RUTH: Where? *(She sees it.)* Oh, it is! And that one hadn't bloomed yet! I wonder—It wasn't broken when I— *(Ruth turns accusingly to Hester.)* Hester!

HESTER *(Returns look calmly. Coldly)*:   Yes?

RUTH: Hester, did you—

BRUCE *(Going over to the fire)*:   Oh, Ruth, don't make such a fuss about it. It can't be helped.

HESTER: I'll take care of the milk. *(She takes the small lamp from the window.)*

RUTH: I'll do it.

HESTER *(Moving toward the kitchen)*: You turn the separator so slow the cream's as thin as water.

RUTH *(Stung to reply)*: That's not true. You never give me a chance to—

BRUCE *(Irritably)*: For God's sake, don't quarrel about it. *(He sits in the chair by the stove.)*

HESTER: I don't intend to quarrel. *(She goes into the kitchen.)*

(Ruth follows Hester to the door. The sound of the separator comes from the kitchen. Ruth turns wearily, takes up the pot of hyacinths, and places them on the stand near the stove. Then sits on the footstool.)

RUTH: It's always that way.

BRUCE *(Gazing moodily at the stove)*: Why don't you two try to get along?

(A silence.)

RUTH: Did you put the stock in? *(The question is merely something to fill the empty space of silence between them.)*

BRUCE: Yes. That black mare may foal tonight. I'll have to look at her later on.

RUTH: It's bitter weather for a little colt to be born.

BRUCE: Yes.

(Another silence. Finally Ruth, to throw off the tension between them, gets up and moves her footstool over to his chair.)

RUTH: I'm glad you're here. I've been lonesome for you.

BRUCE *(Putting his hand on hers)*: I'm glad to be here.

RUTH: I thought of you out at the barn, trying to work in this cold.

BRUCE: I was all right. I'd hate to walk far tonight, though. You can't see your hand before your face.

RUTH *(After a look at the kitchen)*: Hester's been so strange again these last few days, Bruce.

BRUCE: I know it's hard, Ruth.

RUTH: It's like it was when I first came here. At everything I touch, she cries out like I'd hurt her somehow.

BRUCE:　Hester has to do things her own way. She's always been like that.

RUTH:　If only she could like me a little. I think she almost does sometimes, but then—

BRUCE:　You think too much about her

RUTH:　Maybe it's because we've been shut in so close. I'm almost afraid of her lately.

BRUCE:　She's not had an easy life, Ruth.

RUTH:　I know that. She's talked about your father almost constantly today.

BRUCE:　His death hit us both hard. Dad ran the farm, decided everything.

RUTH:　It's been six years, Bruce.

BRUCE:　There are things you don't count out by years.

RUTH:　He wouldn't want you to go on remembering forever.

BRUCE *(Looking at the floor)*:　No.

RUTH:　You should get free of this house. It's not good for you to stay here. It's not good for Hester. *(Getting up, she crosses to the sideboard and returns with the deed of sale, which she hands to Bruce.)* Mr. Manning left this for you. He's coming back tomorrow for it, when you've signed it.

BRUCE *(Takes the papers. Annoyed by her assurance)*:　He doesn't need to get so excited. I haven't decided to sign yet. He said he wouldn't need to know till spring. *(He goes over to the lamp at the table and studies the document.)*

RUTH:　His company gave him orders to close the deal this week or let it go.

BRUCE:　This week?

RUTH:　That's what he said.

BRUCE:　Well. I'll think about it.

RUTH:　You'll have to decide tonight, Bruce. No one else will offer you as much. Five thousand dollars and an irrigated farm a mile from town seems a good price.

BRUCE:　I'm not complaining about the deal. It's fair.

RUTH *(Urgently)*:　You're going to take it, aren't you, Bruce?

BRUCE:　I don't know. God, I don't know. *(He throws the document on the table.)* I don't want to sell, Ruth. I think I'll try it another year.

RUTH: Bruce, you've struggled here too long now. You haven't had a crop, a good crop, in five years.

BRUCE: I need to be told that!

RUTH: It's not your fault. But you've told me you ought to give it up, that it's too dry here.

BRUCE: We may get a crop this year. We're due for one.

RUTH: If you take this offer, we'll be nearer town. We'll have water on the place. We can have a garden, and trees growing.

BRUCE: That's about what those irrigated farms are—gardens.

RUTH: And, Bruce, it wouldn't be so lonely there, so cruelly lonely.

BRUCE: I told you how it was before you came.

RUTH *(Resenting his tone)*: You didn't tell me you worshipped a house. That you made a god of a house and a section of land. You didn't tell me that!

BRUCE *(Angrily)*: You didn't tell me that you'd moon at a window for your old friends, either. *(He stands up and throws the deed of sale on the table.)*

RUTH: How could I help it here?

BRUCE: And you didn't tell me you'd be afraid of having a child. What kind of a woman are you that you don't want your child?

RUTH: That's not true.

BRUCE: No? You cried when you knew, didn't you?

RUTH: Bruce!

BRUCE *(Going blindly on)*: What makes you feel the way you do, then? Other women have children without so much fuss. Other women are glad.

RUTH *(Intensely angry)*: Don't speak to me like that. Keep your land. Eat and sleep and dream land, I don't care!

BRUCE *(Turning to the portrait of his father)*: My father came out here and took a homestead. He broke the prairie with one plough and a team of horses. He built a house to live in out of the sod. You didn't know that, did you? He and Mother lived here in a sod shanty and struggled to make things grow. Then they built a one-roomed shack; and when the good years came, they built this house. The finest in the country! I thought my son would have it.

RUTH *(Moving to him)*: What is there left to give a son? A house that stirs with ghosts! A piece of worn-out land where the rain never comes.

BRUCE: That's not all. I don't suppose you can understand.

RUTH *(Turning away from him, deeply hurt)*: No. I don't suppose I can. You give me little chance to know how you feel about things.

BRUCE *(His anger gone)*: Ruth, I didn't mean that. But you've always lived in town. *(He goes to the window and stands looking out for a moment, then turns.)* Those rocks along the fence out there, I picked up every one of them with my own hands and carried them with my own hands across the field and piled them there. I've ploughed that southern slope along the coulee every year since I was twelve. *(His voice is torn with a kind of shame for his emotion.)* I feel about the land like Hester does about the house, I guess. I don't want to leave it. I don't want to give it up.

RUTH *(Gently)*: But it's poor land, Bruce.

(Bruce sits down, gazing gloomily at the fire, Hester comes in from the kitchen with the small lamp and places it on the sideboard. Then she sits at the table, taking up her knitting. As Bruce speaks, she watches him intently.)

BRUCE: Yes, it's strange that in a soil that won't grow trees a man can put roots down, but he can.

RUTH *(At his side)*: You'd feel the same about another place, after a little while.

BRUCE: I don't know. When I saw the wind last spring blowing the dirt away, the dirt I'd ploughed and harrowed and sowed to grain, I felt as though a part of myself was blowing away in the dust. Even now, with the land three feet under snow, I can look out and feel it waiting for the seed I've saved for it.

RUTH: But if we go, we'll be nearer other people, not cut off from everything that lives.

BRUCE: You need people, don't you?

HESTER: Yes. She needs them. I've seen her at the window looking toward the town. Day after day she stands there.

(Bruce and Ruth, absorbed in the conflict between them, had forgotten Hester's presence. At Hester's words, Ruth turns on them both, flaming with anger.)

RUTH: You two. You're so *perfect!*

HESTER *(Knitting)*: We could always stand alone, the three of us. We didn't need to turn to every stranger who held his hand out.

RUTH: No! You'd sit in this husk of a house, living like shadows, until these four walls closed in on you, buried you.

HESTER: I never stood at a window, looking down the road that leads to town.

RUTH *(The pent-up hysteria of the day and the longing of months breaks through, tumbling out in her words)*: It's not for myself I look down that road, Hester. It's for the child I'm going to have. You're right, Bruce. I am afraid. It's not what you think, though, not for myself. You two and your father lived so long in this dark house that you forgot there's a world beating outside, forgot that people laugh and play sometimes. And you've shut me out! *(There is a catch in her voice.)* I never would have trampled on your thoughts if you'd given them to me. But as it is, I might as well not be a person. You'd like a shadow better that wouldn't touch your house. A child would die here. A child can't live with shadows.

BRUCE *(Much disturbed, Bruce rises and goes to her)*: Ruth! I didn't know you hated it so much.

RUTH: I thought it would change. I thought I could change it. You know now.

BRUCE *(Quietly)*: Yes.

RUTH *(Pleading)*: If we go, I'll *want* this child, Bruce. Don't you see? But I'm not happy here. What kind of a life will our child have? He'll be old before he's out of school. *(She looks at the hyacinth on the stand.)* He'll be like this hyacinth that's broken before it bloomed.

BRUCE *(Goes to the table and stands looking down at the deed of sale. His voice is tired and flat, but resolved)*: All right. I'll tell Manning I'll let him have the place.

HESTER *(Turning quickly to Bruce)*: What do you mean?

BRUCE: I'm going to sell the farm to Manning. He was here today.

HESTER *(Standing up, her eyes blazing)*: You can't sell this house.

BRUCE *(Looking at the deed of sale)*: Oh, Ruth's right. We can't make a living on the place. *(He sits down, leafing through the document.)* It's too dry. And too far from school.

HESTER: It wasn't too far for you to go, or me.

BRUCE *(Irritably)*: Do you think I want to sell?

HESTER: *She* does. But she can't do it. *(Her voice is low.)* This house belongs to me.

BRUCE: Hester, don't start that again! I wish to God the land had been divided differently, but it wasn't.

HESTER: Father meant for us to stay here and keep things as they were when he was with us.

BRUCE: The soil wasn't blowing away when he was farming it.

HESTER: He meant for me to have the house.

RUTH: You'll go with us where we go, Hester.

HESTER *(To Ruth)*: You came here. You plotted with him to take this house from me. But it's mine!

BRUCE *(His voice cracks through the room)*: Stop that, Hester! I love this place as much as you do, but I'm selling it. I'm selling it, I tell you. *(As he speaks, he gets up abruptly and, taking up his coat, puts it on.)*

(Hester sinks slowly into the chair, staring. Ruth tries to put her hand on Bruce's arm.)

RUTH: Bruce! Not that way! Not for me. If it's that way, I don't care enough.

BRUCE *(Shaking himself free)*: Oh, leave me alone!

RUTH: Bruce!

BRUCE *(Going to the door)*: I'll be glad when it's over, I suppose.

RUTH: Where are you going?

BRUCE *(Taking his cap and gloves)*: To look at that mare.

RUTH: Bruce!

(But he has gone.)

HESTER *(Getting up, she goes to her father's chair and stands behind it, facing Ruth; she moves and speaks as if she were in a dream)*: This is my house. I won't have strangers in it.

RUTH *(At the table, without looking at Hester)*: Oh, Hester! I didn't want it to be this way. I tried—

HESTER *(As if she were speaking to a stranger)*: Why did you come here?

RUTH: I've hurt you. But I'm right about this. I know I'm right.

HESTER: There isn't any room for you.

RUTH: Can't you see? It's for all of us.

(Hester comes toward Ruth with a strange, blazing anger in her face.)

HESTER: I know your kind. You tempted him with your bright hair.

RUTH: Hester!

HESTER: Your body anointed with jasmine for his pleasure.

RUTH: Hester, don't say such things!

HESTER: Oh, I know what you are! You and women like you. You put a dream around him with your arms, a sinful dream.

RUTH *(Drawing back)*: Hester!

HESTER: You lift your white face to every stranger like you offered him a cup to drink from. *(Turning from Ruth, as if she had forgotten her presence, Hester looks fondly at the room.)* I'll never leave this house.

BRUCE *(Opens the door and comes in quickly and stormily. He goes into the kitchen as he speaks)*: That mare's got out. She jumped the corral. I'll have to go after her.

RUTH *(Concerned)*: Bruce, where will she be?

BRUCE *(Returning with an old blanket)*: She'll be in the snowshed by the coulee. She always goes there when she's about to foal.

(Hester sits in the chair by the stove, her knitting in her hand. She pays no attention to the Others.)

RUTH: But you can't go after her in this storm.

BRUCE: I'll take this old blanket to cover the colt, if it's born yet. Where's the lantern? *(He sees the two lanterns by the kitchen door and, taking one of them to the table, lights it.)*

RUTH: It's three miles, Bruce. You mustn't go on foot. It's dangerous.

BRUCE: I'll have to. She'd never live through the night, or the colt either. *(He turns to go.)* You'd better go to bed. Good-night, Hester.

RUTH: Let me come with you.

BRUCE: No. *(Then, as he looks at her, all resentment leaves him. He puts down the lantern, goes to her, and takes her in his arms.)* Ruth, forget what I said. You know I didn't mean—

RUTH *(Softly)*: I said things I didn't mean, too—

BRUCE: I love you, Ruth. You know it, don't you?

RUTH: Bruce!

(He kisses her, and for a moment their love is a flame in the room.)

BRUCE: Don't worry. I won't be long.

RUTH: I'll wait.

(Bruce goes out. Ruth follows him to the door, and, as it closes, she stands against it for a moment. There is a silence. Hester is slowly unravelling her knitting but is unaware of it. The black wool falls in spirals about her chair.)

HESTER *(Suddenly)*: It's an old house. I was born here. *(Then in a strange, calm voice that seems to come from a long distance.)* You shouldn't let Bruce be so much alone. You lose him that way. He comes back to *us* then. He'll see you don't belong here unless you keep your hand on him all the time.

(Ruth looks curiously at Hester but does not give her all her attention.)

(Hester suddenly becomes harsh.) This is my house. You can't change it.

(Ruth starts to say something but remains silent.)

Father gave it to me. There isn't any room for you. *(In a high, childlike tone, like the sound of a violin string breaking.)* No room. *(She shakes her head gravely.)*

RUTH *(Aware that something is wrong)*: Hester—

HESTER *(As if she were telling an often-recited story to a stranger)*: I stayed home when Mother died and kept house for my little brother and my father. *(Her voice grows stronger.)* I was very beautiful, they said. My hair fell to my knees, and it was black as a furrow turned in spring. *(Proudly.)* I can have a husband any time I want, but my duty is here with Father. You see how it is. I can't leave him.

RUTH *(Goes quickly to Hester. With anxiety and gentleness)*: Hester, what are you talking about?

HESTER: That's Father's chair, I'll put his Bible out. *(She starts from her chair.)*

RUTH *(Preventing her)*: Hester, your father's not here—not for six years. You speak of him as if you thought—Hester—

HESTER *(Ignoring Ruth but remaining seated)*: When I was a girl I always filled the lanterns after supper. Then I was ready for his coming.

RUTH *(In terror)*:   Hester, I didn't fill them! I didn't fill the lanterns! *(She runs to the kitchen door and takes up the remaining lantern.)*

HESTER *(Calmly)*:   Father called me the wise virgin then.

RUTH: Hester, Bruce took one! He thought I'd filled them. It will burn out and he'll be lost in the blizzard.

HESTER: I always filled them.

RUTH *(Setting the lantern on the table)*:   I've got to go out after Bruce. If he gets down to the coulee and the lantern goes out, he'll never find the way back. I'll have to hurry! Where's the coal oil?

(Ruth goes to the kitchen and returns with a can of coal oil and a pair of galoshes. Hester watches her closely. As Ruth comes in with the oil, Hester slowly rises and goes to her.)

HESTER: I'll fill the lantern for you, Ruth.

RUTH *(Trying to remove the top of the can)*:   I can't get the top off. My hands are shaking so.

HESTER *(Taking the oil can from Ruth)*:   I'll fill it for you.

RUTH: Please, Hester. While I get my things on! *(Giving Hester the oil can, Ruth runs to the footstool and hurriedly puts on her galoshes.)* I'm afraid that lantern will last just long enough to get him out there. He'll be across the field before I even get outside. *(She runs up the stairs.)*

HESTER *(Standing motionless, the oil can in her hand)*:   You're going now. That's right. I told you you should go.

(Ruth disappears up the stairs. Hester moves a step toward the lantern, taking off the top of the coal oil can. She hesitates and looks for a long moment after Ruth. With the strange lucidity of madness, slowly, deliberately, she places the top back again on the can and, moving behind the table, sets it on the floor without filling the lantern. Ruth hurries down the stairs excited and alarmed. She has on heavy clothes and is putting on her gloves.)

RUTH: Is it ready?

(Hester nods.)

Will you light it for me, Hester? Please.

(Hester lights the lantern.)

I'll put the light at the window. *(She crosses with the small lamp and places it at the window.)* Hurry, Hester! *(With a sob.)* Oh, if only I can find him!

(Hester crosses to Ruth and gives her the lantern, Ruth takes the lantern and goes out. A gust of wind carries the snow into the room and blows shut the door after her. Hester goes to the window.

HESTER *(Her voice is like an echo)*: The snow lies deep on the summer fallow—The snow is a moving shroud—a winding-sheet that the wind lifts and raises and lets fall again. *(Turning from the window.)* They've gone. They won't be back now. *(With an intense excitement, Hester blows out the lamp at the window and pulls down the shades. Her eyes fall on the bowl of hyacinths in the corner. Slowly she goes to it, takes it up and, holding it away from her, carries it to the door. Opening the door, she sets the flowers outside. She closes the door and locks it. Her eyes blazing with excitement, she stands with her arms across the door as if shutting the world out. Then softly she moves to the door of her father's bedroom, unlocks it, and goes in, returning at once with a pair of men's bedroom slippers. Leaving the bedroom door open, she crosses to the sideboard, takes up the Bible and, going to her father's chair, places the slippers beside it. She speaks very softly.)* I put your slippers out. *(She draws the footstool up to the chair.)* Everything will be the same now, Father. *(She opens the Bible.)* I'll read to you, Father. I'll read the one you like. *(She reads with quiet contentment.)* "And the winds blew, and beat upon the house; and it fell not: for it was founded upon a rock."

—*1939*

Arthur Miller (b. 1915) *gained a reputation as a major American dramatist with his second play, and continues to be productive in his mid 80s. Miller was born in Harlem, the son of prosperous Jewish immigrants who suffered badly during the Depression. He studied drama at the University of Michigan and was for a time employed by the Federal Theatre Project, a Roosevelt-era government program dedicated to bringing drama with social themes to audiences in areas outside New York. His first success was* All My Sons *(1947), an Ibsenesque problem play (Miller later adapted Ibsen's* An Enemy of the People *for the New York stage) about a manufacturer who profited during World War II by knowingly supplying defective parts that caused airplanes to crash.* All My Sons, *following closely on the heels of investigations of wartime profiteering, easily found appreciative audiences.* Death of a Salesman *(1949) won Miller a Pulitzer Prize. Originally a short story based to some degree on one of Miller's uncles,* Death of a Salesman *evolved into its final form over many years. When Miller finally sat down at the typewriter to write the play, he said, "All I had was the first two lines and a death." During the height of the play's success, Miller wrote a famous essay titled "Tragedy and the Common Man," in which he dismisses the ancient "rule" that true tragedy can concern only the lives and fates of the famous. "I believe," he said, "that the common man is as apt a subject for tragedy in its highest sense as kings were. . . . If the exaltation of tragic action were truly a property of the high-bred character alone, it is inconceivable that the mass of mankind should cherish tragedy above all other forms, let alone be capable of understanding it." Miller's fame was further increased by* The Crucible *(1953), a play about the Salem witch trials that had obvious contemporary political overtones, drawing on Miller's own McCarthy-era investigations by the House Un-American Activities Committee into his past political affiliations. Miller risked a jail term for his refusal to cooperate with the committee. His marriage to Marilyn Monroe, which is in part the subject of* After the Fall *(1964), ended unhappily shortly after Miller completed work on the screenplay of* The Misfits, *which proved to be her final film. Other important plays include* A View from the Bridge *(1955), which has been revived several times on Broadway and also exists in an operatic version;* Incident at Vichy *(1964), a play about the Holocaust;* The Price *(1968);* Broken Glass, *another play about anti-Semitism; and* Ride Down Mount Morgan *(1998), which starred Patrick Stewart in its Broadway production. Miller's autobiography,* Timebends, *was published in 1987. In it he proudly recounts his experiences in 1983 directing a Chinese production of* Death of a Salesman *in Beijing, the first contemporary American play produced in China.*

Arthur Miller
Death of a Salesman

CHARACTERS

Willy Loman
Linda
Biff
Happy
Bernard
The Woman
Charley
Uncle Ben
Howard Wagner
Jenny
Stanley
Miss Forsythe
Letta

Scene: *The action takes place in Willy Loman's house and yard and in various places he visits in the New York and Boston of today.*

ACT 1

Scene: *A melody is heard, played upon a flute. It is small and fine, telling of grass and trees and the horizon. The curtain rises.*

Before us is the Salesman's house. We are aware of towering, angular shapes behind it, surrounding it on all sides. Only the blue light of the sky falls upon the house and forestage; the surrounding area shows an angry glow of orange. As more light appears, we see a solid vault of apartment houses around the small, fragile-seeming home. An air of the dream clings to the place, a dream rising out of reality. The kitchen at center seems actual enough, for there is a kitchen table with three chairs, and a refrigerator. But no other fixtures are seen. At the back of the kitchen there is a draped entrance, which leads to the living room. To the right of the kitchen, on a level raised two feet, is a bedroom furnished only with a brass bedstead and a straight chair. On a shelf over the bed a silver athletic trophy stands. A window opens onto the apartment house at the side.

Behind the kitchen, on a level raised six and a half feet, is the boys' bedroom, at present barely visible. Two beds are dimly seen, and at the back of the room a dormer window. (This bedroom is above the unseen living room.) At the left a stairway curves up to it from the kitchen.

The entire setting is wholly or, in some places, partially transparent. The roof-line of the house is one-dimensional; under and over it we see the apartment buildings. Before the house lies an apron, curving beyond the forestage into the orchestra. This forward area serves as the back yard as well as the locale of all Willy's imaginings and of his city scenes. Whenever the action is in the present the actors observe the imaginary wall-lines, entering the house only through its door at the left. But in the scenes of the past these boundaries are broken, and characters enter or leave a room by stepping "through" a wall onto the forestage.

From the right, Willy Loman, the Salesman, enters, carrying two large sample cases. The flute plays on. He hears but is not aware of it. He is past sixty years of age, dressed quietly. Even as he crosses the stage to the doorway of the house, his exhaustion is apparent. He unlocks the door, comes into the kitchen, and thankfully lets his burden down, feeling the soreness of his palms. A word-sigh escapes his lips—it might be "Oh, boy, oh, boy." He closes the door, then carries his cases out into the living room, through the draped kitchen doorway.

Linda, his wife, has stirred in her bed at the right. She gets out and puts on a robe, listening. Most often jovial, she has developed an iron repression of her exceptions to Willy's behavior—she more than loves him, she admires him, as though his mercurial nature, his temper, his massive dreams and little cruelties, served her only as sharp reminders of the turbulent longings within him, longings which she shares but lacks the temperament to utter and follow to their end.

LINDA (*hearing Willy outside the bedroom, calls with some trepidation*): Willy!

WILLY: It's all right. I came back.

LINDA: Why? What happened? (*Slight pause.*) Did something happen, Willy?

WILLY: No, nothing happened.

LINDA: You didn't smash the car, did you?

WILLY (*with casual irritation*): I said nothing happened. Didn't you hear me?

LINDA: Don't you feel well?

WILLY: I'm tired to the death. (*The flute has faded away. He sits on the bed beside her, a little numb.*) I couldn't make it. I just couldn't make it, Linda.

LINDA (*very carefully, delicately*): Where were you all day? You look terrible.

WILLY: I got as far as a little above Yonkers. I stopped for a cup of coffee. Maybe it was the coffee.

LINDA: What?

WILLY (*after a pause*): I suddenly couldn't drive any more. The car kept going off onto the shoulder, y'know?

LINDA (*helpfully*): Oh. Maybe it was the steering again. I don't think Angelo knows the Studebaker.

WILLY: No, it's me, it's me. Suddenly I realize I'm goin' sixty miles an hour and I don't remember the last five minutes. I'm—I can't seem to—keep my mind to it.

LINDA: Maybe it's your glasses. You never went for your new glasses.

WILLY: No, I see everything. I came back ten miles an hour. It took me nearly four hours from Yonkers.

LINDA (*resigned*): Well, you'll just have to take a rest, Willy, you can't continue this way.

WILLY: I just got back from Florida.

LINDA: But you didn't rest your mind. Your mind is overactive, and the mind is what counts, dear.

WILLY: I'll start out in the morning. Maybe I'll feel better in the morning. (*She is taking off his shoes.*) These goddam arch supports are killing me.

LINDA: Take an aspirin. Should I get you an aspirin? It'll soothe you.

WILLY (*with wonder*): I was driving along, you understand? And I was fine. I was even observing the scenery. You can imagine, me looking at scenery, on the road every week of my life. But it's so beautiful up there, Linda, the trees are so thick, and the sun is warm. I opened the windshield and just let the warm air bathe over me. And then all of a sudden I'm goin' off the road! I'm tellin' ya, I absolutely forgot I was driving. If I'd've gone the other way over the white line I might've killed somebody. So I went on again—and five minutes later I'm dreamin' again, and I nearly . . . (*He presses two fingers against his eyes.*) I have such thoughts, I have such strange thoughts.

LINDA: Willy, dear. Talk to them again. There's no reason why you can't work in New York.

WILLY: They don't need me in New York. I'm the New England man. I'm vital in New England.

LINDA: But you're sixty years old. They can't expect you to keep traveling every week.

WILLY: I'll have to send a wire to Portland. I'm supposed to see Brown and Morrison tomorrow morning at ten o'clock to show the line. Goddammit, I could sell them! (*He starts putting on his jacket.*)

LINDA (*taking the jacket from him*): Why don't you go down to the place tomorrow and tell Howard you've simply got to work in New York? You're too accommodating, dear.

WILLY: If old man Wagner was alive I'd a been in charge of New York now! That man was a prince, he was a masterful man. But that boy of his, that Howard, he don't appreciate. When I went north the first time, the Wagner Company didn't know where New England was!

LINDA: Why don't you tell those things to Howard, dear?

WILLY (*encouraged*): I will, I definitely will. Is there any cheese?

LINDA: I'll make you a sandwich.

WILLY: No, go to sleep. I'll take some milk. I'll be up right away. The boys in?

LINDA: They're sleeping. Happy took Biff on a date tonight.

WILLY (*interested*): That so?

LINDA: It was so nice to see them shaving together, one behind the other, in the bathroom. And going out together. You notice? The whole house smells of shaving lotion.

WILLY: Figure it out. Work a lifetime to pay off a house. You finally own it, and there's nobody to live in it.

LINDA: Well, dear, life is a casting off. It's always that way.

WILLY: No, no, some people—some people accomplish something. Did Biff say anything after I went this morning?

LINDA: You shouldn't have criticized him, Willy, especially after he just got off the train. You mustn't lose your temper with him.

WILLY: When the hell did I lose my temper? I simply asked him if he was making any money. Is that a criticism?

LINDA: But, dear, how could he make any money?

WILLY (*worried and angered*): There's such an undercurrent in him. He became a moody man. Did he apologize when I left this morning?

LINDA: He was crestfallen, Willy. You know how he admires you. I think if he finds himself, then you'll both be happier and not fight any more.

WILLY: How can he find himself on a farm? Is that a life? A farm hand? In the beginning, when he was young, I thought, well, a young man, it's good for him to tramp around, take a lot of different jobs. But it's more than ten years now and he has yet to make thirty-five dollars a week!

LINDA: He's finding himself, Willy.

WILLY: Not finding yourself at the age of thirty-four is a disgrace!

LINDA: Shh!

WILLY: The trouble is he's lazy, goddammit!

LINDA: Willy, please!

WILLY: Biff is a lazy bum!

LINDA: They're sleeping. Get something to eat. Go on down.

WILLY: Why did he come home? I would like to know what brought him home.

LINDA: I don't know. I think he's still lost, Willy. I think he's very lost.

WILLY: Biff Loman is lost. In the greatest country in the world a young man with such—personal attractiveness, gets lost. And such a hard worker. There's one thing about Biff—he's not lazy.

LINDA: Never.

WILLY (*with pity and resolve*): I'll see him in the morning; I'll have a nice talk with him. I'll get him a job selling. He could be big in no time. My God! Remember how they used to follow him around in high school? When he smiled at one of them their faces lit up. When he walked down the street . . . (*He loses himself in reminiscences.*)

LINDA (*trying to bring him out of it*): Willy, dear, I got a new kind of American-type cheese today. It's whipped.

WILLY: Why do you get American when I like Swiss?

LINDA: I just thought you'd like a change . . .

WILLY: I don't want a change! I want Swiss cheese. Why am I always being contradicted?

LINDA (*with a covering laugh*): I thought it would be a surprise.

WILLY: Why don't you open a window in here, for God's sake?

LINDA (*with infinite patience*): They're all open, dear.

WILLY: The way they boxed us in here. Bricks and windows, windows and bricks.

LINDA: We should've bought the land next door.

WILLY: The street is lined with cars. There's not a breath of fresh air in the neighborhood. The grass don't grow any more, you can't raise a carrot in the back yard. They should've had a law against apartment houses. Remember those two beautiful elm trees out there? When I and Biff hung the swing between them?

LINDA: Yeah, like being a million miles from the city.

WILLY: They should've arrested the builder for cutting those down. They massacred the neighborhood. (*Lost.*) More and more I think of those days, Linda. This time of year it was lilac and wisteria. And then the peonies would come out, and the daffodils. What fragrance in this room!

LINDA: Well, after all, people had to move somewhere.

WILLY: No, there's more people now.

LINDA: I don't think there's more people. I think . . .

WILLY: There's more people! That's what's ruining this country! Population is getting out of control. The competition is maddening! Smell the stink from that apartment house! And another one on the other side . . . How can they whip cheese?

On Willy's last line, Biff and Happy raise themselves up in their beds, listening.

LINDA: Go down, try it. And be quiet.

WILLY (*turning to Linda, guiltily*): You're not worried about me, are you, sweetheart?

BIFF: What's the matter?

HAPPY: Listen!

LINDA: You've got too much on the ball to worry about.

WILLY: You're my foundation and my support, Linda.

LINDA: Just try to relax, dear. You make mountains out of molehills.

WILLY: I won't fight with him any more. If he wants to go back to Texas, let him go.

LINDA: He'll find his way.

WILLY: Sure. Certain men just don't get started till later in life. Like Thomas Edison, I think. Or B. F. Goodrich. One of them was deaf. (*He starts for the bedroom doorway.*) I'll put my money on Biff.

LINDA: And Willy—if it's warm Sunday we'll drive in the country. And we'll open the windshield, and take lunch.

WILLY: No, the windshields don't open on the new cars.

LINDA: But you opened it today.

WILLY: Me? I didn't. (*He stops.*) Now isn't that peculiar! Isn't that a remarkable . . . (*He breaks off in amazement and fright as the flute is heard distantly.*)

LINDA: What, darling?

WILLY: That is the most remarkable thing.

LINDA: What, dear?

WILLY: I was thinking of the Chevvy. (*Slight pause.*) Nineteen twenty-eight . . . when I had that red Chevvy . . . (*Breaks off:*) That funny? I coulda sworn I was driving that Chevvy today.

LINDA: Well, that's nothing. Something must've reminded you.

WILLY: Remarkable. Ts. Remember those days? The way Biff used to simonize that car? The dealer refused to believe there was eighty thousand miles on it. (*He shakes his head.*) Heh! (*To Linda.*) Close your eyes, I'll be right up. (*He walks out of the bedroom.*)

HAPPY (*to Biff*): Jesus, maybe he smashed up the car again!

LINDA (*calling after Willy*): Be careful on the stairs, dear! The cheese is on the middle shelf. (*She turns, goes over to the bed, takes his jacket, and goes out of the bedroom.*)

Light has risen on the boys' room. Unseen, Willy is heard talking to himself; "Eighty thousand miles," and a little laugh. Biff gets out of bed, comes downstage a bit, and stands attentively. Biff is two years older than his brother Happy, well built, but in these days bears a worn air and seems less self-assured. He has succeeded less, and his dreams are stronger and less acceptable than Happy's. Happy is tall, powerfully made. Sexuality is like a visible color on him, or a scent that many women have discovered. He, like his brother, is lost, but in a different way, for he has never allowed himself to turn his face toward defeat and is thus more confused and hard-skinned, although seemingly more content.

HAPPY (*getting out of bed*):   He's going to get his license taken away if he keeps that up. I'm getting nervous about him, y'know, Biff?

BIFF: His eyes are going.

HAPPY: No, I've driven with him. He sees all right. He just doesn't keep his mind on it. I drove into the city with him last week. He stops at a green light and then it turns red and he goes. (*He laughs.*)

BIFF: Maybe he's color-blind.

HAPPY: Pop? Why he's got the finest eye for color in the business. You know that.

BIFF (*sitting down on his bed*):   I'm going to sleep.

HAPPY: You're not still sour on Dad, are you, Biff?

BIFF: He's all right, I guess.

WILLY (*underneath them, in the living room*):   Yes, sir, eighty thousand miles—eighty-two thousand!

BIFF: You smoking?

HAPPY (*holding out a pack of cigarettes*):   Want one?

BIFF (*taking a cigarette*):   I can never sleep when I smell it.

WILLY: What a simonizing job, heh!

HAPPY (*with deep sentiment*):   Funny, Biff, y'know? Us sleeping in here again? The old beds. (*He pats his bed affectionately.*) All the talk that went across those beds, huh? Our whole lives.

BIFF: Yeah. Lotta dreams and plans.

HAPPY (*with a deep and masculine laugh*):   About five hundred women would like to know what was said in this room. (*They share a soft laugh.*)

BIFF: Remember that big Betsy something—what the hell was her name—over on Bushwick Avenue?

HAPPY (*combing his hair*):   With the collie dog!

BIFF: That's the one. I got you in there, remember?

HAPPY: Yeah, that was my first time—I think. Boy, there was a pig. (*They laugh, almost crudely.*) You taught me everything I know about women. Don't forget that.

BIFF: I bet you forgot how bashful you used to be. Especially with girls.

HAPPY: Oh, I still am, Biff.

BIFF: Oh, go on.

HAPPY: I just control it, that's all. I think I got less bashful and you got more so. What happened, Biff? Where's the old humor, the old confidence? (*He shakes Biff's knee. Biff gets up and moves restlessly about the room.*) What's the matter?

BIFF: Why does Dad mock me all the time?

HAPPY: He's not mocking you, he . . .

BIFF: Everything I say there's a twist of mockery on his face. I can't get near him.

HAPPY: He just wants you to make good, that's all. I wanted to talk to you about Dad for a long time, Biff. Something's—happening to him. He—talks to himself.

BIFF: I noticed that this morning. But he always mumbled.

HAPPY: But not so noticeable. It got so embarrassing I sent him to Florida. And you know something? Most of the time he's talking to you.

BIFF: What's he say about me?

HAPPY: I can't make it out.

BIFF: What's he say about me?

HAPPY: I think the fact that you're not settled, that you're still kind of up in the air . . .

BIFF: There's one or two other things depressing him, Happy.

HAPPY: What do you mean?

BIFF: Never mind. Just don't lay it all to me.

HAPPY: But I think if you just got started—I mean—is there any future for you out there?

BIFF: I tell ya, Hap, I don't know what the future is. I don't know—what I'm supposed to want.

HAPPY: What do you mean?

BIFF: Well, I spent six or seven years after high school trying to work myself up. Shipping clerk, salesman, business of one kind or another. And it's a measly manner of existence. To get on that subway on the hot mornings in summer. To devote your whole life to keeping stock, or making phone calls, or selling or buying. To suffer fifty weeks of the year for the sake of a two-week vacation, when all you really desire is to be outdoors, with your shirt off. And always to have to get ahead of the next fella. And still—that's how you build a future.

HAPPY: Well, you really enjoy it on a farm? Are you content out there?

BIFF (*with rising agitation*): Hap, I've had twenty or thirty different kinds of jobs since I left home before the war, and it always turns out the same. I just realized it lately. In Nebraska when I herded cattle, and the Dakotas, and Arizona, and now in Texas. It's why I came home now, I guess, because I realized it. This farm I work on, it's spring there now, see? And they've got about fifteen new colts. There's nothing more inspiring or—beautiful than the sight of a mare and a new colt. And it's cool there now, see? Texas is cool now, and it's spring. And whenever spring comes to where I am, I suddenly get the feeling, my God, I'm not gettin' anywhere! What the hell am I doing, playing around with horses, twenty-eight dollars a week! I'm thirty-four years old, I oughta be makin' my future. That's when I come running home. And now, I get here, and I don't know what to do with myself. (*After a pause.*) I've always made a point of not wasting my life, and everytime I come back here I know that all I've done is to waste my life.

HAPPY: You're a poet, you know that, Biff? You're a—you're an idealist!

BIFF: No, I'm mixed up very bad. Maybe I oughta get married. Maybe I oughta get stuck into something. Maybe that's my trouble. I'm like a boy. I'm not married, I'm not in business, I just—I'm like a boy. Are you content, Hap? You're a success, aren't you? Are you content?

HAPPY: Hell, no!

BIFF: Why? You're making money, aren't you?

HAPPY (*moving about with energy, expressiveness*): All I can do now is wait for the merchandise manager to die. And suppose I get to be merchandise manager? He's a good friend of mine, and he just built a terrific estate on Long Island. And he lived there about two months and sold it, and now he's building another one. He can't enjoy it once it's finished. And I know that's just what I would do. I don't know what the hell I'm workin' for. Sometimes I sit in my apartment—all alone. And I think of the rent I'm paying. And it's crazy. But then, it's what I always wanted. My own apartment, a car, and plenty of women. And still, goddammit, I'm lonely.

BIFF (*with enthusiasm*): Listen, why don't you come out West with me?

HAPPY: You and I, heh?

BIFF: Sure, maybe we could buy a ranch. Raise cattle, use our muscles. Men built like we are should be working out in the open.

HAPPY (*avidly*): The Loman Brothers, heh?

BIFF (*with vast affection*): Sure, we'd be known all over the counties!

HAPPY (*enthralled*): That's what I dream about, Biff. Sometimes I want to just rip my clothes off in the middle of the store and outbox that goddam merchandise manager. I mean I can outbox, outrun, and outlift anybody in that store, and I have to take orders from those common, petty sons-of-bitches till I can't stand it any more.

BIFF: I'm tellin' you, kid, if you were with me I'd be happy out there.

HAPPY (*enthused*): See, Biff, everybody around me is so false that I'm constantly lowering my ideals . . .

BIFF: Baby, together we'd stand up for one another, we'd have someone to trust.

HAPPY: If I were around you . . .

BIFF: Hap, the trouble is we weren't brought up to grub for money. I don't know how to do it.

HAPPY: Neither can I!

BIFF: Then let's go!

HAPPY: The only thing is—what can you make out there?

BIFF: But look at your friend. Builds an estate and then hasn't the peace of mind to live in it.

HAPPY: Yeah, but when he walks into the store the waves part in front of him. That's fifty-two thousand dollars a year coming through the revolving door, and I got more in my pinky finger than he's got in his head.

BIFF: Yeah, but you just said . . .

HAPPY: I gotta show some of those pompous, self-important executives over there that Hap Loman can make the grade. I want to walk into the store the way he walks in. Then I'll go with you, Biff. We'll be together yet, I swear. But take those two we had tonight. Now weren't they gorgeous creatures?

BIFF: Yeah, yeah, most gorgeous I've had in years.

HAPPY: I get that any time I want, Biff. Whenever I feel disgusted. The only trouble is, it gets like bowling or something. I just keep knockin' them over and it doesn't mean anything. You still run around a lot?

BIFF: Naa. I'd like to find a girl—steady, somebody with substance.

HAPPY: That's what I long for.

BIFF: Go on! You'd never come home.

HAPPY: I would! Somebody with character, with resistance! Like Mom, y'know? You're gonna call me a bastard when I tell you this. That girl Charlotte I was with tonight is engaged to be married in five weeks. (*He tries on his new hat.*)

BIFF: No kiddin'!

HAPPY: Sure, the guy's in line for the vice-presidency of the store. I don't know what gets into me, maybe I just have an over-developed sense of competition or something, but I went and ruined her, and furthermore I can't get rid of her. And he's the third executive I've done that to. Isn't that a crummy characteristic? And to top it all, I go to their weddings! (*Indignantly, but laughing.*) Like I'm not supposed to take bribes. Manufacturers offer me a hundred-dollar bill now and then to throw an order their way. You know how honest I am, but it's like this girl, see. I hate myself for it. Because I don't want the girl, and, still, I take it and—I love it!

BIFF: Let's go to sleep.

HAPPY: I guess we didn't settle anything, heh?

BIFF: I just got one idea that I think I'm going to try.

HAPPY: What's that?

BIFF: Remember Bill Oliver?

HAPPY: Sure, Oliver is very big now. You want to work for him again?

BIFF: No, but when I quit he said something to me. He put his arm on my shoulder, and he said, "Biff, if you ever need anything, come to me."

HAPPY: I remember that. That sounds good.

BIFF: I think I'll go to see him. If I could get ten thousand or even seven or eight thousand dollars I could buy a beautiful ranch.

HAPPY: I bet he'd back you. 'Cause he thought highly of you, Biff. I mean, they all do. You're well liked, Biff. That's why I say to come back here, and we both have the apartment. And I'm tellin' you, Biff, any babe you want . . .

BIFF: No, with a ranch I could do the work I like and still be something. I just wonder though. I wonder if Oliver still thinks I stole that carton of basketballs.

HAPPY: Oh, he probably forgot that long ago. It's almost ten years. You're too sensitive. Anyway, he didn't really fire you.

BIFF: Well, I think he was going to. I think that's why I quit. I was never sure whether he knew or not. I know he thought the world of me, though. I was the only one he'd let lock up the place.

WILLY (*below*): You gonna wash the engine, Biff?

HAPPY: Shh!

Biff looks at Happy, who is gazing down, listening. Willy is mumbling in the parlor.

HAPPY: You hear that?

They listen. Willy laughs warmly.

BIFF (*growing angry*): Doesn't he know Mom can hear that?

WILLY: Don't get your sweater dirty, Biff!

A look of pain crosses Biff's face.

HAPPY: Isn't that terrible? Don't leave again, will you? You'll find a job here. You gotta stick around. I don't know what to do about him, it's getting embarrassing.

WILLY: What a simonizing job!

BIFF: Mom's hearing that!

WILLY: No kiddin', Biff, you got a date? Wonderful!

HAPPY: Go on to sleep. But talk to him in the morning, will you?

BIFF (*reluctantly getting into bed*): With her in the house. Brother!

HAPPY (*getting into bed*): I wish you'd have a good talk with him.

The light on their room begins to fade.

BIFF (*to himself in bed*): That selfish, stupid . . .

HAPPY: Sh . . . Sleep, Biff.

Their light is out. Well before they have finished speaking, Willy's form is dimly seen below in the darkened kitchen. He opens the refrigerator, searches in there, and takes out a bottle of milk. The apartment houses are fading out, and the entire house and surroundings become covered with leaves. Music insinuates itself as the leaves appear.

WILLY: Just wanna be careful with those girls, Biff, that's all. Don't make any promises. No promises of any kind. Because a girl, y'know, they always believe what you tell 'em, and you're very young, Biff, you're too young to be talking seriously to girls.

Light rises on the kitchen. Willy, talking, shuts the refrigerator door and comes downstage to the kitchen table. He pours milk into a glass. He is totally immersed in himself, smiling faintly.

WILLY: Too young entirely, Biff. You want to watch your schooling first. Then when you're all set, there'll be plenty of girls for a boy like you. (*He smiles broadly at a kitchen chair.*) That so? The girls pay for you? (*He laughs.*) Boy, you must really be makin' a hit.

Willy is gradually addressing—physically—a point offstage, speaking through the wall of the kitchen, and his voice has been rising in volume to that of a normal conversation.

WILLY: I been wondering why you polish the car so careful. Ha! Don't leave the hubcaps, boys. Get the chamois to the hubcaps. Happy, use newspaper on the windows, it's the easiest thing. Show him how to do it, Biff! You see, Happy? Pad it up, use it like a pad. That's it, that's it, good work. You're doin' all right, Hap. (*He pauses, then nods in approbation for a few seconds, then looks upward.*) Biff, first thing we gotta do when we get time is clip that big branch over the house. Afraid it's gonna fall in a storm and hit the roof. Tell you what. We get a rope and sling her around, and then we climb up there with a couple of saws and take her down. Soon as you finish the car, boys, I wanna see ya. I got a surprise for you, boys.

BIFF (*offstage*): Whatta ya got, Dad?

WILLY: No, you finish first. Never leave a job till you're finished— remember that. (*Looking toward the "big trees."*) Biff, up in Albany I saw a beautiful hammock. I think I'll buy it next trip, and we'll hang it right between those two elms. Wouldn't that be something? Just swingin' there under those branches. Boy, that would be . . .

Young Biff and Young Happy appear from the direction Willy was addressing. Happy carries rags and a pail of water. Biff, wearing a sweater with a block "S," carries a football.

BIFF (*pointing in the direction of the car offstage*): How's that, Pop, professional?

WILLY: Terrific. Terrific job, boys. Good work, Biff.

HAPPY: Where's the surprise, Pop?

WILLY: In the back seat of the car.

HAPPY: Boy! (*He runs off.*)

BIFF: What is it, Dad? Tell me, what'd you buy?

WILLY (*laughing, cuffs him*): Never mind, something I want you to have.

BIFF (*turns and starts off*): What is it, Hap?

HAPPY (*offstage*): It's a punching bag!

BIFF: Oh, Pop!

WILLY: It's got Gene Tunney's signature on it!

Happy runs onstage with a punching bag.

BIFF: Gee, how'd you know we wanted a punching bag?

WILLY: Well, it's the finest thing for the timing.

HAPPY (*lies down on his back and pedals with his feet*): I'm losing weight, you notice, Pop?

WILLY (*to Happy*): Jumping rope is good too.

BIFF: Did you see the new football I got?

WILLY (*examining the ball*): Where'd you get a new ball?

BIFF: The coach told me to practice my passing.

WILLY: That so? And he gave you the ball, heh?

BIFF: Well, I borrowed it from the locker room. (*He laughs confidentially.*)

WILLY (*laughing with him at the theft*): I want you to return that.

HAPPY: I told you he wouldn't like it!

BIFF (*angrily*): Well, I'm bringing it back!

WILLY (*stopping the incipient argument, to Happy*): Sure, he's gotta practice with a regulation ball, doesn't he? (*To Biff.*) Coach'll probably congratulate you on your initiative!

BIFF: Oh, he keeps congratulating my initiative all the time, Pop.

WILLY: That's because he likes you. If somebody else took that ball there'd be an uproar. So what's the report, boys, what's the report?

BIFF: Where'd you go this time, Dad? Gee we were lonesome for you.

WILLY (*pleased, puts an arm around each boy and they come down to the apron*): Lonesome, heh?

BIFF: Missed you every minute.

WILLY: Don't say? Tell you a secret, boys. Don't breathe it to a soul. Someday I'll have my own business, and I'll never have to leave home any more.

HAPPY: Like Uncle Charley, heh?

WILLY: Bigger than Uncle Charley! Because Charley is not—liked. He's liked, but he's not—well liked.

BIFF: Where'd you go this time, Dad?

WILLY: Well, I got on the road, and I went north to Providence. Met the Mayor.

BIFF: The Mayor of Providence!

WILLY: He was sitting in the hotel lobby.

BIFF: What'd he say?

WILLY: He said, "Morning!" And I said, "Morning!" And I said, "You got a fine city here, Mayor." And then he had coffee with me. And then I went to Waterbury. Waterbury is a fine city. Big clock city, the famous Waterbury clock. Sold a nice bill there. And then Boston— Boston is the cradle of the Revolution. A fine city. And a couple of other towns in Mass., and on to Portland and Bangor and straight home!

BIFF: Gee, I'd love to go with you sometime, Dad.

WILLY: Soon as summer comes.

HAPPY: Promise?

WILLY: You and Hap and I, and I'll show you all the towns. America is full of beautiful towns and fine, upstanding people. And they know me, boys, they know me up and down New England. The finest people. And when I bring you fellas up, there'll be open sesame for all of us, 'cause one thing, boys: I have friends. I can park my car in any street in New England, and the cops protect it like their own. This summer, heh?

BIFF AND HAPPY (*together*): Yeah! You bet!

WILLY: We'll take our bathing suits.

HAPPY: We'll carry your bags, Pop!

WILLY: Oh, won't that be something! Me comin' into the Boston stores with you boys carryin' my bags. What a sensation!

Biff is prancing around, practicing passing the ball.

WILLY: You nervous, Biff, about the game?

BIFF: Not if you're gonna be there.

WILLY: What do they say about you in school, now that they made you captain?

HAPPY: There's a crowd of girls behind him everytime the classes change.

BIFF (*taking Willy's hand*): This Saturday, Pop, this Saturday—just for you, I'm going to break through for a touchdown.

HAPPY: You're supposed to pass.

BIFF: I'm takin' one play for Pop. You watch me, Pop, and when I take off my helmet, that means I'm breakin' out. Then you watch me crash through that line!

WILLY (*kisses Biff*): Oh, wait'll I tell this in Boston!

Bernard enters in knickers. He is younger than Biff, earnest and loyal, a worried boy.

BERNARD: Biff, where are you? You're supposed to study with me today.

WILLY: Hey, looka Bernard. What're you lookin' so anemic about, Bernard?

BERNARD: He's gotta study, Uncle Willy. He's got Regents next week.

HAPPY (*tauntingly, spinning Bernard around*): Let's box, Bernard!

BERNARD: Biff! (*He gets away from Happy.*) Listen, Biff, I heard Mr. Birnbaum say that if you don't start studyin' math he's gonna flunk you, and you won't graduate. I heard him!

WILLY: You better study with him, Biff. Go ahead now.

BERNARD: I heard him!

BIFF: Oh, Pop, you didn't see my sneakers! (*He holds up a foot for Willy to look at.*)

WILLY: Hey, that's a beautiful job of printing!

BERNARD (*wiping his glasses*): Just because he printed University of Virginia on his sneakers doesn't mean they've got to graduate him, Uncle Willy!

WILLY (*angrily*): What're you talking about? With scholarships to three universities they're gonna flunk him?

BERNARD: But I heard Mr. Birnbaum say . . .

WILLY: Don't be a pest, Bernard! (*To his boys.*) What an anemic!

BERNARD: Okay, I'm waiting for you in my house, Biff.

Bernard goes off. The Lomans laugh.

WILLY: Bernard is not well liked, is he?

BIFF: He's liked, but he's not well liked.

HAPPY: That's right, Pop.

WILLY: That's just what I mean. Bernard can get the best marks in school, y'understand, but when he gets out in the business world, y'understand, you are going to be five times ahead of him. That's why I thank Almighty God you're both built like Adonises. Because the man who makes an appearance in the business world, the man who creates personal interest, is the man who gets ahead. Be liked and you will never want. You take me, for instance. I never have to wait in line to see a buyer. "Willy Loman is here!" That's all they have to know, and I go right through.

BIFF: Did you knock them dead, Pop?

WILLY: Knocked 'em cold in Providence, slaughtered 'em in Boston.

HAPPY (*on his back, pedaling again*): I'm losing weight, you notice, Pop?

Linda enters as of old, a ribbon in her hair, carrying a basket of washing.

LINDA (*with youthful energy*): Hello, dear!

WILLY: Sweetheart!

LINDA: How'd the Chevvy run?

WILLY: Chevrolet, Linda, is the greatest car ever built. (*To the boys.*) Since when do you let your mother carry wash up the stairs?

BIFF: Grab hold there, boy!

HAPPY: Where to, Mom?

LINDA: Hang them up on the line. And you better go down to your friends, Biff. The cellar is full of boys. They don't know what to do with themselves.

BIFF: Ah, when Pop comes home they can wait!

WILLY (*laughs appreciatively*): You better go down and tell them what to do, Biff.

BIFF: I think I'll have them sweep out the furnace room.

WILLY: Good work, Biff.

BIFF (*goes through wall-line of kitchen to doorway at back and calls down*): Fellas! Everybody sweep out the furnace room! I'll be right down!

VOICES: All right! Okay, Biff.

BIFF: George and Sam and Frank, come out back! We're hangin' up the wash! Come on, Hap, on the double! (*He and Happy carry out the basket.*)

LINDA: The way they obey him!

WILLY: Well, that's training, the training. I'm tellin' you, I was sellin' thousands and thousands, but I had to come home.

LINDA: Oh, the whole block'll be at that game. Did you sell anything?

WILLY: I did five hundred gross in Providence and seven hundred gross in Boston.

LINDA: No! Wait a minute. I've got a pencil. (*She pulls pencil and paper out of her apron pocket.*) That makes your commission . . . Two hundred—my God! Two hundred and twelve dollars!

WILLY: Well, I didn't figure it yet, but . . .

LINDA: How much did you do?

WILLY: Well, I—I did—about a hundred and eighty gross in Providence. Well, no—it came to—roughly two hundred gross on the whole trip.

LINDA (*without hesitation*):   Two hundred gross. That's . . . (*She figures.*)

WILLY: The trouble was that three of the stores were half-closed for inventory in Boston. Otherwise I woulda broke records.

LINDA: Well, it makes seventy dollars and some pennies. That's very good.

WILLY: What do we owe?

LINDA: Well, on the first there's sixteen dollars on the refrigerator . . .

WILLY: Why sixteen?

LINDA: Well, the fan belt broke, so it was a dollar eighty.

WILLY: But it's brand new.

LINDA: Well, the man said that's the way it is. Till they work themselves in, y'know.

They move through the wall-line into the kitchen.

WILLY: I hope we didn't get stuck on that machine.

LINDA: They got the biggest ads of any of them!

WILLY: I know, it's a fine machine. What else?

LINDA: Well, there's nine-sixty for the washing machine. And for the vacuum cleaner there's three and a half due on the fifteenth. Then the roof, you got twenty-one dollars remaining.

WILLY: It don't leak, does it?

LINDA: No, they did a wonderful job. Then you owe Frank for the carburetor.

WILLY: I'm not going to pay that man! That goddam Chevrolet, they ought to prohibit the manufacture of that car!

LINDA: Well, you owe him three and a half. And odds and ends, comes to around a hundred and twenty dollars by the fifteenth.

WILLY: A hundred and twenty dollars! My God, if business don't pick up I don't know what I'm gonna do!

LINDA: Well, next week you'll do better.

WILLY: Oh, I'll knock 'em dead next week. I'll go to Hartford. I'm very well liked in Hartford. You know, the trouble is, Linda, people don't seem to take to me.

They move onto the forestage.

LINDA: Oh, don't be foolish.

WILLY: I know it when I walk in. They seem to laugh at me.

LINDA: Why? Why would they laugh at you? Don't talk that way, Willy.

Willy moves to the edge of the stage. Linda goes into the kitchen and starts to darn stockings.

WILLY: I don't know the reason for it, but they just pass me by. I'm not noticed.

LINDA: But you're doing wonderful, dear. You're making seventy to a hundred dollars a week.

WILLY: But I gotta be at it ten, twelve hours a day. Other men—I don't know—they do it easier. I don't know why—I can't stop myself—I talk too much. A man oughta come in with a few words. One thing about Charley. He's a man of few words, and they respect him.

LINDA: You don't talk too much, you're just lively.

WILLY (*smiling*): Well, I figure, what the hell, life is short, a couple of jokes. (*To himself:*) I joke too much! (*The smile goes.*)

LINDA: Why? You're . . .

WILLY: I'm fat. I'm very—foolish to look at, Linda. I didn't tell you, but Christmas time I happened to be calling on F. H. Stewarts, and a salesman I know, as I was going in to see the buyer I heard him say something about—walrus. And I—I cracked him right across the face. I won't take that. I simply will not take that. But they do laugh at me. I know that.

LINDA: Darling . . .

WILLY: I gotta overcome it. I know I gotta overcome it. I'm not dressing to advantage, maybe.

LINDA: Willy, darling, you're the handsomest man in the world . . .

WILLY: Oh, no, Linda.

LINDA: To me you are. (*Slight pause.*) The handsomest.

From the darkness is heard the laughter of a woman. Willy doesn't turn to it, but it continues through Linda's lines.

LINDA: And the boys, Willy. Few men are idolized by their children the way you are.

Music is heard as behind a scrim, to the left of the house; The Woman, dimly seen, is dressing.

WILLY (*with great feeling*): You're the best there is. Linda, you're a pal, you know that? On the road—on the road I want to grab you sometimes and just kiss the life outa you.

The laughter is loud now, and he moves into a brightening area at the left, where The Woman has come from behind the scrim and is standing, putting on her hat, looking into a "mirror" and laughing.

WILLY: 'Cause I get so lonely—especially when business is bad and there's nobody to talk to. I get the feeling that I'll never sell anything again, that I won't make a living for you, or a business, a business for the boys. (*He talks through The Woman's subsiding laughter; The Woman primps at the "mirror."*) There's so much I want to make for . . .

THE WOMAN: Me? You didn't make me, Willy. I picked you.

WILLY (*pleased*): You picked me?

THE WOMAN (*who is quite proper-looking, Willy's age*): I did. I've been sitting at that desk watching all the salesmen go by, day in, day out. But you've got such a sense of humor, and we do have such a good time together, don't we?

WILLY: Sure, sure. (*He takes her in his arms.*) Why do you have to go now?

THE WOMAN: It's two o'clock . . .

WILLY: No, come on in! (*He pulls her.*)

THE WOMAN: . . . my sisters'll be scandalized. When'll you be back?

WILLY: Oh, two weeks about. Will you come up again?

THE WOMAN: Sure thing. You do make me laugh. It's good for me. (*She squeezes his arm, kisses him.*) And I think you're a wonderful man.

WILLY: You picked me, heh?

THE WOMAN: Sure. Because you're so sweet. And such a kidder.

WILLY: Well, I'll see you next time I'm in Boston.

THE WOMAN: I'll put you right through to the buyers.

WILLY (*slapping her bottom*):   Right. Well, bottoms up!

THE WOMAN (*slaps him gently and laughs*):   You just kill me, Willy. (*He suddenly grabs her and kisses her roughly.*) You kill me. And thanks for the stockings. I love a lot of stockings. Well, good night.

WILLY: Good night. And keep your pores open!

THE WOMAN: Oh, Willy!

The Woman bursts out laughing, and Linda's laughter blends in. The Woman disappears into the dark. Now the area at the kitchen table brightens. Linda is sitting where she was at the kitchen table, but now is mending a pair of her silk stockings.

LINDA: You are, Willy. The handsomest man. You've got no reason to feel that . . .

WILLY (*coming out of The Woman's dimming area and going over to Linda*):   I'll make it all up to you, Linda, I'll . . .

LINDA: There's nothing to make up, dear. You're doing fine, better than . . .

WILLY (*noticing her mending*):   What's that?

LINDA: Just mending my stockings. They're so expensive . . .

WILLY (*angrily, taking them from her*):   I won't have you mending stockings in this house! Now throw them out!

Linda puts the stockings in her pocket.

BERNARD (*entering on the run*):   Where is he? If he doesn't study!

WILLY (*moving to the forestage, with great agitation*):   You'll give him the answers!

BERNARD: I do, but I can't on a Regents! That's a state exam! They're liable to arrest me!

WILLY: Where is he? I'll whip him, I'll whip him!

LINDA: And he'd better give back that football, Willy, it's not nice.

WILLY: Biff! Where is he? Why is he taking everything?

LINDA: He's too rough with the girls, Willy. All the mothers are afraid of him!

WILLY: I'll whip him!

BERNARD: He's driving the car without a license!

The Woman's laugh is heard.

WILLY: Shut up!

LINDA: All the mothers . . .

WILLY: Shut up!

BERNARD (*backing quietly away and out*): Mr. Birnbaum says he's stuck up.

WILLY: Get outa here!

BERNARD: If he doesn't buckle down he'll flunk math! (*He goes off.*)

LINDA: He's right, Willy, you've gotta . . .

WILLY (*exploding at her*): There's nothing the matter with him! You want him to be a worm like Bernard? He's got spirit, personality . . .

As he speaks, Linda, almost in tears, exits into the living room. Willy is alone in the kitchen, wilting and staring. The leaves are gone. It is night again, and the apartment houses look down from behind.

WILLY: Loaded with it. Loaded! What is he stealing? He's giving it back, isn't he? Why is he stealing? What did I tell him? I never in my life told him anything but decent things.

Happy in pajamas has come down the stairs; Willy suddenly becomes aware of Happy's presence.

HAPPY: Let's go now, come on.

WILLY (*sitting down at the kitchen table*): Huh! Why did she have to wax the floors herself? Everytime she waxes the floors she keels over. She knows that!

HAPPY: Shh! Take it easy. What brought you back tonight?

WILLY: I got an awful scare. Nearly hit a kid in Yonkers. God! Why didn't I go to Alaska with my brother Ben that time! Ben! That man was a genius, that man was success incarnate! What a mistake! He begged me to go.

HAPPY: Well, there's no use in . . .

WILLY: You guys! There was a man started with the clothes on his back and ended up with diamond mines!

HAPPY: Boy, someday I'd like to know how he did it.

WILLY: What's the mystery? The man knew what he wanted and went out and got it! Walked into a jungle, and comes out, the age of twenty-one, and he's rich! The world is an oyster, but you don't crack it open on a mattress!

HAPPY: Pop, I told you I'm gonna retire you for life.

WILLY: You'll retire me for life on seventy goddam dollars a week? And your women and your car and your apartment, and you'll retire me for life! Christ's sake, I couldn't get past Yonkers today! Where are you guys, where are you? The woods are burning! I can't drive a car!

Charley has appeared in the doorway. He is a large man, slow of speech, laconic, immovable. In all he says, despite what he says, there is pity, and, now, trepidation. He has a robe over pajamas, slippers on his feet. He enters the kitchen.

CHARLEY: Everything all right?

HAPPY: Yeah, Charley, everything's . . .

WILLY: What's the matter?

CHARLEY: I heard some noise. I thought something happened. Can't we do something about the walls? You sneeze in here, and in my house hats blow off.

HAPPY: Let's go to bed, Dad. Come on.

Charley signals to Happy to go.

WILLY: You go ahead, I'm not tired at the moment.

HAPPY (*to Willy*): Take it easy, huh? (*He exits.*)

WILLY: What're you doin' up?

CHARLEY (*sitting down at the kitchen table opposite Willy*): Couldn't sleep good. I had a heartburn.

WILLY: Well, you don't know how to eat.

CHARLEY: I eat with my mouth.

WILLY: No, you're ignorant. You gotta know about vitamins and things like that.

CHARLEY: Come on, let's shoot. Tire you out a little.

WILLY (*hesitantly*): All right. You got cards?

CHARLEY (*taking a deck from his pocket*): Yeah, I got them. Someplace. What is it with those vitamins?

WILLY (*dealing*): They build up your bones. Chemistry.

CHARLEY: Yeah, but there's no bones in a heartburn.

WILLY: What are you talkin' about? Do you know the first thing about it?

CHARLEY: Don't get insulted.

WILLY: Don't talk about something you don't know anything about.

They are playing. Pause.

CHARLEY: What're you doin' home?

WILLY: A little trouble with the car.

CHARLEY: Oh. (*Pause.*) I'd like to take a trip to California.

WILLY: Don't say.

CHARLEY: You want a job?

WILLY: I got a job, I told you that. (*After a slight pause.*) What the hell are you offering me a job for?

CHARLEY: Don't get insulted.

WILLY: Don't insult me.

CHARLEY: I don't see no sense in it. You don't have to go on this way.

WILLY: I got a good job. (*Slight pause.*) What do you keep comin' in here for?

CHARLEY: You want me to go?

WILLY (*after a pause, withering*): I can't understand it. He's going back to Texas again. What the hell is that?

CHARLEY: Let him go.

WILLY: I got nothin' to give him, Charley, I'm clean, I'm clean.

CHARLEY: He won't starve. None a them starve. Forget about him.

WILLY: Then what have I got to remember?

CHARLEY: You take it too hard. To hell with it. When a deposit bottle is broken you don't get your nickel back.

WILLY: That's easy enough for you to say.

CHARLEY: That ain't easy for me to say.

WILLY: Did you see the ceiling I put up in the living room?

CHARLEY: Yeah, that's a piece of work. To put up a ceiling is a mystery to me. How do you do it?

WILLY: What's the difference?

CHARLEY: Well, talk about it.

WILLY: You gonna put up a ceiling?

CHARLEY: How could I put up a ceiling?

WILLY: Then what the hell are you bothering me for?

CHARLEY: You're insulted again.

WILLY: A man who can't handle tools is not a man. You're disgusting.

CHARLEY: Don't call me disgusting, Willy.

Uncle Ben, carrying a valise and an umbrella, enters the forestage from around the right corner of the house. He is a stolid man, in his sixties, with a mustache and an authoritative air. He is utterly certain of his destiny, and there is an aura of far places about him. He enters exactly as Willy speaks.

WILLY: I'm getting awfully tired, Ben.

Ben's music is heard. Ben looks around at everything.

CHARLEY: Good, keep playing; you'll sleep better. Did you call me Ben?

Ben looks at his watch.

WILLY: That's funny. For a second there you reminded me of my brother Ben.

BEN: I only have a few minutes. (*He strolls, inspecting the place. Willy and Charley continue playing.*)

CHARLEY: You never heard from him again, heh? Since that time?

WILLY: Didn't Linda tell you? Couple of weeks ago we got a letter from his wife in Africa. He died.

CHARLEY: That so.

BEN (*chuckling*): So this is Brooklyn, eh?

CHARLEY: Maybe you're in for some of his money.

WILLY: Naa, he had seven sons. There's just one opportunity I had with that man . . .

BEN: I must make a train, William. There are several properties I'm looking at in Alaska.

WILLY: Sure, sure! If I'd gone with him to Alaska that time, everything would've been totally different.

CHARLEY: Go on, you'd froze to death up there.

WILLY: What're you talking about?

BEN: Opportunity is tremendous in Alaska, William. Surprised you're not up there.

WILLY: Sure, tremendous.

CHARLEY: Heh?

WILLY: There was the only man I ever met who knew the answers.

CHARLEY: Who?

BEN: How are you all?

WILLY (*taking a pot, smiling*): Fine, fine.

CHARLEY: Pretty sharp tonight.

BEN: Is Mother living with you?

WILLY: No, she died a long time ago.

CHARLEY: Who?

BEN: That's too bad. Fine specimen of a lady, Mother.

WILLY (*to Charley*): Heh?

BEN: I'd hoped to see the old girl.

CHARLEY: Who died?

BEN: Heard anything from Father, have you?

WILLY (*unnerved*): What do you mean, who died?

CHARLEY (*taking a pot*): What're you talkin' about?

BEN (*looking at his watch*): William, it's half-past eight!

WILLY (*as though to dispel his confusion he angrily stops Charley's hand*): That's my build!

CHARLEY: I put the ace . . .

WILLY: If you don't know how to play the game I'm not gonna throw my money away on you!

CHARLEY (*rising*): It was my ace, for God's sake!

WILLY: I'm through, I'm through!

BEN: When did Mother die?

WILLY: Long ago. Since the beginning you never knew how to play cards.

CHARLEY (*picks up the cards and goes to the door*): All right! Next time I'll bring a deck with five aces.

WILLY: I don't play that kind of game!

CHARLEY (*turning to him*): You ought to be ashamed of yourself!

WILLY: Yeah?

CHARLEY: Yeah! (*He goes out.*)

WILLY (*slamming the door after him*): Ignoramus!

BEN (*as Willy comes toward him through the wall-line of the kitchen*): So you're William.

WILLY (*shaking Ben's hand*): Ben! I've been waiting for you so long! What's the answer? How did you do it?

BEN: Oh, there's a story in that.

Linda enters the forestage, as of old, carrying the wash basket.

LINDA: Is this Ben?

BEN (*gallantly*): How do you do, my dear.

LINDA: Where've you been all these years? Willy's always wondered why you . . .

WILLY (*pulling Ben away from her impatiently*): Where is Dad? Didn't you follow him? How did you get started?

BEN: Well, I don't know how much you remember.

WILLY: Well, I was just a baby, of course, only three or four years old . . .

BEN: Three years and eleven months.

WILLY: What a memory, Ben!

BEN: I have many enterprises, William, and I have never kept books.

WILLY: I remember I was sitting under the wagon in—was it Nebraska?

BEN: It was South Dakota, and I gave you a bunch of wild flowers.

WILLY: I remember you walking away down some open road.

BEN (*laughing*): I was going to find Father in Alaska.

WILLY: Where is he?

BEN: At that age I had a very faulty view of geography, William. I discovered after a few days that I was heading due south, so instead of Alaska, I ended up in Africa.

LINDA: Africa!

WILLY: The Gold Coast!

BEN: Principally diamond mines.

LINDA: Diamond mines!

BEN: Yes, my dear. But I've only a few minutes . . .

WILLY: No! Boys! Boys! (*Young Biff and Happy appear.*) Listen to this. This is your Uncle Ben, a great man! Tell my boys, Ben!

BEN: Why, boys, when I was seventeen I walked into the jungle, and when I was twenty-one I walked out. (*He laughs.*) And by God I was rich.

WILLY (*to the boys*): You see what I been talking about? The greatest things can happen!

BEN (*glancing at his watch*): I have an appointment in Ketchikan Tuesday week.

WILLY: No, Ben! Please tell about Dad. I want my boys to hear. I want them to know the kind of stock they spring from. All I remember is a man with a big beard, and I was in Mamma's lap, sitting around a fire, and some kind of high music.

BEN: His flute. He played the flute.

WILLY: Sure, the flute, that's right!

New music is heard, a high, rollicking tune.

BEN: Father was a very great and a very wild-hearted man. We would start in Boston, and he'd toss the whole family into the wagon, and then he'd drive the team right across the country; through Ohio, and Indiana, Michigan, Illinois, and all the Western states. And we'd stop in the towns and sell the flutes that he'd made on the way. Great inventor, Father. With one gadget he made more in a week than a man like you could make in a lifetime.

WILLY: That's just the way I'm bringing them up, Ben—rugged, well liked, all-around.

BEN: Yeah? (*To Biff.*) Hit that, boy—hard as you can. (*He pounds his stomach.*)

BIFF: Oh, no, sir!

BEN (*taking boxing stance*): Come on, get to me! (*He laughs.*)

WILLY: Go to it. Biff! Go ahead, show him!

BIFF: Okay! (*He cocks his fists and starts in.*)

LINDA (*to Willy*): Why must he fight, dear?

BEN (*sparring with Biff*): Good boy! Good boy!

WILLY: How's that, Ben, heh?

HAPPY: Give him the left, Biff!

LINDA: Why are you fighting?

BEN: Good boy! (*Suddenly comes in, trips Biff, and stands over him, the point of his umbrella poised over Biff's eye.*)

LINDA: Look out, Biff!

BIFF: Gee!

BEN (*patting Biff's knee*): Never fight fair with a stranger, boy. You'll never get out of the jungle that way. (*Taking Linda's hand and bowing.*) It was an honor and a pleasure to meet you, Linda.

LINDA (*withdrawing her hand coldly, frightened*): Have a nice—trip.

BEN (*to Willy*): And good luck with your—what do you do?

WILLY: Selling.

BEN: Yes. Well . . . (*He raises his hand in farewell to all.*)

WILLY: No, Ben, I don't want you to think . . . (*He takes Ben's arm to show him.*) It's Brooklyn, I know, but we hunt too.

BEN: Really, now.

WILLY: Oh, sure, there's snakes and rabbits and—that's why I moved out here. Why, Biff can fell any one of these trees in no time! Boys! Go right over to where they're building the apartment house and get some sand. We're gonna rebuild the entire front stoop right now! Watch this, Ben!

BIFF: Yes, sir! On the double, Hap!

HAPPY (*as he and Biff run off*): I lost weight, Pop, you notice?

Charley enters in knickers, even before the boys are gone.

CHARLEY: Listen, if they steal any more from that building the watchman'll put the cops on them!

LINDA (*to Willy*): Don't let Biff . . .

Ben laughs lustily.

WILLY: You shoulda seen the lumber they brought home last week. At least a dozen six-by-tens worth all kinds a money.

CHARLEY: Listen, if that watchman . . .

WILLY: I gave them hell, understand. But I got a couple of fearless characters there.

CHARLEY: Willy, the jails are full of fearless characters.

BEN (*clapping Willy on the back, with a laugh at Charley*): And the stock exchange, friend!

WILLY (*joining in Ben's laughter*): Where are the rest of your pants?

CHARLEY: My wife bought them.

WILLY: Now all you need is a golf club and you can go upstairs and go to sleep. (*To Ben.*) Great athlete! Between him and his son Bernard they can't hammer a nail!

BERNARD (*rushing in*):   The watchman's chasing Biff!

WILLY (*angrily*):   Shut up! He's not stealing anything!

LINDA (*alarmed, hurrying off left*):   Where is he? Biff, dear! (*She exits.*)

WILLY (*moving toward the left, away from Ben*):   There's nothing wrong. What's the matter with you?

BEN: Nervy boy. Good!

WILLY (*laughing*):   Oh, nerves of iron, that Biff!

CHARLEY: Don't know what it is. My New England man comes back and he's bleedin', they murdered him up there.

WILLY: It's contacts, Charley, I got important contacts!

CHARLEY (*sarcastically*):   Glad to hear it, Willy. Come in later, we'll shoot a little casino. I'll take some of your Portland money. (*He laughs at Willy and exits.*)

WILLY (*turning to Ben*):   Business is bad, it's murderous. But not for me, of course.

BEN: I'll stop by on my way back to Africa.

WILLY (*longingly*):   Can't you stay a few days? You're just what I need, Ben, because I—I have a fine position here, but I—well, Dad left when I was such a baby and I never had a chance to talk to him and I still feel—kind of temporary about myself.

BEN: I'll be late for my train.

They are at opposite ends of the stage.

WILLY: Ben, my boys—can't we talk? They'd go into the jaws of hell for me, see, but I . . .

BEN: William, you're being first-rate with your boys. Outstanding, manly chaps!

WILLY (*hanging on to his words*):   Oh, Ben, that's good to hear! Because sometimes I'm afraid that I'm not teaching them the right kind of—Ben, how should I teach them?

BEN (*giving great weight to each word, and with a certain vicious audacity*):   William, when I walked into the jungle, I was seventeen. When I walked out I was twenty-one. And, by God, I was rich! (*He goes off into darkness around the right corner of the house.*)

WILLY: . . . was rich! That's just the spirit I want to imbue them with! To walk into a jungle! I was right! I was right! I was right!

Ben is gone, but Willy is still speaking to him as Linda, in nightgown and robe, enters the kitchen, glances around for Willy, then goes to the door of the house, looks out and sees him. Comes down to his left. He looks at her.

LINDA: Willy, dear? Willy?

WILLY: I was right!

LINDA: Did you have some cheese? (*He can't answer.*) It's very late, darling. Come to bed, heh?

WILLY (*looking straight up*): Gotta break your neck to see a star in this yard.

LINDA: You coming in?

WILLY: Whatever happened to that diamond watch fob? Remember? When Ben came from Africa that time? Didn't he give me a watch fob with a diamond in it?

LINDA: You pawned it, dear. Twelve, thirteen years ago. For Biff's radio correspondence course.

WILLY: Gee, that was a beautiful thing. I'll take a walk.

LINDA: But you're in your slippers.

WILLY (*starting to go around the house at the left*): I was right! I was! (*Half to Linda, as he goes, shaking his head.*) What a man! There was a man worth talking to. I was right!

LINDA (*calling after Willy*): But in your slippers, Willy!

Willy is almost gone when Biff, in his pajamas, comes down the stairs and enters the kitchen.

BIFF: What is he doing out there?

LINDA: Sh!

BIFF: God Almighty, Mom, how long has he been doing this?

LINDA: Don't, he'll hear you.

BIFF: What the hell is the matter with him?

LINDA: It'll pass by morning.

BIFF: Shouldn't we do anything?

LINDA: Oh, my dear, you should do a lot of things, but there's nothing to do, so go to sleep.

Happy comes down the stair and sits on the steps.

HAPPY: I never heard him so loud, Mom.

LINDA: Well, come around more often; you'll hear him. (*She sits down at the table and mends the lining of Willy's jacket.*)

BIFF: Why didn't you ever write me about this, Mom?

LINDA: How would I write to you? For over three months you had no address.

BIFF: I was on the move. But you know I thought of you all the time. You know that, don't you, pal?

LINDA: I know, dear, I know. But he likes to have a letter. Just to know that there's still a possibility for better things.

BIFF: He's not like this all the time, is he?

LINDA: It's when you come home he's always the worst.

BIFF: When I come home?

LINDA: When you write you're coming, he's all smiles, and talks about the future, and—he's just wonderful. And then the closer you seem to come, the more shaky he gets, and then, by the time you get here, he's arguing, and he seems angry at you. I think it's just that maybe he can't bring himself to—to open up to you. Why are you so hateful to each other? Why is that?

BIFF (*evasively*): I'm not hateful, Mom.

LINDA: But you no sooner come in the door than you're fighting!

BIFF: I don't know why. I mean to change. I'm tryin', Mom, you understand?

LINDA: Are you home to stay now?

BIFF: I don't know. I want to look around, see what's doin'.

LINDA: Biff, you can't look around all your life, can you?

BIFF: I just can't take hold, Mom. I can't take hold of some kind of a life.

LINDA: Biff, a man is not a bird, to come and go with the spring time.

BIFF: Your hair . . . (*He touches her hair.*) Your hair got so gray.

LINDA: Oh, it's been gray since you were in high school. I just stopped dyeing it, that's all.

BIFF: Dye it again, will ya? I don't want my pal looking old. (*He smiles.*)

LINDA: You're such a boy! You think you can go away for a year and . . . You've got to get it into your head now that one day you'll knock on this door and there'll be strange people here . . .

BIFF: What are you talking about? You're not even sixty, Mom.

LINDA: But what about your father?

BIFF (*lamely*): Well, I meant him too.

HAPPY: He admires Pop.

LINDA: Biff, dear, if you don't have any feeling for him, then you can't have any feeling for me.

BIFF: Sure I can, Mom.

LINDA: No. You can't just come to see me, because I love him. (*With a threat, but only a threat, of tears.*) He's the dearest man in the world to me, and I won't have anyone making him feel unwanted and low and blue. You've got to make up your mind now, darling, there's no leeway any more. Either he's your father and you pay him that respect, or else you're not to come here. I know he's not easy to get along with—nobody knows that better than me—but . . .

WILLY (*from the left, with a laugh*): Hey, hey, Biffo!

BIFF (*starting to go out after Willy*): What the hell is the matter with him? (*Happy stops him.*)

LINDA: Don't—don't go near him!

BIFF: Stop making excuses for him! He always, always wiped the floor with you. Never had an ounce of respect for you.

HAPPY: He's always had respect for . . .

BIFF: What the hell do you know about it?

HAPPY (*surlily*): Just don't call him crazy!

BIFF: He's got no character—Charley wouldn't do this. Not in his own house—spewing out that vomit from his mind.

HAPPY: Charley never had to cope with what he's got to.

BIFF: People are worse off than Willy Loman. Believe me, I've seen them!

LINDA: Then make Charley your father, Biff. You can't do that, can you? I don't say he's a great man. Willy Loman never made a lot of money. His name was never in the paper. He's not the finest character that ever lived. But he's a human being, and a terrible thing is happening to him. So attention must be paid. He's not to be allowed to fall into his grave like an old dog. Attention, attention must be finally paid to such a person. You called him crazy . . .

BIFF: I didn't mean . . .

LINDA: No, a lot of people think he's lost his—balance. But you don't have to be very smart to know what his trouble is. The man is exhausted.

HAPPY: Sure!

LINDA: A small man can be just as exhausted as a great man. He works for a company thirty-six years this March, opens up unheard-of territories to their trademark, and now in his old age they take his salary away.

HAPPY (*indignantly*): I didn't know that, Mom.

LINDA: You never asked, my dear! Now that you get your spending money someplace else you don't trouble your mind with him.

HAPPY: But I gave you money last . . .

LINDA: Christmas time, fifty dollars! To fix the hot water it cost ninety-seven fifty! For five weeks he's been on straight commission, like a beginner, an unknown!

BIFF: Those ungrateful bastards!

LINDA: Are they any worse than his sons? When he brought them business, when he was young, they were glad to see him. But now his old friends, the old buyers that loved him so and always found some order to hand him in a pinch—they're all dead, retired. He used to be able to make six, seven calls a day in Boston. Now he takes his valises out of the car and puts them back and takes them out again and he's exhausted. Instead of walking he talks now. He drives seven hundred miles, and when he gets there no one knows him any more, no one welcomes him. And what goes through a man's mind, driving seven hundred miles home without having earned a cent? Why shouldn't he talk to himself? Why? When he has to go to Charley and borrow fifty dollars a week and pretend to me that it's his pay? How long can that go on? How long? You see what I'm sitting here and waiting for? And you tell me he has no character? The man who never worked a day but for your benefit? When does he get the medal for that? Is this his reward—to turn around at the age of sixty-three and find his sons, who he loved better than his life, one a philandering bum . . .

HAPPY: Mom!

LINDA: That's all you are, my baby! (*To Biff.*) And you! What happened to the love you had for him? You were such pals! How you used to talk to him on the phone every night! How lonely he was till he could come home to you!

BIFF: All right, Mom. I'll live here in my room, and I'll get a job. I'll keep away from him, that's all.

LINDA: No, Biff. You can't stay here and fight all the time.

BIFF: He threw me out of this house, remember that.

LINDA: Why did he do that? I never knew why.

BIFF: Because I know he's a fake and he doesn't like anybody around who knows!

LINDA: Why a fake? In what way? What do you mean?

BIFF: Just don't lay it all at my feet. It's between me and him—that's all I have to say. I'll chip in from now on. He'll settle for half my paycheck. He'll be all right. I'm going to bed. (*He starts for the stairs.*)

LINDA: He won't be all right.

BIFF (*turning on the stairs, furiously*): I hate this city and I'll stay here. Now what do you want?

LINDA: He's dying, Biff.

Happy turns quickly to her, shocked.

BIFF (*after a pause*): Why is he dying?

LINDA: He's been trying to kill himself.

BIFF (*with great horror*): How?

LINDA: I live from day to day.

BIFF: What're you talking about?

LINDA: Remember I wrote you that he smashed up the car again? In February?

BIFF: Well?

LINDA: The insurance inspector came. He said that they have evidence. That all these accidents in the last year—weren't—weren't—accidents.

HAPPY: How can they tell that? That's a lie.

LINDA: It seems there's a woman . . . (*She takes a breath as:*)

BIFF (*sharply but contained*): What woman?

LINDA (*simultaneously*):   . . . and this woman . . .

LINDA: What?

BIFF: Nothing. Go ahead.

LINDA: What did you say?

BIFF: Nothing. I just said what woman?

HAPPY: What about her?

LINDA: Well, it seems she was walking down the road and saw his car. She says that he wasn't driving fast at all, and that he didn't skid.

She says he came to that little bridge, and then deliberately smashed into the railing, and it was only the shallowness of the water that saved him.

BIFF: Oh, no, he probably just fell asleep again.

LINDA: I don't think he fell asleep.

BIFF: Why not?

LINDA: Last month . . . (*With great difficulty.*) Oh, boys, it's so hard to say a thing like this! He's just a big stupid man to you, but I tell you there's more good in him than in many other people. (*She chokes, wipes her eyes.*) I was looking for a fuse. The lights blew out, and I went down the cellar. And behind the fuse box—it happened to fall out—was a length of rubber pipe—just short.

HAPPY: No kidding!

LINDA: There's a little attachment on the end of it. I knew right away. And sure enough, on the bottom of the water heater there's a new little nipple on the gas pipe.

HAPPY (*angrily*): That—jerk.

BIFF: Did you have it taken off?

LINDA: I'm—I'm ashamed to. How can I mention it to him? Every day I go down and take away that little rubber pipe. But, when he comes home, I put it back where it was. How can I insult him that way? I don't know what to do. I live from day to day, boys. I tell you, I know every thought in his mind. It sounds so old-fashioned and silly, but I tell you he put his whole life into you and you've turned your backs on him. (*She is bent over in the chair, weeping, her face in her hands.*) Biff, I swear to God! Biff, his life is in your hands!

HAPPY (*to Biff*): How do you like that damned fool!

BIFF (*kissing her*): All right, pal, all right. It's all settled now. I've been remiss. I know that, Mom. But now I'll stay, and I swear to you, I'll apply myself. (*Kneeling in front of her, in a fever of self-reproach.*) It's just—you see, Mom, I don't fit in business. Not that I won't try. I'll try, and I'll make good.

HAPPY: Sure you will. The trouble with you in business was you never tried to please people.

BIFF: I know, I . . .

HAPPY: Like when you worked for Harrison's. Bob Harrison said you were tops, and then you go and do some damn fool thing like whistling whole songs in the elevator like a comedian.

BIFF (*against Happy*):   So what? I like to whistle sometimes.

HAPPY: You don't raise a guy to a responsible job who whistles in the elevator!

LINDA: Well, don't argue about it now.

HAPPY: Like when you'd go off and swim in the middle of the day instead of taking the line around.

BIFF (*his resentment rising*):   Well, don't you run off? You take off sometimes, don't you? On a nice summer day?

HAPPY: Yeah, but I cover myself!

LINDA: Boys!

HAPPY: If I'm going to take a fade the boss can call any number where I'm supposed to be and they'll swear to him that I just left. I'll tell you something that I hate to say, Biff, but in the business world some of them think you're crazy.

BIFF (*angered*):   Screw the business world!

HAPPY: All right, screw it! Great, but cover yourself!

LINDA: Hap, Hap!

BIFF: I don't care what they think! They've laughed at Dad for years, and you know why? Because we don't belong in this nuthouse of a city! We should be mixing cement on some open plain or—or carpenters. A carpenter is allowed to whistle!

Willy walks in from the entrance of the house, at left.

WILLY: Even your grandfather was better than a carpenter. (*Pause. They watch him.*) You never grew up. Bernard does not whistle in the elevator, I assure you.

BIFF (*as though to laugh Willy out of it*):   Yeah, but you do, Pop.

WILLY: I never in my life whistled in an elevator! And who in the business world thinks I'm crazy?

BIFF: I didn't mean it like that, Pop. Now don't make a whole thing out of it, will ya?

WILLY: Go back to the West! Be a carpenter, a cowboy, enjoy yourself!

LINDA: Willy, he was just saying . . .

WILLY: I heard what he said!

HAPPY (*trying to quiet Willy*):   Hey, Pop, come on now . . .

WILLY (*continuing over Happy's line*):   They laugh at me, heh? Go to Filene's, go to the Hub, go to Slattery's, Boston. Call out the name Willy Loman and see what happens! Big shot!

BIFF: All right, Pop.

WILLY: Big!

BIFF: All right!

WILLY: Why do you always insult me?

BIFF: I didn't say a word. (*To Linda.*) Did I say a word?

LINDA: He didn't say anything, Willy.

WILLY (*going to the doorway of the living room*):   All right, good night, good night.

LINDA: Willy, dear, he just decided . . .

WILLY (*to Biff*):   If you get tired hanging around tomorrow, paint the ceiling I put up in the living room.

BIFF: I'm leaving early tomorrow.

HAPPY: He's going to see Bill Oliver, Pop.

WILLY (*interestedly*):   Oliver? For what?

BIFF (*with reserve, but trying; trying*):   He always said he'd stake me. I'd like to go into business, so maybe I can take him up on it.

LINDA: Isn't that wonderful?

WILLY: Don't interrupt. What's wonderful about it? There's fifty men in the City of New York who'd stake him. (*To Biff.*) Sporting goods?

BIFF: I guess so. I know something about it and . . .

WILLY: He knows something about it! You know sporting goods better than Spalding, for God's sake! How much is he giving you?

BIFF: I don't know, I didn't even see him yet, but . . .

WILLY: Then what're you talkin' about?

BIFF (*getting angry*):   Well, all I said was I'm gonna see him, that's all!

WILLY (*turning away*):   Ah, you're counting your chickens again.

BIFF (*starting left for the stairs*):   Oh, Jesus, I'm going to sleep!

WILLY (*calling after him*):   Don't curse in this house!

BIFF (*turning*):   Since when did you get so clean?

HAPPY (*trying to stop them*):   Wait a . . .

WILLY: Don't use that language to me! I won't have it!

HAPPY (*grabbing Biff, shouts*):   Wait a minute! I got an idea. I got a feasible idea. Come here, Biff, let's talk this over now, let's talk some sense here. When I was down in Florida last time, I thought of a great idea to sell sporting goods. It just came back to me. You and

I, Biff—we have a line, the Loman Line. We train a couple of weeks, and put on a couple of exhibitions, see?

WILLY: That's an idea!

HAPPY: Wait! We form two basketball teams, see? Two water-polo teams. We play each other. It's a million dollars' worth of publicity. Two brothers, see? The Loman Brothers. Displays in the Royal Palms—all the hotels. And banners over the ring and the basketball court: "Loman Brothers." Baby, we could sell sporting goods!

WILLY: That is a one-million-dollar idea!

LINDA: Marvelous!

BIFF: I'm in great shape as far as that's concerned.

HAPPY: And the beauty of it is, Biff, it wouldn't be like a business. We'd be out playin' ball again.

BIFF (*enthused*): Yeah, that's . . .

WILLY: Million-dollar . . .

HAPPY: And you wouldn't get fed up with it, Biff. It'd be the family again. There'd be the old honor, and comradeship, and if you wanted to go off for a swim or somethin'—well, you'd do it! Without some smart cooky gettin' up ahead of you!

WILLY: Lick the world! You guys together could absolutely lick the civilized world.

BIFF: I'll see Oliver tomorrow. Hap, if we could work that out . . .

LINDA: Maybe things are beginning to . . .

WILLY (*wildly enthused, to Linda*): Stop interrupting! (*To Biff.*) But don't wear sport jacket and slacks when you see Oliver.

BIFF: No, I'll . . .

WILLY: A business suit, and talk as little as possible, and don't crack any jokes.

BIFF: He did like me. Always liked me.

LINDA: He loved you!

WILLY (*to Linda*): Will you stop! (*To Biff.*) Walk in very serious. You are not applying for a boy's job. Money is to pass. Be quiet, fine, and serious. Everybody likes a kidder, but nobody lends him money.

HAPPY: I'll try to get some myself, Biff. I'm sure I can.

WILLY: I see great things for you kids, I think your troubles are over. But remember, start big and you'll end big. Ask for fifteen. How much you gonna ask for?

BIFF: Gee, I don't know . . .

WILLY: And don't say "Gee." "Gee" is a boy's word. A man walking in for fifteen thousand dollars does not say "Gee!"

BIFF: Ten, I think, would be top though.

WILLY: Don't be so modest. You always started too low. Walk in with a big laugh. Don't look worried. Start off with a couple of your good stories to lighten things up. It's not what you say, it's how you say it—because personality always wins the day.

LINDA: Oliver always thought the highest of him . . .

WILLY: Will you let me talk?

BIFF: Don't yell at her, Pop, will ya?

WILLY (*angrily*): I was talking, wasn't I?

BIFF: I don't like you yelling at her all the time, and I'm tellin' you, that's all.

WILLY: What're you, takin' over this house?

LINDA: Willy . . .

WILLY (*turning to her*): Don't take his side all the time, goddammit!

BIFF (*furiously*): Stop yelling at her!

WILLY (*suddenly pulling on his cheek, beaten down, guilt ridden*): Give my best to Bill Oliver—he may remember me. (*He exits through the living room doorway.*)

LINDA (*her voice subdued*): What'd you have to start that for? (*Biff turns away.*) You see how sweet he was as soon as you talked hopefully? (*She goes over to Biff.*) Come up and say good night to him. Don't let him go to bed that way.

HAPPY: Come on, Biff, let's buck him up.

LINDA: Please, dear. Just say good night. It takes so little to make him happy. Come. (*She goes through the living room doorway, calling upstairs from within the living room.*) Your pajamas are hanging in the bathroom, Willy!

HAPPY (*looking toward where Linda went out*): What a woman! They broke the mold when they made her. You know that, Biff.

BIFF: He's off salary. My God, working on commission!

HAPPY: Well, let's face it: he's no hot-shot selling man. Except that sometimes, you have to admit, he's a sweet personality.

BIFF (*deciding*): Lend me ten bucks, will ya? I want to buy some new ties.

HAPPY: I'll take you to a place I know. Beautiful stuff. Wear one of my striped shirts tomorrow.

BIFF: She got gray. Mom got awful old. Gee, I'm gonna go in to Oliver tomorrow and knock him for a . . .

HAPPY: Come on up. Tell that to Dad. Let's give him a whirl. Come on.

BIFF (*steamed up*): You know, with ten thousand bucks, boy!

HAPPY (*as they go into the living room*): That's the talk, Biff, that's the first time I've heard the old confidence out of you! (*From within the living room, fading off*) You're gonna live with me, kid, and any babe you want just say the word . . . (*The last lines are hardly heard. They are mounting the stairs to their parents' bedroom.*)

LINDA (*entering her bedroom and addressing Willy, who is in the bathroom. She is straightening the bed for him*): Can you do anything about the shower? It drips.

WILLY (*from the bathroom*): All of a sudden everything falls to pieces. Goddam plumbing, oughta be sued, those people. I hardly finished putting it in and the thing . . . (*His words rumble off.*)

LINDA: I'm just wondering if Oliver will remember him. You think he might?

WILLY (*coming out of the bathroom in his pajamas*): Remember him? What's the matter with you, you crazy? If he'd've stayed with Oliver he'd be on top by now! Wait'll Oliver gets a look at him. You don't know the average caliber any more. The average young man today—(*he is getting into bed*)—is got a caliber of zero. Greatest thing in the world for him was to bum around.

Biff and Happy enter the bedroom. Slight pause.

WILLY (*stops short, looking at Biff*): Glad to hear it, boy.

HAPPY: He wanted to say good night to you, sport.

WILLY (*to Biff*): Yeah. Knock him dead, boy. What'd you want to tell me?

BIFF: Just take it easy, Pop. Good night. (*He turns to go.*)

WILLY (*unable to resist*): And if anything falls off the desk while you're talking to him—like a package or something—don't you pick it up. They have office boys for that.

LINDA: I'll make a big breakfast . . .

WILLY: Will you let me finish? (*To Biff.*) Tell him you were in the business in the West. Not farm work.

BIFF: All right, Dad.

LINDA: I think everything . . .

WILLY (*going right through her speech*): And don't undersell yourself. No less than fifteen thousand dollars.

BIFF (*unable to bear him*): Okay. Good night, Mom. (*He starts moving.*)

WILLY: Because you got a greatness in you, Biff, remember that. You got all kinds of greatness . . . (*He lies back, exhausted. Biff walks out.*)

LINDA (*calling after Biff*): Sleep well, darling!

HAPPY: I'm gonna get married, Mom. I wanted to tell you.

LINDA: Go to sleep, dear.

HAPPY (*going*): I just wanted to tell you.

WILLY: Keep up the good work. (*Happy exits.*) God . . . remember that Ebbets Field game? The championship of the city?

LINDA: Just rest. Should I sing to you?

WILLY: Yeah. Sing to me. (*Linda hums a soft lullaby.*) When that team came out—he was the tallest, remember?

LINDA: Oh, yes. And in gold.

Biff enters the darkened kitchen, takes a cigarette, and leaves the house. He comes downstage into a golden pool of light. He smokes, staring at the night.

WILLY: Like a young god. Hercules—something like that. And the sun, the sun all around him. Remember how he waved to me? Right up from the field, with the representatives of three colleges standing by? And the buyers I brought, and the cheers when he came out— Loman, Loman, Loman! God Almighty, he'll be great yet. A star like that, magnificent, can never really fade away!

The light on Willy is fading. The gas heater begins to glow through the kitchen wall, near the stairs, a blue flame beneath red coils.

LINDA (*timidly*): Willy dear, what has he got against you?

WILLY: I'm so tired. Don't talk any more.

Biff slowly returns to the kitchen. He stops, stares toward the heater.

LINDA: Will you ask Howard to let you work in New York?

WILLY: First thing in the morning. Everything'll be all right.

Biff reaches behind the heater and draws out a length of rubber tubing. He is horrified and turns his head toward Willy's room, still dimly lit, from which the strains of Linda's desperate but monotonous humming rise.

WILLY (*staring through the window into the moonlight*):   Gee, look at the moon moving between the buildings! (*Biff wraps the tubing around his hand and quickly goes up the stairs.*)

Act 2

Scene: Music is heard, gay and bright. The curtain rises as the music fades away. Willy, in shirt sleeves, is sitting at the kitchen table, sipping coffee, his hat in his lap. Linda is filling his cup when she can.

WILLY: Wonderful coffee. Meal in itself.

LINDA: Can I make you some eggs?

WILLY: No. Take a breath.

LINDA: You look so rested, dear.

WILLY: I slept like a dead one. First time in months. Imagine, sleeping till ten on a Tuesday morning. Boys left nice and early, heh?

LINDA: They were out of here by eight o'clock.

WILLY: Good work!

LINDA: It was so thrilling to see them leaving together. I can't get over the shaving lotion in this house!

WILLY (*smiling*):   Mmm . . .

LINDA: Biff was very changed this morning. His whole attitude seemed to be hopeful. He couldn't wait to get downtown to see Oliver.

WILLY: He's heading for a change. There's no question, there simply are certain men that take longer to get—solidified. How did he dress?

LINDA: His blue suit. He's so handsome in that suit. He could be a— anything in that suit!

Willy gets up from the table. Linda holds his jacket for him.

WILLY: There's no question, no question at all. Gee, on the way home tonight I'd like to buy some seeds.

LINDA (*laughing*):   That'd be wonderful. But not enough sun gets back there. Nothing'll grow any more.

WILLY: You wait, kid, before it's all over we're gonna get a little place out in the country, and I'll raise some vegetables, a couple of chickens . . .

LINDA: You'll do it yet, dear.

Willy walks out of his jacket. Linda follows him.

WILLY: And they'll get married, and come for a weekend. I'd build a little guest house. 'Cause I got so many fine tools, all I'd need would be a little lumber and some peace of mind.

LINDA (*joyfully*):   I sewed the lining . . .

WILLY: I could build two guest houses, so they'd both come. Did he decide how much he's going to ask Oliver for?

LINDA (*getting him into the jacket*):   He didn't mention it, but I imagine ten or fifteen thousand. You going to talk to Howard today?

WILLY: Yeah. I'll put it to him straight and simple. He'll just have to take me off the road.

LINDA: And Willy, don't forget to ask for a little advance, because we've got the insurance premium. It's the grace period now.

WILLY: That's a hundred . . . ?

LINDA: A hundred and eight, sixty-eight. Because we're a little short again.

WILLY: Why are we short?

LINDA: Well, you had the motor job on the car . . .

WILLY: That goddam Studebaker!

LINDA: And you got one more payment on the refrigerator . . .

WILLY: But it just broke again!

LINDA: Well, it's old, dear.

WILLY: I told you we should've bought a well-advertised machine. Charley bought a General Electric and it's twenty years old and it's still good, that son-of-a-bitch.

LINDA: But, Willy . . .

WILLY: Whoever heard of a Hastings refrigerator? Once in my life I would like to own something outright before it's broken! I'm always in a race with the junkyard! I just finished paying for the car and it's on its last legs. The refrigerator consumes belts like a goddam maniac. They time those things. They time them so when you finally paid for them, they're used up.

LINDA (*buttoning up his jacket as he unbuttons it*):   All told, about two hundred dollars would carry us, dear. But that includes the last payment on the mortgage. After this payment, Willy, the house belongs to us.

WILLY: It's twenty-five years!

LINDA: Biff was nine years old when we bought it.

WILLY: Well, that's a great thing. To weather a twenty-five year mortgage is . . .

LINDA: It's an accomplishment.

WILLY: All the cement, the lumber, the reconstruction I put in this house! There ain't a crack to be found in it any more.

LINDA: Well, it served its purpose.

WILLY: What purpose? Some stranger'll come along, move in, and that's that. If only Biff would take this house, and raise a family . . . (*He starts to go.*) Good-by, I'm late.

LINDA (*suddenly remembering*):   Oh, I forgot! You're supposed to meet them for dinner.

WILLY: Me?

LINDA: At Frank's Chop House on Forty-eighth near Sixth Avenue.

WILLY: Is that so! How about you?

LINDA: No, just the three of you. They're gonna blow you to a big meal!

WILLY: Don't say! Who thought of that?

LINDA: Biff came to me this morning, Willy, and he said, "Tell Dad, we want to blow him to a big meal." Be there six o'clock. You and your two boys are going to have dinner.

WILLY: Gee whiz! That's really somethin'. I'm gonna knock Howard for a loop, kid. I'll get an advance, and I'll come home with a New York job. Goddammit, now I'm gonna do it!

LINDA: Oh, that's the spirit, Willy!

WILLY: I will never get behind a wheel the rest of my life!

LINDA: It's changing, Willy, I can feel it changing!

WILLY: Beyond a question. G'by, I'm late. (*He starts to go again.*)

LINDA (*calling after him as she runs to the kitchen table for a handkerchief*):   You got your glasses?

WILLY (*feels for them, then comes back in*):   Yeah, yeah, got my glasses.

LINDA (*giving him the handkerchief*):   And a handkerchief.

WILLY: Yeah, handkerchief.

LINDA: And your saccharine?

WILLY: Yeah, my saccharine.

LINDA: Be careful on the subway stairs.

She kisses him, and a silk stocking is seen hanging from her hand. Willy notices it.

WILLY: Will you stop mending stockings? At least while I'm in the house. It gets me nervous. I can't tell you. Please.

Linda hides the stocking in her hand as she follows Willy across the forestage in front of the house.

LINDA: Remember, Frank's Chop House.

WILLY (*passing the apron*): Maybe beets would grow out there.

LINDA (*laughing*): But you tried so many times.

WILLY: Yeah. Well, don't work hard today. (*He disappears around the right corner of the house.*)

LINDA: Be careful!

As Willy vanishes, Linda waves to him. Suddenly the phone rings. She runs across the stage and into the kitchen and lifts it.

LINDA: Hello? Oh, Biff! I'm so glad you called, I just . . . Yes, sure, I just told him. Yes, he'll be there for dinner at six o'clock, I didn't forget. Listen, I was just dying to tell you. You know that little rubber pipe I told you about? That he connected to the gas heater? I finally decided to go down the cellar this morning and take it away and destroy it. But it's gone! Imagine? He took it away himself, it isn't there! (*She listens.*) When? Oh, then you took it. Oh—nothing, it's just that I'd hoped he'd taken it away himself. Oh, I'm not worried, darling, because this morning he left in such high spirits, it was like the old days! I'm not afraid any more. Did Mr. Oliver see you?. . . Well, you wait there then. And make a nice impression on him, darling. Just don't perspire too much before you see him. And have a nice time with Dad. He may have big news too!. . . That's right, a New York job. And be sweet to him tonight, dear. Be loving to him. Because he's only a little boat looking for a harbor. (*She is trembling with sorrow and joy.*) Oh, that's wonderful, Biff, you'll save his life. Thanks, darling. Just put your arm around him when he comes into the restaurant. Give him a smile. That's the boy . . .

Good-by, dear. . . . You got your comb?. . . That's fine. Good-by, Biff dear.

In the middle of her speech, Howard Wagner, thirty-six, wheels in a small typewriter table on which is a wire-recording machine and proceeds to plug it in. This is on the left forestage. Light slowly fades on Linda as it rises on Howard. Howard is intent on threading the machine and only glances over his shoulder as Willy appears.

WILLY: Pst! Pst!

HOWARD: Hello, Willy, come in.

WILLY: Like to have a little talk with you, Howard.

HOWARD: Sorry to keep you waiting. I'll be with you in a minute.

WILLY: What's that, Howard?

HOWARD: Didn't you ever see one of these? Wire recorder.

WILLY: Oh. Can we talk a minute?

HOWARD: Records things. Just got delivery yesterday. Been driving me crazy, the most terrific machine I ever saw in my life. I was up all night with it.

WILLY: What do you do with it?

HOWARD: I bought it for dictation, but you can do anything with it. Listen to this. I had it home last night. Listen to what I picked up. The first one is my daughter. Get this. (*He flicks the switch and "Roll Out the Barrel" is heard being whistled.*) Listen to that kid whistle.

WILLY: That is lifelike, isn't it?

HOWARD: Seven years old. Get that tone.

WILLY: Ts, ts. Like to ask a little favor if you . . .

The whistling breaks off, and the voice of Howard's daughter is heard.

HIS DAUGHTER: "Now you, Daddy."

HOWARD: She's crazy for me! (*Again the same song is whistled.*) That's me! Ha! (*He winks.*)

WILLY: You're very good!

The whistling breaks off again. The machine runs silent for a moment.

HOWARD: Sh! Get this now, this is my son.

HIS SON: "The capital of Alabama is Montgomery; the capital of Arizona is Phoenix; the capital of Arkansas is Little Rock; the capital of California is Sacramento . . ." (*and on, and on.*)

HOWARD (*holding up five fingers*): Five years old, Willy!

WILLY: He'll make an announcer some day!

HIS SON (*continuing*): "The capital . . ."

HOWARD: Get that—alphabetical order! (*The machine breaks off suddenly.*) Wait a minute. The maid kicked the plug out.

WILLY: It certainly is a . . .

HOWARD: Sh, for God's sake!

HIS SON: "It's nine o'clock, Bulova watch time. So I have to go to sleep."

WILLY: That really is . . .

HOWARD: Wait a minute! The next is my wife.

They wait.

HOWARD'S VOICE: "Go on, say something." (*Pause.*) "Well, you gonna talk?"

HIS WIFE: "I can't think of anything."

HOWARD'S VOICE: "Well, talk—it's turning."

HIS WIFE (*shyly, beaten*): "Hello." (*Silence.*) "Oh, Howard, I can't talk into this . . ."

HOWARD (*snapping the machine off*): That was my wife.

WILLY: That is a wonderful machine. Can we . . .

HOWARD: I tell you, Willy, I'm gonna take my camera, and my bandsaw, and all my hobbies, and out they go. This is the most fascinating relaxation I ever found.

WILLY: I think I'll get one myself.

HOWARD: Sure, they're only a hundred and a half. You can't do without it. Supposing you wanna hear Jack Benny, see? But you can't be at home at that hour. So you tell the maid to turn the radio on when Jack Benny comes on, and this automatically goes on with the radio . . .

WILLY: And when you come home you . . .

HOWARD: You can come home twelve o'clock, one o'clock, any time you like, and you get yourself a Coke and sit yourself down, throw the switch, and there's Jack Benny's program in the middle of the night!

WILLY: I'm definitely going to get one. Because lots of times I'm on the road, and I think to myself, what I must be missing on the radio!

HOWARD: Don't you have a radio in the car?

WILLY: Well, yeah, but who ever thinks of turning it on?

HOWARD: Say, aren't you supposed to be in Boston?

WILLY: That's what I want to talk to you about, Howard. You got a minute? (*He draws a chair in from the wing.*)

HOWARD: What happened? What're you doing here?

WILLY: Well . . .

HOWARD: You didn't crack up again, did you?

WILLY: Oh, no. No . . .

HOWARD: Geez, you had me worried there for a minute. What's the trouble?

WILLY: Well, tell you the truth, Howard. I've come to the decision that I'd rather not travel any more.

HOWARD: Not travel! Well, what'll you do?

WILLY: Remember, Christmas time, when you had the party here? You said you'd try to think of some spot for me here in town.

HOWARD: With us?

WILLY: Well, sure.

HOWARD: Oh, yeah, yeah. I remember. Well, I couldn't think of anything for you, Willy.

WILLY: I tell ya, Howard. The kids are all grown up, y'know. I don't need much any more. If I could take home—well, sixty-five dollars a week, I could swing it.

HOWARD: Yeah, but Willy, see I . . .

WILLY: I tell ya why, Howard. Speaking frankly and between the two of us, y'know—I'm just a little tired.

HOWARD: Oh, I could understand that, Willy. But you're a road man, Willy, and we do a road business. We've only got a half-dozen salesmen on the floor here.

WILLY: God knows, Howard. I never asked a favor of any man. But I was with the firm when your father used to carry you in here in his arms.

HOWARD: I know that, Willy, but . . .

WILLY: Your father came to me the day you were born and asked me what I thought of the name Howard, may he rest in peace.

HOWARD: I appreciate that, Willy, but there just is no spot here for you. If I had a spot I'd slam you right in, but I just don't have a single solitary spot.

He looks for his lighter. Willy has picked it up and gives it to him. Pause.

WILLY (*with increasing anger*): Howard, all I need to set my table is fifty dollars a week.

HOWARD: But where am I going to put you, kid?

WILLY: Look, it isn't a question of whether I can sell merchandise, is it?

HOWARD: No, but it's business, kid, and everybody's gotta pull his own weight.

WILLY (*desperately*): Just let me tell you a story, Howard . . .

HOWARD: 'Cause you gotta admit, business is business.

WILLY (*angrily*): Business is definitely business, but just listen for a minute. You don't understand this. When I was a boy—eighteen, nineteen—I was already on the road. And there was a question in my mind as to whether selling had a future for me. Because in those days I had a yearning to go to Alaska. See, there were three gold strikes in one month in Alaska, and I felt like going out. Just for the ride, you might say.

HOWARD (*barely interested*): Don't say.

WILLY: Oh, yeah, my father lived many years in Alaska. He was an adventurous man. We've got quite a little streak of self-reliance in our family. I thought I'd go out with my older brother and try to locate him, and maybe settle in the North with the old man. And I was almost decided to go, when I met a salesman in the Parker House. His name was Dave Singleman. And he was eighty-four years old, and he'd drummed merchandise in thirty-one states. And old Dave, he'd go up to his room, y'understand, put on his green velvet slippers—I'll never forget—and pick up his phone and call the buyers, and without ever leaving his room, at the age of eighty-four, he made his living. And when I saw that, I realized that selling was the greatest career a man could want. 'Cause what could be more satisfying than to be able to go, at the age of eight-four, into twenty or thirty different cities, and pick up a phone, and be remembered and loved and helped by so many different people? Do you know? when he died—and by the way he died the death of a salesman, in his green velvet slippers in the smoker of the New York, New Haven and Hartford, going into Boston—when he died, hundreds of salesmen and buyers were at his funeral. Things were sad on a lotta trains for months after that. (*He stands up, Howard has not looked at him.*) In those days there was personality in it, Howard. There was respect, and comradeship, and gratitude in it. Today, it's all cut and dried, and there's no chance for bringing friendship to bear—or personality. You see what I mean? They don't know me any more.

HOWARD (*moving away, to the right*): That's just the thing, Willy.

WILLY: If I had forty dollars a week—that's all I'd need. Forty dollars, Howard.

HOWARD: Kid, I can't take blood from a stone, I . . .

WILLY (*desperation is on him now*): Howard, the year Al Smith was nominated, your father came to me and . . .

HOWARD (*starting to go off*): I've got to see some people, kid.

WILLY (*stopping him*): I'm talking about your father! There were promises made across this desk! You mustn't tell me you've got people to see—I put thirty-four years into this firm, Howard, and now I can't pay my insurance! You can't eat the orange and throw the peel away—a man is not a piece of fruit! (*After a pause.*) Now pay attention. Your father—in 1928 I had a big year. I averaged a hundred and seventy dollars a week in commissions.

HOWARD (*impatiently*): Now, Willy, you never averaged . . .

WILLY (*banging his hand on the desk*): I averaged a hundred and seventy dollars a week in the year of 1928! And your father came to me—or rather, I was in the office here—it was right over this desk—and he put his hand on my shoulder . . .

HOWARD (*getting up*): You'll have to excuse me, Willy, I gotta see some people. Pull yourself together. (*Going out.*) I'll be back in a little while.

On Howard's exit, the light on his chair grows very bright and strange.

WILLY: Pull myself together! What the hell did I say to him? My God, I was yelling at him! How could I? (*Willy breaks off, staring at the light, which occupies the chair, animating it. He approaches this chair, standing across the desk from it.*) Frank, Frank, don't you remember what you told me that time? How you put your hand on my shoulder, and Frank . . . (*He leans on the desk and as he speaks the dead man's name he accidentally switches on the recorder, and instantly*)

HOWARD'S SON: ". . . of New York is Albany. The capital of Ohio is Cincinnati, the capital of Rhode Island is . . ." (*The recitation continues.*)

WILLY (*leaping away with fright, shouting*): Ha! Howard! Howard! Howard!

HOWARD (*rushing in*): What happened?

WILLY (*pointing at the machine, which continues nasally, childishly, with the capital cities*): Shut it off! Shut it off!

HOWARD (*pulling the plug out*): Look, Willy . . .

WILLY (*pressing his hands to his eyes*): I gotta get myself some coffee. I'll get some coffee . . .

Willy starts to walk out. Howard stops him.

HOWARD (*rolling up the cord*): Willy, look . . .

WILLY: I'll go to Boston.

HOWARD: Willy, you can't go to Boston for us.

WILLY: Why can't I go?

HOWARD: I don't want you to represent us. I've been meaning to tell you for a long time now.

WILLY: Howard, are you firing me?

HOWARD: I think you need a good long rest, Willy.

WILLY: Howard . . .

HOWARD: And when you feel better, come back, and we'll see if we can work something out.

WILLY: But I gotta earn money, Howard. I'm in no position to . . .

HOWARD: Where are your sons? Why don't your sons give you a hand?

WILLY: They're working on a very big deal.

HOWARD: This is no time for false pride, Willy. You go to your sons and you tell them that you're tired. You've got two great boys, haven't you?

WILLY: Oh, no question, no question, but in the meantime . . .

HOWARD: Then that's that, heh?

WILLY: All right, I'll go to Boston tomorrow.

HOWARD: No, no.

WILLY: I can't throw myself on my sons. I'm not a cripple!

HOWARD: Look, kid, I'm busy this morning.

WILLY (*grasping Howard's arm*): Howard, you've got to let me go to Boston!

HOWARD (*hard, keeping himself under control*): I've got a line of people to see this morning. Sit down, take five minutes, and pull yourself together, and then go home, will ya? I need the office, Willy. (*He starts to go, turns, remembering the recorder, starts to push off the table holding the recorder.*) Oh, yeah. Whenever you can this week, stop by and drop off the samples. You'll feel better, Willy, and then come back and we'll talk. Pull yourself together, kid, there's people outside.

Howard exits, pushing the table off left. Willy stares into space, exhausted. Now the music is heard—Ben's music—first distantly, then closer, closer. As Willy speaks, Ben enters from the right. He carries valise and umbrella.

WILLY: Oh, Ben, how did you do it? What is the answer? Did you wind up the Alaska deal already?

BEN: Doesn't take much time if you know what you're doing. Just a short business trip. Boarding ship in an hour. Wanted to say good-by.

WILLY: Ben, I've got to talk to you.

BEN (*glancing at his watch*): Haven't the time, William.

WILLY (*crossing the apron to Ben*): Ben, nothing's working out. I don't know what to do.

BEN: Now, look here, William. I've bought timberland in Alaska and I need a man to look after things for me.

WILLY: God, timberland! Me and my boys in those grand outdoors!

BEN: You've a new continent at your doorstep, William. Get out of these cities, they're full of talk and time payments and courts of law. Screw on your fists and you can fight for a fortune up there.

WILLY: Yes, yes! Linda, Linda!

Linda enters as of old, with the wash.

LINDA: Oh, you're back?

BEN: I haven't much time.

WILLY: No, wait! Linda, he's got a proposition for me in Alaska.

LINDA: But you've got . . . (*To Ben.*) He's got a beautiful job here.

WILLY: But in Alaska, kid, I could . . .

LINDA: You're doing well enough, Willy!

BEN (*to Linda*): Enough for what, my dear?

LINDA (*frightened of Ben and angry at him*): Don't say those things to him! Enough to be happy right here, right now. (*To Willy, while Ben laughs.*) Why must everybody conquer the world? You're well liked, and the boys love you, and someday—(*To Ben*)—why, old man Wagner told him just the other day that if he keeps it up he'll be a member of the firm, didn't he, Willy?

WILLY: Sure, sure. I am building something with this firm, Ben, and if a man is building something he must be on the right track, mustn't he?

BEN: What are you building? Lay your hand on it. Where is it?

WILLY (*hesitantly*): That's true, Linda, there's nothing.

LINDA: Why? (*To Ben.*) There's a man eighty-four years old . . .

WILLY: That's right, Ben, that's right. When I look at that man I say, what is there to worry about?

BEN: Bah!

WILLY: It's true, Ben. All he has to do is go into any city, pick up the phone, and he's making his living and you know why?

BEN (*picking up his valise*): I've got to go.

WILLY (*HOLDING BEN BACK*): Look at this boy!

Biff, in his high school sweater, enters carrying suitcase. Happy carries Biff's shoulder guards, gold helmet, and football pants.

WILLY: Without a penny to his name, three great universities are begging for him, and from there the sky's the limit, because it's not what you do, Ben. It's who you know and the smile on your face! It's contacts, Ben, contacts! The whole wealth of Alaska passes over the lunch table at the Commodore Hotel, and that's the wonder, the wonder of this country, that a man can end with diamonds here on the basis of being liked! (*He turns to Biff.*) And that's why when you get out on that field today it's important. Because thousands of people will be rooting for you and loving you. (*To Ben, who has again begun to leave.*) And Ben! when he walks into a business office his name will sound out like a bell and all the doors will open to him! I've seen it, Ben, I've seen it a thousand times! You can't feel it with your hand like timber, but it's there!

BEN: Good-by, William.

WILLY: Ben, am I right? Don't you think I'm right? I value your advice.

BEN: There's a new continent at your doorstep, William. You could walk out rich. Rich! (*He is gone.*)

WILLY: We'll do it here, Ben! You hear me? We're gonna do it here!

Young Bernard rushes in. The gay music of the Boys is heard.

BERNARD: Oh, gee, I was afraid you left already!

WILLY: Why? What time is it?

BERNARD: It's half-past one!

WILLY: Well, come on, everybody! Ebbets Field next stop! Where's the pennants? (*He rushes through the wall-line of the kitchen and out into the living room.*)

LINDA (*to Biff*): Did you pack fresh underwear?

BIFF (*who has been limbering up*): I want to go!

BERNARD: Biff, I'm carrying your helmet, ain't I?

HAPPY: No, I'm carrying the helmet.

BERNARD: Oh, Biff, you promised me.

HAPPY: I'm carrying the helmet.

BERNARD: How am I going to get in the locker room?

LINDA: Let him carry the shoulder guards. (*She puts her coat and hat on in the kitchen.*)

BERNARD: Can I, Biff? 'Cause I told everybody I'm going to be in the locker room.

HAPPY: In Ebbets Field it's the clubhouse.

BERNARD: I meant the clubhouse. Biff!

HAPPY: Biff!

BIFF (*grandly, after a slight pause*): Let him carry the shoulder guards.

HAPPY (*as he gives Bernard the shoulder guards*): Stay close to us now.

Willy rushes in with the pennants.

WILLY (*handing them out*): Everybody wave when Biff comes out on the field. (*Happy and Bernard run off.*) You set now, boy?

The music has died away.

BIFF: Ready to go, Pop. Every muscle is ready.

WILLY (*at the edge of the apron*):   You realize what this means?

BIFF: That's right, Pop.

WILLY (*feeling Biff's muscles*):   You're comin' home this afternoon captain of the All-Scholastic Championship Team of the City of New York.

BIFF: I got it, Pop. And remember, pal, when I take off my helmet, that touchdown is for you.

WILLY: Let's go! (*He is starting out, with his arm around Biff, when Charley enters, as of old, in knickers.*) I got no room for you, Charley.

CHARLEY: Room? For what?

WILLY: In the car.

CHARLEY: You goin' for a ride? I wanted to shoot some casino.

WILLY (*furiously*):   Casino! (*Incredulously.*) Don't you realize what today is?

LINDA: Oh, he knows, Willy. He's just kidding you.

WILLY: That's nothing to kid about!

CHARLEY: No, Linda, what's goin' on?

LINDA: He's playing in Ebbets Field.

CHARLEY: Baseball in this weather?

WILLY: Don't talk to him. Come on, come on! (*He is pushing them out.*)

CHARLEY: Wait a minute, didn't you hear the news?

WILLY: What?

CHARLEY: Don't you listen to the radio? Ebbets Field just blew up.

WILLY: You go to hell! (*Charley laughs. Pushing them out.*) Come on, come on! We're late.

CHARLEY (*as they go*):   Knock a homer, Biff, knock a homer!

WILLY (*the last to leave, turning to Charley*):   I don't think that was funny, Charley. This is the greatest day of his life.

CHARLEY: Willy, when are you going to grow up?

WILLY: Yeah, heh? When this game is over, Charley, you'll be laughing out of the other side of your face. They'll be calling him another Red Grange. Twenty-five thousand a year.

CHARLEY (*kidding*):   Is that so?

WILLY: Yeah, that's so.

CHARLEY: Well, then, I'm sorry, Willy. But tell me something.

WILLY: What?

CHARLEY: Who is Red Grange?

WILLY: Put up your hands. Goddam you, put up your hands!

Charley, chuckling, shakes his head and walks away, around the left corner of the stage. Willy follows him. The music rises to a mocking frenzy.

WILLY: Who the hell do you think you are, better than everybody else? You don't know everything, you big, ignorant, stupid . . . Put up your hands!

Light rises, on the right side of the forestage, on a small table in the reception room of Charley's office. Traffic sounds are heard. Bernard, now mature, sits whistling to himself. A pair of tennis rackets and an old overnight bag are on the floor beside him.

WILLY (*offstage*): What are you walking away for? Don't walk away! If you're going to say something say it to my face! I know you laugh at me behind my back. You'll laugh out of the other side of your goddam face after this game. Touchdown! Touchdown! Eighty thousand people! Touchdown! Right between the goal posts.

Bernard is a quiet, earnest, but self-assured young man. Willy's voice is coming from right upstage now. Bernard lowers his feet off the table and listens. Jenny, his father's secretary, enters.

JENNY (*distressed*): Say, Bernard, will you go out in the hall?

BERNARD: What is that noise? Who is it?

JENNY: Mr. Loman. He just got off the elevator.

BERNARD (*getting up*): Who's he arguing with?

JENNY: Nobody. There's nobody with him. I can't deal with him any more, and your father gets all upset every time he comes. I've got a lot of typing to do, and your father's waiting to sign it. Will you see him?

WILLY (*entering*): Touchdown! Touch—(*He sees Jenny.*) Jenny, Jenny, good to see you. How're ya? Workin'? Or still honest?

JENNY: Fine. How've you been feeling?

WILLY: Not much any more, Jenny. Ha, ha! (*He is surprised to see the rackets.*)

BERNARD: Hello, Uncle Willy.

WILLY (*almost shocked*): Bernard! Well, look who's here! (*He comes quickly, guiltily, to Bernard and warmly shakes his hand.*)

BERNARD: How are you? Good to see you.

WILLY: What are you doing here?

BERNARD: Oh, just stopped by to see Pop. Get off my feet till my train leaves. I'm going to Washington in a few minutes.

WILLY: Is he in?

BERNARD: Yes, he's in his office with the accountant. Sit down.

WILLY (*sitting down*): What're you going to do in Washington?

BERNARD: Oh, just a case I've got there, Willy.

WILLY: That so? (*Indicating the rackets.*) You going to play tennis there?

BERNARD: I'm staying with a friend who's got a court.

WILLY: Don't say. His own tennis court. Must be fine people, I bet.

BERNARD: They are, very nice. Dad tells me Biff's in town.

WILLY (*with a big smile*): Yeah, Biff's in. Working on a very big deal, Bernard.

BERNARD: What's Biff doing?

WILLY: Well, he's been doing very big things in the West. But he decided to establish himself here. Very big. We're having dinner. Did I hear your wife had a boy?

BERNARD: That's right. Our second.

WILLY: Two boys! What do you know!

BERNARD: What kind of a deal has Biff got?

WILLY: Well, Bill Oliver—very big sporting-goods man—he wants Biff very badly. Called him in from the West. Long distance, carte blanche, special deliveries. Your friends have their own private tennis court?

BERNARD: You still with the old firm, Willy?

WILLY (*after a pause*): I'm—I'm overjoyed to see how you made the grade, Bernard, overjoyed. It's an encouraging thing to see a young man really—really . . . Looks very good for Biff—very . . . (*He breaks off, then.*) Bernard . . . (*He is so full of emotion, he breaks off again.*)

BERNARD: What is it, Willy?

WILLY (*small and alone*): What—what's the secret?

BERNARD: What secret?

WILLY: How—how did you? Why didn't he ever catch on?

BERNARD: I wouldn't know that, Willy.

WILLY (*confidentially; desperately*):   You were his friend, his boyhood friend. There's something I don't understand about it. His life ended after that Ebbets Field game. From the age of seventeen nothing good ever happened to him.

BERNARD: He never trained himself for anything.

WILLY: But he did, he did. After high school he took so many correspondence courses. Radio mechanics; television; God knows what, and never made the slightest mark.

BERNARD (*taking off his glasses*):   Willy, do you want to talk candidly?

WILLY (*rising, faces Bernard*):   I regard you as a very brilliant man, Bernard. I value your advice.

BERNARD: Oh, the hell with the advice, Willy. I couldn't advise you. There's just one thing I've always wanted to ask you. When he was supposed to graduate, and the math teacher flunked him . . .

WILLY: Oh, that son-of-a-bitch ruined his life.

BERNARD: Yeah, but, Willy, all he had to do was go to summer school and make up that subject.

WILLY: That's right, that's right.

BERNARD: Did you tell him not to go to summer school?

WILLY: Me? I begged him to go. I ordered him to go!

BERNARD: Then why wouldn't he go?

WILLY: Why? Why! Bernard, that question has been trailing me like a ghost for the last fifteen years. He flunked the subject, and laid down and died like a hammer hit him!

BERNARD: Take it easy, kid.

WILLY: Let me talk to you—I got nobody to talk to. Bernard, Bernard, was it my fault? Y'see? It keeps going around in my mind, maybe I did something to him. I got nothing to give him.

BERNARD: Don't take it so hard.

WILLY: Why did he lay down? What is the story there? You were his friend!

BERNARD: Willy, I remember, it was June, and our grades came out. And he'd flunked math.

WILLY: That son-of-a-bitch!

BERNARD: No, it wasn't right then. Biff just got very angry, I remember, and he was ready to enroll in summer school.

WILLY (*surprised*):   He was?

BERNARD: He wasn't beaten by it at all. But then, Willy, he disappeared from the block for almost a month. And I got the idea that he'd gone up to New England to see you. Did he have a talk with you then?

Willy stares in silence.

BERNARD: Willy?

WILLY (*with a strong edge of resentment in his voice*): Yeah, he came to Boston. What about it?

BERNARD: Well, just that when he came back—I'll never forget this, it always mystifies me. Because I'd thought so well of Biff, even though he'd always taken advantage of me. I loved him, Willy, y'know? And he came back after that month and took his sneakers—remember those sneakers with "University of Virginia" printed on them? He was so proud of those, wore them every day. And he took them down in the cellar, and burned them up in the furnace. We had a fist fight. It lasted at least half an hour. Just the two of us, punching each other down the cellar, and crying right through it. I've often thought of how strange it was that I knew he'd given up his life. What happened in Boston, Willy?

Willy looks at him as at an intruder.

BERNARD: I just bring it up because you asked me.

WILLY (*angrily*): Nothing. What do you mean, "What happened?" What's that got to do with anything?

BERNARD: Well, don't get sore.

WILLY: What are you trying to do, blame it on me? If a boy lays down is that my fault?

BERNARD: Now, Willy, don't get . . .

WILLY: Well, don't—don't talk to me that way! What does that mean, "What happened?"

Charley enters. He is in his vest, and he carries a bottle of bourbon.

CHARLEY: Hey, you're going to miss that train. (*He waves the bottle.*)

BERNARD: Yeah, I'm going. (*He takes the bottle.*) Thanks, Pop. (*He picks up his rackets and bag.*) Good-by, Willy, and don't worry about it. You know, "If at first you don't succeed . . ."

WILLY: Yes, I believe in that.

BERNARD: But sometimes, Willy, it's better for a man just to walk away.

WILLY: Walk away?

BERNARD: That's right.

WILLY: But if you can't walk away?

BERNARD (*after a slight pause*):   I guess that's when it's tough. (*Extending his hand.*) Good-by, Willy.

WILLY (*shaking Bernard's hand*):   Good-by, boy.

CHARLEY (*an arm on Bernard's shoulder*):   How do you like this kid? Gonna argue a case in front of the Supreme Court.

BERNARD (*protesting*):   Pop!

WILLY (*genuinely shocked, pained, and happy*):   No! The Supreme Court!

BERNARD: I gotta run. 'By, Dad!

CHARLEY: Knock 'em dead, Bernard!

Bernard goes off.

WILLY (*as Charley takes out his wallet*):   The Supreme Court! And he didn't even mention it!

CHARLEY (*counting out money on the desk*):   He don't have to—he's gonna do it.

WILLY: And you never told him what to do, did you? You never took any interest in him.

CHARLEY: My salvation is that I never took any interest in anything. There's some money—fifty dollars. I got an accountant inside.

WILLY: Charley, look . . . (*with difficulty.*) I got my insurance to pay. If you can manage it—I need a hundred and ten dollars.

Charley doesn't reply for a moment; merely stops moving.

WILLY: I'd draw it from my bank but Linda would know, and I . . .

CHARLEY: Sit down, Willy.

WILLY (*moving toward the chair*):   I'm keeping an account of everything, remember. I'll pay every penny back. (*He sits.*)

CHARLEY: Now listen to me, Willy.

WILLY: I want you to know I appreciate . . .

CHARLEY (*sitting down on the table*): Willy, what're you doin'? What the hell is going on in your head?

WILLY: Why? I'm simply . . .

CHARLEY: I offered you a job. You make fifty dollars a week. And I won't send you on the road.

WILLY: I've got a job.

CHARLEY: Without pay? What kind of a job is a job without pay? (*He rises.*) Now, look, kid, enough is enough. I'm no genius but I know when I'm being insulted.

WILLY: Insulted!

CHARLEY: Why don't you want to work for me?

WILLY: What's the matter with you? I've got a job.

CHARLEY: Then what're you walkin' in here every week for?

WILLY (*getting up*): Well, if you don't want me to walk in here . . .

CHARLEY: I'm offering you a job.

WILLY: I don't want your goddam job!

CHARLEY: When the hell are you going to grow up?

WILLY (*furiously*): You big ignoramus, if you say that to me again I'll rap you one! I don't care how big you are! (*He's ready to fight.*)

Pause.

CHARLEY (*kindly, going to him*): How much do you need, Willy?

WILLY: Charley, I'm strapped. I'm strapped. I don't know what to do. I was just fired.

CHARLEY: Howard fired you?

WILLY: That snotnose. Imagine that? I named him. I named him Howard.

CHARLEY: Willy, when're you gonna realize that them things don't mean anything? You named him Howard, but you can't sell that. The only thing you got in this world is what you can sell. And the funny thing is that you're a salesman, and you don't know that.

WILLY: I've always tried to think otherwise, I guess. I always felt that if a man was impressive, and well liked, that nothing . . .

CHARLEY: Why must everybody like you? Who liked J. P. Morgan? Was he impressive? In a Turkish bath he'd look like a butcher. But with his pockets on he was very well liked. Now listen, Willy, I know you don't like me, and nobody can say I'm in love with you, but I'll give you a job because—just for the hell of it, put it that way. Now what do you say?

WILLY: I—I just can't work for you, Charley.

CHARLEY: What're you, jealous of me?

WILLY: I can't work for you, that's all, don't ask me why.

CHARLEY (*angered, takes out more bills*): You been jealous of me all your life, you damned fool! Here, pay your insurance. (*He puts the money in Willy's hand.*)

WILLY: I'm keeping strict accounts.

CHARLEY: I've got some work to do. Take care of yourself. And pay your insurance.

WILLY (*moving to the right*): Funny, y'know? After all the highways, and the trains, and the appointments, and the years, you end up worth more dead than alive.

CHARLEY: Willy, nobody's worth nothin' dead. (*After a slight pause.*) Did you hear what I said?

Willy stands still, dreaming.

CHARLEY: Willy!

WILLY: Apologize to Bernard for me when you see him. I didn't mean to argue with him. He's a fine boy. They're all fine boys, and they'll end up big—all of them. Someday they'll all play tennis together. Wish me luck, Charley. He saw Bill Oliver today.

CHARLEY: Good luck.

WILLY (*on the verge of tears*): Charley, you're the only friend I got. Isn't that a remarkable thing? (*He goes out.*)

CHARLEY: Jesus!

Charley stares after him a moment and follows. All light blacks out. Suddenly raucous music is heard, and a red glow rises behind the screen at right. Stanley, a young waiter, appears, carrying a table, followed by Happy, who is carrying two chairs.

STANLEY (*putting the table down*): That's all right, Mr. Loman, I can handle it myself. (*He turns and takes the chairs from Happy and places them at the table.*)

HAPPY (*glancing around*): Oh, this is better.

STANLEY: Sure, in the front there you're in the middle of all kinds of noise. Whenever you got a party, Mr. Loman, you just tell me and I'll put you back here. Y'know, there's a lotta people they don't like it private, because when they go out they like to see a lotta action around them because they're sick and tired to stay in the house by theirself. But I know you, you ain't from Hackensack. You know what I mean?

HAPPY (*sitting down*): So how's it coming, Stanley?

STANLEY: Ah, it's a dog life. I only wish during the war they'd a took me in the Army. I coulda been dead by now.

HAPPY: My brother's back, Stanley.

STANLEY: Oh, he come back, heh? From the Far West.

HAPPY: Yeah, big cattle man, my brother, so treat him right. And my father's coming too.

STANLEY: Oh, your father too!

HAPPY: You got a couple of nice lobsters?

STANLEY: Hundred per cent, big.

HAPPY: I want them with the claws.

STANLEY: Don't worry, I don't give you no mice. (*Happy laughs.*) How about some wine? It'll put a head on the meal.

HAPPY: No. You remember, Stanley, that recipe I brought you from overseas? With the champagne in it?

STANLEY: Oh, yeah, sure. I still got it tacked up yet in the kitchen. But that'll have to cost a buck apiece anyways.

HAPPY: That's all right.

STANLEY: What'd you, hit a number or somethin'?

HAPPY: No, it's a little celebration. My brother is—I think he pulled off a big deal today. I think we're going into business together.

STANLEY: Great! That's the best for you. Because a family business, you know what I mean?—that's the best.

HAPPY: That's what I think.

STANLEY: 'Cause what's the difference? Somebody steals? It's in the family. Know what I mean? (*Sotto voce.*) Like this bartender here. The boss is goin' crazy what kinda leak he's got in the cash register. You put it in but it don't come out.

HAPPY (*raising his head*): Sh!

STANLEY: What?

HAPPY: You notice I wasn't lookin' right or left, was I?

STANLEY: No.

HAPPY: And my eyes are closed.

STANLEY: So what's the . . . ?

HAPPY: Strudel's comin'.

STANLEY (*catching on, looks around*):   Ah, no, there's no . . .

He breaks off as a furred, lavishly dressed Girl enters and sits at the next table. Both follow her with their eyes.

STANLEY: Geez, how'd ya know?

HAPPY: I got radar or something. (*Staring directly at her profile.*) Oooooooo . . . Stanley.

STANLEY: I think that's for you, Mr. Loman.

HAPPY: Look at that mouth. Oh, God. And the binoculars.

STANLEY: Geez, you got a life, Mr. Loman.

HAPPY: Wait on her.

STANLEY (*going to the Girl's table*):   Would you like a menu, ma'am?

GIRL: I'm expecting someone, but I'd like a . . .

HAPPY: Why don't you bring her—excuse me, miss, do you mind? I sell champagne, and I'd like you to try my brand. Bring her a champagne, Stanley.

GIRL: That's awfully nice of you.

HAPPY: Don't mention it. It's all company money. (*He laughs.*)

GIRL: That's a charming product to be selling, isn't it?

HAPPY: Oh, gets to be like everything else. Selling is selling, y'know.

GIRL: I suppose.

HAPPY: You don't happen to sell, do you?

GIRL: No, I don't sell.

HAPPY: Would you object to a compliment from a stranger? You ought to be on a magazine cover.

GIRL (*looking at him a little archly*):   I have been.

Stanley comes in with a glass of champagne.

HAPPY: What'd I say before, Stanley? You see? She's a cover girl.

STANLEY: Oh, I could see, I could see.

HAPPY (*to the Girl*):   What magazine?

GIRL: Oh, a lot of them. (*She takes the drink.*) Thank you.

HAPPY: You know what they say in France, don't you? "Champagne is the drink of the complexion"—Hya, Biff!

Biff has entered and sits with Happy.

BIFF: Hello, kid. Sorry I'm late.

HAPPY: I just got here. Uh, Miss . . . ?

GIRL: Forsythe.

HAPPY: Miss Forsythe, this is my brother.

BIFF: Is Dad here?

HAPPY: His name is Biff. You might've heard of him. Great football player.

GIRL: Really? What team?

HAPPY: Are you familiar with football?

GIRL: No, I'm afraid I'm not.

HAPPY: Biff is quarterback with the New York Giants.

GIRL: Well, that is nice, isn't it? (*She drinks.*)

HAPPY: Good health.

GIRL: I'm happy to meet you.

HAPPY: That's my name. Hap. It's really Harold, but at West Point they called me Happy.

GIRL (*now really impressed*):   Oh, I see. How do you do? (*She turns her profile.*)

BIFF: Isn't Dad coming?

HAPPY: You want her?

BIFF: Oh, I could never make that.

HAPPY: I remember the time that idea would never come into your head. Where's the old confidence, Biff?

BIFF: I just saw Oliver . . .

HAPPY: Wait a minute. I've got to see that old confidence again. Do you want her? She's on call.

BIFF: Oh, no. (*He turns to look at the Girl.*)

HAPPY: I'm telling you. Watch this. (*Turning to the Girl.*) Honey? (*She turns to him.*) Are you busy?

GIRL: Well, I am . . . but I could make a phone call.

HAPPY: Do that, will you, honey? And see if you can get a friend. We'll be here for a while. Biff is one of the greatest football players in the country.

GIRL (*standing up*):   Well, I'm certainly happy to meet you.

HAPPY: Come back soon.

GIRL: I'll try.

HAPPY: Don't try, honey, try hard.

The Girl exits. Stanley follows, shaking his head in bewildered admiration.

HAPPY: Isn't that a shame now? A beautiful girl like that? That's why I can't get married. There's not a good woman in a thousand. New York is loaded with them, kid!

BIFF: Hap, look . . .

HAPPY: I told you she was on call!

BIFF (*strangely unnerved*): Cut it out, will ya? I want to say something to you.

HAPPY: Did you see Oliver?

BIFF: I saw him all right. Now look, I want to tell Dad a couple of things and I want you to help me.

HAPPY: What? Is he going to back you?

BIFF: Are you crazy? You're out of your goddam head, you know that?

HAPPY: Why? What happened?

BIFF (*breathlessly*): I did a terrible thing today, Hap. It's been the strangest day I ever went through. I'm all numb, I swear.

HAPPY: You mean he wouldn't see you?

BIFF: Well, I waited six hours for him, see? All day. Kept sending my name in. Even tried to date his secretary so she'd get me to him, but no soap.

HAPPY: Because you're not showin' the old confidence, Biff. He remembered you, didn't he?

BIFF (*stopping Happy with a gesture*): Finally, about five o'clock, he comes out. Didn't remember who I was or anything. I felt like such an idiot, Hap.

HAPPY: Did you tell him my Florida idea?

BIFF: He walked away. I saw him for one minute. I got so mad I could've torn the walls down! How the hell did I ever get the idea I was a salesman there? I even believed myself that I'd been a salesman for him! And then he gave me one look and—I realized what a ridiculous lie my whole life has been! We've been talking in a dream for fifteen years. I was a shipping clerk.

HAPPY: What'd you do?

BIFF (*with great tension and wonder*): Well, he left, see. And the secretary went out. I was all alone in the waiting room. I don't know what came over me, Hap. The next thing I know I'm in his office—paneled walls, everything. I can't explain it. I—Hap. I took his fountain pen.

HAPPY: Geez, did he catch you?

BIFF: I ran out. I ran down all eleven flights. I ran and ran and ran.

HAPPY: That was an awful dumb—what'd you do that for?

BIFF (*agonized*): I don't know, I just—wanted to take something, I don't know. You gotta help me, Hap. I'm gonna tell Pop.

HAPPY: You crazy? What for?

BIFF: Hap, he's got to understand that I'm not the man somebody lends that kind of money to. He thinks I've been spiting him all these years and it's eating him up.

HAPPY: That's just it. You tell him something nice.

BIFF: I can't.

HAPPY: Say you got a lunch date with Oliver tomorrow.

BIFF: So what do I do tomorrow?

HAPPY: You leave the house tomorrow and come back at night and say Oliver is thinking it over. And he thinks it over for a couple of weeks, and gradually it fades away and nobody's the worse.

BIFF: But it'll go on forever!

HAPPY: Dad is never so happy as when he's looking forward to something!

Willy enters.

HAPPY: Hello, scout!

WILLY: Gee, I haven't been here in years!

Stanley has followed Willy in and sets a chair for him. Stanley starts off but Happy stops him.

HAPPY: Stanley!

Stanley stands by, waiting for an order.

BIFF (*going to Willy with guilt, as to an invalid*): Sit down, Pop. You want a drink?

WILLY: Sure, I don't mind.

BIFF: Let's get a load on.

WILLY: You look worried.

BIFF: N-no. (*To Stanley.*) Scotch all around. Make it doubles.

STANLEY: Doubles, right. (*He goes.*)

WILLY: You had a couple already, didn't you?

BIFF: Just a couple, yeah.

WILLY: Well, what happened, boy? (*Nodding affirmatively, with a smile.*) Everything go all right?

BIFF (*takes a breath, then reaches out and grasps Willy's hand*): Pal . . . (*He is smiling bravely, and Willy is smiling too.*) I had an experience today.

HAPPY: Terrific, Pop.

WILLY: That so? What happened?

BIFF (*high, slightly alcoholic, above the earth*): I'm going to tell you everything from first to last. It's been a strange day. (*Silence. He looks around, composes himself as best he can, but his breath keeps breaking the rhythm of his voice.*) I had to wait quite a while for him, and . . .

WILLY: Oliver?

BIFF: Yeah, Oliver. All day, as a matter of cold fact. And a lot of—instances—facts, Pop, facts about my life came back to me. Who was it, Pop? Who ever said I was a salesman with Oliver?

WILLY: Well, you were.

BIFF: No, Dad, I was a shipping clerk.

WILLY: But you were practically . . .

BIFF (*with determination*): Dad, I don't know who said it first, but I was never a salesman for Bill Oliver.

WILLY: What're you talking about?

BIFF: Let's hold on to the facts tonight, Pop. We're not going to get anywhere bullin' around. I was a shipping clerk.

WILLY (*angrily*): All right, now listen to me . . .

BIFF: Why don't you let me finish?

WILLY: I'm not interested in stories about the past or any crap of that kind because the woods are burning, boys, you understand? There's a big blaze going on all around. I was fired today.

BIFF (*shocked*): How could you be?

WILLY: I was fired, and I'm looking for a little good news to tell your mother, because the woman has waited and the woman has suffered. The gist of it is that I haven't got a story left in my head, Biff. So don't give me a lecture about facts and aspects. I am not interested. Now what've you got to say to me?

Stanley enters with three drinks. They wait until he leaves.

WILLY: Did you see Oliver?

BIFF: Jesus, Dad!

WILLY: You mean you didn't go up there?

HAPPY: Sure he went up there.

BIFF: I did. I—saw him. How could they fire you?

WILLY (*on the edge of his chair*): What kind of a welcome did he give you?

BIFF: He won't even let you work on commission?

WILLY: I'm out! (*Driving.*) So tell me, he gave you a warm welcome?

HAPPY: Sure, Pop, sure!

BIFF (*driven*): Well, it was kind of . . .

WILLY: I was wondering if he'd remember you. (*To Happy.*) Imagine, man doesn't see him for ten, twelve years and gives him that kind of a welcome!

HAPPY: Damn right!

BIFF (*trying to return to the offensive*): Pop, look . . .

WILLY: You know why he remembered you, don't you? Because you impressed him in those days.

BIFF: Let's talk quietly and get this down to the facts, huh?

WILLY (*as though Biff had been interrupting*): Well, what happened? It's great news, Biff. Did he take you into his office or'd you talk in the waiting room?

BIFF: Well, he came in, see, and . . .

WILLY (*with a big smile*): What'd he say? Betcha he threw his arm around you.

BIFF: Well, he kinda . . .

WILLY: He's a fine man. (*To Happy.*) Very hard man to see, y'know.

HAPPY (*agreeing*): Oh, I know.

WILLY (*to Biff*): Is that where you had the drinks?

BIFF: Yeah, he gave me a couple of—no, no!

HAPPY (*cutting in*): He told him my Florida idea.

WILLY: Don't interrupt. (*To Biff.*) How'd he react to the Florida idea?

BIFF: Dad, will you give me a minute to explain?

WILLY: I've been waiting for you to explain since I sat down here! What happened? He took you into his office and what?

BIFF: Well—I talked. And—and he listened, see.

WILLY: Famous for the way he listens, y'know. What was his answer?

BIFF: His answer was—(*He breaks off, suddenly angry.*) Dad, you're not letting me tell you what I want to tell you!

WILLY (*accusing, angered*): You didn't see him, did you?

BIFF: I did see him!

WILLY: What'd you insult him or something? You insulted him, didn't you?

BIFF: Listen, will you let me out of it, will you just let me out of it!

HAPPY: What the hell!

WILLY: Tell me what happened!

BIFF (*to Happy*): I can't talk to him!

A single trumpet note jars the ear. The light of green leaves stains the house, which holds the air of night and a dream. Young Bernard enters and knocks on the door of the house.

YOUNG BERNARD (*frantically*): Mrs. Loman, Mrs. Loman!

HAPPY: Tell him what happened!

BIFF (*to Happy.*): Shut up and leave me alone!

WILLY: No, no! You had to go and flunk math!

BIFF: What math? What're you talking about?

YOUNG BERNARD: Mrs. Loman, Mrs. Loman!

Linda appears in the house, as of old.

WILLY (*wildly*): Math, math, math!

BIFF: Take it easy, Pop!

YOUNG BERNARD: Mrs. Loman!

WILLY (*furiously*): If you hadn't flunked you'd've been set by now!

BIFF: Now, look, I'm gonna tell you what happened, and you're going to listen to me.

YOUNG BERNARD: Mrs. Loman!

BIFF: I waited six hours . . .

HAPPY: What the hell are you saying?

BIFF: I kept sending in my name but he wouldn't see me. So finally he . . . (*He continues unheard as light fades low on the restaurant.*)

YOUNG BERNARD: Biff flunked math!

LINDA: No!

YOUNG BERNARD: Birnbaum flunked him! They won't graduate him!

LINDA: But they have to. He's gotta go to the university. Where is he? Biff! Biff!

YOUNG BERNARD: No, he left. He went to Grand Central.

LINDA: Grand—You mean he went to Boston!

YOUNG BERNARD: Is Uncle Willy in Boston?

LINDA: Oh, maybe Willy can talk to the teacher. Oh, the poor, poor boy!

Light on house area snaps out.

BIFF (*at the table, now audible, holding up a gold fountain pen*): . . . so I'm washed up with Oliver, you understand? Are you listening to me?

WILLY (*at a loss*): Yeah, sure. If you hadn't flunked . . .

BIFF: Flunked what? What're you talking about?

WILLY: Don't blame everything on me! I didn't flunk math—you did! What pen?

HAPPY: That was awful dumb, Biff, a pen like that is worth—

WILLY (*seeing the pen for the first time*): You took Oliver's pen?

BIFF (*weakening*): Dad, I just explained it to you.

WILLY: You stole Bill Oliver's fountain pen!

BIFF: I didn't exactly steal it! That's just what I've been explaining to you!

HAPPY: He had it in his hand and just then Oliver walked in, so he got nervous and stuck it in his pocket!

WILLY: My God, Biff!

BIFF: I never intended to do it, Dad!

OPERATOR'S VOICE: Standish Arms, good evening!

WILLY (*shouting*): I'm not in my room!

BIFF (*frightened*): Dad, what's the matter? (*He and Happy stand up.*)

OPERATOR: Ringing Mr. Loman for you!

WILLY: I'm not there, stop it!

BIFF (*horrified, gets down on one knee before Willy*): Dad, I'll make good, I'll make good. (*Willy tries to get to his feet. Biff holds him down.*) Sit down now.

WILLY: No, you're no good, you're no good for anything.

BIFF: I am, Dad, I'll find something else, you understand? Now don't worry about anything. (*He holds up Willy's face.*) Talk to me, Dad.

OPERATOR: Mr. Loman does not answer. Shall I page him?

WILLY (*attempting to stand, as though to rush and silence the Operator*): No, no, no!

HAPPY: He'll strike something, Pop.

WILLY: No, no . . .

BIFF (*desperately, standing over Willy*):   Pop, listen! Listen to me! I'm telling you something good. Oliver talked to his partner about the Florida idea. You listening? He—he talked to his partner, and he came to me . . . I'm going to be all right, you hear? Dad, listen to me, he said it was just a question of the amount!

WILLY: Then you . . . got it?

HAPPY: He's gonna be terrific, Pop!

WILLY (*trying to stand*):   Then you got it, haven't you? You got it! You got it!

BIFF (*agonized, holds Willy down*):   No, no. Look, Pop. I'm supposed to have lunch with them tomorrow. I'm just telling you this so you'll know that I can still make an impression, Pop. And I'll make good somewhere, but I can't go tomorrow, see.

WILLY: Why not? You simply . . .

BIFF: But the pen, Pop!

WILLY: You give it to him and tell him it was an oversight!

HAPPY: Sure, have lunch tomorrow!

BIFF: I can't say that . . .

WILLY: You were doing a crossword puzzle and accidentally used his pen!

BIFF: Listen, kid, I took those balls years ago, now I walk in with his fountain pen? That clinches it, don't you see? I can't face him like that! I'll try elsewhere.

PAGE'S VOICE: Paging Mr. Loman!

WILLY: Don't you want to be anything?

BIFF: Pop, how can I go back?

WILLY: You don't want to be anything, is that what's behind it?

BIFF (*now angry at Willy for not crediting his sympathy*):   Don't take it that way! You think it was easy walking into that office after what I'd done to him? A team of horses couldn't have dragged me back to Bill Oliver!

WILLY: Then why'd you go?

BIFF: Why did I go? Why did I go! Look at you! Look at what's become of you!

Off left, The Woman laughs.

WILLY: Biff, you're going to go to that lunch tomorrow, or . . .

BIFF: I can't go. I've got no appointment!

HAPPY: Biff, for . . . !

WILLY: Are you spiting me?

BIFF: Don't take it that way! Goddammit!

WILLY (*strikes Biff and falters away from the table*): You rotten little louse! Are you spiting me?

THE WOMAN: Someone's at the door, Willy!

BIFF: I'm no good, can't you see what I am?

HAPPY (*separating them*): Hey, you're in a restaurant! Now cut it out, both of you! (*The girls enter.*) Hello, girls, sit down.

The Woman laughs, off left.

MISS FORSYTHE: I guess we might as well. This is Letta.

THE WOMAN: Willy, are you going to wake up?

BIFF (*ignoring Willy*): How're ya, miss, sit down. What do you drink?

MISS FORSYTHE: Letta might not be able to stay long.

LETTA: I gotta get up very early tomorrow. I got jury duty. I'm so excited! Were you fellows ever on a jury?

BIFF: No, but I been in front of them! (*The girls laugh.*) This is my father.

LETTA: Isn't he cute? Sit down with us, Pop.

HAPPY: Sit him down, Biff!

BIFF (*going to him*): Come on, slugger, drink us under the table. To hell with it! Come on, sit down, pal.

On Biff's last insistence, Willy is about to sit.

THE WOMAN (*now urgently*): Willy, are you going to answer the door!

The Woman's call pulls Willy back. He starts right, befuddled.

BIFF: Hey, where are you going?

WILLY: Open the door.

BIFF: The door?

WILLY: The washroom . . . the door . . . where's the door?

BIFF (*leading Willy to the left*): Just go straight down.

Willy moves left.

THE WOMAN: Willy, Willy, are you going to get up, get up, get up, get up?

Willy exits left.

LETTA: I think it's sweet you bring your daddy along.

MISS FORSYTHE: Oh, he isn't really your father!

BIFF (*at left, turning to her resentfully*): Miss Forsythe, you've just seen a prince walk by. A fine, troubled prince. A hardworking, unappreciated prince. A pal, you understand? A good companion. Always for his boys.

LETTA: That's so sweet.

HAPPY: Well, girls, what's the program? We're wasting time. Come on, Biff. Gather round. Where would you like to go?

BIFF: Why don't you do something for him?

HAPPY: Me!

BIFF: Don't you give a damn for him, Hap?

HAPPY: What're you talking about? I'm the one who . . .

BIFF: I sense it, you don't give a good goddam about him. (*He takes the rolled-up hose from his pocket and puts it on the table in front of Happy.*) Look what I found in the cellar, for Christ's sake. How can you bear to let it go on?

HAPPY: Me? Who goes away? Who runs off and . . .

BIFF: Yeah, but he doesn't mean anything to you. You could help him—I can't! Don't you understand what I'm talking about? He's going to kill himself, don't you know that?

HAPPY: Don't know it! Me!

BIFF: Hap, help him! Jesus . . . help him . . . Help me, help me, I can't bear to look at his face! (*Ready to weep, he hurries out, up right.*)

HAPPY (*starting after him*): Where are you going?

MISS FORSYTHE: What's he so mad about?

HAPPY: Come on, girls, we'll catch up with him.

MISS FORSYTHE (*as Happy pushes her out*): Say, I don't like that temper of his!

HAPPY: He's just a little overstrung, he'll be all right!

WILLY (*off left, as The Woman laughs*): Don't answer! Don't answer!

LETTA: Don't you want to tell your father . . .

HAPPY: No, that's not my father. He's just a guy. Come on, we'll catch Biff, and, honey, we're going to paint this town! Stanley, where's the check! Hey, Stanley!

They exit. Stanley looks toward left.

STANLEY (*calling to Happy indignantly*):   Mr. Loman! Mr. Loman!

Stanley picks up a chair and follows them off. Knocking is heard off left. The Woman enters, laughing. Willy follows her. She is in a black slip; he is buttoning his shirt. Raw, sensuous music accompanies their speech:

WILLY: Will you stop laughing? Will you stop?

THE WOMAN: Aren't you going to answer the door? He'll wake the whole hotel.

WILLY: I'm not expecting anybody.

THE WOMAN: Whyn't you have another drink, honey, and stop being so damn self-centered?

WILLY: I'm so lonely.

THE WOMAN: You know you ruined me, Willy? From now on, whenever you come to the office, I'll see that you go right through to the buyers. No waiting at my desk any more, Willy. You ruined me.

WILLY: That's nice of you to say that.

THE WOMAN: Gee, you are self-centered! Why so sad? You are the saddest, self-centeredest soul I ever did see-saw. (*She laughs. He kisses her.*) Come on inside, drummer boy. It's silly to be dressing in the middle of the night. (*As knocking is heard.*) Aren't you going to answer the door?

WILLY: They're knocking on the wrong door.

THE WOMAN: But I felt the knocking. And he heard us talking in here. Maybe the hotel's on fire!

WILLY (*his terror rising*):   It's a mistake.

THE WOMAN: Then tell him to go away!

WILLY: There's nobody there.

THE WOMAN: It's getting on my nerves, Willy. There's somebody standing out there and it's getting on my nerves!

WILLY (*pushing her away from him*):   All right, stay in the bathroom here, and don't come out. I think there's a law in Massachusetts about it, so don't come out. It may be that new room clerk. He looked very mean. So don't come out. It's a mistake, there's no fire.

The knocking is heard again. He takes a few steps away from her, and she vanishes into the wing. The light follows him, and now he is facing Young Biff, who carries a suitcase. Biff steps toward him. The music is gone.

BIFF: Why didn't you answer?

WILLY: Biff! What are you doing in Boston?

BIFF: Why didn't you answer? I've been knocking for five minutes, I called you on the phone . . .

WILLY: I just heard you. I was in the bathroom and had the door shut. Did anything happen home?

BIFF: Dad—I let you down.

WILLY: What do you mean?

BIFF: Dad . . .

WILLY: Biffo, what's this about? (*Putting his arm around Biff.*) Come on, let's go downstairs and get you a malted.

BIFF: Dad, I flunked math.

WILLY: Not for the term?

BIFF: The term. I haven't got enough credits to graduate.

WILLY: You mean to say Bernard wouldn't give you the answers?

BIFF: He did, he tried, but I only got a sixty-one.

WILLY: And they wouldn't give you four points?

BIFF: Birnbaum refused absolutely. I begged him, Pop, but he won't give me those points. You gotta talk to him before they close the school. Because if he saw the kind of man you are, and you just talked to him in your way, I'm sure he'd come through for me. The class came right before practice, see, and I didn't go enough. Would you talk to him? He'd like you, Pop. You know the way you could talk.

WILLY: You're on. We'll drive right back.

BIFF: Oh, Dad, good work! I'm sure he'll change it for you!

WILLY: Go downstairs and tell the clerk I'm checkin' out. Go right down.

BIFF: Yes, sir! See, the reason he hates me, Pop—one day he was late for class so I got up at the blackboard and imitated him. I crossed my eyes and talked with a lithp.

WILLY (*laughing*): You did? The kids like it?

BIFF: They nearly died laughing!

WILLY: Yeah? What'd you do?

BIFF: The thquare root of thixthy twee is . . . (*Willy bursts out laughing; Biff joins.*) And in the middle of it he walked in!

Willy laughs and The Woman joins in offstage.

WILLY (*without hesitation*): Hurry downstairs and . . .

BIFF: Somebody in there?

WILLY: No, that was next door.

The Woman laughs offstage.

BIFF: Somebody got in your bathroom!

WILLY: No, it's the next room, there's a party . . .

THE WOMAN (*enters, laughing; she lisps this*): Can I come in? There's something in the bathtub, Willy, and it's moving!

Willy looks at Biff; who is staring open-mouthed and horrified at The Woman.

WILLY: Ah—you better go back to your room. They must be finished painting by now. They're painting her room so I let her take a shower here. Go back, go back . . . (*He pushes her.*)

THE WOMAN (*resisting*): But I've got to get dressed, Willy, I can't . . .

WILLY: Get out of here! Go back, go back . . . (*Suddenly striving for the ordinary.*) This is Miss Francis, Biff, she's a buyer. They're painting her room. Go back, Miss Francis, go back . . .

THE WOMAN: But my clothes, I can't go out naked in the hall!

WILLY (*pushing her offstage*): Get outa here! Go back, go back!

Biff slowly sits down on his suitcase as the argument continues offstage.

THE WOMAN: Where's my stockings? You promised me stockings, Willy!

WILLY: I have no stockings here!

THE WOMAN: You had two boxes of size nine sheers for me, and I want them!

WILLY: Here, for God's sake, will you get outa here!

THE WOMAN (*enters holding a box of stockings*): I just hope there's nobody in the hall. That's all I hope. (*To Biff.*) Are you football or baseball?

BIFF: Football.

THE WOMAN (*angry, humiliated*): That's me too. G'night. (*She snatches her clothes from Willy, and walks out.*)

WILLY (*after a pause*): Well, better get going. I want to get to the school first thing in the morning. Get my suits out of the closet. I'll get my valise. (*Biff doesn't move.*) What's the matter! (*Biff remains motionless, tears falling.*) She's a buyer. Buys for J. H. Simmons. She lives down the hall—they're painting. You don't imagine—(*He breaks off. After a pause.*) Now listen, pal, she's just a buyer. She sells merchandise in her room and they have to keep it looking just so . . . (*Pause. Assuming command.*) All right, get my suits. (*Biff doesn't move.*) Now stop crying and do as I say. I gave you an order. Biff, I gave you an order! Is that what you do when I give you an order? How dare you cry! (*Putting his arm around Biff.*) Now look, Biff, when you grow up you'll understand about these things. You mustn't—you mustn't overemphasize a thing like this. I'll see Birnbaum first thing in the morning.

BIFF: Never mind.

WILLY (*getting down beside Biff*): Never mind! He's going to give you those points. I'll see to it.

BIFF: He wouldn't listen to you.

WILLY: He certainly will listen to me. You need those points for the U. of Virginia.

BIFF: I'm not going there.

WILLY: Heh? If I can't get him to change that mark you'll make it up in summer school. You've got all summer to . . .

BIFF (*his weeping breaking from him*): Dad . . .

WILLY (*infected by it*): Oh, my boy . . .

BIFF: Dad . . .

WILLY: She's nothing to me, Biff. I was lonely, I was terribly lonely.

BIFF: You—you gave her Mama's stockings! (*His tears break through and he rises to go.*)

WILLY (*grabbing for Biff*): I gave you an order!

BIFF: Don't touch me, you—liar!

WILLY: Apologize for that!

BIFF: You fake! You phony little fake! You fake! (*Overcome, he turns quickly and weeping fully goes out with his suitcase. Willy is left on the floor on his knees.*)

WILLY: I gave you an order! Biff, come back here or I'll beat you! Come back here! I'll whip you!

Stanley comes quickly in from the right and stands in front of Willy.

WILLY (*shouts at Stanley*): I gave you an order . . .

STANLEY: Hey, let's pick it up, pick it up, Mr. Loman. (*He helps Willy to his feet.*) Your boys left with the chippies. They said they'll see you home.

A second waiter watches some distance away.

WILLY: But we were supposed to have dinner together.

Music is heard, Willy's theme.

STANLEY: Can you make it?

WILLY: I'll—sure, I can make it. (*Suddenly concerned about his clothes.*) Do I—I look all right?

STANLEY: Sure, you look all right. (*He flicks a speck off Willy's lapel.*)

WILLY: Here—here's a dollar.

STANLEY: Oh, your son paid me. It's all right.

WILLY (*putting it in Stanley's hand*): No, take it. You're a good boy.

STANLEY: Oh, no, you don't have to . . .

WILLY: Here—here's some more, I don't need it any more. (*After a slight pause.*) Tell me—is there a seed store in the neighborhood?

STANLEY: Seeds? You mean like to plant?

As Willy turns, Stanley slips the money back into his jacket pocket.

WILLY: Yes. Carrots, peas . . .

STANLEY: Well, there's hardware stores on Sixth Avenue, but it may be too late now.

WILLY (*anxiously*): Oh, I'd better hurry. I've got to get some seeds. (*He starts off to the right.*) I've got to get some seeds, right away. Nothing's planted. I don't have a thing in the ground.

Willy hurries out as the light goes down. Stanley moves over to the right after him, watches him off. The other waiter has been staring at Willy.

STANLEY (*to the waiter*): Well, whatta you looking at?

The waiter picks up the chairs and moves off right. Stanley takes the table and follows him. The light fades on this area. There is a long pause, the sound of the flute coming over. The light gradually rises on the kitchen, which is empty. Happy appears at the door of the house, followed by Biff. Happy is carrying a large bunch of long-stemmed roses. He enters the kitchen, looks around for Linda. Not seeing her, he turns to Biff, who is just outside the house door, and makes a gesture with his hands, indicating "Not here, I guess." He looks into the living room and freezes. Inside, Linda, unseen, is seated, Willy's coat on her lap. She rises ominously and quietly and moves toward Happy, who backs up into the kitchen, afraid.

HAPPY: Hey, what're you doing up? (*Linda says nothing but moves toward him implacably.*) Where's Pop? (*He keeps backing to the right, and now Linda is in full view in the doorway to the living room.*) Is he sleeping?

LINDA: Where were you?

HAPPY (*trying to laugh it off*):   We met two girls, Mom, very fine types. Here, we brought you some flowers. (*Offering them to her.*) Put them in your room, Ma.

She knocks them to the floor at Biff's feet. He has now come inside and closed the door behind him. She stares at Biff, silent.

HAPPY: Now what'd you do that for? Mom, I want you to have some flowers . . .

LINDA (*cutting Happy off, violently to Biff*):   Don't you care whether he lives or dies?

HAPPY (*going to the stairs*):   Come upstairs, Biff.

BIFF (*with a flare of disgust, to Happy*):   Go away from me! (*To Linda.*) What do you mean, lives or dies? Nobody's dying around here, pal.

LINDA: Get out of my sight! Get out of here!

BIFF: I wanna see the boss.

LINDA: You're not going near him!

BIFF: Where is he? (*He moves into the living room and Linda follows.*)

LINDA (*shouting after Biff.*):   You invite him for dinner. He looks forward to it all day—(*Biff appears in his parents' bedroom, looks *around, and exits)*—and then you desert him there. There's no stranger you'd do that to!

HAPPY: Why? He had a swell time with us. Listen, when I—(*Linda comes back into the kitchen*)—desert him I hope I don't outlive the day!

LINDA: Get out of here!

HAPPY: Now look, Mom . . .

LINDA: Did you have to go to women tonight? You and your lousy rotten whores!

Biff re-enters the kitchen.

HAPPY: Mom, all we did was follow Biff around trying to cheer him up! (*To Biff.*) Boy, what a night you gave me!

LINDA: Get out of here, both of you, and don't come back! I don't want you tormenting him any more. Go on now, get your things together! (*To Biff.*) You can sleep in his apartment. (*She starts to pick up the flowers and stops herself.*) Pick up this stuff, I'm not your maid any more. Pick it up, you bum, you!

Happy turns his back to her in refusal. Biff slowly moves over and gets down on his knees, picking up the flowers.

LINDA: You're a pair of animals! Not one, not another living soul would have had the cruelty to walk out on that man in a restaurant!

BIFF (*not looking at her*): Is that what he said?

LINDA: He didn't have to say anything. He was so humiliated he nearly limped when he came in.

HAPPY: But, Mom, he had a great time with us . . .

BIFF (*cutting him off violently*): Shut up!

Without another word, Happy goes upstairs.

LINDA: You! You didn't even go in to see if he was all right!

BIFF (*still on the floor in front of Linda, the flowers in his hand; with self-loathing*): No. Didn't. Didn't do a damned thing. How do you like that, heh? Left him babbling in a toilet.

LINDA: You louse. You . . .

BIFF: Now you hit it on the nose! (*He gets up, throws the flowers in the wastebasket.*) The scum of the earth, and you're looking at him!

LINDA: Get out of here!

BIFF: I gotta talk to the boss, Mom. Where is he?

LINDA: You're not going near him. Get out of this house!

BIFF (*with absolute assurance, determination*): No. We're gonna have an abrupt conversation, him and me.

LINDA: You're not talking to him.

Hammering is heard from outside the house, off right. Biff turns toward the noise.

LINDA (*suddenly pleading*): Will you please leave him alone?

BIFF: What's he doing out there?

LINDA: He's planting the garden!

BIFF (*quietly*): Now? Oh, my God!

Biff moves outside, Linda following. The light dies down on them and comes up on the center of the apron as Willy walks into it. He is carrying a flashlight, a hoe, and a handful of seed packets. He raps the top of the hoe sharply to fix it firmly, and then moves to the left, measuring off the distance with his foot. He holds the flashlight to look at the seed packets, reading off the instructions. He is in the blue of night.

WILLY: Carrots . . . quarter-inch apart. Rows . . . one-foot rows. (*He measures it off.*) One foot. (*He puts down a package and measures off.*) Beets. (*He puts down another package and measures again.*) Lettuce. (*He reads the package, puts it down.*) One foot—(*He breaks off as Ben appears at the right and moves slowly down to him.*) What a proposition, ts, ts. Terrific, terrific. 'Cause she's suffered, Ben, the woman has suffered. You understand me? A man can't go out the way he came in, Ben, a man has got to add up to something. You can't, you can't—(*Ben moves toward him as though to interrupt.*) You gotta consider now. Don't answer so quick. Remember, it's a guaranteed twenty-thousand-dollar proposition. Now look, Ben, I want you to go through the ins and outs of this thing with me. I've got nobody to talk to, Ben, and the woman has suffered, you hear me?

BEN (*standing still, considering*): What's the proposition?

WILLY: It's twenty thousand dollars on the barrelhead. Guaranteed, gilt-edged, you understand?

BEN: You don't want to make a fool of yourself. They might not honor the policy.

WILLY: How can they dare refuse? Didn't I work like a coolie to meet every premium on the nose? And now they don't pay off? Impossible!

BEN: It's called a cowardly thing, William.

WILLY: Why? Does it take more guts to stand here the rest of my life ringing up a zero?

BEN (*yielding*): That's a point, William. (*He moves, thinking, turns.*) And twenty thousand—that is something one can feel with the hand, it is there.

WILLY (*now assured, with rising power*): Oh, Ben, that's the whole beauty of it! I see it like a diamond, shining in the dark, hard and rough, that I can pick up and touch in my hand. Not like—like an appointment! This would not be another damned-fool appointment, Ben, and it changes all the aspects. Because he thinks I'm nothing, see, and so he spites me. But the funeral . . . (*Straightening up.*) Ben, that funeral will be massive! They'll come from Maine, Massachusetts, Vermont, New Hampshire! All the old-timers with the strange license plates—that boy will be thunder-struck, Ben, because he never realized—I am known! Rhode Island, New York, New Jersey—I am known, Ben, and he'll see it with his eyes once and for all. He'll see what I am, Ben! He's in for a shock, that boy!

BEN (*coming down to the edge of the garden*): He'll call you a coward.

WILLY (*suddenly fearful*): No, that would be terrible.

BEN: Yes. And a damned fool.

WILLY: No, no, he mustn't, I won't have that! (*He is broken and desperate.*)

BEN: He'll hate you, William.

The gay music of the Boys is heard.

WILLY: Oh, Ben, how do we get back to all the great times? Used to be so full of light, and comradeship, the sleigh-riding in winter, and the ruddiness on his cheeks. And always some kind of good news coming up, always something nice coming up ahead. And never even let me carry the valises in the house, and simonizing, simonizing that little red car! Why, why can't I give him something and not have him hate me?

BEN: Let me think about it. (*He glances at his watch.*) I still have a little time. Remarkable proposition, but you've got to be sure you're not making a fool of yourself.

Ben drifts off upstage and goes out of sight. Biff comes down from the left.

WILLY (*suddenly conscious of Biff, turns and looks up at him, then begins picking up the packages of seeds in confusion*): Where the hell is that seed? (*Indignantly.*) You can't see nothing out here! They boxed in the whole goddam neighborhood!

BIFF: There are people all around here. Don't you realize that?

WILLY: I'm busy. Don't bother me.

BIFF (*taking the hoe from Willy*): I'm saying good-by to you, Pop. (*Willy looks at him, silent, unable to move.*) I'm not coming back any more.

WILLY: You're not going to see Oliver tomorrow?

BIFF: I've got no appointment, Dad.

WILLY: He put his arm around you, and you've got no appointment?

BIFF: Pop, get this now, will you? Everytime I've left it's been a—fight that sent me out of here. Today I realized something about myself and I tried to explain it to you and I—I think I'm just not smart enough to make any sense out of it for you. To hell with whose fault it is or anything like that. (*He takes Willy's arm.*) Let's just wrap it up, heh? Come on in, we'll tell Mom. (*He gently tries to pull Willy to left.*)

WILLY (*frozen, immobile, with guilt in his voice*): No, I don't want to see her.

BIFF: Come on! (*He pulls again, and Willy tries to pull away.*)

WILLY (*highly nervous*): No, no, I don't want to see her.

BIFF (*tries to look into Willy's face, as if to find the answer there*): Why don't you want to see her?

WILLY (*more harshly now*): Don't bother me, will you?

BIFF: What do you mean, you don't want to see her? You don't want them calling you yellow, do you? This isn't your fault; it's me, I'm a bum. Now come inside! (*Willy strains to get away.*) Did you hear what I said to you?

Willy pulls away and quickly goes by himself into the house. Biff follows.

LINDA (*to Willy*): Did you plant, dear?

BIFF (*at the door, to Linda*): All right, we had it out. I'm going and I'm not writing any more.

LINDA (*going to Willy in the kitchen*): I think that's the best way, dear. 'Cause there's no use drawing it out, you'll just never get along.

Willy doesn't respond.

BIFF: People ask where I am and what I'm doing, you don't know, and you don't care. That way it'll be off your mind and you can start brightening up again. All right? That clears it, doesn't it? (*Willy is silent, and Biff goes to him.*) You gonna wish me luck, scout? (*He extends his hand.*) What do you say?

LINDA: Shake his hand, Willy.

WILLY (*turning to her, seething with hurt*): There's no necessity—to mention the pen at all, y'know.

BIFF (*gently*): I've got no appointment, Dad.

WILLY (*erupting fiercely*): He put his arm around . . . ?

BIFF: Dad, you're never going to see what I am, so what's the use of arguing? If I strike oil I'll send you a check. Meantime forget I'm alive.

WILLY (*to Linda*): Spite, see?

BIFF: Shake hands, Dad.

WILLY: Not my hand.

BIFF: I was hoping not to go this way.

WILLY: Well, this is the way you're going. Good-by.

Biff looks at him a moment, then turns sharply and goes to the stairs.

WILLY (*stops him with*): May you rot in hell if you leave this house!

BIFF (*turning*): Exactly what is it that you want from me?

WILLY: I want you to know, on the train, in the mountains, in the valleys, wherever you go, that you cut down your life for spite!

BIFF: No, no.

WILLY: Spite, spite, is the word of your undoing! And when you're down and out, remember what did it. When you're rotting somewhere beside the railroad tracks, remember, and don't you dare blame it on me!

BIFF: I'm not blaming it on you!

WILLY: I won't take the rap for this, you hear?

Happy comes down the stairs and stands on the bottom step, watching.

BIFF: That's just what I'm telling you!

WILLY (*sinking into a chair at a table, with full accusation*): You're trying to put a knife in me—don't think I don't know what you're doing!

BIFF: All right, phony! Then let's lay it on the line. (*He whips the rubber tube out of his pocket and puts it on the table.*)

HAPPY: You crazy . . .

LINDA: Biff! (*She moves to grab the hose, but Biff holds it down with his hand.*)

BIFF: Leave it there! Don't move it!

WILLY (*not looking at it*): What is that?

BIFF: You know goddam well what that is.

WILLY (*caged, wanting to escape*): I never saw that.

BIFF: You saw it. The mice didn't bring it into the cellar! What is this supposed to do, make a hero out of you? This supposed to make me sorry for you?

WILLY: Never heard of it.

BIFF: There'll be no pity for you, you hear it? No pity!

WILLY (*to Linda*): You hear the spite!

BIFF: No, you're going to hear the truth—what you are and what I am!

LINDA: Stop it!

WILLY: Spite!

HAPPY (*coming down toward Biff*): You cut it now!

BIFF (*to Happy*): The man don't know who we are! The man is gonna know! (*To Willy.*) We never told the truth for ten minutes in this house!

HAPPY: We always told the truth!

BIFF (*turning on him*): You big blow, are you the assistant buyer? You're one of the two assistants to the assistant, aren't you?

HAPPY: Well, I'm practically . . .

BIFF: You're practically full of it! We all are! and I'm through with it. (*To Willy.*) Now hear this, Willy, this is me.

WILLY: I know you!

BIFF: You know why I had no address for three months? I stole a suit in Kansas City and I was in jail. (*To Linda, who is sobbing.*) Stop crying. I'm through with it.

Linda turns away from them, her hands covering her face.

WILLY: I suppose that's my fault!

BIFF: I stole myself out of every good job since high school!

WILLY: And whose fault is that?

BIFF: And I never got anywhere because you blew me so full of hot air I could never stand taking orders from anybody! That's whose fault it is!

WILLY: I hear that!

LINDA: Don't, Biff!

BIFF: It's goddam time you heard that! I had to be boss big shot in two weeks, and I'm through with it!

WILLY: Then hang yourself! For spite, hang yourself!

BIFF: No! Nobody's hanging himself, Willy! I ran down eleven flights with a pen in my hand today. And suddenly I stopped, you hear me? And in the middle of that office building, do you hear this? I stopped in the middle of that building and I saw—the sky. I saw the things that I love in this world. The work and the food and time to sit and smoke. And I looked at the pen and said to myself, what the hell am I grabbing this for? Why am I trying to become what I don't want to be? What am I doing in an office, making a contemptuous, begging fool of myself, when all I want is out there, waiting for me the minute I say I know who I am! Why can't I say that, Willy? (*He tries to make Willy face him, but Willy pulls away and moves to the left.*)

WILLY (*with hatred, threateningly*): The door of your life is wide open!

BIFF: Pop! I'm a dime a dozen, and so are you!

WILLY (*turning on him now in an uncontrolled outburst*): I am not a dime a dozen! I am Willy Loman, and you are Biff Loman!

Biff starts for Willy, but is blocked by Happy. In his fury, Biff seems on the verge of attacking his father.

BIFF: I am not a leader of men, Willy, and neither are you. You were never anything but a hard-working drummer who landed in the ash can like all the rest of them! I'm one dollar an hour, Willy! I tried seven states and couldn't raise it. A buck an hour! Do you gather my meaning? I'm not bringing home any prizes any more, and you're going to stop waiting for me to bring them home!

WILLY (*directly to Biff*): You vengeful, spiteful mutt!

Biff breaks from Happy. Willy, in fright, starts up the stairs. Biff grabs him.

BIFF (*at the peak of his fury*): Pop! I'm nothing! I'm nothing, Pop. Can't you understand that? There's no spite in it any more. I'm just what I am, that's all.

Biff's fury has spent itself and he breaks down, sobbing, holding on to Willy, who dumbly fumbles for Biff's face.

WILLY (*astonished*): What're you doing? What're you doing? (*To Linda.*) Why is he crying?

BIFF (*crying, broken*): Will you let me go, for Christ's sake? Will you take that phony dream and burn it before something happens? (*Struggling to contain himself, he pulls away and moves to the stairs.*) I'll go in the morning. Put him—put him to bed. (*Exhausted, Biff moves up the stairs to his room.*)

WILLY (*after a long pause, astonished, elevated*): Isn't that—isn't that remarkable? Biff—he likes me!

LINDA: He loves you, Willy!

HAPPY (*deeply moved*): Always did, Pop.

WILLY: Oh, Biff! (*Staring wildly.*) He cried! Cried to me. (*He is choking with his love, and now cries out his promise.*) That boy—that boy is going to be magnificent!

Ben appears in the light just outside the kitchen.

BEN: Yes, outstanding, with twenty thousand behind him.

LINDA (*sensing the racing of his mind, fearfully, carefully*): Now come to bed, Willy. It's all settled now.

WILLY (*finding it difficult not to rush out of the house*):   Yes, we'll sleep. Come on. Go to sleep, Hap.

BEN: And it does take a great kind of a man to crack the jungle.

In accents of dread, Ben's idyllic music starts up.

HAPPY (*his arm around Linda*):   I'm getting married, Pop, don't forget it. I'm changing everything. I'm gonna run that department before the year is up. You'll see, Mom. (*He kisses her.*)

BEN: The jungle is dark but full of diamonds, Willy.

Willy turns, moves, listening to Ben.

LINDA: Be good. You're both good boys, just act that way, that's all.

HAPPY: 'Night, Pop. (*He goes upstairs.*)

LINDA (*to Willy*):   Come, dear.

BEN (*with greater force*):   One must go in to fetch a diamond out.

WILLY (*to Linda, as he moves slowly along the edge of the kitchen, toward the door*):   I just want to get settled down, Linda. Let me sit alone for a little.

LINDA (*almost uttering her fear*):   I want you upstairs.

WILLY (*taking her in his arms*):   In a few minutes, Linda. I couldn't sleep right now. Go on, you look awful tired. (*He kisses her.*)

BEN: Not like an appointment at all. A diamond is rough and hard to the touch.

WILLY: Go on now. I'll be right up.

LINDA: I think this is the only way, Willy.

WILLY: Sure, it's the best thing.

BEN: Best thing!

WILLY: The only way. Everything is gonna be—go on, kid, get to bed. You look so tired.

LINDA: Come right up.

WILLY: Two minutes.

Linda goes into the living room, then reappears in her bedroom. Willy moves just outside the kitchen door.

WILLY: Loves me. (*Wonderingly.*) Always loved me. Isn't that a remarkable thing? Ben, he'll worship me for it!

BEN (*with promise*):   It's dark there, but full of diamonds.

WILLY: Can you imagine that magnificence with twenty thousand dollars in his pocket?

LINDA (*calling from her room*):   Willy! Come up!

WILLY (*calling into the kitchen*):   Yes! Yes. Coming! It's very smart, you realize that, don't you, sweetheart? Even Ben sees it. I gotta go, baby. 'By! 'By! (*Going over to Ben, almost dancing.*) Imagine? When the mail comes he'll be ahead of Bernard again!

BEN: A perfect proposition all around.

WILLY: Did you see how he cried to me? Oh, if I could kiss him, Ben!

BEN: Time, William, time!

WILLY: Oh, Ben, I always knew one way or another we were gonna make it, Biff and I.

BEN (*looking at his watch*):   The boat. We'll be late. (*He moves slowly off into the darkness.*)

WILLY (*elegiacally, turning to the house*):   Now when you kick off, boy, I want a seventy-yard boot, and get right down the field under the ball, and when you hit, hit low and hit hard, because it's important, boy. (*He swings around and faces the audience.*) There's all kinds of important people in the stands, and the first thing you know . . . (*Suddenly realizing he is alone.*) Ben! Ben, where do I . . . ? (*He makes a sudden movement of search.*) Ben, how do I . . . ?

LINDA (*calling*):   Willy, you coming up?

WILLY (*uttering a gasp of fear, whirling about as if to quiet her*):   Sh! (*He turns around as if to find his way; sounds, faces, voices, seem to be swarming in upon him and he flicks at them, crying.*) Sh! Sh! (*Suddenly music, faint and high, stops him. It rises in intensity, almost to an unbearable scream. He goes up and down on his toes, and rushes off around the house.*) Shhh!

LINDA: Willy?

There is no answer. Linda waits. Biff gets up off his bed. He is still in his clothes. Happy sits up. Biff stands listening.

LINDA (*with real fear*):   Willy, answer me! Willy!

There is the sound of a car starting and moving away at full speed.

LINDA: No!

BIFF (*rushing down the stairs*):   Pop!

As the car speeds off the music crashes down in a frenzy of sound, which becomes the soft pulsation of a single cello string. Biff slowly returns to his bedroom. He and Happy gravely don their jackets. Linda slowly walks out of her room. The music has developed into a dead march. The leaves of day are appearing over everything. Charley and Bernard, somberly dressed, appear and knock on the kitchen door. Biff and Happy slowly descend the stairs to the kitchen as Charley and Bernard enter. All stop a moment when Linda, in clothes of mourning, bearing a little bunch of roses, comes through the draped doorway into the kitchen. She goes to Charley and takes his arm. Now all move toward the audience, through the wall-line of the kitchen. At the limit of the apron, Linda lays down the flowers, kneels, and sits back on her heels. All stare down at the grave.

REQUIEM

CHARLEY: It's getting dark, Linda.

Linda doesn't react. She stares at the grave.

BIFF: How about it, Mom? Better get some rest, heh? They'll be closing the gate soon.

Linda makes no move. Pause.

HAPPY (*deeply angered*):   He had no right to do that. There was no necessity for it. We would've helped him.

CHARLEY (*grunting*):   Hmmm.

BIFF: Come along, Mom.

LINDA: Why didn't anybody come?

CHARLEY: It was a very nice funeral.

LINDA: But where are all the people he knew? Maybe they blame him.

CHARLEY: Naa. It's a rough world, Linda. They wouldn't blame him.

LINDA: I can't understand it. At this time especially. First time in thirty-five years we were just about free and clear. He only needed a little salary. He was even finished with the dentist.

CHARLEY: No man only needs a little salary.

LINDA: I can't understand it.

BIFF: There were a lot of nice days. When he'd come home from a trip; or on Sundays, making the stoop; finishing the cellar; putting on the new porch; when he built the extra bathroom; and put up the garage. You know something, Charley, there's more of him in that front stoop than in all the sales he ever made.

CHARLEY: Yeah. He was a happy man with a batch of cement.

LINDA: He was so wonderful with his hands.

BIFF: He had the wrong dreams. All, all, wrong.

HAPPY (*almost ready to fight Biff*): Don't say that!

BIFF: He never knew who he was.

CHARLEY (*stopping Happy's movement and reply; to Biff*): Nobody dast blame this man. You don't understand: Willy was a salesman. And for a salesman, there is no rock bottom to the life. He don't put a bolt to a nut, he don't tell you the law or give you medicine. He's a man way out there in the blue, riding on a smile and a shoeshine. And when they start not smiling back—that's an earthquake. And then you get yourself a couple of spots on your hat, and you're finished. Nobody dast blame this man. A salesman is got to dream, boy. It comes with the territory.

BIFF: Charley, the man didn't know who he was.

HAPPY (*infuriated*): Don't say that!

BIFF: Why don't you come with me, Happy?

HAPPY: I'm not licked that easily. I'm staying right in this city, and I'm gonna beat this racket! (*He looks at Biff, his chin set.*) The Loman Brothers!

BIFF: I know who I am, kid.

HAPPY: All right, boy. I'm gonna show you and everybody else that Willy Loman did not die in vain. He had a good dream. It's the only dream you can have—to come out number-one man. He fought it out here, and this is where I'm gonna win it for him.

BIFF (*with a hopeless glance at Happy, bends toward his mother*): Let's go, Mom.

LINDA: I'll be with you in a minute. Go on, Charley. (*He hesitates.*) I want to, just for a minute. I never had a chance to say good-by.

Charley moves away, followed by Happy. Biff remains a slight distance up and left of Linda. She sits there, summoning herself. The flute begins, not far away, playing behind her speech.

LINDA: Forgive me, dear. I can't cry. I don't know what it is, but I can't cry. I don't understand it. Why did you ever do that? Help me, Willy, I can't cry. It seems to me that you're just on another trip. I keep expecting you. Willy, dear, I can't cry. Why did you do it? I search and search and I search, and I can't understand it, Willy. I made the last payment on the house today. Today, dear. And there'll be nobody home. (*A sob rises in her throat.*) We're free and clear. (*Sobbing mournfully, released.*) We're free. (*Biff comes slowly toward her.*) We're free . . . We're free . . .

Biff lifts her to her feet and moves out up right with her in his arms. Linda sobs quietly. Bernard and Charley come together and follow them, followed by Happy. Only the music of the flute is left on the darkening stage as over the house the hard towers of the apartment buildings rise into sharp focus and the curtain falls.

—1949

Samuel Beckett (1906–1989) *was born near Dublin, Ireland. As a young man he enjoyed sports, studied French and Italian, and discovered the silent films of Buster Keaton and Charlie Chaplin, whose influence can be seen in his work. Teaching English in Paris in the 1920s, he joined the circle of fellow Irish writer James Joyce. He began to write novels and travelled in Europe, finally settling in Paris in 1937, where he later worked for the French Resistance during World War II. Most of his plays and novels were originally written in French, including his most famous play,* Waiting for Godot *(1953), in which two lost characters endlessly wait, though they are not sure for what or whom. Other important plays include* Endgame *(1957) and* Happy Days *(1961). Beckett's search to portray the bare essentials of the human condition meant that his plays became increasingly spare.* Act Without Words I: A Mime for One Player, *as the title suggests, dispenses with language entirely, and like other examples of the "theatre of the absurd," conveys a sense of incoherence and improvisation that represents modern life. As the solitary and silent character reaches for various tools, they are withdrawn from him until he no longer reacts, a response that can be interpreted as despair or defiance. This "mime" was first produced in Paris in April 1957 as an afterpiece to* Endgame. *Beckett was awarded the Nobel Prize in 1969 and is considered one of the most original and influential writers of the twentieth century.*

Samuel Beckett
Act Without Words I

A Mime for One Player

Desert. Dazzling light.

The man is flung backwards on stage from right wing. He falls, gets up immediately, dusts himself, turns aside, reflects.

Whistle from right wing.

He reflects, goes out right.

Immediately flung back on stage he falls, gets up immediately, dusts himself, turns aside, reflects.

Whistle from left wing.

He reflects, goes out left.

Immediately flung back on stage he falls, gets up immediately, dusts himself, turns aside, reflects.

Whistle from left wing.

He reflects, goes towards left wing, hesitates, thinks better of it, halts, turns aside, reflects.

A little tree descends from flies, lands. It has a single bough some three yards from ground and at its summit a meager tuft of palms casting at its foot a circle of shadow.

He continues to reflect.

Whistle from above.

He turns, sees tree, reflects, goes to it, sits down in its shadow, looks at his hands.

A pair of tailor's scissors descends from flies, comes to rest before tree, a yard from ground.

He continues to look at his hands.

Whistle from above.

He looks up, sees scissors, takes them and starts to trim his nails.

The palms close like a parasol, the shadow disappears.

He drops scissors, reflects.

A tiny carafe, to which is attached a huge label inscribed WATER, descends from flies, comes to rest some three yards from ground.

He continues to reflect.

Whistle from above.

He looks up, sees carafe, reflects, gets up, goes and stands under it, tries in vain to reach it, renounces, turns aside, reflects.

A big cube descends from flies, lands.

He continues to reflect.

Whistle from above.

He turns, sees cube, looks at it, at carafe, reflects, goes to cube, takes it up, carries it over and sets it down under carafe, tests its stability, gets up on it, tries in vain to reach carafe, renounces, gets down, carries cube back to its place, turns aside, reflects.

A second smaller cube descends from flies, lands.

He continues to reflect.

Whistle from above.

He turns, sees second cube, looks at it, at carafe, goes to second cube, takes it up, carries it over and sets it down under carafe, tests its stability, gets up on it, tries in vain to reach carafe, renounces, gets down, takes up second cube to carry it back to its place, hesitates, thinks better of it, sets it down, goes to big cube, takes it up, carries it over and puts it on small one, tests their stability, gets up on them, the cubes collapse, he falls, gets up immediately, brushes himself, reflects.

He takes up small cube, puts it on big one, tests their stability, gets up on them and is about to reach carafe when it is pulled up a little way and comes to rest beyond his reach.

He gets down, reflects, carries cubes back to their place, one by one, turns aside, reflects.

A third still smaller cube descends from flies, lands.

He continues to reflect.

Whistle from above.

He turns, sees third cube, looks at it, reflects, turns aside, reflects.

The third cube is pulled up and disappears in flies.

Beside carafe a rope descends from flies, with knots to facilitate ascent.

He continues to reflect.

Whistle from above.

He turns, sees rope, reflects, goes to it, climbs up it and is about to reach carafe when rope is let out and deposits him back on ground.

He reflects, looks around for scissors, sees them, goes and picks them up, returns to rope and starts to cut it with scissors.

The rope is pulled up, lifts him off ground, he hangs on, succeeds in cutting rope, falls back on ground, drops scissors, falls, gets up again immediately, brushes himself, reflects.

The rope is pulled up quickly and disappears in flies.

With length of rope in his possession he makes a lasso with which he tries to lasso carafe.

The carafe is pulled up quickly and disappears in flies.

He turns aside, reflects.

He goes with lasso in his hand to tree, looks at bough, turns and looks at cubes, looks again at bough, drops lasso, goes to cubes, takes up small one, carries it over and sets it down under bough, goes back for big one, takes it up and carries it over under bough, makes to put it on small one, hesitates, thinks better of it, sets it down, takes up small one and puts it on big one, tests their stability, turns aside and stoops to pick up lasso.

The bough folds down against trunk.

He straightens up with lasso in his hand, turns and sees what has happened.

He drops lasso, turns aside, reflects.

He carries back cubes to their place, one by one, goes back for lasso, carries it over to cubes and lays it in a neat coil on small one.

He turns aside, reflects.

Whistle from right wing.

He reflects, goes out right.

Immediately flung back on stage he falls, gets up immediately, brushes himself, turns aside, reflects.

Whistle from left wing.

He does not move.

He looks at his hands, looks around for scissors, sees them, goes and picks them up, starts to trim his nails, stops, reflects, runs his finger along blade of scissors, goes and lays them on small cube, turns aside, opens his collar, frees his neck and fingers it.

The small cube is pulled up and disappears in flies, carrying away rope and scissors.

He turns to take scissors, sees what has happened.

He turns aside, reflects.

He goes and sits down on big cube.

The big cube is pulled from under him. He falls. The big cube is pulled up and disappears in flies.

He remains lying on his side, his face towards auditorium, staring before him.

The carafe descends from flies and comes to rest a few feet from his body.

He does not move.

Whistle from above.

He does not move.

The carafe descends further, dangles and plays about his face.

He does not move.

The carafe is pulled up and disappears in flies.

The bough returns to horizontal, the palms open, the shadow returns.

Whistle from above.

He does not move.

The tree is pulled up and disappears in flies.

He looks at his hands.

Curtain

—1957

Tomson Highway (b. 1951) was born on a remote island in Maria Lake near the Brochet Reserve in northern Manitoba. His father was a trapper, fisherman, and champion dog-sled racer, and he spent his early life in a nomadic existence as the eleventh of twelve children. At age six, he was legally required to go to residential school in The Pas, which expanded his educational horizons, especially in the area of music, but separated him from his family and cultural roots and exposed him to traumatic abuse. He eventually went to England, where he studied to be a concert pianist, and later completed his Bachelor of Music at the University of Western Ontario. It was there that he met and studied with playwright James Reaney, and was exposed to the work of Michel Tremblay, whose influence can be seen in Highway's plays. Highway then worked as a social worker in Native communities and became artistic director of an Aboriginal theatre company entitled Native Earth, which co-produced his first major play, The Rez Sisters, *with Theatre Passe Muraille in 1986. This play won the Dora Mavor Moor Award for Best New Play, and was nominated for the Governor General's Award.* The Rez Sisters, *along with its sequel,* Dry Lips Oughta Move to Kapuskasing *(1989), brought Highway to national prominence. Tracing the efforts of seven remarkable women to win The BIGGEST BINGO IN THE WORLD, the text of* The Rez Sisters *is sprinkled with Cree and Ojibway and features the Trickster figure of Native mythology in the guise of Nanabush, who "straddles the consciousness of man and that of God, the Great Spirit." Highway has also written a novel,* Kiss of the Fur Queen *(1998), and books for children.*

Tomson Highway

The Rez Sisters

A Note on Nanabush

The dream world of North American Indian mythology is inhabited by the most fantastic creatures, beings, and events. Foremost among these beings is the "Trickster," as pivotal and important a figure in the Native world as Christ is in the realm of Christian mythology. "Weesageechak" in Cree, "Nanabush" in Ojibway, "Raven" in others, "Coyote" in still others, this Trickster goes by many names and many guises. In fact, he can assume any guise he chooses. Essentially a comic, clownish sort of character, he teaches us about the nature and the meaning of existence on the planet Earth; he straddles the consciousness of man and that of God, the Great Spirit.

Some say that "Nanabush" left this continent when the whiteman came. We believe he is still here among us—albeit a little the worse for wear and tear—having assumed other guises. Without him—and without the spiritual health of this figure—the core of Indian culture would be gone forever.

CAST OF CHARACTERS

Pelajia Patchnose, 53
Philomena Moosetail, 49, sister of Pelajia
Marie-Adele Starblanket, 39, half-sister of Pelajia & Philomena
Annie Cook, 36, sister of Marie-Adele & half-sister of the other two
Emily Dictionary, 32, sister of Annie & ditto
Veronique St. Pierre, 45, sister-in-law of all the above
Zhaboonigan Peterson, 24, mentally disabled adopted daughter of Veronique
Nanabush—who plays the Seagull (the dancer in white feathers), the Nighthawk (the dancer in dark feathers), and the Bingo Master.

Time: *Late summer, 1986.*
Place: *The Wasaychigan Hill Indian Reserve, Manitoulin Island, Ontario. (Note: "Wasaychigan" means "window" in Ojibway.)*

ACT ONE

It is mid-morning of a beautiful late August day on the Wasaychigan Hill Indian Reserve, Manitoulin Island, Ontario. Pelajia Patchnose is alone on the roof of her house, nailing shingles on. She wears faded blue denim men's cover-alls and a baseball cap to shade her eyes from the sun. A brightly-colored square cushion belonging to her sister, Philomena Moosetail, rests on the roof beside her. The ladder to the roof is off-stage.

PELAJIA: Philomena. I wanna go to Toronto.
PHILOMENA (*From offstage*):   Oh, go on.
PELAJIA: Sure as I'm sitting away up here on the roof of this old house. I kind of like it up here, though. From here, I can see half of Manitoulin Island on a clear day. I can see the chimneys, the tops of apple trees, the garbage heap behind Big Joey's dumpy little house.

I can see the seagulls circling over Marie-Adele Starblanket's white picket fence. Boats on the North Channel I wish I was on, sailing away somewhere. The mill at Espanola, a hundred miles away . . . and that's with just a bit of squinting. See? If I had binoculars, I could see the superstack in Sudbury. And if I were Superwoman, I could see the CN Tower in Toronto. Ah, but I'm just plain old Pelajia Rosella Patchnose and I'm here in plain, dusty, boring old Wasaychigan Hill . . . Wasy . . . waiting . . . waiting . . . nailing shining shingles with my trusty silver hammer on the roof of Pelajia Rosella Patchnose's little two-bedroom welfare house. Philomena. I wanna go to Toronto.

Philomena Moosetail comes up the ladder to the roof with one shingle and obviously hating it. She is very well-dressed, with a skirt, nylons, even heels, completely impractical for the roof.

PHILOMENA: Oh, go on.

PELAJIA: I'm tired, Philomena, tired of this place. There's days I wanna leave so bad.

PHILOMENA: But you were born here. All your poop's on this reserve.

PELAJIA: Oh, go on.

PHILOMENA: You'll never leave.

PELAJIA: Yes, I will. When I'm old.

PHILOMENA: You're old right now.

PELAJIA: I got a good 30 years to go . . .

PHILOMENA: . . . and you're gonna live every one of them right here beside me . . .

PELAJIA: . . . maybe 40 . . .

PHILOMENA: . . . here in Wasy.

Tickles Pelajia on the breasts.

Chiga-chiga-chiga.

PELAJIA (*Yelps and slaps Philomena's hand away*): Oh, go on. It's not like it used to be.

PHILOMENA: Oh, go on. People change, places change, time changes things. You expect to be young and gorgeous forever?

PELAJIA: See? I told you I'm not old,

PHILOMENA: Oh, go on. You.

PELAJIA: "Oh, go on. You." You bug me like hell when you say that.

PHILOMENA: You say it, too. And don't give me none of this "I don't like this place. I'm tired of it." This place is too much inside your blood. You can't get rid of it. And it can't get rid of you.

PELAJIA: Four thirty this morning, I was woken by . . .

PHILOMENA: Here we go again.

PELAJIA: . . . Andrew Starblanket and his brother, Matthew. Drunk. Again. Or sounded like . . .

PHILOMENA: Nothing better to do.

PELAJIA: . . . fighting over some girl. Heard what sounded like a baseball bat landing on somebody's back. My lawn looks like the shits this morning.

PHILOMENA: Well, I like it here. Myself, I'm gonna go to every bingo and I'm gonna hit every jackpot between here and Espanola and I'm gonna buy me that toilet I'm dreaming about at night . . . big and wide and very white . . .

PELAJIA: Aw-ni-gi-naw-ee-dick.[1]

PHILOMENA: I'm good at bingo.

PELAJIA: So what! And the old stories, the old language. Almost all gone . . . was a time Nanabush and Windigo and everyone here could rattle away in Indian fast as Bingo Betty could lay her bingo chips down on a hot night.

PHILOMENA: Pelajia Rosella Patchnose. The sun's gonna drive you crazy.

And she descends the ladder.

PELAJIA: Everyone here's crazy. No jobs. Nothing to do but drink and screw each other's wives and husbands and forget about our Nanabush.

From offstage Philomena screams. She fell down the ladder.

Philomena!

As she looks over the edge of the roof.

What are you doing down there?

PHILOMENA: What do you think? I fell.

PELAJIA: Bring me some of them nails while you're down there.

---

[1] **Oh, go on.** (Ojibway)

PHILOMENA (*Whining and still from offstage, from behind the house*): You think I can race up and down this ladder? You think I got wings?

PELAJIA: You gotta wear pants when you're doing a man's job. See? You got your skirt ripped on a nail and now you can see your thighs. People gonna think you just came from Big Joey's house.

PHILOMENA (*She comes up the ladder in a state of disarray*): Let them think what they want. That old cow Gazelle Nataways . . . always acting like she thinks she's still a spring chicken. She's got them legs of hers wrapped around Big Joey day and night . . .

PELAJIA: Philomena. Park your tongue. My old man has to go the hundred miles to Espanola just to get a job. My boys. Gone to Toronto. Only place educated Indian boys can find decent jobs these days. And here I sit all broken-hearted.

PHILOMENA: Paid a dime and only farted.

PELAJIA: Look at you. You got dirt all over your backside.

Turning her attention to the road in front of her house and standing up for the first and only time.

And dirt roads! Years now that old chief's been making speeches about getting paved roads "for my people" and still we got dirt roads all over.

PHILOMENA: Oh, go on.

PELAJIA: When I win me that jackpot next time we play bingo in Espanola ...

PHILOMENA (*Examining her torn skirt, her general state of disarray, and fretting over it*): Look at this! Will you look at this! Ohhh!

PELAJIA: . . . I'm gonna put that old chief to shame and build me a nice paved road right here in front of my house. Jet black. Shiny. Make my lawn look real nice.

PHILOMENA: My rib-cage!

PELAJIA: And if that old chief don't wanna make paved roads for all my sisters around here . . .

PHILOMENA: There's something rattling around inside me!

PELAJIA: . . . I'm packing my bags and moving to Toronto.

Sits down again.

PHILOMENA: Oh, go on.

She spies Annie Cook's approach a distance up the hill.

Why, I do believe that cloud of dust over there is Annie Cook racing down the hill, Pelajia.

PELAJIA: Philomena. I wanna go to Toronto.

PHILOMENA: She's walking mighty fast. Must be excited about something.

PELAJIA: Never seen Annie Cook walk slow since the day she finally lost Eugene to Marie-Adele at the church 19 years ago. And even then she was walking a little too fast for a girl who was supposed to be broken-heart . . . (*Stopping just in time and laughing*) . . . heartbroken.

Annie Cook pops up the top of the ladder to the roof.

ANNIE (*All cheery and fast and perky*): Halloooo! Whatchyou doing up here?

PELAJIA: There's room for only so much weight up here before we go crashing into my kitchen, so what do you want?

ANNIE: Just popped up to say hi.

PELAJIA: And see what we're doing?

ANNIE: Well . . .

PELAJIA: Couldn't you see what we're doing from up where you were?

ANNIE (*Confidentially, to Philomena*): Is it true Gazelle Nataways won the bingo last night?

PHILOMENA: Annie Cook, first you say you're gonna come with me and then you don't even bother showing up. If you were sitting beside me at that bingo table last night you would have seen Gazelle Nataways win that big pot again with your own two eyes.

ANNIE: Emily Dictionary and I went to Little Current to listen to Fritz the Katz.

PELAJIA: What in God's name kind of a band might that be?

ANNIE: Country rock. My favorite. Fritz the Katz is from Toronto.

PELAJIA: Fritzy . . . ritzy . . . Philomena! Say something.

PHILOMENA: My record player is in Espanola getting fixed.

ANNIE: That's nice.

PHILOMENA: Good.

ANNIE: Is it true Gazelle Nataways plans to spend her bingo money to go to Toronto with . . . with Big Joey?

PHILOMENA: Who wants to know? Emily Dictionary?

ANNIE: I guess so.

PELAJIA: That Gazelle Nataways gonna leave all her babies behind and let them starve to death?

ANNIE: I guess so. I don't know. I'm asking you.

PELAJIA AND PHILOMENA: We don't know.

ANNIE: I'm on my way to Marie-Adele's to pick her up.

PELAJIA: Why? Where you gonna put her down?

Pelajia and Philomena laugh.

ANNIE: I mean, we're going to the store together. To the post office. We're going to pick up a parcel. They say there's a parcel for me. They say it's shaped like a record. And they say it's from Sudbury. So it must be from my daughter, Ellen . . .

PELAJIA AND PHILOMENA: . . . "who lives with this white guy in Sudbury" . . .

ANNIE: How did you know?

PHILOMENA: Everybody knows.

ANNIE: His name is Ray*mond*. Not *Ray*mond, But Ray*mond*. Like in Bon Bon.

Philomena tries out "bon bon" to herself.

He's French.

PELAJIA: Oh?

ANNIE: Garage mechanic. He fixes cars. And you know, talking about Frenchmen, that old priest is holding another bingo next week and when I win . . . (*To Philomena.*) Are you going?

PELAJIA: Does a bear shit in the woods?

ANNIE: . . . when I win, I'm going to Espanola and play the bingo there. Emily Dictionary says that Fire Minklater can give us a ride in her new car. She got it through Ray*mond*'s garage. The bingo in Espanola is bigger. And it's better. And I'll win. And then I'll go to Sudbury, where the bingos are even bigger and better. And then I can visit my daughter, Ellen . . .

PELAJIA: . . . "who lives with this white guy in Sudbury" . . .

ANNIE: . . . and go shopping in the record stores and go to the hotel and drink beer quietly—not noisy and crazy like here—and listen to the live bands. It will be so much fun. I hope Emily Dictionary can come with me.

PHILOMENA: It's true. I've been thinking . . .

PELAJIA: You don't say.

PHILOMENA: It's true. The bingos here are getting kind of boring . . .

ANNIE: That old priest is too slow and sometimes he gets the numbers all mixed up and the pot's not big enough.

PHILOMENA: And I don't like the way he calls the numbers. (*Nasally.*) B 12, 0 64.

ANNIE: When Little Girl Manitowabi won last month . . .

PHILOMENA: She won just enough to take a taxi back to Buzwah.

ANNIE: That's all.

Both Annie and Philomena pause to give a quick sigh of yearning.

PHILOMENA: Annie Cook, I want that big pot.

ANNIE: We all want big pots.

PELAJIA: Start a revolution!

PHILOMENA AND ANNIE: Yes!

ANNIE: All us Wasy women. We'll march up the hill, burn the church hall down, scare the priest to death, and then we'll march all the way to Espanola, where the bingos are bigger and better . . .

PHILOMENA: We'll hold big placards!

ANNIE: They'll say: "Wasy women want bigger bingos!"

PELAJIA: And one will say: "Annie Cook Wants Big Pot!"

PHILOMENA: . . . and the numbers at those bingos in Espanola go faster and the pots get bigger by the week. Oh, Pelajia Patchnose, I'm getting excited just thinking about it!

ANNIE: I'm going.

PELAJIA: You are, are you?

ANNIE: Yes. I'm going. I'm running out of time. I'm going to Marie-Adele's house and then we'll walk to the store together to pick up the parcel—I'm sure there'll be a letter in it, and Marie-Adele is expecting mail, too—and we'll see if Emily Dictionary is working today and we'll ask her if Fire Minklater has her new car yet so we can go to Espanola for that big pot.

She begins to descend the ladder.

PELAJIA: Well, you don't have much to do today, do you?

ANNIE: Well. Toodle-oo!

And she pops down the ladder and is gone.

PELAJIA: Not bad for someone who was in such a hurry to get her parcel. She talks faster than she walks.

Noticing how dejected and abandoned Philomena looks, she holds up her hammer.

Bingo money. Top quality. $24.95.

PHILOMENA: It's true. Bingos here in Wasy are getting smaller and smaller all the time. Especially now when the value of the dollar is getting lesser and lesser. In the old days, when Bingo Betty was still alive and walking these dirt roads, she'd come to every single bingo and she'd sit there like the Queen of Tonga, big and huge like a roast beef, smack-dab in the middle of the bingo hall. One night, I remember, she brought two young cousins from the city—two young women, dressed real fancy, like they were going to Sunday church—and Bingo Betty made them sit one on her left, with her three little bingo cards, and one on her right, with her three little ones. And Bingo Betty herself sat in the middle with 27 cards. Twenty seven cards! Amazing.

Pelajia starts to descend the ladder, and Philomena, getting excited, steps closer and closer to the edge of the roof.

And those were the days when they still used bingo chips, not these dabbers like nowadays, and everyone came with a little margarine container full of these bingo chips. When the game began and they started calling out the numbers, Bingo Betty was all set, like a horse at the race-track in Sudbury, you could practically see the foam sizzling and bubbling between her teeth. Bingo Betty! Bingo Betty with her beady little darting eyes, sharp as needles, and her roly-poly jiggledy-piggledy arms with their stubby little claws would go: chiga-chiga-chiga-chiga-chiga-chiga arms flying across the table smooth as angel's wings chiga-chiga-chiga-chiga-chiga-chiga-woosh! Cousin on the left chiga-chiga, cousin on the right chiga, chiga-eeee!

She narrowly misses falling off the roof and cries out in terror.

PELAJIA: Philomena!

PHILOMENA (*Scrambling on hands and knees to Pelajia, and coming to rest in this languorous pose, takes a moment to regain her composure and catch her breath*):   And you know, to this very day, they say that on certain nights at the bingo here in Wasy, they say you can see Bingo Betty's ghost, like a mist, hovering in the air above the bingo tables, playing bingo like it's never been played before. Or since.

PELAJIA: Amazing! She should have gone to Toronto.

Black-out.

The same day, same time, in Wasaychigan Hill. Marie-Adele Starblanket is standing alone outside her house, in her yard, by her 14-post white picket fence. Her house is down the hill from Pelajia Patchnose's, close to the lake. A seagull watches her from a distance away. He is the dancer in white feathers. Through this whole section, Nanabush (i.e. Nanabush in the guise of the seagull), Marie-Adele, and Zhaboonigan play "games" with each other. Only she and Zhaboonigan Peterson can see the spirit inside the bird and can sort of (though not quite) recognize him for who he is. A doll belonging to a little girl lies on the porch floor. Marie-Adele throws little stones at the seagull.

MARIE-ADELE: Awus! Wee-chee-gis. Ka-tha pu-g'wun-ta oo-ta pee-wee-sta-ta-gu-mik-si. Awus! Neee. U-wi-nuk oo-ma kee-tha ee-tee-thi-mi-soo-yin holy spirit chee? Awus! Hey, maw ma-a oop-mee tay-si-thow u-wu seagull bird. I goo-ta poo-goo ta-poo. Nu-gu-na-wa-pa-mik. Nu-gu-na-wa-pa-mik.

NANABUSH: As-tum.

MARIE-ADELE: Neee. Moo-tha ni-gus-kee-tan tu-pi-mi-tha-an. Moo-tha oo-ta-ta-gwu-na n'tay-yan. Chees-kwa. (*Pause.*) Ma-ti poo-ni-mee-see i-goo-ta wee-chi-gi-seagull bird come shit on my fence one more time and you and anybody else look like you cook like stew on my stove. Awus![2]

[2]**Marie-Adele:** Go away! You stinking thing. Don't coming messing around here for nothing. Go away! Neee. Who the hell do you think you are, the Holy Spirit? Go away! Hey, but he won't fly away, this seagull bird. He just sits there. And watches me. Watches me.
Nanabush: Come.
Marie-Adele: Neee. I can't fly away. I have no wings. Yet. (*Pause.*) Will you stop shitting all over the place you stinking seagull bird etc. (Cree).
(Note: "Neee" is a very common Cree expression with the approximate meaning of "Oh you.")

Veronique St. Pierre "passes by" with her adopted daughter Zhaboonigan Peterson.

VERONIQUE: Talking to the birds again, Marie-Adele Starblanket?

MARIE-ADELE: Aha. Veronique St. Pierre. How are you today?

VERONIQUE: Black Lady Halked's sister-in-law Fire Minklater, Fire Minklater's husband, just bought Fire Minklater a car in Sudbury.

MARIE-ADELE: New?

VERONIQUE: Used. They say he bought it from some Frenchman, some garage. Cray-*on*.

MARIE-ADELE: Ray*mond*.

VERONIQUE: These Frenchmen are forever selling us their used cars. And I'm sure that's why Black Lady Halked has been baring those big yellow teeth of hers, smiling all over the reserve recently. She looks like a hound about to pounce on a mouse, she smiles so hard when she smiles. I'd like to see her smile after plastic surgery. Anyway. At the bingo last night she was hinting that it wouldn't be too long before she would be able to go to the bingo in Espanola more frequently. Unfortunately, a new game started and you know how Black Lady Halked has to concentrate when she plays bingo— her forehead looks like corduroy, she concentrates so hard—so I didn't get a chance to ask her what she meant. So. Fire Minklater has a used car. Imagine! Maybe I can make friends with her again. NO! I wouldn't be caught dead inside her car. Not even if she had a brand-new Cadillac. How are your children? All 14 of them.

MARIE-ADELE: Okay, I guess.

VERONIQUE: Imagine. And all from one father. Anyway. Who will take care of them after you . . . ahem . . . I mean . . . when you go to the hospital?

MARIE-ADELE: Eugene.

ZHABOONIGAN: Is he gentle?

MARIE-ADELE: Baby-cakes. How are you?

ZHABOONIGAN: Fine. (*Giggles.*)

VERONIQUE: She's fine. She went berry-picking yesterday with the children.

ZHABOONIGAN: Where's Nicky?

MARIE-ADELE: Nicky's down at the beach.

ZHABOONIGAN: Why?

MARIE-ADELE: Taking care of Rose-Marie.
ZHABOONIGAN: Oh.
MARIE-ADELE: Yup.
ZHABOONIGAN: Me and Nicky, ever lots of blueberries!
MARIE-ADELE: Me and Nicky picked lots of blueberries.
ZHABOONIGAN: I didn't see you there.
MARIE-ADELE: When?
ZHABOONIGAN: Before today.
MARIE-ADELE: How come Nicky didn't come home with any?
ZHABOONIGAN: Why?

Marie-Adele shrugs. Zhaboonigan imitates this, and then pretends she is stuffing her mouth with berries.

MARIE-ADELE: Aw, yous went and made pigs of yourselves.
ZHABOONIGAN: Nicky's the pig.
MARIE-ADELE: Neee.
ZHABOONIGAN: Are you going away far?
MARIE-ADELE: I'm not going far.
ZHABOONIGAN: Oh. Are you pretty?

Marie-Adele, embarrassed for a moment, smiles and Zhaboonigan smiles, too.

MARIE-ADELE: You're pretty, too.

Zhaboonigan tugs at Marie-Adele's shoelaces.

Oh, Zhaboonigan. Now you have to tie it up. I can't bend too far cuz I get tired.

Zhaboonigan tries to tie the shoelaces with great difficulty. When she finds she can't she throws her arms up and screams.

ZHABOONIGAN: Dirty trick! Dirty trick!

She bites her hand and hurts herself.

MARIE-ADELE: Now, don't get mad.
VERONIQUE: Stop it. Stop it right now.
ZHABOONIGAN: No! No!
MARIE-ADELE: Zha. Zha. Listen. Listen.
ZHABOONIGAN: Stop it! Stop it right now!

MARIE-ADELE: Come on Zha. You and I can name the koo-koos-suk.[3] All 14 of them.

ZHABOONIGAN: Okay. Here we go.

Marie-Adele leads Zhaboonigan over to the picket fence and Veronique follows them.

ZHABOONIGAN (*To Veronique*): No.

Veronique retreats, obviously hurt.

MARIE-ADELE (*Taking Zhaboonigan's hand and counting on the 14 posts of her white picket fence*): Simon, Andrew, Matthew, Janie, Nicky, Ricky, Ben, Mark, Ron, Don, John, Tom, Pete, and Rose-Marie. There.

Underneath Marie-Adele's voice, Zhaboonigan has been counting.

ZHABOONIGAN: One, two, three, four, five, six, seven, eight, nine, ten, eleven, twelve, thirteen, fourteen. (*Giggles.*)

MARIE-ADELE: Ever good counter you, Zhaboonigan.

ZHABOONIGAN: Yup.

VERONIQUE: This reserve, sometimes I get so sick of it. They laugh at me behind my back, I just know it. They laugh at me and Pierre St. Pierre because we don't have any children of our own. "Imagine, they say, she's on her second husband already and she still can't have children!" They laugh at Zhaboonigan Peterson because she's crazy, that's what they call her. They can't even take care of their own people, they'd rather laugh at them. I'm the only person who would take Zhaboonigan after her parents died in that horrible car crash near Manitowaning on Saturday November 12 1964 may they rest in peace (*She makes a quick sign of the cross without skipping a beat.*) I'm the only one around here who is kind enough. And they laugh at me. Oh, I wish I had a new stove, Marie-Adele. My stove is so old and broken down, only two elements work anymore and my oven is starting to talk back at me.

MARIE-ADELE: Get it fixed.

VERONIQUE: You know that Pierre St. Pierre never has any money. He drinks it all up.

She sighs longingly.

---

[3]The little pigs. (Cree)

Some day! Anyway. Zhaboonigan here wanted to go for a swim so I
thought I'd walk her down—drop by and see how you and the children are doing—it will do my weak heart good, I was saying to
myself.

MARIE-ADELE: Awus!

*As she throws a pebble at the seagull on the stone, Veronique, for a
second, thinks it's her Marie-Adele is shooing away. There is a brief
silence broken after awhile by Zhaboonigan's little giggle.*

VERONIQUE: Anyway. I was walking down by that Big Joey's shame-
less little shack just this morning when guess who pokes her nose
out the window but Gazelle Nataways—the nerve of that woman. I
couldn't see inside but I'm sure she was only half-dressed, her
hairdo was all mixed up and she said to me: "Did you know,
Veronique St. Pierre, that Little Girl Manitowabi told me her
daughter, June Bug McLeod, just got back from the hospital in
Sudbury where she had her tubes tied and told her that THE
BIGGEST BINGO IN THE WORLD is coming to Toronto?"

MARIE-ADELE: When?

VERONIQUE: I just about had a heart attack.

MARIE-ADELE: When?

VERONIQUE: But I said to Gazelle anyway: Is there such a thing as a
BIGGEST BINGO IN THE WORLD? And she said: Yes. And she
should know about these things because she spends all her waking
and sleeping hours just banging about in bed with the biggest thing
on Manitoulin Island, I almost said.

MARIE-ADELE: This bingo. When?

VERONIQUE: She didn't know. And now that I think of it, I don't
know whether to believe her. After all, who should believe a woman
who wrestles around with dirt like Big Joey all night long leaving
her poor babies to starve to death in her empty kitchen? But if it's
true, Marie-Adele, if it's true that THE BIGGEST BINGO IN THE
WORLD is coming to Toronto, I'm going and I want you to come
with me.

MARIE-ADELE: Well . . .

VERONIQUE: I want you to come shopping with me and help me
choose my new stove after I win.

MARIE-ADELE: Hang on . . .

VERONIQUE: They have good stoves in Toronto.

MARIE-ADELE: Let's find out for sure. Then we start making plans.

VERONIQUE: Maybe we should go back and ask that Gazelle Nataways about this. If she's sure.

MARIE-ADELE: Maybe we should go and ask June Bug McLeod herself.

VERONIQUE: We can't walk to Buzwah and I'm too old to hitch-hike.

MARIE-ADELE: There's Eugene's van. He'll be home by six.

VERONIQUE: I want to find out NOW. But what if people see us standing at Big Joey's door?.

MARIE-ADELE: What do you mean? We just knock on the door, march right in, ask the bitch, and march right out again.

VERONIQUE: Zhaboonigan dear, wait for me over there.

She waits until Zhaboonigan is safely out of earshot and then leans over to Marie-Adele in a conspiratorial whisper.

Anyway. You must know, Marie-Adele, that there's all kinds of women who come streaming out of that house at all hours of the day and night. I might be considered one of them. You know your youngest sister, Emily Dictionary, was seen staggering out of that house in the dead of night two nights ago?

MARIE-ADELE: Veronique St. Pierre, what Emily Dictionary does is Emily's business.

Annie Cook enters, walking fast, and comes to a screeching halt.

ANNIE: Hallooooo! Whatchyou doin'?

VERONIQUE (*Giving Annie the baleful eye*): How are you?

ANNIE: High as a kite. Just kidding. Hi, Zha.

ZHABOONIGAN: Hi.

Giggles. She runs toward Marie-Adele, bumping into Annie en route.

ANNIE: Hey, Marie-Adele.

ZHABOONIGAN: Marie-Adele. How's your cancer?

Giggles and scurries off laughing.

VERONIQUE: Shkanah, Zhaboonigan, sna-ma-bah . . .[4]

---

[4]Shush, Zhaboonigan, don't say that. (Ojibway)

MARIE-ADELE: Come on, before the post office closes for lunch.

VERONIQUE: You didn't tell me you were going to the store.

ANNIE: Well, we are. (*To Marie-Adele.*) Hey, is Simon in? I'm sure he's got my Ricky Skaggs album. You know the one that goes (*Sings.*) "Honeee!"

Calling into the house.

Yoo-hoo, Simon!

MARIE-ADELE: He's in Espanola with Eugene.

VERONIQUE: Expecting mail, Annie Cook?

ANNIE: A parcel from my daughter, Ellen, who lives with this white guy in Sudbury . . .

VERONIQUE: So I've heard.

ANNIE: And my sister here is expecting a letter, too.

VERONIQUE: From whom?

ANNIE: From the doctor, about her next check-up.

VERONIQUE: When?

MARIE-ADELE: We don't know when. Or where. Annie, let's go.

ANNIE: They say it's shaped like a record.

VERONIQUE: Maybe there'll be news in that parcel about THE BIGGEST BINGO IN THE WORLD!

Shouts toward the lake, in a state of great excitement.

Zhaboonigan! Zhaboonigan! We're going to the store!

ANNIE: THE BIGGEST BINGO IN THE WORLD?

VERONIQUE: In Toronto. Soon. Imagine! Gazelle Nataways told me. She heard about it from Little Girl Manitowabi over in Buzwah who heard about it from her daughter June Bug McLeod who just got back from the hospital in Sudbury where she had her tubes tied I just about had a heart attack!

ANNIE: Toronto?

MARIE-ADELE: We gotta find out for sure.

ANNIE: Right.

MARIE-ADELE: We could go to Big Joey's and ask Gazelle Nataways except Veronique St. Pierre's too scared of Gazelle.

VERONIQUE: I am not.

ANNIE: You are too.

MARIE-ADELE: We could wait and borrow Eugene's van . . .

VERONIQUE: I am not.

ANNIE: . . . drive over to Buzwah . . .

MARIE-ADELE: . . . and ask June Bug McLeod . . .

ANNIE: . . . but wait a minute! . . .

MARIE-ADELE AND ANNIE: Maybe there IS news in that parcel about this BIGGEST BINGO IN THE WORLD!

MARIE-ADELE: Come on.

VERONIQUE (*Shouting toward the lake*): Zhaboonigan! Zhaboonigan!

ANNIE: And here I was so excited about the next little bingo that old priest is holding next week. Toronto! Oh, I hope it's true!

VERONIQUE: Zhaboonigan! Zhaboonigan! Zhaboonigan! Dammit! We're going to the store!

And the "march" to the store begins, during which Nanabush, still in the guise of the seagull, follows them and continues to play tricks, mimicking their hand movements, the movement of their mouths, etc. The three women appear each in her own spot of light at widely divergent points on the stage area.

ANNIE: When I go to THE BIGGEST BINGO IN THE WORLD, in Toronto, I will win. For sure, I will win. If they shout the B 14 at the end, for sure I will win. The B 14 is my lucky number after all. Then I will take all my money and I will go to every record store in Toronto. I will buy every single one of Patsy Cline's records, especially the one that goes (*Sings.*) "I go a-walking, after midnight," oh I go crazy every time I hear that one. Then I will buy a huge record player, the biggest one in the whole world. And then I will go to all the taverns and all the night clubs in Toronto and listen to the live bands while I drink beer quietly—not noisy and crazy like here—I will bring my daughter Ellen and her white guy from Sudbury and we will sit together. Maybe I will call Fritz the Katz and he will take me out. Maybe he will hire me as one of his singers and I can (*Sings.*) "Oooh," in the background while my feet go (*Shuffles her feet from side to side.*) while Fritz the Katz is singing and the lights are flashing and the people are drinking beer and smoking cigarettes and dancing. Ohhh, I could dance all night with that Fritz the Katz. When I win, when I win THE BIGGEST BINGO IN THE WORLD!

MARIE-ADELE: When I win THE BIGGEST BINGO IN THE WORLD, I'm gonna buy me an island. In the North Channel, right smack-dab in the middle—eem-shak min-stik[5]—the most beautiful island in the world. And my island will have lots of trees—great big bushy ones—and lots and lots and lots of sweetgrass. MMMMM! And there's gonna be pine trees and oak trees and maple trees and big stones and little stonelets—neee—and, oh yeah, this real neat picket fence, real high, long and very, very, very white. No bird shit. Eugene will live there and me and all my Starblanket kids. Yup, no more smelly, stinky old pulp and paper mill in Espanola for my Eugene—pooh!—my 12 Starblanket boys and my two Starblanket girls and me and my Eugene all living real nice and comfy right there on Starblanket Island, the most beautiful incredible goddamn island in the whole goddamn world. Eem-shak min-stik! When I win THE BIGGEST BINGO IN THE WORLD!

VERONIQUE: Well, when I win THE BIGGEST BINGO IN THE WORLD. No! After I win THE BIGGEST BINGO IN THE WORLD, I will go shopping for a brand-new stove. In Toronto. At the Eaton Centre. A great big stove. The kind Madame Benoit has. The kind that has the three different compartments in the oven alone. I'll have the biggest stove on the reserve. I'll cook for all the children on the reserve. I'll adopt all of Marie-Adele Starblanket's 14 children and I will cook for them. I'll even cook for Gazelle Nataways' poor starving babies while she's lolling around like a pig in Big Joey's smelly, sweaty bed. And Pierre St. Pierre can drink himself to death for all I care. Because I'll be the best cook on all of Manitoulin Island! I'll enter competitions. I'll go to Paris and meet what's-his-name Cordon Bleu! I'll write a cookbook called "The Joy of Veronique St. Pierre's Cooking" and it will sell in the millions! And I will become rich and famous! Zhaboonigan Peterson will wear a mink while she eats steak tartare-de-frou-frou! Madame Benoit will be so jealous she'll suicide herself. Oh, when I win THE BIGGEST BINGO IN THE WORLD!

Zhaboonigan comes running in from swimming, "chasing" after the other three women, counting to herself and giggling.

---

[5]A great big island. (Cree)

ZHABOONIGAN: One, two, three, four, five, six, seven, eight, nine, ten, eleven, twelve, thirteen, fourteen.

At the store. Annie Cook, Marie-Adele Starblanket, Veronique St. Pierre, and Zhaboonigan Peterson have arrived. Emily Dictionary makes a sudden appearance, carrying a huge bag of flour on her shoulder. She is one tough lady, wearing cowboy boots, tight blue jeans, a black leather jacket—all three items worn to the seams—and she sports one black eye.

EMILY (*In a loud, booming voice that paralyzes all movement in the room while she speaks*):   Zhaboonigan Peterson! What in Red Lucifer's name ever possessed you to be hangin' out with a buncha' dizzy old dames like this?

Bag of flour hits the floor with a "doof."

MARIE-ADELE: Emily. Your eye.

EMILY: Oh, bit of a tussle.

VERONIQUE: With who?

EMILY: None of your goddamn business.

MARIE-ADELE: Emily, please.

ANNIE (*Following Emily about the store while Veronique tries, in vain, to hear what she can*):   I wasn't able to find out from Pelajia Patchnose or Philomena Moosemeat if Gazelle Nataways is going to Toronto this weekend with . . . Big Joey . . . they didn't know . . . Gazelle did win the bingo last night though.

EMILY: Aw shit. Veronique St. Pierre, you old bag. Is it true Gazelle Nataways is takin' off for Toronto with that hunk Big Joey?

VERONIQUE: It WAS you coming out of that house two nights ago. I walked by as quickly as I could . . .

EMILY: . . . shoulda come out and nailed your big floppy ears to the door . . .

VERONIQUE: . . . and I would have called the police but I was too scared Big Joey might come after me and Zhaboonigan later . . .

EMILY: . . . yeah, right.

ZHABOONIGAN: Yeah, right.

VERONIQUE: . . . and I have a weak heart, you know? Who hit you? Big Joey? Or Gazelle Nataways?

EMILY: The nerve of this woman.

VERONIQUE: Well?

EMILY (*Calls Zhaboonigan, who is behind the counter, on the floor, playing with the merchandise*):   Zhaboonigan Peterson! Where in Red Lucifer's name is that dozy pagan?

VERONIQUE: You keep hanging around that house and you're gonna end up in deep trouble. You don't know how wicked and vicious those Nataways women can get. They say there's witchcraft in their blood. And with manners like yours, Emily Dictionary, you'd deserve every hex you got.

EMILY: Do I know this woman? Do I know this woman?

VERONIQUE (*During this speech, Marie-Adele and Annie sing "Honeee" tauntingly*):   I'm sorry I have to say this in front of everyone like this but this woman has just accused my daughter of being a pagan. I didn't call her Zhaboonigan. The people on this reserve, who have nothing better to do with their time than call each other names, they called her that. Her name is Marie-Adele. Marie-Adele Peterson. You should talk. I should ask you where in Red . . . Red . . . whatever, you got a circus of a name like Emily Dictionary.

Emily grabs Veronique and throws her across the room. Veronique goes flying right into Pelajia, who has entered the store during the latter part of this speech.

PELAJIA: Veronique St. Pierre! Control yourself or I'll hit you over the head with my hammer.

VERONIQUE (*Blows a "raspberry" in Pelajia's face*):   Bleah!

ANNIE: No, Pelajia, no.

EMILY: Go ahead, Pelajia. Make my day.

ANNIE: Down, put it down.

PHILOMENA (*As she comes scurrying into the store.*):   I have to use the toilet.

Running to Emily.

I have to use your toilet.

And goes scurrying into the toilet.

ANNIE (*To Pelajia*):   Remember, that's Veronique St. Pierre and if you get on the wrong side of Veronique St. Pierre she's liable to spread rumors about you all over kingdom come and you'll lose every bit of respect you got on this reserve. Don't let those pants you're wearing go to your head.

PELAJIA (*Catching Annie by the arm as she tries to run away*): Annie Cook! You got a mouth on you like a helicopter.

ANNIE: Veronique's mad at you, Emily, because you won't tell her what happened the other night at Big Joey's house. And she's jealous of Gazelle Nataways because Gazelle won the bingo again last night and she hopes you're the one person on this reserve who has the guts to stand up to Gazelle.

VERONIQUE (*Making a lunge at Annie, who hides behind Emily*): What's that! What's that! Ohhh! Ohhh!

ANNIE: Leave me alone, you old snoop. All I wanna know is this big bingo really happening in Toronto.

VERONIQUE: Annie Cook. You are a little suck.

EMILY (*To Veronique*): Someday, someone oughta stick a great big piece of shit into that mouth of yours.

PELAJIA (*To Emily*): And someday, someone ought to wash yours out with soap.

PHILOMENA (*Throwing the toilet door open, she sits there in her glory, panties down to her ankles*): Emily Dictionary. You come back to the reserve after all these years and you strut around like you own the place. I know Veronique St. Pierre is a pain in the ass but I don't care. She's your elder and you respect her. Now shut up, all of you, and let me shit in peace.

And slams the washroom door. Veronique, scandalized by this, haughtily walks through toward the door, bumping into Pelajia en route.

PELAJIA: Philomena. Get your bum out here. Veronique St. Pierre is about to lose her life.

She raises her hammer at Veronique.

VERONIQUE (*To Pelajia*): Put that hammer away. And go put a skirt on, for heaven's sake, you look obscene in those tight pants.

ANNIE: Hit her. Go on. Hit the bitch. One good bang is all she needs.

EMILY: Yeah, right. A gang-bang is more like it.

And a full-scale riot breaks out, during which the women throw every conceivable insult at each other. Emily throws open the toilet

*door and Philomena comes stomping out, pulling her panties on
and joining the riot. All talk at the same time, quietly at first, but
then getting louder and louder until they are all screaming.*

PHILOMENA (*To Annie*): What a slime. Make promises and then you
go do something else. And I always have to smile at you. What a
slime. (*To Emily.*) All that tough talk. I know what's behind it all.
You'll never be big enough to push me around. (*To Marie-Adele.*)
Fourteen kids! You look like a wrinkled old prune already. (*To
Pelajia.*) At least I'm a woman. (*To Veronique.*) Have you any idea
how, just how offensive, how obnoxious you are to people? And that
halitosis. Pooh! You wouldn't have it if you didn't talk so much.

EMILY (*To Philomena*): So damned bossy and pushy and sucky. You
make me sick. Always wanting your own way. (*To Veronique.*)
Goddamned trouble-making old crow. (*To Pelajia.*) Fuckin' self-
righteous old bitch. (*To Marie-Adele.*) Mental problems, that's what
you got, princess. I ain't no baby. I'm the size of a fuckin' church.
(*To Annie.*) You slippery little slut. Brain the size of a fuckin' pea.
Fuck, man, take a Valium.

VERONIQUE (*To Emily*): You have no morals at all. You sick pervert.
You should have stayed where you came from, where all the other
perverts are. (*To Pelajia.*) Slow turtle. Talk big and move like Jell-o.
(*To Annie.*) Cockroach! (*To Philomena.*) You big phony. Flush
yourself down that damned toilet of yours and shut up. (*To Marie-
Adele.*) Hasn't this slimy little reptile (*Referring to Annie.*) ever told
you that sweet little Ellen of hers is really Eugene's daughter? Go
talk to the birds in Sudbury and find out for yourself.

PELAJIA (*To Veronique*): This reserve would be a better place without
you. I'm tired of dealing with people like you. Tired. (*To Marie-
Adele.*) You can't act that way. This here's no time to be selfish. You
spoiled brat. (*To Philomena.*) You old fool. I thought you were com-
ing back to help me and here you are all trussed up like a
Thanksgiving turkey, putting on these white lady airs. (*To Annie.*)
Annie Cook. Move to Kapuskasing! (*To Emily.*) "Fuck, fuck, fuck!"
Us Indian women got no business talking like that.

MARIE-ADELE (*To Pelajia*): You don't have all the answers. You can't
fix everything. (*To Annie.*) White guys. Slow down a minute and see
how stupid you look. (*To Emily.*) Voice like a fog-horn. You ram

through everything like a truck. You look like a truck. (*To
Veronique*.) Some kind of insect, sticking insect claws into everybody's business. (*To Philomena*.) Those clothes. You look like a
giant Kewpie doll. You make me laugh.

ANNIE (*To Marie-Adele*):   You always make me feel so . . . small . . .
like a little pig or something. You're no better than me. (*To
Philomena*.) Why can't you go to bingo by yourself, you big baby?
At least I got staying power. Piss off. (*To Veronique*.) Sucking off
everybody else's life like a leech because you got nothing of your
own. Pathetic old coot. Just buzz off. (*To Emily*.) You call me
names. I don't call you names. You think you're too smart. Shut up.
(*To Pelajia*.) "Queen of the Indians," you think that's what you are.
Well, that stupid hammer of yours doesn't scare me. Go away. Piss
me off.

*Then Pelajia lifts her hammer with a big loud "Woah"! And they
come to a sudden dead stop. Pause. Then one quick final volley, all
at once, loudest of all.*

PHILOMENA (*To Annie*):   You slimy buck-toothed drunken worm!
EMILY (*To Veronique*):   Fuckin' instigator!
VERONIQUE (*To Marie-Adele*):   Clutching, clinging vine!
PELAJIA (*To Veronique*):   Evil no-good insect!
MARIE-ADELE (*To Veronique*):   Maggot-mouthed vulture!
ANNIE (*To Philomena*):   Fat-assed floozy, get off the pot!

*Marie-Adele, stung to the quick, makes a vicious grab for Veronique
by the throat. In a split-second, all freeze. Lights out in store interior.
Lights on on Zhaboonigan, who has run out in fright during the riot,
outside the store. Nanabush, still in his guise as the seagull, makes a
grab at Zhaboonigan. Zhaboonigan begins talking to the bird.*

ZHABOONIGAN: Are you gentle? I was not little. Maybe. Same size as
now. Long ago it must be? You think I'm funny? Shhh. I know who
you are. There, there. Boys. White boys. Two. Ever nice white
wings, you. I was walking down the road to the store. They ask me
if I want ride in car. Oh, I was happy I said, "Yup." Took me far
away. Ever nice ride. Dizzy. They took all my clothes off me. Put
something up inside me here. (*Pointing to her crotch, underneath
her dress*.) Many, many times. Remember. Don't fly away. Don't go.

I saw you before. There, there. It was a. Screwdriver. They put the screwdriver inside me. Here. Remember. Ever lots of blood. The two white boys. Left me in the bush. Alone. It was cold. And then. Remember. Zhaboonigan. Everybody calls me Zhaboonigan. Why? It means needle. Zhaboonigan. Going-through-thing. Needle Peterson. Going-through-thing Peterson. That's me. It was the screwdriver. Nice. Nice. Nicky Ricky Ben Mark. (*As she counts, with each name, feathers on the bird's wing.*) Ever nice. Nice white birdie you.

During this last speech, Nanabush goes through agonizing contortions. Then lights change instantly back to the interior of the store. The six women spring back into action. Philomena stomps back into the toilet.

MARIE-ADELE (*To Veronique*):   Fine. And the whole reserve knows the only reason you ever adopted Zhaboonigan is for her disability cheque.

ANNIE: You fake saint.

Annie, Marie-Adele, and Emily start pushing Veronique, round-robin, between the three of them, laughing tauntingly until Veronique is almost reduced to tears.

VERONIQUE (*Almost weeping*):   Bastards. The three of you.

Marie-Adele grabs Veronique by the throat and lifts her fist to punch her in the face. But the exertion causes her body to weaken, almost to the point of collapse, from her illness. At this point, Philomena emerges from the toilet.

PHILOMENA (*Crinkling her nose*):   Emily. Your toilet.
WOMEN: Shhhh.
MARIE-ADELE (*Holding her waist, reeling, barely audible*):   Oh, shit.
PHILOMENA: I can't get it to flush.
WOMEN: Shhhh.
PELAJIA (*Rushing to Marie-Adele*):   Marie-Adele. You're not well.
MARIE-ADELE (*Screams*):   Don't touch me.

Complete silence from all while Marie-Adele weaves and struggles to keep herself from collapsing. Annie scurries offstage, to the back part of the store, where the post office would be.

EMILY (*To Veronique*):   You f'in' bitch!

PHILOMENA: What did I just tell you? Who did that to your eye?

VERONIQUE: Big Joey.

EMILY (*To Veronique*):   Look here, you old buzzard. I'll tell you a few things. You see this fist? You see these knuckles? You wanna know where they come from? Ten years. Every second night for 10 long ass-fuckin' years that goddamn Yellowknife asshole Henry Dadzinanare come home to me so drunk his eyes was spittin' blood like Red Lucifer himself and he'd beat me purple.

VERONIQUE: I wish I'd been there to see it all.

EMILY: Yeah, scumbag. I wish you'd been there to watch me learn to fight back like you've never seen a woman fight for her life before. Take a look at this eye. I earned it, Veronique St. Pierre, I earned it.

PHILOMENA: Henry Dadzinanare, Big Joey. They're all the same. Emily, use your brains.

EMILY: Use my brains. Yeah, right. I used them alright the night he came at me with an axe and just about sank it into my spine, I grabbed one bag, took one last look at the kids and walked out of his life forever.

ANNIE (*From offstage*):   And she took the bus to San Francisco.

PHILOMENA: And gets herself mixed up with a motorcycle gang, for God's sake.

EMILY (*Now addressing all in the room*):   Rosabella Baez, Hortensia Colorado, Liz Jones, Pussy Commanda. And me. The best. "Rose and the Rez Sisters," that's us. And man, us sisters could weave knuckle magic.

VERONIQUE: So why did you bother coming back?

PHILOMENA: You stay out of this.

EMILY: Come back to the Rez for a visit, get all wedged up with that hunk Big Joey one night . . . (*Grunts.*)

PHILOMENA: I give up.

EMILY: . . . and I was hooked. Couldn't leave. Settlin' back on a coupla beers with Big Joey the other night when Gazelle Nataways come sashayin' in like she's got half the Rez squished down the crack of her ass. She was high. I was high. Hell, we were all high, Get into a bit of a discussion, when she gets me miffed and I let fly, she let fly, Big Joey let fly, misses that nympho and lands me one in the eye instead.

VERONIQUE: So it was Big Joey.

EMILY: Damn rights. And that's as close as he got cuz I put him out for the night right then and there. Just one of these. (*Brandishing her fist.*) One. That's all it took.

Veronique runs off to look for Zhaboonigan.

ANNIE AND PHILOMENA: Emily Dictionary.

Philomena with exasperation, Annie with adulation, from offstage.

ANNIE: You're amazing!

EMILY: Not Dictionary. Dadzinanare. Henry Dadzinanare. The man who made me learn to fight back. Never let a man raise one dick hair against me since.

VERONIQUE (*Calling out to Zhaboonigan*): Zhaboonigan. Don't you be talking to the birds like that again. You're crazy enough as it is.

ANNIE (*As she comes running back in from the post office with her parcel, already unwrapped, and two letters, one for herself, already unfolded, and one still in its envelope*): See? I told you. It's a record. Patsy Cline.

PHILOMENA: Never mind Patsy Cline.

ANNIE (*As she hands Marie-Adele the letter in the envelope*): Hey, Marie-Adele.

EMILY: Read your friggin' letter, Annie Cook.

ANNIE: Listen to this.

Zhaboonigan walks back in as Annie reads her own letter very haltingly.

Dear Mom: Here is the record you wanted. I thought you'd like the picture of Patsy Cline on the cover. (*Annie shows off her record.*) See? It's Patsy Cline. (*Returns to her letter.*) I also thought you might like to know that there is a bingo called THE BIGGEST BINGO IN THE WORLD. Can you fu . . . ture that?

EMILY (*Who has been looking over Annie's shoulder*): Feature. Feature.

ANNIE: Can you . . . feature . . . that? . . . that's coming to Toronto. The jackpot is $500,000. It's on Saturday, September 8. Raymond's

Mom was in Toronto. Aunt Philomena will hit the roof when she hears this. Much love, your daughter Ellen.

Annie announces once more.

There is a brief electric silence followed by an equally electric scream from all the women. Even Zhaboonigan screams. Excitement takes over completely.

VERONIQUE: So it's true! It's true!

PHILOMENA: The Espanola bingo. Piffle. Mere piffle.

VERONIQUE: My new stove!

PHILOMENA: My new toilet! White! Spirit white!

EMILY (*Grabbing Zhaboonigan and dancing around the room with her*): I'd take the money, come back to the Rez, beat the shit out of Gazelle Nataways and take you down to Frisco with me. Whaddaya think?

ZHABOONIGAN : Yup.

MARIE-ADELE (*In the background, where she has been reading her letter quietly to herself*): September 10.

ANNIE (*Taking the letter from Marie-Adele*): Look, Pelajia. Marie-Adele's tests are in Toronto just two days after THE BIGGEST.

There is a brief embarrassed silence.

MARIE-ADELE: Kill two birds with one stone.

To Nanabush.

I wanna go.

To Pelajia and Philomena.

I wanna go.

VERONIQUE: Goood!

EMILY (*Mimicking Veronique*): Goood! Now how the hell are you guys gonna get down to Toronto? You're all goddamn welfare cases.

ANNIE: Fire Minklater.

VERONIQUE: Mary, mother of Jesus! I refuse, I absolutely refuse to be seen anywhere near that sorceress! We'll chip in and rent a car.

EMILY: Zhaboonigan Peterson here gonna chauffeur you down?

ZHABOONIGAN: Yup.

VERONIQUE: Don't you make fun of my daughter.

EMILY: What kind of stove you gonna buy, Veronique St. Pierre? Westinghouse? Electrolux? Yamaha? Kawasaki?

VERONIQUE: Oh my god, Marie-Adele, I never thought about it. They will have so many stoves in Toronto, I'll get confused.

ANNIE: If you go to Toronto and leave Wasy for even one day, Emily, you'll lose Big Joey forever . . .

VERONIQUE: To that witch!

ANNIE: . . . and then whose thighs will you have to wrestle around with in the dead of night? You'll dry up, get all puckered up and pass into ancient history.

EMILY: Annie Cook. I don't know what the fuck you're yatterin' on about now but I'd like to hear you say two words of French to that white guy in Sudbury you're so damn proud of.

ANNIE: Oh my god, Marie-Adele, she's right. I won't know what to say to this Ray*mond.* I've never met him. I can't speak French. All I can say in French is Ray*mond* and Bon Bon and I don't even know what that means. I can't go and live with them, not even after I win THE BIGGEST BINGO IN THE WORLD. What am I gonna do?

She collapses on the floor and rolls around for a bit.

EMILY: And Philomena Moosemeat's so fulla shit she'd need five toilets to get it all out.

PHILOMENA (*Going at Emily.*): And just who do you think you're talking to, Miss Dictionary, just who the hell do you think you're talking to?

With a resounding belly butt from Emily, they begin to wrestle.

PELAJIA (*Banging her hammer on the counter*): Alright, alright. It's obvious we've got a problem here.

EMILY (*Throwing Philomena off to the side*): I'll say.

MARIE-ADELE: It's true. None of us has any money.

But Veronique, standing behind Pelajia, winks at the others and makes a hand motion indicating that Pelajia, for one, does have money. All the other women slowly surround Pelajia. But Pelajia catches the drift and quickly collects herself to meet the onslaught. During Pelajia's speech, the women respond at periodic intervals with a "yoah" and "hmmm," etc., as when a chief speaks at a council meeting.

PELAJIA: I say we all march down to the Band Office and ask the Band Council for a loan that will pay for the trip to this bingo. I know how to handle that tired old chief. He and I have been arguing about paved roads for years now. I'll tell him we'll build paved roads all over the reserve with our prize money. I'll tell him the people will stop drinking themselves to death because they'll have paved roads to walk on. I'll tell him there'll be more jobs because the people will have paved roads to drive to work on. I'll tell him the people will stop fighting and screwing around and Nanabush will come back to us because he'll have paved roads to dance on. There's enough money in there for everyone, I'll say. And if he doesn't lend us the money, I'll tell him I'm packing my bags and moving to Toronto tomorrow.

EMILY: That oughta twist his arm but good.

PELAJIA: And if he still says no, I'll bop him over the head with my hammer and we'll attack the accountant and take the money ourselves. Philomena, we're going to Toronto!

The seven women have this grand and ridiculous march to the band office, around the set and all over the stage area, with Pelajia leading them forward heroically, her hammer just a-swinging in the air. Nanabush trails merrily along in the rear of the line. They reach the "band office"—standing in one straight line square in front of the audience. The "invisible" chief "speaks": cacophonous percussion for about seven beats, the women listening more and more incredulously. Finally, the percussion comes to a dead stop.

PELAJIA: No?

Pelajia raises her hammer to hit the "invisible" chief, Nanabush shrugs a "don't ask me, I don't know," Emily fingers a "fuck you, man." Blackout. End of Act One.

ACT TWO

All seven women are holding a meeting in the basement of Pelajia Patchnose's house. This is a collection of chairs and stools off to the side of the stage area. The only light comes from an old, beat-up trilight pole lamp. Some have tea, Emily and Annie a beer.

VERONIQUE: We should have met at the priest's house.

PELAJIA: No! We're gonna work this out on our own. Right here. Emily Dictionary, you chair.

And she lends Emily her hammer.

VERONIQUE: She's good at ordering people around.

PHILOMENA: Shut up.

EMILY: First. When are we leaving? (*She bangs the hammer regularly throughout the meeting.*)

VERONIQUE: How much is the trip going to cost?

EMILY: When are we leaving?

PHILOMENA: How long to Toronto?

ANNIE: Four hours.

EMILY: When are we leaving?

PHILOMENA: The only human being who can make it in four hours is Annie Cook.

VERONIQUE: I'm not dying on the highway.

PHILOMENA: Eight hours.

PELAJIA: No way we're gonna stop at every toilet on the highway.

MARIE-ADELE: Six hours. Eugene's driven there.

VERONIQUE: Maybe we can borrow his van.

ANNIE: Maybe we can borrow Big Joey's van.

A quick little aside to Pelajia.

Hey, can I have another beer?

PELAJIA: No.

VERONIQUE: What about Gazelle Nataways?

EMILY: We're gonna borrow his van, not his buns, for Chris'sakes.

MARIE-ADELE: The only thing we have to pay for is gas.

ANNIE: Philomena's got gas.

EMILY: Right! Six hours. Eugene's van.

MARIE-ADELE: We still don't know when we're leaving.

PHILOMENA: Bingo's on Saturday night.

ANNIE: Leave Saturday morning.

VERONIQUE: Oh! I'll be so tired for the bingo. I'll get confused. Wednesday. Rest on Thursday.

ANNIE: And rest again on Friday? Too much resting. I can't go for that.

PELAJIA: And we can't afford such a long stay.

PHILOMENA: Where are we gonna stay?

EMILY: Whoa!

Pause.

PELAJIA: Friday night.

EMILY: Right. Leave Friday night. Next.

PHILOMENA: Coming home right after the bingo.

MARIE-ADELE: And leave me behind? Remember my tests Monday morning.

EMILY: Right. Monday noon, we come back. Next.

VERONIQUE: Don't go so fast. My mind is getting confused.

EMILY: Goood! Next.

MARIE-ADELE: Where are we gonna stay?

ANNIE: The Silver Dollar!

MARIE-ADELE: You can't stay there.

ANNIE: There's rooms upstairs.

PELAJIA: You wanna sleep in a whorehouse?

VERONIQUE: Zhaboonigan! Don't listen to this part.

PELAJIA: There's room at my son's.

PHILOMENA: Two washrooms! He's got a wonderful education.

EMILY: Next.

VERONIQUE: Who's going to drive?

ANNIE: Emily. She can drive anything.

VERONIQUE: I believe it.

ANNIE: But I can drive, too.

VERONIQUE: Oh my god.

ANNIE: Long as I don't have to drive in the city. You drive the city.

VERONIQUE: Me?

ANNIE AND MARIE-ADELE: No!

PELAJIA: Long as you don't drive too fast, Annie Cook.

PHILOMENA: And we'll pack a lunch for the trip and then eat in restaurants. Chinese.

PELAJIA: Can't afford it. We chip in, buy groceries and cook at my son's.

VERONIQUE: I'll give $10.

EMILY: You old fossil. You want us to starve?

PHILOMENA: $50 a day. Each.

EMILY: Philomena Moosemeat! That's $50 times seven people times four days. That's over $1,000 worth of groceries.

VERONIQUE: Imagine!

MARIE-ADELE: Okay. Veronique St. Pierre. You cook. $20 apiece. Right?

EMILY: Right. Next.

PHILOMENA: Anybody writing this down?

ANNIE: I'm gonna go to Sam the Recordman.

MARIE-ADELE: I'll make the grocery list.

PELAJIA: How much for gas?

VERONIQUE (*Still in dreamland over the groceries*): $1,000!

PHILOMENA (*Flabbergasted*): Nooo! You goose.

ANNIE: $40.

EMILY: $150. Period. Next.

PELAJIA: We got 10 days to find this money.

MARIE-ADELE: What's it cost to get into the bingo?

VERONIQUE: All the Indians in the world will be there!

PHILOMENA: $50.

ANNIE: And we're gonna be the only Indians there.

PELAJIA: Silence.

There is a long, thoughtful silence, broken only after awhile by a scream from Zhaboonigan. Nanabush has knocked her off her stool. The women laugh.

Can't think of anything else.

PHILOMENA: Add it up. (*She hands a pencil to Emily.*)

EMILY (*Calculates*): $1,400. You guys need $200 each.

VERONIQUE: Where am I going to get $400?

EMILY: Make it. End of meeting.

And the women start their fundraising activities with a vengeance. The drive is underlined by a wild rhythmic beat from the musician, one that gets wilder and wilder with each successive beat, though always underpinned by this persistent, almost dance-like pulse. The movement of the women covers the entire stage area, and like the music, gets wilder and wilder, until by the end it is as if we are looking at an insane eight-ring circus, eight-ring because through all this, Nanabush, as the seagull, has a holiday, particularly with

Marie-Adele's lines of laundry, as Marie-Adele madly strings one line of laundry after another all over the set, from Pelajia's roof to Emily's store, etc. For the garage sale, Annie sells off Pelajia's lamp, chairs, etc., so that Pelajia's "basement" simply dissolves into the madness of the fundraising drive.

Beat one.

Pelajia is hammering on the roof.
Emily is at the store cash register and rings up each sale as Annie, Philomena, Marie-Adele, Zhaboonigan, and Veronique stand shoulder to shoulder and pass the following from one side of the stage to the other:
seven large sacks marked "FLOUR"
two giant tubs marked "LARD"
one bushel of apples

Beat two.

Zhaboonigan brings small table on and puts it stage left.
Annie brings table on and puts it stage right.
Philomena brings a basket full of beer bottles to centre and empties it. She has a baby attached to her.
Veronique comes on with cloth and Windex and starts "cleaning windows" rhythmically, listening to whatever gossip she can hear.
Marie-Adele strings two lines of clothing across the stage.
Pelajia hammers on her roof.
Emily brings on several empty beer cases and fills them with Philomena's bottles.

Beat three.

Zhaboonigan brings in six quarts of blueberries and then takes over window cleaning from Veronique.
Annie brings on basket of old clothes and a broken kitchen chair.
Philomena brings on another basket full of beer bottles, empties it. She now has two babies attached to her, like a fungus.
Emily fills beer cases rapidly, expertly.

Pelajia gets down off roof, hammering everything until she is on hands and knees, hammering the floor.

Marie-Adele strings third and fourth lines of laundry across the stage.

Veronique comes in burdened with seven apple pies and puts them on Annie's table.

Beat four.

Pelajia hammers as she crawls across the floor.

Zhaboonigan washes windows like a person possessed.

Emily runs and rings up a sale on the cash register and then brings on more empty beer cases and loads them up.

Philomena brings on a third load of bottles. Three babies are now attached to her.

Annie brings on an old trilight pole lamp and an old record player, which she opens and stacks alongside the rest of her stuff.

Annie and Emily sing a line of their song with very bad harmony.

Marie-Adele strings fifth and sixth lines of laundry across stage.

Veronique comes on with seven loaves of bread and puts them neatly by the pies.

Beat five.

Pelajia hammers as she crawls across the floor, hammering everything in sight. The women protect their poor feet.

Zhaboonigan washes windows even faster; she's starting to cry.

Emily and Philomena work together filling the empty beer cases as fast as they can. Emily runs to the register, rings in seven sales and sings a bit of song with Annie, better this time. Philomena now has four kids attached to her body.

Annie comes on with a small black and white TV with rabbit ears and an old toaster.

Veronique comes on with six dozen buns and dumps them out of their tins all over the table.

Pelajia hammers faster and faster.

Zhaboonigan is now working like a maniac and is sobbing.

Marie-Adele strings seventh and eighth lines of laundry across stage.

Beat six.

Emily goes to cash register and tallies their earnings; she works the register with tremendous speed and efficiency all this beat. Zhaboonigan continues washing windows. Philomena sticks a sign in beer bottles: World's Biggest Bottle Drive. She now has five babies attached to her. Veronique sticks a sign on her table: World's Biggest Bake Sale. Annie sticks a sign up around her stuff: World's Biggest Garage Sale. Marie-Adele sticks a sign up on Zha's table: Big Blueberries and Laundry While You Wait. Pelajia begins hammering the air. She may have lost her marbles.

Beat Seven.

EMILY: Whoa!

The "music" comes to a sudden stop. The women all collapse. The women look at each other. They then quickly clear the stage of everything they've brought on as Pelajia speaks, consulting her list. By the end of Pelajia's speech, the stage area is clear once more, except for a microphone stand that one of the women has brought on as part of the "clean-up" activities.

PELAJIA: Bottle drive. Ten cents a bottle, 24 bottles a case, equals two dollars and 40 cents. 777 bottles collected divided by 24 is 32 cases and nine singles that's 32 times $2.40 equals $77.70. Blueberries equals $90. Good pickin' Zha and the Starblanket kids. Washing windows at $5.00 a house times 18 houses. Five eights are 40, carry the four and add the five is 90 bucks less two on account of that cheap Gazelle Nataways only gave three dollars. That's $88. Household repairs is four roofs including the Chief's and one tiled floor is $225. Garage sale brung in $246.95, the bake sale equals $83 after expenses, we make 110 bucks on doing laundry, 65 bucks babysitting, 145 from Emily doing a double shift at the store and I have generously donated $103 from my savings. That brings us to a grand total of $1233.65. So!

Emily and Annie move forward as the music starts up. They are lit only by tacky floor flood-lighting, and are, in effect, at the Anchor Inn, Little Current. Emily speaks into the microphone.

EMILY: Thank-you. Thank-you, ladies and gentlemen. I thank you very much. And now for the last song of the night, ladies and gents, before we hit the road. A song that's real special to me in my heart. A song I wrote in memory of one Rosabella Baez, a Rez Sister from way back. And Rose baby, if you're up there tonight, I hope you're listenin' in. Cuz it's called: "I'm Thinkin' of You." Here goes . . .

Emily and Annie grab their microphones; Emily sings lead, Annie sings backup. And it's "country" to the hilt.

I'm thinkin' of you every moment,
As though you were here by my side;
I'll always remember the good times,
So darlin' please come back to me.

I'm dreamin' of you every night,
That we were together again;
If time can heal up our partin'
Then love can remove all this pain.

Instrumental—dance break

If love is the secret of livin',
Then give me that love, shinin' light;
When you are again by my side,
Then livin' will once more be right.

The audience claps. Emily says, "Thank-you." And then she and Annie join the other women, who have, during the song, loaded themselves, their suitcases, and their lunches into the "van." This van consists of three battered old van seats stuck to the walls of the theatre, on either side and up high. The back seat is on the "stage left" side of the theatre and the other two are on the other side, the middle seat of the van towards the back of the theatre, the front seat, complete with detachable steering wheel, just in front and "stage right" of the stage area. Each seat is lit by its own light.

EMILY: How much did me and Annie take in singin' at the Anchor Inn?

PELAJIA: $330 at the door.

MARIE-ADELE: Solid packed house, eh? Shoulda charged more.

ANNIE: Fifty bucks for the oom-chi-cha machine. Twenty bucks for Ronnie's guitar. That's our only costs.

EMILY: Ha! We're laughin'.

A cappella reprise of a verse of their song, which fades into highway sounds, and they drive, for a few moments, in silence.

In the van, driving down the highway to Toronto, at night. The women have intimate conversations, one on one, while the rest are asleep or seated at the other end of the van. Annie is driving. Emily sits beside her listening to her Walkman, while Marie-Adele is "leaning" over Annie's shoulder from her place in the middle seat. Veronique sits beside Marie-Adele, sleeping. Pelajia and Philomena are in the very back seat with Zhaboonigan between them.

MARIE-ADELE: Nee, Annie, not so fast.

Pause. Annie slows down.

So. You couldn't get Ellen and *Ray*mond to come along? I'd like to meet this *Ray*mond someday.

ANNIE (*Angrily insisting on the correct pronunciation*): Ray*mond!* Ellen says he's got a whole library full of cassette tapes.

MARIE-ADELE: Annie. You ever think about getting married again?

ANNIE: Not really. I can hear the band at the Silver Dollar already.

MARIE-ADELE: Do you still think about . . . Eugene?

ANNIE: What're you talkin' about? Of course, I think about him, he's my brother-in-law, ain't he?

MARIE-ADELE: He made his choice.

ANNIE: Yeah. He picked you.

MARIE-ADELE: Annie. I never stole him off you.

ANNIE: Drop dead. Shit! I forgot to bring that blouse. I mean. In case I sing. Shit.

MARIE-ADELE: If I'm gone and Eugene if he starts drinkin' again. I see you going for him.

ANNIE: Why would I bother? I had my chance 20 years ago. Christ!

MARIE-ADELE: Twenty years ago, I was there.

ANNIE: Why would I want 14 kids for?

MARIE-ADELE: That's exactly what I'm scared of. I don't want them kids to be split up. You come near Eugene you start drinking messing things up me not here I come back and don't matter where you are . . .

ANNIE: I don't want him. I don't want him. I don't want him. I don't want him. I don't want him.

EMILY: Put us all in the fuckin' ditch!

PELAJIA: Hey, watch your language up there.

ANNIE: Shit! I don't care. There's nothing more to say about it. Why don't you take your pills and go to sleep.

Pelajia and Philomena begin talking.

PHILOMENA: September 8 again.

PELAJIA: Hmmm? What about September 8?

PHILOMENA: You don't remember?

PELAJIA: What?

PHILOMENA: How could you?

PELAJIA: Mama died?

PHILOMENA: No! Remember?

PELAJIA: I can't remember. Got so much on my mind. So many things to forget.

ZHABOONIGAN (*To Philomena*): You like me?

PHILOMENA: Yes, Zhaboonigan. I like you.

ZHABOONIGAN: I like the birdies.

PHILOMENA: You like talking to the birdies?

ZHABOONIGAN: Yup.

She falls asleep.

PHILOMENA: Zhaboonigan . . . sometimes I wonder . . .

PELAJIA: It's dark . . . warm . . . quiet . . .

PHILOMENA: Toronto. Had a good job in Toronto. Yeah. Had to give it all up. Yeah. Cuz mama got sick. Philomena Margaret Moosetail. Real live secretary in the garment district. He'd come in and see my boss. Nice man, I thought. That big, red, fish-tail Caddy. Down Queen Street. He liked me. Treated me like a queen. Loved me. Or I thought he did. I don't know. Got pregnant anyway. Blond, blue-eyed, six foot two. And the way he smelled. God! His wife walks in on us.

Long silence.

He left with her.

Long silence.

I don't even know to this day if it was a boy or a girl. I'm getting old. That child would be . . . 28 . . . 28 years old. September 8. You know what I'm gonna do with that money if I win? I'm gonna find a lawyer. Maybe I can find that child. Maybe I wouldn't even have to let him . . . her . . . know who I am. I just . . . want to see . . . who . . .

PELAJIA: I hope you win.

Annie and Emily, at the front of the van with Annie driving, are laughing and singing, "I'm a little Indian who loves fry bread." From time to time, they sneak each other a sip of this little bottle of whiskey Annie has hidden away inside her purse.

I'm a little Indian who loves fry bread,
Early in the morning and when I go to bed;
Some folks say I'm crazy in the head,
Cuz I'm a little Indian who loves fry bread.

Now, some folks say I've put on a pound or two,
My jeans don't fit the way they used to do;
But I don't care, let the people talk,
Cuz if I don't get my fry bread, you'll hear me squawk.

ANNIE: So tell me. What's it like to go to a big bar like . . . I mean like . . . the Silver Dollar.

EMILY: Lotta Nishnawbs.[6]

ANNIE (*Disappointed*): Yeah? Is the music good?

EMILY: Country rock.

ANNIE (*Screams gleefully*): Yee-haw! Maybe the band will ask me up to sing, eh? I'll sing something fast.

EMILY: You would, too.

ANNIE (*Sings real fast*): "Well, it's 40 below and I don't give a fuck, got a heater in my truck and I'm off to the rodeo. Woof!" Something like that.

EMILY: Yup. That's pretty fast.

---

[6]Indians. (Ojibway)

ANNIE: Hey. Maybe Fritz the Katz will be there. Never know. Might get laid, too, eh? Remember Room 20 at the Anchor Inn? Oh, that Fritz! Sure like singin' with him. Crazy about the way . . .

EMILY (*Starts singing Patsy Cline's famous "Crazy . . . crazy for feelin' so lonely . . ." all the way through Annie's next speech.*)

ANNIE: . . . he stands there with his guitar and his 10-gallon hat. Is that what you call them hats? You know the kind you wear kind of off to the side like this? That's what he does. And then he winks at me. (*Sings.*) "Crazy ..." Oooh, I love, just love the way the lights go woosh woosh in your eyes and kinda' wash all over your body. Me standing there shuffling my feet side to side, dressed real nice and going (*Sings.*) "Oooh darlin' . . ." with my mike in my hand just so. Oh! And the sound of that band behind me. And Fritz. (*Sings.*) "Crazy, crazy for feelin' so lonely . . ."

EMILY: Yeah. You look good on stage.

ANNIE: Yeah?

EMILY: How come you're so keen on that guy anyway?

ANNIE: Sure Veronique St. Pierre isn't just pretending to be asleep back there?

Emily and Marie-Adele check Veronique in the middle seat.

MARIE-ADELE: Nah. Out like a lamp.

EMILY: Hey! We'll get her drunk at the Silver Dollar and leave her passed out under some table. Take two beers to do that.

ANNIE: Hey. Too bad Big Joey had to come back from Toronto before we got there, eh?

EMILY: Man! That dude's got buns on him like no other buns on the face of God's entire creation. Whooo! Not to mention a dick that's bigger than a goddamn breadbox.

Annie screams gleefully.

How about Fritz? What's his look like?

ANNIE (*After an awkward pause*): He's Jewish, you know.

EMILY (*Laughing raucously*): World's first Jewish country singer!

ANNIE: Don't laugh. Those Jews make a lot of money, you know.

EMILY: Not all of them.

ANNIE: Fritz buys me jeans and things. I'm gonna be one of them Jewish princesses.

EMILY: What's wrong with being an Indian princess?

ANNIE: Aw, these white guys. They're nicer to their women. Not like Indian guys. Screw you, drink all your money, and leave you flat on your ass.

EMILY: Yeah, right. Apple Indian Annie. Red on the outside. White on the inside.

ANNIE: Emily!

EMILY: Keep your eye on the road.

ANNIE: Good ol' highway 69.

EMILY: Hey. Ever 69 with Fritz?

MARIE-ADELE: Neee.

ANNIE: White guys don't make you do things to them. You just lie there and they do it all for you. Ellen's real happy with her Ray*mond.* You can tell the way she sounds on the phone. Maybe someday I'll just take off with a guy like Fritz.

EMILY: Then what? Never come back to the rez?

Annie is cornered. Emily then slaps her playfully on the arm.

Hey. Know what?

Sings.

When I die, I may not go to heaven,
I don't know if they let Indians in;
If they don't, just let me go to Wasy, lord,
Cuz Wasy is as close as I've been.

ANNIE: Lots of white people at this Silver Dollar?

EMILY: Sometimes. Depends.

ANNIE: How much for beer there?

EMILY: Same as up here. Nah! Don't need money, Annie Cook. You just gotta know how to handle men. Like me and the Rez Sisters down in Frisco.

ANNIE: Yeah?

EMILY: I'll take care of them.

ANNIE: Maybe we can find a party, eh? Maybe with the band.

EMILY: Whoa! Slow down, Annie Cook! Easy on the gas!

MARIE-ADELE: Annie!

Pow. Black-out. They have a flat tire.

The flat tire. Everything now happens in complete darkness.

VERONIQUE: Bingo!

PHILOMENA: What was that? What happened?

ANNIE: I don't know. Something just went "poof"!

EMILY: Alright. Everybody out. We got a fuckin' flat.

They all climb out of the van.

VERONIQUE: Oh my god! We'll never get to the bingo.

ZHABOONIGAN: Pee pee.

PELAJIA: I can't fix a flat tire.

ANNIE: Emily can.

PELAJIA: Get the jack. Spare tire.

ANNIE: Philomena's wearing one.

ZHABOONIGAN: Pee pee.

PHILOMENA: This is all your fault, Annie Cook.

MARIE-ADELE: It's in the back.

ANNIE: So what do we do?

PELAJIA: What's the matter with Zha?

PHILOMENA: Gotta make pee pee.

VERONIQUE: I knew there was something wrong with this van the moment I set eyes on it. I should have taken the bus.

PHILOMENA: Oh shut up. Quack, quack, quack.

ANNIE: Don't look at me. It's not my fault the tires are all bald.

PHILOMENA: Nobody's blaming you.

ANNIE: But you just did.

PHILOMENA: Quack, quack, quack.

VERONIQUE: Where are we?

ANNIE: The Lost Channel. This is where you get off.

VERONIQUE (*Groans*): Ohhh!

EMILY: Yeah, right.

PHILOMENA: Shhh!

PELAJIA: Jack's not working too well.

EMILY: Okay. Everybody. Positions.

VERONIQUE: Not me. My heart will collapse.

EMILY: You wanna play bingo?

VERONIQUE (*Groans.*): Ohhhh!

ANNIE: Hurry up! Hurry up!

EMILY: Okay. One, two, three lift.

Everybody lifts and groans.

PELAJIA: Put the jack in there.

All lift, except Marie-Adele and Zha, who wander off into the moonlit darkness. Dim light on them.

ZHABOONIGAN: Ever dark.

MARIE-ADELE: You'll be fine, Zhaboonigan.

Suddenly, a nighthawk—Nanabush, now in dark feathers— appears, darting in the night.

ZHABOONIGAN: The birdies!

MARIE-ADELE: Yes, a birdie.

ZHABOONIGAN: Black wings!

Marie-Adele begins talking to the bird, almost as if she were talking to herself. Quietly, at first, but gradually—as the bird begins attacking her—growing more and more hysterical, until she is shrieking, flailing, and thrashing about insanely.

MARIE-ADELE: Who are you? What do you want? My children? Eugene? No! Oh no! Me? Not yet. Not yet. Give me time. Please. Don't. Please don't. Awus! Get away from me. Eugene! Awus! You fucking bird! Awus! Awus! Awus! Awus! Awus!

And she has a total hysterical breakdown.

Zhaboonigan, at first, attempts to scare the bird off by running and flailing her arms at it. Until the bird knocks her down and she lies there on the ground, watching in helpless astonishment and abject terror. Underneath Marie-Adele's screams, she mumbles to herself, sobbing.

ZHABOONIGAN: One, two, three, four, five, six, seven . . . Nicky Ricky Ben Mark . . . eight, nine, ten, eleven, twelve . . .

Until the other women come running. Total darkness again.

EMILY: What the . . .

ANNIE: Marie-Adele!

PELAJIA: Stop her! Hold her!

VERONIQUE: What's happening?

PHILOMENA: Marie Adele. Now, now . . . come . . . come . . .

EMILY (*In the background*): Stop that fucking screaming will ya, Marie-Adele!

PHILOMENA: Emily. There's no need to talk to her like that now.

PELAJIA: Help us get her in the van.

PHILOMENA: Come . . . come, Marie-Adele . . . everything's fine . . . you'll be fine . . . come . . . shhh . . . shhh . . .

And they ease Marie-Adele back into the van. Once all is beginning to settle down again:

PELAJIA: Everything okay now?

PHILOMENA: Yes. She's fine now.

PELAJIA: Emily, take over.

VERONIQUE: Yes. I don't trust that Annie Cook. Not for one minute.

EMILY: All set?

MARIE-ADELE: What time is it?

PELAJIA: Twenty after four.

ANNIE: Oh! We're over two hours behind schedule. Hurry up. Hurry up.

VERONIQUE: I'll be exhausted for the bingo tomorrow night. Maybe I should just take 15 cards.

EMILY: You can rest your heart. And your mouth. All day tomorrow. All set?

And she starts up the van. The van lights come back on.

The dialogues resume. Marie-Adele now sits in the front with Emily, who is driving. Zhaboonigan sits between them. Pelajia and Philomena are now in the middle seat, Annie and Veronique in the back.

EMILY: You scared the shit out of me out there.

Silence.

Don't do that again.

Silence.

Feeling better now?

Silence.

MARIE-ADELE: I could be really mad, just raging mad just wanna tear his eyes out with my nails when he walks in the door and my whole body just goes "k-k-k-k". . . . He doesn't talk, when something goes wrong with him, he doesn't talk, shuts me out, just disappears. Last night he didn't come home. Again, it happened. I couldn't sleep. You feel so ugly. He walks in this morning. Wanted to be alone, he said. The curve of his back, his breath on my neck, "Adele, ki-sa-gee-ee-tin oo-ma,"[7] making love, always in Indian, only. When we still could. I can't even have him inside me anymore. It's still growing there. The cancer. Pelajia, een-pay-seek-see-yan.[8]

PELAJIA: You know one time, I knew this couple where one of them was dying and the other one was angry at her for dying. And she was mad because he was gonna be there when she wasn't and she had so much left to do. And she'd lie there in bed and tell him to do this and do that and he'd say "Okay, okay." And then he'd go into the kitchen and say to me, "She's so this and she's so that and she's so damned difficult." And I watched all this going on. That house didn't have room for two such angry people. But you know, I said to her, "You gotta have faith in him and you gotta have faith in life. He loves you very much but there's only so much he can do. He's only human." There's only so much Eugene can understand, Marie-Adele. He's only human.

EMILY: Fuckin' right. Me and the Rez Sisters, okay? Cruisin' down the coast highway one night. Hum of the engine between my thighs. Rose. That's Rosabella Baez, leader of the pack. We were real close, me and her. She was always thinkin' real deep. And talkin' about bein' a woman. An Indian woman. And suicide. And alcohol and despair and how fuckin' hard it is to be an Indian in this country. (*Marie-Adele shushes her gently.*) No goddamn future for them, she'd say. And why, why, why? Always carryin' on like that. Chris'sakes. She was pretty heavy into the drags. Guess we all were. We had a fight. Cruisin' down the coast highway that night. Rose in the middle. Me and Pussy Commanda off to the side. Big 18-wheeler come along real fast and me and Pussy Commanda get out of the way. But not Rose. She stayed in the middle. Went head-on

[7]Adele, I love you. (Cree)
[8]Pelajia, I'm scared to death. (Cree)

into that truck like a fly splat against a windshield. I swear to this day I can still feel the spray of her blood against my neck. I drove on. Straight into daylight. Never looked back. Had enough gas money on me to take me far as Salt Lake City. Pawned my bike off and bought me a bus ticket back to Wasy. When I got to Chicago, that's when I got up the nerve to wash my lover's dried blood from off my neck. I loved that woman, Marie-Adele, I loved her like no man's ever loved a woman. But she's gone. I never wanna go back to San Francisco. No way, man.

MARIE-ADELE (*Comforting the crying Emily*): You should get some rest. Let Annie take over.

EMILY: I'll be fine. You go to sleep. Wake you up when we get to Toronto.

Emily puts her Walkman on and starts to sing along quietly to "Blue Kentucky Girl" by Emmylou Harris with its "I swear I love you . . ." while Marie-Adele leans her head against the "window" and falls asleep.

After a few moments, Zhaboonigan, who has been dozing off between Emily and Marie-Adele in the front seat, pokes her head up and starts to sing along off-key. Then she starts to play with Emily's hair.

EMILY (*Shrugging Zhaboonigan's hand off*): Don't bug me. My favorite part's comin' up.

Initiated by Zhaboonigan, they start playing "slap." The game escalates to the point where Emily almost bangs Zhaboonigan over the head with her elbow.

EMILY: Yeah, right. You little retard.

Mad at this, Zhaboonigan hits Emily in the stomach.

Don't hit me there, you little . . . Hey, man, like ummm . . . I'm sorry, Zha.

ZHABOONIGAN: Sorry.

EMILY (*Emily feels her belly thoughtfully. After a brief silence*): You gonna have kids someday, Zha?

ZHABOONIGAN: Ummm . . . buy one.

EMILY: Holy! Well, kids were alright. Aw geez, Zha, that man treated me real bad. Ever been tied to a bed post with your arms up like this? Whoa!

Grabbing the steering wheel.

Maybe you should drive.

ZHABOONIGAN: Scary.

EMILY: Aw, don't be scared. Fuck.

ZHABOONIGAN: Fuck.

EMILY: Zhaboonigan Peterson! Your ma'll give me a black eye.

Zhaboonigan turns her head toward the back seat, where Veronique sits sleeping, and says one more time, really loud.

ZHABOONIGAN: Fuck!

EMILY: Shhh! Look, Zha. You don't let any man bother you while we're down in T.O. You just stick close to me.

ZHABOONIGAN: Yup.

EMILY: We're sisters, right? Gimme five.

They slap hands.

Alright. Bingo!!!

Instantly, the house lights come on full blast. The Bingo Master— the most beautiful man in the world—comes running up centre aisle, cordless mike in hand, dressed to kill: tails, rhinestones, and all. The entire theatre is now the bingo palace. We are in: Toronto!!!!

BINGO MASTER: Welcome, ladies and gentlemen, to the biggest bingo the world has ever seen! Yes, ladies and gentlemen, tonight, we have a very, very special treat for you. Tonight, ladies and gentlemen, you will be witness to events of such gargantuan proportions, such cataclysmic ramifications, such masterly and magnificent manifestations that your minds will reel, your eyes will nictitate, and your hearts will palpitate erratically.

Because tonight, ladies and gentlemen, you will see the biggest, yes, ladies and gentlemen, the very biggest prizes ever known to man, woman, beast, or appliance. And the jackpot tonight? The jackpot, ladies and gentlemen, is surely the biggest, the largest, the hugest, and the most monstrous jackpot ever conceived of in the entire history of monstrous jackpots as we know them. $500,000!

Yes, ladies and gentlemen, $500,000 can be yours this very night! That's half a million—A HALF MILLION SMACKEROOS!!! IF you play the game right.

And all you have to do, ladies and gentlemen, is reach into your programs and extract the single bingo card placed therein. Yes, ladies and gentlemen, the single bingo card placed therein, which bingo card will entitle you to one chance at winning the warm-up game for a prize of $20. $20! And all you have to do is poke holes in that single bingo card. Yes, ladies and gentlemen, just poke holes in that single bingo card and bend the numbers backward as the numbers are called. And don't forget the free hole in the middle of the card. Twenty dollars, ladies and gentlemen, that's one line in any direction. That means, of course, ladies and gentlemen, that the first person to form one line, just one straight line in any direction on their card, will be the very lucky winner of the $20 prize. $20! Are you ready, ladies and gentlemen? Are you ready? Then let the game begin! Under the G 56. Etc. . . .

The audience plays bingo, with the seven women, who have moved slowly into the audience during the Bingo Master's speech, playing along. Until somebody in the audience shouts, "Bingo!"

BINGO MASTER: Hold your cards, ladies and gentlemen, bingo has been called.

The Bingo Master and the assistant stage manager check the numbers and the prize money is paid out.

BINGO MASTER: And now for the game you've all been waiting for, ladies and gentlemen. Now for the big game. Yes, ladies and gentlemen, get ready for THE BIGGEST BINGO IN THE WORLD! For the grand jackpot prize of $500,000! Full house, ladies and gentlemen, full house! Are you ready? Are you ready? Then let the game begin!

The house lights go out. And the only lights now are on the bingo balls bouncing around in the bingo machine—an eerie, surreal sort of glow—and on the seven women who are now playing bingo with a vengeance on centrestage, behind the Bingo Master, where a long bingo table has magically appeared with Zhaboonigan at the table's centre banging a crucifix Veronique has brought along for good luck. The scene is lit so that it looks like "The Last Supper."

The women face the audience. The bingo table is covered with all the necessary accoutrements: bags of potato chips, cans of pop, ashtrays (some of the women are smoking), etc. The Bingo Master calls out number after number—but not the B 14—with the women improvising responses. These responses—Philomena has 27 cards!—grow more and more raucous: "B 14? Annie Cook? One more number to go! The B 14! Where is that B 14?! Gimme that B 14! Where the fuck is that B 14?!!!" *etc. Until the women have all risen from the table and come running downstage, attacking the bingo machine and throwing the Bingo Master out of the way. The women grab the bingo machine with shouts of:* "Throw this fucking machine into the lake! It's no damn good!" *etc. And they go running down centre aisle with it and out of the theatre. Bingo cards are flying like confetti. Total madness and mayhem. The music is going crazy.*

And out of this chaos emerges the calm, silent image of Marie-Adele waltzing romantically in the arms of the Bingo Master. The Bingo Master says "Bingo" into her ear. And the Bingo Master changes, with sudden bird-like movements, into the nighthawk, Nanabush in dark feathers. Marie-Adele meets Nanabush.

During this next speech, the other women, one by one, take their positions around Marie-Adele's porch, some kneeling, some standing. The stage area, by means of "lighting magic," slowly returns to its Wasaychigan Hill appearance.

MARIE-ADELE: U-wi-nuk u-wa? U-wi-nuk u-wa? Eugene? Neee. U-wi-nuk ma-a oo-ma kee-tha? Ka. Kee-tha i-chi-goo-ma so that's who you are . . . at rest upon the rock . . . the master of the game . . . the game . . . it's me . . . nee-tha . . . come . . . come . . . don't be afraid . . . as-tum . . .come . . . to . . . me . . . ever soft wings . . . beautiful soft . . . soft . . . dark wings . . . here . . . take me . . . as-tum . . . as-tum . . . pee-na-sin . . . wings . . . here . . . take me .. take . . . me . . . with . . . pee-na-sin . . .[9]

---

[9]Marie-Adele: Who are you? Who are you? Eugene? Nee. Then who are you really? Oh. It's you, so that's who you are ... at rest upon the rock . . . the master of the game . . . the game . . . it's me . . . me . . . come . . . come . . . don't be afraid . . . come . . . come . . . to . . . me . . . ever soft wings . . . beautiful soft . . . soft . . . dark wings . . . here . . . take me . . . come . . . come . . . come and get me . . . wings here . . . take me . . . take . . . me . . . with . . . come and get me . . .   (Cree)

As Nanabush escorts Marie-Adele into the spirit world, Zhaboonigan, uttering a cry, makes a last desperate attempt to go with them. But Emily rushes after and catches her at the very last split second. And the six remaining women begin to sing the Ojibway funeral song. By the beginning of the funeral song, we are back at the Wasaychigan Hill Indian Reserve, at Marie-Adele's grave.

WOMEN:

Wa-kwing, wa-kwing,
Wa-kwing nin wi-i-ja;
Wa-kwing, wa- kwing,
Wa-kwing nin wi-i-ja.[10]

At Marie-Adele's grave. During Pelajia's speech, the other women continue humming the funeral song until they fade into silence. Pelajia drops a handful of earth on the grave.

PELAJIA: Well, sister, guess you finally hit the big jackpot. Best bingo game we've ever been to in our lives, huh? You know, life's like that, I figure. When all is said and done. Kinda' silly, innit, this business of living? But. What choice do we have? When some fool of a being goes and puts us Indians plunk down in the middle of this old earth, dishes out this lot we got right now. But. I figure we gotta make the most of it while we're here. You certainly did. And I sure as hell am giving it one good try. For you. For me. For all of us. Promise. Really. See you when that big bird finally comes for me.

Whips out her hammer one more time, holds it up in the air and smiles.

And my hammer.

Back at the store in Wasaychigan Hill. Emily is tearing open a brand-new case of the small cans of Carnation milk, takes two cans out and goes up to Zhaboonigan with them.

EMILY: See, Zha? The red part up here and the white part down here and the pink flowers in the middle?

[10]Women: Heaven, heaven, heaven, I'm going there; Heaven, heaven, heaven, I'm going there. (Ojibway)

ZHABOONIGAN: Oh.

EMILY: Carnation milk.

ZHABOONIGAN: Carnation milk.

EMILY: And it goes over here where all the other red and white cans are, okay?

ZHABOONIGAN: Yup.

Zhaboonigan rushes to Emily and throws her arms around her affectionately. Emily is embarrassed and struggles to free herself. Just then, Annie enters. She's lost some of her speed and frenetic energy. There's obviously something wrong with her.

ANNIE: Hallooo! Whatchyou doing.

EMILY: Red Lucifer's whiskers! It's Annie Cook.

ANNIE: Well, we seem to have survived the biggest bingo in the world, eh? Well . . . ummm . . . not all of us . . . not Marie-Adele . . . but she knew she was . . . but we're okay. (*Laughs.*) . . . us? . . .

EMILY: Annie Cook. Sometimes you can be so goddamn ignorant. (*Pause.*) Too bad none of us won, eh.

ANNIE: Philomena Moosemeat won $600. That's something.

EMILY: Yup. That's one helluva jazzy toilet she's got there, eh?

ANNIE: She's got eight-ply toilet paper. Dark green. Feels like you're wiping your ass with moss!

EMILY: Holy!

ANNIE: I'm singing back-up for Fritz weekends. 25 bucks a gig. That's something, eh?

EMILY: Katz's whore . . .

ANNIE: What?

EMILY: You heard me.

ANNIE: The Katz's what?

EMILY: Chris'sakes. Wake up.

ANNIE: I love him, Emily.

EMILY: You been drinkin'.

ANNIE: Please, come with me tonight.

EMILY: Have to wait for the old buzzard to come pick up this dozy daughter of hers and that's not 'til seven.

ANNIE: Okay?

EMILY: Alright. But we're comin' right back to the Rez soon as the gig's over. Hear?

ANNIE: Thanks. Any mail today?

EMILY: Sorry.

ANNIE: That's okay. See you at seven.

And she exits.

ZHABOONIGAN: Why . . . why . . . why do you call me that?

EMILY: Call you what?

ZHABOONIGAN: Dozy dotter.

Awkward silence, broken after awhile by Zhaboonigan's little giggle.

EMILY: Look, Zha. Share a little secret with you, okay?

ZHABOONIGAN: Yup.

EMILY: Just you and me, promise?

ZHABOONIGAN: Yup.

EMILY: Gazelle Nataways'll see fit to kill . . . but I'm gonna have a baby.

ZHABOONIGAN (*Drops the Carnation milk cans she's been holding all this time and gasps*):   Ohhh! Big Joey!

EMILY (*In exasperation*):   This business of having babies . . .

And the last we see of them is Zhaboonigan playfully poking Emily in the belly and Emily slapping Zhaboonigan's hand away.

At Eugene Starblanket's house. Veronique St. Pierre is sitting on the steps, glowing with happiness, looking up at the sky as though looking for seagulls. She sees none so she picks up the doll that lies under her chair and cradles it on her lap as though it were a child. At this point, Annie Cook enters.

ANNIE: Hallooo!

Surprised to see Veronique sitting there.

Veronique St. Pierre. What are you doing here?

VERONIQUE: Annie Cook. Haven't you heard I'm cooking for Eugene and the children these days? It's been four days since the funeral as you know may she rest in peace (*Makes a quick sign of the cross without missing beat.*) but I was the only person on this reserve who was willing to help with these 14 little orphans.

ANNIE: That's nice. But I came to see if Simon Star . . .

VERONIQUE: The stove is so good. All four elements work and there is even a timer for the oven. As I was saying to Black Lady Halked at the bingo last night, "Now I don't have to worry about burning the fried potatoes or serving the roast beef half-raw."

ANNIE: Well, I was about to . . .

VERONIQUE: Yes, Annie Cook. I bought a roast beef just yesterday. A great big roast beef. Almost 16 pounds. It's probably the biggest roast beef that's been seen on this reserve in recent years. The meat was so heavy that Nicky, Ricky, Ben, and Mark had to take turns carrying it here for me. Oh, it was hard and slippery at first, but I finally managed to wrestle it into my oven. And it's sitting in there at this very moment just sizzling and bubbling with the most succulent and delicious juices. And speaking of succulent and delicious juices, did you come to call on Eugene? Well, Eugene's not home.

ANNIE: Yeah, right. I came to see if Simon had that new record.

VERONIQUE: Why?

ANNIE: I'm singing in Little Current tonight and I gotta practice this one song.

VERONIQUE (*Contemptuously*): That Ritzie Ditzie character.

ANNIE: It's Fritz the Katz, Veronique St. Pierre. FREDERICK STEPHEN KATZ. He's a very fine musician and a good teacher.

VERONIQUE: Teacher?! Of what?! As I was saying to Little Girl Manitowabi and her daughter June Bug McLeod at the bingo last night, "You never know about these non-Native bar-room types." I said to them, "We have enough trouble right here on this reserve without having our women come dragging these shady white characters into the picture." Before you know it, you will end up in deep trouble and bring shame and disrespect on the name of Pelajia Patchnose and all your sisters, myself included.

ANNIE: Myself included, my ass! Veronique St. Pierre. I wish you would shut that great big shitty mouth of yours at least once a year!

VERONIQUE (*Stunned into momentary silence. Then*): Simon Starblanket is not home.

With this, she bangs the doll down viciously.

ANNIE: Good day, Veronique St. Pierre.

And exits.

Veronique, meanwhile, just sits there in her stunned state, mouth hanging open and looking after the departing Annie.

On Pelajia Patchnose's roof. As at the beginning of the play, Pelajia is alone, nailing shingles on. But no cushion this time.

PELAJIA: Philomena. Where are those shingles?

PHILOMENA (*From offstage*): Oh, go on. I'll be up in just a minute.

PELAJIA (*Coughs*): The dust today. It's these dirt roads. Dirt roads all over. Even the main street. If I were chief around here, that's the very first thing I would do is . . .

PHILOMENA (*Coming up the ladder with one shingle and the most beautiful pink, lace-embroidered, heart-shaped pillow you'll ever see*): Oh, go on. You'll never be chief.

PELAJIA: And why not?

PHILOMENA: Because you're a woman.

PELAJIA: Bullshit! If that useless old chief of ours was a woman, we'd see a few things get done around here. We'd see our women working, we'd see our men working, we'd see our young people sober on Saturday nights, and we'd see Nanabush dancing up and down the hill on shiny black paved roads.

Annie Cook pops up at the top of the ladder.

ANNIE: Pelajia for chief! I'd vote for you.

PHILOMENA: Why, Annie Cook. You just about scared me off the edge of this roof.

PELAJIA: Someday, we'll have to find you a man who can slow you down. So what do you want this time, Annie Cook?

ANNIE: Well, to tell you the truth, I came to borrow your record player, Philomena Moosemeat . . . I mean, Moosetail. I'm going to practice this one song for tonight. Emily Dictionary is coming to Little Current to watch me sing with the band.

PELAJIA: It's back from Espanola.

PHILOMENA (*To Pelajia*): Pelajia Rosella Patchnose!

To Annie.

It's still not working very well. There's a certain screeching, squawking noise that comes out of it every time you try to play it.

PELAJIA: That's okay, Philomena. There's a certain screechy, squawky noise that comes out of Annie Cook every time she opens her mouth to sing anyway.

PHILOMENA: Yes, Annie Cook. You can borrow it. But only for one night.

ANNIE: Good. Hey, there's a bingo in Espanola next week and Fire Minklater is driving up in her new car. There might be room.

To Philomena.

Would you like to go?

PELAJIA: Does a bear shit in the woods?

PHILOMENA (*Glares at Pelajia first*):   Yes.

Then quickly to Annie.

Make . . . make sure you don't leave me behind.

ANNIE: I'll make sure. Well. Toodle-oo!

And she pops down the ladder again, happy, now that she's finally got her record player.

PELAJIA: That Annie Cook. Records and bingo. Bingo and records.

PHILOMENA: You know, Pelajia, I'd like to see just what this Fritz looks like. Maybe he IS the man who can slow her down, after all.

PELAJIA: Foolishness! Annie Cook will be walking fast right up until the day she dies and gets buried beside the two of us in that little cemetery beside the church.

PHILOMENA: Oh, go on.

Pause. As Philomena sits down beside her sister, leaning with her elbow on her heart-shaped pillow.

So, Pelajia Patchnose. Still thinking about packing your bags and shipping off to Toronto?

PELAJIA: Well . . . oh . . . sometimes. I'm not so sure I would get along with him if I were to live down there. I mean my son Tom. He was telling me not to play so much bingo.

PHILOMENA: His upstairs washroom. Mine looks just like it now.

PELAJIA: Here we go again.

PHILOMENA: Large shining porcelain tiles in hippity-hoppity squares of black and white . . . so clean you can see your own face, like in a mirror, when you lean over to look into them. It looks so nice. The shower curtains have a certain matching blackness and whiteness to them—they're made of a rich, thick plasticky sort of material—and they're see-through in parts. The bathtub is beautiful, too. But the best, the most wonderful, my absolute most favorite part is the toilet bowl itself. First of all, it's elevated, like on a sort of . . . pedestal, so that it makes you feel like . . . the Queen . . . sitting on her royal throne, ruling her Queendom with a firm yet gentle hand. And the bowl itself—white, spirit white—is of such a shape, such an exquisitely soft, perfect oval shape that it makes you want to cry. Oh!!! And it's so comfortable you could just sit on it right up until the day you die!

After a long, languorous pause, Philomena snaps out of her reverie when she realizes that Pelajia, all this time, has been looking at her disbelievingly and then contemptuously. Pelajia cradles her hammer as though she'd like to bang Philomena's head with it. Philomena delicately starts to descend the ladder. The last we see of her is her Kewpie-doll face. And beside it, the heart-shaped pillow, disappearing like a setting sun behind the edge of the roof. Once she's good and gone, Pelajia dismisses her.

PELAJIA: Oh, go on!

Then she pauses to look wistfully at the view for a moment.

Not many seagulls flying over Eugene Starblanket's house today.

And returns once more to her hammering on the roof as the lights fade into black-out. Split seconds before complete black-out, Nanabush, back once more in his guise as the seagull, "lands" on the roof behind the unaware and unseeing Pelajia Patchnose. He dances to the beat of the hammer, merrily and triumphantly.

—1986

Judith Thompson (b. 1954) *was born in Montreal but grew up in Kingston, Ontario, graduating from Queen's University and the acting program at the National Theatre School. Her first major success as a playwright was* Crackwalker *(1980), later published along with three other plays in* The Other Side of the Dark *(1989), a collection that won the Governor General's Award, as did her play* White Biting Dog *(1984). With* I am Yours *(1987) and* Lion in the Streets *(1990), she continued to earn respect for her gritty explorations of the dark side of human experience. Though teaching at the University of Guelph and writing increasingly for television and film, Thompson continues to write plays, including* Perfect Pie *(2000) and* Habitat *(2001). Disturbing and controversial, her plays tackle some of the most brutal and beautiful acts that humans are capable of committing, and* Sled, *nominated for the Governor General's Award in 1997, is no exception. Here Thompson dramatizes murder and manipulation, violence and victimization, ideology and identity. Various ethnic backgrounds are represented in the play, including French Canadian, Irish Gaelic, Italian, and Cree. Though the character of Evangeline is Cree, her name alludes to the exile of the Acadians, and most of the characters are haunted by some kind of exile. In a play Thompson described as "a long operatic dream about the forming of Canada and of the self," she uses the streets of Toronto and the Ski-Doo trails of Northern Ontario to explore the wild without and within.*

Judith Thompson
Sled

Playwright's Production Notes

The play should run no longer than 2 hours and 15 minutes (not counting the intermissions). The audience should be out no later than 10:50 pm, given an 8:00 pm curtain. The key to a good pace, other than in the playing, is in the transitions between scenes which should, in almost every case, be instantaneous—the last word of one scene immediately followed by the first word of the next. The designer, of course, can facilitate the speedy transitions.

CHARACTERS

Annie Delaney
Jack
Joe
Evangeline
Kevin
Volker, Mike, Jason, M.C.
Mother, Marsha, Carmella

Setting: *The present, Toronto; a lodge in Northern Ontario and its snowmobile trails; a wilderness farther north.*

ACT ONE

SCENE 1

White birches, snow, a great snowy owl, and a trail, with a hill, running around behind or through the audience. Annie appears walking fast and hard, out of breath through deep snow and birches. The music is mounting, ominous like a heart beating harder and faster but moving towards a dark euphoria; Annie, walks the trail around or through the audience and climbs the hill. At the top of the hill, she looks down over the scene. The music for "Oh heavenly time of day" plays. She sings:

ANNIE: Oh heavenly time of day
the snow and the quiet
the birch
white pine
so high and so high
Shall I sink in the snow and just lie there for hours
alone there for hours
til dark night
erases me?
Oh heavenly time of day

Annie breathes in the air. There is the sound of a wolf howling. She sings.

ANNIE: lie on the white snow and
stare at the dark sky
the sky full of stars
who are people who died
maybe people I know
hello Maeve O'Hara
my mother's mother's
mother's mother's
motherrrr . . . hello!

A wolf howls. She makes her way down the hill.

SCENE 2

A residential street, with mostly red brick houses with high pointed roofs, some three-storey, but most, two-storey workers' houses. The houses, however, look as though they are in the middle of a forest. The birches remain.

JOE: *"America Bella! Si abbandonare a me!"* That's what she used to say whenever things were—fallin' apart. My mother, I don't think she ever said the word "Canada." It was always "America." *"America bella."* This here used to be a cow path. The whole of what you see now, of Clinton Street, wasn't nothin' but a cow path. My mother an' father and the nine of us kids we were livin' south of College, that was about 1918, my dad workin' at the slaughter-house at Clinton and Bloor. It's still there to this day, they won't move it; we'd come up here to the pastures and we'd watch as the cows walked down the cow path to the slaughterhouse, to become ground meat. Led always by the great black bull. Course we'd never see the meat, nor the milk, never saw milk till I went in the Air Force. But I loved sittin' on the fence and watchin' all these cows walkin' down. And all the Italian ladies, they would chase after these cows, to catch the manure they dropped on the way. For their gardens. And my mother, Carmella? She would be the first. She would always be first.

SCENE 3

The Lounge Dining Room at Pickerel and Jack Lake Lodge. A warm fire crackles in the fireplace. There is a trophy on the wall, a deer with antlers. Volker, the proprietor, has a German accent.

VOLKER: Good evening everybody. My name is Volker, and this is my lovely wife Marsha. Welcome to Pickerel and Jack Lake Lodge: The snowmobiling mecca of North America. Marsha and me hope you are really enjoying your stay and that you have seen the 500 kilometres of snowmobile trails out there, and have wind-burned faces, but now it's time to warm up, yes? So we have brought for your entertainment tonight a great honour, a beautiful diva, the sexy singer of Toronto nightclubs, the very interesting and I think such a good singer, the great Annie Delaney. Let's give her a warm hand, yes?

Annie Delaney steps out of the shadows in a beautiful red dress with long red velvet gloves and performs a simple transformation or act of magic, as she sings:

ANNIE: Oh heavenly time of day . . . the fog and the quiet . . .
the mist
no sun
I move out of my dream and into this day as the fog
it clears so slowly away to
reveal . . .
to reveal . . .
to reveal . . .

Kevin enters, interrupting. An awkward silence. He sits down.

VOLKER: Isn't she fantastic?

ANNIE: I saw a fox this morning. On the green trail. The long one? Early this morning. I was walking along, thinking: there's still snow here. It's all melting down there, in the city. Mud rivers running everywhere. But here: snow, spruce, evergreens. I was walking toward a heart-stopping stand of birch, and I saw a fox. A red fox. We looked at each other, for a moment. A wonder. At dawn; a secret time of day.

My son, Jason, was born at dawn; that time of day gives me hope. Whereas, the hour *before* dawn? In the winter? The job that degraded day after day, that picked at my being. It was dark when I rose and I walked down the empty cold street and I am nauseous just before dawn I wake up, with dread. My heart beating very fast. I know I will die just before dawn.

She sings one again: "Thursday in November."

Thursday in November
at that duskish time of day
Walking west on Bloor Street. Past Italian groceries, Korean fruit and flowers, Hungarian deli . . . I feel a sharp pain in my knee a red dog, no, a fox, has bitten me . . .

(*spoken*) It's a fox.

(*sung*) At Bloor and Bathurst my downtown
in the rushing
A red fox
Is here and
has bitten my knee and it stands and it stares back at me.
And we all
go down on our—knees on the spit covered
sidewalk and say
Oh heavenly time of day
ohhh heavenly time of day
A fox on the street
the geese in the V twisting this way and that
The lights through the dark clouds the blues and the
indigos, breathe in the chatter, the down to the
subway and buses to homes
See the fox on the street
grab a paper, a Mars bar, a *People*, and rest your head
Let the thoughts drift like I did on Pickerel Lake.
Just drift
Oh Heavenly time of day
Gives me some hope
And I do, believe that I'll stay
For a while
With this fox
On this street

A red coat
For a while
with its dusk
With its eyes

SCENE 4

Lodge dining room lounge: Mike Head and Kevin Dorner are eating dinner at one table. Annie sits down and immediately Jack praises her.

JACK: Beautiful. That was beautiful. Never heard that one before. It's something.

Annie rests for a moment.

ANNIE: How's the dinner? Are you enjoying it?

JACK: Beautiful roast of beef.

He offers her a bite, she turns her head away.

ANNIE: What did you mean "something."

JACK: What?

ANNIE: You said "It's something." My song. As if it was deranged.

JACK: I liked it. It was good.

ANNIE: But . . . ?

JACK: You're not gonna get a fox on Bloor Street.

ANNIE: Well. I saw a fox in Trinity Bellwoods Park once. Early in the morning.

JACK: You did?

ANNIE: Yes. I did. I told you about that—

JACK: Shit. Shit I forgot to cancel the paper. What a fucking idiot I am.

ANNIE: Shhhh, don't worry, Joe will do it.

JACK: Joe?

ANNIE: Old Joe from across the street.

JACK: Oh yeah, Joe. Ace.

ANNIE: He'll pick them up for us. He knows we're going away. He's my pal.

JACK: Why does he sit there watchin everybody all day? Doesn't he have anything better to do?

ANNIE: Give him a break, he worked like a dog for fifty years, he's earned his rest. Besides, it's great for us: He never misses a thing on that street.

He touches her knee under the table. She enjoys it.

Jack.

He takes her hand.

JACK: So I never asked you, what'd you do Thursday, did you swim?

ANNIE: Seventy-three lengths.

JACK: You're amazing. But you like that, don't you, just thinkin' your thoughts.

ANNIE: Actually I don't think at all. I just don't have a thought in all that green water.

JACK: You are looking incredibly beautiful tonight.

ANNIE: To your eyes only.

JACK: You're the most beautiful woman in this room.

ANNIE: You look very handsome yourself. That jacket does look nice on you.

JACK: It better for thirteen hundred bucks. Hey. That was very wonderful last night. Last night you were all . . .

ANNIE: Shhhh.

JACK: I did pretty good with the hand last night, eh? You had, how many, four fireworks last night, didn't you? You are so unpredictable. My quiet woman.

He touches her. She looks at his fingers on her arm.

ANNIE: Jack? How long do someone's fingerprints . . . last? Say, in a house?

JACK: Ten years. Give or take. Less they're wiped off.

ANNIE: So if I don't clean, if I don't polish, my mother and father; their fingerprints will stay with us for ten more years after they . . .

JACK (*nods*): Annie. I won't talk about hockey. If you don't talk about death. Deal?

ANNIE: "Behold I shall tell you a mystery. We shall not all sleep but we shall all be changed." I wish I believed that. For even a minute.

JACK: Hey. Look at the fire. You love fires.

At the other table, Kevin, and Mike are getting rowdy.

KEVIN: Sunday roast beef dinner, eh? Just like my old lady used to make.

MIKE: Right. Sunday my old lady would open a box of potato flakes. Throw some boiling water on 'em. There's Sunday dinner. I'm not fucking kidding.

KEVIN: Look at that waitress. Fuck, man, looks like she swallowed the Skydome.

MIKE: This beef is fine, man.

KEVIN: But where's the Yorkshire pudding? I want my fuckin' Yorkshire pudding.

MIKE: Yeah. Yorkshire fucking pudding.

On the other side of the room.

ANNIE: Is it working, Jack? This weekend? You think things are going to be alright? With us?

JACK: It's working. I haven't seen you like this in months. Maybe it's the nature, the snow, whatever. You're actually, I don't know, happy.

ANNIE: Yes. I am, aren't I.

JACK: Yes. You are.

KEVIN: HEY. WAITRESS.

MARSHA: Were you born in a barn? Or was it a sewer?

KEVIN: Sewer. That's good, that's good. You're Big Marsha aren't ya? Didn't you used to work at The Keg in Huntsville?

MARSHA: Yes I worked at The Keg. I think I tossed you out a couple of times, did I not? What can I get for you boys?

KEVIN: I was just wondering . . . um, like . . . did I fuck you?

MARSHA: That's not funny. I don't think that's funny at all. You're out of here.

Marsha leaves their table.

KEVIN: I'm sorry.

MIKE: We didn't mean nothin'.

MARSHA: Everything okay here, folks?

ANNIE: Yes, thank you, wonderful.

JACK: My compliments to the chef. The roast is excellent.

MARSHA: Well thank you. I made the roast myself tonight. Chef was off sick, he's got some kinda kidney trouble. So Volker says,

"Marsha you're doin' the roast beef." And I don't cook, eh, generally, so I said, "Volker I can't cook a roast of beef." Volker hands me some garlic and some paprika and says, "Rub it on, Marsha, like lotion on a baby's bottom." So there you are, it's not so bad.

ANNIE: Looks very good.

MARSHA: It's very good, I know. Hey. I meant to tell you, I like your singing. It's unusual. Different.

ANNIE: Thank you.

KEVIN: Waitress. Excuse me, not to bother you or anything, but like, we were wondering. Like where's our Yorkshire pudding. It says on the menu "Yorkshire pudding." Pardon my French.

MARSHA: That is Yorkshire pudding.

MIKE: Where? Am I like, buh-lind?

MARSHA: On your plate. There.

Kevin points to the Yorkshire pudding.

KEVIN: THAT? You are tellin' me that THAT is Yorkshire pudding?

MIKE: No fuckin' way.

MARSHA: Yes, that is Yorkshire pudding. I made it myself.

KEVIN: Looks like my grandmother's tit, man.

MARSHA: That is it.

Marsha exits. They laugh hysterically. Jack and Annie exchange a look. Annie is pleading with him silently not to do anything.

KEVIN: Look at those two, they are pissed.

MIKE: Excuse me, miss? No, you, big guy's woman.

ANNIE: Are you talking to me?

MIKE: Like, how did you get so tall and skinny anyways? Did you, like, eat the CN Tower?

Note: If the actress does not fit this physical description, replace the lines with "How'd you get so homely lookin' anyways? Did you, like, eat Yonge Street?"

They laugh even harder. Jack stands up, furious.

KEVIN: And that guy over there, he ate Exhibition Stadium, man.

They laugh some more, knocking over some plates etc. Jack walks over.

JACK: Before we go any further, I would like you both to go down on your knees and apologize, to my wife, NOW.

ANNIE: It doesn't matter, Jack. Let's go.

JACK: You are going to get an apology. Do it boys. Do it now.

Silence.

KEVIN: It's a free country, sir, I believe. And I would like to keep eatin' my supper.

MIKE: I'm really enjoying these green beans. Deliciooooso.

JACK: You are going to apologize to my wife and to every other diner in this establishment, or I will make you sorry.

MIKE: What the fuck? Is this, like, a Sylvester Stallone movie or something?

KEVIN: He's a cop, man. I see it in the white of his fuckin' eyes. He's one of those, that shoves ya up against the car and bangs your head over and over.

JACK: *Diablo.*

KEVIN: What?

JACK: Just do what I told you to do.

ANNIE: Jack.

JACK: Everything's gonna be just fine, Annie. Just stay where you are.

There is a long pause. Kevin and Mike laugh and start eating again.

KEVIN: So as I was saying, Mike, I wouldn't fuck that wife of his if you paid me a fuckin' million, like fuckin' the railroad tracks, right? She likely smells down there, anyways, right? Like a fuckin' can of sardines.

Mike is laughing like a kid, snorting.

Jack slams Mike's head into the table, knocking him out.

JACK: I have had just about enough out of you, you piece of fucking trash—you fucking apologize NOW.

Jack drags Kevin to his table, forces him to his knees and into a bow. Kevin goes for his hunting knife strapped to his belt but Jack pins Kevin's arm behind him, pressing hard.

Now learn some goddamned respect.

Scene 5

Joe sits, rocks on the porch.

JOE: I used to have the satellite. Because I enjoyed the television quite a bit. Because I was a TV salesman at Eaton's for forty-three years. That was my profession. So I enjoyed my television. But since Essie got sick, I can't watch it no more. I turn it on, and I just can't watch it. Because I got to watch the street. That is what I am here for. Now that my kids are grown and gone. To watch the street. Trouble is, a kind of strange thing is happening to me. I'll sit here, sippin' on my coffee, and instead of watchin' out for how things are, right now, like if little Claire and Joshua two doors up come home from school on time, or if too many people seem to be livin' in the house on the corner, instead of those urgent things, I keep seeing: what has already happened.

Scene 6

Hotel room. Music: sexy like Santana.[1] Presumably coming from radio.

Jack and Annie. They start at some distance from each other and move slowly together dancing in response to the music.

Scene 7

Kevin and Mike in enclosed shack getting ready to go out sledding. Kevin loads his gun.

KEVIN: Fuckin' cocksucker. I'll kill that cocksucker.

MIKE: Forget it, man, you know what cops are like.

KEVIN: Nobody does that to me. NOBODY.

MIKE: Well somebody did. A fuckin' psycho cop did. And it could have been a hell of a lot worse, we coulda been dead, he'd get away with it. Now let's get over it and go man. Let's go do what we're here for, we fuckin' risked our necks gettin' this sled, let's shoot us a moose!

---

[1]Latin Rock band, led by guitarist Carlos Santana.

KEVIN: MOOSE!

MIKE: Whoooo!

They whoop and bark like dogs as they run out.

SCENE 8

Annie and Jack's room. He is asleep. She is lying next to him, looking out the window. An owl hoots. She sees the owl and the owl sees her.

ANNIE: Ohhh.

She turns, excited.

Jack? Are you awake? It's an owl, a great snowy owl. I'm going to go for a walk. I'm gonna go and walk until dawn. Wait for the light. Sweet dreams.

SCENE 9

It is a dark night lit only by a mass of stars, A night bird sings ominously. We are looking at a snowmobile trail in Northern Ontario. A green or pink neon sign in handwriting overhead says: "Pickerel and Jack Lake Lodge: Snowmobiling Mecca of North America!" And then in small letters, underneath, in a different colour of neon, it says: "50 km. of Pristine X-country ski trails!" The cross-country ski trail is zig-zagging through a stand of birches. Annie walks by the sign and heads down a steep hill. It is very steep. She edges down it, grabbing onto trees occasionally, slipping.

ANNIE: All alone, in the woods, in the dark. In the middle of Northern Ontario by myself at night. I've never swam across Lake Ontario. I've never run across the 401. I've never driven across the frozen ice. But I am here.

She sings briefly in Gaelic. A shimmering, strange music. She sees a vision in the distance.

I see her again. The girl. On the ship. A dark, battered, dying ship. In Gaelic, my blood tongue, say: *Long an bhais* [pronounced: Long on vache] Big holes in the mast. The crashing of fifty foot waves.

Maeve. The raining. Maeve O'Hara, born in Connemara,[2] December 6, 1791. Praying. Standing on the mast of the ship. Praying to our Lord Jesus Christ. And everybody else down under, is dead. Of fever. Babies and mothers and fathers and families, all dead, piled together. They threw them overboard, one by one, wrapped up in sheets, until there was nobody left to throw them. Only Maeve, to say prayers for the dead. And she looks out to sea. For land, or whales, or fairies of the sea. In Gaelic, say: *Si na farraige*. And a cold wind comes up, cold and strong and she hangs on, she doesn't fall but her hair, her hair stands straight up. I know this is true. I know this girl is my great-great-grandmother. I know this girl is me.

She hears the sound of breaking branches. The shadow of a moose appears. They stare at one another for a moment.

She reaches up to touch the moose.

Oh. God. What is it? It couldn't be. Oh my God it is. A moose. I don't believe this. Hello. You are so big. Hey I'm not going to hurt you. Wait!

The moose runs. A snowmobile approaches. Annie stands, terrified in the moonlight.

Oh my God. This is all I need.

The snowmobile's light beams on her. There are birches between her and the snowmobile. There is a stand of birches blocking their view of her.

KEVIN: Hey hey shut off shut off. I see somethin' through those trees.

He shuts it off.

ANNIE: Hello. Hello.

Kevin motions Mike to stay back. Mike keeps his sunglasses and headphones on. He is drunk. Kevin moves in.

KEVIN: Well look at that. We got ourselves a she moose.
MIKE: Moose. Fuck.

---

[2] a county in northwest Ireland

ANNIE: Hey, fellows! It's not a moose. It's me from the lodge. The singer. Hey. Can you hear me!

MIKE: Shoot her, man, before she takes off.

KEVIN: Right cornered she is.

MIKE: Fuckin' shoot it.

ANNIE: No! No! Please answer me, guys. Hello! I'm here, through the bushes. What, are you wearing headphones? Take off your headphones.

KEVIN: Let's cut open her belly, and if there's a calf there, we pull out the calf.

MIKE: Where is she man, I can't fuckin see her.

Annie gasps and goes into shock.

ANNIE: This is not funny. Will you answer me please. Please. PULL OUT YOUR HEADPHONES.

KEVIN: Let's pull out the calf. Just shoot her, cut her open, and pull out the calf. Take it to a vet, leave it on the steps, whatever.

MIKE: Did you shoot it?

KEVIN: Just pull the calf right out. Alright.

Kevin moves through the brush until he has quite a clear view of Annie.

ANNIE: My husband will kill you.

KEVIN: I want the antlers.

ANNIE: I'm sorry about the thing at the lodge, my husband went too far. He will apologize to you.

KEVIN: We split the meat. Shove it in the freezer, that's supper all winter. Moose and chips, moose and fries, moose and rice, moose and Yorkshire pudding.

ANNIE: Please.

MIKE: Why isn't she movin', man? What's wrong with her?

KEVIN: She's froze; in the light of the sled. She's froze.

MIKE: I can't fuckin' see her!

KEVIN: *Ek skal skjota ther huortu I gegnum* [This is Norse and pronounced: Yeg skal skeeota tear hertu ee gagnum]. Let's shoot her man. Right through the heart.

Two shots. Blackout.

SCENE 10

Evangeline comes out on her porch and looks around with great ex-
pectation. She is looking for another neighbour's tame pigeons. She
sees them, flying in circles. She follows them with her eyes. They
make quite a racket.

EVANGELINE: Morning Joe.

JOE: Morning.

EVANGELINE: See the pigeons?

JOE: Where? Oh yeah. A whole flock of 'em.

EVANGELINE: Have you noticed they do this every day at this time?
Fly around in a circle, from here to the Loblaws over to the Food
City, and down to Fiesta Farms and back.

JOE: Now that you mention it. I do see 'em flying around every day. I
didn't think nothing of it. Don't care for pigeons.

EVANGELINE: They belong to a guy over on Grace. 'Parently he races
them, down in the States every spring. They're in training.

JOE: Training?

EVANGELINE: For the races.

JOE: Well well.

EVANGELINE: How's Essie today, Joe?

JOE: I tried to cut her toenails for her and I couldn't. They're too hard.
And yellow. Don't know what that means. I'm gonna have to give
the doctor a call. Get that mobile foot clinic over here.

EVANGELINE: I could come do them later Joe. Before I go to work.

JOE: It's a nasty job, Ev.

EVANGELINE: Agh.

Evangeline looks at Annie and Jack's house. The house looks omi-
nous to her.

Ooooh. That house give me the shivers today. Looks empty.

JOE: Workin' holiday for Annie up north. Singin' in a lodge up there.
She's a lounge singer. The two of them went for the weekend.

EVANGELINE: You know I don't think I've ever seen him.

JOE: Long hours. He's a police detective. 14 Division.

EVANGELINE: So they're way up north.

JOE: Don't tell nobody though. 'Specially that nosey check-out, over at Fiesta Farms.

EVANGELINE: Hah. She's always askin' me when I'm getting married. Next time, I'm gonna just tell her "It's none of your business, you potato-faced grocery girl." HAH. That'd be funny.

JOE: I'd like to see that.

EVANGELINE: Joe.

JOE: Yeah.

EVANGELINE: Will you think I'm crazy?

JOE: No.

EVANGELINE: I heard footsteps last night. And the night before that. On the street. Real clear, like it was summer. And I thought I heard someone climbing the steps and coming up on the porch. When I looked out the window, I didn't see anyone.

JOE: Maybe you should get a dog. Although they do shed something terrible. Our Dory she was a piece of work; she would get up on the couch soon as we went up to bed. One night my stomach was bad, I come down for a Brio, I'm half asleep and I think I see my mother sittin on our couch. I go "now what are you doin' comin' back from the dead and sittin' on my couch in my parlour when you never let me so much as touch that precious couch of yours" and Dory she kinda whimpers and jumps off. Ha. Oh, I felt a fool.

EVANGELINE: Joe? Do you think, maybe, I mean, don't you think, there is some possibility that it might be him?

JOE: Who?

EVANGELINE: You know. Kevin. My brother. Joe? Do you think:?

JOE: Oh dear.

EVANGELINE: Well, it's possible.

JOE: I don't see how, Evangeline. It's been 20 years.

EVANGELINE: But maybe he—found out somehow, about who he was. That he belongs right here. On Clinton Street. Like maybe she got sick and she wanted to just tell him the truth, people do that, you know, they get tired of keepin' somethin' buried.

JOE: Even if he did know the truth, Ev, what makes you think he's gonna come back here? This is not home to him no more, not since he was took. He was only four years old, remember. He's got a life there, wherever that woman stole him to, could be Australia for all we know, he likely has a job, a girlfriend—

EVANGELINE: But don't you think he'll want to come and find his real sister? And mother? I mean everyone wants to know their real family.

JOE: I don't know about that.

EVANGELINE: He'll be real disappointed when I tell him Mama's dead.

JOE: Evangeline, dear. Please don't count on him comin'.

EVANGELINE: I heard those footsteps. Joe? I know I did. Are you sure you didn't hear nothing?

JOE: Well . . .

EVANGELINE: You did? You did Joe? You heard them too?

JOE: More than likely it's just some drunkard comin' home from the Tasty's Tavern.

EVANGELINE: I'm going to stay awake all night tonight, and watch out the window. Then I'll be sure not to miss him.

JOE: Evy, there's no point in you losing a good night's sleep.

EVANGELINE: He's gonna want to know everything about Mama, about our life before he was took. I gotta be ready. Tell me, Joe. Tell me about like, how she used to keep the house so nice. Before. Before she got sick.

JOE: She made apple crisp. That's the mother you should remember.

EVANGELINE: She made apple crisp? With brown sugar on top? With what kind of apple, Joe?

JOE: I'm not so sure about that . . .

EVANGELINE: But what kind do you think . . . like . . . MacIntosh?

JOE: Yes, that's what it was. It was MacIntosh.

EVANGELINE: Oh. MacIntosh!

Scene 11

Trail at night. Annie, in her red dress, lies in the snow before a towering tree. Sound of an owl hooting. Annie slowly wakes up looks up at the owl.

ANNIE: This is very strange. This is very strange. My heart is not beating, the blood is pouring, gushing out of me—In my Gaelic, *Vee a mer egg foil vache* [this is the phonetic spelling] I am dying. I will be buried. Deep, unmoving inside a box under the ground, eyes never moving my tongue curling up mouldy inside my mouth these hands folded, living only in dreams, and thoughts, and hurried conversations in front of Steven's Milk, with dogs pulling at the leash and kids dancing round, "Did you hear who died?" or at the skating rink, flirting, buying hot dogs, "Did you hear?" less and less, and less, present only in my recycled clothes, hanging at the Goodwill, in the hairs I have left in the brushes all over the house, in my fingerprints which will fade in ten years, she disappeared; they the neighbours they will go on for years Valerie Pratt rushing her three children out the door at two minutes to nine, every day, for years and years to come, Joe will sit on his porch the Sikh men will deliver flyers to our door every Sunday and the kids will play road hockey and I will have left so little; I wish to leave more on this earth, more than I have, (*big raspy breath*) oh let me go back, to lie naked in the wet cement, to spray paint my name in blue all over my city, (another big breath) to French kiss the men lying in doorways and stinking of urine, to run from rooftop to steeple, to stand on a speeding train and r-r-r-rave (*breathing becomes more difficult and shallower*). I have made such a faint impression in the world a bird alighting on a branch (*breath*) I want to go back and resume my life and just be be be (*breath*) with my son, my husband, just walk, breathe just breathe again in the leaves in the snow, walk (*breath*) and the snow can cover my footprints the blue light of the snow dropping bare feet on burning sand (*breath*) the August humidity wrapping around me, diving into murky lakes with weeds the rough of my husband's cheek (*breath*) the smell of his neck in the summer, the breath of my child, with a cold, (*breath*) the smell of his head his head in the night oh! let me resume—

Final breath.
She lies, still.
The owl hoots.

Scene 12

Jack in the hotel room.

JACK: Annie? You in the bath? You enjoy your bath. I won't bother you. I know how you love your long bath. I was thinking about what you were talking about, my temper. Like my . . . anger. The local punks callin' me *"Diablo."* What I did to those kids tonight and that thing with Pochinshky on Eglinton. I was thinking—I have to tell you something I haven't told you yet.

Remember, we ran into that—Jemma? The legal secretary from Brantford, blonde with the moussed hair—in February. Remember? At Yorkdale Mall? And remember how uncomfortable you said you felt? The way she looked at you? You said you thought there was something . . .

I used to . . . get very pissed at Jemma. Sometimes I think it was because she was blonde. And she was so big breasted. I, like, I wanted to own her. I would leave you at home reading in your nightgown, tellin' you I had to work all night and I would drive to Brantford to see Jemma, to have sex with her four, five times every which way. I did things to her that . . . and then I would drive home and slide into bed next to you and we would talk that sweet night talk and you were so trusting—I was an animal. I was out of control. I still don't get it. I don't get why it happened. I didn't tell you before because I was afraid you wouldn't forgive me; maybe you won't forgive me, maybe you'll get outta the bath and say you want a separation, I wouldn't blame you. But I love you so much I wanted to tell you the whole truth. I was good as golden right up till I was nine. You know? The perfect kid. I would give my dad the paper, ask him if he wanted a beer, go get it for him, help my Mama with the table, change my baby sister. Sundays, I would put on the little suit, and we'd go to church. My sister and I would get under a blanket on the couch and watch cartoons all morning. I'd talk French with my gramma, sing songs with her; I played every sport goin', hockey, baseball, soccer, everything. I slept with my football. And then this kid, at school, he started to pick on me. Take off my hat, in the winter, throw it around. Say I was cheating in ball hockey. I never cheated. But he was a grade older, bigger, and said I couldn't play ball hockey. And I would sit there, on the side, and hope to be asked.

It was around then, I got—angry at home. I put holes in the walls with my fists. I wouldn't talk French wouldn't eat French, if my mother put tortière and sugar pie on the table I would throw 'em on the floor, "You stupid bitch, I want a hamburger and a fuckin' popsicle not this frog shit, not this. . . ." I never kissed a woman till you, Annie. I would turn away. I would say, I'm not one for kissing. Because kissing meant . . . I don't know. Being there. Goin' inside like an underwater cave with someone, swimmin' in, hand in hand, and you're under the water, inside the cave, with this person, and so much so much could go wrong. You're not the first woman I slept with, as you know, and maybe not the last, as you also know, but you are the first, and the last woman I will ever kiss. Annie?

SCENE 13

Evangeline's house. She is in a slip, about to get dressed for her job at Fran's. The ghost of her mother stands behind her.

MOTHER: Evangeline. My lovely girl.

EVANGELINE: Oh Mama, I am so lonely. I am missing you so much.

MOTHER: I'm all around you, Vange.

EVANGELINE: I've been waitin' so long for Kevy I've forgotten how to make friends.

MOTHER: I can see him coming, like a storm, my love.

EVANGELINE: My Kevin? My brother? Is coming back?

MOTHER: Oh. My lovely child. Just . . .

Mother is trying to warn her.

SCENE 14

The two snowmobilers walk through the brush towards Annie's fallen body. They do not see her yet.

MIKE: Wait'll my dad sees all this moose meat in his freezer. He's always after me sayin' I never bring home nothin' he will go freaky when he sees a pair of antlers sittin' on his kitchen table.

KEVIN: Hey. I'm getting the antlers. I'm the one that . . .

Mike sees Annie lying in the snow.

MIKE: Oh my God. Oh my fucking God.

KEVIN: The lady from the lodge.

Mike vomits and throws down the earphones.

MIKE: I told you we shouldn't wear these fucking things. Fuck. I'm blind in one eye, man, I didn't fuckin' see her through all them trees. What's your fuckin' excuse? Eh? Eh? Why didn't you see her?

KEVIN: I did see her. And so did you, Mike.

MIKE: What? What do you mean you did see her? What are you talking about?

KEVIN: Mike.

MIKE: What do you mean "Mike." WHAT THE HELL?

KEVIN: We were gettin' back at the cop, right?

MIKE: You are saying you knew it was her? You saw it was a lady, man? Why didn't you tell me?

KEVIN: I thought you were jokin' around, man. I thought you could see.

MIKE: No!

KEVIN: We messed him up good, man.

MIKE: I don't give a fuck about that, Kevin.

KEVIN: You know and I know we followed her here. Mike.

MIKE: I'm tellin' you I didn't see her. I can't see without my glasses, man. I thought she was an animal.

KEVIN: We only meant to scare her, Mike. We didn't mean to kill her.

MIKE: But we did kill her. We shot her. YOU shot her.

KEVIN: We shot her. Right through the heart.

MIKE (*pushes Kevin to ground*): Why didn't you say nothin', asshole. Why didn't you fuckin' say nothin'? You want to end up in fucking Millhaven?[3] Do you know what that fuckin' place is like? It's a rat's fuckin asshole, man, it's worse than any fuckin' hell in any fuckin' bible. I heard stories, man, see what happened to Kendal? Kendal got knifed in three days man, the place is a fuckin' hellhole. I'll kill you man, I'll fuckin' kill you if we get sent down.

(*Mike unpins Kevin.*)

KEVIN: Mike.

MIKE: What?

KEVIN: Do you feel it?

MIKE: What?

---

[3]maximum security prison, Kingston, Ontario

KEVIN: The rush.

MIKE: That's the devil, Kevin. That's the devil, shakin' your hand.

SCENE 15

Jack walks along the trail, pointing the flashlight in various directions.

JACK (*passing close by Annie*): Annie? Annie? Annie?

SCENE 16

Evangeline is getting into her waitress uniform.

EVANGELINE: I like working the graveyard shift at Fran's. Because it's quiet. And people who come in, mostly just want to think. They have scrambled eggs and toast with butter, ice cream and chocolate sauce, macaroni and cheese. And always coffee. They always have their coffee. With cream. With sugar. They are very much alone. I can see it in their eyes. Looking down. Smoking. Lately I been thinkin' about things. Last things. Many people say they don't believe in God or life after death or heaven or hell but I have seen God. I have seen God in the deep brown eyes of the smoking people who ask for rice pudding at three forty-five in the morning. The Indians, teasing me, "Hey Apple," whatever that means, watching me.

And I have seen hell in their raw dirty hands. The boy prostitutes from Grosvenor Street. Talking. Together. Lookin' around the room, never resting. Smoking. Joking around with me. Want fries. Jesus Christ. In their voices. The way their voices sing. In the way their hair falls over their eyes. Sons of God. I touch their shoulders, sometimes. And in those times, I know . . . I know . . . that . . . I have seen . . .

Kevin starts taking Annie's dress off

I hope Patty's working tonight she always has the best stories. She's got this great big family out in Etobicoke, like six brothers and sisters and fourteen cousins and her mother and father and they have these big, funny dinners. And the way she tells it, she keeps saying everything is "so fabulous" and "so hideous" and she is just so funny.

And every time after she tells me a story I think it's that much more possible that when I get home . . .

SCENE 17

Night trail with Kevin beside Annie's body. Mike is watching in shock as Kevin takes dress off the body.

MIKE: I don't fuckin' know you man.

Mike picks up his gun and exits. Kevin finishes and stuffs the dress into his jacket. Sound of owl. Jack walks into clearing.

JACK (*off, shouting*): Annie?

Kevin hears him, takes off, and hides.

Annie. Oh my God.

He walks over to her. He kneels, he shakes her. He tries to give her the kiss of life, sees she is dead. He sees the bullet holes. He puts his coat over her. He picks her up.

Annie!

SCENE 18

JOE: I was there. At the table, in the kitchen. Sittin' on the boarder's knee. About to eat my pepper and egg. When I saw my father killed by his own brother. Shot through the heart. With the gun from the garden. They'd had to dig up my mother's climbing yellow roses to get it, it was hid, ya see, under the roses. They had dug it up from the ground to scare some Irish fellows that were botherin' them at all hours, askin' for whores and for whisky. My uncle, he was sittin' at one head of the table, across from my father, and he was cleaning the gun. My mother, she says "get the *pistola* offa my table." My father he tells her, "be quiet" and he and my uncle they are joking around about this and that and boom. My father falls back. Blood. Spraying out of him. Over the walls. Over me. Her face. She falls to her knees. And she cries: "*America Bella, se abbandonare ah meeeeeeeeee!*" I still hear her sometimes, just outta nowhere, I'll be

bringing home a bag of groceries from Fiesta Farms, or walkin' to
the bus up on Dupont . . .

Scene 19

*On the trail. Dawn. Mike is sitting, drinking. We hear the sound of
Kevin's snowmobile and we see the beams of its headlights. Kevin
enters, the headlights lighting his way.*

KEVIN: Beautiful night. Clear.

MIKE: Kev?

KEVIN: Yeah, Mike.

MIKE: What was that . . . shit you said . . . before you . . . shot her?
That fuckin . . . "Ek skal" . . . what was that?

Kevin laughs.

KEVIN: English teacher back home. Fag. Used to buy me cigarettes,
CD's, down jackets, whatever I fuckin' wanted. Knew all these, like,
ancient languages. Said I woulda been Norse, like a thousand years
ago. Took me hunting. Deer. Taught me how to say *"Ek skal skjota
ther huorti geognum,"* "Let's shoot her man, right through the
heart." You like that?

MIKE: I'm turning myself in.

KEVIN: What?

MIKE: To the O.P.P[4] First for the stolen sled. And then for the
manslaughter.

KEVIN: WHAT?

MIKE: You can't stop me, man.

KEVIN: I'll fuckin' stop you, Mike.

MIKE: Kev, look. It was an accident. These things happen all the time
up here. My uncle, he got shot in the Kap[5]—I'm gettin' married for
Christ sake, Kevin. I don't want this on my conscience, Kev. Come
with me. If we own up we get manslaughter at the worst. That's
nothin'.

KEVIN: You're not gettin' out of these woods, Mike. I got things goin'
on, things—waitin' on me—

MIKE: Don't play asshole with me, Kev. I can beat your ass.

[4]Ontario Provincial Police
[5]Kapuskasing area of northern Ontario.

KEVIN: Oh yeah?

Mike moves to Kevin who then points his rifle at Mike.

I couldn't take the green paint, man. In the jail. All the jail's a kind of green to make you sick to your stomach, never seen another green like that to make you feel less than a piece of shit crawlin' with maggots, they'll put me in with the Jamaicans again man, cause they hate me, the cops already hate me; living with that green, a kind of green that gets into your mouth, turns all your food rancid, I'm not livin' in the green again, not because of your fuckin' conscience.

Kevin shoots him. Mike is felled. As he dies, Kevin talks to him.

During the following speech, the Northern Lights appear in the sky, lighting up Kevin and darkening him, flashing across his face and body.

Mike, I'm gonna tell you about the greatest sled of my life. My ride through the Northwest Territories. It was this friendship thing I was hired on: promotional. I replaced the guy who owned the Bombardier[6] dealership I was workin' in Thunder Bay, you know Pierre, he was sick, right, he knew I was keen and he seen how I handle a sled, so he sends me on this fuckin' ride. First off, everything you have heard about the toughness of pullin' off a ride in the interior of NWT is totally true. On the other hand, it happens to be the most beautiful place on this earth. From the Bering Strait to the tundra there it's like nothing you've ever seen, Mike. And all that wind, and snow and nothin' like nothin' for miles and miles and no trees and you are, well, very much alone. But you're not, Michael, you're not really alone, right? Cause come nightfall, you'll be sittin' there, and . . . Mike? (*pulling out his hunting knife*)
have you ever seen . . .?
the lights?
You know, (*drawing his knife across Mike's throat*) the Northern Lights?

Northern Lights on Kevin, as Mike dies.

---

[6]maker of the original Ski-Doo snowmobile.

ACT TWO

SCENE 1

The North. Under music. Kevin is running, breathless, away from the scene of his crime, on the trail. A light and music change. Kevin, with his bag, is in Toronto, walking up Clinton Street, searching for his house. The ghost of his mother appears, full of sadness, for she senses what horror is to come.

MOTHER: Kevin. Oh Kevin. I remember the day you were born. My water broke on the Bathurst streetcar, goin' down Bathurst to Queen, and there I was, stretched over the back seat; my waters gushing out of me, pouring out, like a fast stream, over everybody's boots and shopping bags. Well when the car stopped at Queen I somehow got off, crossed the street, everyone staring, staring at me and into Galaxy Donuts. The front of my dress is soaked and I'm there with the donuts. The chocolate sprinkle, the sugared, the iced, and smell of coffee overpowering and BOOM I pass out and the next thing I know you're crowning and the nurse said she said she said "would you like to feel your baby's head?" and I reached down and then I pushed and I pushed and whoooooooo there you were, Kevin, all wet and blue and bloody and they put you on my tummy and oh my goodness you had such a wise little face. I have never forgotten your wise little face. Kevin? Ohhhhhh Kevin. Please—*(disappearing)*

Kevin walks up the street and stops in front of her house. He stares at the house. He looks at the next house. Evangeline calls out.

EVANGELINE: Um Excuse me? Hello?

He turns.

Are you looking for somebody in particular? I uh—know the neighbourhood pretty well.

KEVIN: Yeah. Yeah I am.

He searches in his bag for a notebook with the particulars written on it. He finds it and reads her name.

I'm lookin' for a—uh—a woman called Evangeline Melnyk? The street number got blurred, right? But the name, I can read. Is there anyone of that name who lives around here? Or did? With her mother, name of—Crystal—? But, then, the mother, I was told she passed away sometime last year, so this Evangeline, she would be livin' alone now. If she was still here.

She is in shock so he doesn't see a response in her face.

It must be other side of Bloor then. Okay, *thanks* for your *help*, have a good day!

He heads down the road. She lets him go till he is almost out of sight.

EVANGELINE: Kevin?

He turns, slowly. They look at one another. They know. During Joe's speech, they slowly make their way inside.

SCENE 2

Joe is at the grocery store. We see the fruit and vegetable stand. He calls in to the owner, and then walks home.

JOE: *Grazie, Vincente! Ciao!* (*he starts his walk home*) I don't read Italian and I don't write Italian. But I can speak it. Pretty well. I grew up speakin' it. To my mother. To the fella who ran this store. To a couple of neighbours. To everyone else, I spoke English. You have to bury all that. Once you're here. In Canada. My father, Carlo, he arrived at Union Station in 1909, all by himself. He gets off the train and he leaves the station and he walks up Yonge Street. What else is he gonna do? He sees a man selling bananas, he goes up to him he says *"Paesano,* can you tell me where I might get a room, and a job." The guy sellin' bananas he's Calabrese, and he tells him he can work on the railroad for 7 cents an hour, or sell bananas, then he asks my father if he has a gun, a *pistola,* and my father says "Yeah," and then the guy says to him "Bury your gun." Like, in the garden. He tells him if the cops catch you with a gun, you're on the next boat back.

I speak Italian when I get together with my brothers and sisters, you know, a mix of Italian and Canadian, I speak it to old Annunciata, down the street. But to tell you the truth, I'm always behind, translating, back into English in my head. So I guess I don't really speak it. My children, they don't speak it at all.

SCENE 3

In the sitting room.

KEVIN: Until a few months ago, I thought I'd never been to Toronto. I thought I was born in North Bay and I thought Diane was my true mother.

EVANGELINE: Kevin. Oh Kevin.

KEVIN: So she's in hospital with cancer last year and she calls me to her bedside and she tells me that she's not my mother at all. She says she had been my babysitter and she had stole me away from my home in Toronto when I was four years old. At first I thought she was delirious, right? With the morphine, eh? I didn't think nothin' of it.

EVANGELINE: It's true. She stole you away from us Kevin. We nearly died of it, the whole city was lookin' for you, flowers on our porch every day, hundreds and hundreds of cards, the police, the whole city—

Kevin goes into his backpack and pulls out a wind-up music box from home.

KEVIN (*winding the music box*): Then I had to be in T.O. on business. And . . . I found the name and address she gave me, right? So I thought I'd check it out.

He gives it to her. It plays.

EVANGELINE: Oh Kevin. I've been waiting for you for so long.

KEVIN: I'd forgotten about you. And my real mother. Everything. Because I was so young . . . when she . . . fuck. This is fucking . . .

An awkward silence.

EVANGELINE: And Diane, did she—Was she—?

He sees Evangeline is wondering if he was ill-treated. He was, so he can't answer.

KEVIN: Huh? Yeah . . . What are the—uh—balloons and that for?

He is starting to get edgy, looking through the curtains out into the street, nervous that cops might have followed him.

EVANGELINE: Just—your birthday.

KEVIN: It's not—Oh yeah?

EVANGELINE: March 27th. Didn't—?

KEVIN: No. She didn't.

EVANGELINE: You're twenty-four, right?

KEVIN: Yeah. Today. I guess.

EVANGELINE: I always wished you Happy Birthday. Every year.

KEVIN: Cool.

EVANGELINE: You're shaking. Kevin? What's the matter?

KEVIN: Crashed. Snowmobile. White snow, dark, and—

EVANGELINE: What, a moose? A deer? Kev? You crashed into a moose?

Scene 4

Joe is working in his garden. Sound of a car driving up to the back. Door slamming. Jack walks along the side path to the front of the house, with luggage. He ignores Joe and carries the luggage up the front steps.

JOE: Jack. How was your holiday? Still got snow up there?

Jack just stares.

Everything okay? Jack?

Jack appears frozen. He tries to get his keys.

I got your papers, if you want 'em. You forgot to cancel. I know what that's like, I'm forgetful too. Where's Annie?

Sound of robins.

Oh listen to that. First robin. First robin of the year.

JACK: There uh . . . there was . . .

Silence.

JACK: I didn't know how to give her the kiss. If I'd known how to give her the kiss, she would be alive today.

JOE: Oh my God.

JACK: They go into the woods. For deer meat. They're jittery, they been drinking, they been there for days, nights, seen nothing. They see a shape. They shoot. Guy told me it happens a lot up there. People get shot. Mistaken for deer, usually. Should never go walking at night. I told Volker he should have put up a sign. It's very dangerous in the woods up there. Annie thought, people think it's like a . . . conservation area so they are safe. They think because they are in the woods, in their own country, and there is a warm fire back at the lodge, they are safe. They're not safe.

Joe nods.

There was . . . the poacher, he has something of hers, her dress, her red. . . . I am going to find him, if I have to spend the rest of my life doing it, Joe. I am going to find him, and I am going to tear him apart.

JOE: *Si abbandonare ah me.*

JACK: What?

JOE: I said if there's anything we can do, please, just let us know. I mean that, Jack.

JACK: Yeah uh thanks. I don't exactly . . .

Silence. Jack goes into the house.

JOE (*an echo of Carmella*): *Si abbandonare ah me.*

Scene 5

Evangeline's house: Kevin crouched on the floor of his room stares at Annie's dress hanging there. In his underwear, he sits on a diagonal from the dress in the corner, shivering. He puts on the dress. Evangeline is calling to him while she makes dinner:

EVANGELINE: You know what, guess what? I was thinkin' we could start like a business?

Annie's ghost appears. She is a little wonky, as this is her first visit back to her home and neighbourhood since her death. She moves slowly. She stares at her home with longing, and she turns and sees

Evangeline. She sees the horror Evangeline faces, and she reaches for her to give her the strength on her journey.

Cause like I know the ladies at the bank of Montreal up at Christie and Dupont really well, they're really, really nice to me, especially Gloria. (*Evangeline becomes aware of Annie's presence and stops talking for a moment.*) I think if we saved up my tips from Fran's, and you start workin soon, we could save up and then go and ask 'em for a loan and then just start up our own business. I was thinking maybe a bed and breakfast. After all we have the house, it's paid for. It's got the six bedrooms. Alls it needs is well, quite a bit of work, but we could do a lot of it ourselves, hire some students, and . . .

Evangeline looks directly at Annie's ghost, and she knows something has happened. She is deeply shaken.

In his room, Kevin is putting on Annie's dress. It is very clingy, sexy. He looks in the mirror, terrified.

Evangeline walks almost in a trance outside to Joe, who is standing on his porch.

EVANGELINE: What happened? Did something happen? To Annie Delaney?

JOE: A poacher. In the woods. Shootin' after deer. A terrible accident.

She stands, leaning against the porch, in shock.

Annie's ghost appears as Kevin's reflection in the mirror.

Scene 6

Jack's place. He makes some calls.

JACK: Yeah, Hello, is this The Bay credit office? I'm calling about my payment? Just to let you know that my cheque is in the mail, I put it in Friday. Yes, okay.

He lays out some clothes for Annie in her coffin. He lays out a red dress and shoes in the image of her body on the floor.

Meanwhile, Kevin has heard from Evangeline about Annie. He looks out his window at Jack's house. He initially thinks of leaving, but decides he would like to stay. In the danger.

JACK: Yeah, can I have the number of the Bank of Montreal on Dupont and Christie. Hello. Yeah is Gloria there. Gloria. It's Jack Prevost. Fine fine how are you. Yeah. I was phoning about locking money in that high yielding account because my wife she she is in the morgue, on a cold in a cold her body is on / her heart isn't beating / a slab they are cutting / the coroner / her blood isn't running / is cutting to see the insides how the insides she isn't even thinking her quiet thoughts her quiet quiet—

He drops the phone.

SCENE 7

JOE (*to audience*): I ran; when he was shot and I ran out the door and for blocks and blocks all the way over to Yonge Street, where I found myself by the movie theatre, with the celluloid they used to throw out, after the show, I picked it up, rolls and rolls of it, put it in my pocket and I held it to the sun, so I could watch it burst into flames, it always calmed me, doin' that, I sat on the curb and held it and I watched as the fire flamed and then travelled around and around and into my pocket and fwoof I was fire, burning, red, my father, blood, spraying hot, hot and like it was like it—snowed, and white, holy white surrounded me, and it was white and it was quiet and there was only the smell of sweet bread. And then I passed out. In and out, in a cloud of white flour. Because the baker next door, he had seen me, on fire, from his window, where he was pounding dough, and he had run with a giant bag of flour and emptied it over me, over the fire, and surrounded me with his sweet-smelling arms.

SCENE 8

Evangeline with a candle lit for Annie. She prays and cries. Kevin watches her silently.

KEVIN: I know what you're goin' through. I lost people too. Blurry snowfall, can't see too well. I'm walkin' towards this figure I seen, on the ice, on the lake, hearing the wind, the figure don't move. I get closer and I see it's a man. It's a frozen man. His hand, like, out. Stretched. He doesn't look human any more I'm tellin' you. And I'm just starin' at him and then I hear, like a breath. And his, one of his eyes, like was lookin'. At me. He's alive. And I look over into the bush and I see his sled crashed, and I walked up real close and I breathed my hot breath onto his face, to try to . . . he breathed in some air one more time and then his eye went dead like the other one and he was just froze. He was the frozen man.

EVANGELINE: When someone's dead they're dead forever. So long . . .

Kevin goes to her and comforts her.

KEVIN: Hey now, don't cry. Don't cry.

His actions become sexual. Evangeline breaks away.

EVANGELINE: What are you doing? Kevin, what are you doing?
KEVIN: Givin' you some brotherly love.
EVANGELINE: It's not right.
KEVIN: Uncut nine inches, babe.

Evangeline throws him across the room. She is very strong.

EVANGELINE: You are my brother. And you're in shock. That's all. You're not right because of your crash. So I will forgive you this once. But you must never ever ever do this again. You mustn't ever.
KEVIN: Harsh me out why don't ya.
EVANGELINE: We're brother and sister.

Kevin approaches her.

No!

She slaps him. Kevin moves away from her and sits down, crying.

It's not right. It's not right for you to talk to me like that.
KEVIN: Not right, not right. Nothing's been right since she took me away from you, my whole life, nothing. I should just go and fuckin' die. That's what I'm gonna do, I'm gonna fuckin' walk right down Bathurst Street into the lake and I'll be outta your way and bother you no more.

Kevin puts on his coat and goes to leave. She tries to stop him.

EVANGELINE: Kevin please.

(He goes to leave again.)

Kevin.

He comes back in. He undoes his jeans and rubs himself against her breasts until he ejaculates. [Whether this is seen or not is optional.] He then holds her tightly. She is confused. Kevin moves away.

KEVIN: Anyways, don't worry about it. It's not like we have the same father.

She looks at him amazed.

Well, look at your hair. Look at your hair, and then look at my hair. Oh, by the way, I been lookin' over our accounts? And we gotta get you makin' some cash.

SCENE 9

The North. Annie walks very close to Evangeline, and gives her solace with a touch or a look. The following speech is in reaction to what has happened.

ANNIE: I am a silent woman. That is what they say about me. When they have to say something about me. Oh, Annie, she's . . . quiet. When she's not on stage, singing her quirky songs or telling her strange stories she is . . . quiet. Jack, he really liked my silences. That's why he married me.

When I was a child, I would lie in my bed and hear the voices of my parents fighting, underneath me, night after night. All their words like a claw in my chest; I would go for days without talking, days and nights and days and there was only one place I found peace and that was . . . under my dear grandmother's skirts. A kind of chapel, there. Blossom was her name, her real name was Catherine but they called her Blossom. It was dark and fragrant under there, 4711 I think, lemonish scent, and I loved to look at her veiny legs. Beautiful blue worms. Tea and toast. Sweet wine. Falling asleep, together. She lived with us, she spent her time looking out the window, and doing watercolours of birds, and my mother was always exasperated with her. "Mother, will you just get OUT of my kitchen?" "Mother, do you need to go to the toilet?" When she fell and broke her hip, she was moved to a home for the aged. It smelled of Phisohex[7] and creamed corn. The look on her face, when we left her there, on a cold autumn morning, sitting on her designated bed. She held onto her coat her brown coat and the look of . . . there is no word; I stood there, treachery, looking at the floor. A few weeks later, my grandmother walked out of the home with a razor blade she had stolen from one of the old men and into the Rosedale ravine and she cut her wrists and she walked and walked through the brown and yellow leaves and she turned in circles and then bowed, deeply, I think.

Annie grabs the curtain behind her, or an imaginary dress and wraps herself in it.

Ahhhhhhh! Ohhh there she is. Waiting for me. Huge. With her big skirt......
This silence is perfect.
This is silence exquisite.
This is . . .

SCENE 10

Evangeline in a nightie, remembering. Her mother's ghost is there, and speaks, slightly drunkenly.

MOTHER: Oh babe you woulda loved Nathan. He was a dreamer, like you, always . . . tellin' me his funny stories in that deep sexy voice, wearing that tall black hat, with his black glossy hair, long: Him and me we made this seafood soup with the, the shrimp and the whitefish and after we lay in the backyard under the lilac tree . . .

Evangeline walks over to Joe's porch and checks to find him rocking in his chair.

JOE: Everything okay?
EVANGELINE: I couldn't sleep.
JOE: Nope. Me neither.

---

[7]antibacterial soap

EVANGELINE: Joe. Do you mind if I ask you something?

JOE: Go right ahead.

EVANGELINE: Did you know my father?

JOE: Sure, I knew Bert, when he was around. Worked up at the TTC.[8] Nice fella. Till he took to the bottle. But that's not his fault, really.

EVANGELINE: And Bert was my father. My real and natural father.

Joe is silent.

Joe? Do you know anything that I don't know?

Silence.

Joe? I always knew I looked well not like my mother and father but I figured I must be some you know, genetic throwback to like an Indian or Spanish great grandmother, somethin' like that; my mother when she was drinking she used to say something about . . . a man named Nathan?

Silence.

Joe?

JOE: There was a guy. Used to come around. Before she married Bert.

Silence.

EVANGELINE: Did she have me before she married Bert? Joe, please, just tell me the truth.

JOE: Bert, he didn't seem to mind. I always figured she had told you.

EVANGELINE: No.

JOE: I don't think she told the guy neither.

EVANGELINE: His name was Nathan?

JOE: Yes, yes I think it was. He was a nice enough fellow. Tall, with the long hair, an Indian fellow I believe. You know, Canadian Indian.

EVANGELINE: Indian? Oh my goodness. Indian?

JOE: He said . . . somethin' about he was teaching book writing at George Brown.[9] He had a couple of books you could buy in the bookstores. And your Mom she was going for the cooking, to become a chef. She brought him home one night. I could hear the two of them laughing from two blocks away. Your mom told me

---

[8]Toronto Transit Commission
[9]George Brown College, Toronto.

they stayed up all night cooking and laughing. Oh he brought out the woman's laugh. She stopped laughing when she married Bert.

EVANGELINE: Nathan was my father.

JOE: I think that's what your mom told Essie.

EVANGELINE (*touching her hair*): And you say he was Indian? Joe?

They sit in silence.

Scene 11

JOE: After he was killed, my mother became nervous. She was nervous of me. Second son. Because she blamed me. Second son. For the shooting. She thought my playing with the pepper and egg distracted my uncle, caused him to shoot off the gun. And kill my father. Second son. The way she looked at me when he fell . . . it is a look—I wish I had never . . .

Scene 12

Evangeline and Kevin walking down the street. She wears spiked high heels that he has given her.

KEVIN: Beautiful. Remember: smile, talk nice.

EVANGELINE: I don't know what to say.

KEVIN: Don't say nothin'. I'll say.

EVANGELINE: Only for a couple weeks, right? Just till we get up the money for the roof.

KEVIN: You're wobbling.

EVANGELINE: I am not.

KEVIN: Don't fucking wobble. If you wobble you won't get the fucking job.

EVANGELINE: Well maybe I don't want the job, you bad-breath pimp. Whoremonger. (*as Kevin walks away*) I'm sorry. I'm sorry okay, your breath is fine, I didn't mean it.

KEVIN: You're tryin' to make me feel bad, aren't you?

EVANGELINE: No.

KEVIN: Don't try to make me feel bad, Evangeline, I'm just tryin' to keep us alive here. Okay? Let me tell you something: There is only one thing in this world I ever ever did that I feel bad about and that is—

Joe appears on his porch.

EVANGELINE (*cutting him off*):   Kevin. C'mere, I want you to meet somebody.

They move to Joe's porch.

JOE: Hello. Good morning.

EVANGELINE: Joe? I would like you to meet my brother Kevin. Again.

JOE: Kevin. It's a huge pleasure. And a very big surprise. Ev told me this morning on the phone and I almost fell to the floor! I remember you very well indeed. You would climb up our stairs and you would stand in front of the door and say "Open." "Open." Curly blonde hair. Essie would say "That kid is too cute for words." She'd laugh.

KEVIN: A long time ago.

JOE: "Even the fox must sleep," that's what Essie would say when we seen you sleepin' on the porch.

KEVIN: Oh yeah?

JOE: Well you've made your sister very happy.

KEVIN: That's nice.

JOE: Gonna stay for a while? Get some work?

Jack enters onto his porch for a breath of air.

KEVIN: I'll stay for a while.

JOE: It's good to have you back.

KEVIN: Even the fox must sleep.

Joe waves to Jack. When Kevin sees him we hear the sound of the bullet that killed Annie.

C'mon, we gotta go.

Evangeline and Kevin leave.

JOE: Bye now.

Joe watches Evangeline wobble up the road. This reminds him of the past. Joe's mother, Carmella, comes up the road with a shoe in her hand and a broom.

CARMELLA: Joe.

JOE: Mama!

CARMELLA: I told you not to go climbing fences and playing rough. We can't afford another pair of shoes. What are you trying to do?

JOE: Ya can't get me a pair of shoes?

CARMELLA: We can't afford nothing. We can't afford a loaf of bread for the ten of us, Joe. You know that. You do this on purpose, to make me cry, don't you, you bad, bad . . .

She hits him with her broom.

JOE: Ask the priest, Mama. The priest always helps us.

CARMELLA: I canno go that priest again, Joey. I canno do that.

JOE: Mama. Please. What am I going to wear?

She is silent.

Mama.

Carmella takes off her Depression-era widow shoes and presents them.

CARMELLA: You will wear my shoes to school.

JOE: But Mama, I can't. I can't wear your shoes.

CARMELLA: If you want shoes so bad, you wear my shoes. Put them on.

JOE: No.

CARMELLA: Put them on

JOE: NO.

Carmella hits him hard. He cries and slowly puts the shoes on. He is totally humiliated. They are way too big. He walks, with difficulty, across the stage. His mother is very upset for him, but cannot show it.

Scene 13

Jack dusts the house for fingerprints. They come up very clear. He spots Annie's, and puts his hand on her prints. If the theatre is unable to do this just drop it.

SCENE 14

Funeral music.

JACK: Thank you all very much for coming. Annie and I used to place bets who'd get a bigger turnout at their funeral. It's clear she's the winner. Annie, I'll pay you later. Ummm, Annie, she was afraid of getting old. And now she never will be getting old. (*Long pause.*) I don't know if you heard this already or not. Anyway, I wanted to play it.

Annie, the ghost, appears. Song: "My mother and father."

ANNIE: my father and mother
           are getting old
           I and my brother
           were sad when they sold
           our old house
           with its sagging porch
           and kitchen mouse
           and view of the forks
           of the Credit River
           we were puppies biting at their heels
           now they are old
           don't finish their meals

           They were big bright so perfect
           now they are old
           not as happy somehow
           not as quick
           not as clean
           can't sleep very long
           they get up before dawn
           sit in the dark
           Watch the dew
           on the grass
           My mother and father are old
           When I say good-bye after Thanksgiving dinner
           They have tears in their eyes
           so do I.

for something lost
Something lost. And gone.
Am I saying good-bye to ghosts
(*spoken*) oh no.
(*sung*) my mother and father
Are getting old.

SCENE 15

Joe's house.

JOE: My older sister, Annabella, married young, seventeen, very young, to get away from my mother. Niko, her husband, he was older, in his forties, but he was good to her. The problem was that he couldn't see. He couldn't see. And it was the Depression. Who had money for glasses? And when she was crying in pain with her menstrual cramps, eh? Niko goes to get her medicine. And he thinks he's gettin' like a Alka-Seltzer and he puts the tablet in water and he gives it to her. It was athlete's foot medicine. It killed her in two days. I'm playin' ball in the schoolyard, I refused to go see her in hospital. I didn't like hospitals. Her body looked so stiff. In the coffin. The ring on her finger. Her face . . . with the terrible makeup . . . her lips and fingernails inky blue.

God forgive me, Annabella.

(*seeing a ball land on his lawn*) GET THAT BALL OFFA MY LAWN. I'M GOING TO CUT IT INTO LITTLE BITS NEXT TIME THAT BALL LANDS ON MY LAWN, YOU HEAR ME? DO YOU HEAR WHAT I'M SAYING?

SCENE 16

Zanzibar strip club. Evangeline as a Mother Superior. Jack walks in mid-dance and stands at the back, electrified by her. She directs most of her dance to him. She throws her garter to him. Back stage: Kevin is in the dressing room, waiting, watching and notices that she is dancing for Jack. He is enraged. She comes in and covers herself with a bathrobe.

M.C.: Let's have a big hand, gents for Sister Fantasia, our Lady of Perpetual Love!

Evangeline gives Kevin six twenties.

KEVIN: Seen you flashin' that cop out there. I told you to stay away from him, Evangeline.

EVANGELINE: Are you coming home tonight?

KEVIN: If I see you lookin' at him again you know what I'm gonna do.

EVANGELINE: Shall I thaw the chicken? Make some chicken curry?

KEVIN: And another thing. You're not bringing home cash. You gotta show more pussy, I tole ya. Flash a little candy floss.

EVANGELINE: Go to hell.

KEVIN: The house is fallin' down, Evy, we need the money. If we don't start workin' on it, we may have to leave it.

EVANGELINE (*after a silence, loud*): Ha! Ha! Ha! Ha! Ha! Ha!

KEVIN: What's so funny?

EVANGELINE: This. It's—it's—it's—it's like something out of Charles Dickens. *Little Dorrit.*

KEVIN: What?

EVANGELINE: You know, you comin' back here, forcing me into a life of . . . ill-repute . . . but you know what? To tell you the truth I love it. I love fancy dancing. EXOTIC DANCING. Takin' my clothes off. I love the griminess of the place and the men's hungry faces. I love watching them jack off to the sight of my swaying hips. I'm Lucifer, I'm bringing them light, and I just think it's so funny that you think you're this bad dude and I'm this poor little—

M.C.: And coming up in a few minutes, the pure and lovely Fantasia, guys, she is just getting herself ready for you as we speak . . .

KEVIN: Are you makin' fun of me?

She looks at him, kisses him. Aroused, he pursues it.

M.C.: And now . . . the temperature rises, the temperature soars. What's happening? Are we moving closer to the sun? Oh no, my friends, we have a furnace here. A furnace named FANTASIA. Gentlemen, please will you put your filthy hands together for Fantasia.

KEVIN: Now you get out there. And remember, your brother loves you.

She leaves. Kevin watches her dance towards Jack and shouts.

Always!!

ACT THREE

SCENE 1

Jack, in his dressing gown, remembers. He enters his and Annie's living room. She is reading on the couch.

JACK: I got us a movie.
ANNIE: Oh. What did you get?
JACK: A special movie. You know. Romantic.
ANNIE: Oh.
JACK: I think you'll like this one. The girl . . . is very good.
ANNIE: Ohhhkay. If you say so.
JACK: Listen, if you don't want me to put it on, just say so. I just thought something . . . erotic might be fun. Help me forget the shitty day I had.
ANNIE: No, no, it's okay. Actually I'm kind of interested.

Jack puts in the videotape. The porno type of music starts up. They watch. Annie is amused at first. Jack is also amused but the amusement turns to arousal.

JACK: Look at that one. The blonde.
ANNIE: You like her?
JACK: I just think she's good. She's a good actress. I don't know. She really seems to be liking . . . all the guys at once. I don't think she's acting. Do you know what I mean?
ANNIE: Hmm.

They both become aroused. Jack begins to kiss her. They begin to make love in an almost violent way. Jack cannot keep his eyes off the screen, and both times he looks at it he is more violent with her.

Suddenly, Annie gets up and covers herself.

JACK: What's wrong, you okay?
ANNIE: I just . . . I just don't feel so well.
JACK: Yeah? What is it.

The porno music blares.

Is it the movie?

ANNIE: No, no, I think I'm getting sick, that's all. I had a headache before.

JACK: Are you sure it's not the movie?

ANNIE: Yeah.

JACK: Okay. Do you want me to get you something? An Alka Seltzer?

Annie shakes her head. He turns back to the movie.

ANNIE: Would you mind, turning down the volume?

He turns down the volume but still looks at the screen.

Would you . . . take it out, please? Take it out of the machine. Take it out of the machine.

He does so. He puts it down on the table.

JACK: I thought you were enjoying it.

Silence.

ANNIE: All those men, crowding around her . . .

JACK: You shoulda said something. How come you didn't say nothing?

ANNIE: Their faces: dogs.

JACK: Oh come on. You were enjoying it at first. I know you were.

ANNIE: Crowding her.

JACK: But honey, it was what she wanted. She was the one that asked them all . . .

ANNIE: No.

JACK: Annie.

ANNIE: No.

JACK: Would you relax? It's just a movie. A sexy movie. Sex between consenting adults. What's the big deal?

Annie is silent. She is deeply distressed, Jack doesn't know what to do.

There was no violence, I made sure of that. I just thought, something different . . .

Annie begins an activity she always begins when she goes into one of her silences.

Please. Don't go into one of your silences. This is not a good time for me.

ANNIE: I'm going to go—for a walk.

JACK: A walk? At this time of night?

ANNIE: I need a walk. When I return I want it to be out of our house.

JACK: I'll put it out with the garbage tomorrow.

ANNIE: Tonight. Take it out of our house tonight. I'm not coming back till it's out of the house. I'll walk the streets all night if I have to.

JACK: Oh for God's sake.

ANNIE: Out of our house!

JACK: Alright. You go for your walk and I will take the movie out of the house. I'll take it right out of the neighbourhood. Will that make you happy?

Annie slams the door.

ANNIE: OUT OF MY HOUSE!

JACK: I want to make you happy, Annie.

Scene 2

The North. Kevin is in the dark. In the woods. In the spot where he killed Mike. Mike is frozen there, like a statue. Kevin has driven all the way up north. He approaches Mike's frozen body.

KEVIN: Two and a half hours, 120 all the way, Mike. You shoulda seen these bozo's from Quebec playin' chicken with me I pushed em off the road man, they're still waitin' for a tow.

Kevin covers Mike's body with evergreen boughs as he speaks.

I can't believe they didn't find ya, Mike, fuckin' search party probably walked right by you I'm sittin' there down in Toronto thinkin' I gotta bury Mike. He's my best friend in the whole world and I will not have his body torn apart by wolves. Goodnight Michael, I'll be thinkin' about you.

He covers him up. Annie appears behind him, in the same position as she was when he shot her. He faces her.

He runs away from Annie.

SCENE 3

Joe and Evangeline on Joe's porch.

EVANGELINE: Tell me more about my father?

JOE: Well, like I said, he was funny.

EVANGELINE: Funny? How? How was he funny?

JOE: Like TV. Very funny. Make ya laugh out loud kind of funny.

EVANGELINE: Did he talk much about . . . his people?

JOE: He never said. Well, once he said somethin' about he could never do the sun dance. He didn't have the patience. And he said his mother lived out at some reserve in Manitoba. He'd go out to see her once in a while. I think he said he was of the Cree nation. I think.

EVANGELINE: Cree. So that's why I've always felt so—apart from . . . Cree? Will I ever know him, Joe?

JOE: You may. You may not.

EVANGELINE: I just feel things are going in a certain way. And there's nothin' I can do to stop them. Like I'm in a sled, right? In a runaway sled goin down a mountain of ice, faster and faster and if I tip over I will break my neck and bones for sure but if I keep going, what's at the bottom, what's at the bottom Joe is the lake. I'll crack through the foot-thick ice in a moment and down into the frigid waters, stopping my heart and my breath . . .

JOE: I know the feeling.

EVANGELINE: My very life is shaken, Joe. If you know what I mean.

JOE: Yeah. I know what you mean

SCENE 4

Evangeline's house. Kevin goes into the bedroom and looks out the window. She wakes.

KEVIN: Hold me, baby. Please hold me.

She moves to the window and puts her arms around him.

I missed you so much. I missed you so fuckin' much.

EVANGELINE: Hardly seen ya in the last few weeks, Kevin. I was gettin' worried.

KEVIN: That cop from across the street—has he been around?

EVANGELINE: Haven't noticed, really.

KEVIN: Just hold me.

EVANGELINE: Steer escaped from the slaughterhouse today. Ran right up the street.

KEVIN: Yeah? Fuck. What . . . happened?

EVANGELINE: They shot it through the head and dragged it back down the street. Blood all over the street.

Kevin opens the window.

KEVIN: Fucking—dogs.

EVANGELINE: You know what he was sayin'? The guy that runs the video store?

KEVIN: What?

EVANGELINE: That the earth is gonna get hit by a comet. Like, soon.

KEVIN: How does he know?

EVANGELINE: The scientists, the astronomers have said, soon. What will we do when that happens? What will we do, Kev?

KEVIN: We fill up a needle. And we shoot ourselves into deep dark space.

EVANGELINE: So we won't feel the quaking. The fires.

KEVIN: We don't feel sweet nothin'. Just like that steer. He's not afraid any more. He's not anything.

SCENE 5

Jack's house. He is sitting in the dark, in his dressing gown. He walks over to a table where Annie is sitting, doing some translating.

ANNIE: (*Gaelic*) *Ghiomar ag fail bhais den ocras in Eirinn.* [Pronounced: Vee a mer egg foil vagh den ocras in Airinn.] We—were—getting death—of the hunger—in Ireland. I want to go to Ireland. To Connemara, to look at the graves.

JACK: Why? What for?

ANNIE: I want to know—

JACK: Who you are.

ANNIE: Yes.

JACK: You and about three hundred thousand American tourists a year.

ANNIE: Jack, I want to hear my natural language.

JACK: They hate you over there. They have no interest in you whatsoever. They don't see you as family, they see you as American.

ANNIE: I don't believe it. If I were to meet a Delaney I know it would be . . . a very beautiful . . . it would help me, Jack.

JACK: I have absolutely no desire ever to visit France, or even Quebec. Just because my name is Prevost? And my grandfather grew up in Rimouski? I have nothing to do with those people. *Oh tabernaque, je me souviens je suis très* fuckin' *triste* and pissed off that Wolfe *il triumph de Montcalm* on the fuckin' Plains of Abraham and *je suis triste vive le Quebec libre vive le Quebec libre* that was my ancestors, on both sides, two generations ago, but that is not me do you ever see me watch the French station? No! No! I am this now, THIS.

ANNIE: I am going to Ireland. In the spring.

JACK: And leave me alone?

ANNIE: I need to go.

JACK: And if I ask you not to?

Annie is silent.

If I ask you not to?

ANNIE: And why would you do that, Jack?

JACK: Because . . . I would worry about you, over there all by yourself. The IRA is everywhere—

ANNIE: The IRA? Why are you LYING Jack you are a LIAR you are not worried about me being shot by the IRISH REPUBLICAN ARMY you are worried about me doing something that has nothing to do with you; the way you were with your girlfriend Jemma; (*she prods and hits him*) you gonna hit me too? Throw me up against the wall and then fuck me up the ass and piss on me the way you did with her?

JACK (*breathless*): Annie.

ANNIE: You are just like the pathetic husband in the story of the selkie, the half-woman half-seal, terrified his beautiful wife he stole from the sea would find her seal skin, her true skin because he knows if she finds it then nothing, not children, not love, not any amount of pleading, will keep her from the sea. YOU WANT TO KEEP ME FROM THE SEA.

She collapses.

JACK (*in the present*): Annie, you didn't know about Jemma then, I hadn't told you, this isn't fair, this isn't . . .

Annie weeps.

ANNIE: But of course I knew, I knew in—here.

She pounds her gut.

JACK: I even said I'd go, I said if you feel that strongly about it, let's just . . . wait till my holidays in August, and we'll go together. What about that? Do one of those walking tour things you like.

ANNIE: No.

JACK: Why not for God's sake? Hey it's quite a sacrifice for me even goin' there, you know I like Trinidad and Tobago, or St. Lucia, I love to lie in the sun I HATE the rain. I mean, Annie, Ireland is just like fuckin' New Brunswick. And who wants to go there?

Annie glares at him.

ANNIE: You don't understand at all, do you?

He looks at her.

JACK: I'm trying to, Annie. I'm really really trying to. I just thought if we went together, maybe—

ANNIE: I need to go alone. And you will have to accept that.

JACK: How long have you been sleeping with him?

ANNIE: WHO?

JACK: Whoever it is you are meeting there, Annie. This is classic—

She laughs.

A lot of things are making sense now.

ANNIE: What are you talking about?

JACK: Your coldness. In the last few months.

ANNIE: What?

JACK: Like making love to a fucking corpse.

ANNIE: Go to hell. And fucking burn there.

JACK: You don't make a sound, you don't move. I don't remember the last time you gave me a back massage.

Annie turns away.

What is his name? Annie? Who is it? Do you do for him what you haven't done for me in five years?

ANNIE: Jack. First of all, I swear on my life there is nobody else. And secondly, I am your wife not your concubine. NOT your concubine! If I am like a—corpse—

JACK: Worse than a corpse because you lie there and you send out these waves, these waves of like, hatred.

ANNIE: And that hasn't stopped you, has it? Maybe you like that, maybe you like—fucking a dead woman.

JACK: Get the fuck out of here. Go to fucking Ireland and suck your boyfriend's dick dry.

ANNIE: Aghhhhhhhh! (*She attacks, they struggle.*)

JACK: Please don't lie to me. If you have any respect for me.

ANNIE: There is no one else. But I have been cold. I've been feeling— very—cold. I feel as though I may never get warm again.

JACK: And may I ask why?

ANNIE: I don't . . . know. I don't know.

JACK: Okay. Can I take a guess? You've ah . . . fallen out of—love with me. After twenty years. It's okay, I mean it happens. And I'm not exactly any great catch. You always much preferred the company of your son to my company, the two of you ignore me when he's here, home from college, maybe you're longing for his Daddy, your one night stand from where was it? The El Mocambo?[10] I would just like to know for certain, okay? And once I know, I would appreciate the chance to to to . . .

ANNIE: Jack, Jack, it's it's listen. It's just sometimes I'm not sure who you are. I hear these rumours about you being a brutal cop, being called *Diablo* by the local kids and—

---

[10]Toronto nightclub on Spadina Avenue.

JACK: So you're saying I'm like a stranger. Like someone you might brush past on the subway. Twenty years wiped out, like that.

ANNIE: I'm going to work on it, I promise, I don't know, maybe if we go away, north to the country—

JACK: My brothers said this would happen. They said you were too good for me, too educated, too—swish. I'm a cop from Mississauga with a grade twelve education. They would go "What the hell is she doin' with you?"

ANNIE: No Jack, it's not any of that, believe me, our differences, I love, they kept things electric for so long.

JACK: So what's happened? WHAT has happened?

ANNIE: I have been having this dream. For the last year or so. And I am having it more and more. In the dream, you are walking towards me with an aluminum bucket in your hand. And in that bucket is a rattlesnake. (*makes rattle sound*) And I'm saying "Please, Jack, please don't come closer," (*makes rattle sound*) and you are humming to yourself and you keep approaching . . . you have this rattlesnake in this bucket and I think the dream it is something to do with I don't know, with me sensing or my body sensing that you have . . .

JACK: Secrets.

Annie nods. Jack is silent. He does some cleaning.

Well we all have secrets. Don't we? (*exiting*)

SCENE 6

Zanzibar. Music: Evangeline does a table dance for Jack. Their eyes meet. They have connected in a way that transcends the grotty environment. She gives him a bracelet.

SCENE 7

Joe's porch.

JOE: I risked my life for this country! That's the thing. I was a belly gunner. In a Lancaster. Seventeen missions. It's cold, man, on your belly, you better believe it at 20,000 feet. They were always shooting at us, I shit my pants twice. It's the coldest I ever was in the

belly there. Most belly gunners didn't last three missions. Because
the Messhershmitt, they wiped us out. And the Night Fighters. I
remember this one. We're moving along. And there's a Messhershmitt coming that way, and the other way. Well soon enough the
pilot's dead, the second dicky's dead, he was a boy of nineteen on
his second mission, and the nose gunner's dead (*taking a moment to
recover from the memory*). When the war was over I come back to
Toronto. And Eatons, they got signs up everywhere "We want vets."
"Vets please apply." Well I went down to apply, with a few of my
buddies, other vets. We filled out the application. And under religion, I put Catholic. Because I was. Well all the other vets I knew,
they were Protestant. They all got the job, right off. They were
called the next day. I didn't get any calls, nothing. I said to one, "I
wonder how come I never got called." He looked at me, he says,
"You didn't say you were Catholic?" "Well, yes," I says. He says
"You'll never get a job if you're Catholic. Not in Toronto. Not in
Ontario." So I went to an Anglican priest and I told him my
predicament. I told him I wanted to change religions and he was
very accommodating. He made me an Anglican. So I went back
down, and I filled out the form again. And this time where it said
"Religion" I wrote down Anglican. And I got the job the next day.
But to tell you the truth, although I was an Anglican, I was still a
Catholic. You always are.

SCENE 8

A piano bar at night with cocktails.

JACK: How did you think up a dance like that? 'Cause that is really
exotic.

EVANGELINE: Oh. I don't know. I just got bored with the same old
thing.

JACK: So you came up with this?

EVANGELINE: You think it's okay?

JACK: It's . . . enchanting.

EVANGELINE: It's a kind of a . . .

JACK: What?

EVANGELINE: Nothing.

JACK: No, what were you going to say?

EVANGELINE: Prayer. In a way. You think I'm crazy.

JACK: No, I don't. I think that's cool. I pray too. By driving fast. Seriously. In a chase. Chasin' some guy who's just robbed a bank, or knocked down a kid, hit and run. It's like a prayer.

EVANGELINE: Because the other kind of prayer, on your knees and putting your palms together? And repeating words you learned in Sunday school? Those don't work.

JACK: I know, I used to try it. Please GOD make my brother get run over by a truck so my dad and I can get Swiss Chalet Christmas dinner. Please GOD let the guy not have a gun on him, please GOD let my wife have a heartbeat. It never—

EVANGELINE: You okay? You're trembling, aren't you? Here, let me—

She puts her jacket on him

JACK: They should turn the goddamn heat up in here. What are they trying to do, freeze us out?

She is silent.

So how do you like the boss, is he okay? I heard this one he doesn't treat the girls so well.

EVANGELINE: No.

JACK: Well . . . do you . . . like working there?

Evangeline laughs.

EVANGELINE: You're asking me if I like working there?

JACK: Isn't there . . . isn't there . . . anything else that you wanted to do? With your life?

She turns to him. There is so much to say that there is not much point in saying anything.

So why do you stay there?

EVANGELINE: You don't understand.

Evangeline smiles.

I've seen you. You live in my neighbourhood.

JACK: Where do you live.

EVANGELINE: Clinton just south of Dupont.

JACK: Oh. That's close to me. I'm closer to Follis.

EVANGELINE: You're a policeman.

JACK: Is that bad?

EVANGELINE: Your wife. Annie Delaney. The singer.

JACK: Yeah.

EVANGELINE: "As a hart yearns for channels of water, so my soul yearns for thee."

JACK: Oh you've heard Annie's— (*Evangeline nods.*) It's hard at night. (*Annie's ghost enters.*) Sometimes I just get up, go out, for a walk. Sit in some all-night donut place. Keep away the thoughts.

EVANGELINE: I know what that's like.

JACK: At work, and at the bar, I can almost forget, you know, distracted. But as soon as I get home.

EVANGELINE: Yeah.

JACK: Get into bed. That bed. It's like . . . I swear to God I've seen her. In the house.

EVANGELINE: I've seen my mother.

JACK: Yeah?

EVANGELINE: You loved her. Annie Delaney.

Silence. Evangeline nods, smiles.

JACK: Annie would have liked you. She would have liked you a lot.

EVANGELINE: I said "Hi" to her a few times on the sidewalk. We even talked about the weather. Our gardens. You think so?

JACK: Yeah.

Evangeline caresses his face.

EVANGELINE: I like those lines from the ends of your eyes.

JACK: You do? I hate them. Reminds me I'm getting old. Hey. Am I too old for you?

Evangeline is embarrassed.

Because I would like to, I don't know. Hang out with you. Go to the Botanical Gardens, you ever been to the Botanical Gardens?

Evangeline shakes her head.

Oh you'll love the Botanical Gardens.

Evangeline kisses him. He kisses her back.

Do you mind if I tell you, I find you very beautiful?

EVANGELINE: Me?

JACK: And mysterious. A forest. In winter.

EVANGELINE: No.

JACK: Would you like to dance?

He touches her, caresses her.

The ghost Annie sings. They dance to Annie's music. They dance politely, and then more and more sensually.

SCENE 9

Song: "Morning in bright fall."

ANNIE: A morning in bright fall
In Caledon Hills

Maple leaves my bouquet
I had chills

Oh my day (*pause*)
from my lips to my knees
Love (*small pause*)
You were stung by a bumblebee
the ringing of bells
Your cheek swelled
as you said (*pause*)

Till death us do part
Clear eyes and clean consciences
Oh when did this start
This painful infection (*pause*)
Of our strong our red heart?

Oh when did this start?
Are, (*tiny pause*) we so far apart? (*pause*)

That morning in bright fall
Maple leaves—my bouquet
You were my prince
And now what you say
Makes me sad (*pause*)
Makes me fear

You said you were the sun dear
And I was the sky
But are you the gun dear
I carry inside?
Waiting to fire
To kill your tall bride

Oh when did this start
Are we so far apart
Are we so far apart?

SCENE 10

Dawn breaks. Jack and Evangeline are on Clinton Street, looking at the stars.

JACK: You see that there? That's the North Star.

EVANGELINE: *Keeweetinok Atchak.* In Cree. I'm half Cree.

JACK: Yeah?

EVANGELINE: That star stays still. The other stars, they swirl around but that one stays just still.

JACK: You know it.

EVANGELINE: I studied the stars. The stars and some Cree. Songs, a few phrases. I got books from the library.

JACK: Wow. I like that, I like it that you studied the stars, and the Cree, that's elegant.

EVANGELINE: Your eyes—like a sea of glass.

She laughs, and kisses him. From inside Kevin sees, and, drunk, wanders out.

KEVIN: What the hell are you doing, Evangeline?

They start and turn.

EVANGELINE: You'd better go.

JACK: Who are you? Are you the brother?

KEVIN: Who the fuck are you?

EVANGELINE: Kev, please.

JACK: Jack, pleased to meet you. I'm just walking Evangeline home.

KEVIN: You come near her again and I'll kill you. Now get the fuck off my property.

JACK: Is this your house?

EVANGELINE: Kevy please don't talk to my friend that way. He's been very nice to me.

KEVIN: Get offa my property. Fuckin' now.

JACK: Evangeline is an adult, Kevin. And what she does is none of your business.

KEVIN: Evy, get inside.

EVANGELINE: I can do what I want to do, Kev. You can't stop me anymore.

KEVIN: I said GET INSIDE.

JACK: Hey you don't—

Kevin hits her. Jack hits him. They fight. Kevin is trying to escape Jack and the fight moves inside, and towards Kevin's bedroom. Evangeline tries to stop them, crying "Please." "Stop it." and "Don't." They are there squaring off, when Jack sees the red dress hanging in Kevin's room. He looks back at Kevin, and back again at the dress. He touches the dress. They freeze.

Annie!

He turns to Kevin. Kevin laughs.

KEVIN: We thought she was an animal, man.

EVANGELINE: Kevin?

KEVIN: We couldn't see through the branches. In the dark. It happens.

Jack attacks Kevin hard.

EVANGELINE: No. Stop it. Stop it you two. I'll call the cops. Stop it. You're hurting him.

They are fighting, Jack is about to kill Kevin by strangling him. Evangeline grabs the gun.

Stop it or I'll shoot. I swear to God I'll shoot.

Evangeline has a moment of terrible indecision, but then her need for her brother, for family, wins out and she kills Jack. The sound of the bullet is naturalistic this time, to avoid comic melodrama. He falls to the ground. Music should come in right away.

Kevin gets up, takes the gun, then steals the money out of Jack's pockets and takes off.

Evangeline has blood all over her hands. She is in shock. She puts on the red dress. She sings a Cree song of lamentation over Jack's body [see music for "Evangeline's Lament" at end of play].

She walks outside. JOE sees her.

Help me.

JOE: What happened? What happened child?

Evangeline staggers down Clinton Street.

SCENE 11

Night. Kevin appears out of Joe's front door, rifling though Essie's purse and throwing it away. Joe is on the porch.

JOE: Who's that? Who's there?

KEVIN: Cover your face. Cover your face or I fuckin' kill you.

JOE: My wife is not well. Please don't hurt her. You can have anything you want.

KEVIN: Shut the fuck up, Joe.

JOE: Kevin. What are you doing here? Where's Evangeline?

KEVIN: Where's your wallet? Where is your fuckin' wallet, old man.

JOE: It's okay. Now calm down Kevin, you're welcome to anything you want. It's right here, in my jacket.

KEVIN: Okay, now what's your PIN number? Tell me the wrong one, I come back and shoot your fuckin' head off.

JOE: Okay. It's—uh . . . 6?

KEVIN: NOW. NOW!

JOE: 6 . . . 5, no 4 . . . no, 5, 7, 9. Yes, that's it.

KEVIN: 6579.

JOE: Kevin? It's not too late to give yourself up.

KEVIN: Are you tellin' me what to fuckin do? YOU, who sat on your fuckin' porch and watched as I was dragged away from my home only four years old? You sat and you rocked and you didn't do nothing. You didn't do nothing.

JOE: Kevin.

KEVIN: I remember the sound of the chair. The sound of the rocking. I remember it, man. I have nightmares.

JOE: I thought she was takin' you down to Christie Pits, to play on the big airplane. You loved that big airplane.

KEVIN: Bullshit.

JOE: It's God's truth.

KEVIN: Bullshit.

Kevin goes to leave.

JOE: Kevin. May God forgive you.

KEVIN: Fuck that.

Kevin leaves.

SCENE 12

Night. Bloor Street. Fruit and vegetable stand. Streetlight shines on it. Evangeline is standing still among the fruit and vegetables. We can see Honest Ed's neon signs flashing across the street.

EVANGELINE (*whispers*): Hail Oh Hail Annie full of Grace we are soaked we are soaked in our neighbour's blood my brother and I the Law the Law is with thee. Come to me, I wait here, behind the apples and avocados and oranges sweet, I will wait for you to guide me are you here? Are you—

Annie appears.

Annie. Hey. Have you come to smote me down? I wouldn't blame you. I am murder see my hands? *Geen-sa. Ni nipbo* [I have killed somebody. I am death] Soaked in blood His blood—

ANNIE: Evangeline, walk.

EVANGELINE: Walk?

Annie swings around and points north.

ANNIE: *Keeweetinok Atchak.* The North Star to the northern star walk you'll reach the dark forest where the air is clear you lie on the moss you will have your baby on moss not a grimy jail floor; clean your baby with clear water not infected jail water you go, and walk and disappear. It happens in Canada all the time, a disappearing woman, nobody minds. Just walk. Disappear.

EVANGELINE: Oh. Annie. Will you ever sing to me again?

Annie disappears.

You know my baby? I'm callin' her after you, Annie.

Evangeline fills her bag with oranges and apples. Kevin, meanwhile, is all over the neighbourhood looking for her.

KEVIN: We gotta take off, babe, cause they're comin' after us. There's buses every hour we can be outta here in twenty minutes.

She starts to walk up the street.

EVANGELINE: We are walking.

KEVIN: Walking? (*pausing and watching her walk*) Walking.

They walk together into the horizon, up Yonge Street. We see Joe's rocking chair, a yellow police ribbon around Evangeline's house. About halfway through the speech we see Kevin and Evangeline, in the woods, in a sled or on a stump. He seems to be sleeping, in a sleeping bag beside her. She is heavily pregnant.

EVANGELINE: *Tansi niskneeksqueem* [hello my daughter] dear my darling daughter.

Happy eighth birthday Annie Northstar. *Kisageetin ooma* that means I love you, baby, in Cree; the language of your blood I hope this finds you happy and strong. My dear friend Patty is giving you this letter. Patty is your mother now and I know she is tellin' you funny stories and bringing home rice pudding from Fran's for ya, and taking real good care of you. I wanted more than life itself to keep you, love, but I had to send you down to Patty to keep you safe, because I am doomed to walk, forever. And that's no way for you to live. Your feet would get tired. I want you to have school, and friends, and gymnastic classes and all of that. I do not know what lies ahead, on my travels. I know one thing only, and that is that you will see me, in the North Star, because, the North Star, in Cree: "*kewe tinok atchak,*" is always there in the sky, Annie, and guides us.

Nell, whatever people may tell you about your father, I want you to know that what you are is a long summer evening, Nell, Clinton Street, kids playing outside our window my friend Joe cutting his roses, talking with the neighbours, and we lined up barefoot for soft ice cream and Kevin he got a vanilla with hot chocolate dip and I got the warm butterscotch and we brought them inside and we sat in the dark and we licked them faster and as the ice cream melted his face melted too, melted along with the ice cream we had no fans, Nell our house was so hot, and the laughing boy was there underneath, that boy who said park and I saw him again and he was gentle and sweet and your father, my love, was not the man but the sweet heavenly child.

Kisageetin ooma, I love you so, *kisageetin ooma*.

SCENE 13

EVANGELINE:　Oh I wish I could be near you, Annie, while you read this, touching the lights in your soft hair, wish it were possible but I know that it isn't, for the bone in the air it has broke I am doomed to walk till I cannot walk more till I fall on my knees to the ground till I fall on my—

Kisageetin ooma, I love you so, *kisageetin ooma kisageetin ooma kisageetin ooma*

daughter

Kev? Kev, come on, wake up.

KEVIN:　Leave me alone. I gotta sleep.

EVANGELINE:　Kevin it's time. We have to walk.

KEVIN:　Fuckin' cold, fuckin' wolves, howlin' in my ear—

EVANGELINE:　You're going to be fine. Come on.

They walk together for a while along the trail. They struggle.

KEVIN:　My foot is killin' me, Ev. I can't fuckin' walk no more. Don't make me, don't—

He falls.

EVANGELINE:　No resting, Kevin. If we rest we fall into the fires! We burn. Forever. Now come on. You can do it. Come on. Stand. Up. Now. One foot in front of the other. Come on.

She tries to make him walk, like a puppet.

KEVIN:　Have some mercy, woman. Mer-cy. Can't you see I'm dyin' here? I'm goin' blind. Left eye is worse. Everything's startin' to look shimmery. Just the way it happened with the right one.

He buckles.

EVANGELINE:　Keeeevin!!

KEVIN: And the cold. Ev. I can't take the cold no more, I never felt such cold. This fuckin' country. How come you don't feel the cold?

EVANGELINE: Come on.

KEVIN: Take me home. I want to go home.

EVANGELINE: We have no home! You know that.

KEVIN: Then I'll go to fucking Millhaven. At least there's television there. Regular food.

EVANGELINE: Kevin. Kevin look at me.

KEVIN (*he laughs*): What are you going to do, have the baby out here? In the bush? And then keep walkin' with her? What do you do when it's time to put her in school?

EVANGELINE: I have plans for Annie, Kevin. Annie will be just fine. Now can you please try to walk?

Evangeline decides to carry him. She lifts him over her shoulder. She sings to him, a Cree lullaby [see music for "Evangeline Carries Kevin" at end of play]. She lifts him onto her back and they climb the hill where Annie was killed. Kevin wakes, a final burst of energy before dying. He hears wolves.

The Northern Lights light up the sky.

KEVIN: Wha's that sound? 'Vangeline, it's the wolves. Oh yes. There they are. In the blizzard, can you see them?

EVANGELINE: Oh, no, my little brother. No! It's something else. Something kind. Yes. Cheepyuk Neemeetowuk. They've finally come for us. Oh. Dancing spirits. Yes. They're every bit as lovely as you said, Kev.

His breathing has become shallow, quick, as breathing often does before death. The Northern Lights surround them. Annie sings:

ANNIE: Oh heavenly time of day . . .
the fog and the quiet.
The mist, no sun. I move out of my dream and into
this day as
the fog it clears so slowly away to reveal . . . to reveal . . .

The snowy owl hoots.

Evangeline's Lament for Jack

Evangeline Carries Kevin

—1997

Credits

Index of Critical Terms